Gathered at the River

GRAND RAPIDS, MICHIGAN, AND ITS
PEOPLE OF FAITH

Gathered at the River

GRAND RAPIDS, MICHIGAN, AND ITS PEOPLE OF FAITH

James D. Bratt and Christopher H. Meehan
for the Grand Rapids Area Council
for the Humanities

Foreword by
Martin E. Marty

The Grand Rapids Area Council for the Humanities
William B. Eerdmans Publishing Company

Jacket and frontispiece photos: Paul Crouse

Printed in the United States of America

Library of Congress Cataloging-in-Publication Data

Bratt, James D., 1949–
Gathered at the river : Grand Rapids, Michigan, and its people of faith / James D.
Bratt and Christopher H. Meehan for the Grand Rapids Area Council for the
Humanities ; foreword by Martin E. Marty.
p.   cm.
Includes bibliographical references.
ISBN 0–8028–7054–6
1. Grand Rapids (Mich.) — Church history.   2. Grand Rapids (Mich.) — Religion
I. Meehan, Christopher H., 1949– . II. Title.
BR560.G69B73   1993
277.74'56 — dc20   93–26656
CIP

To

All people of faith whose lives have nurtured
their congregations and our city.

Contents

CHAPTER 4 FURNITURE AND FAITH 65

Time: 1875–1910
Topic: The rapid development of the furniture industry brought thousands of Europeans, particularly Dutch and Poles, into Grand Rapids. Religion gave the immigrants a new home but also became the focus of intra- and inter-group conflict. Meanwhile, one church of the native-born took over the city's political leadership.

CHAPTER 5 TAMING THE INDUSTRIAL CITY 89

Time: 1906–1920
Topic: This era saw Grand Rapids, like the nation at large, trying to manage the tensions of urban-industrial growth. Fountain Street Baptist Church took the lead in this process, as it fought the furniture strike of 1911, sponsored the municipal charter revision of 1916, and led the patriotic fervor of World War I. Local Catholics and Dutch Reformed resisted these crusades with mixed success.

CHAPTER 6 THE FUNDAMENTALIST CRUSADE 107

Time: 1920s
Topic: Grand Rapids took a notable role in the nationwide "civil war" between liberal and fundamentalist Protestants. It also saw a parallel battle in the Dutch Reformed community. These put stress on older, established congregations in the community.

Maps

The congregations featured in the text are located on one or more maps in their respective chapters. Each map fits the time period of the chapter; particular attention was given in the first five maps to reflect changes in the city's landscape. The city reorganized the street numbering system in 1912 at which time many streets changed names. In the early maps, the original street name is used with the present-day name in parentheses. The map on this page shows the 1993 city limits and how the maps in the suburbs relate to those downtown.

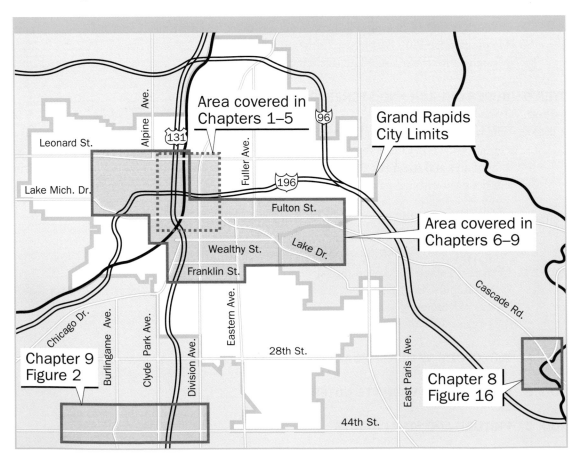

Acknowledgments

Bringing centuries of religious history to life is a task that requires the work, support and inspiration of many individuals and organizations. When the building blocks for such a project materialize, significant accomplishment can follow. So it was with *Gathered at the River*.

The project began with the inspiration of Norbert Hruby, president emeritus of Aquinas College and president of the board of directors of the Grand Rapids Area Council for the Humanities. His vision challenged and sustained all the participants through the three years of labor this book represents.

The Humanities Council also is indebted to a host of people throughout the Grand Rapids area who compiled the histories of their own congregations after receiving training through the Council. Their enthusiastic efforts provided a foundation for this book.

The staff of the Local Historical Collections at the Grand Rapids Public Library, The Grand Rapids *Press* and its editor Mike Lloyd, and the Catholic Diocese of Grand Rapids enhanced the book's visual richness by opening their photo files to us. Institutional assistance came from the Grand Rapids Public Library and from Provost Gordon L. Van Harn of Calvin College who granted author James D. Bratt research leave that helped keep book production on schedule. Special thanks go to Gordon L. Olson, city historian of Grand Rapids; Richard H. Harms, archivist at the Grand Rapids Public Library; and Herbert J. Brinks, archivist at Calvin College, for pointing to resources that helped strengthen the walls of this project.

Myriad angels gave the financial support to build a roof over this house. In particular, we are grateful to the Michigan Humanities Council, long-time supporters of the Grand Rapids Council. It provided initial funding for the training of volunteer church historians and supported the project generously through its duration. Other major benefactors included the Steelcase Foundation, which provided the initial challenge grants; the Sebastian Foundation; Meijer Inc.; the Frey Foundation; the Burke E. Porter Foundation; the Keller Foundation; the Tom and Mickie Fox Family Fund of the Grand Rapids Foundation; the Boersma Charitable Foundation; the Cook Charitable Foundation; the Robert L. and Judith S. Hooker Foundation; and Mazda Great Lakes. Without their support, *Gathered at the River* would have been an idea that simply gathered dust.

A foundation, walls, and roof do not make a finished structure. The heart of the book is found in the talents and commitment of the six-member team: three writers, an editor, an artist, and a photographer.

James D. Bratt, a Calvin College history professor and author of the acclaimed *Dutch Calvinism in Modern America*, provided the scholarship and understanding that wove the fabric for *Gathered at the River*. Christopher H. Meehan, a veteran reporter and former religion editor at The Grand Rapids *Press*, crafted the two dozen vignettes that vividly demonstrate how religion touched particular people. The Rev. Dennis W. Morrow, pastor at SS. Peter & Paul Catholic Church, painstakingly sifted through decade upon decade of Grand Rapids city directories and called on the persistence of volunteer assistants — particularly Ruth Stellino, Henry Ippel, Mary Rosendall, and Regina Waldon — to produce a comprehensive directory of extant and extinct congregations. As editor, Andrew N. Angelo, metro editor of The *Press*, wove everyone's contributions into a coherent product with a consistent style. Aaron Phipps, a graphic artist at The *Press*, created the maps and laid out the text and photos into a lively package, then applied his technological wizardry to produce the book on a Macintosh computer in the comfortable confines of his Walker apartment. Paul Crouse, a photographer at The *Press*, helped gather the historical photos and took modern-day photos of various congregations throughout the city.

Finally, thanks go to Bill Eerdmans, Jr., president of the William B. Eerdmans Publishing Company for believing in the project and agreeing to act as co-publisher of the book with the Grand Rapids Area Council for the Humanities while giving the Council full editorial control. In particular, Sandra DeGroot, production manager, stood by the book through publication.

We hope *Gathered at the River* pleases our benefactors and backers alike, and that readers come away with a greater appreciation of the vital role religion plays in the life of one community.

— Linda Samuelson
Project director and executive director of the
Grand Rapids Area Council for the Humanities

This project funded, in part, by

MICHIGAN HUMANITIES COUNCIL

HUMANITIES COUNCIL
G R A N D   R A P I D S

Introduction

Grand Rapids, Michigan has often called itself the city of churches. Of course, many places, from Portland to Peoria, make the same claim. Which one best deserves the title may be impossible to tell. It is better to think about why so many have made the claim in the first place; better, that is, to plumb the roles religion plays in a city's life.

This book tries to do just that in a preliminary way for Grand Rapids. Preliminary because the city has so many religious organizations, each with its own intricate history, each also enmeshed in the life of the city at large, that to try telling the whole story at once would require more research than any scholar would carry out and a heavier book than any reader could hold. Nonetheless, a portrait gallery has to start somewhere, and this volume offers a canvas painted from the palette of 25 congregations.

The 25 were selected not by some measure of absolute importance but as a fair cross-section — denominationally, geographically, chronologically — of Grand Rapids' religious development. They are placed where they are in the chapters because of the significant role they played at a particular stage in the city's history. Whether as forceful actors or more reflective mirrors, they all stood at the cutting edge of the era they are assigned.

Given these selections, what threads bind them? As to method, readers will encounter here more the sociology than the psychology of religion, more ethics than spirituality, more politics than personal prayer. Of course, the two sets build on each other and are equally vital and valid. That this account has the one focus rather than the other reflects my own interests and abilities; I trust someone else will write the book that evens the balance.

My own interests also have made migration the chief organizing theme of the volume. Migration includes successive waves of new immigrants coming to town, rebuilding their lives, changing the city's texture and shape. But migration also includes native-born people experiencing dislocation or social mobility on a changing city scene and looking to redefine — maybe even to refind — themselves in consequence. In both processes, I believe, religion provided vital resources and so gained remarkable significance in lives private and public. Believers themselves might be more conscious of their faith's bearings upon an eternal journey, of the meaning it supplies amid the confusions of time and the promise it offers of a better world to come. Given the long argument between critics and believers as to what religion finally is — a social function or a transcendent quest — I can only confess that it seems to be both at once, sometimes in ironic, sometimes in inspiring, but always in intriguing combination.

The book proceeds on two levels at the same time. People like myself, who approach local materials from the vantage of the nation's religious history, will find many of its trends coming through here. Those better acquainted with Grand Rapids history will find some new twists and greater depth in a story they already know. Grand Rapids both has conformed to and put a special spin on national developments. Readers can therefore treat this book as a sort of primer in American religious history and as the profile of an under-explored dimension of a unique city.

Surely the one fact that makes Grand Rapids different is the large Dutch Reformed presence in town. The pages that follow give that tradition just measure. Yet — surprising to many — Grand Rapids has long been half Roman Catholic, early on had a Jewish mayor and congressional representative (Michigan's first), and today counts one Pentecostal congregation as its largest and another as its best known. Another surprise to many: the majority in Grand Rapids' congregations is today, as always, female. The research for this volume shows how substantial a role women have taken in local religious life, from financing buildings to crusading for moral politics to training the young, greasing the wheels of sociability, and — of late — proclaiming from the pulpit. With such suggestions, this book hopes future studies will give this part of the story the full amplification it deserves.

While it is the first book devoted to Grand Rapids religion as a whole, *Gathered at the River* rests on the labors of many people who have studied one aspect or another of its subject. The end-notes acknowledge some of them — from professional scholars to amateur chroniclers, some long dead, others still active. All of these, and others, deserve our gratitude. Special praise goes to the Rev. Peter Moerdyk who wrote the religion section of Albert Baxter's 1891 *History of the City of Grand Rapids, Michigan*. Many of the references to "Baxter," therefore, could just as well read "Moerdyk." Anyone who writes about Grand Rapids' religious history stands on his tall shoulders; may our vision be as clear, broad, and impartial as his.

If the present volume offers an equivalent of Moerdyk's work, it is in the Directory of Congregations compiled by Father Dennis Morrow. So far as the available sources let us know, this is a comprehensive listing of every religious assembly that has ever existed in Grand Rapids. It confirms the amazing variety of the city's religious life and will give invaluable assistance to generations of historians to come.

All the contributors to this book have tried — whether successfully or not, the reader may decide — to keep their own faith commitments from distorting the account. We hope the congregations treated here find ours to be a plausible telling of their story. We hope even more that readers will recognize how many other stories — and other interpretations of those given here — remain to be told and then begin the process of telling them.

And so this project ends where it began — with a training session on the writing of local congregational history. That more than 100 people turned out on a hot June evening in 1990 to attend the session, and that many of them completed the 20-page manual they received that night, argues that Grand Rapids really *is* a city of churches. We hope they see this book as a fruit of their labors and that others take it as their own training session to go out and do likewise.

— James D. Bratt

Foreword

"Tell me your landscape, and I will tell you who you are."

Spanish philosopher Jose Ortega y Gasset's words written decades ago hold true today. Tell me you are from a small Utah town, and I am likely to know a good deal about you. Tell me that you are an African American in rural Alabama and that your parents were sharecroppers, and a certain image and expectation form in the mind. Tell me that your parents were Jews on New York's Lower East Side and that you never moved far away, and I shall expect a different outlook than if you grew up in the Dakotas on a Native American reservation.

As with the general outlook, so it is with the spiritual, the subject *Gathered at the River* describes in respect to the cityscape of Grand Rapids. The people of the West Michigan city could certainly have been gathered, saved, or called to service in a million other places. They do not have to argue that their place is better than others for the spirit, though many do; they do not have to complain that it is worse, as some do. It is simply different; it carries its own stamp. And being in Grand Rapids provides its own coloration to the faith as practiced.

How does one get a handle on the genius, the ethos, the peculiar story of Grand Rapids, especially in respect to things of the spirit? We would have learned little had this book concentrated on the individual pilgrimage of a maverick here or a path-breaker there. I doubt if we would have learned much had the historical committee and authors James D. Bratt and Christopher H. Meehan only made a hop-skip-jump tour of the several hundred congregations listed in the directory at the back of this volume.

Instead, authors Bratt and Meehan give lessons on how to tell the living history of the city's religious life. They always set the congregations into the web of reality created by the lives of their members in Grand Rapids. By choosing a few congregations in each period to illustrate response to main events, they build drama and suspense into the tale. Had the authors worked on "equal time" or a phone book Yellow Pages sort of venture, we would be bored by page three. By using a wider angle lens and then doing a few close-ups in each period, they succeed in orienting us without then disorienting us by telling too many stories out of context.

Bratt and Meehan are gifted storytellers. One completes the book "knowing" Grand Rapids religious life. In many senses, this may become a landmark book on how to discern the genius of congregations in their cityscape.

But are there some marks of religious distinctiveness in Grand Rapids? The city always has stood for "Reformed" and "furniture" in the public mind. Of course, that does not mean that the Reformed of Dutch extraction statistically predominate. As is the case with most northern U.S. cities, Catholics come in first. Then come two Reformed denominations second and third, one at half the size of the Catholic community and the other half the size of number two. Then come Lutherans and African-American Baptists and more. We are down to sixth or seventh before we come to heirs of the English-speaking Protestant world that dominated in earlier America. After these United Church of Christ and United Methodist congregational totals, it is still further down before Episcopalians and Presbyterians (the other two of the colonial big three) or the Christian Church (Disciples of Christ) or Baptists of the Northern movements (the other two of the frontier big three) show up.

Here emerges part of a profile: Grand Rapids religion does not follow the Anglomorphic (British Isles-rooted) pattern of so much of American religion, especially in its middle-size cities.

The authors show how influential Baptist missions and Congregational, Episcopal, and Presbyterian congregations were in the early years. These helped shape the old Grand Rapids elite. But one has to say that "they were influential beyond their numbers," because the numbers instead came from Catholic, Reformed, and Lutheran parts of the European continent. They came not speaking English and many developed "enclave" cultures. They were not fated to interact, either positively or negatively, as citizens were where most of them spoke English from day one.

Whether or not the authors intended to make this point, I think that words in the chapter titles suggest this organization of life. Mission. Settlers. Shelter. Soul. Religion in a culture of enclaves is somewhat different from that where the interaction always exists.

From this picture emerges an image that we might call "cozy" to much of Grand Rapids religion until recent decades. The two volumes on my shelves that direct people to pilgrimage sites in America do not suggest any Kent County spots. In Michigan, St. Ignace and Mackinaw City make it, as do various Native American chapel and mission sites; Greenfield Village is there in all its artificial American splendor, and Frankenmuth and Holland are cozier-yet places chosen to show off German Lutheran and Dutch Reformed cultures. Grand Rapids has more of a practical, "furniture-making" image, and that carries into religion, too.

But if you wanted to make a pilgrimage out of conservative Protestantism to publishing houses, Grand Rapids would be the first stop, and probably the best one anywhere. I have been with evangelicals and moderates in Cape Town and Kyoto, and they know the Grand Rapids zip code for names like Eerdmans and Zondervan and Baker. The conservative Protestant world, and some beside it, know Calvin College, though there are also representative higher education institutions of other traditions. And, perhaps as a maverick expression, a Protestant safety-valve, there emerged in Grand Rapids one of the Midwest's better known theologically liberal churches, Fountain Street Baptist Church, so well described in Chapter Five and one of the few congregations that engaged in battles with other denominations on any large scale.

The two largest churches, Roman Catholic and Christian Reformed, and then a sizable Lutheran body, historically have been the most stand-offish groups, so far as joint worship and activity are concerned, in American religion. That changed for Catholicism after the Second Vatican Council more than a generation ago, and the change did much for the new Grand Rapids climate. The Christian Reformed are so big and so influential that they can be relaxed about sharing civic responsibility and religious energies. Thus, if Grand Rapids religion often has been of the "enclave" sort, it acquired less of a mean cast than we find in many places.

From these sites and the many others treated in this book, one senses the serious spiritual quest of people who love God, their congregations, often their denomination; who have real concerns about the education of their young and the dissemination in print and by radio of their message. Theirs has not been a highly politicized religious front. Instead, they have religiously politicized their denominational and congregational abodes.

And in that non-mean, dutiful, devotional context of Grand Rapids religion it came about that as pluralism grew, so did hospitality toward the stranger, or at least readiness to get along with others. One evidence of that is the fact that in unprecedented ways, in connection with the Grand Rapids Area Council for the Humanities, the churches across the city pooled their resources and trusted good historians to tell a story that reveals more of a common narrative than one would have thought possible. The grand theme: people have liked their Grand Rapids environment and, in serving God in their separate ways, have helped build a livable city, one that holds considerable promise for the future.

Martin E. Marty
The University of Chicago

The Odawa Missions   1

FEBRUARY 1827. THE INDIAN VILLAGE NESTLED AT THE rapids of the river that white people call the Grand is quiet in the midwinter cold. Villagers await the promise of the growing season ahead. Two hundred acres will be planted with corn, squash and beans, or enclosed with rail fences for cattle grazing. Orchards planted to the north and west will yield a fine harvest.

Life is improving for the Odawa who have converted to Christianity. Besides the land, the white government in Washington has provided log homes. Isaac McCoy, the missionary and government emissary who has arranged all this, lives nearby in his own house. He holds services in a 500-square-foot pine church, and he teaches 30 students in a 400-square-foot schoolhouse. The lumber for the buildings comes from a sawmill powered by the river rapids. Nails and tools come from the smithy on site.[1]

On the river's east side, white trader Louis Campau has been set up for three months now and is looking forward to a good year of business, taking hides and furs in exchange for clothing, tools, and household goods. If some liquor slips into the bargain, he will not protest. Business is business; people — even Indians — should be free to get what they want, even if it breaks the law.

Nawequageezhig (Chief Noonday, as whites call him), the leader of the village, views all this with mixed emotions. The farms and orchards are not new; his people have been tending them for years. Mills and smithies are new, but their products are welcome. The church is interesting; he himself one day will go into the river to be baptized. The school might be good for the children; it is necessary, anyway. Campau's liquor is bad for everyone but seems irresistible. The whole white way, for better or worse, beckons. Yet the old ways were good.

His people's ancestors, when of such mixed mind, would wait for a dream or sign to sort it out. Nawequageezhig received his on Feb. 11, 1827, when a blazing meteor split the night sky and exploded nearby in thunder. The next morning he went to McCoy for an interpretation. Superstitious nonsense, the missionary declared; it means nothing.[2] The ancestors might have told Nawequageezhig better. The split sky signaled division, and so it was on earth: McCoy suspicious of Campau, and Nawequageezhig at odds with Kewaycooshcum (Chief Blackskin), leader of the village a mile down the river. The thunderclap spelled destruc-

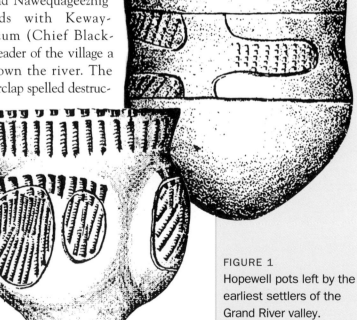

FIGURE 1
Hopewell pots left by the earliest settlers of the Grand River valley.

tion, and so it would be for the native presence on the Grand; McCoy foresaw it even as he preached there. The explosive light prophesied the brief, bright presence that Frederic Baraga, Michigan's most famous missionary, would have on the Grand six years later.

That such a portent came at this place and time was fitting. The rapids of the Grand in the winter of 1826–27 was the crossroads of the region's future. Competing visions of that future confronted each other across the water; they also divided the people on either side. Those visions must be understood in terms of religion.

A SPIRITUAL WORLD

Nawequageezhig's people were not the first to live in the Grand River valley. Wandering hunters likely moved into the area from the south as the glaciers of the last Ice Age receded between 12,000 and 8,000 B.C., and permanent human habitation seems to have begun here around the time of Christ. These settlers are known as the Hopewell people — more colloquially as the Mound Builders, after the large burial sites which distinguished their civilization. More than 30 such mounds once lined the west bank of the river in present-day downtown Grand Rapids. These were all leveled by white settlers, but 17 more still stand southwest of the city along Indian Mounds Drive. In them, the Hopewell interred their dead along with pots, tools, food, and clothing to ease the deceaseds' way into the afterlife. Modern anthropologists have used these items to reconstruct the Hopewells' earthly life. Whatever the Hopewells' intentions, their graves have given them one sort of afterlife — preservation in human memory. But for their religion, they would be lost to history.[3]

After the demise of Hopewell civilization, villages did not reappear along the Grand River until the 1700s. These belonged to a people from the north known as the Odawa, remembered by whites as the Ottawa.[4] According to their oldest traditions, the group started as a cluster of four clans in the interior of present-day Ontario.

By the time of their first contact with Europeans in 1608, they were settled on the northeastern shores and islands of Lake Huron. Significantly, the contact was with Samuel de Champlain, who was busy establishing a trading network along the St. Lawrence River ahead of his Dutch and English rivals. This competition would push the Odawa ever further south and west until, in the 1830s, they took a last stand for their lands in the Grand River valley.

The fur trade pressed all the peoples it

touched to hunt animal species to the point of extermination, then to fight each other for wider hunting grounds. The process caught up with the Odawa in 1641 when the Iroquois, bearing firearms from their Dutch and English partners, launched a war of conquest on their western neighbors by annihilating the Huron at Georgian Bay. The Odawa fled west, were repulsed by the Sioux, then led a counterattack that eventually pushed the Iroquois back south of the Great Lakes. Taking over the Huron role as middlemen in the French trading network, they settled at the strategic Straits of Mackinac. The French gradually replaced them with their own traders, however, so the Odawa spread across lower Michigan, setting up permanent villages at Detroit (1701), Saginaw (1712), the Grand River (1740s), and their new center, L'Arbre Croche (Harbor Springs 1742).[5]

For all its impact, fur trading held but a secondary place in the Odawa economy. Farming was their key to survival, while fishing and gathering maple sap and wild foods provided crucial supplements. The Odawa lived in tandem with nature but also with each other. Their society was first and last communal. Land was held by the village, not by individuals. The harvest aimed at supplying enough food for everyone to survive until the next season. Sharing and reciprocity were their deepest values, balance and proportion their reigning ideals.[6]

In this system religion was nothing and everything. On the one hand, the Odawa had no equivalent for the Western concept of faith. They recognized no natural-supernatural dichotomy, no impersonal forces, no fixed separations between the living and the dead, the visible and invisible. On the other hand, religion was enmeshed as the tone, texture, and framework of their whole round of life. Their creation story taught that water once covered the earth until the otter (alternatively, the muskrat or the turtle) plunged to the deep to bring up a grain of sand which Nanabozo, a god-like figure, made into land for all the animals to live on. From their dead bodies he fashioned the first humans, who generated clans named accordingly (otter, bear, etc.). In the Odawa universe every being and object had, or could have, a spirit — manitou — as well as a body. Manitous were powerful, could readily change form or embodiment, could be used for good or evil, and had to be treated with care and respect.[7]

Children had their own manitous revealed to them in rituals undertaken at puberty. The clans had their collective visions, too — stories descended from "the ancient ones," recounting the origins of the earth and the tribe, their own journeys and triumphs. Down through the years, these stories would be retold at great ceremonial gatherings. As dreams linked the visible and invisible, ritual stories connected the living and the dead. Mastering these visions was a vital skill, and some of the Odawa had a special proficiency at it. Contact with Europeans led them to organize more formally than they

had before, so that by 1700 lodges of midewiwin, or medicine society, emerged as a priestly order of healers and diviners. They became custodians of tribal legend and ritual and initiated prospects into the "killing" and "curing" properties of various elements.[8]

Such powers were in high demand since European contacts disrupted traditional ways. The customary goals of warfare and hunting changed from getting even to conquest, from keeping balances to extermination. Worse yet, European diseases decimated native populations. By 1600, Iroquois and Huron numbers had fallen 33 to 50 percent.[9] This ripped the fabric of kinship and continuity vital to the tribal world view. Native religion could suffer as well as prosper by its close fit with traditional life. But that suffering fostered less a conversion to Christianity than a reassertion of the old ways, particularly those aspects that struck Europeans as magical or pagan.

Ultimately, Odawa fortunes followed those of their European partners. Some of their warriors joined the French in routing British General Edward Braddock and George Washington in western Pennsylva-

FIGURE 5
Louis Campau set up his trading operation in the Grand River valley in 1826. He is shown here with his wife, Sophie Marsac.

FIGURE 6
The Rev. Isaac McCoy wanted to "save" the Odawa by separating them from the white man.

nia in 1755, but the eventual British triumph in this war confronted the Odawa with a less friendly regime. At first they fought back behind their leader Pontiac, who launched a full-scale assault on the British frontier in 1763. But a few years later, the Odawa generally sided with the British during the American Revolution. Again, they chose a distant partner against a closer and hungrier threat, and again they suffered the consequences. Their last armed resistance came in the War of 1812 when the Odawa followed the Shawnee chief Tecumseh against the Americans. Though the Indians proved the stoutest warriors of this campaign, they lost with their British allies at the battle of the Thames on Oct. 5, 1813, in southwestern Ontario. One of the leaders who carried Tecumseh's body from the field was Nawequageezhig, who soon returned to his village on the Grand.[10]

Amid all these contests the Odawa had settled in growing numbers in lower Michigan. They

had long been working the Grand River valley during their winter hunts but now established farming villages there as well. By 1782, these numbered 1,200 people and constituted one of the four principal Odawa centers. By 1830 they were tending 2,500 acres of corn and 3,000 apple trees up and down the valley, harvesting fish at the rapids and the Lake Michigan outlet, and carrying on trade at various posts.[11] The first belonged to Rix Robinson, who bought an existing French store at present-day Ada in 1821. Louis Campau followed at the rapids in 1826. The traders formed the vanguard of the white tide that flowed into the upper Midwest following Tecumseh's defeat. To sanction this movement, the 1821 Treaty of Chicago acquired all land south of the Grand River for the United States government at the cost of $1,000 a year.

MISSIONARY McCOY

Besides its benefits for whites, the Treaty of Chicago granted an annuity for a teacher and blacksmith to work among the Odawa. While the government called this the "civi-

lization fund," in fact the jobs could be primitive. That combination attracted the Rev. Isaac McCoy, a Baptist minister of immense energy, zeal, and ambition, and one of the most important figures in American-Indian relations before the Civil War.[12] McCoy figures in this history ironically, for while he set up a station at the rapids, he hardly intended to stay there. His greater design was to save the Odawa, and all other Indians, by moving them beyond the Missouri, far — and as he thought, permanently — from white contact. The other two parties at the rapids resisted: the Odawa rejected the temporal and eternal salvation he offered, while Louis Campau's clan could not doubt whom McCoy had in mind when he denounced the "heathen whites" who made the civilizing process so difficult.

McCoy was born in 1784 in Uniontown, Pa., but moved with his parents to Kentucky soon after. Though of Scots-Irish Presbyterian stock, his father, William, became a Baptist preacher on the frontier. He held Calvinist doctrine in honor but had only contempt for professional clergy and their ecclesiastical machinery. Isaac must have

FIGURE 7
One of Rix Robinson's main contributions to the Indian settlement in Grand Rapids was whiskey.

angered his father already at age 19 when he married and set out to become a missionary, on salary. Isaac dreamed of following the white tide to Missouri, but when his sponsors failed to fund his quest he turned to the Indians closer to home. He set up a mission among the Miami in western Indiana, then began badgering the Baptist mission board for more money, greater publicity, greener pastures. That practice lasted a lifetime. So did a pattern of constant relocation, political excursions, and long separations from his family. Through them all, McCoy somehow managed to father 13 children. His wife, Christiana Polke, who married him when she was 16, had to endure burying 10 of the youngsters, five in Isaac's absence.[13]

McCoy's adventures peaked in an eight-year flurry that saw him move from Indiana to the Grand to Kansas. It began in 1820 when he relocated to Fort Wayne. In 1822 he won the government teaching commission among the Potawatomi on the St. Joseph River, where, at present-day Niles, Mich., he established another mission. He named it after William Carey, the legendary Baptist missionary to India. The commission gave McCoy some leeway with his board

FIGURE 8
Cattle graze on an island in the Grand River in 1865.

THE ODAWA MISSIONS **5**

Caught Between Cultures, Rejected By Both

Adoniram Judson sat at the feet of Baptist missionary Isaac McCoy and for a stretch of his life dedicated himself to becoming part of the white man's world. Born of Potawatomi parents, Adoniram turned from his culture to learn more about the one McCoy presented him.

At McCoy's urging, Judson left West Michigan in 1826 to attend the Literary and Theological Institute at Hamilton, N.Y. He exchanged the buckskins of his fathers for the clothes handed down to him by white men. At the institute, he learned the ways of the people who back home were taking over his ancestral lands.

Upon graduation, Judson returned to the Grand Rapids area to spread the white man's word. He was seen as a forerunner of his tribe; he would span the cultural gap. He would bring his people out of the dark ages and into a new world dominated by whites.

"I went home among my people full of purpose and sanguine expectation," he told a reporter from the New York *Christian Union*.

Accompanied by his friend and fellow theological school pupil George Dana Boardman, Judson wanted to build churches and schools. He pledged to teach his fellow Indians farming and how to fix machines. He wanted them to have all the "blessings of civilization."

The optimism which had carried him through school and brought him back was soon shaken.

"Our people did not want such things. They turned from us with contempt and derision," he said.

The clothing he and Boardman wore was a sign that they had forsaken the native culture for the oppressive ways of whites. Soon, he found himself an outsider, neither white nor Indian.

"We gave up in despair. Our own people fairly drove us away from them as useless and disagreeable members of their society," he recalled.

But he didn't disappear into the woods or hide himself in some larger city — yet. He heard of a teaching job as principal of a school near what is today Prairieville, south of Grand Rapids. Teaching other Indians and some whites at a mission site there, he found himself happy and fulfilled.

Again, however, the rift between the cultures became clear when he fell in love with one of his pupils, a white girl. Drawn to her beauty and intelligence, he courted her. When he proposed marriage, the impossibility of the life he had chosen became painfully clear.

The girl's father said to his proposal: "What! You, an Indian, presume to address our daughter! Our daughter marry an Indian? You are crazy. She might as well marry a Negro. You will never be anything but an Indian for all of your education."

Crushed to the core, he resigned his job the next day. He gave away his suit and boots. He put on moccasins, leggings and blanket, and returned to the woods.

"I shall thus live and die among my own people," he told the reporter. "This was three years ago, and for the future I can only be an Indian, as God has made me."

FIGURE 9

Adoniram Judson was born a Potawatomi but took up the ways of white people. He eventually returned to his roots.

but it still was not enough. He immediately began working his government contacts for the Odawa commission, too. He journeyed to Detroit to lobby Gov. Lewis Cass and to Washington, D.C., where he huddled with Secretary of War John C. Calhoun. McCoy did not set up at Carey Mission until December 1822 and had to wait until the next spring to visit the Odawa.[14]

He finally arrived at the rapids on May 30, 1823. His reception was hostile. Many Odawa were drinking and few responded to his call for a council. After some inquiries McCoy learned that the majority regarded the 1821 treaty as fraudulent and viewed his visit as an attempt to trick them into ratifying it.[15] Just three days later McCoy left, quite discouraged. This would be the fourth mission he had started and, by the looks of it, the fourth time his labors would be in vain. Through white deception and the blandishments of liquor, the Odawa, too, were losing their lands, their pride, their dignity. The prospects of Christian civilization were being washed away in a flood of white corruption — more exactly, as McCoy often repeated, by the low-class depravities which fur traders everywhere represented. It was on his journey home from the Grand in early June 1823, McCoy's memoirs record, that he "... *formed the resolution that I would, Providence permitting, thenceforward keep steadily in view, and endeavour to promote a plan for colonizing the natives in a country to be made forever theirs, west of the state of Missouri, and from that time until the present I have considered the promotion of this design as the most important business of my life."*

He immediately set to work, writing Cass and his old friend Richard Johnson, U.S. senator from Kentucky. In January 1824 he went to Washington again and had an audience with President James Monroe.[16]

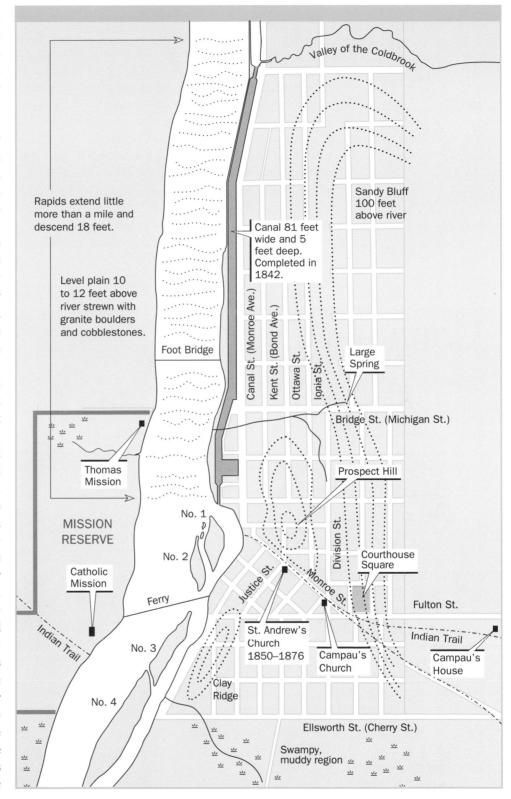

FIGURE 10
The map combines the 1842 plat map of Grand Rapids with some of the prominent geographical features of the area.

McCoy's grievances were not imaginary. John Jacob Astor's American Fur Company, which Rix Robinson represented at Ada, was landing 5,800 gallons of whiskey a year at its Mackinac post alone.[17] All pronouncements to the contrary, the government's Indian agents either could not or would not disrupt this trade. And McCoy's plan had a certain nobility. He envisioned Kansas and Oklahoma as sovereign Indian preserves where, aided by white missionaries and led by their own newly educated children, the tribes would build farms, towns, manufactories. They also would form new political associations among themselves and eventually enter the Union as full-fledged states. Above all, they would keep their integrity, joining their virtues to the best of white civilization while avoiding the worst.[18]

Amid such dreaming and scheming, actually working with the Odawa was delayed. In June 1824 an Odawa delegation showed up at Carey Mission apologizing for the previous year's fiasco. Then in November more Odawa came down, "earnestly requesting" a visit. So McCoy left Carey on Nov. 24 and four days later met Nawequageezhig at Gun Lake.[19] There followed a semi-comic process by which the first permanent white habitation was established at the rapids.

Confusing Baptism

From the shore, high above the river, many in the crowd called: "Yahi tah yal, kitchee mokomon!"

Lining the banks of the Grand, the Odawa were enjoying what appeared to be a wrestling match between their chief and the kindly Baptist missionary.

In English, they were saying: "Hurrah, hurrah, the white man got him down first."

In the water were two men — one white, probably garbed in dark clothes, and one tall, dark-haired, powerfully built, with angular features and well along in years.

The white man punctuated the air with some hand gestures, leaned over and pulled the other into the river. As the chief disappeared, the cheer went up.

Those on the west bank of the Grand, not far from the fast-moving rapids, loved a contest. No one was too concerned that their leader, Chief Noonday, had seemingly been bested by the Rev. Leonard Slater, the village's new Baptist missionary.

As the chief emerged, water dripping from his shoulders, he may have looked puzzled at his cheering brethren. Didn't they know he and this preacher weren't fighting? Noonday, also known as Nawequageezhig, had just been initiated into the white man's faith.

It was a ritual, performed sometime in the summer of 1827, that would put the chief and his people in a better position to receive the many goods that the whites were bringing. With this, the whites would see that the Odawa were serious. They wanted to be a part of the white world. The old way was ending. Chief Noonday, veteran of the War of 1812, had just been baptized.

FIGURE 11
The Rev. Leonard Slater baptized Chief Noonday in the summer of 1827.

Although neither was fluent in the other's language, the chief managed to convey that he wished to escort the missionary on the last leg of his journey, a two-day hike to the northwest. McCoy welcomed the offer but had to confess to a more immediate need: whether from the food, the weather, or the rigors of his four-day trek through the snow, he had developed a severe case of dysentery. Together, McCoy's autobiography recalled, the two "found vegetable remedies in the forest" and the next morning proceeded on their way. The slow going allowed McCoy to note the lush variety of game and hardwoods in the region and to take some language lessons from Nawequageezhig.

On Dec. 1, the party reached the top of the later-named Prospect Hill, from which they could hear welcoming drumbeats in the village and see the Grand curving in from the north, nearly a quarter mile wide. To cross it, Noonday brought out from the brush on shore a canoe "smaller," McCoy thought, *"than I had ever seen before … placing it in the river [Noonday] directed me to lie down in it, as in a sitting posture there would be danger of capsizing. When I was thus adjusted, he said he believed he could get me across as I did not appear to be so heavy as a deer he had once taken over in the same canoe."* [20] The Grand wasn't quite the Jordan, but McCoy and Noonday landed safely on the other side.

Noonday took special pains to give McCoy a tour — in a sleet storm — of the area's potential facilities and points of interest. These included a salt spring and gypsum rocks that the Odawa considered sacred and that betokened one of the future city's key industries. Noonday's pains, however, were not McCoy's: The Grand Rapids scenery "would have been more interesting in pleasant weather and in better health." [21] More interested in nursing his bowels than in tourism, McCoy left the next day, but he did deliver on the promised blacksmith shop by the spring thaw.

He next visited in September 1825 to find his sponsors helpful but other Odawa drinking again. In fact, one of the former had earlier saved McCoy's delegate from one of the latter who charged him, gun in hand. McCoy now knew what his employees at the smithy had been going through for months, but he managed to steel them to their duty. He delivered to his allies the government-issued "ploughs, yokes, chains, and other farming utensils" he had promised, most of which, "as too often happens in such cases, were not of good quality. By such delinquencies the confidence of the Indians is impaired, and the obstacles to the success of missionary labors are increased." [22] None of this was calculated to change his mind about the necessity of transplantation. Building on the Grand still pointed at resettlement beyond the Missouri.

In any case it took McCoy a year more to settle at the rapids. On Nov. 28, 1826, Isaac, Christiana, and their sick child set out in a driving snow on an eight-day journey north. Their wagon bogged down in the mud, teetered on slippery hills, and was always exposed to a dangerously cold wind. Finally, on Dec. 5 they arrived at the rapids and McCoy formally opened Thomas Mission (named after another Baptist hero in India). He chose Christmas Day 1826 to open his school which, along with the smithy and a chapel, constituted the three

FIGURE 12
Louis Campau's homestead. It later was the site of the William Gay home, 422 E. Fulton St.

FIGURE 13 The Rev. Frederic Baraga founded the Catholic outpost along the Grand River.

Wild Whiskey

From a letter written by Frederic Baraga on Feb. 1, 1834:

"A few days ago there were many drunken savages in our village. A fur trader had brought them such quantities of whiskey that they kept on drinking four days and four nights. Our Christians were much saddened at this and were in danger themselves, and one of my best men almost lost his life. A drunken wretch came to his house, denounced his religion, and finally wanted to stab him. Only with the greatest difficulty the Christian averted the calamity.

During the same days, I, myself, had a nocturnal visit from these inebriated savages. While they were yet a great distance away their terrible shouting aroused me from sleep. When they came to my door, they tried to enter and shouted terribly, but I could not understand anything they said. I remained quiet, trusting in the providence of God, and when they realized that they could not get in, they went away howling. Whenever I notice that there are drunken savages in the locality, I lock my doors as soon as it gets dark."

parts of his complex. Two weeks later he held his first full council with the Odawa.[23] There he could put together the puzzle of the past three years.

The local Odawa turned out to be divided. McCoy had set up at Noonday's village, on the west bank near present-day Bridge Street. A mile south, below today's Fulton, stood the village of Kewaycooshcum/Blackskin, who had given McCoy the cold shoulder in June 1823. Noonday had endorsed the Treaty of 1821; Blackskin had opposed it. Noonday was affiliated with Rix Robinson, his sister's husband, while Blackskin favored Campau, across the river. Noonday would convert to McCoy's Baptist Christianity; Blackskin would join Campau in bringing in a Catholic mission. At bottom, the two chiefs were cultivating different sets of resources and patronage to keep their own leadership strong. Perhaps the rivalry made things uncomfortable for McCoy; it undoubtedly showed a tear in Odawa communality.[24]

McCoy's sojourn at Thomas Mission lasted just six months. In May 1827 the Rev. Leonard Slater arrived from Boston as missionary-teacher; McCoy departed for bigger things, yet professing to be more hopeful for Thomas than he had ever been about a mission. From December 1827 through February 1828 he was back in Washington, lobbying for his colonization bill. That June he headed a federal survey of Kansas, plotting likely spots for Indian relocation. He took along three Potawatomi leaders from Carey and three Odawa, including Noonday. When he returned to Thomas, in March 1828 and July 1829, he found things to be sadly "retrograding." The school was closed, the model farm unattended, "the whole establishment … in a state of dilapidation." [25]

What had changed to dim the mission's promise? Probably less in fact than in McCoy's sentiments. First, the Baptist mission board had appointed

Slater without consulting McCoy and with some digs at his government stipend. Second, and more important, Slater disagreed with McCoy's relocation scheme. He wished to nurture the Odawa on their home site and foresaw that no place, not even Kansas and Oklahoma, would remain immune from white influence. Third, Slater took a different approach to mission work. McCoy viewed the Odawa as a factor in a grand historical process; Slater saw their ordinary human needs. Where McCoy turned to government funding, Slater relied more on church donations. Slater lived as close to the people as possible, respected their customs, and learned the Odawa language, which McCoy never mastered because of the press of business. Slater favored village day schools over McCoy's boarding school model. Slater did the teaching and preaching himself, which McCoy often delegated to others. Finally, Slater seems to have always stressed gospel preaching, "soul-winning," whereas McCoy increasingly attended to social reform.[26]

For all these differences, however, the purpose of Thomas Mission remained the same. Converting the Indians to Christianity entailed "civilizing" them, often as a precondition. McCoy and Slater, like their counterparts among other tribes, demanded of the Odawa not just a new deity, cosmology, and ritual but new social relations built on the nuclear family, new land-holding practices more personal than communal, new gender roles (men would do the farming instead of women), a new education, and sooner or later a new language.[27] The demands proved too high, which explains why so few Odawa followed Noonday into the river to be baptized.

Nor did conversion bring earthly compensations worth the price. As the press of white settlers intensified, a new treaty was drawn up in 1836 ceding the lands north of the Grand to the American government. Slater closed Thomas Mission and led one-third of the village's 150 families south to Barry County. They left behind all the

FIGURE 14
The Catholic Indian chapel on the west bank of the Grand River was built in 1833 by the Rev. Frederic Baraga.

improvements they had made: farms, orchards, cattle pens, and a sawmill that turned out the lumber for the new white town on the Grand. Slater's party took along only their dismantled chapel. They re-erected it near Gun Lake, a site the tribe considered sacred, where Noonday had welcomed McCoy just 12 years before.[28]

PLANTER OF CATHOLICISM

If McCoy named his missions after legendary Baptists, the Catholic outpost on the Grand was founded by a legend himself. At this writing, Frederic Baraga is under consideration for canonization by the Vatican, but he is already memorialized by a huge statue at the courthouse of the Upper Peninsula county named after him. This "apostle to the Chippewa" — or Ojibwa — however, began in the United States as a missionary to the Odawa and as the planter of Catholicism in the Grand River valley.

Father Baraga was born in 1797 to a prosperous family in Slovenia, then a part of the Austrian empire, later the northwestern region of Yugoslavia. He received a sterling

> " ... our holy religion alone is capable of making them Christians and good men."
>
> — The Rev. Frederic Baraga

education at the University of Vienna, which would help him become an authority on the Odawa and Ojibwa languages. Ordained to the priesthood in 1823, Baraga served two Slovenian parishes until 1830 when he dedicated himself to American Indian missions under the auspices of the Austrian Leopoldine society. He arrived in New York City on Old Year's Day 1830 and at the Odawa headquarters in Harbor Springs the next May.[29] For two years he built up the mission there, then decided to extend his work southward. On June 15, 1833, he began a three-week tour of the Grand River valley that proved a smashing success. He baptized 86 Odawa at four different sites, including 46 at the south village on the rapids. Encouraged by Chief Blackskin and Louis Campau, he returned there to formally open the Mission of the Blessed Virgin Mary on Sept. 22. For worship he used a yellow frame house, complete with windows and dormers, built by a carpenter imported from Detroit.[30]

In numbers of converts, Baraga enjoyed much greater success than Thomas Mission. "The non-Catholics," he wrote his Austrian supporters, "cannot make any considerable gain among the Indians … Oh, what a glorious triumph of the truth that we profess. Praise and adoration to the Good Shepherd who so lovingly looks after His lost sheep!" He specifically invoked his mission's patron "Mary, to whom it is given to root out all heresies of the world … to destroy the false

[i.e. Protestant] teachings with which some of the poor Indians are already infected, and suffer only His gospel to reign everywhere." [31] Part of Baraga's advantage lay in the long acquaintance of the Odawa with Catholicism, which dated from Father Jacques Marquette's mission at St. Ignace in 1671. Besides, he had the good sense to appeal to their ceremonial sensibility. Where McCoy would mark Christmas Day by opening a school, Baraga used it as a winter religious festival that gathered the Odawa from miles around. Then, too, Baraga's conversion requirements were lower than the Protestants': not the full load of "civilization" but basic confession and proper ritual observance. Baraga did not disparage the civilizing process but was sure that "our holy religion alone is capable of making them Christians and good men." [32]

Even so, Baraga found talk easier than achievement on this point. Alcoholism afflicted the Grand River Odawa worse than those up north, frustrating his mission and even imperiling his life. In response, Baraga took a vow of abstinence and stepped up his campaign against the liquor trade.[33] This put him in a pinch. He knew as well as McCoy that the white fur traders were the problem, and not least the Campau clan, his local welcoming committee. His relations with Campau worsened when Baraga discovered that Louis, for all his French descent, was more anti-Protestant than positively Catholic and that in any case the family

FIGURE 15
Louis Campau had this yellow building moved across the river on the ice in the winter of 1834. Relocated from the west side to the east side just south of Pearl Street, the former chapel was used as a warehouse.

wanted the church to serve their community, not the Odawa.

In October 1833, Baraga proved his intent to stay on the Indian side of the river by beginning construction of a regular chapel there. Campau responded with his first — it would not be the last — fit of ecclesiastical spite. When winter came and the river had frozen over, he paid another legendary pioneer, Barney Burton, to haul the old yellow church across the ice to the east side, where Louis' brother, Toussaint, used it as a fur warehouse.[34] Baraga called on Austrian funding to finish his chapel. It was 50-by-30-feet with a proper steeple and an altar adorned by candelabra. Most strikingly, its walls were decorated with 18 paintings donated by noted Slovenian artist Matej Langus. The building was dedicated in an impressive ceremony on April 20, 1834. By then, Baraga could claim 26 more baptisms and a school of 33 pupils. He also regularly toured the Grand River valley and established a prosperous station at Masch-Kigong (Muskegon).[35]

Still, Baraga felt nearly as restless as McCoy. Sometimes his work seemed terribly discouraging. During his bout with Campau he wrote his sponsors:

"The condition of an Indian missionary, particularly of a new mission, is exceedingly hard and difficult. If it were not for the desire and hope to save a few unfortunate souls ... nothing in the world could persuade me to remain here, where paganism is so deeply rooted with all its vices ...." [36]

Moreover, he heard persistent rumors of a new treaty that would implement McCoy's relocation scheme. The Odawa did, too. The Harbor Springs and Grand River branches held a council at the rapids in 1834 to plan their resistance, and Baraga fully supported them. But the tide was running against them. The same year that Baraga came south (1833), a colony of New Yorkers also arrived at the rapids. By 1837 the local white population reached 500. So it was with "indescribable joy" that Baraga reported the arrival of a replacement, Andreas Viszoczky, and received his bishop's permission to start another Indian mission, this time on Lake Superior.[37] There Baraga went on to great fame; Viszoczky stayed to

gradually transform the Odawa mission into a white parish.

The transition was rough but Viszoczky handled it honorably. Born in Hungary in 1796, Viszoczky too had felt a call to the Indian missions. In 1834, his first year in the new country, the raw frontier tested his health and patience. At Grand Rapids he also was forced to cope with the second stage of progress. As long as any Odawa remained on the west bank, Viszoczky preached to them in their own chapel and in their own language. He also preached to the whites on the east side — in English, French, and German.[38] Then came *his* fight with Campau. Louis built a church on the east side — on the site of present-day City Centre — in 1837, out of gratitude for his enormous profits at land speculation. But he refused to deed the building to the bishop as church law required. Finally, one Sunday, Viszoczky vented his displeasure with the situation from the pulpit, removed his vestments, packed up the communion vessels, and invited the true Catholics in attendance to join him at the west-bank Indian chapel. All but the Campaus paddled over to finish the service there, leaving the east-side building permanently vacant.[39] Perhaps by way of judgment, Campau lost his fortune in the panic of 1837 and signed the church over to his mother. She sold it to the local Congregationalists in 1841.

FIGURE 16
The Rev. Andreas Viszoczky, here shown in death in his casket, succeeded the Rev. Frederic Baraga at the Catholic mission along the Grand River.

⌘

NEW FRONTIERS

The aftermath of the mission era brought its principals frustration, tragedy, and some worthy legacies. Louis Campau survived the crash of 1837 to die an honored 80-year-old man in 1871. The people of First (Park) Congregational Church used his building for

FIGURE 17
The iron cross from Louis Campau's church as it stands today in St. Andrew's cemetery.

27 years until they moved into their current structure in 1869; Campau's building perished in flames the morning of Nov. 26, 1872.[40] The rivalry between the two missions reached its sad, symbolic conclusion in the disposition of the iron cross that had adorned the old steeple. Over the protests of the Congregational minister, Madame Campau had excepted the cross from the sale of the building in 1841. When carpenters finally — on June 24, 1846 — got around to removing it, the cross toppled, killing one man.[41] Doubtless, the Catholics in town muttered about sacrilege, Protestants about obstinacy. Repaired, the cross stands today in St. Andrew's cemetery at Madison Avenue and Prince Street SE.

In 1847, Father Viszoczky began holding services on the east side again in a frame house purchased from layman Richard Godfroy with some of the $8,000 the government paid for the old

mission lands. While a new church was being erected on the rest of the lot, a fire destroyed the old house and the parish records. Viszoczky and his valet escaped only by jumping from a second-story window, but the assistant pastor's mother and sister, both named Catherine Kilroy, perished in the flames.[42] The new church, built of Grand River limestone, was consecrated seven months later, Aug. 11, 1850, on which occasion Viszoczky renamed the parish for St. Andrew, his namesake. From this has descended today's cathedral of the Diocese of Grand Rapids. At his death in 1853, therefore, Viszoczky left a vital foundation. Meanwhile, far to the north Frederic Baraga labored tirelessly as "the snowshoe priest," establishing churches along the Lake Superior shore. He became the founding bishop of the Diocese of Marquette and died in that office in 1868.

By contrast, Grand Rapids' Baptists had to start all over. In 1842 they founded the congregation that evolved by fits and starts into Fountain Street Baptist Church. Leonard Slater carried on with his Indian mission near Gun Lake until it was dispersed in 1852, leaving as its trace the grave of Noonday, who died there in 1840. Slater

FIGURE 18
The church that Louis Campau built in 1837 was sold to the Congregationalists in 1841.

moved to Kalamazoo, where he ministered to an African-American group and helped found Kalamazoo College in 1853. He served as a hospital chaplain in Tennessee during the Civil War and died at Kalamazoo in 1866.[43]

McCoy suffered in exact proportion to his grander dreams. President Andrew Jackson signed an Indian removal bill in 1830 but was candidly cynical about McCoy's proposals for Indian autonomy and statehood. These were never implemented. Nor did McCoy, for all his politicking, attain the high office he craved in the Indian territories. He finally set up his own mission board in 1842 but could find few missionaries willing to submit to his demanding rule. Worn out by 40 years of frontier trials, in 1846 he joined 10 of his children in premature death.[44] His life's work mirrored its Grand Rapids phase: for the Indians, but never by or of them.

The aftermath of the mission era brought its principals frustration, tragedy, and also some worthy legacies.

The local Odawa began to disperse after the 1836 treaty was ratified. Although they ceded their lands, they did retain hunting and fishing rights and managed to resist the McCoy-Jackson removal scheme. A few wound up in Kansas, some at the Ojibwa reservation near Mount Pleasant, more at the tribe's ancestral grounds near Harbor Springs and on Georgian Bay. Others took title to lands that a final treaty signed in 1855 allocated for them near Pentwater. Keeping title proved difficult, however, as fraud, inexperience, and the incompatibility of family farming with tribal tradition took their toll. Grand Rapids saw its last great Odawa gathering in 1857 when the government dispensed the final annuity payment owed under the Treaty of 1836. The transaction took place in the yellow frame building where Father Baraga had first gathered his flock and where Louis Campau had stored their fleece.[45]

Big Yankees, Little Yankees, and the Irish

VILLAGE FOUNDERS, 1835 – 1875

WHAT GOD WAS TO JOB, THE RIVER WAS TO THE FIRST inhabitants of Grand Rapids: it gave and it took away. The Grand gave settlers their prospects and their village its name, but in spring 1838 an unusually severe flood nearly washed them all away. Virtually every house was inundated and ice chunks floated through the streets.

Another flood was more metaphorical but no less threatening. That same spring, the tidal wave of bank failures that had begun in the East the previous summer reached Grand Rapids, wiping out its wildcat banks and several paper fortunes that had been made in local real estate speculation. The stream of westward migration shifted to Illinois and Wisconsin, and the village — literally and figuratively — barely held its head above water. Prosperity returned only in the late 1840s when immigration from overseas brought in a new wave of settlers and when a channel was dug along the east bank of the river to provide power for mills and factories.

The metaphors of deluge and drought, of flux and swirl, applied everywhere on the American frontier, of course, and dramatize the challenge facing people who would be remembered by quite another language — as settlers and founders, bearing stability and order. In Grand Rapids as elsewhere, the pioneers turned to religion as much as to government for that purpose, but even there had to struggle amid turbulence. To recall the river's character, churches first served as islands of security in a threatening sea, later

FIGURE 1
This early 1900s photo, looking west along the Bridge Street bridge, shows how winter ice would build up and cause ice jams.

as channels for directing the social flux to desired ends.

But churches also were conduits connecting the settlers with their past. Contrary to American mythology, the pioneers did not re-invent themselves or fashion a whole new world in the wilderness; rather, they tried to remake — or make good on the promise of — the places they had left. No sooner had the necessities of survival been secured on the Grand than the lines of class, culture, and ethnic origin reappeared.

Grand Rapids' three oldest congregations show the pattern clearly. First (Park) Congregational Church comprised a New England-New York band that carried on a centuries-old tradition of Puritanism and grasped the reins of city leadership. First Methodist Church attracted people of like background but from lower on the social scale, pursuing America's promise for common people. And St. Andrew's Church, the Roman Catholic parish descended from Baraga's mission, turned increasingly into a haven for Irish newcomers who sensed that, somehow, they had not yet really arrived.

THE PURITAN WAY

On Sept. 18, 1838, nearly two dozen people gathered in the dining room of Myron and Emily Hinsdill's house on Monroe Avenue.

Present besides the hosts and their three children were Myron's cousin, Hiram, with his wife, Roxalany, and their daughter; William and Hulda Henry, who ran the apothecary next door; newlyweds Kendall and Eliza Woodward; carpenter Samuel and Sophia Howland; Sally Winsor, the postmaster's wife, and her daughter-in-law; and a few others. After some discussion about religious matters, the group covenanted with each other to enter the bonds of Christian fellowship, pledging themselves to a common doctrine and mutual discipline. They solemnized the occasion with a communion service, passing the bread on a dinner plate and the wine in an ordinary tumbler.[1]

Thus was formed Grand Rapids' First Congregational Church. But so also had the Puritan settlers of New England organized their fellowships 200 years before, and their ancestors in old England for two generations before that. The people covenanting in the Hinsdill house shared more than belief and behavior. Despite their youth (Hiram Hinsdill and Sally Winsor, in their mid-40s, were the oldest) and recent relocation, they all had deep roots in New England and intended to replicate its Puritan culture as thoroughly as possible on the banks of the Grand. In that effort they were partially successful and irrepressibly earnest.

The Puritan heritage behind the Hinsdill

FIGURE 2
The Hinsdills owned the National Hotel, pictured in 1870, and it served as the first meeting place for First (Park) Congregational Church.

gathering has been caricatured a dozen different ways but followed out of a few basic principles. Historically, it had adhered to strict Calvinistic theology; demanded a proven, personal conversion; worshipped in a spare, intellectual style; and contended always and everywhere for public as well as private righteousness. Its group-mindedness showed up in its covenanting rituals and in the tribalism that marked New England's towns and families. Their God being foremost a lawgiver, New Englanders were not shy about trying to enforce His rules on all comers, regardless of popular majorities. They also were passionate for education, flooding New England and the West with a bevy of schools, an army of teachers. Finally, their disciplined lives made them successful at business, just as their religion made them wary of the hazards of wealth. Wherever Puritanism spread, the magistrate, schoolmaster, and merchant strode alongside the minister, a righteous ruling class in the making, eager to shape this world as closely as possible to the mandates of heaven.

By the 1830s, this heritage had lost some of its hard edges but not its soul. Over the previous two generations New Englanders had shown their mettle by disciplining the frontier of upstate New York.[2] Now some of these "Yorker" transplants were joining their home-grown Yankee cousins in settling the Midwest. First Congregational's membership list in the early years amounts to a register of this migration. To cite only the more influential names: from Vermont came the Hinsdill clan in 1835; Abel Page and Stephen Hinsdill, joining his relatives, in 1837; and the Solomon Withey family in 1838. From upstate New York came William and Sally Haldane (1836), Wilder Foster (1838), Martin L. Sweet (1846), Noyes Avery (1850), and Harvey J. Hollister (1850), a descendant of 1642 settlers in Connecticut. The congregation tapped this source for ministers, too. In its first 100 years, all of its pastors but one had a New England birth and education, and the exception was born to Yankee missionaries in Thailand.[3]

The congregation's first minister was James Ballard, a Williams College graduate, a schoolmaster, and a son-in-law of Stephen Hinsdill, whom he accompanied here in 1837. Paid $200 a year by a New England missionary society, Ballard had to supplement his church work with farming to get by, but he was determined to have First Congregational set the lead in town. He got his chance when the village's only recognizable church structure, Campau's deserted building, came on the market. The Congregationalists were delighted to seize the prize from their ancient Catholic enemies and sent Ballard and Stephen Hinsdill to scour New England for the necessary funds. They came back with enough to secure the building, to add the town's first big bell (a 1,000-pounder), and to install an organ. To fill the seats Ballard held revivals, including a 40-day run in the terrible winter of 1842–1843. To soul-winning he added

FIGURE 3
The Rev. James Ballard was First (Park) Congregational's first minister.

FIGURE 4
The Rev. Stephen S.N. Greeley served as a Civil War chaplain.

political agitation, campaigning for the abolition of slavery and of alcoholic beverages. When financial strain wore him down, he returned to his earlier career, becoming the first principal of both the East Side (1850–1853) and West Side (1853–1857) schools. Among his teachers were Mary and Celestia Hinsdill and other Yankee settlers.[4]

First Congregational's mix of religion and politics reached a boil under her Civil War minister, Stephen S.N. Greeley. He used Sundays for fiery sermons on the Union, weekdays to exhort young men to their duty and to watch them drill on the square. Eventually Greeley himself went to war as chaplain of the Sixth Michigan Cavalry. The church's women were no less active, raising $6,000 for soldiers' aid, sewing a mountain of bedding and bandages, and opening a pickle factory that shipped 5,000 pounds of product to the front. One of their

number, Annette Henry, who had been a babe in arms at the church's chartering, honored the cause on her wedding day by dressing her bridesmaids in red and blue to complement her bridal white, then sending her groom, Russell Alger, off to the fray.[5] He returned a brigadier general and went on to become a lumber baron, Michigan's governor, and a U.S. senator — all testimony, First Congregational people would agree, to the glory that crowns righteousness.

With the war's end, the city held a gigantic celebration, then roared into a business frenzy. In 1865 and again in 1868 the city passed $100,000 bond issues for railroad construction. First Congregational took a full share of the profits. Its new minister, J. Morgan Smith, a cousin of New York financier J.P. Morgan, brought with him a top 10 standing in his Yale class, a new theology, and plans for a new building. As to the theology, Smith turned from revivalism and Puritan orthodoxy to themes of progress and nurture. The warm glow of family affection, he taught, ought so to bathe children that they would grow up never knowing a time when they had not been Christians, loving, upright, and honorable.[6] Responsibility for this task lay with women — with mothers in the home and with teachers like Lizzie Hanchett, who for years taught the boys in Sunday school with the same devotion and much the same message as she dealt out in the city's public schools.

As to the building, between 1867 and 1869 the church erected a $75,000 "Gothic structure, dignified, correct, and beautiful," across from Fulton (now Veterans) Park. The congregation raised $20,000 before construction began and paid off the balance by 1879, despite the depression of 1873–1877. Again the ladies took the lead, shifting their fund-raising from Civil War relief to sanctuary decoration. With the building completed, First Congrega-

FIGURE 5
Russell Alger: Civil War veteran, Michigan governor, and U.S. senator.

FIGURES 6,7
The Rev. and Mrs. J. Morgan Smith.

tional had 1,025 seats to accommodate the 660 new members it gained during Smith's pastorate (1863–1883).[7] It also held a familiar, and significant, location: just like New England, Grand Rapids had a Congregational church fronting the village green, the symbol of grace over the central public space.

The church's women had ample energy left for civic leadership. Mrs. J. Morgan Smith, "a woman of charming personality and a New England conscience," helped organize an educational mission among the freed people of the South immediately after the Civil War; First Congregational's first minister, James Ballard, ended his career in that enterprise.[8] Marian Hinsdill Withey, a little girl at the church's chartering in her parents' house, turned into Grand Rapids' leading philanthropist. She not only led the fund-raising for First Congregational's new building but organized the city's premier women's guild, the Ladies Literary Club, managed the merger of smaller collections into a new public library, and helped start the United Benevolent Association Hospital (later Blodgett Memorial Medical Center), aided by her visit to Florence Nightingale in England.[9]

Park's women showed some militancy, too. They allied with Fountain Street Baptist's women in an anti-drinking crusade that dominated the city's political agenda in the mid-1870s. The campaign combined daily prayer meetings at the Baptist church during the spring and summer of 1874 with leafleting, vigils at alcoholics' homes, lobbying visits to lawyers and landlords, and a boycott of all liquor-selling grocers. The city council refused to dry up the city but did levy high license fees and strict regulations on saloons. The result was a partial victory for the church women: the number of bars increased nearly five-fold from 25 to 115 between 1859 and 1888, but the population rose eight-fold from

8,000 to 65,000 in the same stretch.[10]

Still, crusading zeal declined in the church over time. First Congregational's women reorganized as the United Workers in 1888, deployed in smaller cadres (the Tens) that continue to this day. For most of their existence these groups have worked at raising money for church improvements. Their records tell of quilting bees, picnics, rummage sales, strawberry festivals, Christmas bazaars, and bake sales that had the desired pecuniary effect but also served as strong female-bonding agencies. As one of their chroniclers summarized it: "Thus has gone the history of our cherished organization ... nothing spectacular, but years of steady service to our beloved church, and happy companionship and love for one another." [11] Family nurture continued then and to the present in First Congregational's persistently strong programs of youth educa-

FIGURE 8
The new First (Park) Congregational Church across from Fulton Street Park.

FIGURE 9
First Church's "great lady," Marian Hinsdill Withey.

Church Women Helped Heal the Needy, Sick

One night in the late 1840s, Mrs. Wealthy M. Morrison was summoned from her bed by a knock on the door. Answering, she was told a family was in desperate need of food, clothing and medical supplies. Mrs. Morrison left to help — as she often did as one of the organizing members of the Female Union Charitable Association.

Mrs. Morrison's agency was among the first efforts of Grand Rapids church women to help the community's sick and needy. Efforts like hers led to the creation of a home for the homeless and to a hospital that later became Blodgett Memorial Medical Center.

Similar efforts led to the formation of two other hospitals in Grand Rapids: Butterworth Hospital, the medical edifice atop Michigan Street hill, and Saint Mary's Hospital, a Catholic hospital begun by three nuns from Big Rapids.

Each of the three hospitals neared the 21st century as state-of-the-art medical institutions. But each had a special beginning that arose out of the faith commitment of a handful of people, primarily church women.

Not only in Grand Rapids but across the United States, the need for social services grew in the 1840s. Immigrants poured into cities; work in factories and other businesses was often hazardous. Conditions in the cities also led to outbreaks of cholera, smallpox and tuberculosis. Formal hospitals began to spring up across America.

In Grand Rapids, the Female Union Charitable Association — later the United Benevolent Association — opened a hospital in 1848.

The aid society took its mission seriously from the start. On Jan. 18, 1848, the members decided to help "three destitute families and one colored woman." A week later, the group met at the home of Mrs. Finnery and voted to help Mrs. Cassin, a widow living in Alpine Township who had lost all her belongings when her house burned down. That same afternoon the women in the society sewed new clothes for the widow.

Not 10 years after forming, the society bought a home for orphans near the corner of LaGrave Avenue and Oakes Street SE. The name it adopted was the Orphan Asylum Association. Other homes eventually were opened. A hospital was added in 1886. In 1916, that hospital, which became Blodgett, was moved to its current site at Wealthy Street and Plymouth Avenue SE.

Butterworth Hospital also traces its history to a body of believers. In this case, the faithful came from St. Mark's Episcopal Church.

FIGURE 10

United Benevolent Association Home in 1888. It's now the site of Fountain Elementary School.

In late 1872, two elderly members of the church approached St. Mark's leaders and asked for help. They had no home, no food, few clothes. The Rev. Samuel Sharp, then rector of St. Mark's, made a pulpit plea on their behalf. Soon after, a church home was established for the destitute members and for others. This home was only temporary, however, because Mr. and Mrs. E.P. Fuller, a couple in the church, decided to donate a permanent place for the homeless in their congregation.

The first year, six elderly women were cared for in St. Mark's Church Home.

In 1875, a larger home was opened to care for a growing number of sick and homeless persons. In 1876, a medical staff and house physician were hired. And soon the home also became a hospital.

But that home at 110 Weston St. SE proved inadequate. Grand Rapids' population was increasing, business-

FIGURE 11   St. Mark's Home.

es were locating here, and more people were experiencing medical problems. Another building was needed.

In an appeal for money to build a new structure, Mrs. George W. Fitch wrote to church members to remind them that what they were doing was being done in the name of the Lord. Her appeal was heard in 1887 by another church member, industrialist Richard Butterworth. He offered a site at Michigan Street and Bostwick Avenue NE for a new hospital. His gift of more than $40,000 led to the construction of a 65-bed hospital.

Standing atop the hill, the hospital was a testament to the faith of St. Mark's members and the benevolence of the man who made his fortune mining gypsum deposits nearby on the banks of the Grand River.

Almost in the shadow of the new Butterworth Hospital, reflecting yet another religious movement's desire to care for the sick, was a health care institution started by the Sisters of Mercy. The Roman Catholic order of nuns was founded in Dublin, Ireland, by Mother Catherine McAuley in 1831. Twelve years later, the sisters came to Pittsburgh, whence they pushed on to points west, including Grand Rapids.

The sisters came here in 1873 when Mother Mary Joseph Lynch, a nurse in the Crimean War, was asked to start a school by the Rev. P.J. McManus, then pastor of St. Andrew's Church. The sisters taught children here for several years before a few of them went on to Big Rapids to start a hospital for lumbermen.

Women were not allowed in this hospital until 1890. A unique dimension of this health care facility was the ability of a lumberjack to get comprehensive treatment by paying the sisters $5 a year.

In 1893, the Most Rev. Henry J. Richter, bishop of the Grand Rapids Diocese, asked the sisters to return to start a hospital here. He gave them a home at 225 Lafayette Ave. SE that had been donated to the diocese by the McNamara family. The 15-bed hospital was named Saint Mary's in honor of Mary McNamara, the pious widow who had given the home to the diocese.

Sister Mary Ignatius McCord, Sister Mary Anthony McMullen and Sister Mary Baptist Feldner arrived in Grand Rapids from the north on Aug. 17, 1893. The women set about right away cleaning the home, hiring carpenters to expand the structure, and finding equipment to use in their new hospital.

Whereas the hospital in Big Rapids served the needs of men in the lumber industry, this institution was open to all. Early on, Saint Mary's had two wards on the first floor costing the patient $1 a day for a bed. There were five private rooms on the second floor that went for $10 to $20 per week, and two in the attic. By the end of the first year, the three sisters who had started the hospital had cared for 69 patients. And they showed a profit of 65 cents.

Eventually, the sisters purchased the whole block. Over the years the entire site, as well as another nearby block, were taken up by the hospital. Today, a nearly $53 million structure stands on the same corner to which the three sisters came so many years ago from ministering to sick and injured lumbermen in the north.

FIGURE 12   Saint Mary's Hospital.

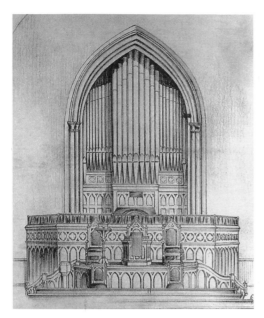

FIGURE 13
Drawing by C. Bjorncrontz of
First Park Church's organ in
1868.

tion. In fact, the tribal instinct was strong enough by the 1890s to trump theology. When a daughter of the church, Jessie Smith, married Charles Garfield, the groom applied for membership despite his forthright Universalist convictions. Confronted with this most un-Calvinistic prospect, the church board thought a moment, then assented to one deacon's declaration: "If Charlie Garfield is good enough for our Jessie Smith, he's good enough for Park Church." [12]

Prosperity also had its effects. Between 1904 and 1912, the church purchased 12 Tiffany windows that today constitute its most notable possession. In 1916, Charles Merriam began an 18-year pastorate that would move the congregation toward a high-church liturgy at marked variance with the Puritan tradition. The sanctuary was remodeled on a medieval Catholic plan by Ralph Adams Cram, the nation's leading church architect. A British visitor one Sunday morning recognized the resulting oddity. He watched as the ushers came forward, the congregation sang the Gloria, the minister turned to the altar and bowed his head to the cross, and in the ensuing silence, the organist rang a bell three times. But these were not Catholics consecrating the host; rather, Protestants taking the offering. Puritanism was breaking down in pastimes, too. The congregation which had in the 1850s and 1860s denounced theaters and dancing as "utterly inconsistent with the Christian profession," in the 1910s showed movies for neighborhood youth on Sunday afternoons in the sanctuary and in the 1920s sponsored a young couples' club that met for a weekly dance in the church hall. [13]

Through all these changes, the Puritan tradition of public leadership stayed strong. If First Park Church women led in the voluntary sector, its men held official posts with remarkable persistence, power, and tribal loyalties. When Solomon Withey's son, Solomon L., finished his education, he entered a law partnership with the famous pioneer, New Hampshire-born John Ball, and married Myron and Emily Hinsdill's daughter, Marian. After President Lincoln named him the first justice of West Michigan's federal court, Withey hired his brother-in-law, Chester Hinsdill, as court administrator. Stephen Hinsdill's daughter married James Ballard; his granddaughter married W. Millard Palmer, Grand Rapids' mayor from 1902 to 1904. Palmer was the

FIGURE 14
The Morton House was
built in 1873 on the site of
the National Hotel.

third First Church man to hold that office. Wilder Foster had served there before, then went on to Congress, as would Park Church's Carl Mapes. Solomon L. Withey was followed on the federal bench by Park Churchers Arthur Dennison and Fred M. Raymond. The congregation also sired three U.S. senators besides their adopted Russell Alger: John Patton, William Alden Smith, and Arthur Vandenberg.[14]

As to business, Myron Hinsdill's house was big enough for the church's charter meeting because it doubled as the city's first hotel. This developed into the Morton House which in its time matched the hotel of Park Church member (and former mayor) Martin Sweet as the city's premier public accommodation. Before that enterprise, Sweet began the area's largest flour mill and the city's leading bank, the First National. The bank's manager was Park Church deacon and Sunday school superintendent Harvey J. Hollister. On the board of directors sat Solomon L. Withey and another Park Church trustee, J.H. Martin. Hollister also managed this firm's successor, Old National Bank, under much the same board. His daughter, Mary, married Grand Rapids lawyer and Park Church member McGeorge Bundy. The marriage produced Harvey Hollister Bundy, who took the family name back East and into the highest echelons of national power. After graduating from Yale in 1909 and clerking with Judge Oliver Wendell Holmes, Jr., Bundy married into Boston's Lowell clan and entered a lifelong

collaboration with Secretary of State, later of War, Henry Stimson. Bundy's son, thus Harvey Hollister's great-grandson, was the more famous McGeorge, ghostwriter of Stimson's memoirs and architect of President John F. Kennedy's Vietnam policy. To bring things full circle, such foreign interventionism had long been anathema to Stimson's Washington rival, First Church's Senator Arthur Vandenberg.[15]

The later McGeorge Bundy's exploits were, arguably, as far removed from Puritanism as his consciousness was from Grand Rapids, and some of Park's movers and shakers doubtless used their church membership as a convenience. But the integrity among many others was unmistakable. Harvey Hollister, for instance, put as much stock by his church posts as by his banking. To his mind economic power and prosperity survived only so long as he observed the truths of the Gospel and the unshakable moral law it taught. More poignantly, William Haldane, the city's pioneer furniture maker and a member at Park since 1837, always went by his church title, Deacon. For all his cabinetry, he took greatest

FIGURES 15, 16
Photos of Park Church member Martin Sweet's hotel. Photo on the left was taken during his years as mayor in the mid-1860s. Photo on the right is from the mid-1870s.

FIGURE 17
Prominent Park Church layman and furniture industry pioneer, William "Deacon" Haldane.

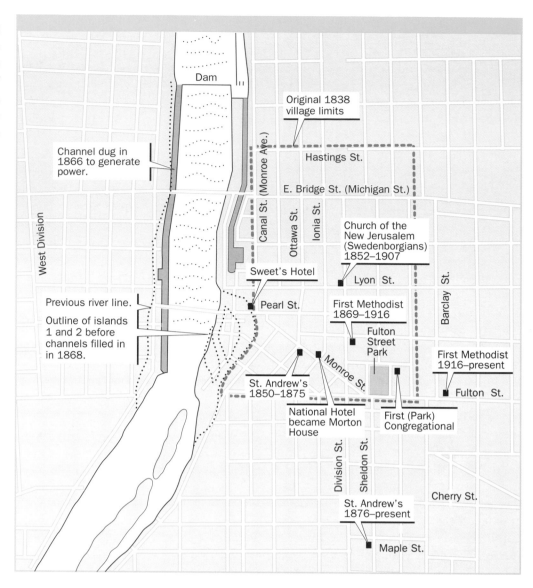

FIGURE 18
Many modifications were made to the river banks with the filling in of channels around islands No. 1 and 2 and the building of the West Side power canal.

pride in serving communion — for many years, the wine pressed from his own grapes, the bread baked Saturday afternoons by his wife, Sally. As late as the 1890s, William helped distribute the elements at worship, tottering up and down the aisles while the congregation waited breathless for the plates to crash to the floor. They never did.[16] Haldane died in 1898 at 90 years of age, his happiest achievement being 50 years a Park Church deacon.

❧

GOD'S COMMON FOLK

If the Congregationalists could claim preeminence in public service, the Methodists left them behind on other counts. They came first, organizing the earliest Protestant church in the state in 1818 and the first non-Indian Protestant gathering in Grand Rapids. They also grew the fastest. In Grand Rapids their 27 members of 1835 doubled to 55 by 1839 and reached 151 a year later. Statewide, Methodists numbered one out of 40 white Michigan residents in 1830, one out of 18 in 1840; and that despite a 700 percent increase in the population.[17]

Such phenomenal growth resulted from the Methodists' well-tested combination of a plain message, organizational genius, democratic appeal, and the sacrificial devotion that made their circuit-riding preachers a legend on the American frontier. When first organized in 1835, the Grand River circuit stretched from Portland to Grand Haven. Two men were each expected to cover this territory every four weeks, traveling on horseback without benefit of roads, preaching daily to whatever scattered farmers they might be able to gather, sleeping in houses when such were available, in barns, under the stars, or in the rain when necessary. After a year of this, they could count on being transferred to another circuit to start all over. For such labors, one of the Grand Valley preachers for 1839–1840, Allen Staples, received $54.75 in salary and $6.75 in expenses. Staples worked himself to death in 10 years at this job, bringing 1,300 sheep into the fold.[18] Congregationalists might wait for those rooted in their tradition to gather of their own accord; Methodists went out into every byway to compel the rootless to come in.

The Methodist message was basic, direct, and unavoidable: repent and live straight. While its preachers hardly underestimated sin, they insisted — unlike the Calvinists — on the ability, the duty, of each listener to come to conversion by an act of free will.

Neither the circuit-riders nor their listeners were well-educated or theologically subtle. The Methodist message was basic, direct, and unavoidable: repent and live straight. While its preachers hardly underestimated sin, they insisted — unlike the Calvinists — on the ability, the duty, of each listener to come to conversion by an act of free will. Thereafter, the converted were to band together in weekly classes under the guidance of a pious lay leader, monitoring each other's behavior by exacting standards of morality. Every three months members of the local stations on the circuit were to gather for the Quarterly Meeting at which the Presiding Elder would hold baptism and communion. Every summer as many as could attended the camp meeting, where night and day the message of conversion and consecration would be leveled with great power and with the emotional, sometimes frenzied response for which Methodism was (in)famous.

Methodists were unpretentious and proud of it. They claimed no public role, at first had little social vision, and suspected high-toned folks like Congregationalists who did. Methodism had originated in protest against fancy, established churches, and it spread by appealing directly to the potential of the common people. Yet its organization was tight, even authoritarian. Presiding Elders shifted circuit-riders at will and brooked no scandal or laziness. Local class leaders mobilized group conscience against the wayward. One such mentor in Grand Rapids earned the reputation of being, in the city historian's words, "a conspicuous exemplar of perpendicular and conscientious integrity." [19] In short, Methodists bought their freedom with discipline — personal, moral, organizational — believing that the frontier's promise could be achieved only under strict order.

But no district was immune to temptation. Such staggered the Grand Rapids group twice in its early years. Their circuit-rider for 1836–1837 fell into adultery somewhere along the trail and was promptly suspended, leaving his stations unattended for the duration. Into this crisis entered the inimitable Mehitable Stone. She promised Michigan's Presiding Elder, Henry Colclazer (who also happened to be her brother-in-law), to provide room and board for a sufficiently tested preacher. She got her wish in autumn 1837, when an official Methodist mission was organized for Grand Rapids at a meeting in her living room. By 1840 the group could buy a lot at Division Avenue and Fountain Street NE for $200, and in June 1843 they moved into their own building, described by

FIGURE 19
Mehitable Stone played a major role in Methodist revivals in the 1850s.

FIGURES 20, 21
First Methodist laymen,
Luman Atwater, near right.
Gaius Deane, far right.

the congregation's historian as "a plain, straight meeting house for a plain, straight people." In 1849, however, the congregation was rocked by a sizable secession to the local Swedenborgian society, a body of dubious orthodoxy by any Christian standard. Three of the church's trustees defected, while the minister fled the other way to join the Congregationalists.[20]

Resuscitation came at the hands of the Rev. Andrew Jackson Eldred, who arrived in town in 1852, only 27 but already a preacher for 11 years. Eldred knew his business and within a year had a revival going that electrified the town. Schools were closed; people of all persuasions, and none, attended nightly services that went on for weeks on end. One participant, the Episcopalian and future mayor Peter R.L. Peirce, later recalled that the real power at the meetings belonged not to Eldred or any other man but to a woman "whose shout was of more value than any preaching — Mehitable Stone!"[21] When it was over, the revival was said to have brought 300 of the city's 3,000 residents to conversion, 79 of them into Methodist ranks.

By 1858, the year the Odawa left town and the first railroad and telegraph line arrived, the Methodists were numerous enough to have planted a second congregation, on the West Side, and still have 200 members in the first church. The same year, First Methodist admitted the young Julius Berkey, who would play a powerful role in the city's future as a captain of the furniture industry. A Ladies Social Society was also in place to raise money for church beautification. The building received its first coat of paint in 1860, earning it the title of "the Old White Church."[22]

All these were signs of the respectability that Methodists had long craved and always feared. Their dilemma arose from the very character of the movement, for while Methodism attracted people of humble means, it instilled in them a dedication that naturally bred success. Besides, in its modest way First Methodist duplicated Park Church's background; it interlinked "little Yankees," New Englanders of humbler origins but with the same tribal instincts. For instance, two of its first trustees, Luman Atwater and Gaius Deane, grew up together in Vermont, came to Michigan together in 1837, and founded an iron foundry here into which they took as partner Henry G. Stone, son of the shouting Mehitable. Other Vermonters who joined the congregation included Knowlton S. Pettibone, 40 years a

FIGURE 22
The Rev. Andrew
Jackson Eldred.

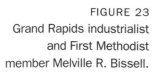

local surveyor and civil engineer, and Leonard G. Baxter, who arrived in 1835 and married into the first New York family (the Guilds) on the scene. Upstate New York also sent charter members James and Louise Ewing and Erastus U. Knapp, a farmer on the northeast end. Another titan of local industry, Melville R. Bissell, came to town from Hartwick, N.Y., via Wisconsin. While his main enterprise was carpet sweepers, he joined with his fellow First Methodist trustees Julius Berkey and Oscar R. Wilmarth (insurance) on the board of a felt-shoe company run by still another trustee, E.G. Studley.[23]

In the early years, the First Methodists accepted their lower status. Where the Congregationalists' first building cost $3,700, theirs barely totaled $1,000. Farmers, blacksmiths, stonemasons, and small shopkeepers filled their ranks, and their public offices rated a couple notches below the Congregationalists': constable, alderman, city undertaker. After the Civil War, they began a conscious effort to catch up. In exact coincidence with the Congregationalists, they built a new church on their established site. They moved into the basement rooms New Year's Day 1869 and dedicated the completed structure that June. Still, the building cost less than half of their rivals' — $33,000 — and saddled them with a debt that proved harder to work off. The Methodist ladies, too, learned fund raising, scoring a coup at the 1867 city fair where they monopolized the food concession and served up potables and edibles contributed by Methodist farmers. The 1873–1877 depression so hurt the membership that in 1882 the church still needed $15,000 to pay off its bonds. Julius Berkey contributed $5,000 out of his furniture profits; others covered the rest. Evidently the new building reflected the church's overreaching, for its dozen minarets earned it the nickname, "Church of the Holy Toothpicks." [24]

For the next 30 years, the congregation oscillated between its heritage and its ambition. They joined Park Churchers and Baptists to clean up the public sector, serving on the boards of the Kent County Bible Society, the YMCA, the Women's Christian

FIGURE 24
First Methodist's financier and furniture executive, Julius Berkey.

FIGURE 25
First Methodist Church's second building earned the nickname "Church of the Holy Toothpicks" because of its dozen minarets.

Radicals and Atheists

The American frontier offered room for every radical and eccentric brand of religion to bloom. And then there was Calvin Hinds. If not the village atheist, Hinds was certainly the town scoffer and skeptic. City historian Albert Baxter painted Hinds as a "a man of some education, of peculiar humor, witty and sometimes severely satirical."

Hinds lived out of town, west of the river. He had been unlucky at commerce, and somehow believed Deacon Stephen Hinsdill of First Congregational Church was the root cause of his financial misfortune. He made the contention most pointedly when inebriated.

As Baxter recounts:

"On one occasion when he was very noisy, some young men, one of their number acting in the guise of an officer, arrested and took him 'to jail.' Their 'jail' was an apartment under the rear of the Congregational church. It was closed with a strong door and a padlock, and, having locked him in, the boys retired a short distance. After exhausting his vocabulary of epithets upon his tormentors, he threw himself against the door, burst it from its hinges, took it upon his shoulders, and marched down Monroe, shouting: 'Here I come, with the gates of Gaza on my back!' ... While Deacon Hinsdill was in his last sickness, in his house a little south of the Division Street Methodist Church, Mr. Hinds came along in front of the place, one balmy evening, quite late, knelt down upon the grass, and prayed with great fervor and apparent earnestness for the man whom he regarded as his enemy ... closing with the invocation: 'O Lord, may his last hours be peaceful, and his soul, redeemed, be taken with the blest into Thy kingdom, if it be consistent with Thy will — but, O Lord, we awfully fear that it isn't!' Strangely in keeping with

his life was the death of Mr. Hinds, which occurred soon after. He said to several whom he met, when leaving the village one evening, that he had a 'summons to appear as a witness in the Court of Heaven' on the morrow, and that he should never come to this side of the river again. The next morning he was dead."

Calvin Hinds wasn't the only Grand Rapids settler who was decidedly unorthodox in religion.

According to Baxter, Isaac Turner, a respected millwright on the West Side, was "a firm believer in Spiritualism," a movement practicing communication with the

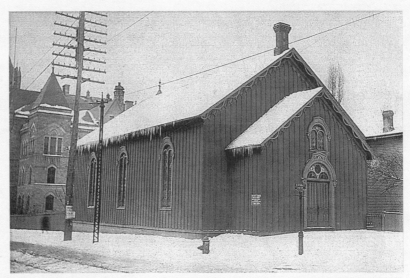

FIGURES 26, 27   Church of the New Jerusalem: exterior above, interior below.

dead and favoring radical experimentation with gender roles and social arrangements generally. Head of the local Spiritualist fellowship was Wright Coffinberry, city and state surveyor, inventor, archaeologist, Civil War officer, Mason, "unswerving Republican," and "life-long temperance man." Lucius Lyon, the surveyor who first

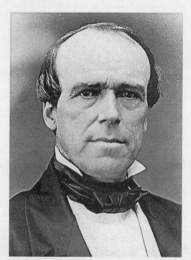

platted out the Grand Rapids area, led the local Church of the New Jerusalem, better known as Swedenborgians after their founder, a Swedish scientist-mystic.

Drawing on his visits to the angelic world, Swedenborg developed an elaborate allegory of the spiritual qualities of terrestrial objects. The group attracted free-

FIGURE 28   Lucius Lyon

thinkers and religious experimentalists of all sorts, though many soon moved on to something else. This affiliation hardly damaged Lyon's reputation, however. He was Michigan's territorial delegate to Congress and the state's first U.S. senator. He founded the local chapter of the Washingtonians, a secular temperance society, and also donated the land for his sect's church. Ironically, this building was more often rented out to other fledgling groups than used by its own.

The Second Congregational Church, Westminster Presbyterian, a Christian Reformed band, the Free Will Baptists, and the Disciples of Christ used it as a house of worship.

FIGURE 29   Wright Coffinberry

Temperance Union, the Anti-Saloon League. They held annual winter revivals, once hiring "the Boy Preacher" Thomas Harrison with conspicuous success. But they also accommodated their increasingly wealthy parishioners — Bissell; Berkey; his brother, William Berkey, also a furniture executive; John Widdicomb, vice president of the local furniture cartel; and James Lowe, a British immigrant who combined a profound piety with the business acumen that made his iron foundry one of Michigan's largest. By 1906 the Ladies Society had carpeted the Sunday school rooms and purchased silver service for the church kitchen.[25]

In 1913 the church made its decisive move. It sold its Division Avenue site to Keeler Brothers for a furniture exhibition building and worshiped in the St. Cecilia auditorium while raising what it claimed would be "Grand Rapids' Protestant Cathedral," an English Gothic complex at the corner of Fulton Street and Barclay Avenue NE. Being now in Park Church's neighbor-

hood, First Methodist also tried to match it in taste. The new building cost $205,000 exclusive of the Tiffany windows in the chancel and narthex. The speakers at its dedication services in April 1916 were advertised as scholarly, cultured, and Phi Beta Kappa. At the inaugural organ recital,

FIGURE 30
Laying the cornerstone for First Methodist's new building on April 21, 1915. The Masonic Temple is under construction in the background.

however, the Methodists' distinctly middle-brow tastes came through, as the new sanctuary echoed to the "William Tell Overture," the Bridal Chorus from "Lohengrin," and Victorian parlor songs.[26]

Unstable as that mix might seem, it served First Methodist well for another generation. The new building was paid off already in 1919, and the congregation's membership more than doubled from 700 in that year to 1,500 by 1926. At the same time the church increased its staff, its organizational efficiency, and its activities for young people to shield them from the raucous lures of the 1920s. These were all marks of the new American Protestant "mainline" that was first defined in that decade. First Methodist took pride in cooperating with its prominent downtown neighbors at Park Congregational, Central Reformed, and Fountain Street Baptist. For the less fortunate, already in the 1920s it opened the Methodist Community House on Wealthy Street SW to provide social and educational services among the mostly Syrian immigrant population.[27]

After the Crash of 1929, First Methodist felt some financial pressures of its own but not enough to keep it from completing the installation of a dozen stained-glass windows in the sanctuary in 1938. Donated by affluent members and dedicated to such themes as faith, prayer, and humanitarianism, the windows symbolized a congregation that stood figuratively as well as geographically in the center of the city. First Methodist could claim Grand Rapids' mayor, Elvin Swarthout, in the later 1920s, and the presidents of the three major downtown service clubs — Rotary, Optimist, and Kiwanis — in 1940. The congregation's long-time (1935–1957) pastor, Lester Kilpatrick, was one of the trio and chaplain to the Saladin Temple Shrine besides. As a 33rd-degree Mason, Kilpatrick showed the church's ease with the Masonic Temple that flanked its building on the east.[28] All this spelled a comfortable collusion between Methodist and middle-American identities; in the interwar era, the two seemed one.

That ease continued for a time after World War II. In contrast to Methodism's original rigors, First Church in the 1950s attired its ushers in morning coats, while Wesley Hall, its social facility, hosted dinner dances for the couples' club. Then the bills came due. As the automobile culture drew more people to the suburbs, a downtown location lost some prestige. The 1960s' youth revolt struck the Protestant mainline especially hard as young people from

FIGURE 31
The new First Methodist Church, at Fulton Street and Barclay Avenue NE, was dedicated in 1916.

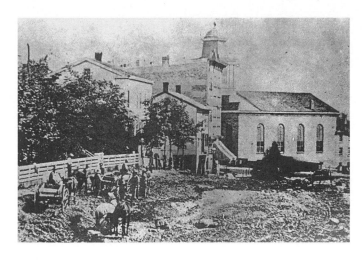

such churches increasingly let their birthright memberships lapse. First Methodist responded by co-founding the Grand Rapids Youth Ministry with its counseling and housing for runaway teens. It also widened its ecumenical orbit by opening dialogue with Temple Emanuel and with Father Hugh Michael Beahan, the cherubic emissary of local Catholicism.[29]

By the mid-1980s, mainline Protestant churches had stanched their membership hemorrhage, yet had clearly and permanently lost their old preeminence in American society. A congregation like First Methodist may find its new situation bearing some resemblance to its original circumstances. Set between downtown street people to the south and west and the college and singles population to the north and east, called to speak with people of other faiths (and none) but at the same time to renew its Methodist heritage, First Methodist today occupies a new spiritual and geographical frontier. Appropriately, its denomination is particularly open to women clergy. These might do well to recapture Mehitable Stone's vigor.

❧

MANY PLAIN, FEW FANCY

Given the numbers and energy of the valley's Yankee pioneers, Grand Rapids' Catholic roots are easy to forget. Yet the first white settlers at the rapids were of French descent, adhering to the Catholicism that had long been the only Christianity in the territory. Moreover, these settlers — the Campaus and their Marsac in-laws — could claim as venerable a North American lineage as any New

Englander, tracing their roots back to 17th century Quebec. At the signing of the Treaty of 1836, the 200 white inhabitants east of the river included as many Catholics as Protestants. That percentage dipped over the next decades, but by the 1906 federal religious census Catholicism had regained its original share, registering 49 percent of the city's church members.[30]

The low Catholic profile in the city's early annals must therefore be explained in other terms. First, Catholic social status seems to have been humbler than even the Methodists'. To run ahead of our story a bit: of the 25 men listed as sponsors of St. Andrew's new edifice in 1876 — therefore probably the most affluent members of the parish — barely half showed up in Albert Baxter's city history, which catalogued every local proprietor, professional, tradesman, and politician of note and a good many lesser still.[31] Secondly, the Constitution notwithstanding, Protestantism functioned as the United States' established religion in the 19th century, dominating the nation's politics, public schools, culture, and customs. In a real sense, Catholics did not count, whatever the census might say. As a "typical American city," Grand Rapids "had to be" Protestant. Thirdly, local Catholics at the start made it easy to forget them. For a dozen years after the

FIGURES 32, 33
The best photo of St. Andrew's original building, seen in background, on Monroe. At top right, a sketch of the building.

FIGURE 34
The Rev. Patrick Joseph McManus was the force behind building St. Andrew's Cathedral.

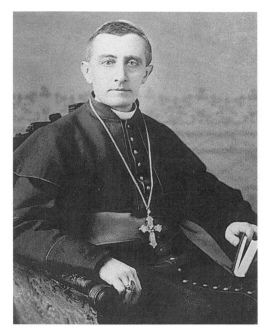

1836 treaty, their parish waned just as the Protestants' rose.

Their troubles began with the 1837 fiasco over the Campau church. The faithful who wanted services had to ford the river every Sunday for the next nine years to attend the Odawa chapel. Not that many took the trouble. As Father Viszoczky complained to his Austrian benefactors:

"The French, despite their higher civilization, neglect too often their religious duties, rarely appear in church on Sundays and holy days, are negligent with regard to the sacraments, and indulge in all manner of vices and excesses notwithstanding my warning and preaching .... I have a miserable little wooden church and a room for a school which resembles a stable rather than a human habitation. There can be no question of a parsonage since I can only live as a poor tenant." [32]

Viszoczky also had to battle the better-connected Baptists to get his share of the proceeds from the sale of the mission lands on the West Side. At first the federal government allotted $6,000 to the Baptists, $300 to the Catholics. Only a petition signed by Protestants and Catholics alike righted the matter, so that the Grand Rapids parish ended up with $8,000 (the Baptists with $12,000).[33]

With these funds Viszoczky came back to the East Side. He bought the Godfroy house at Monroe and Ottawa NW in 1846 and announced plans to erect a church on the site. Construction began June 10, 1849, using limestone quarried from the Grand. But the tragic fire of Jan. 14, 1850, damaged the new structure as well as destroying the old. When the bishop finally dedicated the new church that August, however, Grand Rapids' Catholics had, in their 80-by-40-foot, cupola-domed structure, the city's largest and finest building. Viszoczky used the occasion to change the parish name from Baraga's St. Mary to that of his own patron, St. Andrew.[34]

The new building signaled a revival of Catholic fortunes. The massive Irish and German immigration that began in 1845 brought hundreds of the faithful to West Michigan. Many of these were farmers, so St. Andrew's pastors and assistants had to undertake some circuit-riding of their own. From Yankee Springs to Ludington, from Ionia to Muskegon they toured four times a year, establishing parishes in cities, villages, and rural townships. They apparently suffered Methodistic burnout, too, as most of St. Andrew's clergy in the late 1850s and the 1860s served but two-year terms. With the French sector in the city declining and with the Germans starting their own church in 1857, St. Andrew's became more and more an Irish parish. It gradually added to its services: an altar society in 1855, a benevolent society in 1856, Stations of the Cross in 1858, a parochial school the same year. Next door to the church, Luce Hall thrived as a Catholic social center, offering a 1,000-seat

facility for rallies, concerts, and plays.[35]

These activities were supported by families of modest means: Jacob Nagel, small hotelier; Anthony Rusche, bootmaker; Patrick McGuinn, stonemason; William Riordan, bootmaker, constable, and eventually alderman. Bigger names slowly came on the list. John Clancy founded a wholesale grocery in town, shifted into lumbering in the north country, and died wealthy enough to leave $60,000 for St. John's orphanage on Leonard Street NE. His protege, John Caulfield, arrived from Ireland in 1858, took over the grocery business, added on real estate development, and built a palatial Victorian home at 110 Sheldon Ave. SE. John Killean moved to town from Buffalo during the Civil War and rose from groceries to politics, being elected alderman in 1882 and 1884, state representative in 1886 and 1888, and mayor in 1889.[36]

By 1870 the many plain and the few fancy were so crowding St. Andrew's stone sanctuary that a new building became necessary. To guide that enterprise the parish received the ebullient "Father Mack," Patrick Joseph McManus, an Irish immigrant and a grand success at building the huge frame church in Grattan Township. McManus bought $10,000 worth of property on Sheldon "Boulevard," the cutting edge of the city's prime Catholic neighborhood. On the site he erected a new school for $15,000, a convent for the Sisters of Charity who taught there (another $15,000), and finally the church itself ($50,000). The cornerstone was laid on May 30, 1875, before a crowd that a local newspaper deemed "the largest assemblage of people ever gathered in the city." [37] They were attracted, no doubt, by a massive parade featuring a detachment of the city police, the Germania Cornet Band, a West Side Irish group, a local Polish detachment, the Centennial Guards, the mayor and city council, and taking pride of place, the St. Patrick Benevolent Society, sponsors of the day, resplendent in new green and gold uniforms purchased for the occasion. This group did not fare as well in the novel competition McManus held to raise funds for the structure. For $1 a vote, parishioners could decide the name of the new building; St. Patrick lost out at the last minute to St. Andrew's loyalists. Fittingly, McManus had limestone carted from the old building to set in the foundations of the new. At its dedication on Dec. 19, 1876, St. Andrew's could boast of a 1,138-seat sanctuary to serve its 4,000-member parish, a wor-

FIGURE 37
Students of St. Andrew's School, May 19, 1886.

FIGURE 38
New bells come to St. Andrew's, April 11, 1909.

A Tale of Two Churches

The well-to-do woman from First (Park) Congregational Church was astonished to see large numbers of children at play as she traveled through the outskirts of the growing city one Sunday in early 1874.

This part of Grand Rapids — east of South Division Avenue near Franklin Street SE — was sparsely populated. The Kent County Fairgrounds, located on a tree-shaded plot nearby, was the area's main attraction. A horse-drawn streetcar line ended at Hall Street.

Stopping to talk to a man, the woman inquired: "Is there no church or Sunday school nearby that these children could attend?"

The woman was deeply disturbed to find children roaming so freely on the Lord's day.

"Isn't there any place of worship for any of the people in this vicinity?" she persisted.

"No, ma'am," the man replied and went on his way.

The name of this woman is not recorded. But she returned to her home and soon convinced several Park churchgoers that they had to do something to bring religion to this supposedly "heathen" part of town.

She and her cohorts soon learned that this neglected part of town was indeed served by a church. But it was for blacks. Located near Franklin and Sheldon streets, St. Luke's Zion (Colored) Church was the worship home for ex-slaves and railroad workers.

The woman and others from Park Church decided to ask the Rev. David Butler, pastor of St. Luke's, if he would rent them space in his church's basement. He agreed.

Soon, with Park matrons at the makeshift podium, the neighborhood's white children had a place to learn the Bible. The Sunday school would stay there until eventually moving out and becoming South Congregational Church.

"Our church was there and had been serving the needs of our people when they started looking for their Sunday school," said Mary Edmond, historian for St. Luke's.

Edmond said that once the surprise that the black church was there and was so active had diminished, and once the rental agreement was made, the two

churches began a "a friendship that has endured."

The Zion church did not boast wealthy patrons. In many ways St. Luke's members found themselves grateful to have a church roof over their heads.

The handful of worshippers came from families that moved here mainly from the South in the Civil War era when Grand Rapids was a minor spur on the Underground Railroad. Fleeing slaves did not normally come through this community, although a few did come to Grand Rapids for one reason or another.

Enough ex-slaves and other blacks had gathered here by 1854 to found St. Luke's, which affiliated itself with the African Methodist Episcopal Zion Church of America, itself established in New York City in 1796.

In its early years, St. Luke's members met in local homes. A history of the congregation states: "This local church holds the distinction of being the 'Mother of Zionism' in Michigan. It is the oldest such church in the state and was instrumental in the organization of the Michigan and Canadian Conference, the name given to the division formed in 1877."

The denomination was founded by ex-slaves and abolitionists as a vehicle to promote "the struggle for freedom in the larger society." Once in Grand Rapids, black men and women continued their battle for self-determination by beginning the church. In the late 1800s, there were probably fewer than 1,000 blacks in this area. Few

FIGURE 39   St. Luke's AME on Delaware Street SE.

were members of the church.

Following the lead of the denominational founders, members of St. Luke's wanted more than just a place to worship from the start.

"The purpose of this church was not only to attend to the spiritual edification of a people," Mary Edmond said. "Even more crucial was to attend to the totality of people. They were not just thinking of serving God in a classic way, but also serving humanity."

Renting the drafty basement to the church women from Park, as well as helping to start other congregations as Ames Methodist Episcopal Church, were examples of this outreach.

Never a large church, this AME Zion congregation nonetheless played a role in the formation of the city and its social conscience. The Rev. A.P. Miller, a member of the Negro Academy of America and a former missionary to Africa, became pastor here in 1901 and spoke out forcefully and passionately on the "race question" from the pulpit and at forums.

Evidence of the church's commitment to local causes came in 1914 when St. Luke's members raised money to keep open the Richard Allen Home for girls — a halfway

FIGURE 40   Mary Edmond

house for unwed mothers. And in 1926, the Rev. Moses Jones took to the pulpit and became active in many community and church affairs.

The history of St. Luke's and what had become South Congregational Church again intersected in 1950.

That year members of South put their church on Delaware Street SE up for sale and prepared to move into a $170,000 structure at Madison Avenue and Alger Street SE.

Needing a new home themselves but in no position to build one, representatives from St. Luke's were now the ones to make the offer. A deal was struck and St. Luke's congregation took over the building from South.

Members of both congregations were pleased that, so many years later, members of the white church were able to return a favor. A spirit that began with that first Sunday school agreement prevailed. In some ways, said Mary Edmond, it is a tale of two churches which have bridged the racial gap.

"We've had a dialogue going between the two churches for many, many years," said Edmond. "There has always been an understanding between us, a common history that began with that first Sunday school class."

thy competitor for the new Park Congregational (1869), First Methodist (1869), and Fountain Street Baptist (1877) edifices.[38]

The church gained even more dignity when it was made the cathedral of the new diocese which the Vatican carved out for West Michigan in 1882. But its parishioners and first bishop, Henry Joseph Richter, still felt at odds with the prevailing culture. Suspicious of the Protestantism being purveyed in the public schools by the likes of Lizzie Hanchett, Richter urged every parish in his diocese to build its own school. At his death in 1916, 86 out of 108 of them had. By 1895 St. Andrew's School enrolled 456 pupils; by 1916, 654. The parish also housed the new high school that the city's Catholics opened in 1906, and three years later it harbored the diocesan seminary, St. Joseph's.[39] This mas-

sive educational enterprise testified to the parishioners' upward mobility but also to a determination to nurture their youth in a distinct world view, whatever the cost.

The feeling of estrangement deepened under the pastorate of John A. Schmitt, who served St. Andrew's for 28 years, 1889–1917. Schmitt was known for three qualities: a quick pen that churned out popular tracts; a tireless spirit for the poor; and — as the diocese's historian put it — a "strong, zealous, often undiplomatic, sometimes rigid" manner in defending the faith. Not that he lacked for grievances. A local anti-Catholic organization was strong enough during the 1890s to earn denunciations even from Park Congregational's minister.[40] Schmitt's pastorate was followed by the 34-year term (1917–1951) of Dennis

Malone, whose first challenges were facing down the local chapter of the Ku Klux Klan and helping to fight a proposed amendment to the state constitution that would have forced all children to attend public schools. Malone received support from his bishop, Edward D. Kelly (1919–1926), who had handled many an objection as Catholic chaplain at the University of Michigan.[41]

The 1920s were not a happy time for any faith in America, and several of them responded by retreating into religious fortresses. Grand Rapids' Catholics witnessed the process in 1926 when their new bishop, Joseph Pinten, insisted on being "enthroned" at the Cathedral in an elaborate pontifical high Mass without a complementary civil ceremony. But the 1920s were also the palmiest decade of Malone's pastorate, St. Andrew's golden age. Its parishioners could walk to church from their solidly middle-class neighborhood along Sheldon Avenue or drive up from the suburbs "in Cadillacs and New Yorkers." [42] Even in tougher times, St. Andrew's felt a new sense of attainment. Francis J. Haas was appointed bishop in 1943, arriving from Washington, D.C., where he had served as dean at Catholic University and chair of President Franklin Roosevelt's Committee on Fair Employment Practices. As familiar with the corridors of power as were Park Congregational's eminences, Haas had worked to resolve labor disputes and contributed to American Catholicism's notable social witness during the hard Depression years.[43]

Tugged between prosperity and marginality, St. Andrew's lived in the paradox of American Catholicism from the 1920s until the Second Vatican Council in the 1960s. Vatican II tried to reduce that tension by renovating the faith from within and reconciling it to the modern world without. In fact, St. Andrew's anticipated both moves. Its renovation was physical as well as spiritual, for the parish began a major building project in 1961, the year before the Council convened. Besides replacing dangerously weak beams and faulty wiring, the remodeling brought the altar forward facing the people and attached hymnal racks to the pews, inviting better congregational participation in worship as Vatican II would mandate. Eventually the confessional gave way to a "reconciliation room" and the

FIGURE 41
Father Dennis Malone, pastor of St. Andrew's, 1917-1951.

FIGURE 42
St. Andrew's Cathedral was renovated in the 1960s.

baptismal font was brought back into the sanctuary, too. Parishioner Catherine Rose gave the greatest aid to the project by donating $100,000 for a new chapel and additional funds toward a complete, in-house television studio, the first in any American parish. Under the direction of Father Hugh Michael Beahan, it made St. Andrew's a lively witness to the entire state of Michigan.[44]

While renovation exacted a high monetary cost — some $800,000 — reconciliation proved more challenging. Vatican II's liturgical reforms disturbed many, some to the point of leaving the church, and its breaching the wall between church and world seemed to sap the commitment of others. By this time St. Andrew's membership rolls also had been drained by the white exodus from the neighborhood. The parish addressed both difficulties at once by reaching out to its new Hispanic and African-American neighbors. This involved special worship services but, even more, a radical change at St. Andrew's School, which became one of the city's pioneers at multicultural education and something of a laboratory of pedagogical experimentation. For young adults raised under the old rigor of "the sisters," the change might have seemed bewildering but welcome. Welcome also were the new measures Vatican II prescribed for parish life: a stronger lay council, including women members; liturgical variety ranging from majestic traditional to folksy charismatic; and small-group prayer and discussion meetings in members' homes.[45]

Vatican II tried to reduce that tension within the Catholic Church by renovating the faith from within and reconciling it to the modern world without.

Reflecting these changes within and without, St. Andrew's, along with Catholicism as a whole, fully and finally arrived in America. Its reward has been mixed, for it is as venerable and vulnerable as its downtown neighbors at First Methodist and First (Park) Congregational. Born in the boom and bust of the 1830s and ensconced in majestic buildings by the time that cycle returned in the 1870s, the three churches earned their title of founders and set a standard which later comers would have to emulate or consciously resist. If the three have recently sailed choppy waters, they did the same at the start. They can chart their course by looking to the past, but the pioneers they see there would have them set their eyes on the frontiers of our own time, and on a kingdom to come.

City Settlers: 3
The Dutch and Germans
1840 – 1875

IN 1857 THE ODAWA GATHERED FOR THE LAST TIME IN GRAND Rapids to receive their annuity under the Treaty of 1836. The next year the railroad and telegraph came to town. The two events marked an epoch in the city's development, as contemporaries were quick to note.

They allowed themselves a nostalgic tear for "the noble red man" of the past, then turned to rhapsodies about the future. Grand Rapids Mayor Gilbert M. McCray inaugurated the telegraph line with this message to Detroit: "The Valley City shakes hands with the city of Detroit … [to] congratulate each other that distant parts are joined together by that mysterious agent which makes all nations one and mankind a brotherhood. Peace and prosperity to the city of Detroit, and may her noble-hearted citizens ever enjoy the blessings of civil and religious liberty." [1] Detroit's mayor replied in kind.

Perhaps harmony was dawning across the miles that year, but near neighbors posed a tougher test. Consider the tragicomedy that played at Second Reformed Church, Sunday morning, Jan. 25, 1857. The minister entered the sanctuary to take the pulpit only to find some church elders barring his way. The pastor appealed, loudly, to the assembly; the officers shouted back. People rushed in and out of the building. Finally, another elder appeared at the rear of the hall to usher the

minister and half the congregation out of the church.[2] Worship was postponed for the day on account of stormy weather. But this was no passing squall. Out of the fracas emerged the Christian Reformed Church, whose presence — in fact, headquarters — in Grand Rapids more than anything else has distinguished the city's religious landscape.

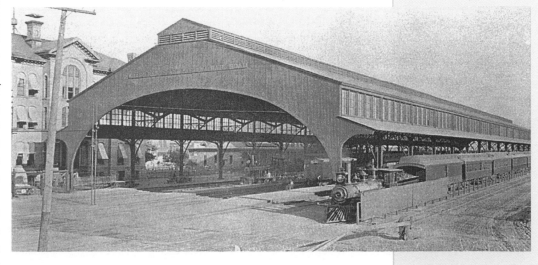

Of course, the telegraph and railroad did not bring in the mayor's promised peace. In a few years Americans would be engaged in the Civil War, the greatest bloodletting of their history, its carnage made worse by the advanced technology used to fight it. Nor did religion always descend into brawling; church sanctuaries usually remained just that.

But the notable churches founded in

FIGURE 1
Train shed of the Grand Rapids & Indiana Railroad with GR&I building in background at left.

these years show that Grand Rapids was facing the test of the mayor's ideals. The people of other nations were not staying at comfortable, telegraphic distance but walked the city streets. Prominent among them were Germans, who founded the Immanuel Lutheran congregation in 1856 and St. Mary's Roman Catholic Church in 1857, and the Dutch, some of whom remained at Second Reformed (founded 1849) while others, who left on that memorable January 1857 Sunday, organized Spring Street Christian Reformed Church, which was later renamed First CRC.

These four churches highlight the crucial role immigrants played in Grand Rapids' early years, and at every stage to come. At the same time, the fact of immigration profoundly shaped the congregations' lives. Their early records — of quarrels, short budgets, growing numbers, and resolute commitment — bear poignant testimony to the uncertainties of transplantation. While the immigrants seized the economic opportunities the city had to offer, they also were busy laying insulation in church, home, and school against the new land's cultural climate. By all evidence, many of them did not come to the new country to pursue a new way of life, as American mythology said they should, but to keep as much as they could of an old way of life — traditions their native

lands were threatening but which America gave them space to continue.

If the Dutch and Germans noticed the mayor's telegram at all, it was probably with a raised eyebrow. "Civil liberty" America did offer. "Religious liberty" — real, full religious liberty — was another matter; Immanuel, St. Mary's, and Spring Street all felt compelled to create their own schools, at enormous cost, to educate their children as their faith demanded. Nor did they hold much with the "mysterious agent" of technical progress. Their trust lay with a God who could lead down difficult paths but who offered a nobler destination than a world of new machines.

THE DUTCH COME TO TOWN

At the head of the Fulton Street hill, looking west over the river valley that holds Grand Rapids' downtown, stands Central Reformed Church. Its location gives the church the sort of eminence its founders had in mind more than 150 years ago. But it attained that position only after some brutal disappointments and with help from an unexpected quarter. Furthermore, its stature has come less from shaping Grand Rapids affairs, as its founders might have hoped, than from being a unique meeting ground for old Dutch-Americans and new, and for

FIGURE 2
The view of downtown looking northwest at the turn of the century. Second Reformed Church is in the foreground. Visible in the background, from left to right: the old post office, city hall, county courthouse, police headquarters, and the tower of the Berkey and Gay Co., which burned in 1943.

both with the American environment.

The first Dutch presence in Grand Rapids came not directly from the Netherlands but from the 17th century Dutch settlement in the Hudson River valley. George Young, a descendant of New Netherland, came to town in 1837 with other New Yorkers and prevailed on some old friends in Albany to sponsor a Dutch Reformed congregation here. The venture opened by drawing three families (that is, 25 percent) of the infant Congregational church who preferred the Reformed mode of church organization. They chartered First Protestant Reformed Dutch Church on Aug. 12, 1840, at the home of their pastor, Hart E. Waring, the only other member of Dutch descent. Their worship was a movable feast between the village schoolhouse and various stores until revival meetings in February 1841 boosted their numbers to 75 and made them consider building. They accepted a free lot some local land developers donated at Ottawa Avenue and East Bridge Street NW, and in autumn 1842 moved into a finished basement there that was constructed of 18-inch-thick Grand River limestone. The basement would last until the city's 1966 urban renewal project.[3]

Nothing else in the enterprise was as solid. George Young canvassed the East that winter for money to complete the building (he bumped into Myron Hinsdill doing the same for First Congregational) but returned with only $943 already owed in back debt. For the next 19 years, the congregation stayed in the basement, the superstructure roughed in but unfinished. Part of the problem was that the Bridge Street corridor became the axis of the German community, isolating First Reformed from its natural clientele. Worse, the spring 1843 revival brought more dissension than growth as the congregation divided over the church's direction and Dutch identity. In August, Waring resigned and First Reformed began a steady descent from the promising to the pathetic. By 1860 the church had gone 12 years without a pastor, dwindling to seven members and staying alive only out of the wallets of Young and the erstwhile Congregationalists Samuel Butler and Hezekiah Osborn.[4]

FIGURES 3, 4
Mr. and Mrs. George Young, founders of First Reformed Church.

But First Reformed did provide a signal service for a new Dutch flood that began to pour into Grand Rapids in 1848. Dutch immigration to the United States had commenced in earnest in 1846, owing to crop failures and hard times in the Netherlands. But the movement also drew off religious unrest. In the 1830s, some 130 congregations had left the Netherlands Reformed Church in protest against doctrinal liberalism, liturgical innovations, and state interference in church affairs. The government had punished these Seceders with fines and prison terms. A disproportionate number of the Seceders entered the immigrant stream, and the founders of the principal Dutch-American settlements were Seceder pastors or prominent laymen.[5] The most eminent in West Michigan was the Rev. Albertus C. van Raalte, spiritual, legal, and financial leader of the Ottawa County "kolonie." His followers found the liberty they were seeking easier to come by than the prosperity. Many of them, particularly young singles, took work in

FIGURE 5
Sketch of the building that First Reformed built over its limestone basement in the 1860s.

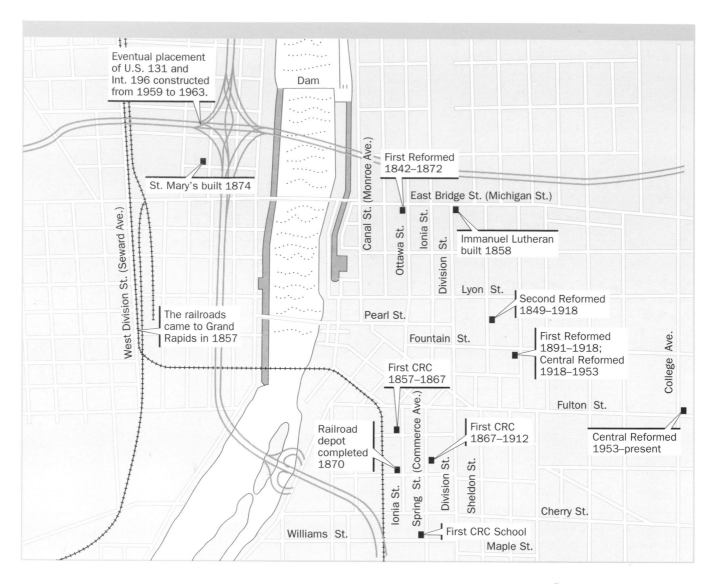

Eventual placement
of U.S. 131 and
Int. 196 constructed
from 1959 to 1963.

Dam

First Reformed
1842–1872

St. Mary's built 1874

Canal St. (Monroe Ave.)

East Bridge St. (Michigan St.)

Ottawa St.

Ionia St.

Division St.

Immanuel Lutheran
built 1858

West Division St. (Seward Ave.)

Lyon St.

Second Reformed
1849–1918

Pearl St.

First Reformed
1891–1918;
Central Reformed
1918–1953

Fountain St.

The railroads
came to Grand
Rapids in 1857

First CRC
1857–1867

College Ave.

Fulton St.

Railroad
depot
completed
1870

Spring St. (Commerce Ave.)

First CRC
1867–1912

Central Reformed
1953–present

Ionia St.

Division St.

Sheldon St.

Cherry St.

Williams St.

First CRC School

Maple St.

FIGURE 6
The map reflects the
addition of the railroads
and the eventual
placement of the freeways
in the 1960s.

FIGURE 7
The Rev. Albertus C.
van Raalte was the founder
of the West Michigan
Dutch "kolonie."

Grand Rapids as maids or laborers to supplement the family income. First Reformed lent them its basement room for Dutch-language services.[6] Eventually, their English-speaking children would return to fill First Reformed.

The man who organized these newcomers was Frans van Driele, an immigrant himself who shared the pattern of impoverished childhood and Seceder conviction. In summer 1847, van Driele took ship for New York where he worked nine months as a canal digger for money to get to Michigan. Once here, a month of felling trees in Ottawa County convinced him to try city life, so he came to Grand Rapids in June 1848. After four months of digging in the Grand River canal, he took a job at a flour mill. He learned the trade well enough to go into business for himself in 1863, and lived until 1900, a prosperous, respected businessman.[7]

But van Driele's real vocation was as a religious shepherd. Just six months in town, he was gathering five families, a score of young men, and more than 100 single women for worship three times a Sunday in First Reformed's basement. Van Driele married a widow from a village in the kolonie; to save money, the couple lived in the church basement. Already the next summer van Raalte formally organized the group as Second Reformed Church. By 1854 the congregation could claim 200 members, erect a pretty, brick church on Bostwick Avenue near Lyon Street NE, and call a full-time pastor, the 1849 immigrant Hendrik G. Klyn.[8]

Nothing among the local Dutch Reformed could go altogether smoothly, however. At the battle for Second Church's pulpit in 1857, Klyn was the minister barred and van Driele the stoutest barrier. But in contrast to First Reformed, Second quickly rebounded from its crisis, fed by the immigrant stream. A second wave poured into the country between 1865 and 1873, then a third, the largest of all, in the 1880s. In response, the church in 1870 put up a new $34,000, 1,000-seat edifice next

to the old one (which van Driele converted to a flour warehouse). Five years later, with its adult membership at 600, Second Reformed spun off two daughter congregations, in 1886 another still. These were named, with typical Dutch flair, Third, Fourth, and Fifth Reformed.[9]

This growth did not come by lax standards. The Reformed in Grand Rapids would long have the reputation of being looser than their Christian Reformed rivals, but the term is entirely relative to the latter's strictness. The ministers at Second Reformed preached consistent Calvinism in the Dutch fashion and in the Dutch language. The minutes of the church council record a number of would-be members turned down for insufficient knowledge of the catechism. The same records testify to an exacting moral code. Members were disciplined for working on Sunday, for excessive party-going, for drunkenness and gossip, for belonging to the Masons or other secret societies.[10] Frans van Driele, the "liberal" in the 1857 argument and later, in another battle at Fourth Reformed, was a man of profound piety,

FIGURE 8
Local Dutch pioneer,
Frans van Driele

FIGURE 9
The Rev. Hendrik G. Klyn

FIGURE 10
First Reformed building on Fountain Street and Barclay Avenue NE. It became Central Reformed after First and Second Reformed merged in 1918.

FIGURE 11
Re-builder of First
Reformed Church, the
Rev. Peter Moerdyk

FIGURES 12, 13
Picture on left shows the
burning Second Reformed
building just before the
steeple fell May 23, 1895.
Burned-out interior at right.

constant in prayer, keen in theology, and death on worldliness. In one of his last speeches, delivered at the 50th anniversary of Dutch settlement in West Michigan, he lowered the boom against the younger generation for enjoying the new land's economic plenty:

"And yet all [our] progress is not without its dark side. On [Lake Macatawa] today steamboats, on Sunday as well as on week days, are carrying hundreds of people to the parks dishonoring the Lord's day by boating, diving, swimming, etc. Possibly among these groups of pleasure seekers are to be found some of our younger children of the Covenant .... Possibly you are asking, 'How are these young people getting along, are they sending their earnings to their parents in the Kolonie?' Answer: Not many farmers' children are to be found in Grand Rapids, nor in other places, for necessity no longer urges them. And besides, those who nowadays are earning wages here and there themselves need their money very much, for if they want to be well dressed and follow the fashions, that costs money. Hence the complaints that the younger folk make only slight contributions to the church, for the poor, and for God's kingdom. This they appear to leave to the older folk, to the married people ...." [11]

A slightly softer touch revitalized First Reformed Church.

After sporadic attempts to revive the congregation in the 1860s had yielded little, the young and energetic pastor Peter Moerdyk arrived in 1873 to set a new course. Moerdyk, then 29, had been a toddler in the company that Pastor Klyn brought to America in 1849, and was among the first products of the kolonie's educational system, having gathered degrees from Hope College and Western Theological Seminary in Holland. He needed all the zest of the pioneers in his new role, to build the first English-speaking church in the immigrant circle. Moerdyk had little patience for Dutch parochialism but even less for the wavering path First Reformed had followed for too long. "I was profoundly convinced," he recalled later, "that this city had no need of us, and the Lord no mission for us, unless we became an unadulterated Reformed church." As Americanizing youth flocked to his church, Moerdyk drilled them in Reformed doctrine and quickened them to Calvinistic activism. The membership grew from 29 in 1873 to 140 by 1880, the year First Reformed finally weaned itself from denominational subsidies. [12]

The church had been liberated already in 1872 by the loss to fire of the albatross on East Bridge Street. During part of Moerdyk's pastorate, First Reformed worshipped in the Division Avenue building which its recent Baptist tenants had left for a new home on Fountain Street and which St. Mark's Epis-

copal Church had originally constructed in 1840. Upon Moerdyk's departure in 1891, the congregation was in the throes of another building project, this time at Fountain Street and Barclay Avenue NE. They stayed in its basement for three years, on Sept. 9, 1894, dedicating a lavish structure that featured a 700-seat sanctuary, a 100-foot tower, and stained-glass windows provided by the estate of Mary Ball, a long-time member and the wife of Grand Rapids' legendary pioneer, John Ball.[13]

What First Reformed gained, Second lost in a conflagration on Ascension Day, May 23, 1895. It rebuilt on the same site, a move some protested as equally foolish as First's mistake a half century before. With the two churches so close together, Second's reason for being was the Dutch language, and it had begun to phase that out in 1886. From two evening services a month, English expanded to take over all evenings by 1896, to the crucial morning service in 1903, and to the elimination of Dutch entirely in 1905.[14] Other signs of Americanism were rife as well. Prohibition, the dearest cause of Anglo Protestantism, had long held a privileged spot at First Reformed; by 1902 it was getting special Sundays at Second. In 1907 the two groups held exploratory merger talks, broke them off for a time, but finally

reached agreement in the atmosphere of World War I patriotism. On April 23, 1918, First and Second combined to become Central Reformed Church; they kept First's building, Second's parsonage, and sold the extra church to the Salvation Army.[15]

With the merger, immigrant memories were left behind; this was to be the Dutch flagship of the American mainline. For a pastor, the group turned to Grand Rapids native John A. Dykstra, a graduate of Grand Rapids Central High School, Hope College, and Princeton Seminary. The choice proved immensely popular, as membership doubled to 1,000 by 1940. Dykstra stayed on until his retirement in 1954. Under his leadership the congregation assumed the tone and social status befitting a downtown church. Drama guilds, literary evenings, and professional musi-

FIGURE 14
After the fire of 1895, Second Reformed erected the building shown above. This is also the building shown in the foreground of Figure 2 in this chapter.

FIGURE 15
The interior of Second Reformed Church at the turn of the century, decorated in honor of its 50th anniversary.

FIGURE 16
Central Reformed Church
fire of Feb. 10, 1953. This
is the same building shown
in Figure 10 of this chapter.

cianship blended with the positive-thinking sermons that Dykstra offered in imitation of the Reformed Church's East Coast lion, Norman Vincent Peale.[16]

Yet the Calvinist God still had some fire left, particularly the blaze that destroyed the church building and all its contents on the morning of Feb. 10, 1953. After some deliberation, the members decided to stay downtown and erected their present structure at Fulton Street and College Avenue NE.[17] Their course since then has followed that of their mainline neighbors at Park Congregational and First Methodist: confidence in the early 1960s, doubt and eroding influence in the 1970s. Sometimes the congregation responded with more peace-of-mind preachments, sometimes with bold political proclamations. Always, however, it could count on an influx of newcomers raised Christian Reformed but unhappy with the customs or demands that upbringing entailed. For such, Central Reformed has offered a body in touch with the Reformed heritage, yet well-tuned to the American world. Of late, the church has even revived some classic themes of Calvinist theology, combined with a service outreach to the displaced and homeless in the city's Heartside neighborhood. Frans van Driele would recognize the pattern.

FIGURE 17
Gysbert Haan

THE CRC TAKES ROOT

By the standards of polite society, Second Reformed took the high road of Americanization, First Christian Reformed the low. Its members had a gloomy view of the new country, held on 20 years longer to the Dutch language, and passed through more theological quarrels. But in the long run this path was more popular. Even though the Seceder share of Dutch immigration steadily declined over time, more Dutch newcomers affiliated with Christian Reformed than with Reformed congregations. First CRC's history shows why this was so.

As at Second Reformed, a zealous, self-trained layman figured large in the church's origins. Gysbert Haan arrived in America in 1849, two years after Frans van Driele. Haan came with his own family of wife and nine children and five other clans in tow. Haan tarried longer in New York, and in the process soaked up two years' exposure to the Reformed churches in Albany. The experience left him distinctly unimpressed, so when he arrived in Ottawa County in 1851, he immediately began criticizing the immigrant churches' affiliation with "the East." Van Raalte was strong enough in the kolonie to thwart the attack there, but Haan found better success after relocating to Grand Rapids.[18] Since van Driele was orga-

Church Building Boom of the 1870s

After the Civil War, Grand Rapids entered a building boom. Its population doubled and the assessed valuation of its property tripled. It started a streetcar system, sold bonds to lure in more railroads, and saw the furniture industry take off.

The city's churches kept pace. From 1867 to 1882, a dozen congregations raised new edifices, some costly, some remarkably inexpensive, all of them large. New immigrants as well as old settlers took part in the process. The buildings served as houses of worship but also as objects of pride, as competitive measures of status and influence. Above all, the new spires on the skyline and the stone fortresses along downtown streets asserted that the churches, like the city, were settled and mature. The claim to permanence was sound: seven of these buildings still stand today, six are still in use by the original congregation.

CHURCH	DATE	$ COST	SEATING	LOCATION
Spring Street CRC	1867	7,000	1,300	Commerce SW south of Weston
First (Park) Congregational	1869	75,000	1,025	East Park at Library NE
First Methodist	1870	33,000	800	Division at Fountain NE
Second Reformed	1870	34,000	1,000	Bostwick near Lyon NE
St. James Roman Catholic	1872	45,000	750	Bridge near Straight NW
St. Mark's Episcopal	1872	36,000	1,300†	Division opposite Pearl NW
St. Mary's Roman Catholic	1874	50,000	600	Turner at First NW
St. Andrew's Roman Catholic	1876	50,000	1,138	Sheldon at Maple SE
Fountain Street Baptist	1877	90,000	1,100	Fountain at Bostwick NE
Grace Episcopal	1878	10,000	340	Cherry at Lafayette SE
Westminster Presbyterian	1875–85	60,000	1,000	LaGrave at Weston SE
Temple Emanuel	1882	15,000	300	Ransom at Fountain NE

† St. Mark's Episcopal was remodeled and enlarged in the 1870s

SOURCE: Albert Baxter, *History of the City of Grand Rapids*

nizing the same audience for the pro-van Raalte side, Grand Rapids, with its prominent lay leaders, held much of Dutch America's future.

Haan soon joined van Driele on the governing council at Second Reformed. There and at every meeting of the Dutch churches' regional assembly (Classis) he agitated his cause. The denomination they had joined, Haan complained, offered communion to non-Reformed people, neglected core Reformed doctrines like predestination, baptized children privately rather than at public worship, and sang man-made hymns to the neglect of God-delivered Psalms. Haan also seems to have circulated his charges by letter back to the Netherlands. For this "trampling underfoot the brethren" the Classis was about to censure him in April 1856 when Haan's pastor, Hendrik G. Klyn, suggested a special day of prayer. No one could oppose that proposal, but Haan did boycott the services, then left Second Reformed entirely. John Gelok and several others left with him; Pastor Klyn was left in tears.[19]

Perhaps Klyn's emotions reflected his own uncertainties; in any case, he proceeded on an erratic course that left no one happy. In January 1857 he decided to join the Haan-Gelok faction, but van Driele got wind of the plan and decided to block it, leading to the battle for the pulpit. While Klyn followed Haan and half the assembly out of Second Reformed that Sunday, six months later he returned — again in tears — to the Reformed Church, which accept-

FIGURE 18
First CRC building on
Spring Street, present-day
Commerce Avenue.

ed him and packed him off to a church in Kalamazoo. The dissenters fumed at this "faithlessness" but hardly proved immune to it themselves. One of their elders, John Gezon, went back in 1860. Haan took the same route in 1861, angry that his new congregation made him stand for re-election to his eldership. He reversed himself again in 1867 before ending his days out of town, independent of all church relations.[20]

From such beginnings grew the denomination which, first having no name, then passing through a series of permutations on True, Dutch, and Reformed, eventually became known as the Christian Reformed Church. Its original congregations included the Grand Rapids band and three groups in Ottawa County, but they had only one minister among them, saw their members — sometimes whole churches — come and go, and in general suffered so meager and erratic progress as to make their survival an open question.

The answer came from a cadre of devoted laity who stayed the course and pointedly maintained certain traditions of the home country. While both denominations drew in orthodox Calvinists, the Christian Reformed generally won favor among immigrants who originated in the northern and western parts of the Netherlands, the Reformed among those from the south and east. For the first group, real Calvinism meant precise doctrine; for the second, it meant pious experience. Van Raalte and van Driele shared the latter priority and could join the East Coast Reformed Church in America because it honored the same. Haan, Gelok, and the dissenters held to the other and so took a separate road. As the source of emigration in the Netherlands

shifted northward and toward the doctrinalist school after the Civil War, the CRC stood to benefit.[21]

In the meantime, the Grand Rapids band started building. By fall 1857 it had erected a single-story frame church at Ionia Avenue and Weston Street SW, where it also housed a Christian school that had originated at Second Reformed two years before. Ten years later a 1,300-seat brick edifice on Spring Street (present-day Commerce Avenue) was built, adding in 1869 a new school building around the corner on Williams Street.[22] With these decisions the local CRC put itself squarely by the city's future train station, transient housing, and premier red-light district. It had tough luck in pastors as well. The congregants had no minister at all until 1863, lost their first to a Christian Reformed group in New Jersey after only four years, and lost their second after three to the Reformed Church. Their next pastor, Gerrit Boer, proved to be such a workhorse as the denomination's treasurer and magazine editor that after only two years (1874–1876) at Spring Street he was named professor (the sole professor) at the CRC's new theological seminary. The congregation contributed significantly to Grand Rapids' educational future by offering the

FIGURE 19
The Rev. Gerrit Boer

upper floor of the Williams Street school to the seminary rent-free and by paying one-third of Boer's salary to keep the institution — and with it, eventually, Calvin College — from being relocated to Holland in Ottawa County.[23]

Under its next pastor, Jon Kremer, Spring Street CRC suffered a schism of its own. A number of laity, complaining that his preaching, like Boer's, underplayed predestination, left to form the Netherlands Reformed Church on the West Side. Again, the spiritual got physical for on Nov. 14, 1878, the church council decided that "because of scandalous things happening in front of and in the church, we should ask our city government to appoint our janitor as a special policeman."[24] Kremer departed the opposite way from his foes, taking a Reformed Church pastorate in 1879.

The tenure of the Rev. Johannes H. Vos (1881–1900) finally gave the congregation some stability, but no

less controversy. Vos led the opposition to the founding of Grand Rapids' first English-language Christian Reformed congregation, on LaGrave Avenue in 1886, out of fears that orthodoxy would be lost in the language change. Some of his own congregation disagreed, including John Gelok, a founding elder at Spring Street who transferred to LaGrave CRC to play a similar role there.[25] For Vos the problem soon came home, literally. His son, Geerhardus, one of the best minds the CRC has ever produced, returned to Grand Rapids from a sterling theological education in Europe to teach at the denomination's seminary. To it he introduced English-language instruction, progressive Calvinism, and his Methodist wife.

All these strains should not hide from view the vibrancy of the congregation's life. If Spring Street's members were deadly serious about theology, they also were common folk seeking things eternal in time-bound ways. The glory of God sometimes came in comic dress among them, as long-time member John Hage recalled of the congregation's a capella singing:

"They would sing … from the bottom of their lungs with 100 pounds of air pressure. And if perchance they would have to sing a psalm a little strange, then nearly every one had a tune of his own and the man with the strongest voice and who could sing the loudest was the best singer regardless whether he would keep in tune or not. And how they would flat. The voorzinger [song-leader] would start with a very

FIGURE 20
The Rev. Johannes H. Vos

FIGURE 21
In 1869, Christian Reformed Church leaders built the Williams Street School.

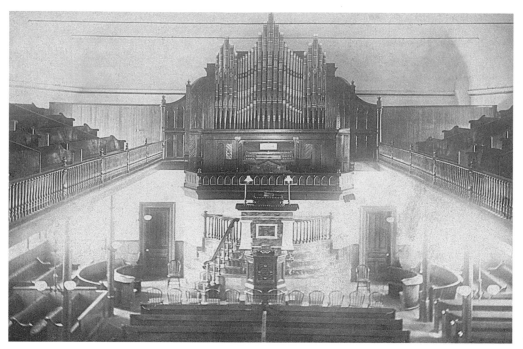

'niet slapen, hoor!' [no sleeping, hear?] Bert straightened up and paid close attention to the sermon for the rest of the evening. But it happened two or three weeks later that Bert's eyes wandered through the church, and up toward the throne, and lo and behold, the king was asleep. Bert gets up, marches through the aisle, takes a firm grip on the king's shoulder and says, 'niet slapen, hoor!'" [26]

high pitch, but the audience would flat, flat, until they would get to the bottom, and then how they would scrape the bottom, and when they would have to sing a second verse, the voorzinger would start five or six notes higher, but always with the same result."

Hage especially enjoyed the peculiar Christian Reformed custom of allowing the young people to sit together in the balcony at evening service.

"How I used to beg my father to sit up there! Then I could look down upon that vast audience, for I thought nearly the whole human race was gathered there. And I remember that … against the wall above the back gallery was a small seat for one man, which we boys called 'the throne' and very naturally the man occupying a throne is a king. Now the king was the sexton, a Mr. Vander Vliet, a square built, stern man. When seated upon his throne his eyes would wander through the church, and woe unto the young man creating any disturbance, the king would march down the aisle and would very likely give the culprit a cuff on the ear, which would make him sit up and take notice.

"… one evening there was a young man by the name of Bert Boer, oldest son of Professor Boer, sitting in the end of the pew … [who] had fallen asleep. Soon the eagle eye of the king discovered him and he descended from his throne, marched down the aisle, took a firm hold of Bert's shoulder and shook him violently and said

Outside the sanctuary, developments were no less incongruous. In 1906 the church had to buy a new parsonage since prostitution on the now aptly named Commerce Avenue made the old one unfit for a minister's family. The next year, at its 50th anniversary celebration, the church was debating changing locations entirely. Resistance prevailed for a time, but in March 1912 the congregation moved under its present name into its present building at Bates Street and Henry Avenue SE, in the heart of the Dutch Southeast Side.[27] Then the language question reappeared. Worship in English was first proposed in 1914 but rejected; tried out in the evening service during spring 1917 but discontinued; reinstituted twice a month in April 1918 and, finally, kept. Undoubtedly, World War I propaganda against things foreign tilted the balance. By March 1919 the church was holding one Dutch and two English services per Sunday, and 10 years later, on Sept. 8, 1929, it discontinued Dutch altogether.[28]

With that, First CRC's adoption of and by America was at last complete. Now it had to decide its place in the American family; given English, what would it say? First Church's response typified the CRC. On the one hand, its pastor in the 1920s, Edward J. Tanis, was a leading voice for the more positive Calvinism which many in the denomination wanted to give America: less judgmental of other faiths, more engaged in social and political concerns. Tanis wrote weekly commentary on current events from this perspective for the denomination's English-language periodical. the Banner. On the other hand, First's members wished to raise their children in the faith at school as well as at home and church. Tanis helped expand this mission as a founder of, and later Bible teacher at, Grand Rapids Christian High School. First CRC also fueled the denomination's missionary enterprise in the interwar years by sending an evangelist to China.[29]

After World War II it faced a new mission at home. In 1949 First Church helped found an inner city chapel on Buckley Street SE that would grow into the interracial Grace CRC. But with the postwar African-American migration to the North, First's own location soon became "inner city," raising at its 1957 centennial the same question it had faced 50 years before. This time the congregation decided to stay in the neighborhood, a decision that cost it half its membership over the next 15 years. Some of the loss was replaced by an influx of young people whom the 1960s had made hungry for social ministry, for freer-flowing worship, and for greater female participation in church leadership. The church found racially integrated services harder to achieve than expected but has undertaken cooperative ventures with the nearby African-American Messiah Missionary Baptist Church [see Chapter 8] as well as substantial food, medical, and social ministries of its own.[30]

Today, First CRC has the progressive profile of many older Christian Reformed congregations that have stayed in aging, changed neighborhoods. The Spring Street founders would probably not like much of that profile, but they would recognize the location. Spring Street's prostitution has given way to Bates Street's urban problems but, as at its founding, First Church still features an energetic laity committed to maintaining their Calvinistic heritage in the heart of the city, voicing the hope of salvation where too many have despaired.

❧

THE VIEW FROM THE HILL

Americans used to be in the habit of calling Germans "Dutchmen," perhaps from Germans' self-designation as "Deutsch." The error was probably less common in Grand Rapids, given the number of real Hollanders here, but it still might have been understandable, for on several counts the two groups seemed separated by little more than the extra "e." This is particularly true of the city's first German church, the Immanuel Evangelical Lutheran Congregation, UAC [Unaltered Augsburg Confession]. Like the Christian Reformed, Immanuel's Lutherans saw doctrinal orthodoxy as the first part of

FIGURE 23
View of Grand Rapids circa 1860s looking southwest from atop the Michigan Street hill. Immanuel Lutheran's first church is in the foreground at the corner of East Bridge Street (now Michigan Street) and Division Avenue. Also of note, North Division School in front of Immanuel Lutheran, the covered bridge at Pearl Street and, in the distance, the original width of the river before the channels were filled in.

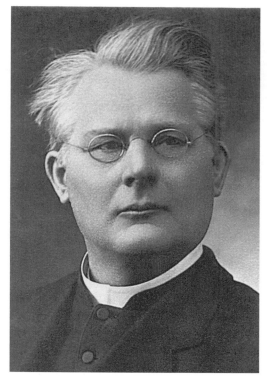

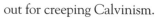

FIGURE 24
The Rev. Frederick W. Richmann was Immanuel Lutheran's first pastor.

FIGURE 25
1889 view of Immanuel Lutheran School built behind the church.

religion: hence the UAC in their title. They, too, insisted on Christian schools for their children, forbade their members from belonging to secret fraternities such as the Masons, and held on to their native tongue until World War I. Immanuel even started out worshipping in the same place as had the immigrant Dutch, in the basement rooms of First Reformed Church.[31]

The two groups followed the same immigration patterns. The Germans also came in three progressively larger waves — 1845 to 1857, 1865 to 1873, 1880 to 1893 — and were mostly farmers who had fallen on hard times. Like the Dutch, the German stream contained many religious conservatives who were rebelling against government meddling in their churches and who were determined to restore their traditions, pure and undefiled, in the new land. At this point, however, their very similarities drove the two groups apart. The act of state interference that loyal Lutherans had most resented in Germany was a forced unification with the Reformed church.[32] Immanuel's founders, in other words, were on the look-

out for creeping Calvinism.

Grand Rapids also presented the two groups with opposite roles from those they played in the country at large. Nationally, the Dutch were negligible while Germans by 1900 constituted a full 10 percent (some 8 million) of the American populace. In Grand Rapids, however, the Dutch-born outnumbered the German-born in 1910 by 11,137 to 4,313, a gap that widened over the next two decades. Still, the local German presence was strong, especially early on. From 1850 to 1900, Germans consistently ranked as the city's third-largest foreign-born group, trailing only the Dutch and Canadians. The 1860 census nearest to Immanuel's founding showed German families contributing more than 10 percent of the city's 8,085 residents.[33]

The German migration to America was far too large to be contained in the religious channels that directed so many of the Dutch. Local Lutherans had to sift through the disaffected and unaffiliated among the newcomers to find the like-minded. By March 1856, however, some 40 men (women and children did not count for this purpose) signed papers formally organizing a congregation and calling a minister, the Rev. Frederick W. Richmann. The parish bought the site it still occupies today, at Michigan Street NE and Division Avenue, and in 1858 moved out of the First Reformed basement into their own building, a 35-by-30-foot, 400-seat Gothic structure.[34] Its 80-foot tower claimed a space on the Grand Rapids skyline; the Christian school in the basement made a claim on the city's future — a claim well-earned, for Immanuel's is the oldest surviving Christian school in town.

Under Richmann's guidance Immanuel also affiliated with the Lutheran Church-Missouri Synod, a denomination whose theological conservatism was matched only by its success at gathering in new immigrants. On both counts it surpassed any of the 60 or so Lutheran synods that appeared on the American map in the later 1800s. The connection confirmed Immanuel in the zeal for orthodoxy and Christian education, the hostility to liberal reformers, and the suspicion of state interference that made its profile so remarkably like that of the Christian Reformed.

The similarity also carried over to disputes and divisions. Just two years after its founding, Immanuel lost a number of charter members but in the opposite direction from the exodus at Second Reformed. Immanuel's dissenters represented the experiential, or heart-religion, wing of the church rather than the doctrinalists, and they were attracted, not repelled, by currents in American Protestantism. At Immanuel the specific question concerned prophecies of the end of the world, common among evangelical revivalists. The Grand Rapids case was just one of many in the Synod, which reacted in 1857 by declaring the new teaching erroneous. With that the dissidents departed to alternative harbors; in Grand Rapids, they joined the German Methodist Church and planted a congregation at Bridge Street and Scribner Avenue NW.[35]

Although some of the dissenters eventually returned, for the moment Immanuel faced extinction. Richmann took a call to Illinois, leaving the church for 15 months without a pastor, without services, and with but 10 members to fill its new building. Immanuel survived only by the efforts of its two leading laymen: Heinrich Bremer, a German-university graduate who built a soap and candle factory here and eventually became city treasurer; and Christoph Kusterer, the city's foremost brewer. The next pastor, William Achenbach, arrived in late 1859, living free at Kusterer's house but also obligated, like many Missouri Synod clergy, to teach the Christian school on top of his ministerial duties. When Achenbach left for the more promising classrooms of a Missouri Synod college in 1863, the Rev. John L. Daib, who replaced him, won release from teaching responsibilities only to take on Lutheran circuit-riding. Three Sundays a month found

him cultivating German enclaves from Grand Haven to Clinton County. Immanuel stabilized when immigration resumed after the Civil War. It grew to 66 voting members (confirmed adult males) and 150 children in school by 1874, and 78 members with 230 students in two schools — the other being on the West Side — in 1884. Even so, Immanuel unwillingly spawned another church in 1880 when members seeking more leniency on doctrine and secret society membership, founded St. John's German Evangelical Church at

FIGURE 26
Interior of Immanuel Lutheran in 1889.

FIGURES 27, 28
From left to right, the Revs. John L. Daib and William Achenbach.

FIGURE 29
The Rev. Charles J.T. Frincke

Mount Vernon Avenue and Bridge Street NW. (see Chapter 8) [36]

Immanuel's golden age came under the 26-year pastorate of Charles J.T. Frincke (1884–1910). Its membership boomed with the city's population and the third wave of German immigration. The two-room schoolhouse next to the church was replaced in 1892 with a $7,300 structure serving 215 students under the tutelage of long-faithful and, one can imagine, long-suffering teachers: Andrew Beyer, who taught from 1871–1904; J. George Nüchterlein, 1882–1907; and Ernest H. Dress, 1892–1912. But the church's boldest venture was the new building it dedicated in 1890 and that has lasted, little changed, for

more than a century. Its unshakable brick, 150-foot steeple, 1,000 seats, and organ testified above the jumbled streets then as it does to freeway traffic today of the fixed theology, rich liturgy, and accomplished status of its parishioners.[37]

The building's $35,250 price tag, much of it borrowed, presented the congregation with a new crisis when the economy fell into depression between 1893 and 1897. With school and church attendance sagging and many parishioners out of work, Immanuel could barely meet its bills, much less address its debts. "Strife and faction" ensued, its historian recalled in 1906, as "discontent, worry, loss of courage, and depression spread in ever-widening circles." But the congregation scraped by until it was in a position to respond to the "fiery sermons" of a 1901 debt-reduction crusade. Revivalistic or not, the measures raised $15,000, and two years later the entire $24,500 debt was paid off.[38]

Their building secured, Immanuel's members had to decide which language to worship in. One pastor had held biweekly English services already in the early 1870s, and Pastor Frincke had resumed the attempt in 1885, again in 1891. But these novelties died under the weight of tradition and of new immigration. Only in 1900 and following the school's lead did the church go bilingual, hiring an English-speaking assistant pastor who preached first on alternate Sunday evenings, later at all the evening and

FIGURE 30
Andrew Beyer's choir in Bailey Park in 1892.

FIGURE 31
J. George Nüchterlein with school children in 1903.

FIGURE 32
View from the Michigan Street hill looking west in 1906 showing the new Immanuel Lutheran building in the center. Just behind it is the Fox Brewery. To the left is the Butterworth Home, on the present-day site of Butterworth Hospital.

half the morning services. Finally, in 1913 Immanuel fostered an English-language congregation, Hope Evangelical Lutheran on the West Side.[39]

The World War that dawned the next year subjected German-Americans to harrowing trials in the court of public opinion. All sorts of German organizations, including churches, were labeled subversive and their members were assaulted with various displays of American patriotism: paint and flagging raids, the banning of German language and music, the destruction of portraits of German poets. Missouri Synod Lutherans, among other supposedly backward Germans, had the pleasure of reminding the nation about civil liberties and the dangers of conformity, words they had been hearing from self-styled progressives for half a century.[40]

World War I concluded on the home front with the prohibition of alcoholic beverages including beer, the German symbol that had long aggravated the nation's Anglo Protestants. In Grand Rapids this ended a 50-year battle that had pitted the Congregational, Baptist, and Methodist ladies (eventually their husbands, too) against local brewers, the most prominent of whom were associated with Immanuel Lutheran. The town's first licensed tavern keeper was a brother of Christian Christ, an Immanuel charter member. The city's largest brewery was founded in 1849 by Immanuel's pillar, Christoph Kusterer, and run by his descendants until Michigan went dry in 1916.[41] Among their properties was the old site of First Reformed Church.

On this issue, too, Missouri Synod conservatism proved remarkably liberal, for Lutheran theology allowed Christians considerable freedom from legalistic scruples, whether religious or political. By the account of city historian Albert Baxter, the German custom also worked wonders for public health. Kusterer and his fellow parishioner Simon Mangold constructed one of Grand Rapids' first fresh water pipelines, bringing spring water from the north side to the city center in 1854. That the same water went into their brewery mattered not, Baxter asserted, for with the coming of German lager, the "chills and shaking ague" which afflicted so many residents miraculously diminished. "It is not the province of the historian to moralize upon these facts," Baxter coyly concluded, "but only to chronicle the coincidence." [42]

A DEVOUT ST. MARY'S

In its heyday, Grand Rapids' Germania was concentrated along the Michigan/Bridge Street artery. Immanuel Lutheran anchored the east end of this corridor; St. Mary's Roman Catholic Church dominated the west end, a block to the north at Turner Avenue and First Street NW. St. Mary's, like Immanuel, still stands on its original site, a testament to the stability its immigrants sought in their new world. Today this testimony has a broader audience because of the ravages of change. The freeways which tore up the German corridor join at St. Mary's front door, making it

Men of Straightforward Dealing

Joseph Houseman had been in Grand Rapids only a few weeks, having fled religious and social persecution in his native Bavaria. He had come to join his cousin, Julius Houseman, in the clothing business. But quickly he found himself involved in a land deal that led to establishment of the first Jewish congregation in Grand Rapids.

It seems a 28-year-old fur trader named Jacob Levy had come to the area from Wingersheim, France, to barter for hides with Indians. Tragically, he died of consumption in September 1857.

A proper Jewish burial place was needed. And it was Joseph — nudged by Julius — who spearheaded the drive to buy for $500 a parcel atop a hill at Union Avenue and Hall Street SE to use for Levy's interment. In doing so, the Jewish Benevolent and Burial Society was created.

Out of the burial society emerged Michigan's first Jewish congregation outside Detroit. Hence, Joseph, as chairman of the society, was the founding official of what later became Temple Emanuel.

Although Joseph Houseman was a central figure in the development of the Reform Jewish congregation, his elder cousin, Julius, also played a significant role in shaping Temple Emanuel's character.

Together, the Houseman cousins became important players in more than just the development of the area's first synagogue. The cousins helped form the city itself. For the last decades of the 19th century, the Houseman cousins were active in civic, political and business affairs.

Of the two, Julius was richer. He was also the better known. In 1883, he served as the U.S. representative in Congress for the Grand Rapids area. This made him for many years Michigan's first and only Jewish representative in Washington, D.C.

As was the case with his cousin, Julius was a man of practical religious persuasion. For him, freedom of worship was closely aligned with the ability to immerse himself unfettered in civic and business affairs. Also having fled persecution in Bavaria, Julius Houseman prospered under U.S. democracy. But even though his financial holdings were vast, Julius Houseman was generous and shared his success.

One time, Julius Houseman was counting bank funds in the back room of the National City Bank, of which he was president, when he gave "Old" Mike Smith a gentle lesson in the management of money. A dark-eyed man with a flowing beard and grandfatherly bearing, Houseman told Smith, the bank's janitor, there was more than $100,000 on the table — money Houseman and the others were tallying as part of their duties as bank directors.

"Now, Mike, if this money were your own, what would you do with it?" Houseman had asked.

Mike replied he would first buy a house, then a horse and buggy, followed by a good suit of clothes for himself and a cloak and dress for his wife. The rest, Smith said, he would probably put in the bank.

At that Julius Houseman smiled. The man to whom many came for guidance would later remark: "Mike's ideas of investments were like those of thousands of others who, having large sums to handle, would not know what to do with the same."

Julius Houseman wasn't one to squander money. When he had a few extra dollars, he knew what to do with them. He became one of the largest holders of real

FIGURES 33, 34 Julius Houseman, above; Joseph Houseman, facing page.

estate in this part of the state and at one time owned huge tracts of timberland across the upper Midwest. But despite being one of the area's first millionaires, he kept offering help of one kind or another to those in need.

Julius Houseman also could be terse and almost unforgiving when it came to business dealings with those he believed had treated him unfairly.

One time a man vying for a top political appointment needed backing from local business people. Since the man had once cheated Houseman out of property, Houseman asked his friends not to help. Only after the man's wife pleaded with Houseman to drop his opposition did he relent. "Ma'am, your husband is a damned scoundrel," he told her. But because she and her children needed his help, he gave it.

Joseph Houseman also was generous. His personality, by most accounts, was less harsh than that of his cousin. Joseph was more apt to listen and offer solutions.

More often than not, Joseph remained in his cousin's shadow. He let Julius take the spotlight while he remained closer to his spiritual roots.

"For years he has been prominent in politics, but although often urged by members of his party to accept office, he has steadfastly refused," the Michigan *Tradesman* wrote of Joseph in July 1902.

Joseph Houseman, however, served on the local school board and helped found the city's first building and loan association. He also helped organize efforts to build the first paved roads through Grand Rapids.

Weaving their faith into the activities of their adopted city, the Housemans had a hand in nearly every significant development in post-Civil War Grand Rapids.

As mayor of Grand Rapids, Julius Houseman helped start the city waterworks. Later, he was one of the principal investors in the effort to bring gas-driven energy to the city.

It was Julius Houseman who gave Temple Emanuel a progressive, Americanized bent upon its founding in October 1871. He believed that in coming to America, it was important to leave behind some of the trappings of the past. He said he wanted the first Jewish congregation in Grand Rapids to hold to the "progressive viewpoint of these Reform Jews." He favored a religion that adapted itself to the new world.

In his later years, Julius Houseman strolled the streets, stopping frequently to talk to friends and business associates, to give advice and offer opinions. When he died in 1891 at the age of 59, his body lay in state in the old city hall on Lyon Street, and more than 10,000 citizens paid homage. Today a street and an athletic field in Grand Rapids bear his name.

As he grew older, Joseph Houseman became more philosophical than his civically active cousin and immersed himself deeply in Temple Emanuel matters.

For example, in 1895, Joseph almost single-handedly saved the congregation from an untimely demise. There was talk of disbanding the synagogue. Services were only sparsely attended. Money wasn't coming in. The progressive branch of Judaism was in danger of disappearing in Grand Rapids. But Joseph Houseman threatened to resign from the board if services weren't held. He demanded that the Temple remain intact. He used all of his influence to guide the congregation beyond that crisis and into the 20th century.

Just before his death in 1905, Joseph Houseman wasn't thinking about his civic accomplishments. They seemed of less importance than the progress he had helped make in spiritual areas. What was on his mind was his faith and the way in which it had become an important part of the local religious scene. He told an interviewer that in his time Judaism and Christianity had grown closer in Grand Rapids.

The congregation he helped found with the purchase of cemetery plots was no fringe element of the society here, he said. Anti-semitism might be rife elsewhere, but here the two religions were at some peace.

"Christianity and Judaism are actually growing nearer together," he told the Michigan *Tradesman*. "The devotees of the Christian faith are not so strongly partisan for their beliefs as not to recognize that there are truths in other forms of religion."

The cousins brought to Grand Rapids a faith that they put into practice. Each had strengths; each had weaknesses. But together, a minister eulogized on the death of Julius, they were "men of straightforward dealing."

FIGURE 35
The Rev. Mathias Marco,
founding pastor of St.
Mary's Church.

FIGURE 36
The Rev. John G.
Ehrenstrasser

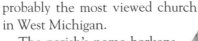

FIGURE 37
St. Mary's in 1875
minus its steeple.

probably the most viewed church in West Michigan.

The parish's name harkens back to Frederic Baraga's Grand River mission, and its existence to a German caucus from St. Andrew's Church that first met at the home of Joseph Emmer on Canal Street in 1855. With a blessing and $900 from the mother parish, St. Mary's was formally organized on Sept. 18, 1857, six months after the Christian Reformed and 18 months after the Lutherans across town. The parish members moved into a 75-by-30-foot wooden sanctuary they had built themselves, where they could hear the gospel in their own tongue from the Rev. Mathias Marco. Much of Marco's labors were typical of immigrant pastors, gathering in newcomers and trying to secure them amid the hazards of a strange environment.

One instrument to this end was familiar to other immigrants in town, a parochial school; St. Mary's founded its own in 1859.[43] Another strategy resembled, of all things, a Protestant revival meeting. Father Marco held such a "mission" before his departure in 1861, and his successor repeated it in 1866. In fact, such services remain a staple of St. Mary's modern history. By the late 1880s the missions were in the hands of the Redemptorists, an order devoted to just this calling and housed locally at St. Alphonsus Church at Leonard Street and Lafayette Avenue NE. By this device many an immigrant, and many a wandering native, followed not the sawdust but the incense trail into the bosom of the church.[44]

St. Mary's membership grew so rapidly that the congregation was ready to take part in Grand Rapids' great church-building boom of the 1870s. Four sodalities (age and gender groups) bore the brunt of fund raising for the cause and of the criticisms it could bring. Summer picnics, for instance, could net $900 apiece but, as the parish historian put it, sometimes "unfortunately were attended by unpleasant excesses" when the beer tent proved too popular. In any case, the new cornerstone was laid on May 25, 1873, and the building opened in all its 142-by-60-by-52-foot Gothic glory on Oct. 18, 1874, before a crowd of 4,000.[45] Some 7,000 pounds of bells were added in 1877 and the present 200-foot tower completed in 1884. Parishioners did most of the construction on this edifice, too, and the young men's and young ladies' sodalities were kept busy for a decade more providing confessionals, furnishings, and trim. These included 20 stained-glass windows, the University of Notre Dame's organ and Bavarian-crafted Stations of the Cross. Such donations and sweat equity kept down the indebted portion of the building's $65,000 price tag. More important, they both symbolized and actualized the parishioners' devotion to their church.[46]

Leadership for this enterprise came from the Rev. John G. Ehrenstrasser. Born in Innsbruck, Austria, in 1835, Ehrenstrasser immigrated to the United States in 1865 to serve a parish in Adrian. His term at St. Mary's lasted from 1870 to Dec. 6, 1886, when he died, perhaps fittingly, while a mission was being conducted at the church. Besides supervising the building project, he

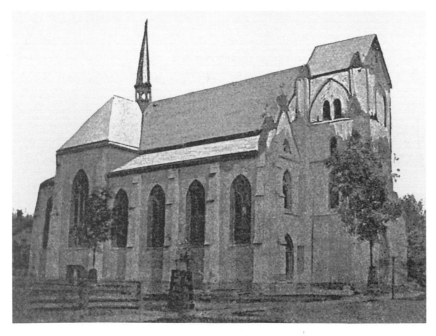

helped guide the potentially disruptive birth of St. Adalbert's, a separate Polish parish, out of St. Mary's in 1881. The congregation also sired a Dutch-language parish, St. Joseph's on the Southwest Side, in 1887. Meanwhile, the School Sisters of Notre Dame continued the reign they had begun over the parish's children in 1866. At Ehrenstrasser's death in 1886, the school housed some 200 pupils in the old church building. A new schoolhouse built in 1891 allowed enrollment to soar beyond 500 by the century's end and gave the Sisters the dubious privilege of living in the old church until 1906, when they finally got a $13,000 home of their own. Wasting nothing, St. Mary's donated the materials of the 1857 building to another daughter parish, St. Anthony's, on the farther northwest end.[47]

The depth of commitment manifest in these projects stirred outsiders' praise, and sometimes their envy or suspicion. Like other Catholics, St. Mary's gave off ambiguous signals in response — sometimes invoking the nation's welfare, then again fearing the culture's threat; appealing here to divine law and there to American rights. At the new school dedication on Feb. 21,

1892, the Rev. James Pulcher from St. James Church, St. Mary's English-language neighbor on Bridge Street NW, gave classic expression to their thinking:

"To an outsider it may seem ridiculous that any class should pay a tax [for public schools] and then pay another [to the parish] for the same purpose — two taxes for one privilege. Yet such is the case with Catholics ... A great many people think that we Catholics are bigots to do this.

"But we hold that the state has no more right to educate our children than to feed them or nurse them .... The family is the supreme and sacred unit. It was in existence first. The state may govern the people as a whole and make laws to govern their conduct, but it has no business with the inherent rights of the family. We are masters of education, and it is wrong to take it from us .... We claim our rights, and

FIGURE 38
St. Mary's in 1888 with the steeple completed.

FIGURE 39
Funeral at St. Mary's for five people who died in a car accident in June 1920. To the right of the church is St. Mary's School.

shall have them in spite of all that united Protestantism can do against us. You must educate your children in your own belief. You can teach children the multiplication table in any school, but you cannot educate the child in the tenets of a religion. Destroy religious teaching in this country, and all you have left is confusion and anarchy. Secular education is not education. We must educate the soul. No power, imperial or otherwise, has the right to say you must educate the heart as we say. This is why the Catholic people pay a double proportion of taxes for education and religion."

Pulcher concluded with what surely was the main point for his audience: *"We can be Americans and still be Catholics."* [48] Bedecked as he was in ecclesiastical robes, yet speaking by an altar overhung with a picture of George Washington, Pulcher showed how conflicted, yet intertwined, those loyalties could be.

The tension showed up most memorably for St. Mary's during the pastorate of Joseph Schrembs (1900–1911). The Grand River flood of March 25, 1904, struck the West Side hard, damaging some 2,500 homes and turning the church into a relief station. Here, St. Mary's and the city were one. But in 1911 a furniture strike shut down the entire city, putting parish members on the

picket line against the Protestant captains of industry and bringing Schrembs to the forefront of public attention as the workers' chief defender. Contrary to common wisdom, this social activism fit well with a pronounced interest in the supernatural. Schrembs regularly lectured the city's Catholics (and Protestant eavesdroppers) on the mystical claims of Rome. In 1902 he established the Archconfraternity of the Most Holy Rosary at St. Mary's which granted plenary indulgences to all who attended Mass on Rosary Sunday. Schrembs brought this style home dramatically on his return from a European tour in 1902. To each parishioner he gave a medal blessed by the pope. To the ladies' societies, he donated pictures of Our Lady of Lourdes which he had touched to the rock of the apparition itself. Most impressively, to the parish as a whole he offered eight small boxes of relics — bones from 87 martyrs of the early church — which were deposited in the sanctuary. [49]

St. Mary's demonstrated its devotion again at its 50th anniversary in 1907. A golden monstrance was made for the occasion, cast in the form of a miniature church complete with side chapels for St. Boniface, the German patron, and the Blessed Virgin, the church's patron. It was decorated with hundreds of jewels donated by parishioners. The parish also commissioned new priestly vestments which depicted the biblical narrative of Mary's life. The church was consecrated on Jubilee Sunday, Sept. 19, 1907, and capped its celebration with a mission

FIGURE 42
Where other churches fell to the wrecking ball in the 1960s to make way for the freeways, St. Mary's was left standing with U.S. 131 at its front door and Int. 196 to the north.

followed by Rosary Sunday services for 1,600 people.[50]

To Protestants in town, all this seemed so much superstition. To Catholics of Irish descent, it could look too ornate. To both, St. Mary's answered with a confident combination of religion and ethnicity, an answer beautifully recorded in the decor of its sanctuary. Compared to — in the words of one parishioner — "that big grey box on Sheldon" (the Irish-toned St. Andrew's), St. Mary's offers a surprisingly intimate space, warm with hues of amber, green, and gold. The three altars honor the Holy Family, underscoring German values of hearth and home. On the right side altar, St. Joseph is flanked by Saints Cyril and Methodius, Slavic missionaries recalling the early Polish presence in the parish. On the left side altar, Mary as Queen of Heaven is flanked by St. Gertrude of Saxony, a writer and teacher, and Elizabeth, Queen of Hungary and friend of the poor. In front of them all stands a mission cross, remembering all those who built a church from the throes of immigration and who have kept it alive amid the pressures of more recent change.[51]

Two changes are most notable. The German presence in the neighborhood has declined; other ethnic groups have moved in. Fittingly, at this writing the parish has an African-American pastor, the Rev. Bernard A. Hall. A more graphic challenge seems to loom in the elevated highways that ring St. Mary's calm with droning traffic. To fleeting glances from a car, St. Mary's somber exterior tells all that is needed of a faith passed by. But inside this and the other churches of the old immigrants runs a story that is still alive and vibrant because it is rooted amid the flux of America's machines.

Furniture and Faith 4

1875 – 1910

I N THE SUMMER OF 1876 THE UNITED STATES MARKED ITS centennial with a great fair in Philadelphia. If the year commemorated political independence, the fair celebrated industry and material progress.

Some 10 million fairgoers ogled reapers and power looms, the newly invented typewriter and telephone, and above all, the 40-foot tall Corliss steam engine, whose 2,500 horsepower ran all 8,000 displays in the 13-acre Machinery Hall. Among the displays was one of Grand Rapids furniture featuring thick, ornately carved bedroom sets decorated with mythological symbolism and patriotic allegories. The display gave Grand Rapids a national reputation and helped make furniture the city's leading industry for decades to come.[1]

The exhibition came just in time. During the depression that had begun with the Panic of 1873, eight out of Grand Rapids' 10 furniture makers had gone bankrupt. After the fair, new orders poured in. New, well-capitalized firms were founded under comfortable relationships with local banks. Soon Grand

Rapids companies opened permanent showrooms in New York City and inaugurated a local semi-annual furniture market which attracted hundreds of salesmen from across the nation. The designer David Kendall moved to town in 1879 and began a popular trend by reproducing old period styles for a mass market. As a result, local furniture production soared. The eight furniture makers and 280 employees of 1870 grew to 15 firms employing 2,279 by 1880, 31 employing 4,347 by 1890, and 54 employing 7,250 by 1910. Already in 1890, the furniture industry employed one-third of all the city's wage earners and, in terms of market value, produced more than had all Kent County manufacturers combined just 10 years before.[2]

Prosperity brought with it striking population growth. The city's 16,500 inhabitants of 1870 nearly doubled to 32,000 by 1880, which almost doubled again to 60,275 by 1890, which soared to 87,500 by 1900 — all in all, more than a five-fold increase in one generation. But so much growth brought worries. Where were all these people coming from? Some filtered in from the Michigan countryside, but many more came from overseas, from Germany, Sweden, Ireland, but especially from the Netherlands and Poland. How would these newcomers sur-

vive their uprooting and adjust to a new climate? From their hosts' point of view, what would make them orderly so as not to disrupt the peace, and content so as not to siphon off too much of the manufacturers' profits? And how would the city's political system deal with such radical change?

A crucial part of the answer to these questions came from religion. The immigrants built churches at a rate that estab-

Christian Soldiers Derail Secular Symbol

The church bell, high in the belfry at Eastern Avenue Christian Reformed Church, began to ring at 10 p.m. on Thursday, May 10, 1888. The pealing bell called church members in the neighborhood into the streets to battle with workers for the Street Railway Company of Grand Rapids.

Within minutes, more than 1,000 people huddled in the dark outside the church. They were irate that a steam-driven engine and 24 open-air cars had rolled past their church and through their neighborhood earlier that day.

Not 24 hours before, many of these same people had been on the streets, trying to keep railroad workers from laying tracks. That effort had failed. The tracks went down and that afternoon the first train arrived in a cloud of hissing steam.

To Eastern Avenue CRC members, the train was a symbol of rampaging secularism. Of particular concern was that the train was scheduled to rattle through the neighborhood on the Lord's day, carrying revelers to nearby Ramona Park where there was drinking, gambling and dancing. They also knew the train would rock their stained glass windows.

The angry Hollanders had tried to convince the railroad company to reroute the tracks. But their arguments to local authorities, buttressed by a petition signed by many who lived in the area, were of no avail.

So on this May night, emotions ran high. It was time to make clear to the workers still at the site that residents wanted no trains interfering in their lives or posing a hazard to playing children. Thus began what came to be known as the "Dummy Line Riot.".

FIGURE 2   A steam-driven engine like the one that rumbled past Eastern Avenue Christian Reformed Church.

Some in the crowd yanked up the steel tracks and flung them into a nearby frog pond. Others began to pelt the railroad workers with rocks. Shots were even fired. A policeman, an engineer and a lantern boy were injured, and arrests were made.

The actions of the faithful that night, a church history states, reflect "not only an outburst of rowdy lawlessness but also an indication of earnestness and piety in not allowing Sabbath peace to be shattered."

In the end, the parishioners prevailed.

Following the outburst on the evening of May 10, a judge issued a temporary injunction that halted the company from operating its steam engine on Eastern Avenue that summer. The next year a permanent injunction was handed down, keeping the road that ran in front of the church, just south of Wealthy Street SE, free from the roar and rumbling of the city's too-worldly train.

lished residents could not match and with a zeal that drew off several sources. Churches could re-create a piece of the homeland, an enclave of the familiar where newcomers could find moral and material support. Amid the harsh conditions of the new life, with its numbing routine of long hours at low wages, of cramped housing and noisy factories, churches afforded spiritual solace, reinvigoration, answers to the big questions of life. Religion also built a base of independence. While on the one hand Dutch and Polish immigrants showed remarkable dedication to family, propriety, and patriotism — the message of the Centennial bedroom sets of 1876 — on the other hand they bristled at the plans "real Americans" made to change and "improve" them. As one Dutch immigrant pastor declared: "We are not and will not be a pretty piece of paper upon which America can write what it pleases." [3]

All this made immigrant religion in Grand Rapids a game of high stakes, marked by amazing sacrifices, marked also by bald conflict. Such themes stand out in the records of two churches founded at the cutting edge of the immigrant wave: Coldbrook Christian Reformed Church among the Dutch, and St. Adalbert's Roman Catholic Church among the Poles. Whatever the city's establishment thought of these ventures, it might have used them as a mirror, for Grand Rapids was changing rapidly enough to make it a new world even for those born there. The native citizens also looked to their churches for leadership in city management, particularly to St. Mark's, the big Episcopal church downtown. Together, these three churches open a window on the public and private worlds of the era when Grand Rapids changed from a small city into a major manufacturing center.

❦

DUTCH ZEAL
Between 1875 and 1893 the Dutch Reformed in Grand Rapids opened 20 new churches — more than one a year.[4] The

FIGURE 3
The Rev. Lammert Jan Hulst moved to Grand Rapids in 1876.

" We are not and will not be a pretty piece of paper upon which America can write what it pleases."

— A Dutch immigrant pastor

mid-1870s brought hard times to the Netherlands, as well as to the United States and Germany, knocking its rural economy into a depression that wouldn't lift for another 20 years. The result was the largest wave of immigration in all Dutch-American history. In the 1880s, some 53,000 Hollanders came to the United States, five times the numbers of the more famous initial wave of the 1850s.[5] Most of the newcomers, being of rural background, hoped to start farms in America. But as land prices soared, more and more of them settled in cities. They chose sites close to established Dutch communities: Chicago; Paterson, N.J.; and especially Grand Rapids, on the edge of the Holland-Zeeland colony. By 1900, Grand Rapids would number 11,000 Dutch-born inhabitants, one-eighth of the city's population, and qualified as the new capital of Dutch America.

New churches to serve this population sprouted in every ward, usually sponsored by established congregations. Second Reformed and Spring Street Christian Reformed Church were particularly active in the process, which meant that their old rivalry would be replicated across the local map. In the formation of Coldbrook Christian Reformed Church, the original battle of 1857 was fought all over again, now with a new issue but with the same dynamics and some of the same personalities.

The process began in 1875 when Second Reformed organized three satellite congregations, among them Fourth Reformed Church on the city's near north side. The old pioneer Frans van Driele himself took the lead in the latter venture only to see his dream again, as in the 1850s, become something of a nightmare. Situated on Ionia Avenue just south of Leonard, hard by factories and warehouses and in the middle of an ethnically mixed neighborhood, the church provided a cockpit for all the turmoil and contrary ideals the new immigrants brought with them. By 1880 it was embroiled in a fight that split the congregation. This time, unlike 1857, the dissenters won. They kept title to the building, renamed it after its Coldbrook location, and affiliated with the Christian Reformed Church. The battle echoed far beyond the neighborhood, however, for it mirrored and widened a breach in the Dutch-American community nationwide and set the religious lines of that community for a long time to come.

A central role in this drama belonged to the congregation's pastor, the Rev. Lammert Jan Hulst.[6] Hulst himself had immigrated from the Netherlands in 1874 to pastor a small RCA congregation in rural Illinois. But he quickly tired of the prairies and jumped at the invitation to become the first pastor at Fourth Reformed. In the centennial summer of 1876, 50 years old himself, Hulst moved to Grand Rapids — just in time for the death of Albertus C. van Raalte, founder of the West Michigan colony. Instantly, Hulst found himself positioned — and thought himself well-qualified — to contend for the succession.

He soon had a cause: a controversy over Freemasonry. Secret fraternal societies like the Masons had been fixtures on the American scene for more than a century. They were apparently respectable, often eminent,

FIGURE 4
Dutch class at Coldbrook Christian School with teacher Helen Flietstra in May 1908.

FIGURE 5
The original Coldbrook Christian Reformed Church building and parsonage. The building today is occupied by Schaafsma Heating Co.

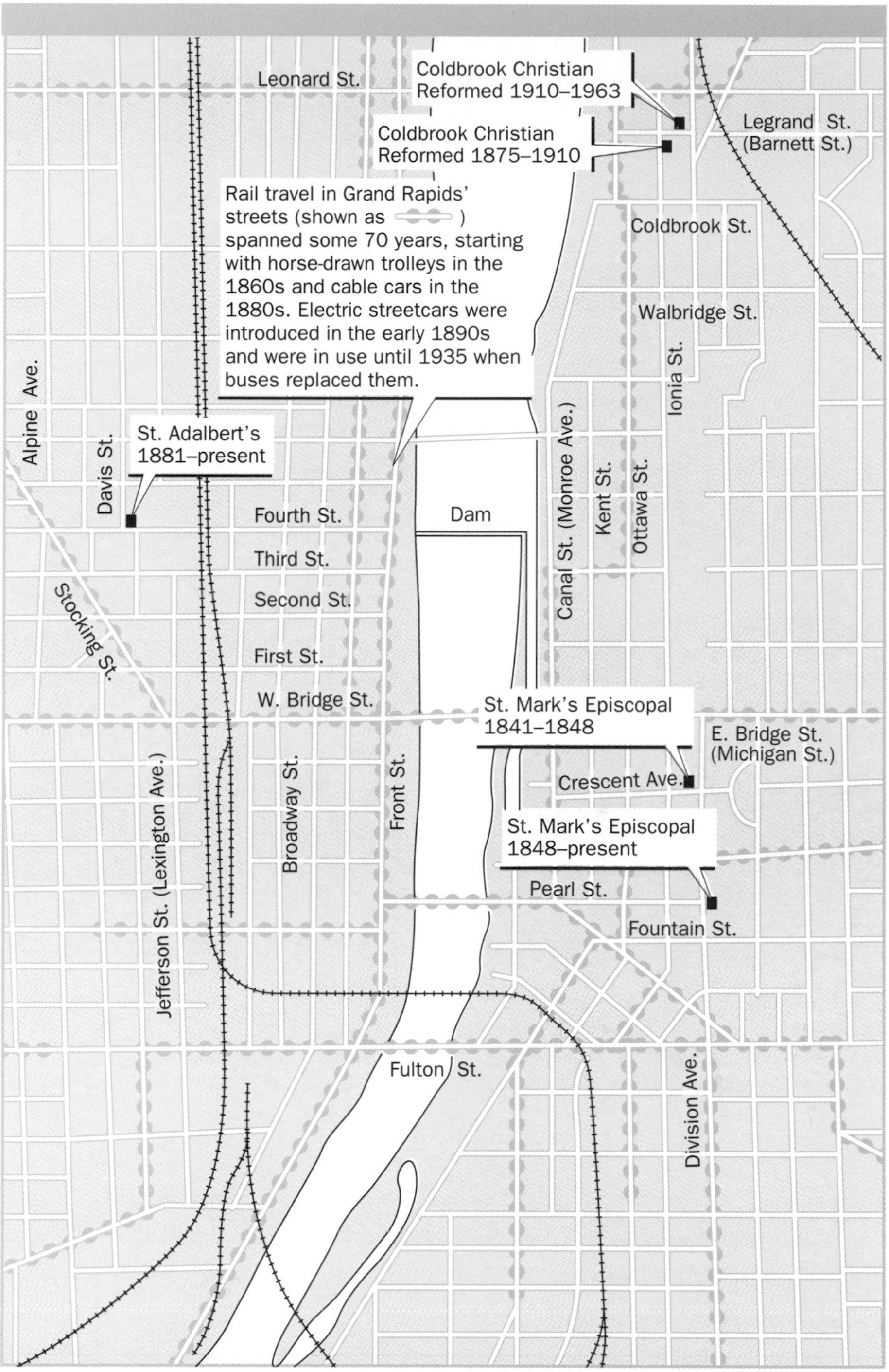

and seemed to offer no worse than innocuous male-bonding rituals among businessmen and professionals. RCA congregations on the East Coast allowed Masons in their membership, even on their governing boards. But the newer immigrants had a different perspective. To devout Christians from continental Europe — to Lutherans and Catholics as well as Calvinists — lodges were dens of skepticism and immorality, a rival religious network sworn to displace the true faith. Already in the 1860s immigrant RCA congregations in the Midwest had petitioned the denomination (unsuccessfully) to bar lodge members from fellowship. In 1879 the agitation started up again, and Fourth Reformed quickly became the Grand Rapids center of the movement. When the church's petitions to the RCA's national assembly went unavailing, the dissenters broke ranks. Six congregations, led by Fourth Reformed, left the denomination for the CRC. Two more soon followed, including van Raalte's old Pillar Church in Holland, the fountainhead of the West Michigan colony. Where whole churches did not withdraw, various families did. Most important, the Masonic controversy reverberated back to the Netherlands, where the conservative Calvinist denomination now instructed its emigrants to join the CRC, not the RCA, upon arrival.[7]

At the start of the largest wave of Dutch immigration, the Christian Reformed Church won a crucial endorsement, several new churches, and vital new leaders such as L.J. Hulst. It bloomed from a rather erratic collection of dissenters into a substantial enterprise. Its 26 churches in 1875 tripled to 79 by 1890 and gave it representation — often dominance — in every Dutch enclave in the country. By 1895 its membership surpassed that of the Midwestern, immigrant sector of the RCA. Simply stated, the Masonic controversy guaranteed

Leonard St.

Coldbrook Christian Reformed 1910–1963

Coldbrook Christian Reformed 1875–1910

Legrand St. (Barnett St.)

Coldbrook St.

Walbridge St.

Ionia St.

Rail travel in Grand Rapids' streets (shown as) spanned some 70 years, starting with horse-drawn trolleys in the 1860s and cable cars in the 1880s. Electric streetcars were introduced in the early 1890s and were in use until 1935 when buses replaced them.

Alpine Ave.

Davis St.

St. Adalbert's 1881–present

Fourth St.

Dam

Canal St. (Monroe Ave.)

Kent St.

Ottawa St.

Third St.

Second St.

First St.

W. Bridge St.

Stocking St.

Broadway St.

Front St.

St. Mark's Episcopal 1841–1848

E. Bridge St. (Michigan St.)

Crescent Ave.

St. Mark's Episcopal 1848–present

Jefferson St. (Lexington Ave.)

Pearl St.

Fountain St.

Fulton St.

Division Ave.

the CRC's future.

The Coldbrook congregation's 50th anniversary booklet described the Fourth-Coldbrook split in telling language: "Just a few families left Rev. Hulst." [8] Numerically this was true: the congregational vote to leave the RCA was 100 to 15. But the RCA loyalists were cast as those leaving; Hulst himself was the center of loyalty and leadership. A Dutch dominie (pastor) he was, with all the title's connotations of domin-

FIGURE 6
The map details the streets that were in use by trolleys and streetcars.

Grand Rapids' Dutch Reformed Family Tree 1840–1900

By 1900, the Dutch had founded 27 churches in Grand Rapids, all but four of them after the sharp upturn in Dutch immigration in the early 1870s and all but five of them affiliated with either the Reformed or Christian Reformed denominations. The dates, places, and sponsors of their founding demonstrate the group's networking and the denominational competition that went with it. The final column indicates whether Dutch (D) or English (E) was the language of worship.

CONGREGATION	FOUNDED	SPONSOR	LOCATION	LANGUAGE
REFORMED CHURCH IN AMERICA				
First	1840		Michigan and Ottawa NW	E
Second	1849	First RCA	Bostwick near Lyon NE	D
Third	1875	Second RCA	Hermitage and Diamond SE	D
Fourth	1875	Second RCA	Ionia near Walbridge NW	D
Fifth	1886	Second RCA	Church near Pleasant SW	D
Oakdale Park	1889	Third RCA	Adams near Kalamazoo SE	D
Seventh	1890	Fourth RCA	Leonard and Jennette NW	D
Eighth	1891	Fifth RCA	Burton near Clyde Park SW	D
Ninth	1892	Second RCA	Deloney and Watson SW	D
Bethany	1893	Third RCA	Baldwin and Eastern SE	E
Grace	1897	Fifth RCA	Caulfield and B St. SW	E
CHRISTIAN REFORMED				
First/Spring Street	1857	Second RCA	Commerce near Oakes SW	D
Eastern Avenue	1879	First CRC	Eastern and Logan SE	D
Coldbrook	1875/82	Fourth RCA	Taylor and Barnett NW	D
Alpine Avenue	1881	First CRC	Alpine and Eleventh NW	D
LaGrave	1886	First CRC	LaGrave near Oakes SE	E
Fifth/Franklin Street	1887	First CRC	Franklin and Oakland SW	D
Crosby Street/West Leonard	1888	Alpine Avenue CRC	Crosby and Garfield NW	D
Oakdale Park	1890	Eastern Avenue CRC	Hancock and West Butler SE	D
Grandville Avenue	1891	Franklin Street CRC	Grandville and Clyde Park SW	D
Dennis Avenue	1893	Eastern Avenue CRC	Dennis near Hermitage SE	D
Broadway Avenue	1893	Alpine Avenue CRC	Broadway near Leonard NW	E
OTHER AFFILIATIONS				
Free Christian Reformed	1870		Division near Michigan NE	D
Netherlands Reformed	1876		Turner near Eleventh NW	D
Unitarian Dutch	1885		Ionia and Michigan NW	D
St. Joseph's Roman Catholic	1887	St. Mary's	Rumsey near Grandville SW	D
Free Dutch Reformed	1889		Clancy near Cedar NE	D

Between 1900 and 1920, the trend toward English accelerated in these circles. Dutch-language congregations introduced some English services in their own parishes and sponsored 11 more English-speaking churches.

CONGREGATION	FOUNDED	SPONSOR	LOCATION
REFORMED CHURCH IN AMERICA			
Bethel	1906	Fourth RCA	Coit and Travis NE
Immanuel	1907	Third and Bethany RCA	Eastern and Thomas SE
Trinity	1908	Seventh RCA	Davis near Leonard NW
Calvary	1915	Third and Bethany RCA	Fulton and Lowell NE
Zion/Garfield Park	1917	Oakdale Park RCA	Burton and Jefferson SE
CHRISTIAN REFORMED			
Burton Heights	1905	LaGrave CRC	Burton and Jefferson SE
Sherman Street	1907	Eastern Avenue CRC	Sherman near Dolbee SE
Bethel	1912	Grandville Avenue/Franklin CRC	Shamrock near Grandville SW
Neland Avenue	1915	Oakdale Park/Sherman Street CRC	Neland and Watkins SE
Creston	1915	Coldbrook CRC	Spencer near Lafayette NE
Twelfth Street	1917	West Leonard/Alpine CRC	Twelfth and Tamarack NW

SOURCES: David Vander Stel, *"The Dutch of Grand Rapids, 1848–1900."* Peter Vandenberge, ed., *Historical Directory of the Reformed Church in America, 1628–1965. Yearbook of the Christian Reformed Church, 1924.*

ion. He presided at Coldbrook for 30 years, until he was 80, and in that time preached three sermons a Sunday, taught 18 catechism classes a week, and led the young people's meeting on Sunday evening. In between, he taught at the CRC's Grand Rapids (later, Calvin) seminary, wrote voluminously for the denomination's magazines, and did much of the sick-calling and counseling — marital, personal, spiritual — in the congregation.[9] Hulst stamped Coldbrook in his own image. Humble before God but proud in public, adamant about doctrine but earnest in pursuing the wayward, hardnosed in church politics but capable of graciousness, Hulst helped set the orthodoxy of the Christian Reformed denomination he was so instrumental in building.

That orthodoxy entailed first of all correct belief. Hulst and a steady line of successors down to the present have insisted on the Bible's strict authority and the Calvinist theology that they took to be its most faithful witness. But piety placed a close second. Hulst himself, in his Netherlands childhood,

had passed through a long, exacting search for salvation, and thereafter kept constant check on the state of his soul.[10] Balancing formal doctrine and inner spirit was no easy task, as Hulst knew from personal experience, so the Coldbrook congregation received plentiful, sensitive advice on the matter. Equally important was keeping this heritage alive. Hulst waxed eloquently on the covenant parents had with God on behalf of their children. Coldbrook helped set a CRC pattern by saturating its children in doctrinal instruction via catechism class — a far better choice than the American Sunday school, in Hulst's estimation. Additionally, in 1890 it began a day school, the forerunner of present-day Creston-Mayfield Christian School, for elementary education.

All this instruction had clear mandates for behavior. Being truly Reformed for Hulst meant keeping clean from "the world," and the world seemed to include everything outside the church circle except for honest, obedient labor at a job. As he declared in the pulpit, the world — particularly the

American world with its human pride, its materialistic greed, its lusts of the flesh — was lost to the faithful, a barrier to God. The Christian life came down to a simple choice: either you conquer the world or the world conquers you.[11]

The lesson held well. As late as the 1920s, the Coldbrook consistory had to decide whether bowling, watching professional baseball, and listening to the radio were permissible activities. 'Yes — with caution!' was the reply. Card-playing, dancing, and theater attendance, however, were taboo.[12]

So also, at Coldbrook, were a church choir and, for a long time, the use of English in worship. Hulst groused when LaGrave CRC was founded in 1886 as the first English-speaking church in the denomination. He opposed the formation of the English-speaking Broadway CRC in 1893 on the West Side because it drained a good number of Coldbrook members. The congregation was a little more gracious after Hulst left (for Eastmanville CRC, where he carried on until rheumatism forced him to retire at age 86) when it authorized the formation of Creston CRC as an English-language daughter church in 1915. But not until 1920 were there English services at Coldbrook itself; then there were two, along with two Dutch services, every Sunday. The ratio changed to 2:1 in 1929, but a Dutch service was held regularly at Coldbrook until 1951.

At bottom, Hulst objected not to English or America as such but to the sins and corruption that threatened Christians everywhere. While the Dutch language gave his flock extra insulation against the temptations at hand, it provided no guarantees. Hulst and many like him, then and since, sniped at the allegedly progressive attitudes they saw developing right in the CRC. To their mind, this was worldliness, too, just dressed up in higher education and respectability and so likely to thrive at such institutions as Calvin Seminary. The truly faithful, by contrast, were the rejected and despised of the world. As Hulst never tired of reminding the denomination: "We must bear in mind that generally the spirit of error begins to develop in the circles of the learned, and comes down ... to the common people. Reformation generally originates with the common folk."[13] Nonetheless, Hulst himself showed strong intellectual cravings. He always regretted his lack of higher education, disciplined himself to a rigorous course of reading (starting each day at his desk by 6 a.m.), and wrote a 1,000-page manuscript on theology and philosophy. Such was the classic Calvinist tension common among the Grand Rapids Dutch: proud, but suspicious, of higher learning; in theory proclaiming God to be the master of this world, but in practice fearing that the devil had dislodged him.

> *The CRC's 26 churches in 1875 tripled to 79 by 1890 and gave it representation — often dominance — in every Dutch enclave in the country.*

FIGURE 7
Coldbrook CRC's massive second building, erected in 1910.

In the early 20th century, however, the tide was shifting toward the progressives. These were orthodox enough theologically and critical enough of American society but far more engaged with public affairs than Hulst ever wanted to be. His sort of Calvinism would flourish in the CRC again after World War I, when worldliness and greed seemed to threaten once more. But the closed uniformity that Hulst desired for his denomination always has remained elusive, from his day to the present.

Meanwhile, the world encroached on Coldbrook in subtler ways. After Hulst left in 1906, the congregation built a new church in the old neighborhood. But the factories and warehouses kept closing in, while Dutch families kept moving out. Coldbrook's neighborhood ranked high among Dutch enclaves in Grand Rapids for transiency, low in home ownership.[14] Hulst's successor built the church up to 250 families (from 180 in 1906); the language split lowered this to 170 by 1935. It grew again to 200 families by 1950, then declined to 130 by 1970, the size it maintains at present. Seeking to arrest this decline, the congregation sold its old building in 1963 to an African-American Church of God congregation and moved farther northeast, where it renamed itself according to its new neighborhood as Beckwith Hills CRC. For all that change, however, the church's centennial book of 1982 proclaims a message of Scriptural faithfulness and sound biblical doctrine that Hulst would recognize. The roster of Beckwith Hills' membership carries a lot of Coldbrook names and maintains some of the remarkable continuity that the old church offered. Hulst himself had not moved at random but followed several families from his old Dutch parish to America. One of his most faithful supporters at Coldbrook, Sipke S. Postma, had not only been his parishioner back in the Netherlands but had witnessed Hulst bury his father there in 1859. Postma was succeeded in Grand Rapids by his son who was organist at Coldbrook from

the day the instrument was installed in 1884 until the last Dutch service in 1951.[15] Such were the ties of faith and blood that helped the Dutch transplant themselves from one homeland to another.

HUMBLE GLORY

As the Dutch battle proceeded on the near north end, a happier event on the West Side announced the arrival of another ethnic presence in Grand Rapids. St. Adalbert's Roman Catholic Church was founded in 1881 as the third urban Polish Catholic parish in Michigan, the 25th in the United States. Polish immigration to Grand Rapids hit flood tide, however, only in the first decade of the 20th century, just when St. Adalbert's gained its landmark status by raising the magnificent edifice that dominates the near West Side to this day. This course of progress had a counterpoint of privation, denigration, and its own set of ecclesiastical quarrels, all of which do not diminish but enrich St. Adalbert's story,

FIGURES 8, 9
Exterior and interior of St. Adalbert's first building.

A Testament to Their Faith

Clothed in his clerical finery and followed by a horde of well-wishers, Bishop Paul Rhode from Chicago stood outside the doors of St. Adalbert's Catholic Church on the morning of June 22, 1913. Sunlight was just starting to filter through the clouds. After six years of construction, the huge stone edifice was being consecrated.

FIGURE 10 Detail of St. Adalbert's Basilica.

Many Poles for whom the domed building was so important stood silently as the bishop struck its front door with the base of his crozier, and called: "Lift up your gates, ye princes and be ye lifted up, ye everlasting doors, and the King of glory shall come in."

From inside, echoing an historic response from the Psalms, a deacon called: "Who is the King of Glory?" Still standing outside, the bishop from Chicago replied: "The Lord of armies. He is the King of Glory."

And with that, the door swung open and the bishop and a small, hand-picked entourage entered the spacious church. Most of the clergy and nearly 200 onlookers had to remain outside as the mysterious rite continued.

At the time of the consecration, the Sandusky limestone structure with its Romanesque domes and stained glass windows was an architectural wonder. Erected at a cost of $150,000 and standing at its highest point 150 feet above the ground, the church was a testament to the faith of a persecuted people. Marbled walls, sturdy, beamed floor, lofted altar, Corinthian columns and oak pews reflected a dedication that required families to go without to build what at the time was Michigan's largest Catholic church outside of Detroit.

Work began on the church in 1907. The cornerstone was laid Aug. 18 of the same year. The semi-Gothic windows, the Stations of the Cross imported from Italy, and the raised canopy above the altar drew proud stares and tear-filled glances on the day of the consecration, which occurred when a church was debt free.

"Building a church of this stature was part of their ethos," said Eduard A. Skendzel, a historian whose father, Adam Paul, played in a Polish military band at the church's consecretion activities. "My dad mentioned the day many times. He knew that this church was an external manifestation of what they could do, of what they believed in."

The church was constructed as a reminder as well of the impoverished and troubled place from which these immigrants came. The church was made as a "beautifully balanced, imposing, profound and lovely building in the northern Romanesque style so characteristic of many churches still standing in Poland," writes Philip Jung in his history of St. Adalbert's parish.

On the day of the consecration, the auxiliary bishop from Chicago was given the duties of performing the rites that would make this officially a Catholic structure. Rhode had come to Grand Rapids the night before. Being of Polish extraction, he was called upon by the pastor, the Rev. Casimir Skory, to perform the consecration. Later that day, Bishop Henry Richter, the German head of the church in Grand Rapids, would arrive to say a high Mass.

Once inside the church and before the German bishop arrived, the bishop from Chicago proceeded down the front aisle. As hymns were chanted, Rhode traced in ashes a cross on the floor. He then blessed and sprinkled holy water on the altar and walls of the church before performing one the most important parts of the consecration ceremony.

"Bishop Rhode pronounced the parts of bones of St. Lawrence and St. Innocent, martyrs, genuine relics," wrote a Grand Rapids *Press* reporter. "He sealed them in a silver box, paraded them around the church, sealed them with 'blessed cement' and placed them in the altar stone of the new church."

These relics had been stored the night before in the old church at Fourth Street and Davis Avenue NW. This wooden church next door would be dismantled and shipped in pieces to a new location in Belmont.

As the bishop from Chicago was finishing the cere-

FIGURE 11
One of the stained glass windows that grace St. Adalbert's.

mony inside the church, a procession of horse-drawn and gas-driven vehicles traveled to the east side of the Grand River to the residence of Bishop Richter to escort him to the church.

The streets on this day were packed. Bands played, children hung from trees and perched atop their parents' shoulders. On the way back to church, many marchers could see its copper domes shining in the distance.

"It was one of the most memorable days of his life," said Lorraine Oatley, a St. Adalbert's parishioner of Walenty Flincinski, her grandfather. Flincinski was at one time treasurer of the St. Adalbert Aid Society, the group that had originally dreamed of building a new church.

What Walenty Flincinski saw in the parade were 1,500 men, many in military regalia with sabres and rifles, moving toward the church.

Once outside the church, the bishop stepped out of his vehicle. Bodies parted and hats were doffed as he entered the church. The bishop had been skeptical and a little critical of plans to build such a Catholic church on the West Side. But looking around the new church, he realized how wrong he had been.

In his homily during the Mass, he said: "I did not believe that you people could complete the undertaking that you have started, but today I see the result of your generosity."

On Feb. 16, 1980, another ceremony occurred within the walls of St. Adalbert's. On that day, the structure was officially designated a basilica, making it the only one in Michigan and only one of a small handful in the nation.

The term basilica derives from the ancient Roman court of law but now designates a Catholic church of unusual architecture and historical significance.

On both counts, St. Adalbert's building has amply fulfilled the dreams of the humble people whose sacrifice erected it.

making it a fit microcosm of the Polish immigrants' venture into a new life.

In 1876, while the United States celebrated a century of independence, Poland neared 100 years of eclipse. Poland's territory had fallen to the Prussian, Austrian, and Russian empires piece by piece in the late 18th century until, politically speaking, there was nothing left. By the 1870s, things had gotten worse. The Russians avenged a Polish uprising in 1863 by launching a Russification policy to suppress Polish language and culture. The Germans, newly unified after 800 years of fragmentation, carried out a similar plan with particular hostility toward the Roman Catholic Church, which they were attacking in all their territories. Austria's Poles were left unmolested but suffered economically in one of the most densely populated, underdeveloped regions in all Europe.[16]

These trials spurred a massive emigration to the United States. Where the Dutch sent thousands, Poland sent millions — in fact, 2.5 million between 1850 and 1920. This meant that the Polish sector of Grand Rapids, while substantial, would be more a miniature than a leader of the Polish community nationwide. The first Poles in the city came from German-ruled regions where industrialization had begun. They often were craftsmen who could find decent positions in the booming furniture trade. By the 1890s Poles from the Austrian and Russian sectors were coming in huge numbers and continued to do so until World War I. These had fewer industrial skills and tended to land grueling jobs in tough industries: mills, mines, and slaughterhouses. In Grand Rapids, they worked the lower rungs of the furniture plants on the northwest end, "the brickyard" near Michigan Street and Fuller Avenue NE, and the gypsum mines on the near Southwest Side. Soon, each of these quarters had its own Polish Catholic parish: respectively, St. Adalbert's (1881), St. Isidore's (1897), and Sacred Heart (1904).[17]

St. Adalbert's was formed in a typical immigrant pattern. The first Grand Rapids Poles worshipped at the German-language St. Mary's but their numbers (25 percent of St. Mary's baptisms by 1880) led them to plan a church of their own. The laity took the lead. From the start Grand Rapids Poles had formed fraternal associations to provide such basics as burial insurance, employment and housing references, friends to talk to. One of

now superior of the School Sisters of Notre Dame who taught at St. Mary's School. With 130 families pledging support, St. Adalbert's came into being in 1881 at Fourth Street and Davis Avenue NW.[18]

The church was the heart of a busy neighborhood. Five religious and four secular associations had their own halls in the area, while corner grocers and saloon-keepers served as its nerve centers. Choral groups, theater troupes, athletic clubs, lecture series, banks and credit unions blossomed, making Grand Rapids Polonia a vibrant and nearly self-sufficient community. In all these, lay people and Polish cultural and patriotic themes loomed large. Just that caused tensions in the church. American Catholicism by now had vested substantial power, including parish property titles and budget supervision, in the hands of the clergy. The Poles were used to more lay control. They also were accustomed to a style of worship that featured everyday language, folk hymns, color, and exuber-

FIGURES 14, 15
Two giants of the Polish West Side: left, Father Ladislaus Krakowski, founding pastor of Sacred Heart Church; below, Father Casimir Skory, pastor of St. Adalbert's, 1905-1935.

these, the St. Adalbert Benevolent Society, became the core of the new parish. News of its intentions disturbed church authorities, however — not so much St. Mary's pastor, Father John G. Ehrenstrasser, who remained neutral toward the proposal, but Bishop Caspar Borgess of Detroit who had experienced enough grief from the five Polish parishes already existing in the state. Crucial support came from Sister Mary Tita Hutsch, a native of the first Polish settlement in America and

FIGURE 16
The 1886 Pulaski Cornet Band.

FURNITURE AND FAITH **77**

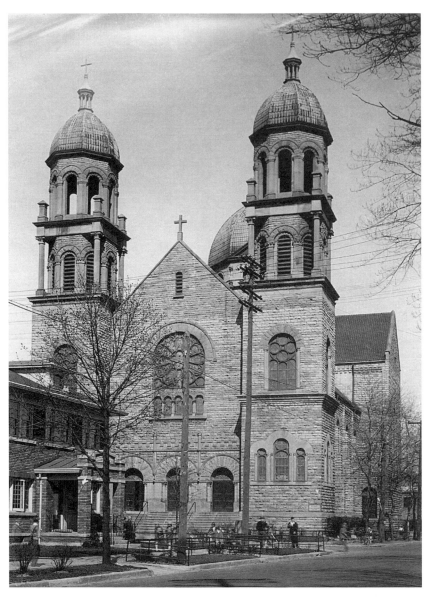

ance, in contrast to the quiet, spare Irish style ("the church of silence," some Poles called it) common to American parishes. These differences could literally be causes of war. In the 1890s Polish factions fought each other in the streets and bishops in the courts of Chicago over control of church buildings. Various dissenters across the country defied the Catholic hierarchy to form the separate Polish National Catholic Church in 1904.[19]

The priests at St. Adalbert's, therefore, had to walk a thin line between patriotism and piety, between their Polish parishioners and (after 1883) their German bishop, Henry Joseph Richter. Father Simon Ponganis did well for much of his pastorate on the West Side from 1886 to 1904 but, eventually, not well enough. He quelled the national separatists by managing to keep his flock Catholics first, Poles second. On the other hand, when the Polish National Alliance at its 1899 national convention in Grand Rapids called for the formation of Polish political clubs, Ponganis agreed. The Kosciuszko Democratic Club organized that year with his blessing to give Poles a common voice in city affairs. Bishop Richter disapproved — what else, Ponganis asked, would you expect from a "Prussian"?[20] But then Richter and Ponganis had already fought in 1897 over the name of the brickyard parish. Ponganis had suggested St.

FIGURE 17
St. Adalbert's was consecrated on June 22, 1913.

Grand Rapids' Roman Catholic Family Tree 1833–1993

From the arrival of the first missionary to the Indians at the Grand River to sprawling suburban churches with acres of blacktopped parking lots, the genealogy of its Catholic churches reflects the growth of the Grand Rapids area. Assimilation of one ethnic group always has been followed by the arrival of another, providing the local Catholic community with a truly international flavor.

CHURCH	DATE	ORIGINAL LOCATION	PARENT CHURCH	ETHNICITY
St. Andrew's	1833	Butterworth and Front SW	Diocese of Detroit	—
Holy Trinity	1848	Five Mile and Baumhoff NW	St. Andrew's	German
St. Mary's	1857	First and Broadway NW	St. Andrew's	German
St. James	1870	Bridge and National NW	St. Andrew's	Irish
St. Adalbert's	1881	Fourth and Davis NW	St. Mary's	Polish
St. Joseph's	1887	Rumsey near Grandville SW	St. Andrew's/St. Mary's	Dutch
St. Alphonsus	1888	Leonard and Lafayette NE	St. Andrew's	—
St. Isidore's	1897	Diamond and Flat NE	St. Adalbert's	Polish
Sacred Heart	1903	Valley and Park SW	St. Adalbert's	Polish
SS. Peter and Paul	1904	Quarry and Myrtle NW	St. Adalbert's	Lithuanian
St. Anthony's	1906	Richmond and Broadway NW	St. Mary's	German
Holy Name	1908	Godfrey and Chicago Drive SW	St. Joseph's	—
Our Lady of Sorrows	1908	St. Andrew's Cathedral	St. Andrew's	Italian
St. Francis Xavier	1914	Brown and Lafayette SE	St. Andrew's	—
St. Stephen's	1924	Rosewood and Franklin SE	St. Andrew's	—
St. Thomas	1924	Wilcox Park and Youell SE	St. Andrew's	—
St. John Vianney	1942	Division and Abbie SE	St. Francis Xavier	—
Blessed Sacrament	1946	Plainfield and Eleanor NE	St. Alphonsus	—
St. Jude	1946	Plainfield and Fuller NE	St. Alphonsus	—
Immaculate Heart	1949	Plymouth and Burton SE	St. Francis Xavier	—
Our Lady of Guadalupe	1950	LaGrave and Maple SE	St. Andrew's	Mexican
Our Lady of Aglona	1951	LaGrave and Maple SE	St. Andrew's	Latvian
St. Robert's	1951	Fulton and Ada Drive SE	St. Francis Xavier	—
Holy Spirit	1952	Lake Mich. Dr. and Edison Park NW	St. Thomas	—
St. Pius X	1953	40th and Wilson SW	Holy Name	—
St. Mary Magdalen	1956	52nd and Christie SE	St. John Vianney	—
St. Paul	1961	Burton and Woodlawn SE	St. Stephen	—
St. Dominic	1974	Division and Abbie SE	St. John Vianney	—
Vietnamese Community	1976	Burton and Union SE	Diocese of GR	Vietnamese
Korean Community	1993	—	Diocese of GR	Korean

Stanislaus; Richter had forbidden any Polish name and mandated St. Isidore instead. A few years later, however, the roles seemed to reverse. When the Poles south of Fulton petitioned for their own parish, Bishop Richter approved, to Father Ponganis' rage

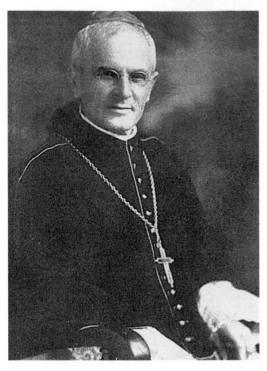

FIGURE 19
Bishop Joseph Pinten,
whose stern German
style aggravated local
Polish Catholics.

("Sooner will hair grow on my palms!"). Perhaps Ponganis feared that the new parish, Sacred Heart, would join the Polish National schism then reaching its peak. Perhaps he suspected Richter of trying to conquer the West Side Poles by dividing them. Perhaps he saw the split as dooming his plans for a magnificent new building at St. Adalbert's. In any case, he was abruptly transferred to St. Mary's in Gaylord, whose pastor, Casimir Skory, was brought to Grand Rapids to replace him. Sacred Heart was duly formed in 1904 with St. Adalbert's assistant, Ladislaus Krakowski, as pastor.[21]

Father Skory served St. Adalbert's until 1935; Father Krakowski was succeeded by Joseph Kaminski, who served at Sacred Heart until 1931. Between them, these pastors built two of Grand Rapids' architectural landmarks. St. Adalbert's new building was under construction from 1907 to 1913 because of Bishop Richter's pay-as-you-go plan, but the delay was worth it. When the first Polish-American bishop, Paul Peter Rhode, came to consecrate it on June 22, 1913, the parish had a 194-by-80-foot building with a 150-foot exterior dome and two 134-foot bell towers. The interior was illuminated with windows telling the life of Christ; those in the apse honored five Polish saints. Wasting nothing, the diocese moved the old building to St. Adalbert's daughter church, Assumption parish in Belmont (then a rural Polish enclave). Sacred Heart's new structure went up much faster. Commissioned in 1920, it was dedicated New Year's Day 1924 as the grandest building on the Southwest Side, its Romanesque interior echoing St. Paul's-Outside-the-Walls in Rome.[22]

Not just the buildings but the ceremonies within and around them reveal the full measure of the Poles' faith. At Sacred Heart's first worship, Christmas Eve 1923, the parish historian records, the new bells and the jubilant Polish carols literally made the building shake; this faith could move mountains. At St. Adalbert's dedication, as on most public occasions in that era, Grand Rapids' Poles marched in dashing color. Six bands and scores of men in drill teams — the King John Sobieski Guards, the Uhlans, the Zouaves, the Polish Guards — dressed in gold-trimmed uniforms, or on horseback with high-plumed helmets, escorted dignitaries from St. Andrew's Cathedral to the West Side in a parade that couldn't help but rivet the whole city's attention.[23] The Poles might live in tiny frame houses, might labor at hard, dirty jobs, might be slandered as drab and no-account, but through their faith they asserted glory in public and found radiance for themselves. For this, the core of their life and community, they would sacrifice. St. Adalbert's was erected debt-free at the cost of $150,000 at a time when the average furniture worker made $12 a week.[24]

These sacrifices could exact a high price. Sacred Heart was built for $250,000, more than half of that borrowed on the assumption that Polish immigration and the 1920s' prosperity would both continue. Neither did. The depression of the 1930s reduced Father Kaminski to door-to-door begging for funds to meet the mortgage. That, together with his insistence on keeping Polish in services when his bishop Joseph Pinten (another "Prussian") wanted English, caused his ouster for "maladministration" in 1931. Father Skory at St. Adalbert's was relieved of his duties soon after. The Polish-American Bank, sanctioned by Sacred Heart's pastor, failed in the Depression just as its successor, St. Matthew's Credit Union, would be caught in the banking vicissitudes of the 1980s.[25]

These crises, however, did not disturb the core values of Grand Rapids' Polonia. Their worship on Sunday translated into a steady, weekday commitment to family, hard work, and parochial education. Already in 1890, St. Adalbert's erected an eight-room schoolhouse to replace the frame structure built in 1884 and three years later a convent to house the School Sisters of Notre Dame who taught there. In 1921 they put up a 27-room building for the 1,450 pupils in attendance. Sacred Heart's school had been expanded in 1918 to accommodate 650 students but enrolled 900 just 10 years later.[26] The city establishment tended to sniff at the large class size and spare resources these numbers imply, but the parents who sent their children there wanted pedagogical sophistication less than a firm foundation in the ethic of their own community. That ethic mistrusted the American cult of upward mobility when such came at the cost of communal loyalty. It did not scorn blue-collar status but taught pride in hard work of every station. It believed that small people could do great things. That belief was amply confirmed just before the parish centennial in 1980 when St. Adalbert's was elevated to basilica status as both an architectural treasure and an historic center of the faith. The official designation came from the Polish Pope, John Paul II.

⁂

THE CHURCH OF MAYORS

In the centennial summer of 1876, when the Dutch dominie L.J. Hulst arrived in town, the mayor of Grand Rapids was Peter R.L. Peirce, a merchant and 18-year member of the ruling council at St. Mark's Episcopal Church on Division Avenue downtown. In 1904, when Sacred Heart Church was founded over Father Ponganis' protest, the mayor was Edwin F. Sweet, a lawyer and another vestryman at St. Mark's. Almost every year in between showed a good chance of a St. Mark's member being in the mayor's chair. Nine of the 19 mayors who served from 1875 to 1906 came from this one church, and they held the office for 20 of these 32 years.[27]

This record can be attributed in part to age and status. In 1876 St. Mark's was one of the oldest and most elite churches in town, an enclave of affluent, Anglo-American business and professional families. But some other congregations had that profile, too. Something about St. Mark's gave it a strategic place in city affairs. Nor was its role simply political. In 1873, when the economy collapsed, the infant furniture industry nearly died, and Peter Peirce was serving his first term as mayor, eight women of St. Mark's organized one of the city's first and longest lasting charitable institutions, a home for the sick and indigent that would

FIGURE 20
Edwin F. Sweet: member of Congress, Grand Rapids mayor, and St. Mark's Church member.

FIGURES 21, 22
St. Mark's Church first building, exterior and interior, circa 1850s.

evolve into Butterworth Hospital. From their heights, St. Mark's men and women could work effectively at the depths and at the center of city life.

For one, they had had a lot of practice, both at struggle and at success. The church had been formally organized by 17 villagers on Oct. 6, 1836, but had floundered without a pastor. It had to be reorganized in November 1839, this time with a minister, the Rev. Melancthon Hoyt. The group managed to gather $800 for a 41-by-27-foot frame building at Division and Crescent NW, consecrated on April 25, 1841, to the accompaniment of a string trio and vocal quartet. But the next year the vestry could not raise the minister's promised salary, so Hoyt regretfully departed. St. Mark's owed its survival through all these jolts to tenacious lay leaders; as Hoyt later recalled: "I have never known a more faithful band of workers." [28]

Only with the arrival in October 1843 of the Rev. Francis H. Cuming did St. Mark's become firmly established. As this was his seventh pioneer parish, Cuming offered St. Mark's plenty of experience at church planting. He also was familiar with the sorts of Yankees that had settled Grand Rapids and knew how to position an Episcopal church among them. Cuming had been pastor in Rochester, the citadel of upstate New York during its

1820s boom, and there, through his family connections with the town's founder and his post as Grand Master of the Masonic Lodge, had made his church the home of the business elite. The congregation also had resisted the tides of evangelical revivalism that swept the area.[29] Similarly in Grand Rapids, where revivals caught up the Methodists, Congregationalists, and Dutch Reformed in the early 1840s, St. Mark's offered a clear alternative: a set, dignified liturgy already 300 years old; an atmosphere of calm elegance; and a reluctance to pry too closely into members' beliefs and behavior so long as these met the forms of respectability and tradition.

In fact, St. Mark's went well beyond respectability to public responsibility. The case of John Almy stands out. Almy was present at the 1836 meeting, at the 1839 reconstitution, at Hoyt's departure and Cuming's arrival. He was equally active in secular affairs, being one of the village's first bankers and land surveyors, four years vil-

FIGURE 23
A veteran planter of frontier Episcopal parishes, the Rev. Francis H. Cuming made St. Mark's flourish from 1843-1862.

FIGURE 24
St. Mark's in 1850 before the towers were added.

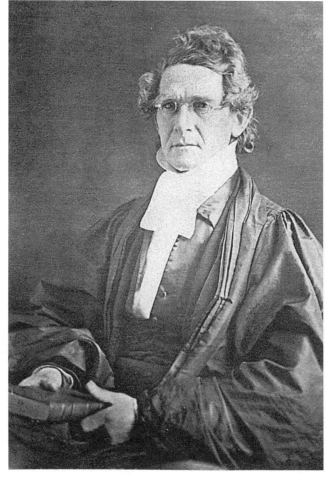

lage president, and a successful state immigration agent.[30] Appointed to the latter post in 1845, he could watch the Dutch, the Germans, and the Irish start to pour into Michigan and the Grand River valley. At this point, too, St. Mark's women played a crucial role. One of the two surviving charter members at St. Mark's semi-centennial in 1886 spent much of his speech testifying to "the holy women who were the founders of this church" and the "foster mothers" of dozens of young people who arrived in the valley alone and unsheltered.[31]

Given, then, a permanent pastor and active laity, the congregation flourished. The core of St. Mark's present building went up already in 1848 — financed in large part by the ladies' sewing circle — and qualified at the time as the state's largest Episcopal church west of Detroit. Its towers were added in 1851, a 1,300-pound bell in 1865, and a $4,000 organ in 1867. The church also ventured boldly into education, founding a girls' prep school and a co-ed college in 1850; the project failed three years later for reasons of cost, not of interest (225 enrolled). The church's leadership was tested again in 1862 when Pastor Cuming became a chaplain in the Civil War army, leaving behind a congregation numbering 300 full members. St.

FIGURE 25
The interior of St. Mark's around World War I.

Mark's carried on well enough to be able to meet the postwar boom by sponsoring three mission centers in outlying Grand Rapids that soon became Episcopal churches in their own right: St. Paul's (1871) at Turner Avenue near Fourth Street NW, Trinity (1873) at Michigan Street and College Avenue NE, and Grace (1875) at Lafayette Avenue and Cherry Street SE. In 1873, besides opening its hospital, St. Mark's hosted the convention which decided to form West Michigan as a separate Episcopal diocese.[32]

The economic depression that began the same year found St. Mark's financially

FIGURE 26
View of St. Mark's in the 1890s with the towers.

overextended from all these projects, not to mention a recent $36,000 refurbishing of its sanctuary. For several years the congregation struggled to lower the debt, then erased it entirely with a single offering of $16,500 on Easter 1881. Since furniture workers at the time were averaging $10 earnings for a 70-hour week, the collection gives an idea of St. Mark's resources.[33] But wealth alone does not explain the church's leadership in city affairs, since the money continued after St. Mark's political role eventually declined. The particular occupations of St. Mark's leaders were significant in that, as lawyers and old-time merchants, they could see the city whole without being immersed in the furniture manufacturers' point of view.[34] As earlier religiously, so now politically, St. Mark's offered an alternative — a leadership separate from the industrialists and able to mediate between management and labor's interests.

This political position had clear religious components. By a numerical standard, Episcopalians have been highly over-represented in American history among business executives and university presidents, federal judges and Cabinet officers, members of Congress, senators, and presidents from George Washington to George Bush. Part of the reason is the particular theological outlook to which St. Mark's memoirs also give ample testimony. The Episcopal tradition claims religious legitimacy by historical descent from the archbishops of England back to the apostolic church, hence to Christ himself. In this argument, institutional continuity and constitutional legality are of the essence and establish a mindset that naturally carries over into secular affairs.[35] With their confidence in law, tradition, and organic growth, St. Mark's leaders could keep their poise amid the city's tumultuous changes in the late 19th century.

Just as important, St. Mark's occupied an intermediate zone between Catholicism and Protestantism. Episcopalians owe no allegiance to Rome and follow basic Protestant doctrine, yet their institutional structure of bishops and dioceses and their liturgy of rich vestments and ritual resemble Catholics'. Exactly this mediating position helped St. Mark's in local politics. In 1906 Catholics constituted 49 percent of Grand Rapids' church population, Protestants (and a very few "others") 51 percent.[36] Catholic and Protestant precincts could elect their own to seats on the city council, but the city-wide post of mayor demanded someone acceptable — or less offensive — to both groups. That St. Mark's offered. Moreover, St. Mark's vestry was heavily Democratic.[37] Their party affiliation therefore appealed to the Polish and native-born working class, while their

FIGURE 27
Restoration of St. Mark's Grand River limestone exterior in 1954.

Secret Societies Versus the Churches

The heavy door slams shut on a tomb-like hall. The initiate, blindfolded and bound in chains, is led around the room—two, five, ten times before he loses count. Then the blindfold is removed. White-robed torch bearers surround him; a black-robed judge stands before him and directs his gaze down to a blood-tinged skeleton lying in a coffin at his feet. Men, all in masks, ring the room; they take up an ancient-sounding chant, then fall silent. The black robe gives a sermon, then the initiate is blindfolded again and subjected to several more rounds of mock ordeal, prayers, and lectures. Finally, to solemn warnings, he takes a blood oath never to reveal what he has learned, always to come to the aid of these, his new brothers, and to abide faithfully by the code of universal fraternity and charity.

FIGURE 28   Arch over Canal Street (Monroe Avenue) welcomes Masons to Grand Rapids.

So proceeded the induction ceremonies of the Odd Fellows, the Masons, the Knights of Pythias, and a dozen other male secret societies which entered their golden age in post-Civil War America. From near extinction in 1840, their membership climbed to 446,000 in 1870, to 854,000 in 1900, to a peak of 3.3 million (12 percent of the eligible population) in 1930. Grand Rapids was no exception to the trend. By 1890 it had 49 lodges, including 10 of the Odd Fellows and 13 of the Masons, the latter numbering 1,700 members. In Grand Rapids as elsewhere, the movement attracted the rich and powerful: bankers, lawyers, and eminences in local politics. Secret societies gained special attention here in the late 1870s when, in successive years, the Masons, Odd Fellows, and Knights of Honor held their state conventions in Grand Rapids.

As a counterattack Edmond Ronayne, an ex-Mason and itinerant lecturer, came to town in 1879 to expose lodge secrets and prove their dangers to religion and the republic. Thus was launched the debate that split not only

In Grand Rapids, the rise of secret societies paralleled the national trend. By 1890, the city had 49 lodges, including 10 of the Oddfellows and 13 of the Masons.

the Dutch Reformed, but the German Lutherans. A group dissatisfied with its prohibition of secret societies left Immanuel Lutheran in 1880 to form St. John's Evangelical Church (see Chapter 8).

Members of fraternal orders argued that the whole uproar was mistaken, that lodges were the friends of Christianity and morality. Recent historians, however, have agreed with the opposition at least on one point: by their ritual, indoctrination, and ethical directives, secret societies did function as religious bodies. The religion might supplement, parallel, or rival Christianity, but the religious dimension itself was the source of the lodges' appeal. Whereas churches tended to be heavily female-influenced, the all-male orders supplied rites and instruction that acclimated young men to the difficult business-professional world they were entering. Dying to their mothers' world, born again amid their new brothers, the initiates were well advised to keep oaths of silence lest it be publicly acknowledged that fraternal societies indeed amounted to "an alternative form of religion, of family, and of social organization ...."

FIGURE 29
One more view of Grand Rapids in the 1870s taken from the Morton House looking northeast. Churches visible in the picture are, from left to right, St. Mark's, Second Reformed, First Methodist and Fountain Street Baptist.

social standing and economic respectability merited the trust of the city elite.

But this formula did not last forever. In 1896 the Democratic Party was taken over by elements that, to St. Mark's eyes, looked radical: angry farmers, populists, easy-money advocates. St. Mark's vestrymen joined the conservative, Gold Democrat faction in response, but the split only guaranteed the Democrats' defeat in 1896 and hastened their decline in the years thereafter. The congregation's politicos lost some of their zeal and most of their local offices.[38] Edwin Sweet left the mayor's office in 1906 and went to Washington — as congressman (1911–13), then as Assistant Secretary of Commerce in the Wilson administration (1913–21). Local power passed to George "Deacon" Ellis, a renegade Methodist who allied East Side, native-born workers and the West Side Polish Catholics under — of all things — a reform-Republican banner. Every two years from 1906 to 1914 Ellis defeated an Episcopalian Democrat opponent for the mayor's chair. Ellis' right-hand man was Stanley Jackowski, a member at St. Adalbert's and head of the Polish-American Bank.[39] Consequently, political loyalties in Episcopalian circles gradually shifted. Gerald Ford, Sr., was a

FIGURE 30
St. Mark's magnificent organ in 1987.

vestryman at St. Mark's, but his son would belong to Grace Church where the vestry was strongly Republican.[40] When Ellis finally encountered an effective opposition, it originated one block south and east of St. Mark's at Fountain Street Baptist Church. There, in 1906, the furniture industrialists joined their new pastor in a crusade for clean government. St. Mark's leaders could only wonder when it had gotten dirty.

St. Mark's and Politics

Members of St. Mark's Episcopal Church dominated the mayor's office in the last quarter of the 19th century but, typically, they held a number of posts on the way to that office and sometimes went on to higher positions as well.

Name	Occupation	Years Mayor	Party	Other Offices Held
Peter R.L. Peirce	Merchant	1873 1875–1876	Republican	City Clerk, 1853–1855 County Clerk, 1854–1868 State Senate, 1869–1870
Francis Letellier	Merchant, lumber	1879	Citizen-Democrat	Board of Public Works, 1890–1897
Edmund B. Dikeman	Jeweler	1882, 1886–87		
John L. Curtiss	Wholesale oil/paper	1885	Democrat Greenback	Alderman, 1878–1879 State Senate, 1885–1886
Isaac Weston	Banking, lumber	1888	Democrat	Democratic state commissioner, 1880–1890 treasurer, 1882–1886 chairman, 1886–1890 Delegate, Democratic National Convention 1888
Edwin F. Uhl	Lawyer, banker	1890–1891	Democrat	Asst. U.S. Secretary of State,1893–1896 U.S. ambassador to Germany, 1896–1897
William J. Stuart	Lawyer	1892–1893	Republican	City attorney, 1880–1884, 1888–1891 Superior Court judge, 1905, 1911, 1915
George R. Perry	Wholesale grocer	1898–1902	Democrat	City treasurer, 1887–1888, 1890 City council, 1915 Lost mayor's race, 1912, 1914 Lost congressional race, 1898
Edwin F. Sweet	Lawyer	1904–1906	Gold-Democrat	Board of Education, 1899–1906, 1923–26 Congress, 1911–1913 Asst. U.S. Secretary Commerce, 1913–21 City Commission, 1926–1928 Lost governor's race, 1916

All these men but two (Letellier, born in Belgium, and Stuart, born in Barry County, Michigan) were natives of New York or New England. Five — Letellier, Curtiss, Weston, Stuart, and Perry — were members of secret societies like the Masons.

SOURCE: Compilations of Philip R. Vander Meer from Grand Rapids city directories, and Albert Baxter, *History of the City of Grand Rapids, Michigan*.

Taming the Industrial City 5

1906 – 1920

THE REV. ALFRED WESLEY WISHART ROARED INTO Grand Rapids in October 1906, ready to crack the whip over his new parishioners at Fountain Street Baptist Church. His object was not the sin in their hearts — for by all estimates, they were righteous enough — but the evils of the city, from its mean streets to its high offices.

Over the next 27 years, Wishart used his pulpit to great effect but with paradoxical results. Preaching brotherhood, he provoked quarrels; lauding democracy, he bolstered the city's elite.

Wishart took over a church that was already well-positioned. Since 1876, Fountain Street could claim the city's most imposing church building; since 1886, its largest congregation; and, since 1896, its most striking minister in the person of John Herman Randall — a tall, athletic pulpiteer of considerable eloquence and powerful mind. On both counts Wishart fell short. He was short, literally: 5-foot-6; he weighed but 122 pounds; his enormous "Texas longhorn" mustache seemed oddly out of place; and his sermons lacked both the rhetorical and intellectual command of Randall's.[1] But Wishart was no fool. He proved feisty and shrewd, full of high ideals, equally full of worldly wisdom, and skilled at blending the two into a crusading spirit that fired the imagination of his listeners. The people who hired Wishart knew they were getting a fighter. They wanted no less.

The most notable crusades came during Wishart's first 12 years in town. He took a commanding position in Grand Rapids' tumultuous furniture strike in 1911. He led the 1910–1916 campaign for a new city charter which altered the power structure of local politics. During World War I he swelled the chorus of militant patriotism that brought dissenting radicals

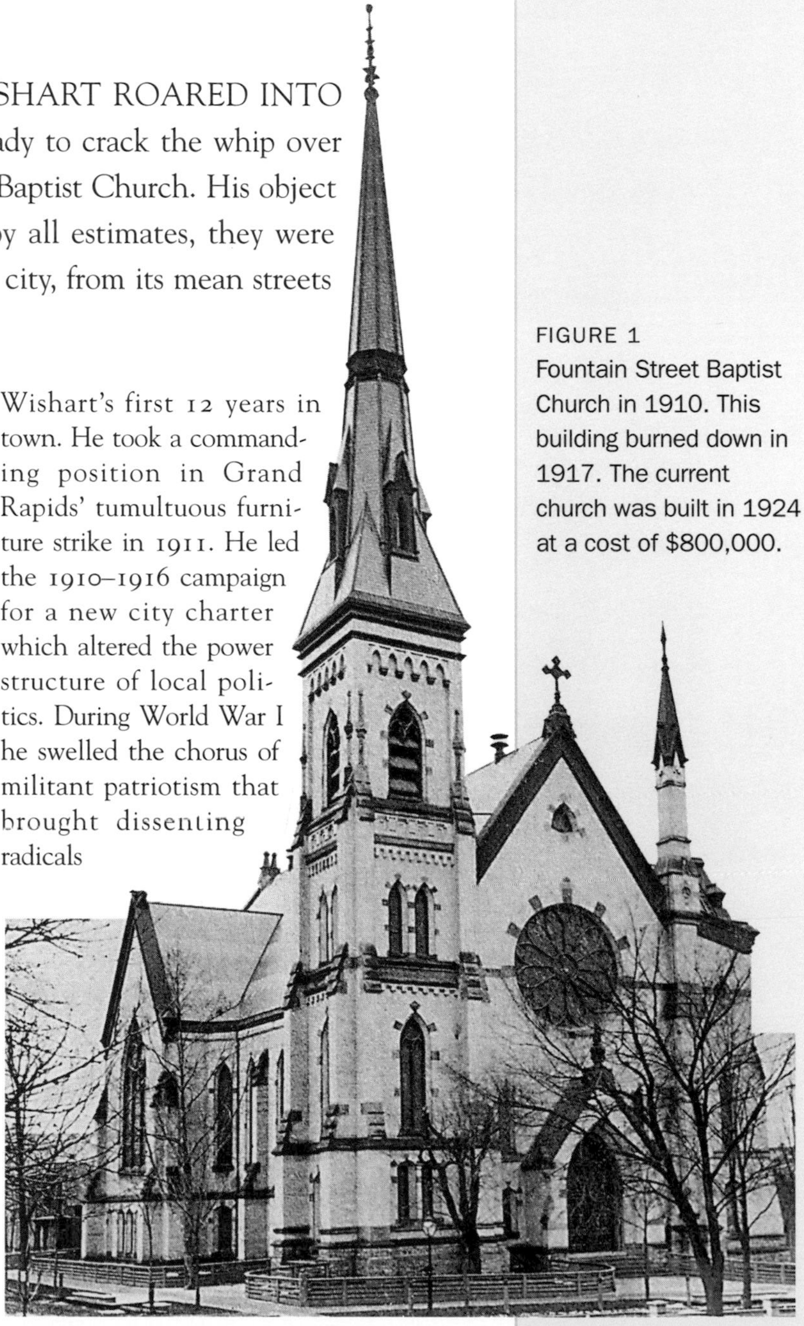

FIGURE 1
Fountain Street Baptist Church in 1910. This building burned down in 1917. The current church was built in 1924 at a cost of $800,000.

FIGURES 2, 3
The Rev. John Herman Randall, left, and the Rev. Alfred W. Wishart led Fountain Street Baptist Church from 1896 to 1933.

and immigrants to heel. All these secular battles grew out of Wishart's "progressive" theology, which earned him the ire of local Catholics, the Dutch Reformed and his fellow Baptists. Like the Apostle Paul, Wishart loved fighting the good fight, finishing the course, and claiming the crown of righteousness. Most everything else of St. Paul he wished to drop — or improve.

A CHALLENGE TO CHURCHES

Wishart came by his spirit naturally, for he was caught up in a great change sweeping the upper reaches of American Protestantism in his generation. Born on Sept. 9, 1865, of Scottish and French Protestant stock in New York City at the close of the Civil War, he was raised on legends of the Grand Crusade in the South while witnessing America's transformation into an industrial giant. After clerking awhile in a law office, he turned to higher education at the new universities endowed by industrial magnates. Probably out of family tradition, Wishart chose Baptist institutions: college at Colgate in upstate New York (B.A. 1889) and some graduate study at the University of Chicago. From these exposures Wishart

drew the two questions that dominated his life. Could the explosive changes of industrialization be smoothed and settled so as to preserve liberty and order? And could Christian faith survive the assault of science and new learning so evident in the universities? Wishart's answer was "yes," with conditions. First, good people had to be mobilized to regain control of public affairs; second, traditional theology had to be radically overhauled. The two, in Wishart's mind, had to go together.

Wishart's ministry at the Central Baptist Church in Trenton, N.J., from 1895 to 1906 took up the first cause in earnest. He sponsored a series of "civic revivals" — special meetings where people were challenged to cast sin not out of themselves but from the city's public life. Trenton's gambling ring, its red-light district, its political system of bribes and collusion all fell to Wishart's assaults from the pulpit and, interestingly, in his two-year editorship of the Trenton *Times.* Doubtless this success helped attract Fountain Street's attention as the church searched for a new pastor in 1906. For Grand Rapids, too, had recently joined the era's hall of shame, the list of cities plagued by trickery and corruption. Over the previous five years a water scandal had unfolded in which half the city council, the city attorney, strategic journalists, and assorted other parties had received bribes from devious entrepreneurs to support a grossly inflated bond issue for a pipeline to Lake Michigan. The project might eventually have pumped fresh water to city faucets; it certainly would have put fresh cash into the conspirators' pockets.[2]

If Grand Rapids' ordinary citizens were bothered by the scandal, the furniture manufacturers had a graver worry. Grand Rapids was their trade name, and water-marked furniture does not sell well. At the same time they sensed here an opportunity. Since the scandal had discredited the reigning politicians (the set of conservative Democrats at St. Mark's), it opened the door for new leadership from another quarter. They wanted that to be Fountain Street, and they wanted their new pastor to lead the way. The committee that brought Wishart to town included two of the city's most powerful furniture executives, William Gay and Charles Hamilton. Two others, Robert Irwin and John Covody, Jr., sat prominently in the pews.[3] They all applauded as Wishart repeated his civic revivals in Grand Rapids, agitating for clean government, more parks and playgrounds, straighter streets and urban beautification. But Wishart also would fulfill their larger dream. Over the next decade his battles provided the furniture elite with the occasions to turn their wealth and prestige into political power.

Wishart also pursued his theological agenda. His first year in town, he called the city's churches to face up to the intellectual challenge of the new century. Traditional Christianity, he declared, tried to deliver individuals out of this world into a supernatural salvation. That explained why American cities could be filled with pious Christians and political corruption. The churches' new calling was to bring salvation in this world, and not just to selected individuals but to the whole society. The kingdom of God was

earthly peace, justice, and progress — nothing more and nothing less. To bring in that kingdom, Wishart insisted, theology had to be drained of its supernatural content. To him Jesus was not divine and human but simply human, but also a perfect human and therefore God. Jesus came not offering an otherworldly escape but an example of conduct, an inspiring ideal that would energize people to reform their own character and the society around them. God was revealed not only in the Bible — which was fallible — but also in science and literature, in the advance of culture and prosperity, in the noblest human deeds and aspirations. People did not need to be converted from a supposed natural wickedness but encouraged to develop the full potential of their personalities. In this way Christianity could be thoroughly reinterpreted to fit with modern thought and to face up to modern, complex society.[4]

Wishart recognized that this "liberal" theology, as it was labeled, had been introduced to Fountain Street by John Herman Randall 10 years before.[5] But he apparently did not see that his congregation had promoted intellectual progress and social service all along. Isaac McCoy's Baptist mission tried to teach the Odawa literacy and farming techniques as much as the gospel. And Samuel Graves, whose ministry from 1870 to 1885 had made Fountain Street the foremost congregation in the city, was an intellectual and social crusader, too. Graves, like Wishart, had graduated from Colgate and had taught at Kalamazoo College besides. Following his Grand Rapids ministry, he would become president of Atlanta Baptist Seminary, a school for freed blacks in the South and the predecessor of More-

"Because I believe in God, I believe in progress. The world is getting better."

— **The Rev. Alfred W. Wishart**

FIGURE 4
The Rev. Samuel Graves was pastor of Fountain Street Baptist Church from 1870 to 1885.

"A Matter of Decency"

Introduced by Grand Rapids' own Mel Trotter, evangelist Billy Sunday took the stage at the city's old Coliseum on Nov. 5, 1916, and railed against the evils of demon rum. Sunday tore off his tie, ripped open his shirt collar and exhorted more than 7,000 people to turn out two days later and vote to rid the town of the evils of alcohol.

The wiry former big league baseball player came to Grand Rapids at the 11th hour from a revival in Detroit to throw his support behind the move toward Prohibition. On the stage, the fiery fundamentalist preacher figuratively lifted his opponent John Barleycorn by the neck and the seat of the pants and wiped him all over the floor.

FIGURE 5   Billy Sunday and his wife eating breakfast at the Pantlind Hotel.

"I'm here on behalf of the greatest cause on earth," the bantamweight Sunday roared. "I'm here to fight that dirty, God-forsaken whiskey gang."

Sunday's one-day booze-bashing crusade in Grand Rapids was followed two days later by a landslide victory in which voters here, as well as across the state, decided overwhelmingly to go dry. Following years of effort on behalf of various religious organizations, churches and Bible-believing orators such as Sunday, the dread alcohol curse was supposedly rid from this West Michigan community. At the time, Grand Rapids was one of the largest cities in the country to side with the temperance people and members of the indefatigable Anti-Saloon League. In the 1916 election, Grand Rapids voters opted to go dry by more than 3,000 votes. Prohibition became a fact.

Billy Sunday's crusade paid off handsomely here, at least in the opinion of the authors of a widely circulated article which appeared in the Nov. 6, 1920, edition of the national magazine, *The Survey*. Grand Rapids, some people said, was blessed gloriously with the fallout from the anti-liquor crusade.

While Michigan voters decided for Prohibition in November 1916, the nation didn't get on the wagon until May 1, 1918. Taking a look at Grand Rapids from that time until late in 1920, *The Survey* authors concluded that this city reflected the very best of what going dry meant to towns across America.

"Here, then, we have in Grand Rapids a friendly, well-conditioned, representative Midwestern community," *The Survey* wrote. "And here in its homes, its factories, its social institutions and more especially its saloons and savings institutions, we have so many barometers on which we may gauge those three forces at work in the common life of a nation — a year without unemployment, without starvation wages and without drink."

It's unclear if Prohibition truly was the cause of the prosperity that swept the community in the years following World War I. *The Survey* authors argued it was. They claimed the health, wealth and general welfare of Grand Rapidians rose markedly as a direct result of the closing of 160 saloons, seven wholesale liquor dealers, three breweries and dozens of ethnic social halls in Grand Rapids. The intense fervor brought to bear by religious forces in West Michigan uprooted an evil that, *The Survey* authors contested, had been festering here for years.

At the time Prohibition went into effect, Grand Rapids was the 48th largest city in the country. Its 1920 census was 137,634. It had never had a financial bust, had never experienced a bank failure and had not had any serious labor disputes since the furniture strike in 1911. With its booze problem licked and happy days on the horizon, the city was on the rise.

Tuberculosis and infant mortality, crime and unemployment were on the way down in the months following the closure of the bars. Calmly moving into a new era of plenty, fueled by the religious convictions of those who believed booze was behind many problems, Grand Rapids workers found that their average daily wage increased by almost 100 percent between 1917 and 1920.

Without hangovers plaguing laborers, absenteeism on the job decreased. Pawnshop transactions were reduced in this period by one-third and businesses found it easier than ever to collect debts.

As the city rolled into the 1920s, people were reading books, buying cars, going on vacations, purchasing clothes and other goods, and putting money in the collection plates at church in record amounts.

But by 1927, a harsher economic forecast was in the air; it was becoming clear that Prohibition wasn't the cure-all for the city's difficulties. Police records showed in 1927 that "there has been a large increase in offences both in felonies and misdemeanors during the arid decade."

Demon rum was here, bootlegged in from Detroit and Toledo and made in stills throughout the community. And people were again breaking the law.

By then wage increases had slowed and more people had moved to Grand Rapids, perhaps adding to the strain. But it seemed clear that booze was again a reason behind arrests. Police records at this time showed that there were 2,150 arrests for drunkenness in 1927, compared with 1,655 in 1917. Police officials in 1927 said one of the regrettable features of Prohibition was the fact that it placed

money in hands of bootleggers who simply circumvented the law to give people what they continued to crave.

Some of the illicit hooch came from unlikely taps.

In the early years of Prohibition, there were certain Dutch families in the Eastern Avenue and Hall Street SE area who dug tunnels between one another's homes. They brewed spirits in these underground places and traveled through the tunnels to share their fermented fare.

Moonshine was made all over the city. Each ethnic neighborhood oversaw production and in some cases import of booze. Police were left to conclude that Prohibition was unenforceable.

When he was here on the eve of the big vote, Billy Sunday said about his effort to crush the sale of booze: "It is simply a matter of decency and manhood, irrespective of politics. It is prosperity against poverty, sobriety against drunkenness, honesty against thieving, heaven against hell. Don't you want to see men sober? Brutal, staggering men transformed into respectable citizens?"

The citizens of Grand Rapids grasped his vision and voted for it. Many probably did undergo some transformation, if only for a time, when the tap was turned off. But before long, religious beliefs notwithstanding, the liquor began to flow again. Billy Sunday's dream of an entirely sober and god-fearing populace was soon overwhelmed by the Depression.

FIGURE 6   A Prohibition demonstration in Sparta.

house College. Under Graves, Fountain Street Baptist hosted lectures by leading social reformers of the day, including Wendell Philips and Frances Willard. But Graves had aligned all these activities with "old-fashioned" revivals, baptizing converts by full immersion in the Grand River as late as 1875. Contrary to Wishart's notions, this was no oddity. For most of the 19th century, such evangelical revivalism had been at the forefront of American reform: the abolition of slavery, prohibition of alcohol, public education, women's rights. This work had been grounded in a supernatural theology and often came with sharp distrust of big money. Graves protested the system of pew rentals (by which the best seats went to the

high bidders) that Fountain Street used to fund its new building in 1876; this was an "aristocratic" device sure to repulse the poor and needy. He denounced dancing, the theater, and ladies' finery as signs of worldly pride and social callousness. And in 1884 he exploded, his son recalled, when people of "marked acquisitive features" in his increasingly well-to-do congregation staged a commercial play in the church sanctuary. A year later Graves was gone in a dispute over church finances.[6]

What had changed in just one generation to make born-again religion seem, by Wishart's day, so out of touch with social realities? In part, Wishart replied, the sheer scale of the modern city. But many in Wishart's generation also had a new view of human nature. Beneath their denunciations of civic evils lay great optimism. In a sermon which the Grand Rapids *Herald* summarized under the headline, "Pastor Sees Life in a Cheery Light," Wishart proclaimed: "Because I believe in God, I believe in progress. The world is getting better. The religion of love and social service and respect for human rights and belief in democracy is more alive than ever. Jesus Christ never had so much influence on mankind as He has today. Never has there been such soul hunger for peace, unity, and brotherhood between all honest souls."[7]

These pronouncements provoked the reaction Wishart might have expected. In 1909, just three years after he came to town, 18 of the 25 Baptist churches in the area left the Grand Rapids Baptist Association in protest of Fountain Street's deviations. Most of the Dutch Reformed churches in town ritually denounced Wishart's liberal theology for decades to come. The city's Catholics had an additional grievance. In 1907 Wishart scorned Catholicism from the Fountain Street pulpit as "the religion of interference" and the "enemy of the true soul of liberty." To him, Catholicism embodied the very worst of the outmoded, otherworldly theology, yet at the same time was a "monstrous Politico-Religious Trust," a corrupt corporation that meddled all too potently in this world's politics.[8]

Talking harmony while inciting argu-

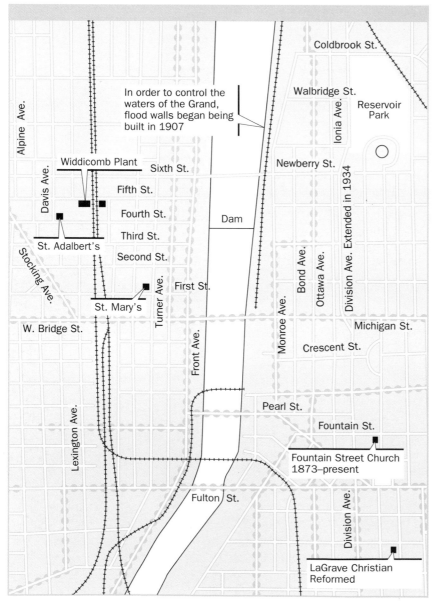

ments was just the first of Wishart's contradictions. The great furniture strike of 1911 brought others into plain view and put fundamental questions to Wishart's vision. Where was peace in the class war of American industry? In the mean streets of the factory district on the near West Side, what did progress mean? Who supervised and thrived off it? Who paid for it? Was liberal theology really necessary, or even helpful, to poor people, given its source (for Randall, Wishart and many others) at the University of Chicago, and built on the Rockefeller fortune? Essentially, Wishart's answer amounted to a proposal that control be entrusted to the "better people" in town, such as he represented. But leaders of the workers, of the Catholic Church, of the Christian Reformed, and even a member of his own staff, had other things to say.

> *"You have the heartihood to say, 'I have always been and always will be a friend of the working man.' May you be forgiven for that statement."*
>
> **— William B. MacFarlane**

FRIEND OF THE WORKING MAN?

The 1911 furniture strike was the greatest civic upheaval Grand Rapids would see until the riots of 1967. Its first stirrings emerged in November 1909 when a delegation of workers petitioned the Oriel Furniture Company management for a 10 percent wage hike to match that year's dramatic rise in the cost of living. Told to come back after Christmas, the workers did, only to find themselves fired as agitators. The next summer the local chapter of the United Brotherhood of Carpenters and Joiners brought the same petition to the local industry cartel, the Furniture Manufacturers Association. Told to return after the July trade show, the local did, only to be informed that the manufacturers would engage in "no collective bargaining under any circumstances."[9] The following February 1911, the union appealed to its national headquarters, and the FMA prepared for a strike. Mayor George Ellis tried to appoint a citizens' committee to arbitrate the dispute, but Wishart — appealing to his experience as a civic leader — persuaded all parties to appear before a less powerful fact-finding commission instead. Two of its five members were from the Board of Trade (essentially the Chamber of Commerce) and Wishart himself wrote the report.

While confirming some of the workers' grievances, the report supported the owners' position. Yes, some workers were not getting a living wage; yes, the 10-hour day could be cut back to nine without loss of production; yes, the piecework system was open to abuse. But no, the FMA did not keep a common record of workers' wages and union attitudes (though the individual factories did); no, the FMA did not set but responded to national industry standards; and therefore, no, the owners could not afford to grant any of the workers' demands. Above all, the implication was clear, workers should not unionize but trust the FMA to do fairly by them and for Grand Rapids as a whole. The union rejected this conclusion and denounced the whole fact-finding process as a management whitewash. Two days after the report was published, April 21, 1911, 5,000 workers (two-thirds of all furniture employees and 20 percent of the city's wage earners) walked out, closing down every furniture plant in town.

For the next three weeks, tensions built steadily. The union posted official, well-dressed pickets at factory gates to try to dissuade those still showing up for work. The owners used their own cars to carry non-strikers into the plants. Some militant laborers started harassing non-strikers, while some owners — especially Harry and William Widdicomb — began taunting pickets and brandishing

FIGURE 8
George "Deacon" Ellis served as mayor of Grand Rapids from 1906 to 1916, the longest tenure of all but one mayor in Grand Rapids history.

firearms. Strikers' families started gathering at factory gates. Then Wishart again intervened. On May 11, he gave the workers a stern sermon in the form of a public letter.[10] For all that they were pinched by high prices and long hours, Wishart declared, the workers needed to face the "cold hard facts" — facts which turned out not to be about their work at all. Fact 1: the strike was hurting Grand Rapids' competitive position (versus New York and Chicago manufacturers). Fact 2: local authorities (meaning Ellis) had so far been derelict in keeping law and order, and probably had encouraged the strike for their own political advantage. Not to worry: the public would find "other means ... to preserve order. Politics may let confusion go on for a while, but politics will have to get out of the way." Above all, Fact 3: "The furniture manufacturers never will enter into agreement or recognize the unions in any way." Conclusion: "Workers, believe me, I am stating in plain English a fact which cannot be successfully denied." And he had only their welfare at heart: "I have always been and always will be the friend of the working man."

In stating that union recognition, which the workers never demanded, was *the* issue of the strike for owners Wishart was entirely correct. In calling the workers simply to surrender to that insistence, he contradicted himself. For in his Labor Day sermon of 1908 Wishart had acknowledged that unions had done a lot of good and called the doctrine of the "free contract" — the core position of the FMA in 1911 — "a fiction." It was a fiction because workers bargaining individually, one-on-one with management was a gross imbalance that would bring neither stability nor justice. And it was a fiction because, in the realities of laboring life, workers were not really free to leave their jobs at will. In any case they had just as much right and need to organize collectively as owners had in forming corporations and cartels.[11]

What made the Wishart of 1911 forget the Wishart of 1908? Nothing so crude as directives from the executives in his congregation; rather, the premises that had always underlaid his social philosophy. To Wishart, a Christianized society would be democratic but a democracy ruled by an elite on behalf of those below them — to change the terms of the Gettysburg Address, a democracy more for the people than of or by them. Only those educated enough to see the big picture and strong enough to set policy could be trusted with ultimate responsibility: a perilous proposition unless the elite was dedicated to humane ideals, as Wishart had been preaching at Fountain Street. Secondly, the good society was a prosperous society, but prosperity depended on efficiency. Society, like industry, had to be smoothly organized and rationally administered according to the best lights of scientific experts. Then America would be a great production machine whose goods would filter down to laborers. Thirdly, local communities had to unify around local leadership. There was no place for discordant factions, no role for "meddling outsiders" such as national labor organizers. From these premises it followed, in Wishart's words, that "society is not wrong in looking to its industrial leaders" to solve industrial crises, and that organized labor, which represented only one piece of the social puzzle, "has very little ... to do with the general advance of human beings

FIGURE 9
A May 12, 1911, edition of the Grand Rapids *News* carried an account of union organizer William B. MacFarlane's denunciation of Wishart.

M'FARLANE MAKES REPLY TO WISHART

G.R. News, May 12, 1911

Declares the Pastor's Letter of Yesterday Tends Further to Prolong the Furniture Workers' Strike

MAKES CLAIM OF PARTISANSHIP

Labor Leader's Answer Is One of the Bitterest Documents Ever Promulgated By Any Person in An Important Industrial Conflict.

Speaks for the Men

WILLIAM B. MACFARLANE.
Organizer of the United Brotherhood of Carpenters and Joiners of America.

W. B. Macfarlane this morning issued the following open letter to Rev. Alfred W. Wishart, in response to the one Mr. Wishart addressed to the strikers yesterday through the Evening Press. In his letter Mr. Wishart advised the men to go back to work, saying, practically, that there was no hope for them to win their strike. Macfarlane's letter is caustic and indicates that distrust of Mr. Wishart,

"3. That the man who encourages the workers to believe that a law may be trampled upon in the interests of the strikers is the enemy and not the friend of the worker.
"4. That the great mass of workers mean to be law abiding.
Where the Two Disagree.
"With the foregoing every furniture worker in Grand Rapids is in full sympathy. However, there are statements in your letter with which the workers beg to differ:
"1. You pose as a friend of the

scientiously differ with you at a disadvantage, that you may, if possible render their criticism of your position valueless by creating prejudice against them in advance thereby further indi-

in this country." [12]

The workers' response to Wishart's advice was quick and bitter. Perhaps they would listen to him, one laborer's wife wrote to the Grand Rapids *News*, when Wishart too could look forward, for all his skill, sweat, and seniority, to the wage of $12 a week.[13] The union's organizer, William B. MacFarlane, answered with an open letter of his own. Your "unfair statements are not unexpected by the workers, all of whom have expected continuance of the partisan activities which you have heretofore shown …. They have not looked to you, nor do they now look to you, for fair consideration of their grievances. They are grateful that you are not also a furniture manufacturer …. You pretend to be a disciple of the Great Friend to mankind, the Carpenter of Nazareth; and yet you oppose those for whom he labored. You have the heartihood to say, 'I have always been and always will be a friend of the working man.' May you be forgiven for that statement. You have done more than any other single individual to prevent the furniture manufacturers from conceding righteous consideration to their employees …." [14]

Wishart and the owners also heard from a prominent church sponsor of the laborers' cause. Joseph Schrembs, auxiliary bishop of the Roman Catholic Diocese of Grand Rapids and pastor of St. Mary's Church on the West Side, spoke for the Polish Catholic workers who, owing to their recent arrival in town, were at the bottom of the totem pole in the factories. By virtue of his office, Schrembs had been a target of Wishart's old insults to Catholicism. As a member of the fact-finding committee, he was privy to Wishart's pre-strike maneuvering on the owners' behalf. In his open letter he brushed Wishart aside and appealed to the owners directly. The fact-finding committee, he pointed out, did call for the nine-hour day and acknowledged the intolerably low wages some workers earned. The owners' refusal even to acknowledge the committee's findings indicated arrogance. Their refusal to countenance unions contradicted the policy of Presidents William Howard Taft and Theodore Roosevelt, hardly flaming radicals. It amounted to refusing to meet the worker on the only ground where he could maintain his dignity. Schrembs could only conclude that the owners wished to intimidate, if need be to starve, the workers into submission. Such a policy was "neither reasonable nor humane, nor will it bring lasting peace or the necessary friendly relation between employer and employee." Schrembs concluded with an appeal to old-fashioned decency. "Gentlemen, I plead with you in the name of justice and humanity. I plead with you even for your own interest, because I know of no mightier school for the promotion of Socialism … than the adamantine insensibility of employers toward the human groanings of their workers." [15]

FIGURE 10

The Aug. 13, 1911, issue of *Grit* from Williamsport, Pa., claimed the "most unusual strike of the century is taking place among the furniture workers of Grand Rapids, Mich., the furniture center of the world."

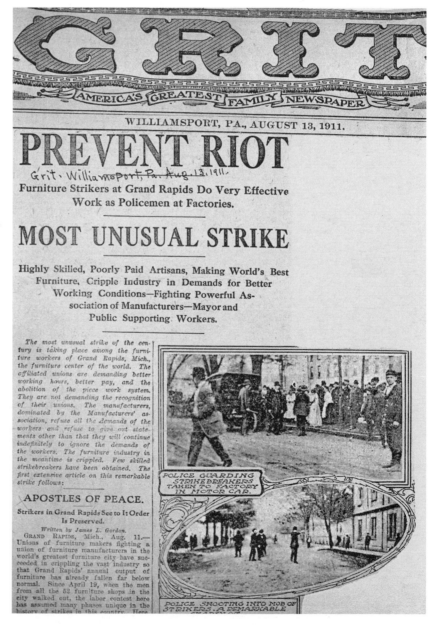

FIGURE 11
The Widdicomb Co. plant at Fifth Street and Seward Avenue NW was the site of a major flare-up in the furniture strike of 1911. St. Adalbert's can be seen in the background.

While the daily papers were carrying on this war of words, violence erupted in the streets. On May 15, the owners preemptorily declared the strike to be over and announced plans to import scab labor from Illinois and Ionia County. The near West Side exploded. A crowd of 2,000 gathered at the Widdicomb plant at Fifth Street and Seward Avenue NW with anger in their voices and stones in hand. Mayor Ellis arrived to appeal for calm; the assembly cheered him but, upon his departure, returned to riot. Firefighters turned their hoses on the crowd, and the police retreated, firing warning shots and using captured rioters as human shields. The night concluded with a rock barrage that broke every window in the Widdicomb plant.

In the ensuing days, Mayor Ellis earned the owners' eternal wrath by deputizing 100 strikers to keep the peace; the union cooperated. Kent County Sheriff William Hurley enlisted non-strikers in response. The impasse continued into midsummer. Then, at the July trade show, national buyers cooperated with the owners by cutting back orders and selecting from back stock. Pressed by scab laborers, a general recession, and the drain on its own resources, the national union withdrew its support on Aug. 1. The union's doom was sealed when the Christian Reformed Church pronounced against it on

Aug. 9. The strike ended on Aug. 19 with a total victory for management.

As the CRC action demonstrated, neither the workers nor Wishart's religious opponents were of one mind. The most radical and hard-pressed of the strikers were Polish, but Poles altogether made up only one-fourth of the furniture work force. The Dutch contingent was twice as large, and their status in the industry was a bit higher due to their earlier arrival in the city.[16] Dutch laborers could sympathize with Poles economically but not religiously. As for Wishart, the Dutch detested his liberal theology, but for all their Calvinistic supernaturalism they were as totally committed as he to working out their faith in every area of life, economics included. In fact, their leaders in 1911 were in the middle of a 20-year debate about labor unions. The CRC was on record against the Knights of Labor, but more as a secret society than as a labor organization. CRC leaders acknowledged the right, even the duty, of workers to organize for the sake of justice and dignity. They strongly supported cooperation and solidarity against the notion of individualism and warned against the spirit of materialism — whether from business or labor — taking over society.[17]

What, then, to do? In April 1911 Dutch

A Different Viewpoint

Higher wages and better working conditions weren't the only issues that led to the furniture strike of 1911. Weaving through the sensibilities and outlooks of the major participants were strongly held religious beliefs and values.

Although she wasn't a striker, Viva Flaherty, social outreach secretary for Fountain Street Baptist Church, is one who closely followed the battle between workers and the bosses. In many ways, she exemplifies the theological position of those who believed workers had a God-given right to demand justice and a bigger slice of the manufacturers' profits.

As a result, Viva Flaherty was acutely troubled during the strike by the fact that her church and its pastor, the Rev. Alfred Wishart, took the other side in the walkout. Wishart espoused an approach that aligned itself with the furniture factory owners at the same time he dubbed himself "a friend of the working man."

Viva found his position so repugnant she decided to write her own detailed account of the strike. The following excerpts give the flavor of how Viva Flaherty viewed what had turned into Grand Rapids' most serious expression of labor strife in the early part of the 20th century.

On the reasons for the strike, Flaherty wrote:

"The men claimed that the present wage was not commensurate with living expenses, that there had been no general increase in wages of late but on the contrary more than one general cut, and that since Grand Rapids dominated the market the employers could afford the increase at this time."

On the support of strikers by Catholic Auxiliary Bishop Joseph Schrembs:

"Such a determined stand for justice taken by a churchman indicates the place which organized Christianity must take in the industrial revolution, or cease to call itself Christian and, instead, worship openly the Almighty God of the Pocketbook, who rules by the divine right of capital."

On the character of the strikers themselves:

"Many of the leaders among the striking furniture workers are deeply religious men with very clear-cut ideas of what was just to their employers. And it is their sense of injustice, with which they feel that they and particularly their less well-equipped comrades have been treated, that led them to determine to organize, in spite of custom and religious scruples, to gain the trade agreement."

On the result of the strike:

"The workers lost the strike. Moral victories do not pay for potatoes and sugar, or secure the rest and relaxation that a hard day's work merits. It was not right that settled this strike and, consequently, industrial peace has not been settled in this strike."

The role of the Christian Reformed Church in the strike:

"It committed a gross injustice to the workers by investigating their organization during the strike while postponing action upon the employers' association to an indefinite date. If it could not have investigated both organizations simultaneously it should not have 'butted in.' This action is only one of many illustrations of the inefficiency of organized Christianity when it attempts to deal with modern social problems."

Referring to her own church's anti-union stance in the strike:

"Organized money is the greatest enemy of social progress; it has no heart and it is determined and unscrupulous. Conciliation and arbitration are not parts of its policy. Yet the workers are blamed for being 'class conscious,' are accused of arousing enmity and stirring up trouble."

FIGURE 12   Viva Flaherty as pictured in the 1904 Grand Rapids Central High School yearbook.

workers had walked out with everyone else. They took up picketing, even when it was not their turn, but shied from militant demonstrations.[18] They listened to the debates in their churches. Finally, they heeded their ministers' decision. At its Aug. 9 meeting, Classis [regional assembly] Grand Rapids West declared that the union was, "by reason of its principles, ritual and funeral ceremony not an association for a thoroughgoing Christian to be a member of." [19] Why this decision? The remarks about ritual and funeral ceremony indicated fears of a secret society. As to the principles involved, the ministers argued that since the union did not explicitly acknowledge the authority of Christ, did not explicitly renounce violence, and set forth only materialistic goals of wages and hours, it was humanistic and probably socialistic. By the same token, of course, so was the FMA and most every corporation in America. The Classis promised to investigate the FMA at an unspecified later date — a promise not fulfilled once the strike was over. It also called for a Christian labor union, which died aborning in Grand Rapids. In short, CRC leaders told their workers to suffer the owners' paternalism, individualism, and materialism but not the union's.

While the CRC wound up supporting the social formula of Wishart, their theological opponent, Wishart's own staff member, Viva Flaherty, vigorously condemned him. Flaherty represented the radical spirit that some of the elite at Fountain Street instilled in their children. Born into an old Grand Rapids family, she graduated from Central High in 1904 and attended Vassar College and the University of Michigan before becoming church social worker in the New York City parish of John Herman Randall, Fountain Street's former pastor. She brought the zeal of that experience back to her home-

> *"Organized money is the greatest enemy of social progress ... it has no heart and it is determined and unscrupulous."*
>
> **— Viva Flaherty**

town in 1911 only to run up against her employers. Hired as the church's social service secretary to work among the poor, she was outraged by the stance Wishart and "the big money interests" in the church took in the strike. A month after it ended, she took her leave by means of a public letter.

"I am resigning because I will no longer be associated with Rev. Alfred W. Wishart .... Large churches are governed now by boards comprised of men selected because of their business or social prominence which is no guarantee of their fitness to direct religious institutions .... 'Big business' is the curse of the country, and the Church of Christ, the Carpenter of Nazareth, raises no voice of protest and condemnation.'"

A few months later she published a booklet, "History of the Grand Rapids Furniture Strike," which combined literary flair, sociological insight, a participant's recall, and moral indignation to drive home the strike's lesson.

"The responsibility for so-called labor wars

FIGURE 13
Robert Irwin was a leading furniture manufacturer and Fountain Street Baptist Church layman.

rests with capital ... when employers reserve for themselves rights and privileges which they deny their employees [namely, the right to organize], the employers are the ones who are responsible for class consciousness." [20]

Wishart never responded publicly to Flaherty, in fact, spoke little about labor issues for the rest of his life. The manufacturers, having broken the back of unionism for 20 years to come, showed some benevolence. Early in December 1911, Grand Rapids executive and Fountain Street member Robert Irwin persuaded the National Association of Furniture Manufacturers to adopt the nine-hour day. After a long speech that honored the owners' role in the Grand Rapids strike, Irwin suddenly changed gears. "The lot of all the workmen at best is none too good," he said, and owners should be "progressive" enough to say so. As "a powerful organization," Irwin's audience was urged to "use what Providence has given us to some end other than one that is purely selfish ... just because [we believe] it is right." [21]

CHARTING A NEW COURSE

Irwin and his pastor at this juncture had more than just economic fish to fry. Their social vision also demanded "cleaner," more dependable politics which could only be accomplished by changing the city's charter. The campaign for charter reform in Grand Rapids registered clear religious and ethnic differences and refought the 1911 strike on political ground. Already in 1910 Irwin headed a citizens' committee to revise the charter along the lines of efficiency, order, and scientific management. Their proposal went to the voters in February 1912 and was roundly defeated, 64 percent to 36 percent. Just as in the strike, working-class Poles and Hollanders headed the opposition, while the elite Hilltop (present-day Heritage Hill) precincts gave the strongest support. Middle-class Dutch and native Protestants were both split down the middle. [22] Undaunted, Wishart at the behest of the Board of Trade soon opened an investigation into waste and inefficiency in city government. This study eventually produced another charter revision which went to voters in 1916 and passed 56 percent to 44 percent. Polish workers still heartily disapproved (69 percent), Dutch workers somewhat less (54 percent). Dutch and native Protestant middle-class voters gave enough approval (58 percent and 54 percent, respectively) to push the city elite's astounding support (88 percent) to victory. [23]

The charter campaign settled scores dating back to the water scandal of 1900; it also avenged the manufacturers on their "betrayal" by Mayor Ellis during the furniture strike. The new charter reduced the number of wards from 12 to three, and the city council from 24 to seven. It reduced the mayor to figurehead status and transferred all executive powers to a commission-appointed manager. All commissioners were to be elected from the city at large, not just by their own wards. The city elite were divided between the second and third wards, making them eligible to run in each. Any number of commissioners were authorized to declare a civic emergency and call out the police to meet it. All in all, the charter was designed to move political power from neighborhoods to the center, and to move it upscale to the well-

FIGURE 14
The Rev. Henry Beets of LaGrave Avenue Christian Reformed Church battled charges that Dutch Americans lacked patriotism.

educated, the well-connected, and the well-to-do.[24] A Christian Reformed attorney, Dorr Kuizema, noted as much at the time: "the new charter was drafted under the supervision of the big men of the city and seeks to ban the small man's influence from government." This put the talk of "democracy" by reformers like Wishart in a new light: "The most wonderful thing of all is, that where men speak so much of returning government to the hands of the people, they use just those means that remove it as much as possible from their hands." [25]

With the charter ratified, Wishart launched one more crusade, to consolidate

FIGURE 15
A fire of unknown origin destroyed Fountain Street Baptist Church early in the morning of May 22, 1917. Until the war was over and re-building could begin, services were held in the Powers Theater.

the community in support of World War I. This time Hollanders were his target. As the United States edged toward war in the winter of 1916–1917, some prominent CRC leaders voiced their opposition in short, bold statements. The war, they charged, was being fought for British imperialism and American commerce, for Mars and Mammon, WASPs and Wall Street. The Grand Rapids *News* attacked these "wagging alien tongues" with the same arguments as Wishart leveled from the Fountain Street pulpit on March 4, 1917. Wishart declared the Christian Reformed were "un-American" because of the obsolete theology and social separatism evident in their belief in biblical infallibility, Calvinistic doctrines, and separate Christian schools.[26]

The CRC's leading local minister, Henry Beets of LaGrave Avenue CRC, went to Fountain Street two weeks later to respond. Beets argued the historical connection between Calvinism and constitutional liberty. He thought that the current war proved rather than contradicted the truth of Calvinists' doctrines of total depravity and original sin, while their trust in God's sovereignty gave comfort in troubled times. He hoped that American freedom allowed for diversity, also in educational options. He showed that more American churches held to the CRC view of the Bible than to Wishart's. And he recalled the American patriotism of the CRC dating back to the Civil War.[27]

But Beets knew that more was needed. For the rest of the war he stumped the CRC for the Liberty Loan (war bonds) and used its magazine, the Banner, to call Dutch Americans to a more fervent display of patriotism. That did not satisfy the "good Americans" of the city. The Michigan *Tradesman*, a staunch ally of the Furniture Manufacturers Association, alleged that "the Christian Reformed churches harbor many preachers who are not loyal to the American flag" and who should be imprisoned or deported. Worse, "Calvin College is a hotbed of treason. ... The professors who are conceded to be anti-American should be stood up against a wall and shot. There is no proper place for them in the land of the free." A campaign of harassment, much of it petty, some of it grievous, spread toward Dutch-Americans as well as German-Americans of suspect loyalty.[28] It also caught up Viva Flaherty. She had left town after the furniture strike to pursue her vocation in Baltimore and New York City, but returned to Grand Rapids in 1917 as a labor and antiwar activist. Flaherty was arrested along with 12 others on charges of sedition. Despite the government's best efforts and a trial that lasted several months, she was acquitted.[29]

The United States entered the conflagration of war in April 1917. The next month a lesser conflagration burned down the Fountain Street church. No cause was determined, though rumor laid the blame variously on those offended by Wishart's liberal theology, by his ardent patriotism, or by his behavior in 1911.[30] Wishart left town for six months service with the YMCA in France. He returned with familiar themes. The German army impressed him by its efficiency, quite in contrast to the "partisan bungling" in Washington.[31] Like Grand Rapids, the national government needed direction by a coalition of experts. Like union organizers, Catholic bishops, and separate Christian schools, antiwar voices represented disruptive factions and should be squashed.

The Great Crusade ended in Europe with America triumphant. Wishart settled back in the 1920s to concentrate on rebuilding Fountain Street's edifice. It was completed in 1924 at the cost of $800,000, featuring stained glass windows, "the finest organ in the Midwest," and a special narthex donated by the Irwin family.[32] Wishart's sermons turned more toward themes of art and beauty, the cultivation of the individual personality. In 1928 he took the conservative side of a theological question for once when he debated renowned trial lawyer Clarence Darrow, the champion agnostic of the age, over whether the science and nature to which people such as

"The more I study the whole situation which confronts us today, the more I am convinced that basically it is a moral and spiritual problem ..."

— The Rev. Alfred W. Wishart in a 1931 sermon

Wishart had fastened their faith left any ground for religious belief. The Fountain Street audience's applause gave the decision to Wishart, although the print record of the debate indicates otherwise.[33]

Events also assaulted him. The Great Depression of the 1930s cast doubt on his confidence in material progress and far-sighted industrialists. "The more I study the whole situation which confronts us today," he declared in a 1931 sermon, "the more I am convinced that basically it is a moral and spiritual problem ... mixed with whatever good there has been in the aims and policies of business and politics and often dominating and overshadowing the good has been a passion for material welfare, and a national and private selfishness, which have brought the world to the edge of ruin .... People should reflect seriously on the need and value of spiritual help in these times."[34]

Wishart would not lead that process of reflection for very long. On April 25, 1933, he died of a heart attack after a steady three-year decline in health. He left a congregation larger than the one he had inherited but quite smaller relative to the city's population growth. Religious increase in the "progressive" 20th century would continue to go to the conservative side.[35] Fountain Street experienced a sharp decline under Wishart's successor, Milton M. McGorrill (1933–1943) but revived with new purpose under the ministry of Duncan Littlefair (1944–1979). That purpose included, as it had for Wishart, city leadership in liberal social causes like the civil rights

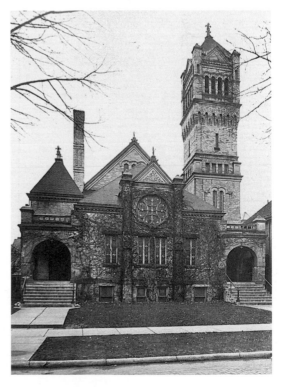

FIGURE 16
The original building of LaGrave Avenue Christian Reformed Church, 1888 to 1960.

movement, Planned Parenthood, and the American Civil Liberties Union. But it accentuated what had earlier been a subordinate theme: freedom of conscience. Fountain Street became the church home of those in the city who were dissatisfied with the orthodoxies of their native traditions, who wanted to carve out their own individual spiritual space in the company of the like-hearted, if not the like-minded. Maintaining a community of prickly individualists is a paradoxical enterprise, made possible, perhaps, only by the heavy conservative weight against which all these individuals are rebelling. The cost of such an arrangement is clear. Where Wishart defended freedom of conscience as the finest feature of Baptist Christianity, Little-

Religion and Politics: 1906–1916

City elections in early 20th century Grand Rapids showed an intriguing, complex blend of class, ethnic, and religious-cultural loyalties. On a strictly economic issue — like the 1914 referendum to give city employees an eight-hour working day — voting clearly followed class lines. And in the 1916 polls on charter reform and Prohibition, Dutch Reformed laborers stood closer to their German co-workers than to their middle-class ethnic kin.

Other times, ethnicity outweighed class. Neither of the Dutch groups supported Mayor George Ellis, but Dutch workers deviated sharply from the average of their class on the matter. Their opposition peaked in 1916 when Ellis ran against the Dutch city comptroller and one-time furniture worker, George Tilma; the Dutch vote against Ellis, even from the working class, exceeded that of the Heritage Hill elite (precinct A).

Ethnicity often but not always entailed religious and cultural values. The Dutch suspected Ellis for his shady business operations and lax enforcement of the city morals code. Their attitude is clear from the remarkable 1906 vote on closer regulation of theaters and other places of entertainment. The Dutch Reformed hostility to "dens of iniquity" was overwhelming and class-blind. The more affluent Dutch Reformed were 50 percent more likely to favor the measure than were their class peers or superiors, while the Calvinist working class gave three times the support of their peers. Shows were one thing, however; beer was another. Though the Dutch were the only working-class segment to favor Prohibition in Grand Rapids in 1916, they lagged notably behind middle-class Dutch on the issue.

When class, ethnicity, and values reinforce each other on both sides of a divide, the result can be a strong, enduring polarity. Just that occurred with the basic opposition in this era's politics — that between the Heritage Hill elite and West Side Polish Catholics. The struggle between these two in the 1911 furniture strike was repeated, less violently, every election, whatever the issue. As a final solution to all the problems of the era, the 1916 city charter won the elite's support far above any other proposal or any other group. The Polish Catholics liked it even less than Prohibition.

All figures are percentages in favor of candidate/measure. See next page for map and description of the precincts.

Precinct	Class	Ethnicity	Mayoral Votes 1906–1916 Ellis/Opponents†	Vote for Mayor 1916 Ellis/Tilma	Theater Regulation 1906	Prohibition 1916	Charter 1916	8-hr day 1914
A	Upper-Middle	Native-born Prot	31/69	34/66	58	75	88	24
B	Middle	Native-born Prot	47/53	54/46	40	54	54	53
C	Middle	Dutch Reformed	38/62	22/78	75	69	58	49
D	Working	Dutch Reformed	38/62	28/72	73	53	46	65
E	Working	German Prot and Catholic	48/52	66/34	24	45	52	63
F	Working	Polish Catholic	51/49	69/31	27	33	31	75
City Totals			44/56	49/51	48	57	56	55

† *Ellis usually faced more than one opponent and so could win without a clear majority.*

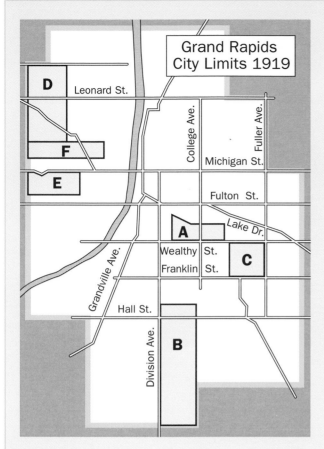

**Grand Rapids
City Limits 1919**

Leonard St.

College Ave.

Fuller Ave.

Michigan St.

Fulton St.

Lake Dr.

Wealthy St.

Franklin St.

Grandville Ave.

Division Ave.

Hall St.

D

F

E

A

C

B

Precincts selected are those in which more than 80 percent of every tenth voter bore its designated characteristics.

PRECINCT A: bound by Cherry-State Streets, Charles Avenue, Wealthy Street, and Jefferson Avenue. Typical church: Fountain Street Baptist.

PRECINCT B: bound by Highland Street, Madison Avenue, Alger Street, and Division Avenue. Served by such churches as First Methodist and Wealthy Street Baptist.

PRECINCT C: bound by Wealthy Street, Fuller Avenue, Franklin Street, and Eastern Avenue. Typical church: Eastern Avenue and First CRC.

PRECINCT D: bound by Richmond Street, Tamarack Avenue, Sixth Street, and Bristol Avenue. Typical church: Seventh Reformed.

PRECINCT E: bound by Bridge Street, Straight Avenue, Lake Michigan Drive, and Bristol Avenue. Typical church: St. Mary's Roman Catholic.

PRECINCT F: bound by Third Street, C&O railroad, Sixth Street, and Bristol Avenue. Typical church: St. Adalbert's Roman Catholic.

SOURCE: Anthony B. Travis, "Mayor George Ellis: Grand Rapids Political Boss and Progressive Reformer," *Michigan History* 58/2 (Summer 1974): 101–30.

fair had to move beyond the Baptist tradition, indeed beyond Christianity altogether. And where Wishart hoped that Fountain Street would lead from the center, the congregation since his time has led — more often dissented — on the margin.

On the political front, however, Wishart's formula lived on for another generation. Wishart's last campaign came early in the Depression when Mayor George Welsh used irregular procedures to give the unemployed food and jobs. Wishart saw the ghost of George Ellis and corrupt, wasteful government. Social welfare, he insisted, needed to be systematic, rational, administered by impartial experts, emergency or no.

This anti-Welsh sentiment culminated in the 1940s' Home Front campaign to restore "clean government" to city hall. Fountain Street parishioners Dorothy Leonard Judd and Paul Goebel led the charge, aided by Dutch Reformed laymen Willard Vermeulen and Joseph Zandstra. The 1916 charter-reform coalition was reborn and triumphed by breaking Welsh's power. One side effect was the birth of Gerald Ford, Jr.'s political career, which 25 years later brought Fountain Street member Philip Buchen to the White House as Counselor to the President. From another world, perhaps, Alfred Wishart looked on with admiration and a little envy.

The Fundamentalist Crusade

6

GRAND RAPIDS CHURCHES IN THE 1920s

PEOPLE LIKE ALFRED WISHART EXPECTED WORLD WAR I TO bring in a harvest of peace and cooperation. The reality was just the opposite. Yes, Germany was defeated abroad, but the U.S. Senate rejected the League of Nations, the cornerstone of the new world order.

Yes, demon rum was exorcised at home, but Prohibition was defied as much as obeyed, triggering the 1920s revolt against Protestant morality. Most astonishing of all, progressives faced an explosion of rage in their own churches, once their safest haven, when conservatives began accusing them of betraying the faith and undermining social morality.

Grand Rapids did not take a back seat in this fundamentalist crusade. One of the country's first fundamentalist organizations was founded by Wealthy Street Baptist Church in

response to the "modern infidelity" reigning at its parent church on Fountain Street. As vigorous as it was uncompromising, Wealthy Street grew into Grand Rapids' most prominent voice for the old-time faith. The Dutch Reformed went through a rift of their own, joining battle just two blocks south of Wealthy Baptist at Eastern Avenue Christian Reformed Church. This congregation split in 1924, producing the First Protestant Reformed Church which, too, became the hub of a national network, this time in

FIGURE 1
Interior of Wealthy Street
Baptist Church.

FIGURE 2
The Rev. Oliver W. Van Osdel, pictured here in the upper right at a Lake Macatawa resort, made Wealthy Street Baptist Church a fundamentalist bastion.

Dutch-American circles. That same year Westminster Presbyterian Church hosted its denomination's national convention. Fundamentalists came to the meeting organized for victory but broke against the resistance of delegates from churches like Westminster. Accordingly, Westminster represented mainline Presbyterian fortunes thereafter, both in prosperity and in decline.

In short, as the wars of the 1920s forged the future of American Protestantism, the local battles permanently changed the religious landscape of Grand Rapids. The history of these three-congregations-become-four shows how this process occurred and why.

⟨✦⟩

DOOM AND BOOM

On Feb. 21, 1909, the Rev. Oliver W. Van Osdel was installed as the eighth pastor at Wealthy Street Baptist Church. This marked Van Osdel's second term there; the first, in 1895–1896, had ended quickly when the congregation balked at his bold building plans. This time, however, the church was ready to cooperate, while Van Osdel, now 62 years old, was

FIGURE 3
Mrs. Ira Remington, a charter member of Wealthy Street Baptist Church.

perhaps expected to make this the grand finale of a career that had already seen him carry out building projects in five previous congregations. But he was welcomed to town for another cause as well. Virtually his first day on the job, Van Osdel was approached by local Baptists alarmed at the modernist message emanating from Fountain Street Baptist Church, and he gratified them by his eagerness to lead a counterattack. The two agendas came together at once. In June 1909, Van Osdel finalized construction plans for Wealthy Street's new edifice; in September, he led 14 congregations out of the Grand Rapids Baptist Association in protest of Fountain Street's betrayal of the "inestimably precious" Baptist heritage. Van Osdel was adding breaking to building: breaking old allegiances that had developed dangerous leaks, and forging new alliances for the sake of the old-time religion. Old as he was, Van Osdel would carry on the crusade from Wealthy Street for another 25 years.

The break of September 1909 severed child from parent. Wealthy Street Baptist Church had begun as a Sunday school in 1875, the first of six missions that Fountain Street Baptist planted around the perimeter of the city between that year and 1894. After 10 years of roving about the neighborhood, the group officially organized as a church on Jan. 5, 1886, counting 19 members and worshipping in a chapel on Charles Avenue near Wealthy. Twelve months later they had grown to 90 members and dedicated a commodious new structure at Wealthy and Eastern.[1] Vigorous evangelism over the next 20 years produced a daughter church, Lake Drive Baptist in East Grand Rapids, and pushed Wealthy Street's own numbers to 350.

Most lived in the immediate neighborhood of laborers and shopkeepers on the city's booming Southeast Side. Economically, Wealthy Baptist's parishioners lived below the Heritage Hill elite of Fountain Street Church but above the denizens of the factory district, who might show up at the rescue mission the two congregations co-sponsored in the 1890s.[2] Ethnically, the church maneuvered between the African-American precinct to the near southwest and the burgeoning Dutch population to the south and east. Messiah Missionary Baptist served the former, and a few of the latter came to Wealthy Baptist, but by and large the church was composed of native-born Protestants. In 1907 it could join its Congregational and Methodist neighbors to sponsor a two-week revival campaign. Its pastor, William P. Lovett, endorsed the Anti-Saloon League slate in local elections. At the same time the church announced plans for an ambitious building project.[3]

In calling back Van Osdel to implement these plans, Wealthy Street received a leader of considerable talent and an all-American career. Born in 1846 to a blacksmith's family in the Hudson River valley, Van Osdel's journey as a pastor had taken him across the continent, from the Midwest to Washington state. He had been preco-cious enough to serve as a teen-aged messenger boy in the Union Army during the Civil War and to earn a divinity degree at the forerunner of the University of Chicago. He was also peculiar, inventing contraptions and various financial schemes, and insisting — when his wife died — that she not be buried but interred in a mausoleum so that he could visit her for conversation and so that she could more readily greet the imminent return of Christ.[4]

A bit of all these traits entered his building project at Wealthy Street. The new structure immediately won city-wide attention for its secular appearance. The congregation's purpose "all along," reported The Grand Rapids Press, "has been to get away as much as possible from the church idea" and make the building serve as a neighborhood gathering place. As evidence one could look

FIGURE 4
Wealthy Street Baptist
Sunday school in 1911.

FIGURE 5
Wealthy Street Baptist's new building was dedicated in 1917 after eight years under construction.

at the gymnasium and banquet hall in the basement, the steel and reinforced-concrete frame, the absence of a spire and other religious trappings. But the slow pace of construction turned fascination into ridicule: "Van Osdel's folly" took eight years to finish, forcing the congregation to worship in a temporary shed, in the basement, then the annex of the new edifice. When the structure was dedicated on Oct. 28, 1917, its parishioners showed all the pride of the middling class. The church could seat 1,300 for worship, house 1,000 Sunday school students, and serve 800 diners. It was thoroughly up-to-date, yet would last 100 years. It cost $90,000, about the valuation of Fountain Street's building. But Wealthy's was "absolutely fireproof" in contrast to Fountain Street's sad experience the previous May.[5]

Such self-conscious comparison to the mother church bore more than class rivalry. Wealthy Street's secular structure would house

true religion, its members vowed, while Fountain Street's churchly appearance masked fatal heresies. Van Osdel's bill of secession from the local Baptist Association specified these errors along with a list of "fundamental" doctrines that all Christians had to believe, including the deity, virgin birth, miracles, vicarious atonement, and bodily resurrection of Jesus. Since the association's by-laws were "inadequate to deal with any church … found teaching error," Wealthy Street and the 13 other dissident churches felt compelled to form their own resolutely orthodox fellowship, the Grand River Valley Baptist Association.[6] Begun together, Van Osdel's two causes came to completion at the same time. In October 1917, with construction on its new building completed, Wealthy Street formally ended its contributions to the state Baptist Association and gave the pulpit at its dedicatory services to William Bell Riley, the nation's first and foremost fundamentalist organizer.[7]

The newspaper columns announcing these developments were ringed with reports on World War I. While Fountain Street's Alfred Wishart turned that into a righteous crusade, Van Osdel stepped up hostilities in the churches. He converted Wealthy Street Baptist's bulletin into a nationally circulat-

FIGURE 6
Entrance to the Baptist Theological Seminary at Wealthy Street Baptist Church in 1950.

FIGURE 7
Baptist Bible Institute senior class April 22, 1958.

ing newsletter, blasting Baptist "apostasy" in virtually every issue. In 1920, the Grand River Valley Baptist Association went statewide as the Michigan Orthodox Baptist Association, earning its dismissal from the mainline Baptists' state and national conventions. Van Osdel, in turn, quickly linked up with other dissenters across the country; together they held caucuses, then full-scale counter-conventions at the time and site of the mainliners'. For a time, Fundamentalists hoped to take over, or at least to flush the liberals out of, the national association. But by 1923 the more radical among them, including Van Osdel, gave up on this strategy and formed a new national fellowship of their own, the Baptist Bible Union (BBU). Van Osdel was on its executive committee and Wealthy Street was a key link in its network. The BBU began to falter, however, when the mainline Baptists repelled its every assault and its leaders were caught in scandal. The worst fiasco involved the BBU's attempt in 1927 to take over Des Moines University as a fundamentalist school. Wealthy Street pledged $100,000 toward the effort, but a student riot in 1929 caused the institution — and with it the BBU — to collapse. Wealthy Street hosted

FIGURE 8
Carl and Anna Gowman, shown here with their children in 1909, were Wealthy Street Baptist Church's first missionaries.

the union's final convention in 1930.[8]

Wracked by this failure, not to mention the simultaneous crash of the national economy, Wealthy Street was fortunate to be able to fall back on its statewide organization. The Michigan Orthodox Baptist Association sent one of the key delegations to forge a new alliance that has lasted, indeed thrived, to the present day: the General Association of Regular Baptist Churches (GARBC). Beginning with fewer than 100 churches in 1934, it has grown to 1,600 churches today, one of the largest fundamentalist affiliations in the country. Van Osdel was the only founder and survivor of the BBU to participate in chartering the new body, and Wealthy Baptist continued its prominent role by periodically hosting GARBC's national meetings. The evening Bible institute the congregation began in its classrooms in 1941 has since grown into Grand Rapids Baptist College and Seminary, one of only six educational institutions the association sanctions nationwide.[9]

But national scope was never closest to Wealthy Baptist's heart. Indeed, the church faulted the mainliners' ambitions on this score, and the centralized administration such bring, almost as much as their lax doctrine. Wealthy Street has treasured the Baptist heritage of local autonomy, seeing individual congregations as the key agencies of God's work. The church has made good on its principles, too. Its membership doubled between 1907 and 1917 to 690, rose to 1,214 by the end of Van Osdel's pastorate in 1934, and crested at 1,717 in 1954. Its growth stemmed from and supported an enormous missionary enterprise. The evangelistic preaching of Van Osdel and his successor, David Otis Fuller,

FIGURE 9
The Rev. and Mrs. David Otis Fuller in December 1954.

One Family, Different Worlds

After more than 25 years of jousting from their respective pulpits, the Rev. David Otis Fuller and the Rev. Duncan Littlefair finally came face to face one afternoon in 1970.

Littlefair, the outspoken liberal preacher from Fountain Street Church, was dabbing his car clean at a car wash on Eastern Avenue SE when a tall, almost gaunt man with a steely glint in his eye approached.

"Dr. Littlefair?" asked the man.

Littlefair nodded.

"I'm David Fuller," was the reply of the preacher from Wealthy Street Baptist Church, a conservative congregation just down the street.

Littlefair extended a hand and said: "I've wanted to meet you for a long time."

For many years these two men had been at theological loggerheads. Despite the fact that both had trained as Baptist preachers, they were as opposed on most subjects as dark and light, as heaven and hell.

Fuller had even written a lengthy, red-bordered diatribe in which he branded Littlefair as being the devil incarnate. At the car wash that day, Fuller was in no mood to make small talk with this preacher of little faith.

"Dr. Littlefair," he responded, "I'd like to be your friend. I like to make friends with people. But as long as you blaspheme my Lord Jesus Christ and make fun of the word of God, I can't do it. I pray for you every day."

With that, the brief encounter ended. They were never to meet again — and yet each remained in many ways the other's nemesis.

Rarely before in Grand Rapids church history had ministers of such solid convictions and passionate persuasions been in such prominent positions at the same time. The ties that bound and split them ran deep.

Both were Baptists, although only nominally in Littlefair's case. Both were men of great verbal skills; both were

FIGURE 10 The Rev. David Otis Fuller

community and church leaders; both came to Grand Rapids to serve churches early in their careers and stayed. The two had almost diametrically opposed views of Christ. And it was this that drove them apart.

From his pulpit in downtown Fountain Street Church, Littlefair promoted what he claimed was a thinking man's Christianity. Soon after arriving in Grand Rapids in September 1944, he launched a series of sermons that challenged the divinity and many of the "supernatural" considerations surrounding the person of Jesus Christ.

At the southeast side Wealthy Street Baptist Church, David Otis Fuller was no less demonstrative in the ways and words with which, week after week, year after year, decade after decade, he championed the faith.

For Fuller, who came to Grand Rapids in 1934, the King James Version of the Bible contained the very bedrock of truth. To him, anyone who did not literally believe in the virgin birth, perfect life and actual resurrection of Christ was following a false, even demonic path.

"We believe the Bible is the infallible word of God and the only complete and final revelation of the will of God to man," he once wrote.

Coming from such unadulterated positions, Fuller and Littlefair represented Grand Rapids religion at its most intense, its most public and its most divisive.

In an interview shortly before he died, Fuller branded Fountain Street Church and its faithful as "sinners" who were "adrift" and presented "a definite threat to Christianity."

He saved some of his most invective statements for the liberals and the Roman Catholics — both had strayed, he believed.

The relativism that Littlefair professed with its heavy emphasis on personal choice and the social gospel was terribly misleading and dangerous, Fuller believed, and he never turned down the opportunity to broadcast that belief in any way possible.

From his side of town, Littlefair frequently lambasted those who held to a "narrow-minded" view of God. Fundamentalists, especially those of Fuller's category, became a subject of his ire.

"That tradition is so absurd," he has said. "The arguments are nonsense to me. I can't believe in a being who created a world like a car in six days."

Although they never publicly debated their stances, Littlefair seemed often to direct his statements, whether in church or at some civic function, at those who, like Fuller, tried to keep God in a "rigid, literalistic box."

"I've tried to explain the fundamental beliefs in a better, larger way," he said. "I wanted to prove something strong and solid to people. I wanted them to know and believe that there was no need for stupid, superstitious beliefs."

While the struggle between the preachers was lengthy and loud, it was by no means the sole focus of either man's ministry.

Reared in Toronto by a "staunch Presbyterian" mother and a "free-thinking" father, Littlefair attended McMaster University in Hamilton, Ontario, the University of Basel in Switzerland, where he studied under theologian Karl Barth, and the University of Chicago, from which he earned a Ph.D.

In his years at Fountain Street, Littlefair rarely shied from controversy. Once, he preached against and called for the resignation of then-mayor George Welsh, a member of his own church. He spoke out often in favor of giving a woman the right to an abortion. And he helped start several organizations, among them Project Rehab, the local chapter of the American Civil Liberties Union, and the Sheldon Complex, a community center.

Ironically, the church of which he was senior pastor was the mother church of Wealthy Street Baptist. And it was Wealthy Street Church members who led a move in the 1910s to oust Fountain Street from the Grand Rapids

FIGURE 11   The Rev. Duncan Littlefair

Baptist Association. Even then, before the coming of Fuller and Littlefair, the churches were at odds over doctrinal matters. Fountain Street remained at least nominally Baptist until 1969 when, under Littlefair, it broke for good from its Baptist roots. Denominational ties were not important to him.

"I always wanted to talk about what was going on today, to deal with the lives of people. I tried to bring religion at its most radical and in a sense its best to Grand Rapids," he said.

Fuller, too, was active in his community and in church affairs.

Born in Brooklyn, N.Y., in 1903 and "saved" at a tent revival in Ashville, N.C., in 1917, Fuller's traditional educational path led him through Wheaton College in Illinois and Princeton Theological Seminary. Wealthy Street was his second and last pastorship.

In his many years in West Michigan, he founded or played a role in organizing a variety of groups and institutions, both local and elsewhere. He began the Which Bible Society, a group that did battle to defend the King James Version of the Bible. He also helped to establish the Grand Rapids Baptist College and Seminary, the Children's Bible Hour, Grand Rapids Baptist Academy, and the Michigan Christian Home. He was the author or editor of 18 books.

Although he and Littlefair remained enemies in principle until the end, he never gave up trying to bring the wayward Baptist from Toronto back into the fold. At least twice a year, he would write the Fountain Street pastor and offer him an opportunity for repentance.

"Boy, when I think of that man!" Fuller once said. "What an account he's got to give before Almighty God. Honest! It sends chills up and down my spine."

When Fuller died in 1988, at the age of 84 and just minutes after teaching his final Sunday school class, Littlefair used the opportunity to assess the "strange" relationship and rivalry that had existed between them.

"I respected him more than I do many of my liberal colleagues," Littlefair said. "He could tell people they would go to hell, but he had a real human caring."

FIGURE 12
Wealthy Street
Baptist's Vacation Bible
School in 1935.

brought hundreds to baptism, and these practiced the sacrificial giving that helped fund 19 missionaries in 1925 (up from zero in 1908), twice that in the 1950s, and 50 in the early 1990s. Wealthy Street's missions and benevolence budget consistently surpassed its operating expenses from World War II through the early 1960s, amounting to $1,450 per week in 1966.[10]

This congregation has exemplified what to outsiders seems fundamentalism's great paradox: fiery condemnation of liberals in the church, loving entreaties to the unsaved in the world. The two are joined at the root of the church's mission, as Wealthy Street Baptist conceived it: to win individual souls for Christ; to bind them in disciplined fellowship, knowledgeable in doctrine, sober in behavior; and then to spring them forth as soul-winners in the world. In this perspective, "modernist trifling" with the Bible cracked the foundations of truth, liberal notions of progress sapped the urgency of salvation, and both together damned souls to hell and society to sin. Social reform would come, Fuller declared, only by multiplying personal conversions. Purely human ventures, even if cloaked in religious talk, could only fail.[11]

The message was familiar to Grand Rapids in the 1920s but nonetheless outrageous in progressive circles. For that reason, Wealthy Street let it sound loud, clear, and continuous. Where Alfred Wishart orated about human potential, Van Osdel proved human depravity from the daily news. The progressives spoke of nature's evolutionary rise; the fundamentalists of nature's remorseless conclusion in death, from which only supernatural salvation gave deliverance. For the former, hope lay in education; for the latter, only in conversion. If Fountain Street discarded creeds and chunks of Scripture, Wealthy Street made the Bible's inerrancy the first item in its statement of faith, and made that statement binding on all its members. In and through it all, where progressives read history as growth toward perfection, fundamentalists saw it as accelerating degeneration, bringing very near Christ's cataclysmic return in judgment. For Americans, events of the 1920s made either reading possible. But to Grand Rapids' native-born Protestants, who saw their morality ridiculed; to laborers and small shopkeepers, pressured by the times; to people accustomed to stability, whose doctrinal anchors the intellectuals would cut — to all these, Wealthy Street's message made eminent sense. The congregation prospered while preaching doom.

If Van Osdel's sermons drew regular crowds, visiting celebrities won the headlines. At the 1923 Baptist Bible Union convention held in the church, William Bell Riley called the 1,100 delegates to "Holy War" against the "lie that is evolution." William Jennings Bryan, three-time Democratic candidate for president, repeated the charge with his incomparable eloquence at an evening service in 1924 that seated 2,000 people — and turned a like number away. In the mid-1930s, the Rev. Bob Jones arrested the audience by flouting the intellectuals with Southern folk humor: "This is the day of Balaam's ass when the Lord is willing to use anybody he can get …. If a hound dog came to my town and began barking for Jesus Christ, I would welcome him into my home; and if he had the mange, I would help him get rid of it." [12]

By the time Van Osdel finally succumbed to old age, New Year's morning 1935, his replacement already had been in the Wealthy Street pulpit for three months. David Otis Fuller came to a city ministry and fundamentalist leadership honestly, having been born in Brooklyn in 1903 and educated at Wheaton College ("the evangelical Harvard") and Princeton Seminary. Like Van Osdel, Fuller was equally at home with elegance and passion and was blessed with longevity. He pastored Wealthy Street Baptist for 40 years and died at 85, only three years short of his predecessor's mark. Arguably, Fuller faced the harder task in having to maintain a huge congregation after its formative battles were over. He did remarkably well, adding 50 percent to the membership in his first 20 years and building his Bible institute into a college and seminary. Under his leadership, Wealthy Street extended its ministry to the opposite ends of the age spectrum. In 1942 it helped found the Children's Bible Hour, a radio program that beamed fundamentalist-style Sunday school lessons into local homes, churched or unchurched. In 1959 it instituted the Michigan Christian Home on Boston Street

SE as a rest home for the elderly in the GARBC network.

To Fuller, these ventures existed not for their own sake, much less for purposes of personal empire, but to proclaim an unchanging faith amid a fast-changing world. Yet he articulated that message so boldly that during his 40-year pastorate he became an eminence in the city, acclaimed or feared but never ignored. Now slashing the liberal enemy, now prodding his sometime allies among the Dutch Reformed, Fuller never let his own congregation become complacent. Every service included a call to salvation for the wavering, the challenge of mission for the committed.

FIGURE 13
Children's Bible Hour broadcast, Feb. 21, 1953.

FIGURE 14
Some examples of games and teaching aids produced by the Children's Bible Hour.

A New Age Religion

With an emphasis not on the blood but the life-enhancing spirit of Jesus Christ, Ida Bailey began a new religious movement in the Grand Rapids area in 1920.

A strong, clear-eyed woman who always wore long dresses in public, Ida Bailey was raised an Episcopalian in the Sparta area. In her life, she saw America progress from candles to electric lights, and from ox carts to airplanes.

Such technological advancements convinced her a new spirit was sweeping the land, bringing men and women out of the darkness into a new world in which every person would realize that he or she was indeed a living, breathing incarnation of God. As a result, she helped to bring to Grand Rapids a faith characterized by some as "New Thought" or "New Age."

"Ida Bailey was a real strong person and very outspoken," said Barbara Fairchild, historian of the West Michigan church founded by Bailey, Unity Church of Practical Christianity. "Through her strength she made you feel you could do things. God was working through her."

Just after World War I, Ida Bailey began the first West Michigan branch of Unity Church out of her home on Coit Avenue NE.

"Ida Bailey was a very educated person and an excellent speaker," said Beverly Pearson, a long-time member who recalls hearing Bailey preach in the early days of the congregation. "The church is what it is because of her."

The Unity movement itself was begun in Kansas City, Mo., by Charles and Myrtle Fillmore. What attracted Ida Bailey to this denomination, she once said, was that it had no stipulated creed. She said she liked the way it taught a combination of "Christianity and psychology, calling it metaphysics."

In 1993, the local Unity Church had about 500 members in its church on Walker Avenue NW. A sister church — the Unity Church of Peace — grew out of that congregation and started meeting in late 1992.

From its start, Unity in Grand Rapids has followed the spirit of its founder and has offered a distinct brand of Christian worship.

"We do believe in God. We believe in prayer and we do use the Bible as our text," said the Rev. Nathaniel R. Carter, co-minister of the church with his wife, Suzanne. "Where we are different, at least in Grand Rapids, is that we are a liberal child of the Holiness movement of the middle to late 19th century."

Unity members believe God resides in everyone; that people are all God. They do not believe in a literal hell. Evil to them is simply the absence of good.

Unity members use the Bible as a guide and text, but much of it is viewed as story and metaphor that reflect various aspects of a human nature we all share, said Carter.

Church members believe in faith healing, positive thinking and allowing members to bring to their worship many varying strains of thought and practice.

"We've got members of fundamentalist churches and people from astrology groups in our church every Sunday," Carter said.

The practical piety at work in Unity is a direct result of the influence of Bailey, a woman whose devotion and faith were evident and strong from an early age.

By the time she was 10, Ida Bailey could recite the New Testament by memory. She was active in the Chautauqua movement, took special studies in speech at the University of West Virginia, and lectured and recited works before audiences all over the country.

She discovered Unity in 1914 and was quickly caught up in a religion that gave expression to her own beliefs in astrology, faith healing and positive Christianity.

FIGURE 15
Ida Bailey

Bailey was married and had grown children when she started offering classes in this faith out of her home. She was ordained a Unity minister in 1934 at the age of 75.

For nearly 25 years, the local congregation, with Ida Bailey at its head, moved from place to place, never solidly rooted in one building. In 1949, the congregation purchased its first permanent home at Scribner Avenue and Second Street NW from Ahavas Israel, a conservative Jewish congregation that was moving.

The structure was paid for within two years and the deed of ownership was presented to Ida Bailey in early 1951, on her 90th birthday. Six months later she died.

Not long before Christmas in 1962, several men and women gathered at the foot of a hill on Walker Avenue NW and began work on their new house of worship. Within two years, the simple structure, surrounded by pines and still in use, was completed.

Making Unity distinct in Grand Rapids has been the powerful spirit of acceptance that Ida Bailey left as her legacy. The church has been a quiet haven for those unhappy with other, usually more theologically rigorous and autocratic denominations.

"Most of our members come because of some life crisis — a divorce, a death in the family, a personal disappointment — in which their traditional beliefs have not been sufficient to meet their needs," the Rev. David Drew, a former pastor, once explained.

In a small, quiet way, the Grand Rapids faction of the Missouri denomination offered a religion that was long on acceptance and short on dogma.

Unity in Grand Rapids, Ida Bailey once said, was helping to usher in a New Age of belief.

"It remains a fact that the new is always becoming, and the old is continually passing," she once preached. "Thus are the New Day and the New Age always with us ... I have spoken so many times of the New Age into which we are moving, and nothing can either stop it or vary its course."

Fuller continued the battle for the Bible by campaigning well into his retirement to have the King James Version recognized as the only translation that carried the divine inspiration of the original.[13] His own calling and his sense of the Christian life as combat were best captured in the title of a collection of evangelical writings he published in 1961, *Valiant for the Truth*. The "chattering sparrows" of popular opinion might "travel in flocks," Fuller declared, but "the eagle soars alone above the clouds and craggy peaks, to brave the storm and scream defiance at the jagged lightning." Doubtless Fuller saw himself in the eagle, and so could draw comfort from the lessons God taught through history: "... it is thrilling to learn that in every age God has had His man, chosen, predestined, and fitted for warfare against the powers of darkness ...." As long as believers held fast to the Bible, whose authority was as "supreme" and "absolute" as "the multiplication table," they could be sure that "neither persecution, banishment, torture, nor death could dislodge or destroy them ...."[14]

But not even Fuller could stop social change. As its neighborhood became increasingly African-American, his church's membership began to fall: from 1,581 in 1959 to 1,211 in 1973. The next year Fuller had to quit his pulpit because of a heart attack, and the congregation decided to move to the suburbs. Blacks were free to join the church but would not feel comfortable there, Fuller explained, and the membership had to be built back up to support the missions budget. After first buying land at Lake Drive and East Paris Avenue SE, the church located on Michigan Street NE instead. They held their last service at Wealthy and Eastern on Sept. 5, 1982; broke ground for a permanent building in their centennial year, 1986; and moved into the finished, $2.5 million complex in 1988 as Wealthy Park Baptist Church.[15]

An African-American version of their old ministry continues at the original site, which the congregation donated to the Community Bible Baptist Church. For their own part, the new site has not brought Wealthy Park the anticipated growth. Sunday attendance averages about 500; membership stands at 825, including some 200 "shut-ins."[16] Perhaps economic prosperity has sapped some of the fundamentalist appeal. Perhaps the media-spread culture of entertainment has rendered their sober, rather formal worship less attractive. But the

FIGURE 16
First building of East Street Christian Reformed Church and its parsonage with the Rev. and Mrs. J. Post standing out front.

voices of wealth and "progress" have counted out such churches as Wealthy Baptist before. They would be foolish to do so again.

THE GRONINGERS' GENERAL

Like the Baptists, the Christian Reformed also began a mission in the Eastern-Wealthy area in the 1870s. Some 80 families who had moved to that edge of town responded to the venture and formally organized as the East Street Dutch Christian Reformed Church in 1879. They acted just in time for the great Dutch immigration of the 1880s. The newcomers who settled in this part of town were mostly displaced farmers and artisans from the northern Netherlands, giving the neighborhood the nickname of Groningen corner after their province of origin.[17] The Christian Reformed resembled their Wealthy Street neighbors economically and, in some respects, religiously. Both congregations frowned on dancing, card playing, and theater. But the Baptists further prohibited alcohol and tobacco use, which the Dutch tolerated, while the latter added on the exacting Calvinist theology for which the northern Netherlands was notable.

So heavy was the immigration that East Street already in 1887 had to build a new 1,200-seat edifice to accommodate the crowd. It took a more momentous step in 1900 by calling as pastor Johannes Groen,

one of the CRC's few American-born clergy and a leader of decidedly progressive views.[18] Progressive Dutch Calvinism, that is. Groen tolerated no liberal theology, insisted on Dutch for worship, and built up the Christian school on Baxter Street. But inspired by the great Dutch statesman-theologian Abraham Kuyper, Groen encouraged his flock to enter vigorously into public life. Christians had a heavenly citizenship, he taught, but also belonged to the organic stream of human life and had to learn to cooperate with the people around them, Christian or not. By the 1910s, this attitude made Groen one of the few local CRC clergy to support women's suffrage and to countenance Christians joining secular labor unions. Those views did not faze the congregation which under Groen's pastorate became the largest in the denomination, numbering 485 families and 2,075 souls. But others took exception. Groen's stance on labor unions elicited a stern rebuke from Herman Hoeksema, a young minister in Holland, Michigan. And Groen's career at Eastern Avenue abruptly ended when he was shot at by one of his parishioners, said to be a deranged man with marital problems. After recuperating from the shock, Groen left for an easier charge in Los Angeles.[19]

It seemed astonishing, then, when East-

FIGURE 17
East Street CRC's new building in 1887.

ern Avenue voted in 1920 to fill its vacant pulpit with … Herman Hoeksema. Perhaps his youth (born 1886) and vigorous Calvinism recalled what Groen had been. But where Groen had seen one organic stream of life, Hoeksema saw two: that of real Christians — the true church — descended from God's decree of election, and that of the lost world — everybody else — bound by the decree of damnation. The two should have nothing to do with each other, Hoeksema argued, since they operated from antithetical loyalties. Nor could they cooperate since they shared no moral ground. Everything the non-saved did promoted, indeed *was*, sin, Hoeksema insisted. All their seemingly good deeds either stemmed from self-interest or served in the long run to build up the resources of unbelief.[20]

Since these views soon earned Hoeksema a reputation as a "monster," it is good to recall the experience in which they made sense. Hoeksema had been born in Groningen to a pious mother beset with an alcoholic, philandering husband. When he deserted them, the family of five was left in poverty. Young Herman took to the streets, stealing bread, running with a gang, defying all order and propriety. His mother's faith eventually turned him around and his blacksmith's training gave him a skill. Following his sister to Chicago in 1904, Herman worked in steel construction. He also displayed brilliant mental and rhetorical gifts in a Christian Reformed young people's group there, and so left for Calvin College and Seminary in 1908. His proficiency put Hoeksema at the head of the class, a position he would seek in every future undertaking. With the status of minister, therefore, Hoeksema could subdue one haunt of his past. His frame of mind answered another. Hoeksema's Calvinism was logical, unswerving, and remorselessly consistent. For him

life was a perilous course which one negotiated either by selfish cunning, as in his boyhood, or under the uncompromising law of the Sovereign Lord. His world offered stark, opposed alternatives. It was a world familiar to hundreds of immigrants.[21]

Hoeksema proclaimed this message boldly from his first pulpit, at 14th Street CRC in Holland. He defied the hysterical patriotism of World War I by refusing to place the American flag in the sanctuary during services; the church was not to be compromised by national symbols. The ensuing uproar, especially among the better folk in town, prompted him to carry a pistol, which he threatened to use one night on some vigilantes near his home. Upon coming to Grand Rapids, Hoeksema, like his new neighbor Van Osdel, poured a wartime spirit into theological questions. He even started with the same issue, attacking Ralph Janssen, professor of Old Testament at Calvin Seminary, for supposedly denying the truthfulness of Scripture. When Janssen countered by faulting Hoeksema's conception of how God works in the world, Hoeksema's own views became implicated in the struggle. For the moment, he won; Janssen was deposed from his post by the CRC Synod of 1922. But then the guns turned, and Hoeksema came under attack.[22]

A war of words ensued, filling the air with pamphlets and counter-pamphlets, articles, and heated street-corner debates. Legal action began on Saturday morning, Jan. 19, 1924,

FIGURE 18
The Rev. Johannes Groen

FIGURE 19
The Rev. Herman Hoeksema

FIGURE 20
Ralph Janssen, professor of Old Testament at Calvin Seminary from 1902 to 1906 and 1914 to 1922.

FIGURE 21
The Christian Reformed Church's annual Synod was held in Kalamazoo in 1924.

when three of his parishioners filed an official complaint against Hoeksema's theology. The Eastern Avenue consistory censured the three on technical grounds; they appealed to the CRC's regional assembly, Classis Grand Rapids East, which urged the consistory to lift the suspension and which passed along the theological question to that summer's Synod, the CRC's highest tribunal. After two weeks' deliberation, the Synod officially declared against Hoeksema and for three points of common grace: God restrained the working of sin on earth among all peoples and showed favor of a non-saving sort to the unregenerate; these were capable therefore of civil (though not divine) righteousness. That said, Synod granted that Hoeksema was properly Reformed on the basics and so did not merit official discipline. It then confused the issue further by issuing a ringing attack upon the "worldliness" of the age.[23]

Back at Eastern Avenue, the three censured members applied for exoneration and, that failing, appealed to the classis. Intricate legal and rhetorical maneuvering followed, to which Hoeksema contributed by blasting Synod in his own recently inaugurated periodical, the *Standard Bearer*. Graffiti for and against Hoeksema appeared on alley fences in the Groningen quarter.[24] In November, the classis ordered the Eastern Avenue consistory to lift the censure and to force Hoeksema to comply with, or at least not publicly defy, the three points. At the classis meeting on Dec. 9, Hoeksema announced the consistory's refusal to do so, delivering a 90-minute rationale in each language. The next day, classis found him guilty of insubordination, deposed the consistory, and called for the congregation's faithful remnant — 800 had signed a petition in favor of Hoeksema, 92 one against him — to organize anew.[25]

Until now the fracas had stayed within Christian Reformed circles. But in February 1925 all Grand Rapids could peek in as the loyalist minority took the Hoeksema faction to Kent County Circuit Court over possession of the church property. Newspapers gave the proceedings front-page coverage. In the courthouse halls, partisans of either side quarreled over the fine points of Reformed theology and passed along rumors that CRC magnates had offered Hoeksema a $40,000 bribe to concede the case. On the stand, a parade of dignified clergymen dueled with the lawyers. The questioning once drove Hoeksema to protest the "ridicul[ing] of … my sacred convictions" and left the president of the 1924 Synod tangled in double-talk and, literally, gasping for air.[26] Upon reading the minutes of their classis meetings, Judge Major L. Dunham commended the Christian Reformed for their meticulous records but professed himself bewildered as to their meaning. The real questions in the case, he concluded, were whether the classis had proper jurisdiction over Eastern Avenue Church and whether the latter's actions — buying property for a new building, financing other dissidents — amounted to an effective withdrawal from the denomination. The answer to

both was yes, Dunham decided, so the church property belonged to the loyalists. Hoeksema's group appealed the decision, but the Michigan Supreme Court upheld it on Dec. 22, 1925. The loyalists immediately took possession, leaving the protesters out in the cold. They held Christmas services in the Franklin [now King] Park lodge, murmuring that, after all, Jesus' stable had been rude and improvised, too.[27]

With these events the First Protestant Reformed Church was born. The congregation comprised 450 of Eastern Avenue's 500 families and on Dec. 22, 1926 — a year to the day from their exile — occupied their huge, new brick structure at Fuller Avenue and Franklin Street SE. They joined with six small groups in other Dutch-American enclaves to form a new denomination. Discord immediately wracked this body, however, as Hoeksema came into conflict with Henry Danhof, his collaborator in the 1924 battle and pastor of the other large Protestant Reformed congregation, in Kalamazoo. By 1926 Danhof and his church had departed, leaving Hoeksema and one other pastor to shepherd their flocks, write the *Standard Bearer*, and conduct the fledgling Protestant Reformed seminary in First Church's basement. By 1935, the school had sent 18 graduates out to parishes across the country.[28]

Only iron convictions and iron discipline enabled Hoeksema to maintain his schedule over the next two decades: preaching three times a Sunday, making up to 500 pastoral calls a year, writing, teaching, turning summer vacations into missionary journeys, and constantly sniping at the CRC. The church

hired an associate pastor in 1939, who soon led some of the members into a daughter congregation — Fourth, later Southeast, PRC on Cambridge Avenue SE — but then added a radio ministry (the Reformed Witness Hour) in 1940. Despite one, then two, more assistants, Hoeksema buckled under the strain. A stroke in June 1947 left him weak, and left an opening for some of the younger clergy to find their own voice. These hoped to bring the more conservative of the post-World War II Dutch immigrants into the Protestant Reformed fold, and they offered to reconsider some theological points in the process. Hoeksema's co-pastor, Hubert De Wolf, did so in the pulpit in 1950, declaring that God's election awaited the individual's consent to take effect. First Church, like the denomination as a whole, fell into factions, then split in 1953.[29] This time Hoeksema led the loyal minority, as two-thirds of the congregation left. Overall, the denomination lost half its ministers and 60 percent of its members in the fray. Hoeksema did better in court, however, as his party was awarded the property. He also got even with attorney Jay Linsey, his nemesis from the 1925 trial. Cross-examin-

FIGURE 22
First Protestant Reformed Church exterior in 1963.

FIGURE 23
Reformed Witness Hour choir doing radio broadcast.

Religious Publishing Was All in the Family

P.J. "Pat" Zondervan burst through the door of his family's farmhouse in Grandville and stood before his surprised mother.

"Why are you coming home? What does this mean?" asked Petronella Zondervan.

Six years before, in 1924, P.J.'s mother had arranged for her oldest son to live with and work for her brother, William B. Eerdmans, owner of a book-selling business in nearby Grand Rapids. P.J. had been home many times in the interim, but his mother suspected something out of the ordinary this day.

"Ma!" P.J. announced. "I just got fired."

P.J. had worked his way up from sweeping the floors to traveling the Midwest as a book salesman. As he came to know the business, the ambitious young man began to ask for more responsibility. His uncle, however, wasn't ready to make room at the top for his 22-year-old nephew. When P.J. pushed, he found himself without a job.

Years later, P.J. would say the firing was a "lucky break" because it nudged him toward starting his own business. He was able to turn the energy and personal drive that got him into trouble with his uncle into what today is one of the largest publishers of evangelical literature and music in the nation.

FIGURE 24   P.J. Zondervan

But the story of P.J. Zondervan's break with his uncle is more than just the tale of a family spat that had a happy ending. Reflected in the firing of the up-and-coming bookseller was the reality that in Grand Rapids in the early decades of the 20th century there were several men for whom spreading the Word of God meant entering the publishing business. The Good News from Grand Rapids was that religious publishing took root here in the early 1900s and despite, or possibly because of, family rivalries has flourished to the present.

A rich Dutch Calvinistic heritage, with a strong emphasis on the written word, helped spawn four religious publishing enterprises.

P.J.'s uncle, Bill Eerdmans, began it all at the turn of the century when, soon after deciding to end his studies for the Christian Reformed Church ministry, he started selling theological books door to door in Grand Rapids. Little did William Eerdmans know that his book-peddling business would beget a religious publishing enterprise, out of which would spring, in the form of his hard-driving nephew, another book-selling business and publishing enterprise. Nor did Eerdmans, who came to this country when he was 20, realize that one of his contemporaries, Louis Kregel, would do the same. Kregel also bartered books door to door in the city's largely Dutch Reformed enclaves. And like Eerdmans before him, he started his own bookstore and hired as an apprentice his nephew, Herman Baker. And, ironically, Herman — as had P.J. — eventually struck out on his own to start another publishing venture.

The firms that sprang from the Eerdmans and Kregel families were: William B. Eerdmans Publishing Co.; Zondervan Inc.; Kregel Publishing Co.; and Baker Book House.

The four publishing houses all took different approaches.

Louis Kregel, with his long love affair with the dusty tomes of old, set up a world-renowned used book business out of the basement of his bookstore on Eastern Avenue SE. In later years, after the founding of the business, his son Robert Kregel would forage bookstalls, antique marts and estate sales around the world in search of hard-to-find, often out-of-print books for his customers. Every year, Christian leaders from all over the United States would browse the aisles of his store, looking for their favorite titles. Kregel also has made a name for his company by republishing books of lasting merit. One such title is the *Book of Josephus*, a look at biblical times by a 2nd century Jewish historian.

"The reason why we got into the business is that we were very serious, devoted Christians interested in books and in bringing what they had to offer to others," said Robert Kregel.

In 1939, almost a decade after P.J. Zondervan and his brother, Bernie, began a business in books, Herman Baker broke from his uncle and opened his store at 1019 Wealthy St. SE. The stock in his first store consisted of hundreds of used books "that he had painstakingly collected over the years, and his equipment consisted of two used desks, a typewriter purchased from the Salvation Army and some homemade shelves."

Although his leaving caused some friction in the families, he, too, longed to reach fellow believers.

Baker, for instance, mixed solid theological scholarship with practical approaches to daily living. The lay reader with a passion to know how God works in his or her world outside church has been the one Baker labored to serve. Popular Baker texts include *The Baker Encyclopedia of the Bible*, *Cruden's Unabridged Concordance* and *Bedtime Stories*, an illustrated collection of Bible tales for children. Baker also expanded his company — a way of making a living that he saw more as a ministry than a business — into bookstores. Baker Book Houses were created to sell Christian books and items across West Michigan.

Following the scholarly lead of its founder, who had a lifelong love for anything related to John Calvin, Eerdmans Publishing Co. evolved into by far the most intellectually diverse and daring of the quartet of local publishers. Moving farther afield in the evangelical arena, Eerdmans has published books on nuclear power, medical ethics, politics in South Africa, abortion, minority rights, and the relationship between contemporary literature and theology. Books coming out of Eerdmans focus often on the issues of the day, seen through the eyes of an evangelical author.

Looming large over the others, however, was the firm begun out of a farmhouse dining room in Grandville. With a wide range of offerings, Zondervan Inc. grew far beyond its Grand Rapids underpinnings.

The company that P.J. Zondervan built eventually included various book lines that ranged from Christian romances to an extremely popular end-of-the-world saga called *The Late Great Planet Earth*. The company's empire also included Family Bookstores scattered throughout the United States. But probably the firm's most lucrative mainstay has been the New International Version of the Bible, a scripture translation for which the company owns exclusive publishing rights. By the 1990s, this translation was overtaking the King James translation as the most popular in English-speaking Christendom.

Becoming such a guiding influence on the evangelical publishing field did not happen without enormous struggle. The company in the early 1980s was the object of several takeover attempts by outside corporations. In 1988, after many offers and rumors of sales, P.J. Zondervan relinquished final control of

the operation when he sold to HarperCollins Publishers, a division of media mogul Rupert Murdoch's international News Corp.

By the time the company was sold, P.J. had semi-retired from the firm. His brother, Bernie, who had helped to build the business, had died. The family book concern was no longer. What began in his mother's home was by then a publicly held corporation spread throughout the city and offering a certain message to the world. P.J. Zondervan died in April 1993.

Although P.J. and his uncle never became close friends, there is a happy ending in that part of the publishing story as well.

In the mid-1960s, P.J. received a call from William Eerdmans, asking if they could meet for lunch. Until then, nephew and his former boss had rarely spoken. But that day in a German restaurant near downtown Grand Rapids, reconciliation occurred.

"Pat," said Uncle Bill. "I want you to know that I don't hold anything against you and wish you every success in your business."

"Believe me, Uncle Bill," P.J. replied. "I don't hold anything against you either. If it had not been for you, I would never have gotten started in this business."

Eerdmans died soon after, leaving the business in the hands of his son, William Eerdmans Jr.

Emerging from the same roots in more ways than one, these four firms, founded by four ambitious men, helped shape the local religious scene for many years. But more than that, the publishing houses these men built continued to touch and influence Bible-based readers everywhere as the 21st century approached.

FIGURE 25

William Eerdmans, right, and son, William Eerdmans Jr.

ing him, Linsey remarked that it had been 30 years since the two had met before. "I wonder what another 30 years will bring," he mused. Hoeksema replied: "I'll be in heaven, Mr. Linsey. Where will you be?" [30]

First Protestant Reformed carried on after the rupture and after Hoeksema's death in 1965. The influx of black neighbors prompted the church, in a close copy of Wealthy Street Baptist, to move out to Michigan Street NE in 1984. The congregation did its part in the publication and educational ministries of the denomination, building the Adams Street Christian School in the early 1950s and supporting the Protestant Reformed's Covenant Christian High School, which opened in 1968. But the location of the high school in Walker, the move of the seminary to Ivanrest Avenue SW in 1973, and First Church's declining numbers reflected the denomination's shift-

ing demographics. In 1950, First Church numbered 1,962, 34 percent of the PRC's total membership; in 1972, 519 for 16 percent; in 1987, 382 for 7 percent. Meanwhile, the membership of Protestant Reformed congregations in Walker, Grandville, and Jenison soared from 385 in 1960 to 675 in 1972 and 1,507 (29 percent of the denomination) in 1987. The Groningen district had emptied to the southwest, and First Church had moved northeast.[31]

Meanwhile, what was left of Eastern Avenue CRC stayed in the old neighborhood, limping through the 1930s, buoyed by new Dutch immigrants after World War II, and re-emerging as a flagship of CRC progressivism in the 1960s. Dozens of young veterans of the reform crusades of that decade flocked to its programs of social ministry and fresh worship. The congregation helped turn Baxter Christian School into

FIGURE 26   Mel Trotter

Mel Trotter's Ordination

Soon after arriving in Grand Rapids to start his mission work, Mel Trotter went before the Grand Rapids presbytery, a local body that at that time certified non-denominational ministers.

"What are your Christian evidences?" he was asked.

"What's that?" replied Trotter.

"Are you saved?"

"You bet."

"How do you know?"

"I was there when it happened, January 19, 1897, 10 minutes past nine, Central time, Pacific Garden Mission, Chicago, Illinois, U.S.A.."

"What do you know about church history?"

"You know more about it than I do."

"What is your doctrine?"

"The Monroe Doctrine."

"Are you Calvinist or Arminian?"

"You can search me; my father is Irish."

At this point in the interview, an elderly minister stood and said: "Who are we to refuse ordination to one God has ordained? God put His hands on this man; the Presbytery of Grand Rapids will follow our Lord."

Mel Trotter was ordained in seven minutes, from the time he went before the ministers until the moment he was officially pronounced a preacher.

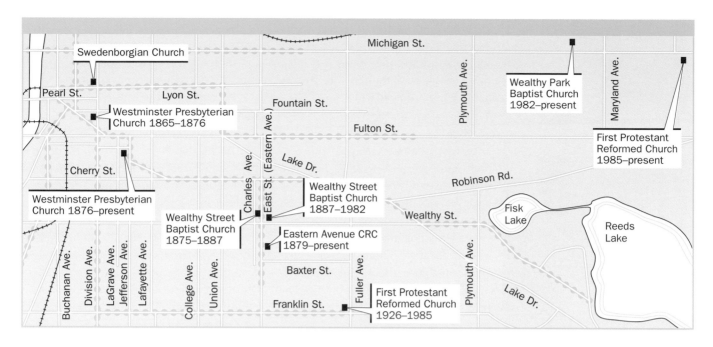

FIGURE 27

The Wealthy Street — Eastern Avenue neighborhood was Grand Rapids' center of religious controversy in the 1920s.

Baxter Community Center, which offers vital social services to its neighborhood. It also led in the founding of the Inner City Christian Federation, a non-profit housing rehabilitation agency. Every week the church distributes two tons of produce and 1,000 loaves of bread at low cost to some 275 people. It also has spawned political activism, claiming — at this writing — a state senator, a state representative, a county commissioner, and a congressional staffer among its members.[32] All this Johannes Groen would salute. More controversially, Eastern Avenue has pressed the cause of women's ordination in the CRC. When the 1992 Synod refused to implement a measure approved two years before to open all church offices to women, Eastern Avenue went ahead and ordained women elders anyway. The substance of this stance Herman Hoeksema would vigorously reject; the style he might recognize.

While the press sometimes gave him the label, Hoeksema never called himself a "fundamentalist." He disliked the free will doctrine implied by that movement's revival campaigns; he disagreed with some of its behavioral prohibitions; and he never, as it could, equated the kingdom of God with the United States. But within the bounds of Reformed doctrine, the Protestant Reformed surely echoed the fundamentalist crusade. Both were militant and uncompromising.

Both demanded unambiguous commitment to the core of their faith. Both scored "liberal apostasy" for teaching false doctrine and for abetting moral chaos. Both wanted to lead lives separated from a degenerate world. More than a mild echo of that message lives on in Protestant Reformed circles today. As Gertrude Hoeksema, Herman's daughter-in-law, wrote on the denomination's 50th anniversary in 1975:

... amid all the increasing apostasy of our present day, when former citadels of the Reformed truths of the Word of God are crumbling, when the Scriptures are being denied as God's infallible Word, when the foundations of the truth are mercilessly being trampled under foot ... [the PRC] remains what it has always been — an institution dedicated to the uncompromising and unadulterated Word of God.[33]

HOSTING THE SHOWDOWN

For all their passion, the arch-conservatives in the 1920s failed to take over any broad denomination such as the Baptists or tighter ones like the CRC. Perhaps the closest they came was at the 1924 Presbyterian General Assembly that met in Grand Rapids. They also failed here, however, for reasons and with results evident in the history of the Assembly's host congregation, Westminster Presbyterian Church.

Westminster was the third Presbyterian

FIGURE 28
The Rev. Courtney Smith,
Westminster's first pastor.

church to be organized in town, the first to prosper. The band that met at Myron Hinsdill's house in 1836 organized under Presbyterian rules before going Congregational two years later. Then a group started meeting at "Dr. Penny's lecture hall" on Bridge Street at the river. From it emerged both Second Methodist and, on Oct. 26, 1855, First Presbyterian Church. Raising some $11,000 in pledges, the Presbyterians boldly contracted for a marble-fronted building in August 1857 — just in time for the economic crash of that fall. Over the next four years, the building's framing timbers were scavenged by neighbors for firewood, and the core of the congregation departed to organize Westminster Presbyterian, on the east side of the river. They took along First's minister, the Rev. Courtney Smith.[34]

The new church was chartered on July 17, 1861, in the first flush of the Civil War. An army encampment lay just north of the Swedenborgian meeting house at Division and Lyon where Westminster worshipped, so Smith had a golden chance for evangelism. That fit the church's inclination in any case, since Westminster belonged to the Presbyterians' New School which favored revivals and social reforms such as abolishing slavery. Their conviction did not run that deep, however, for when the New School assembly dropped Westminster's subsidy and the more Calvinistic Old School picked it up, the congregation switched sides. The issue became moot in 1869 when the two parties healed their rift. By this time the congregation had erected its own little brick church across the street from

their first site, but a few years later they were displaced when the federal government acquired the land for a new post office.[35] Thus, Westminster's first years showed problems of buildings and theology, breaks and healing, all in the shadow of a great national crusade. These were apt signs of the future.

In 1876, the church moved into a chapel at Weston Street and LaGrave Avenue SE and began to collect money for a larger building. It was completed 10 years later at a cost of $40,000 — and suffered such poor acoustics that the sanctuary walls and ceiling had to be covered with canvas. Theologically, these years featured stalwart orthodoxy. The Rev. Sanford Cobb preached scholarly sermons on duty. The Christmas service of 1885 alternated high-toned hymns with strictly biblical responsive readings. Governing its affairs were such laymen as William O. Hughart, president of the Grand Rapids & Indiana Railroad. Hughart observed the strict Sabbath and rock-ribbed morality of his native western Pennsylvania, the Presby-

FIGURE 29
Westminster Presbyterian
Church in 1888.

terian heartland, and after serving variously as elder, trustee, and Sunday school superintendent for 21 years until his death in 1899, left two sons to carry on similarly.[36]

By 1894, however, Cobb was hearing enough complaints to move on. His successors introduced a more dynamic, innovative style that doubled the membership from 374 in 1893 to 765 in 1916. Among the newcomers were entrepreneurs in the furniture industry, such as William and Harry Widdicomb, and socially rising Dutchmen like the banker Henry Idema, who transferred from Second Reformed Church.[37] Westminster began to downplay its doctrinal distinctives; its 1910 bulletin stated: "The sole requirement for admission [to membership] … is an honest confession of Jesus Christ as Lord and Master. We require assent to no creed and impose no obligation, putting each member 'on honor' before his conscience." The church's mission program promoted Americanization of immigrants along with evangelism in Asia, and joined the era's social crusade by sponsoring lectures on topics like "The Minimum Wage," "The Modern Woman," and "Loan Sharking in Grand Rapids."[38] Westminster's Presbyterianism had become piety plus progressive politics. That the "Master" and the nation could be served simultaneously the congregation showed by sending 60 youth into the World War I armed forces.

The post-war tumult did not strike Westminster first of all on points of doctrine but in a more familiar spot. A thorough overhaul in the early 1910s had aimed but failed to resolve the perennial building problem. In February 1920 the trustees voted for relocation by purchasing the Blodgett estate at Madison Avenue and Cherry Street SE, partly for reasons of space, partly because the city was thinking of running State Street through to downtown, right through the current site. The congregation disapproved, however. When the city decided against extension, Westminster voted to stay downtown and erected a $100,000 parish house next to the church for classrooms, recreational facilities, and office space.[39] At the same time the congregation was committed to the New Era Movement, the Presbyteri-

FIGURE 30, 31
Furniture executives and Westminster laymen Harry Widdicomb, left, and William Widdicomb, below.

ans' part of a multimillion-dollar inter-denominational campaign aimed at reforming the world in the image of America. But what did these reforms have to do with Christianity? And could the New York City bureaucrats who ran them be trusted? Against the backdrop of such questions, the fundamentalist movement arose in the Presbyterian Church. It pushed for a showdown in Grand Rapids.

Like their Baptist kin, the Presbyterian fundamentalists suspected that liberal doctrine was rife at their denomination's seminaries, mission fields, and headquarters. Unlike the Baptists, Presbyterians had no fear of creeds. In 1910 they added a five-point rider — including Christ's virgin birth, miracles, and bodily second coming — to their historic standards. The policy was reaffirmed at the General Assembly of 1923 and aimed at the Rev. Harry Emerson Fosdick, the nation's foremost liberal preacher who, though a Baptist, occupied a Presbyterian pulpit in New York City. The Assembly told the New York presbytery, or regional governing body, to take corrective action with Fosdick and to report the next year. When

FIGURE 32
Henry Idema was a banker and Westminster layman.

Soup, Soap, and Salvation

Passing by the Pacific Garden Mission in Chicago on the way to throw himself into the icy waters of Lake Michigan, Mel Trotter felt a divine tug. There was no way the young man could have known that the providential pull would one day take him to Grand Rapids and far beyond to international acclaim as a preacher.

On that night, all he knew is that he was drunk and distraught, and he wanted to die. But instead of continuing on his suicide mission to the lake, he slipped into the mission, propped himself against a wall and listened to another man tell him about the Bible. Within minutes, a spirit moved through him and an important change occurred.

"There is no question in my mind, that the greatest day I have ever lived was on the 19th of January, 1897, when the Lord Jesus Christ came into my life and saved me from sin," Trotter wrote in his autobiography.

Struck sane and cured of his awful obsession to drink, Trotter — after whom a mission in Grand Rapids is named — immediately embarked on a new path. He committed himself and his newfound energy to bring the same spiritual experience that had revolutionized his life to others.

In his autobiography, Trotter said it was after repeated failures, in fact so many that hope was practically gone, that he stumbled into the mission that night. "I am positive sure that that was my day; that God the Father, God the Son and God the Holy Ghost planned it," he recalled in that same book.

Following his conversion, Mel Trotter was to become one of the most renowned mission men in the country. As cities began to fill at the turn of the 20th century with people whose needs were many, it was ministers such as Trotter who brought to them the spiritual and material solace they needed.

Industrialization unleashed many forces in America, among them a degree of urban poverty which had not been experienced before. First in Grand Rapids and then across the country, Trotter offered soup, soap and salvation to the growing number of people who had become the vic-

FIGURE 33   Mel Trotter, who brought the down-and-out the spiritual and material solace they needed, works at his desk.

tims of a society undergoing profound transformation.

"I seriously doubt that any man during Mel Trotter's day excelled him in force of personality, in native ability or in spiritual power," the Rev. Bob Jones, himself a noted preacher, once said of Trotter.

"He painted on his canvas of natural eloquence, the most wonderful picture of Jesus Christ as the up-to-date miracle-working Son of God that I have ever known any man to paint," Jones also said.

Trotter was bombastic. His style, energy and administrative skills made the Grand Rapids mission a model for many others in the country. The annual report for 1911 — the mission's 12th year in existence — reports that Trotter's enterprise that year held an evangelistic service every Friday night that drew an average of 1,600 people. Also in 1911, more than 100 calls were made every month by Trotter and his workers on "poor, miserable, poverty-stricken homes."

Dozens of prisoners worked out their probation at the mission. A well-attended mission picnic was held in July at Jenison Park; baskets were sent out to the destitute at Thanksgiving; and clothing, trees and presents were handed out to the needy at Christmas time. In all, this agency was in 1911 and continued for years to be one of the most active and successful evangelistic missions in the city.

Begun in 1900 by a few local businessmen, the mission was first located at 95 Canal St. (later 317 Monroe Ave. NW), an area filled with shacks and dilapidated structures and known as Bucktown.

Not one for intense book learning, Trotter was a human dynamo of religious fervor. Without the spirit of booze to drag him down, he saw himself filled with another spirit he sought to share with the world.

"The night the mission opened the crowd was four times too big for the place and it was a funny bunch," writes Fred Zarfas, Trotter's biographer.

"The rich and poor, drunken and sober, washed and unwashed, young and old, all in the same room singing the same songs and praying to the same God."

FIGURE 34   Mel Trotter's ministry extended beyond Grand Rapids' streets and into the Kent County Jail.

In the early years, Trotter built a following as much with what he said as by his exploits. Occasionally, he had to wade through an unruly mission crowd and throw a loud, often drunken critic out onto the street. And often these troublemakers returned, only to find themselves repenting and born again themselves.

Trotter's accomplishments were many, but were also attended by controversy.

In 1920, the evangelist's character came under attack when rumors began to circulate that he had fathered an illegitimate child by his secretary, Florence Moody. Two years later, a bitter divorce ensued between Trotter and his wife of many years, Lottie. It was determined by the judge who heard the divorce proceedings that the preacher was not the father of the child. Even so, the rumors and the divorce followed him for many years afterward.

Soon after his divorce was final, Trotter's ministry changed direction. He began to spend an increasing amount of time away from Grand Rapids. Revivals in this country and gospel meetings abroad drew him away again and again.

But he always returned to his mission here. And while here he continued to visit the jails, to speak and minister to the men who wandered into his mission, and to drive his famous Gospel Wagon to street corners in the city, at which he told his story of personal salvation.

Trotter, in many ways a father of the rescue mission movement in America, retired to his home on Lake Macatawa in 1940. At that time, he had helped to start nearly 70 missions in this country. He had visited many countries abroad and his message of salvation had touched innumerable lives.

"He made Grand Rapids known throughout the Christian world," the Rev. Henry Beets, a local minister, said at Trotter's memorial service.

"Everywhere he founded rescue missions. Yet throughout all — notwithstanding all — he remained a humble servant of Christ, ever seeking to advance His cause, always loyal to the Gospel of His Master."

FIGURE 35   Mel Trotter's first mission, shown above, was located at 95 Canal St. in Grand Rapids.

New York did nothing and the Auburn Presbyterian Seminary in that state sponsored a petition for greater theological latitude, the fundamentalists organized to clean house, once and for all.[40] The stage would be Grand Rapids — more specifically, and ironically, Fountain Street Baptist Church, the only local space commodious enough to house the 1,000 delegates plus officers, advisers, and journalists who descended on the city to enact, and report, the fray.[41]

For a week in late May 1924 the Assembly dominated the city's headlines. Special attention went to the speeches of such celebrity delegates as William Jennings Bryan, the fundamentalist champion; Will Hays, former Republican national chairman and current czar of Hollywood; Robert E. Speer, missionary-statesman; and Frank Lowden, former governor of Illinois and presidential hopeful.[42] All the anticipations of a purge seemed confirmed when the fundamentalist candidate for Assembly moderator, Clarence Macartney, defeated the moderate 464–446. That meant that committee chairs also would be conservatives. Bryan's nominating speech for Macartney defined their agenda: the Presbyterian Church ought to be a combat unit, faithful simply and totally to God's word in the war against sin and unbelief.[43]

While the appropriate committee studied the Fosdick case, the Assembly busied itself with moral rectitude. It pleaded for a stricter Sabbath and Prohibition, which it labeled "the greatest moral reform of a generation". It petitioned for a halt to the impending Gibbons-Carpentier heavyweight championship bout in Michigan City, Ind., which motion "passed unanimously amid a roar of applause." It called for firmer control of the entertainment industry whose workings the delegates could observe close at hand. The downtown Regent Theatre ran "Son of the Sahara" during convention week, featuring the "kidnapping of white girls by sheiks" and "dusky oriental beauties." The Majestic had "Burt Earle's California Jazz Maids," while Ramona Park promised a vaudeville show with "the greatest collection of feminine beauty ever assembled with a traveling organization." [44]

Finally came the votes everyone was waiting for. The fundamentalists warmed up by dropping William Merrill, a defender of Fosdick, from the mission board; such an

FIGURE 36
The front page of The Grand Rapids *Press* on May 22, 1924, highlighted the start of the Presbyterian Church's General Assembly.

action was virtually unprecedented and caused an uproar. Then came the Fosdick report which faulted him but on technical, not theological, grounds. A Baptist should not hold a Presbyterian pulpit, the committee advised; Fosdick ought to apply for Presbyterian credentials. The Assembly approved the motion 504–311, averting the fundamentalists' clean kill. Then things got much worse for them as the Assembly decided that it might not impose additional creeds like the five points of 1910 without the concurrence of presbyteries, including the liberals' in New York.[45] The fundamentalists' auspicious run ended in compromise and defeat.

Analysis of the Assembly's voting indicates that the liberal New York and conservative Pennsylvania delegations canceled each other out, leaving the decision with "western" representatives from churches like Westminster. And these voted for peace and tolerance; the Michigan delegation went 34–7 with the moderates.[46] Robert D. Towne, a nationally syndicated columnist, caught the real drift of the convention. Presbyterians, he observed, were most enamored of missionary advance around the world and moral tone at home. Their denomination had become a "huge machine," a "big corporation," run by the "chief engineer" (the Stated Clerk), propagated by 1,545 "traveling salesmen" (missionaries), and offering a $50 million budget for the cause of high ideals. Subsequent Assemblies bore him out. Future fundamentalist complaints were buried in study committees, and the General Assembly sacrificed more of its theological oversight while increasing its administrative control.[47]

But that formula did not always win hearty support at the local level. For

instance, Westminster raised only one-third of its New Era Movement quota in 1921 and 1922, and the 1924 Assembly buried the project, without much notice, in a tomb of a $1 million debt.[48] Probably owing to a change in pastors, Westminster's membership dropped from 866 in 1925 to 672 the next year. Complaints about location, dubious amusements in the church gym, and eroding membership compelled a full review of church operations in the early 1930s. The study found that a few wealthy members

FIGURES 37, 38
Ramona Park at the turn of the century. An ad from The Grand Rapids *Press* of May 24, 1924, touts an upcoming vaudeville show.

FIGURE 39
Mr. and Mrs. G.C.
Shepard. Mrs. Shepard
was secretary of
Westminster's Women's
Missionary Society for
20 years.

moved out of town or, in town, over to Park Congregational, Fountain Street Baptist, or Grace Episcopal. On the other hand, prominent Hollanders moved in: Paul F. Steketee and son, of the department store; Dr. and Mrs. William Vis; Dr. Benjamin H. Masselink, and more Idemas, now connected with the parent firm of Steelcase Inc. as well as with banks. Of Westminster's 103 World War II service-people, 19 had Dutch names.[50]

In most mid-sized cities, Presbyterians would be the voice of Calvinism. Given the Reformed and Christian Reformed presence in Grand Rapids, Westminster could hardly claim that role. Still, it was too loyal to the tradition to jettison it for culture and modernism. To partisans of either side, this left the church halting between two opinions. In its own mind it has occupied a creative boundary, offering harbor to the disaffected from left and right. An apt metaphor of its condition lies in the high profile that building projects hold in its history: fitful, renewing, revising, seeking firm ground in a swirl that this congregation can neither simply ride nor reject. As its closing resolution put it, the 1924 General Assembly could not have had a better host.

were paying most of the bills and that people were leaving for churches with better music programs. So a minister of music was hired, while successive pastors urged the congregation to evangelistic efforts, without much effect. Its 85th anniversary booklet, published in 1946, captured Westminster's spirit of efficient moral routine: "harmony and cohesion" prevailed; "all departments have functioned smoothly and with increasing effectiveness," providing "many activities and congenial groups ... for worthwhile work." [49] A review of additions and departures reveals the high rates of mobility characteristic of the business and professional class. The children of lay leaders often

CHURCHES AND OTHER LANDMARKS

A. Reeds Lake
B. Fountain School, former location of the UBA hospital
C. First Methodist
D. Saint Mary's Hospital
E. Butterworth Hospital
F. Second Reformed
G. St. Mark's Episcopal
H. Fountain Street
I. First (Park) Congregational
J. Westminster Presbyterian
K. Immanuel Lutheran
L. Fox Brewery

M. Crescent Park
N. County Building
O. City Hall
P. McKay Tower
Q. Pantlind Hotel (old Sweets Hotel)
R. Future site of the Welsh Civic Auditorium
S. Rowe Hotel, currently Olds Manor
T. Grand Trunk Railroad terminal on site of present day Post Office
U. Bissell Carpet Sweeper Factory
V. Unity Church
W. First Presbyterian
X. Second Street Methodist
Y. St. Mary's Roman Catholic

FIGURE 40
This aerial view of Grand Rapids taken about 1930 presents a good visual context for the churches and other landmarks mentioned in the text so far. Churches and landmarks are immediately to the left of their denoting letter. Saint Mary's Hospital is shown to the right of its letter.

Harbors in the Storm

1930– 1950

O N MARCH 4, 1929, HERBERT HOOVER WAS SWORN IN AS THE 31st President of the United States. His inaugural address warmly commended the American people for their recent achievements and future prospects.

Business prosperity, the extension of education, and yearnings for peace were the landmarks of the decade just ending, he observed, and they indicated America was about to realize its mission of bringing the whole world to "a real brotherhood of man" under "the reign of justice and reason."

"I have an abiding faith in [Americans'] capacity, integrity, and high purpose," Hoover concluded, and so "have no fear for the future of our country. It is bright with hope." [1]

The very issue of The Grand Rapids *Press* which covered Hoover's inauguration also reported a dramatic speech given the day before. At the morning service of Sunday, March 3, the Rev. Martin R. De Haan of Calvary Reformed Church announced

that he was resigning his pulpit to head a new, independent church where the gospel could be preached without compromise.[2] The new congregation included, in fact, about three-fourths of Calvary Reformed's membership and so was named Calvary Undenominational Church. There De Haan would sound a message sharply at odds with Hoover's. The world was rapidly declining, not getting better. Not peace and prosperity but war, turmoil, and suffering were on the horizon. Christians should look not to the brotherhood of man but to the bosom of their Savior who might at any moment be calling them home.

For secular affairs, De Haan proved the better prophet. The 1930s and 1940s witnessed the United States' worst economic depression, the world's deadliest war, Russia's and Germany's most grievous tyranny, and the near-extermination of Europe's Jews. Hoover should have paid attention to the weather on Inauguration Day. "The President," records the official chronicle, "spoke in a downpour of rain" — an apt forecast of calamities to come.

Amid these storms many in Grand Rapids, as elsewhere, turned to religion for shelter. This chapter will examine three representative havens. Calvary Undenominational Church attracted worried Protestants, especially people of Dutch Reformed background, who found their native churches inadequate to the assaults of the age. To them Calvary gave a clear reading of the signs of the times and reassurance of their own salvation. If the world was going to hell, Calvary looked toward the imminent raptures of heaven. The members of Temple Emanuel, Grand Rapids' oldest Jewish congregation, faced perhaps the ultimate test of faith and hope in light of the Nazi assault in Europe. These trials led them to reconsider their habit of adjusting Judaism to modern life and to find new strength by reviving

some traditions that their forebears had let slip. Though smaller than either of these bodies, St. John Chrysostom Russian Orthodox Church carried on in Grand Rapids' near West Side the ancient liturgy of its distant homeland, a country overtaken by the Bolshevik Revolution during World War I, wasted by the German invasion in World War II, and afflicted with police-state terror in between. In an American world that paid it little notice and in a global scene gone grim and violent, this little flame of tradition kept burning the incense of remembrance and renewal.

FIGURE 2
The Rev. Martin R. De Haan

SIGNS OF THE TIMES

The ministry of Martin R. De Haan at Calvary Reformed Church began in May 1925 under the brightest promise for both parties. Calvary had been founded a decade before as a Reformed Church in America (RCA) extension on East Fulton Street. After a couple of brief pastorates (one ended by a fatal gas explosion in the parsonage), the congregation had stabilized in the early 1920s, erecting a 640-seat sanctuary and expanding the membership to nearly 200. For his part, De Haan also seemed primed for a new beginning. Originally a medical doctor in Byron Center, De Haan had worked himself to success, exhaustion, and borderline alcoholism. A near-deathbed conversion experience in 1921 convinced him to work full-time for the Lord instead. After attending the RCA's Western Theological Seminary in Holland, Mich., he took up Calvary as his first charge.[3]

Charge he did, with a fiery, dramatic pulpit style unusual among the Dutch Reformed. The congregation boomed, doubling its membership and tripling its budget in two years. By 1928 Calvary had grown to 600 adult members and undertaken a $15,000 building expansion that increased its seating capacity to 1,400. Then De Haan reached farther still when he and four laymen bought radio station WASH for $2,500 and began broadcasting eight hours of religious programming a day.[4]

Controversy attended this boom, however, and by January 1929 it surfaced in official

channels. Calvary Reformed's consistory (governing board) had to meet with the RCA's classis (regional assembly) to answer complaints about De Haan's doctrine, specifically his doubts about infant baptism and his unusual teachings about Christ's second coming. The meeting went badly, and after some further investigation, the classis filed formal charges against him. The same day (Feb. 26, 1929), 17 of the consistory's 24 members organized a separate church and called De Haan to be its pastor. That set the stage for De Haan's Inauguration Eve sermon — and for another church dispute to be aired in the daily press. With his resignation De Haan declared himself to be outside the RCA's jurisdiction. The denomination disagreed and proceeded to try him anyway. After several well-publicized exchanges, the classis on April 4 found De Haan guilty of six offenses ranging from heresy to fraud to slander, and formally deposed him with words of "scorching rebuke."[5]

De Haan's group was incensed at this procedure and surprised at what followed. Calvary Reformed was left with but 100 members and $90,000 in debt, a predicament De Haan hoped would lead them to accept his offer to buy the property, debt and all. He

even bought a house in the neighborhood for his new parsonage. But the RCA poured money into the loyal remnant which built itself back up slowly against the financial hardships of the Depression. It would finally pay off its denominational loans in 1951.[6]

Meanwhile, De Haan's group had to scramble for facilities. Members first worshipped at the vacant Orpheum Theatre downtown, where De Haan opened on Sunday, March 10, to a crowd of 1,100. In August they purchased the recently vacated Michigan Street Elementary School, converted it to Sunday school classrooms, added a 2,000-seat auditorium on its east side, and fronted the whole with a new facade. The $120,000 complex was dedicated from Jan. 29 to 31, 1930. There, high on the hill at Michigan and College Avenue NE, Calvary Undenominational Church stood for the next 56 years as a "Lighthouse pointing the way to the Safe Harbor of Salvation."[7]

What made De Haan so attractive — and so controversial? Doubtless his style attracted many in the first place, but it was his substance that brought them back and that brought down charges on his head. De Haan's message was simple: All people, even nice churchgoers, were wretched sinners

FIGURE 3
Calvary Undenominational Church on Michigan Street near College Avenue NE.

FIGURE 4
Hugh Hart, also known as
"Uncle Terry," entertained
children over radio
station WASH.

who needed a direct, personal conversion to be saved. To that end he weekly issued invitations to public repentance, insisted that adults — not infants — should be baptized, and criticized the Dutch Reformed system of creeds, tradition, and formal church structures as a formula for spiritual sloth. In short, De Haan was more a fervent evangelical than traditionally Reformed. He heartily joined the 1920s fundamentalist crusade, denouncing every form of liberalism (including its alleged representatives in the RCA) and demanding moral separation from the world. Above all, he propounded fundamentalism's radical notions of the "last days," away from which the Reformed had steered. Jesus might return at any moment, De Haan tirelessly repeated. That return would involve first the rapture, the taking up to heaven of all true Christians. Then would follow the tribulation, a global war featuring the near-triumph of the Antichrist. Then Jesus would return in person to squash that beast and to reign in Jerusalem for 1,000 years as King of the Jews. Accordingly, De Haan argued against his Reformed mentors, churches had no business meddling with politics and social reform but should devote all their attention to saving souls — as many as possible, as quickly as possible, by whatever means available. Hence his use of radio and outdoor revival meetings, of altar calls and advertising.[8]

De Haan personified the Protestant fundamentalist combination of old-time religion and new-fangled methods. The Reformed, of course, saw nothing "old-time" about it but a serious deviation from their historic faith; by their standards, De Haan's doctrines were as erroneous as his methods were distasteful.[9] Nonetheless, these were appealing. De Haan spoke for hundreds — Reformed, Christian Reformed, and long-time Americans — who believed that recent tumults had introduced an entirely new and foreboding era. They did not wish to adjust to the times, as liberals such as Fountain Street Baptist's Alfred Wishart had suggested. But they also felt their native religious customs to be wholly inadequate to the crisis. World War I, the Bolshevik Revolution, the 1920s' moral upheaval, the emergence of a corporate, consumerist economy all left them grasping for order, for a new message of salvation tied fast to "the Bible

FIGURE 5
The Radio Bible Class
was broadcast in the
1950s from the former
Vogue Theatre at 710
Michigan St. NE.

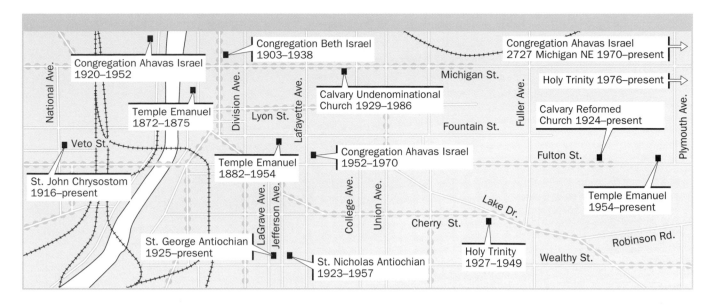

Congregation Ahavas Israel
1920–1952

Congregation Beth Israel
1903–1938

Congregation Ahavas Israel
2727 Michigan NE 1970–present

Michigan St.

Holy Trinity 1976–present

National Ave.

Division Ave.

Lafayette Ave.

Lyon St.

Calvary Undenominational
Church 1929–1986

Fountain St.

Fuller Ave.

Calvary Reformed
Church 1924–present

Plymouth Ave.

Temple Emanuel
1872–1875

Veto St.

St. John Chrysostom
1916–present

Temple Emanuel
1882–1954

Congregation Ahavas Israel
1952–1970

Fulton St.

Temple Emanuel
1954–present

College Ave.

Union Ave.

Lake Dr.

Cherry St.

St. George Antiochian
1925–present

LaGrave Ave.

Jefferson Ave.

St. Nicholas Antiochian
1923–1957

Holy Trinity
1927–1949

Wealthy St.

Robinson Rd.

alone" and secured in the experience of their own hearts.

After breaking with the RCA, De Haan tried to make his church the hub of a larger movement. He joined two other ousted RCA ministers and Harry Bultema, a Muskegon pastor who had left the CRC a decade before in a similar dispute, in publishing *Grace and Glory* magazine to spread the cause in West Michigan Dutch circles. In 1930 Calvary hosted a convention of independent fundamentalist churches from across the Midwest. Disagreements and fail-

ures crippled both these efforts, however, so Calvary turned instead to local evangelism. Its summer Bible school won local headlines for using city buses to transport students to the church; the children simply had to show a Bible to cover their fare. In 1932 the church promoted a city-wide revival, moving the meetings from one neighborhood to another. De Haan's sermons kept him in the headlines as he flailed Fountain Street Baptist for teaching evolution, the Grand Rapids public schools for secularizing the curriculum, and city authorities for allowing airplanes to fly during church hours.[10]

Attention turned to notoriety in 1933, however, when De Haan used his Wednesday night Bible classes to attack President Franklin Roosevelt's New Deal. Reading current events in light of his "last days" scenario, De Haan announced that the New Deal foreshadowed the coming of the Antichrist. The Civilian Conservation Corps was a covert military training program, the National Recovery Administration an attempt to consolidate the nation's economy under dictatorial control. Roosevelt's program would work for a while, De Haan allowed, but only at the cost of depriving the American people "of our individualism and constitutional rights." In the long run it would fail and lead to global war. The whole enterprise was "as red as communism ... [and] closely allied to [the Soviet Union's] five-year plan" because, "though innocently and honestly undertaken by

FIGURE 6
The map details the movement of the major congregations discussed in this chapter.

FIGURE 7
The Rev. M.R. De Haan preaches at the microphone of his Radio Bible Class.

Soldiers and Song

Grand Rapids manufacturer James Lowe was vacationing in Toronto in 1883 when he came across a copy of the *War Cry*, a publication describing the work of a group he had come into contact with a few years earlier in his native England.

Paging through the magazine, the businessman was again struck by the zeal and commitment this group had in translating the Gospel into practical everyday assistance for those in need. Especially interesting to him was the work the group — the Salvation Army — did in trying to transform drunkards.

Back in Grand Rapids, the owner of Lowe & Butterworth Machine shops, located at the site of the current Welsh Auditorium, decided to do what he could

FIGURE 8
The Grand Rapids Temple Corps Band of 1884, the first commissioned Salvation Army band in this country, regularly performed on city streets.

to bring a contingent of the Army to West Michigan. He traveled to England and spoke with William Booth, a Methodist minister who founded the Army in London. He asked that the general dispatch some of his troops to West Michigan. Booth agreed.

On Nov. 25, 1883, the "Salvation Army opened fire on Grand Rapids." A service was held in a hall on Pearl Street. An old stove provided heat; lighting came from dim kerosene lamps. Seats were made of boards, and a bass drum and flags were purchased. Not long after, outreach work began for the first time in this city and in Michigan.

The Army's first convert in Grand Rapids was Casey DeBlond, the drayman who carried the luggage for Capt. Jane McCracken and Lt. Jennie Hall, the first officers to set up camp here. Initially, he wanted no part of the Army, but he attended the first service, where the singing and the preaching overcame his reluctance and he signed on. For

FIGURE 9 Salvation Army Hotel and center in Grand Rapids in 1928. The building at 225 Commerce Ave. SW today houses Mel Trotter Ministries.

many years thereafter he served as a soldier for the cause.

Jacob Vogt, another early convert to the Army's message, described his conversion this way:

"Me drink beer, me smoke pipe and hear dat drink beer and smoke pipe Christians are no Christians at all, so me give beer and smoke pipe to Jesus and me happy, saved and sanctified."

But saving and sanctifying souls was not easy in the beginning in West Michigan. Not everyone accepted the Army's often brash and brassy methods.

"When the Army began its work in Grand Rapids its purpose and methods were misunderstood," a newspaper article written in 1933 stated. "Tough and roughs jostled among the open air crowds and disturbed the (open air) meetings and even followed into the hall."

Adding to the disturbances and eventually landing a few Army members in jail was the nation's first duly commissioned Salvation Army band. The Citadel Band, the

FIGURE 10
Salvation Army Band plays in front of the Tree of Lights in 1972.

Number One Corps for the Army in this country, regularly performed on city streets. Apparently concerned about the raucous clangor the Salvationists made, city fathers passed a law in the late 1880s that banned the band from playing outdoors on Sundays. The Lord's day, city officials believed, was not one for such noise. Salvationists thought otherwise.

"Feeling that the open air was a vital part of their ministry, the officers and soldiers defied the law," reports a history of the Grand Rapids Centennial Temple Corps, the army's first local church.

Both male and female Salvation Army members were taken to jail, but the women were not put behind bars until they insisted that they, too, were part of the supposedly disruptive music ministry. The offensive musicians were soon brought to trial and, with Lowe as one of their prime supporters, cleared. The law was changed and they were allowed to march and sing and bang their tambourines on street corners even on Sunday.

In the early 1920s, Grand Rapids became the Divisional Headquarters and hub of Army services for much of southwestern Michigan and northern Indiana.

Throughout its history in West Michigan, the Army has been deeply involved in social service efforts. It has housed the homeless, helped alcoholics and drug abusers rid themselves of their addictions, clothed the downtrodden, served food to the hungry, taught the poor how to find jobs, and run a summer camp for the disadvantaged. Every Christmas, the Army holds its annual Tree of Lights fund-raiser, in which soldiers and volunteers ring bells and accept donations in the famous Army kettles.

A few principles have guided the Army and remain in force: military discipline for the long-time struggle against sin; equality of women; strong focus on family and marriage; a fundamental reading of the Bible; the importance of conversion; and abstinence from alcohol, mind- or mood-altering drugs.

Although James Lowe never converted to the Army, from his leading position at First Methodist Church he gave it long-lasting, crucial support. He, too, saw it as a necessary mix of faith and good works. Its ministry to body and soul was why he brought it to Grand Rapids and why he stood behind it.

When Lowe died, the Salvation Army went to his home, recited prayers and sang a few of his favorite hymns. The community to this day, many feel, owes the manufacturer a debt for bringing the uniformed Salvation Army forces to town.

FIGURE 11
The Rev. Malcolm Cronk

President Roosevelt," it was "Satanically inspired by a group of Christ-hating Jews." [11]

When reproved by prominent local Protestants and Jews, De Haan tried to explain himself. He had no quarrel with "orthodox Jews," who were "peace-loving, good citizens;" in fact, when these returned to Palestine, as they should, they would become the world's greatest nation. But for "atheistic, communistic, renegade, apostate Jews" De Haan had "nothing but condemnation" and promised to "exhaust my vocabulary" in denouncing them. He repeated his charges on the eve of the 1936 Presidential election when he advised the Republican candidate, Alfred Landon, to guarantee a landslide victory by promising to "drive out, wipe out every vestige of Communism." [12]

The thousands who turned out to hear him in person and the thousands more who tuned in his radio show proved that De Haan had struck a nerve. His addresses breathed the spirit of small-town, small-scale America, of the simple life and plain virtues. He castigated sophistication, luxury, elite educators, big government, big labor, and big business.[13] Yet Landon's landslide loss in

1936 demonstrated that De Haan's model society was gone forever. Hence his fascination with biblical prophecies. The evil turn in the world was all part of God's plan; the Bible was still true, the more clearly accurate the longer events unfolded. The arrogant rulers of the world from the capitols to the laboratories would soon be taken down, and God's plain and righteous ones restored to their rightful place.

But first De Haan ran into trouble closer to home. On April 5, 1938, the Calvary Church board fired Floyd D. Leary, whom De Haan had put in charge of the church's music and youth programs two years before. The board made its move (in fact, had recently been elected) while De Haan was in the South recuperating from heart problems and promoting his radio ministry. In his sermon on Sunday, May 15, De Haan denounced the board's action and called a special congregational meeting to reinstate Leary, to elect a new board, and to amend the church charter to reduce the dissenters' power. These proposals were duly ratified by a 233–143 vote, but the minority protested the moves as unconstitutional and won a court restraining order to protect their financial interests in the church. The next Sunday, May 22, De Haan gave another resignation sermon and walked out.[14] Most of the congregation followed him, reducing Calvary's membership from 2,000 to 200. De

FIGURE 12
The Rev. Louis Lehman

FIGURE 13
The Rev. George Gardiner

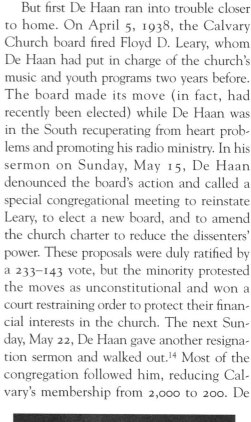

Haan was invited to head yet another "Calvary," this time Calvary Gospel Center, but he had tired of such affairs and opted for full-time radio preaching. He spent the rest of his days (until December 1965) running the nationally broadcast Radio Bible Class from his Grand Rapids headquarters. Things at Calvary Undenominational worsened as its replacement pastor, a flamboyant ex-convict named Thomas Carter, had to be sacked after one year for dallying with his secretary. Calvary Gospel Center in turn suffered its own split as many of its members exited to found Trinity Baptist Church.[15]

The entire sequence demonstrated the perils of charismatic leadership. De Haan excelled at relating to large, anonymous audiences but did poorly one-to-one and especially with authority structures. When he removed himself from church leadership, his followers, cut loose from creed and custom, could drift and divide again. It took more subdued ministers to restore stability at Calvary Undenominational. Malcolm Cronk, the 26-year old pastor of a tiny Wesleyan Methodist church on Grand Rapids' West Side, was brought on in 1940 for an eight-year stint that saw the church co-sponsor a new radio ministry, the Children's Bible Hour, with Wealthy Street Baptist Church. Calvary did not go along with Wealthy's new Bible Institute but began its own, the Grand Rapids School of the Bible and Music. William E. Sampson succeeded

FIGURE 14
The Rev. Edward Dobson

Cronk and brought back many of the people who had left with De Haan. In 1952 Louis Paul Lehman, one-time "boy preacher" from Chicago, began a 12-year pastorate notable for a $390,000 refurbishing of the church's physical plant. And in George E. Gardiner's term from 1970–1983, Calvary took part in the nationwide evangelical resurgence, adding hundreds to its membership and making plans to move to its current complex at East Beltline Avenue and Int. 96.[16]

Through all these changes, however, Calvary's mode and message remained the same. It taught an inerrant Scripture, heard evangelistic preaching, and sang emotionally

FIGURE 15
The Calvary complex as it looked under construction at Int. 96 and East Beltline Avenue in 1985.

"Not Souvlaki Heaven"

Since 1972, the smell of grilled lamb has floated through the air early every June, beckoning visitors to Grand Rapids' downtown Festival to Holy Trinity Greek Orthodox Church's food booth.

Long lines of Festival-goers hungry for the popular sandwiches dwarf the queues at other food booths throughout the weekend arts and food celebration.

The Greeks who founded Holy Trinity are happy their food has brought them attention. But they want people to know there's more meat to their history.

"The name of our church is not Souvlaki Heaven," said Paul Chardoul, a Grand Rapids historian and a Holy Trinity member. "There is an awful lot more to us than that."

Teaching youngsters Greek, supporting missionaries in Africa, bringing in people from abroad for heart surgery, and hosting services with all Orthodox churches in Grand Rapids are the real activities that define this congregation.

"As we've grown and become more integrated, I think our positive influence has spread," said the Rev. James Bogdan, pastor of the church at 330 Lakeside Drive NE. "We have maintained our Orthodox traditions at the same time we've become part of the larger world."

Like other immigrants, Greeks came to West Michigan for various reasons.

The first wave arrived in Grand Rapids in the early 1900s. Some came here because of crop failures, others to escape persecution, and still others to work for a huge boot-blacking operation.

"The Greeks as a group have tended to be hard working and successful. They have one of the highest per capita educational attainments of any ethnic group," Chardoul said.

The Greeks have maintained ties to their past. An important part of this link is the church.

The first church meetings were held at St. Mark's Episcopal Church. The first services, with their floating strands of incense and embroidered clerical robes, took place on the second floor of Woodman Hall on Bostwick Avenue NE. Mostly, though, the early Greeks attended services officiated by local Syrian and Russian Orthodox clergy.

According to "Grand Rapids' Greek Heritage," the city's 26 Greek families by 1925 considered themselves permanent enough to elect a symvoulion, or church council. They were ready to build a house of worship for themselves.

Not only Greeks but Turks, Romanians, Egyptians, Ethiopians, Armenians and Finns have made the Orthodox or "true" church their home over the years.

In the beginning, the church was a rallying point for Greeks who had recently arrived in the new world, Bogdan added.

"The church became a presence in the Grand Rapids area of Orthodox culture as well as ecclesiology (church life)," Bogdan said. "Out of this church has grown a very vibrant Pan-Orthodox community."

According to historian Chardoul, it took two years after the start of their church community for the Greeks to remodel and build an altar for the first Greek Orthodox church in a house at 1000 Cherry St. SE.

"In 1928, the church received its charter from the state of

FIGURE 16
A service at Holy Trinity Greek Orthodox Church in April 1970.

Michigan as an ecclesiastical corporation," he states in his 28-page booklet, compiled in 1986 to commemorate the 60th anniversary of the city's Greek Orthodox community.

Church school, regular services and community events were held in the structure, the first of three to house the church. By 1993, the church had a traditional Byzantine setting, which included a colorful, expansive dome, and hand-painted religious icons.

Homes for the church have included the Cherry Street structure, the former Temple Emanuel on Ransom Avenue and the current, dome-topped edifice set among trees in a residential area on Lakeside NE.

Although it has long been a gathering point for area Greeks, the church was never the sole focal point of Hellenic life, Chardoul said. From the start, the Greeks tried to amalgamate themselves into the larger society. They kept ties to their history even while learning a new language and customs. Nonetheless, Greeks faced discrimination and many difficulties in an attempt to make sense out of and become

FIGURE 17
Holy Trinity parishioners prepare food for World Community Day in 1981.

an accepted part of this new place, he said.

The struggle always has been between preserving Greek heritage while at the same time working to become part of the bigger picture of community life.

"The church has always been a unifying factor," Pastor Bogdan said.

charged music adapted from popular-cultural styles. Above all it emphasized soul-saving: for those present, for their children, for the "unsaved" around the world, whom it tried to reach with an enormous missionary enterprise. Calvary's missions budget skidded during the Depression to less than $4,000; but it rebounded to $35,000 by 1949, to $50,000 by the mid-1950s, $88,000 by the mid-1960s, $132,000 by the mid-1970s, and $900,000 by the early 1990s.[17]

The enormous leap in the last figure reflects Calvary's recent rise to "megachurch" status. Its new sanctuary, dedicated in 1986, can seat 2,200 people and hosts 4,000 for Sunday morning worship. Its 1,800 members raised $8.5 million to finish the complex debt-free and are now planning a $4.2 million addition, also to be paid for in cash. Such figures indicate an affluence quite beyond that of De Haan's flock and

must dilute some of the urgency of looking for Jesus' immediate return. But the economic chaos of the 1930s has since given over to moral and familial breaks, so Calvary today can claim to be carrying on a tradition by working specially with AIDS patients, the divorced, and those suffering from drug- or parental-abuse. The church's "Saturday Night" program, which entertains hard questions from the unchurched in a hard-rock entertainment milieu, is typical of Calvary by being untypical. The current pastor, the Rev. Edward Dobson, bears more than an echo of De Haan's political interests in that he came to Calvary from the side of the Rev. Jerry Falwell, captain of the 1980s Moral Majority crusade. Dobson now foreswears explicit political pronouncements, however, in favor of helping suffering people directly through voluntary efforts.[18]

Whether that suffices for the future

FIGURE 18
The star badge worn in
Germany by a Temple
Emanuel member during
the Nazi era.

FIGURE 19
Julius Houseman

remains to be seen, "should [as De Haan would put it] Jesus tarry." By its size Calvary should be a major player in community life. And it designates itself "the church at the crossroads." [19] But its crossroads, appropriately, lie at the edge of Grand Rapids. Calvary always has been poised halfway between this city and the New Jerusalem to come.

LIGHT TO GENTILES

The storm M.R. De Haan prophesied for the United States in fact fell on Europe, especially on its Jews. World War II claimed some 40 million lives there, including 6 million Jews exterminated at Nazi concentration camps. The Holocaust shook Jews everywhere, even in places where they lived securely. After all, the Germany that gave rise to Nazism had earlier been counted among the most advanced nations in the world, and its Jewish citizens had gladly sought to bear its name, render it service, and adapt their customs to its ways. If such people had been taken to the death camps, where could any Jew be safe?

In Grand Rapids, the members of Temple Emanuel,[20] the city's oldest Jewish congregation, felt the blow particularly. Their founders had come from Germany and had followed the course of assimilation pioneered by German Jewry. They themselves had rendered their city distinguished service. Were they now, too, in jeopardy? What was, or should be, their identity: American? Jewish? Both? Neither? Temple Emanuel decided for "both," but with a difference. In the face of the Holocaust, they fashioned a bolder Judaism, recovering old traditions and reaching out to their suffering kin around the world as they had for so long to needy neighbors in Grand Rapids.

Temple Emanuel traces its origins to the same year as the city's Christian Reformed and German Christian bodies. In 1857 a wandering French Jewish trader died passing through the area. The handful of Jews in town, headed by businessman Julius Houseman, organized a Hebrew Benevolent and Burial Society which bought a half acre of Oakhill Cemetery for such necessities. The group also commenced weekly educational and worship meetings which rotated from home to home.[21] After a hiatus during the Civil War, a larger body gathered and formally incorporated on Oct. 2, 1871, as Temple Emanuel, the second-oldest continuing Jewish congregation in Michigan. They rented a hall at Monroe Avenue and Erie Street NW (present-day Grand Center), counting assets of an ark, a reading desk, the cemetery, and $5,800 in cash. Their membership comprised 12 families and more than 20 single men, all of German descent and mostly involved in business. The

FIGURE 20
Rabbi Emanuel Gerechter

women followed the American pattern by forming a charitable society the same year. The men matched them in 1875 with a chapter of the B'nai B'rith fraternal order.[22] With the help of both and the successful rabbinate of Emanuel Gerechter (1874–1880), the congregation could dedicate its own building, a $15,000 Victorian Gothic structure at Fountain Street and Ransom Avenue NE, on Sept. 15, 1882. In thanking the city's Christians for their gifts toward the venture, Temple president Sidney A. Hart voiced confidence for its future in the city: "… the benign parts of man's nature seem here at least to prevail … neighborly good will [shall guarantee] that bigoted and superstitious people cannot be any detriment to the progress of religious belief." [23]

Certainly Temple Emanuel itself held to no superstitions. From its founding it practiced Reform Judaism, which radically overhauled the faith to make it fit the standards of science and middle-class taste.[24] Kosher diet was optional in this system as was Hebrew in worship. Distinctive garb was absent from the start. Hopes for a literal Messiah and for regathering in geographical Israel were spiritualized into ethical ideals, which ideals tended to overshadow creed and cult. From the start Temple Emanuel did not require head coverings for men at worship. Over time this breach with custom widened and deepened until by World War I the congregation was worshipping in English on Sunday morning, sitting in family (not sex-segregated) pews, looking for all the world like Fountain Street Baptist Church two blocks away, references to Jesus excepted.[25]

Reform Judaism, like liberal Protestantism, was an attempt to save faith by modernizing it. Actual developments proved more complicated. Between 1880 and 1886, Temple Emanuel went through four rabbis. These found the congregation stingy; the congregation found them pompous and insulting. The next decade saw membership and contributions slump badly, bringing the congregation to the verge of eclipse in the depression year of 1895. "Almost singlehandedly," according to the congregation's historian, "Joseph Houseman [Julius' cousin] saved the day" with cash and leadership. Part of the problem, visiting rabbis noted, was "poor esprit de corps" resulting from the experience of "too much cold reform and not enough of the beauty and warmth which characterizes Judaism." [26] Another cause was lack of reinforcements. Jewish immigrants to Grand Rapids after 1880 hailed from eastern Europe, accurately perceived the Germans to be snobbish, and disliked the Reform program. In 1892, 15 of these

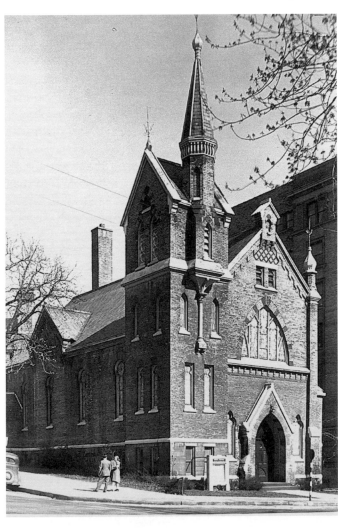

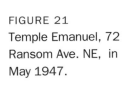

FIGURE 21
Temple Emanuel, 72 Ransom Ave. NE, in May 1947.

families founded the Orthodox congregation Beth Israel near their residential center on the near Northwest Side along the river. This group grew so fast, and quarreled among themselves so vigorously, that by the early 1920s they were supporting two synagogues (Ahavas Achim being more Orthodox still), each with more than 100 families and its own Hebrew day-school.[27]

At the same date Temple Emanuel again faced dissolution. The Reform program had proceeded to the point where many members were worshipping with local Unitarians. The Unitarians needed a building, Temple Emanuel needed funds. It was only natural to consider merging. At this, one of the most dramatic moments in Temple history, Emanuel's "Samuel Braudy arose and broke up the meeting with the stirring words: 'The Lion of Judea is great enough for all of us. We invite all of you to become Jews!'"[28] With that, the merger was thwarted and Temple Emanuel saved, but it still needed to find its mission. Theologically, Reform Judaism did resemble Unitarianism with Christian vestiges removed, and that would not do. Ethnically, the Jewishness of Ahavas Achim and Beth Israel was too embarrassing to Emanuel to be a live option. Politically, it was the former who sponsored Zionism (to restore world Jewry to the biblical homeland), which one Temple Emanuel rabbi pronounced to be both impossible and — so far as American Jews were concerned — undesirable.[29] In effect, Temple Emanuel filled a social niche in the city for two groups: affluent Jews who fit in — so they hoped — on the local scene, and some Orthodox offspring whom upward mobility made hungry for respectability and modern thought. The melding between the two could go roughly, as in 1928 when eastern European women won election to the Temple Sisterhood board. That prompted the elite German president of the Sisterhood to resign in disgust.[30]

The congregation navigated these shoals under the direction of Philip Waterman, whose 1921–1936 rabbinate was its longest to date. Waterman took Reform's rational-ethical principles to their peak, publishing the critical *Story of Superstition* (1929) with the prestigious New York firm Alfred A. Knopf. He saw his congregants through the 1920s' passing of their old leadership corps. He chided them in a most cerebral vocabulary for their niggardly charity. By 1936 he had had enough and retired from the rabbinate. The financial assaults of the Depression contributed to his decision, for they brought the congregation to a painful moment. The city's Jewish community had always taken care of its own needy and others besides, but in the hardest times of the 1930s some Jewish cases, too, had to go on public relief.[31] This embarrassment, coupled with the rise of Hitler abroad, primed Temple Emanuel for a new direction.

It came during the 1937–1947 rabbinate of Jerome D. Folkman. Along with Reform Jews across the

country at the time, Temple Emanuel "felt a spontaneous surge toward … the warmth of traditional ceremonies." Folkman restored services to Friday night, reopened the ark for rites of adoration, and reinstated the lighting of Sabbath candles. He lay particular stress on Judaism's foundation in family observances and made the temple a center both for social occasions and for a network of smaller fellowships: a Boy Scout troop with Mothers' Auxiliary, a Newcomers Club, the Judean Service Guild, a Men's Club, an adult education program, and a rigorous confirmation class for the youth. The program worked wonderfully: Temple membership soared in Folkman's first year from 63 to 150 families.[32] In all domains, from ritual to nurture, from friendship to philosophy, Temple Emanuel learned not only to make the best of a bad situation but to appreciate the warmth and riches of their tradition. If Jews the world labeled them, positively Jewish they would be.

The crises of the 1930s also pushed the other synagogues in town to mend their breach. In 1937 Ahavas Achim and Beth Israel merged into Ahavas Israel, a Conservative (midway between Orthodox and Reform) congregation. And as war descended, Temple Emanuel quietly sponsored the relocation to West Michigan of some 20 Jewish refugee families. Resurgent and recommitted, then, Grand Rapids' Jews could face the shock of the Holocaust as its enormity and full implications unfolded over time. The Temple Emanuel *Bulletin* for Rosh Hashanah (Jewish New Year) 1950 captured the mood well:

"We might as well accept the realities of our contemporary situation. Our world will continue to reel from crisis to crisis; we will be subject to strains and tensions almost beyond human endurance. Our days and nights will be filled with the horror of another worldwide catastrophe … There are no easy solutions or panaceas or magic wands with which to beat off the creeping shadows of disaster. But one thing remains to be done: to present the truth and help people become used to living with it.

Away with illusions! Let us first accept the facts of our anguished pattern of existence in this hour of crisis. There are no other alternatives." [33]

Grand Rapids' Jews responded in the spirit of reconstruction, at home and abroad. New sanctuaries at home were needed to accommodate the membership boom. Temple Emanuel's board first proposed revamping its existing structure, but a 1945–1946 fund drive netting $217,000 made a new building feasible. The congregation doubled their pledges, hired renowned architect Eric Mendelsohn for the job, and dedicated the finished structure, at Fulton Street and Holmdene Avenue NE, in May 1954. The previous year Ahavas Israel completed its move from the West Side to a Heritage Hill mansion (at 44 Lafayette Ave. NE) which they remodeled into a synagogue.[34]

Building abroad involved enormous donations to the new state of Israel. In an emergency campaign of September 1946, Grand Rapids Jews gave $134,000 toward the $100 million American Jewry raised for the survivors

FIGURE 24
Rabbi Jerome D. Folkman was at Temple Emanuel from 1937 to 1947.

FIGURE 25
Renowned architect Eric Mendelsohn designed Temple Emanuel's building at Fulton Street and Holmdene Avenue NE.

FIGURE 26
Ahavas Israel synagogue at
44 Lafayette Ave. NE.

FIGURE 27
Temple Emanuel
moved into its current
building at 1715 E.
Fulton St . in 1954.

ously because of its stable leadership and thriving laity. The congregation has had only five rabbis since 1921. A 1944 community study found its people to be well anchored: 73 percent of Grand Rapids' Jews had lived here more than 10 years, and 59 percent more than 20. They were also well off: 46 percent had graduated from high school and 29 percent from college (both well above city norms), while 50 percent qualified as having "high" or "very high" economic status.[36] In addition, Temple Emanuel's aid to Israel was but the latest expression of a perennial theme. The congregation had begun as a benevolent society, and its charities always had reached beyond Jewish circles. "In one year," according to the congregation's historian, "these 'other-than-Jewish' efforts numbered 17." Typically, Jerome Folkman was a founder and first president of the Kent County Council of Social Agencies; his successor, Rabbi Harry Essrig, was president of the Grand Rapids Child Guidance Clinic; and the current pastor, Rabbi Albert Lewis, helped found Grand Rapids' Hospice chapter.[37]

of the Holocaust. Funds for Israel became the staple of the annual United Jewish Appeal thereafter. Temple Emanuel contributed substantially to the $77,000 Grand Rapids raised in 1960, to the $385,000 raised in 1980, and to the $300,000 and $500,000 raised in Israel's war years of 1967 and 1973.[35] The promotional literature for these campaigns was replete with images of construction and security — putting down roots and putting up homes for a people that had wandered too long.

Temple Emanuel could respond so generously because of its stable leader-

In this light, Julius Houseman Amberg (1890–1951) epitomized Temple Emanuel's

history. The grandson of Julius Houseman and of his wife, Jennie Ringuette, herself the daughter of Louis Campau's business partner, Amberg exemplified Grand Rapids Jewry's deep roots and continuity. As valedictorian at Central High (1908), at Colgate University (1912), and at Harvard Law School (1915), Amberg displayed an early brilliance well-realized in his professional career. He served in the office of the Secretary of War in World War I and World War II, the latter on the same team as fellow Grand Rapids descendant McGeorge Bundy). Amberg established a distinguished law practice in town which he supplemented with community service. He chaired the Kent County Relief Committee in the middle of the Depression, served on the board at Butterworth Hospital for 20 years, headed six annual Community Chest (United Fund) drives, and chaired committees which investigated and reformed city government practices in the early 1930s and late 1940s.[38]

Amberg's legacy still shines, literally, at Temple Emanuel. In his European travels for the War Department in 1945, Julius Amberg visited Zeckendorf, the Bavarian hometown of his grandfather, Julius Houseman. He found the old synagogue in ruins but managed to salvage its ner tamid, the eternal light that burns in every Jewish house of worship. Today this lamp hangs in Temple Emanuel's sanctuary in front of the doors of the ark containing the Torah scrolls. By its light one can see the decorations on the sanctuary's front wall. On one side of the ark twine the grapevine and honeycomb of celebration; on the other, the sheaves of wheat recalling labor and sorrow. According to Judaism, these two together mark the entrance to the full life. Across the wall recur the three crowns of the faith: religion, education, and government. Temple Emanuel's dedication to all three has earned it the fourth diadem, painted above the doors to the ark: the crown of "a good name." [39]

FIGURE 28
Temple Emanuel's ner tamid (eternal light).

FASTING AND FEASTING

In the uproar following World War I, both Temple Emanuel and Calvary Undenominational Church purged themselves of traditional rituals and customs. At the same time another cluster of churches was forming in town dedicated to preserving an ancient liturgy as the essence of true religion. These are Grand Rapids' Orthodox churches: St. George Antiochian (Syrian), founded in 1910; St. John Chrysostom (Russian), founded 1916; St. Nicholas Antiochian (Syrian), founded 1924; and Holy Trinity (Greek), founded 1925. Orthodox Christianity descends from apostolic days but became distinguished as Eastern Ortho-

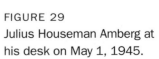

FIGURE 29
Julius Houseman Amberg at his desk on May 1, 1945.

doxy in the year 1054 out of a dispute with Rome, which retained the loyalty of western Catholics. United by creed and ritual, Orthodox churches are differentiated by nationality and by their allegiance to different patriarchs, or head bishops. In Europe and the Middle East these differences might not collide because of believers' fixed locations, but immigration to polyglot America required new, sometimes uneasy, arrangements.

The Orthodox began arriving in Grand Rapids around 1900. Their first public notice came with the purchase of a home at 200 Williams St. SW, where they celebrated Christmas (by the traditional Julian calendar) on Jan. 7, 1909. Their 75 members, largely Syrian (which included Lebanese) and Greek, grew to 700 by 1912 and were served by the Rev. Phillipous Abou-Assaley. In fact, his parish included all of Michigan plus the northern tier of Ohio and Indiana. The hardships of his job were matched by those of his parishioners. As recent immigrants they could choose between peddling, hard manual labor, or running tiny restaurants, clothing repair shops, or grocery stores. The Syrians were crammed into dilapidated shacks along Market Avenue SW and the Greeks found many neighborhoods closed to

them by prejudice. Under such pressures, tempers could flare as on a January Sunday in 1909 when rival Syrian factions fought during worship, prompting Father Abou-Assaley to threaten resignation.[40]

A greater strain emerged in 1915 when the Syrian bishop of North America died, leaving his succession in dispute. St. George divided into Russian and Antiochian factions, nor did the issue die when 20 Russian families on the West Side formed their own congregation, St. John Chrysostom. The case eventually went to the courts which decided for the Antiochian party in 1923. Within a year, Father Abou-Assaley and a large bloc of the congregation were worshiping as St. Nicholas Church in a building purchased from the Seventh-Day Adventists at 328 Cass Ave. SE. Meanwhile, Grand Rapids' Greeks had been meeting in St. Mark's Episcopal parish house. In 1925 they organized their own congregation and in 1927 purchased and remodeled a house at 1000 Cherry St. SE as Holy Trinity Church. Completing these changes, in 1925 the remaining parishioners of St. George built the sanctuary at LaGrave Avenue and Goodrich Street SE where their descendants still worship.[41]

These differences did not break the bonds of faith and paled beside the animosities that buffeted the Orthodox in their homelands. In 1922, for example, one million Greeks were expelled from Asia Minor by the Turkish government — that on top of a collapse in the Greek economy the decades previous. By 1915, an estimated 25 percent of all Greek males aged 15 to 45 had gone to the United States.[42] To the north, the revolutionary Soviet government made life difficult for the Russian Orthodox. To the south and east, Syrian and Lebanese Christians escaped from Turkish domination only to fall under French. Orthodox immigrants to America, then, had often lost their homelands in more ways than

FIGURE 30
A sketch of the current exterior of St. John Chrysostom Russian Orthodox Church.

FIGURE 31
St. George Antiochian Orthodox Church on LaGrave Avenue and Goodrich Street SE.

FIGURE 32
The consecration of St. John Chrysostom on Nov. 28, 1916. From left to right: Father Anthony Diachenko, Father V. Oranosky from Detroit, and Father Kedrousky from Gary, Ind.

usual and so relied on religion for identity in the new country.

Perhaps the parishioners at St. John Chrysostom felt the severance most keenly. They consecrated their church, purchased from the Norwegian Lutherans, at National Avenue and Veto Street NW on Thanksgiving Day 1916 — that is, on the eve of the Russian revolution. Thereafter, Orthodoxy was ideologically suspect in the old country, and anything Russian was politically suspect in the new. That, combined with their small number and their working-class status, made their faith a difficult venture. The congregation's membership rose to 50 families in the 1920s but has slowly diminished since. Members lived several blocks either side of West Fulton Street, within walking distance of the church and of the men's jobs in the tanneries, furniture factories, and construction trades of the West Side. The women took in boarders and, after the children were grown, worked as cooks and cleaning ladies downtown.[43]

Such humble skills served the church well. The men themselves remodeled the building on the Orthodox pattern and, over two years of weekend work, converted its Michigan basement into a social hall and classrooms. In 1942 they added the present Russian-style cupola and belfry with funds raised by selling scrap metal for the war effort. Andrei Boydovsky, a woodworker at

Stickley Furniture Co., carved the frame for the church's icon of the enthroned Jesus and built the catafalque that is placed in the sanctuary during Holy Week. St. John's women helped finance its operations by conducting dinners, dances, wedding parties, and church theatricals at the Jackson Street Hall.[44]

The lay people's contributions to St. John's stand out especially in light of the emphasis Orthodox governance puts on priests and patriarchs. These pass on and certify the apostles' authority to the present day and so are accorded great respect. Over the years a few pastors in particular have won St. John's affections. Father Anthony Diachenko, foster son of Archbishop Platon,

FIGURE 33
The cast of a church play at Jackson Street Hall on the West Side in the 1920s.

Metropolitan (head) of all the Russian Orthodox in North America, married a daughter of the congregation, Vera Lensky, and served as its first resident pastor (1916–1917). Father John Tertichny's term (1919–1928) marked the church's greatest prosperity, while Father Nicholas Bellavin (1928–1938) saw it through the Depression. Many other times, however, St. John's has depended on temporary pastors or on visiting priests from Battle Creek and Lansing. That put the burden of leadership on the laity. In fact, the local chapter of the Russian Orthodox mutual aid society got the church formed in the first place, and while pastors came and went, the same names appeared on the parish board decade after decade: Bolbat, Chernoby, Lomashevich, Mikita, Niewadomski, Novosad, Olesczcuk, Palagin, Peshkun, Pirok, Radik, Slivick. Against all odds they carried on.[45]

Their loyalty doubtless was cemented by the rich liturgy of their tradition. Although the 2½-hour service of the old days has shrunk to 1½, although Old Slavonic has made way for English, although chairs are now provided for the elderly who can no longer stand and kneel on hardwood floors, the essence of the Russian Orthodox service

remains the same. A warm, intimate setting promotes at once spiritual meditation and close community.[46] Incense and candles, unaccompanied singing and chant, and the icons at the altar fill every sense, surround the whole assembly, with palpable awe. The fusion of sensory and spiritual in the ritual reinforces Orthodox theology. All of creation comes from and is in Christ, and all of Christ is in creation; all of Christ is in the faithful, and all of the faithful in Christ; all of creation opens for the faithful, and all the faithful must open for others. Orthodoxy aims at the transfiguration of earthly into heavenly — better, into heavenly earthliness. The weekly service gives a foretaste of the ultimate transfiguration to come.

This message gains special force on Orthodox holy days. St. John's still observes these by the Julian calendar, anywhere between two weeks (at Christmas) and six weeks (at some Easters) later than do other Christians. The celebrations come thick with ancestral customs. Both are preceded by fasting, which gives the feasting to come all the more relish. St. John's Christmas observances in the World War II era began, as one parishioner remembers them, with the congregation setting out for caroling at the sight of the first star on Christmas Eve, no matter what the temperature outside. Then would follow a meal of kutija (a mixed dish of grains, honey, nuts, and raisins), the decoration of the tree (kept behind closed doors), and a full service. At midnight the doors would be opened for the children to see the lighted tree and for all to exchange blessings.[47]

The fasting-feasting cycle is more intense for Easter, the holiest season of the Orthodox year. The 40 days of Lent lead into Passion Week, which is marked by daily church services, cleaning the home, and preparing special foods, particularly eggs dyed red with onion skins to recall Jesus' suffering. Good Friday is solemnized by day-long church ceremonies in which the special catafalque is decorated with flowers for Christ's burial. On Holy Saturday the members prepare special foods for an Easter basket to be taken to church and for Easter breakfast at home. The menu — kielbasa, ham, eggs, farmer's cheese, kulich

FIGURE 36
St. John Chrysostom
sanctuary in 1993.

(sweet bread), and paska (cheesecake) — comes from all the categories forbidden during Lent. Late Saturday night, the members gather at church, standing in the darkness until midnight. Then the pastor lights a candle behind the icon screen. To chanting and clouds of incense, the flame is passed from one member's candle to another until the whole sanctuary is full of light. The congregation then moves outdoors to circle the building three times while the bell tolls the news of Christ's resurrection. A three- to four-hour service follows in which the parishioners again and again repeat the refrain, "Christ is risen, he is risen indeed." After the service, the congregation mingles to exchange blessings and to forgive past grievances. The pastor blesses the baskets and everyone repairs to the ample breakfast which, indeed, breaks the fast, bringing home to body and soul the good news of life, health, and joy.[48]

Light at midnight beaming the promise of new life: St. John Chrysostom's Easter rite

capsulized religion's message for the era of Depression and war. Calvary Undenominational Church, too, set itself as a "Lighthouse," and Temple Emanuel salvaged an eternal light from the destruction of European Jewry. All of Grand Rapids' congregations sought, with these three, to harbor the light of life in a darkening world.

FIGURE 37
A portion of St. John
Chrysostom's congregation
in 1925. Center,
Archbishop Platon; right,
Father John Tertichny.

The Soul of the City and Suburbs

8

1950 – 1970

VICTORY IN WORLD WAR II LEFT THE UNITED STATES triumphant abroad and unsettled at home. To fight the war, millions of Americans had left home for battle stations around the globe or for distant defense plants on the home front.

While the battles ended, the social flux went on. Returning veterans sought a home where life could be normal again, rooted and peaceful. Courtesy of the GI Bill, this translated into the 1950s' famous suburban housing boom. Mobile war workers sought some permanence, too, a chance to call their new place home and to get a share of postwar prosperity. The most dramatic case involved African Americans. Thousands had come north for war work in the 1940s; they were followed by millions more over the next two decades. In one generation the African-American majority changed from rural and Southern to urban and Northern.

"Black core and white fringe" told the story of cities like Grand Rapids in the quarter century after World War II. Grand Rapids numbered 176,515 inhabitants in 1950, up 7.5 percent from 1940; yet its Afro-American population had increased at 20 times that rate, from 2,660 to 6,813, from 1.6 to 3.6 percent of the city's total. In the 1950s, as the city's population increased but 800, its number of African-American residents expanded by nearly 8,000 (to 14,260) to compose 8 percent of the

city's residents. By 1970 Grand Rapids numbered 197,649, but 39,000 of those were gained by territorial annexation. The old boundaries of 1960 held 158,694 of whom 22,296 — or 14 percent — were black. Even an extended Grand Rapids, meanwhile, fell behind the pace of suburban growth. In

157

1940 the city's population was 67 percent of Kent County's. That share fell to 61 percent by 1950, to 49 percent in 1960, and to 41 percent in 1980.[1]

On this altered landscape, churches functioned much as they had in the era of immigration decades before. They gave the unsettled and resettled some stability and direction, a center from which to negotiate the promise and strains of postwar opportunities. Grand Rapids saw its share of America's phenomenal church-building boom in the 1950s as new edifices went up in the suburbs and inner city alike. But the more interesting story might lie in the way long-established churches adapted to new circumstances.

Of particular interest are four such congregations, all of them today more than a century old. Messiah Missionary Baptist Church, in the heart of the city's black community, blended an old-time religion with social services on behalf of newcomers who had to struggle with unfamiliar surroundings and an all-too-familiar racism. Cascade Christian Church, at the other extreme, had to try to make a community out of a flood of white suburbanites. In the process it turned itself from a little country church into a metropolitan giant. Two Protestant churches on the West Side served their traditional ethnic clientele but along opposite paths. St. John's United Church of Christ brought its German parishioners into contact with some of the most cosmopolitan Protestants in the country, while Seventh Reformed Church took a more insular strategy in the conservative reaches of the Dutch community.

❧

DIGNITY, DISCIPLINE, AND HOPE

Of all the individuals to debut on the American scene in the 1950s, the one best remembered was a Southern black Baptist preacher, Martin Luther King, Jr. As the symbolic leader of the civil rights movement, King drew off the resources of the churches that had long been the center of his people's social and political as well as spiritual life. When he was gunned down in 1968, his mantle passed to other Baptist ministers, like Ralph Abernathy and Jesse Jackson. In sum, the African-American

cause took its vision, direction, organization, and leadership from the pulpit.

The pattern applied in the North as well as the South, during quieter times as well as turbulent crusades. A church like Grand Rapids' Messiah Missionary Baptist always has been a communal center, a spiritual refuge, and a spearhead of social witness, led by pastors whose voices have sounded well beyond the sanctuary on Sunday morning.

Just as Martin Luther King's career was launched by the actions of a woman, Rosa Parks, so Messiah was birthed by a mother in Israel, Catherine Carter.[2] Born in Canada, Carter came to Grand Rapids in the 1880s with her husband, Newton, who ran a barber shop on Baxter Street SE, on the edge of the most prestigious of the three Grand Rapids neighborhoods where blacks clustered at the time. The area was dominated by the Dutch immigrants of Eastern Avenue CRC and the Anglo natives at Wealthy Street Baptist, but thanks to Catherine Carter's zeal, the African Americans soon had a church of their own, the third religious pillar of the neighborhood.

Although she joined one of the two black churches in the city, St. Luke's African Methodist Episcopal (AME) Zion, Mrs. Carter longed for her own Baptist tradition and canvassed the neighborhood for potential recruits. By 1889 she was hosting a dozen such in her home, enough to have the Rev. Jacob Holt visit from Amesburg, Ontario, to formally organize them as a Baptist fellowship. The congregation moved through a succession of storefront halls and visiting pastors until the mid-1890s when the Rev. Robert Gillard arrived for a five-year pastorate. Under his leadership Messiah built — largely by its own hand — a 46-by-28-foot wooden frame structure on Henry Avenue near Logan Street SE, a site the congregation still occupies today.

The building project pointed up one of the church's long-term problems. Messiah undertook its own construction because of its members' exceedingly modest means; their leaders, not to mention the rank and file, held such jobs as janitor, coachman, and waiter. This accentuated a second problem, the potentially ruinous lure of the city's attractions and entertainments. Gillard, an ex-slave who had come north in 1865, knew that hard-pressed folk especially needed strict moral discipline to survive. Thus he publicly condemned the cakewalk, a black dance form that whites found especially intriguing, and forbade his parishioners from indulging in it. Its vulgarity besmirched their reputation, Gillard told The Grand Rapids *Press*, and its sensuality took their minds off the higher things needed to improve their lot.[3] It was left to one of Gillard's successors, the Rev. S. Henri Browne (Messiah's pastor 1908–1915), to give further account of their trials. The city's 1,000 blacks, he complained, were trapped

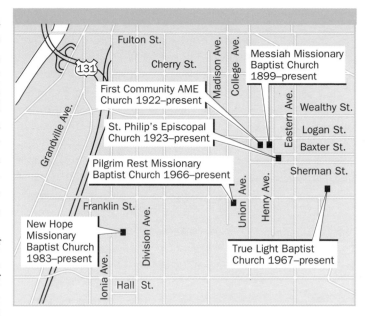

in menial jobs by white prejudice, undercutting incentives to pursue education or raise their status. Personal proof of his charges came within the month when Browne was denied service at a downtown shoe store. Larger-scale confirmation came in the form of street fights in 1912 between local blacks and Syrians over jobs and housing.[4]

Such difficulties did not slow a new flow of African Americans into the city during the open labor market of World War I. Anticipating hundreds from the South in the near future, St. Luke's Church in 1917 proposed to build a $9,000 social center; the (white) Grand Rapids Ministerial Association opposed the campaign in favor of supporting the war effort.[5] The city's black inhabitants in fact increased by 1,700 over the 1920s (from 1,070 to 2,795), triggering a building boom among their local congregations. In 1922 First Community AME Church moved from the near Southwest Side to the more auspicious southeast neighborhood, erecting a $55,000 building adjacent to Messiah's, at James Avenue and Logan. The next year, St. Philip's, begun in 1913 as the first "colored Episcopal" church in West Michigan, laid the cornerstone for its new building two blocks south at Henry and Sherman Street SE.[6]

FIGURE 3
The map shows the locations of several major African-American churches in Grand Rapids' inner city.

FIGURE 4
The first building of Messiah Missionary Baptist Church on Henry Avenue near Logan Street SE.

FIGURE 5
Alfonso Williams,
contractor and builder of
Messiah's second edifice
(Figure 6) in 1922.

Messiah kept up the Baptist side by starting a mission at Bartlett Street and Market Avenue SW in 1922, which evolved into True Light Baptist Church and in turn generated Pilgrim Rest and New Hope Missionary Baptist churches over the next 12 years. On its own site, in 1922 Messiah constructed a new 56-by-36-foot brick veneer building, seating 350 and featuring a pipe organ, pastor's study, and complete kitchen. The congregation raised half of the $20,000 cost out of its own pocket and promoted black contractors by awarding design and construction to Alfonso Williams, a Messiah member. The church's prosperity owed much to the vigorous leadership of the Rev. Wyatt M.J. Northcross who in the first five years of his tenure (1918–1929) raised the membership from 65 to 350, began Bible classes, and built Sunday school and youth-meeting attendance to equal that of morning worship.[7]

As it happened, Northcross left Messiah the year of the stock market crash. The ensuing Great Depression was disastrous for Northern blacks, who occupied the most vulnerable positions in the industrial economy. Grand Rapids' African-American population actually fell by 5 percent (to 2,660) over the 1930s while black unemployment soared well beyond white rates. At the same time this shrunken community was supporting, proportionately, more than twice as many churches as were Grand Rapids' whites.[8] Local black congregations — like the recently expanded Polish Catholic churches on the West Side — felt enormous financial strains. Messiah's debt totaled $12,000 and its resources were so meager that Northcross's two successors had to leave for more promising parishes. Aid from the government came in unequal measure: Grand Rapids' blacks received relatively more local relief funds than did whites but only low-paid federally funded jobs. Self-help did a little better. Five black churches, including Messiah, coordinated large "Tag Day" sales in 1933 and 1934 to alleviate some of their burden, but First AME Church's attempt in 1930 to build a Negro Social Center ran afoul of other black churches' suspicions and general fears of self-segregation.[9]

In these circumstances, powerful leadership was vital. For Messiah it arrived in 1933 in the Rev. Albert Keith, who would serve the church for 36 years. Keith came with a master's degree in philosophy from the University of Michigan (1923) and the benefit of connections he had forged there with other African-American professionals in town, such as attorneys Oliver Green and Floyd Skinner, dentist Cortez English, and physician Eugene Alston.[10] But he also knew the ropes of congregational organization. Keith first of all raised the congregation's religious involvement by starting up choirs and clubs for social, educational, and charitable activities. He also won Messiah a place in the 1940 Community Chest (United Way) drive that liquidated the debt on five black churches. The deacons then set out to raise another $4,500 for building repairs and redecoration. In these efforts Keith had the help of two key men, Alexander Tynes and Tackie G. Scott, who as skilled workers for the Pere Marquette Railroad represented the economic elite in the church but who distinguished themselves equally by their example of prayer, gentlemanly bearing, and community activism. Just as important were women leaders, "mothers" in the congregation such as Ade-

line Jefferson, Catherine Carter's daughter, and Sara Glover, a teacher in her native Virginia who came to Grand Rapids in 1922, began working at Blodgett hospital as a maid, and persisted against prejudice and disbelief to receive training and employment as a nurse.[11]

By the 1940s its own affairs were sufficiently in order to enable Messiah to participate in another, finally successful, attempt at black community organization. The Brough Community Association (BCA) was formed in 1943 by four pastors, including Keith as secretary-treasurer, to coordinate social services, promote citizenship and self-development, and provide wholesome recreation among the city's African Americans. The BCA dedicated its community house at 554 Henry SE that summer, with noticeable effects on delinquency rates in the neighborhood, and joined the national Urban League to conduct surveys of race relations in the city.[12] The study found Grand Rapids to be better than some Northern cities but in need of improvement. The influx of war workers had worsened housing segregation; black educational opportunities lagged behind whites'; and employment patterns were grossly skewed by racism. Of the city government's 1,333 employees in 1940, only 10 were African-American; of the board of education's 1,186, one (a janitor); of the city's 3,700 furniture workers, three; of Globe Knitting's 1,100, none; of Keeler Brass' 940, none; of 1,000 utility workers, three. The city's largest black employer was the Pantlind Hotel, whose 300 staff members included 62 blacks, mostly waiters and maids.[13]

To the great postwar migration then, Grand Rapids showed a double face: pervasive habits of discrimination and vibrant nodes of autonomy, like Messiah Baptist. The discrimination eased some when local auto plants and railroad yards began to hire blacks in production (not just service or custodial) positions. The churches thrived by providing familiarity and encouragement. Most of

Messiah's members in 1950 were less than one generation removed from the South, so newcomers could hear there the chords and cadences they had grown up with. Pastor Keith was something of a power in town — elected the first black president of the Grand Rapids Ministerial Association in 1948 and heading an NAACP drive for 1,000 local members in 1956. But he still combined the multiple roles of the Southern black pastor: moral monitor of the young, visitor to the sick, counselor to the needy, voice of the people, celebrant of the spiritual ritual that every Sunday affirmed hope and dignity in the face of a situation that improved only erratically.[14]

It was the erratic course of progress that most troubled local race relations. Employment opportunities improved, school segregation and housing discrimination worsened. The 1954–1965 civil rights movement

FIGURE 7
The Rev. Albert Keith pastored Messiah Missionary Baptist Church from 1933 to 1969.

FIGURE 8
Mrs. Sara Glover, exemplar of the notable female leadership at Messiah Missionary Baptist Church.

A Preacher Storms City Hall

The Rev. Lyman Parks came to Grand Rapids amid the turbulent 1960s when the community, like many other American cities, faced civil rights struggles.

When the man who would become the city's first black city commissioner and mayor took to the pulpit at First Community AME Church, the community itself was undergoing racial, social and cosmetic changes. Freeways were ripping through neighborhoods; old downtown buildings were being razed; suburban shopping malls were siphoning business from established stores in the heart of the city. But most of all, the life fabric of the community, especially of its growing minority sector, was in transition.

Parks came to Grand Rapids from a church in southeast Michigan. The African Methodist Episcopal pastor decided to assume the pulpit at 500 James Ave. SE not because of high pay, an interest in West Michigan beaches or other benefits. What drew him to this area, he once said, was the fact that the church in Grand Rapids wanted a minister "who was willing to become involved in the community."

Founded in 1874 and organized by Charles R. Pickney, First Community AME is part of a denomination whose first leader was Richard Allen, a former slave who purchased his freedom for $2,000. The group was initially part of the Methodist denomination but broke away and formed its own body in 1816. It was the first African-American denomination in the nation.

Long active in social matters, the denomination has often attracted preachers such as Parks who saw their job as going well beyond the pulpit.

A graduate of Payne Theological Seminary in Wilberforce, Ohio, Parks arrived in Grand Rapids in 1965. In short order, he adhered to the wishes of his flock by immersing himself in affairs outside church. He studied the ebb and flow of local politics and in 1968, the year after the city's dramatic race riot, he was elected the first black city commissioner.

Convinced that his Christian faith dictated that he push for equality and fairness in his adopted community, Parks quickly became a critic and activist whose voice was heard on a variety of matters. These ranged from demanding to know the criminal backgrounds of persons seeking approval for a liquor license to investigating complaints of racial tensions at the city's South High School to seeking solutions to complaints of police brutality.

Parks' probing, sometimes controversial, style won him backers and detractors. Some said he was best at pointing out problems, not at finding solutions.

"My job as I perceived it at that point was being a good PR person, keeping in touch with people, keeping all ethnic groups informed," he recalled.

Combative as he sometimes was, Parks was also

FIGURE 9
The Rev. Lyman Parks in November 1978 in First Community AME sanctuary.

respected enough that he was named mayor when Robert Boelens resigned in 1971. During the next election, Boelens and nine other candidates ran against Parks, who was re-elected.

As a youth, Parks loved to make speeches in the auditorium of his segregated high school in southern Indiana. He enjoyed letting words roll off his tongue as he walked his neighborhood and stood before the mirror at home.

His love for and interest in politics came from his father, a custodian for a time at the state capitol in Indianapolis. Madison Parks introduced his son to state representatives. He also brought Lyman to township board meetings in and around their small community of Lyles Station.

FIGURE 10

The Rev. Lyman Parks is sworn in for another term as mayor on Jan. 3, 1974.

Parks' father also placed great emphasis on education. In college, Parks leaned toward becoming a mortician — one of the few professions open to blacks at that time. A discussion with a professor, however, convinced him to try another occupation open to blacks — the ministry.

Throughout, the emphasis in Parks' family was on hard work and doing without handouts or welfare. In Grand Rapids, Parks became an espoused Republican, a party not popular with most African Americans.

"One of the things that was a driving force and motivation, at least when I came along, was that we were taught and brought along to believe you had to work for what you achieved," he once told an interviewer. "That barrier because of your color was not an excuse to throw up your hands and give up."

As mayor of Grand Rapids, Parks worked hard and pushed his causes. But the firebrand who first came to town grew lukewarm, some said, once his position as mayor solidified.

"It was hoped that stagnation would cease with the mayor's outright election, but thus far nothing seems to have changed," a 1974 Grand Rapids *Press* editorial bemoaned.

Even though his passion for change seemed to dim during his years as mayor, Parks helped obtain police and fire personnel positions for minorities. He also backed construction of low-income housing.

Amid charges and rumors that the preacher/mayor had accepted favors in exchange for his support on certain projects and causes in the city, Parks waged a heated campaign for re-election in 1975. He was defeated by Abe Drasin, a city commissioner.

Parks remained marginally active in civic and state affairs. Much of his energy following his leaving office was devoted to his church.

"He was one of the first political stars on our horizon," said Gene Proctor, a long-time Grand Rapids civil rights activist and head of the Baxter Community Center. "In that point in our growing process, we needed him."

Parks, now a pastor in Chicago, was able to "eradicate a lot of the mentality that suggests we have a limit to our learning capacity. He was an intellect; he was a role model for us," Proctor said.

Mixing religion and politics, heeding the call of AME founder Richard Allen before him, Parks worked to draw together the races in Grand Rapids. Talking to a rally at the Calder Plaza in 1974, Parks made it clear that what he did he did because of his faith. Christianity helped shape who he was and how he conducted his life.

"This is the way our city should go — following the Lord," he said. "This is the (Christian) witness to our city and community. This is what I wanted."

FIGURE 11
A fire rages at Hall Street
and Lafayette Avenue SE
on July 25, 1967, during
the riots in Grand Rapids.

improved the laws, but white attitudes seemed to harden. The social stresses of so large a migration and the inconsistent fulfillment of civil rights hopes combined to trigger the mid-1960s' series of riots across America's inner cities. Grand Rapids had its

trial on July 25–27, 1967, hard on the heels of Detroit's massive conflagration the weekend before. Rumors of discord here moved local black clergy to issue a call on July 24 for a month of white repentance and black calm, but the fuse of unrest was already lit. The explosion left 44 injured, 213 arrested, and $175,000 in fire damage.[15] The riot was universally deplored and followed by much talk and a few key actions: an open-housing ordinance, some school desegregation (notably the closure of South High School and integration-by-busing of Union), and the election of First AME Church's pastor Lyman Parks to the City Commission. An equally noteworthy event was the dedication, one month after the riot's end, of True Light Baptist Church's new sanctuary at Thomas Street and Dolbee Avenue SE. With Pastor Keith aging and True Light expanding to some 1,500 members, the latter's Rev. W.L. Patterson assumed stronger leadership among local black Baptists. As he had with the pre-riot meeting in July 1967, Patterson hosted an open forum in December 1968 to respond to racial fighting at Union High School.[16]

The next Easter Keith resigned his pastorate at Messiah for reasons of age. The committee that sought his replacement showed signs of some upward mobility at the church; instead of the barber, baker, porter, and carpenter of the 1923 building board,

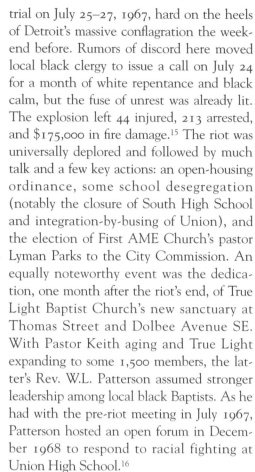

FIGURE 12
A tense stand-off between
police and inner-city youth
at Jefferson Avenue and
Sycamore Street SE
during the July 1967 riots
in Grand Rapids.

FIGURE 13
The Rev. Clifton Rhodes,
Jr., in Messiah's new
building in December 1989.

the search committee featured Russell John-son, a representative of the Michigan Civil Rights Commission; James E. Adams, Jr., principal of Franklin School; and Lewis Johnson, foreman at the John Widdicomb furniture factory.[17] After their choice, I. Joseph Miller, died only two years into his tenure, Messiah looked closer to home and called the Rev. Clifton Rhodes, Jr. Rhodes was himself part of the postwar migration, coming to Grand Rapids from Louisiana as a child with his father. Upon taking Messiah's pulpit in 1972, he duplicated Keith's initia-tive of 40 years before and surpassed his record. The clubs and choirs that galvanized lay participation were revived; new Bible classes and a neighborhood evangelism cam-paign began. Messiah's membership quickly spurted toward the 1,700 mark it holds today, and the congregation acquired four adjacent lots for the new 750-seat building that it dedicated on April 29, 1979.[18]

Messiah's boom stemmed partly from Rhodes' dynamism but mostly, his flock would say, from the truth of the gospel that he preaches with such power. Messiah today might include a half-dozen Ph.D.s, a hun-dred M.A.s, a bevy of school teachers, social workers, and engineers; but on nearby streets drug deals turn to murder, old people go to bed hungry, and single parents struggle to hold families together.[19] In this context

an old-time message makes sense. The mis-sion of Messiah, Rhodes repeats, is soul-sav-ing, first and last. That begins with a call to personal conversion to Christ; leads on to a growing knowledge of Scripture, taken as utterly true and authoritative for all realms of conduct; is expressed in ministering to others in soul and body, that is, by evange-lism and social concern; all to glorify the God who is at once the supernatural Ruler of the cosmos and an immediate felt pres-ence along one's way.[20]

The center of Messiah's life is Sunday worship where these doctrines come alive via preaching, singing, and testimonies that ring with a rhythm centuries old. The proof of its conviction comes out in a dozen pro-grams ranging from visiting the sick and imprisoned to feeding the hungry, clothing the needy, and caring for the children of working parents, black and white. The church today gives special attention to the likeliest casualties of the inner city, youth and black males, who face some of the same perils as did Robert Gillard's flock a hun-dred years ago.[21] If Messiah's current mea-sures are more systematic and programmed, they rely on the same vision of dignity, dis-cipline, and hope that lifted the prayers of its founders in the tiny frame church at Henry and Logan.

FIGURES 14, 15
Zebulon and Edytha Stow,
part of the Alfred Stow
clan that were among the
early settlers of the
Cascade area.

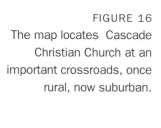

FIGURE 16
The map locates Cascade
Christian Church at an
important crossroads, once
rural, now suburban.

FIGURE 17
Exterior of Cascade
Christian Church in
the 1880s.

THE CRABGRASS FRONTIER

While Grand Rapids' population grew by less than one-half of one percent in the 1950s, Kent County's grew by 26 percent. Clearly, the black migration into the city was surpassed by a flood — a white flood until 1980 — to the suburbs. One of the destinations was Cascade Township, whose numbers rose from 1,266 in 1940 to 3,330 in 1960 to 12,869 today. The 1950s held the key portents of change. Cascade Road was widened to four lanes in 1955; the township's southern tier was acquired for the new airport in 1958; and entrepreneurs began the commercialization of 28th Street that today brings the string of stores unbroken to the intersection of Cascade Road.[22] The sprawl has not obscured, however, the white church spire that has looked over that intersection for more than a century. The steeple represents a parish whose mission, for all the changes in between, resembles that of its founders 125 years ago: to turn a scattering of people into a community.

Cascade Christian Church was founded in 1864 by a cluster of settlers from Stow Corners, Summit County, Ohio. The extended family of Alfred Stow composed 10 of the church's 16 charter members, and the Cascade group represented one of 40 congregations which the original Summit County church helped pioneer across

the Midwest.[23] This network was part of the simple "Christian" (later, Disciples of Christ) movement that was born in the Ohio Valley in the early 19th century, tailor-made for the American frontier.

Amid the chaotic religious competition of the frontier, the Disciples' two founders proclaimed a clear message. Barton Stone called for all believers to unite on the essentials of Christian doctrine, liberally interpreted. Alexander Campbell believed that unity could be found by restoring all and only the original practices of the apostolic church; what the New Testament taught, if literally and rationally applied, would cut through human corruptions and bring all Christians together. The tension between

unity and New Testament purity would trouble the Disciples later, but for the rest of the century they flourished across the heartland of the United States.

The Cascade group faced another sort of difficulty — the lure of the city. In 1874 several of its members formed the nucleus of First Christian Church in Grand Rapids; two of these, Russell Stow and Thomas Haight, founded the table manufactory that became known as Stow & Davis Inc. The Cascade assembly was revived in 1879 by meetings held in the township temperance hall under the leadership of Mrs. T.D. Butler, wife of the Grand Rapids church's pastor, and Elias Sias, the Disciples' Michigan evangelist. A donation of land by George S. Richardson (another Summit County man) enabled the group to erect the white frame chapel that from its dedication on Oct. 8, 1880, until today has represented the center of the Cascade community.[24]

For the next 60 years Cascade Christian followed the course of a small country church. Membership peaked at 175 in 1895, new joiners being baptized by immersion (a Disciples mandate) in the Thornapple River or, later, in the chapel's own rather leaky baptistry. Annual revival meetings held after the autumn harvest

FIGURE 18
The Rev. Elias Sias helped revive Cascade Christian Church in 1880.

FIGURE 19
George S. Richardson donated the land for Cascade Christian's building.

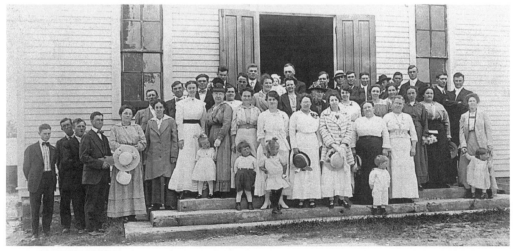

FIGURE 20
Cascade Christian Church congregation in 1916.

FIGURE 21
Women from Cascade
Christian Church play
croquet in 1895.

brought in some souls, but the congregation was largely an assembly of long-settled and inter-related clans: Wrides, Richardsons, Wattersons, Pattersons.[25] Membership dipped to 60 by 1910 as the church suffered a rapid turnover of pastors (nine between 1900 and 1920). But in 1916, when it excavated a basement for use as a social hall, Cascade Christian rediscovered its mission. The chapel became the center of local social life — at least for those who did not run with "the tavern crowd." School programs, ice cream socials, 4th of July festivities, polling booths and election luncheons, weddings, funerals, young folks' theatricals, and the community Christmas party all centered on its building. Whatever welfare work the area needed was coordinated through the church, and the town-

ship's political leadership came mostly from its pews.[26]

The 1920s challenged this status as the auto age eroded Cascade's physical isolation and its hold over the young. Prohibition pushed the tavern crowd underground, possibly a more dangerous location. In response Cascade Christian gave special attention to youth work, offering clubs and recreational activities quite as Grand Rapids' black churches would a generation later. Its adult membership slumped, however: from 135 in 1920 to but 35 a decade later. The Depression taxed this meager band harshly. As with Messiah Missionary Baptist, Cascade Christian stayed alive through sacrificial leadership. From Grand Rapids, where he served as principal of South High School, Lester C. Doerr continued as he had since 1920 to

FIGURES 22, 23, 24
From left to right:
The Revs. Lester C.
Doerr, J. Frank Green, and
Harold S. Chambers.

commute to Cascade every Sunday to lead worship. During the 1930s he did so without salary. When Doerr left to join the World War II Army chaplaincy, two others replaced him: J. Frank Green, the Disciples' state evangelist, and Harold S. Chambers, the superintendent of Godwin Heights, later of Forest Hills, public schools. With its youth emphasis reinforced with leadership by educators, the church's Sunday school flourished even while its adult attendance flagged.[27]

Upon his return in 1949, Lester Doerr pushed the congregation in a new direction. The melting pot of the U.S. Army had given him a vision that fit with the postwar housing boom: Cascade Christian needed to drop some of its specifics (the Disciples' "New Testament purity") for the sake of a broader ministry ("unity"). In particular, Doerr proposed that the church admit new members who had been baptized by rites other than immersion. After considerable controversy, the church accepted the change and began to harvest the suburban migration. Its membership jumped from 65 in 1950 to 340 some 10 years later.[28] Members who worried about losing their distinctiveness were correct to a point but perhaps missed continuities beneath the change. In 1957 the congregation made its first building expansion an educational facility; and in 1958 it called as pastor Raymond Gaylord, who made youth work and community service the twin keys of his 31-year pastorate.

Gaylord hailed from the same parts as had Cascade Christian's pioneers; in fact, he had been baptized in the home church at Stow, Ohio. Arriving at Cascade at the time the township ceded land for the new airport, Gaylord recognized the face of change: "The church stood at the crossroads. It would either broaden to become diverse and metropolitan or stay a country church and die. Everything was a struggle but it changed and thrived."[29] In April 1965 the congregation dedicated a new $200,000 sanctuary, and nearly lost it to that month's Palm Sunday tornado. A fellowship hall and meeting rooms were added in 1972, expanded offices in 1983. These buildings left some members longing for the intimacy of the old chapel, but at least the latter was spared the demolition planned for it by an earlier architect. The facilities have been well used, too. While the Disciples nationally lost nearly half their membership in the 1960s and 1970s, Cascade Christian set and met a goal of adding at least 100 new members per year. The rolls held 760 in 1971, 1,206 in 1981, and 1,350 at Gay-

FIGURE 25
The Rev. Raymond Gaylord, pastor of Cascade Christian from 1958 to 1989.

FIGURE 26
An aerial view of Cascade Christian's current complex.

A Touch of GRACE

Each January during the Week of Prayer for Christian Unity, dozens of people from various faiths file down the center aisle of an area church to share in the Eucharist.

Every May, thousands of men, women and children don sweatshirts and tennis shoes and walk 12 kilometers through Grand Rapids' streets to raise hundreds of thousands of dollars to combat hunger in West Michigan and beyond.

In between these times, other events, services and ministries are also sponsored by an agency that serves as a clearinghouse for ecumenical activity and outreach in Grand Rapids. Called the Grand Rapids Area Council for Ecumenism, the group represents more than 500 churches.

"What we have done for 20 years is given people in this community permission to be cooperative and to be ecumenical," said the Rev. David Baak, co-director of GRACE.

Unlike the Grand Rapids Council of Churches, the organization that preceded it in the 1950s and 1960s, GRACE does not regularly speak out on social matters. From its start, GRACE has worked "to put people on the streets, in pastoral care, in groups in which they can share their faith," Baak said.

Offering help to a person dying from AIDS, providing transportation to the elderly, and publishing an annual yearbook of church addresses and pastors' names, GRACE has been a mostly behind-the-scenes force in Grand Rapids.

"We are a very natural outgrowth of the church council," Baak said. "What people realized in 1973 is that there was a next step to take and that was what we did."

The Grand Rapids Area Council of Churches was founded in 1957. It was part of the national ecumenical movement that grew out of the wreckage brought about by World War II.

Taking its lead from the National Council of Churches and drawing in the process some of the same criticism leveled at the national body, the Grand Rapids Council spoke out regularly and often with controversy. The council saw its role as partly political.

In 1962, for example, the local council offered a series of classes on such topics as "Christianity and Communism" and "Michigan's Proposed Constitution."

Two years later, the Rev. Ray Prescott, council president, helped spearhead an unsuccessful campaign to keep grocery stores closed on Sunday. He and other council members were displeased with a state Supreme Court decision declaring that counties could not keep these stores closed on the Sabbath.

In 1971, the council waded into controversy when it supported the right of farm workers to choose a union and backed men who refused to fight in the Vietnam War out of conscientious objection.

But the council's work was not entirely political. It held an annual Reformation Day rally; programs for the mentally handicapped and chaplain services at area hospitals and jails were established. And in late 1964, the Grand Rapids Area Council of Churches blazed the national ecumenical trail by becoming the second church council in the country to formally accept a Roman Catholic congregation into its fold.

At that time, only the church council in Tulsa, Okla., had taken a similarly bold step.

Nevertheless, the council proved too controversial and eventually dissolved. In its wake, GRACE was born in 1972.

Neither then nor now were members of non-Christian organizations allowed to join either ecumenical group. Mem-

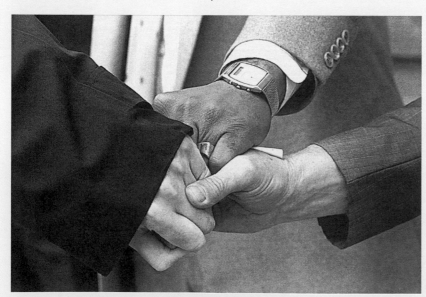

FIGURE 27   The Revs. Dennis Morrow, Clifton Rhodes, Jr., and Morris Greidanus join hands on the Monroe Mall in observance of the National Day of Prayer.

bers of local Jewish synagogues, however, were active in GRACE on various levels from the start.

"At that time (in 1972) 70 percent of the religious community was not participating" in ecumenical activities, Baak said. Notably absent in those early days were the Christian Reformed Church and the Roman Catholic Church.

GRACE came in with a "congregationally based, responsive agenda," Baak said, "consciously trying to include traditions at the level of their gifts and diversity."

Local churches may not have been able to agree on theological matters, but they were willing to band together in outreach. At a time when the ecumenical movement lost focus nationally, GRACE remained rooted in its community and worked to join churches in shared service and worship.

Taking a different approach than the council out of which it was spawned, GRACE has had member denominations from across the Christian spectrum. Catholics, Christian Reformed, Lutherans, Baptists, Methodists and Congregationalists all joined to work under one Christian banner.

"This group (GRACE) has entered a no man's land, fulfilling needs that churches on their own cannot," a former GRACE board member declared when speaking of the Clergy Interracial Forum, some pastors from various ethnic groups who gather frequently for discussions. "It (GRACE) gets down on the street and helps the poor, the unfortunate, those who can't do it on their own."

FIGURE 28
GRACE's annual Hunger Walk in 1992.

lord's retirement in 1989. Today the church facilities host 20 different community meetings a week.[30]

Led by the church's high schoolers, Gaylord in his first year at Cascade stumbled upon the formula for growth on the "crabgrass frontier." Some Boy Scouts in the congregation asked him to supervise their work for the organization's God and Country Award. That work in Bible study, church history, comparative religion, and charitable activities soon expanded into a Church Awards program for girls as well as boys, took on a second year of service projects, and became a model program for national youth organizations. The church provided for children outside its membership as well. It opened a nursery school, a day-care center, and Kent County's first before- and after-school child-care operation. By baby boom rules, where children went, parents followed. These operations, together with visits to new residents by parish women, brought many adults into membership.[31]

Providing for children also led the church to expand its social services. For his first Christmas at Cascade, Gaylord encouraged six college students to deliver food and presents to two destitute families in the area. Since then, Operation Santa Claus has grown under the direction of Cascade Christian's Jane Wood to reach 3,000 families. In the early 1990s, its budget surpassed $25,000 besides $15,000 worth of donated goods; its proceeds went to 227 families plus hundreds of senior citizens, with ample surplus left

and Protestant social charities. Bridging religious divides has of necessity become the congregation's strong suit; the membership today includes people of 50 different denominational backgrounds. The church poses only one doctrinal requirement, that members profess Jesus Christ as Lord and Savior. Within and beyond that lies latitude for personal interpretation and belief.[35] If all this is new, it is also as old as Barton Stone's vision, some 200 years ago, that Christian unity could and must form a charitable community on the frontiers of American life.

over for distribution at Grand Rapids' Mel Trotter Mission.[32] Meanwhile, to extend help over the whole year, the church opened its Second Mile House to distribute food, clothing, and financial assistance to the rural poor. This record made it the natural place to organize ACCESS-6 during the recession of 1982. Through this program, 15 area churches coordinated their help to the needy in six southeast county townships. Over the past 10 years it has given $80,000 in cash for rent and utility emergencies, food to 1,265 families, and clothes — at the rate of 35 tons a year — to nearly as many.[33]

To youth ministry and social care Cascade Christian added ecumenical concern in the 1960s. Previously, Gaylord confessed, he had issued "diatribes" against Catholics and the Christian Reformed in the area, but an emergency in 1965 changed that. Embarrassed at the prospect of offering a Thanksgiving service to an empty new sanctuary, the church invited Father Hugh Michael Beahan as guest speaker. An ample crowd turned up out of curiosity — no Catholic priest had yet occupied a Protestant pulpit in the area — but went away charmed and edified. Beahan returned for the next 15 Thanksgivings until taken by death from cancer in 1980. Gaylord counted it the "greatest single honor" of his career to be asked to offer prayer at Beahan's funeral Mass at St. Andrew's Cathedral.[34]

FIGURE 30
The Rev. Frederick Mueller was St. John's first pastor from 1880 to 1884.

The Beahan series epitomized the new directions of Cascade Christian Church. The proceeds from the Thanksgiving offerings were always divided between Catholic

GERMANS IN THE NATIONAL ORBIT

Postwar America not only challenged local churches to keep up with a mobile population but also led Protestants to undertake new efforts to maintain their historic leadership in national affairs. Longstanding differences diminished as denominations coordinated their activities more closely through the National Council of Churches or, in some cases, merged with each other. This movement was arranged in such power centers as New York City or Washington, D.C., but had to play out in a thousand local communities. Grand Rapids' West Side provided an instance of two opposite reactions to the trend. St. John's United Church of Christ

wholeheartedly endorsed it, while Seventh Reformed resisted it. Both strategies proved successful, perhaps because both were rooted in traditions older than the current age.

Ironically, the ecumenically minded St. John's had originated out of separation from a well-established church. In 1880, some members of Immanuel Lutheran, chafing at its strict rules, particularly against lodge membership, decided to form an alternative for the German Protestants in town. They set up shop at the west end of the local German corridor — on Bridge Street, opposite Immanuel's site on Michigan — and affiliated with a denomination on the other side of the German-American church spectrum. Whereas Immanuel's Missouri Synod stuck to the letter of Lutheranism, the new group's Evangelical Union carried on the attempt, begun in Prussia in 1817, to bring Lutherans and Calvinists together in a single national Protestant church. The Union actually found America a fairer site for this project than Germany, and embarked on a vigorous church extension effort when immigration boomed again in the 1880s. As part of that campaign the Rev. Frederick Mueller officially organized the ex-Immanuelites as St. John's Evangelical Church on June 20, 1880.[36]

St. John's 20 founding families thought big. In little more than a year they had built a 400-seat Gothic edifice on Mount Vernon NW, borrowing two-thirds of its $11,000 cost. By 1890 they had added a $2,000 parsonage, doubled their membership, and started a German-language day-school in the church basement. The depression of the 1890s struck them as hard as it had Immanuel Lutheran, however. Their pastor, David Greiner, had to go about the region lecturing for extra money, perhaps hastening his premature death in 1895. The post-depression years required $25,000 in property improvements, $1,000 of which came from steel magnate

FIGURE 31
A 1930 photo shows the interior of St. John's with the organ purchased with funds from steel magnate Andrew Carnegie.

FIGURE 32
St. John's first building at 348 Mount Vernon Ave. NW was constructed in 1881. It later served as Our Lady of Aglona Church for Latvian Roman Catholics from 1956 until it was removed for the U.S. 131 expressway in 1961.

THE SOUL OF THE CITY AND SUBURBS   **173**

Helping on the Hill

The Rev. Wesley Samuelson was walking near his church on Crescent Street NE one afternoon in the early 1950s when he noticed the dilapidated state of a few homes in the area. As he often did, the pastor of Bethlehem Lutheran Church assumed his neighbors would spruce up their homes when they found the time and money.

But in the next several weeks, the Swedish Augustana Lutheran Synod minister began to notice other buildings in need of paint, shingles and cement work. It finally became clear to Samuelson that something insidious was happening to the area surrounding his church, south of Michigan Street and north of Lyon Street NE in what was even then known as the Hill District.

"It was very subtle, but something was happening and something had to be done," the pastor said.

One of eight churches in the area directly east of downtown Grand Rapids at that time, Bethlehem Lutheran was not a bastion of social activity and concern. From its inception on April 3, 1873, the Swedish church had more or less kept to itself. So it was a little unusual when Samuelson decided to involve himself and eventually members of his church in a long fight with City Hall to preserve the historically distinct part of town.

While Samuelson was not the leader in the effort to maintain the neighborhood and obtain National Register of Historic Places designation, he nonetheless took the unusual step, at least for his church, to become involved in the very political fray.

With commitment and determination, he and his church members worked steadfastly and prayerfully to preserve the flavor, architecture and overall character of the two-square-mile neighborhood. They opened their church for meetings, attended many of the civic gatherings at which the issue was discussed and helped circulate informa-tion about the often difficult preservation process to homes in the neighborhood.

"Bethlehem Lutheran was very supportive of our efforts," said Barbara Roelofs, one of the founders of the Heritage Hill Foundation, the group that battled city officials and in 1971 won the historic designation that served to protect and preserve the neighborhood from further development.

"The Lutheran church showed great sensitivity and did not try to pave their way to paradise like other churches."

A handful of other Hill-area congregations bought up homes, demolished them and slapped down concrete for parking. One church went so far as to hire a bulldozer operator to do his dirty work at midnight, Roelofs said.

"We were happy when a few churches such as Bethlehem stood behind us and didn't just pay lip service to the preservation movement," she said.

The Heritage Hill District, with its expansive lawns and turn-of-the-century mansions, is one of the city's premier neighborhoods. Prestigious lawyers, doctors and local politicians make the area their home, as do college students, single parents and the elderly. Bounded loosely on the north by Michigan Street, on the south by Cherry Street, on the west by Lafayette

FIGURE 33
The Rev. Wesley Samuelson in front of Bethlehem Lutheran.

Avenue and on the east by Union Avenue, the neighborhood comprised in the early 1990s more than 1,200 well-tended homes. As part of the National Register of Historic Places, all homes and buildings are required to undergo a rigorous review by local and federal historic officials before any of the structures can be significantly altered or torn down.

At the time Samuelson first became active in petitioning City Hall to slow its urban expansion plans, the churches in the Hill area included Ahavas Israel on Lafayette south of Fountain; Grace Episcopal at Lafayette and Cherry; First Netherlands Reformed on Crescent at Union; First Church of Christ Scientist on Lafayette south of East Fulton; Central Reformed Church on East Fulton at College; Central Christian Church at Cherry and Madison; Calvary Undenominational on Michigan east of College; and Bethelehem.

Increasing the size of the congregation as well as playing a role in this model preservation effort were among the highlights of his ministry, said Samuelson, who also served on a committee that planned the inte-

> *"The Lutheran church showed great sensitivity and did not try to pave their way to paradise like other churches."*
>
> **— Barbara Roelofs**
> **Heritage Hill Foundation**

gration of city schools in the 1960s. He served the church three decades before retiring in 1978.

But helping maintain the neighborhood was only part of the history of a church, which in the 1970s offered the first federally funded day care program in the city.

Bethlehem from its start was a spiritual home for Swedish immigrants, many of whom traveled to West Michigan to labor as wood workers in local furniture factories. And it eventually spun off three other Lutheran congregations.

Among other things the church had to contend with over the years were doctrinal disputes over whether to hold onto the staunch, old Swedish ways or to adapt to this new world. Adaptation eventually won out. And in the early years, church members more than once had to dig deep in their pockets; some even had to mortgage their own homes to help pay the church's bills. But Bethlehem has remained vibrant to this day.

"Any church is only here and only survives if it has a purpose in the present day. I think so far we have had a purpose," Samuelson said.

Andrew Carnegie for the new pipe organ. When the mountain of debt was finally removed in 1913, St. John's was free to carry on what its historian aptly called "the best of the German state-church traditions": an excellent choir and musical liturgy, societies for both genders and all ages, and a dedication to ennobling life by lifting parishioners' minds toward "higher ideals." [37]

That elevated posture ran into difficulties in World War I. German nationalism was more foundational to the Evangelical Union than to Missouri Synod Lutherans, but was decidedly unwelcome in the America of 1917–1918. Just before and after those years St. John's donated heavily to German war relief; in between they did their duty by the American Red Cross. In 1915 the congregation began alternating English and German in worship and society meetings.[38] There is no public record of persecution toward the church, perhaps because of its genial bearing. Certainly the 40-year pastorate

(1898–1938) of the Rev. F. Robert Schreiber gave stability and continuity over the choppy course of Americanization. Schreiber was in appearance, manner, and office the epitome of German Evangelical character: genial, cultured, pious, and undogmatic, devoted to the flock he led as a friend. He taught loyalty to God, church and country — in that order — and represented that part of the old country that had no quarrel with the new.

Nonetheless, a new quarrel came, this time total in dimension. St. John's faced World War II with its first American-born pastor, Theodore Franke, and a hearty devotion to the American cause. The most moving records in the church's files consist of correspondence with the 85 sons of the church who entered the U.S. armed forces. By these letters Pastor Franke had them all join at midnight, Christmas Eve 1944, in the congregation's service of prayer for their well-being. Some wrote back — from Alaska, the South Pacific, and the Ardennes for-

FIGURE 34
St. John's Women's
Society in 1929.

the corner of Lake Michigan Drive and Covell Avenue NW. The old facility went to a Latvian Roman Catholic parish and, eventually, to demolition for the new expressway. Institutionally, they became joined to the most venerable of American churches. Already in 1934 the Evangelical Union had consolidated with the German Reformed Church in the United States. In 1957 that body merged with the Congregational Christian Churches, themselves a union of some of Barton Stone's old frontier movement and the Congregational descendants of New England's Puritan founders. St. John's was the first Grand Rapids congregation to vote approval of the new denomination, the United Church of Christ (UCC).[40] In a new era, its old unionist impulse held firm.

est — to say how they treasured the moment. Three did not return, having died in battle against their grandparents' countrymen, one of them in the fatherland itself.[39]

After the war the people of St. John's took up a familiar role in what was truly their own nation. German was dropped from worship in 1946, although the oldest ladies' society used it until their 110th year in 1990. The congregation followed the suburban trek out Bridge Street to a new $258,000 building (dedicated in 1956) at

Today, St. John's shows the typical profile of mainline American Protestantism. Its 413 members are older than average and active in local charities, particularly through Smith Memorial UCC and Hall School on the Southwest Side. They pay for but do not always agree with the national headquarters'

FIGURE 35
The Rev. F. Robert Schreiber,
far left, and his family.

FIGURE 36
St. John's double quartet
in the early 1930s.

political liberalism. Tolerance and diversity stand high on their roster of ideals. St. John's prescribes few rules or doctrines beyond basic Scriptural principles, leaving ample room for the exercise of individual conscience which is taken to be the central point of religious life. Deep roots and warm fellowship keep bringing back many who have moved some distance from the old West Side.[41] These often have German names, but even when they do not, they are moving in the orbit of national Protestantism, translated from German to American.

BUILDING THE WALLS OF ZION

In the 1970s the news media stumbled upon "evangelical" Protestantism as a vibrant force in American religion. Their surprise at the discovery said more about their own perception than about the facts of the matter, for while the ecumenical course typified by St. John's UCC got most of the attention in the 1950s and 1960s, the conservative tide had been swelling all along. The purposes and methods of that growth were classically displayed at Seventh Reformed Church.

Seventh Reformed was founded on May 1, 1890, by West Side Hollanders who were tired of making the two-mile trek to Fourth Reformed Church across the river. The booming Dutch population on the West Side made success likely; Seventh joined two Christian Reformed churches already in existence there, and each of the three fostered an English-speaking congregation by 1910. By 1900, Seventh's dozen charter families swelled to 120; its original $700 budget ($400 lent by the denomination) expanded to finance a $3,500 sanctuary with a $1,300 organ. Growth required enlarging and moving the building to the corner of Leonard Street and Jennette Avenue NW, constructing a new parsonage, and spinning off Trinity Reformed Church for the English-speakers in the congregation. Although World War I involved the pastor of Alpine Avenue CRC in controversy over neutrality and patriotism, the Dutch at Seventh Reformed

FIGURE 37
St. John's current building,
erected in 1956.

went untroubled by the fracas. They began an English evening service in 1919, sired another English-speaking congregation (Richmond RCA) in 1925, eliminated their old debt in 1920, took on a new one to refurbish their sanctuary in 1923, and held their own with 223 member families and a Sunday school enrolling 520.[42]

For its first half-century, in short, Seventh seemed a typical, perhaps slightly conservative, congregation of the Reformed Church in America. It was a bit more open to American ways than the average Christian Reformed church — for instance, giving its evening service a looser, evangelistic format. It held but did not accentuate orthodox doctrine. Its emphasis fell, rather, on classic strains of Reformed piety: the believer's humble trust in the God who proved ever reliable, through good times and bad. Ministers came and went every five years. Sundays, the members walked to church. Weekdays, the mothers tended to their neat bungalows, the fathers to their furniture-factory jobs, the children to their games and catechism classes, the latter of which they tried, in ancient Dutch fashion, to spice up with the former.[43]

World War II disrupted this idyll. Seventh Reformed's 275 families sent 130 young people into the armed forces; five never returned. Dutch services ceased in 1947. The creaky old building raised the issue of postwar location, which the congregation answered in 1944 by pur-

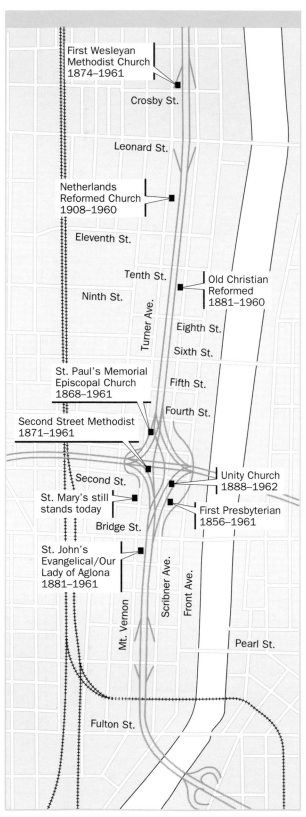

FIGURE 38
The freeways that helped build the suburbs required the demolition of eight historic churches on the near West Side of Grand Rapids.

First Wesleyan Methodist Church 1874–1961

Crosby St.

Leonard St.

Netherlands Reformed Church 1908–1960

Eleventh St.

Tenth St.

Ninth St.

Old Christian Reformed 1881–1960

Turner Ave.

Eighth St.

Sixth St.

St. Paul's Memorial Episcopal Church 1868–1961

Fifth St.

Fourth St.

Second Street Methodist 1871–1961

Second St.

Unity Church 1888–1962

St. Mary's still stands today

First Presbyterian 1856–1961

Bridge St.

St. John's Evangelical/Our Lady of Aglona 1881–1961

Mt. Vernon

Scribner Ave.

Front Ave.

Pearl St.

Fulton St.

FIGURE 39
The Rev. Morris J. Folkert was pastor of Seventh Reformed Church from 1949 to 1957.

chasing the old Widdicomb School property at Leonard and Tamarack Avenue NW. Collecting $15,000 a year, the congregation finished a new building on the site in 1952.[44] Seventh had not moved far geographically; it was not about to budge an inch theologically. When the RCA in the late 1940s entered merger talks with the United Presbyterian Church, Midwestern Reformed churches like Seventh blocked the move. At the same time Seventh objected to the RCA's increasing participation in the Federal (later, National) Council of Churches because of the theological liberalism and looser ethics they suspected would come in the bargain. Under the leadership of Rev. Morris Folkert (pastor from 1949 to 1957), the church began withholding offerings from certain denominational programs.[45]

Such opposition came to define the church's very being during the 1958–1979 pastorate of the Rev. Gordon H. Girod. By virtue of his leadership and the era's shifting demographics, Seventh Reformed changed from being a neighborhood church into the bastion of a particular theology. The broadening trends in mainline Protestantism struck Girod as part of the fuzzy relativism spreading through postwar American culture. Against that he insisted on clear statements, resolute convictions, and demanding discipline. From the pulpit he gave a house packed morning and evening a hard-nosed presentation of traditional Reformed doctrine, not hesitating to

FIGURE 40
The first parsonage of Seventh Reformed Church, corner of Leonard and Jennette NW, around 1910. Shown are Pastor Lubbers and his family.

FIGURE 41
Seventh Reformed Church worshipped at 838 Leonard St. NW from 1892 to 1952.

FIGURE 42
Laying sidewalk in front of the church in 1892.

Father Mike: Messenger for the Masses

On Thanksgiving 1965, ecumenical history was made in the Grand Rapids area when Monsignor Hugh Michael Beahan took to the pulpit and delivered a holiday message at Cascade Christian Church.

For the first time, a Roman Catholic priest had been invited to speak in an official, liturgical capacity to a Protestant flock inside the confines of their church.

"We always appreciated what he had to say. Father Mike was always new, exciting and interesting," the Rev. Raymond Gaylord, Cascade's pastor at the time, said of the sermon, which became an annual event.

"Many of the old divisions and prejudices were still around when we began this service," Gaylord added in a newspaper interview published after Beahan's death from cancer in 1980.

Breaking down religious barriers and particularly bringing a Catholic message to people from other backgrounds and beliefs was a hallmark of the man who for many years

FIGURE 43   Monsignor Hugh Michael Beahan at the controls of his radio show.

was the voice of Catholicism in West Michigan.

In significant ways, Father Mike's annual sermon at Cascade Christian was a symbol of change that had begun to sweep the Catholic Church in the years during and following the Second Vatican Council. Held at the request of Pope John XXIII, the council was a monumental gathering in which many of the church's traditions and stances were examined, altered and modernized.

Although the church itself began a slow turnaround as it shed its more antiquated trappings in the mid- to late-1960s, Father Mike had been speaking about matters of the faith to wide-ranging audiences for years. His sermon before the Protestant church on Thanksgiving was as much a reflection of his own ministry as an example of the changing face of his church.

Ecumenism aside, Father Mike was a communicator. He was one of the first clergymen in any denomination in West Michigan to foresee the power of the mass media, notably television, to reach the masses.

Beahan had been head of the Department of Communications for the Grand Rapids Diocese since 1974, director of radio and television for the diocese starting in 1953 and editor of the weekly newspaper *Western Michigan Catholic* for two years. His weekly television show, "Fifteen with Father," was created in 1953 and aired for 23 years on WOOD-TV. He also served for years as producer, director and narrator of the "Television Mass," which was broadcast first from the WOOD-TV studio and later from St. Andrew's Cathedral, the parish of which he was rector when he died.

"For him, the television cameras were not alien creatures or a necessary inconvenience one has to tolerate," Monsignor Gaspar "Gus" Ancona has written. "They were the wings of the Gospel. He caressed the camera, and the living, speaking image on the tube that showed it."

In his sermons, numerous speeches in communities across the Midwest and on TV, Father Mike presented a Catholic approach to religion that was "friendly, familiar and inviting" to all Christians, added Ancona, who also has served as rector of St. Andrew's.

What Sister Marie Michael Jacobs, principal of St. Andrew's School, remembers most about Father Mike was his voice.

"As soon as you heard it, it attracted your attention,"

FIGURE 44 Father Mike, second from left, at WOOD-TV.

she said. "The voice was very soft, mellow and gentle. But on issues that he strongly believed in it could be firm."

Beyond that, the Dominican sister who worked closely with the priest remembers his slight frame, his smile and his intense work habits. "He never took a day off. He said his ministry was his hobby," she recalled.

Father Mike was born in Ionia in 1920 as the son of the owner of a home improvement business. He graduated from Lowell High School, where he was an award-winning member of the school's oratorical society. He graduated from St. Joseph's Seminary in Grand Rapids in 1941, then attended St. Mary's Seminary in Baltimore where he studied theology. In 1945, which should have been his last year at St. Mary's, he became ill and left school.

Out of the seminary, he landed a job as an announcer and writer at WOOD radio. Although he returned to school in 1946, he never lost interest in the media.

He served a variety of churches in and around Grand Rapids, but by the early 1950s had launched the first of many efforts in bringing the faith to people through TV, radio and the written word.

His first radio venture began out of the coal bin at St. James Catholic Church. From there, he gave listeners a mix of church-sanctioned talk and music, mixing contemporary tunes and an age-old message.

Busy from before dawn until well after dusk tending to the needs of his various and far-flung flocks, Father Mike played a role in community as well as religious affairs. He served as chairman of the United Way of Kent County and spoke at forums about racial problems.

In 1979, Pope John Paul II proclaimed Beahan a protonotary apostolic — the highest honor a priest can receive from the pope short of being made a bishop.

A few years after his death, an ecumenical award was begun in his honor. The Hugh Michael Beahan Award is given annually to a person who exemplifies the ecumenical enthusiasm evident in the life of Father Mike.

As far back as 1965, a time when Catholics and Protestants were practicing a not-so-subtle form of shunning one another, Father Mike called for a uniting of local church bodies.

"It's high time we in the Christian world practice charity toward one another," he told the Grand Rapids Rotary Club on Christmas Eve of that year.

"The greatest effect of the ecumenical movement will be the reuniting of the Christian world in some way. And this will take charity of mind of all people."

Even as he approached death from Hodgkin's disease, Beahan maintained a high profile. He used his illness as a way to continue sharing a message of faith.

In an interview before his death, he said: "If you don't have that faith, I don't know what the hell you do, very frankly. I would just go up the wall."

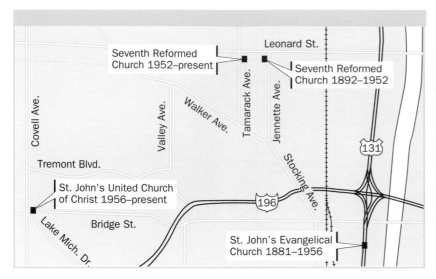

FIGURE 45
Seventh Reformed Church
moved little in this era; St.
John's much farther.

FIGURE 46
The Rev. Gordon H. Girod
at the pulpit and radio
microphone that made him
famous.

FIGURE 47
A full house at Seventh
Reformed Church on a
Sunday morning in 1965.

name heresies and deviations in churches nearby and far away.[46] The message went out well beyond the sanctuary, too, after Seventh acquired the 11 a.m. Sunday slot on WFUR. Hundreds of families driving home from other churches could listen to Girod's sermon and compare it to what they had just heard. Enough preferred him to change membership and offset the losses that Seventh, like other West Side churches, suffered to suburbia.[47]

Seventh became a legend of orthodoxy not just in Grand Rapids but across the RCA. By his sermons, journalism, and books, Girod kept up a steady assault on the National and World Councils of Churches for their theological and political liberalism, and on the RCA headquarters in New York City for being lax and uncaring. Seventh led

the way when the western RCA rejected another proposed merger, this one in the late 1960s with the Southern Presbyterians. But when that proposal threatened to break the RCA apart, east and west, Girod surprised some by dismissing suggestions that RCA conservatives join the CRC. He treasured the autonomy which the RCA constitution granted local congregations, he explained, and which the CRC's "clergy-run hierarchy" would not allow.[48]

With its fast self-definition and commitment, Seventh generated enough revenue to set its own course. Girod presided over the liquidation of the $400,000 building debt in 1962, at the same time working the operations budget up from $70,000 in 1958 to $106,000 in 1963 and the missions budget from $19,000 to $39,000. In 1963 Seventh used conservative Presbyterian channels to build and staff a Christian hospital in Eritrea. When that fell to political insurgents in 1974 (one of Seventh's missionary nurses, Anna Strikwerda, being killed in the process), the church transferred the venture to Kenya. On the Grand Rapids scene, it became a major supporter of a

new Orthodox Presbyterian congregation on the south end and started a mission, Friendship Community Chapel, in the Alpine-Bridge-Richmond-U.S. 131 quadrant. To the RCA headquarters in New York, Seventh contributes only an annual assessment for operational expenses and money for specific programs approved by its own council.[49] Local autonomy and sacrificial giving, this record would attest, work as well as ecumenical methods.

On the other hand, Seventh did not buck the other trend of the postwar era. It undertook youth ministry but in a traditional fashion. It hired a full-time youth pastor in 1962 to coordinate three classes of the Christian Endeavor program that Seventh already had joined as a Dutch church in 1895, the Sunday school that continued to enroll more than 300, and the catechism classes that taught 250. Add to that junior and teen choirs and high (by RCA standards) enrollments in Christian schools, and the youth of Seventh were thoroughly saturated in their religious culture. The results were manifest on special occasions like the Good Friday service in 1964 when 42 made profession of faith, and in long-term loyalties evident in the persistence of family surnames on the church's rolls.

Inevitably, some of these youth would later leave for other denominations, but even then took along biblical knowledge and Calvinist convictions that were deep, keen, and quickening in their new environment. Seventh's habits of heart and mind were not easily broken or forgotten. Thus, among its rebels as well as its loyalists and behind its new posture in the postwar world persisted one theme of the old neighborhood church: a lively sense of generational continuity, of living members worshipping

among a cloud of witnesses who had gone on before, united in the face of an unchanging God.[50]

The pastorates of Gordon Girod and his successor, Charles Krahe (1980–1990), coincide with the tenure of Raymond Gaylord at Cascade Christian Church and with St. John's affiliation with the United Church of Christ. The latter two have followed precisely the course that Seventh Reformed rejects; yet the three have prospered together. At the same time Seventh and Messiah Missionary Baptist Church have earnestly and similarly cultivated conversion, moral discipline, and stout ethnic-religious traditions; yet the two find themselves poles apart on Election Day. If such ironies complicate the picture of recent American religion, they at least refute the charge usually laid against the decade so decisive for all these congregations: apparently the 1950s did not breed conformity.

Super-Church 9
and Storefronts

1970 – 1990

IN THE MIDDLE OF THE 1960S, THE UNITED STATES ENTERED
upon a cultural revolution that is just now coming to an end. Its original signs
are still familiar: long hair on men, short skirts on women, rock music, and dubious drugs. These were the icons of new values, of youthful energy and personal
fulfillment, of experience and expression beyond traditional restraints.

If it all seemed secular and sexual, the movement also embodied a spiritual quest. Suddenly it was easier to soar beyond modern doubts about the supernatural into fervent worship of any number of gods, from Krishna to Jesus. But as any revolution will, this one claimed its casualties — the rock stars and ordinary souls who overdosed on drugs, sex, or "experience" itself. That brought out

a communal impulse which the movement had harbored all along, a yearning for warm bonds of trust and fellowship. Betrayed by their own excesses, but no less by an America bespoiled with riots at home, war in Vietnam, and corruption in the White House, the rising generation looked for a place where they could be themselves and belong.

The two themes of liberation and com-

FIGURE 1
Raising and laying
on hands at First
Assembly of God.

FIGURE 2
A Wyoming church from the start, First Assembly now draws from the entire West Michigan area.

munity have dominated the American scene since. The first is evident in the smorgasbord of lifestyles now available for personal choice and in the rush to talk candidly, ceaselessly, about intimate things. The second is obvious in the search for roots, the celebration of ethnicity, the new awareness that the United States is not just a nation but a collection of tribes. The same forces have reshaped religious bodies. Some have thrived by reclaiming their ethnic past; others have felt called to draw in people from different tribes. All have had to arrange a truce between the new personal freedom and some pattern of discipline. This chapter will explore the ways that three local congregations have responded to that challenge.

By a numerical measure, the First Assembly of God has met the challenge best, for since 1970 it has ballooned from ordinary size to become the largest church in West

Grand Rapids as elsewhere, Pentecostals suffered ridicule owing to their worship style of open exuberance, faith-healing, and speaking in tongues. But now these feed the hunger for intense personal experience, while Pentecostalism's other face — strict Scriptural authority and behavioral standards — provides a clear moral compass. First Assembly has sealed this combination by adopting a key organizational innovation of the past 20 years, blending mega-church scale with small-group intimacy.

While First Assembly is mostly white, Pentecostalism has African-American roots as well; Bethel Pentecostal Church is the city's best known bearer of that legacy. For good reason, the hallmark of its worship and reputation is gospel music. Gospel is traditional and innovative, rooted in the African past but forged in 20th century America. Gospel's message puts universal Christian

FIGURE 3
The Singing Christmas Tree pageant at First Assembly of God, 1983.

themes to the strains of a particular ethnic culture. But most memorably, Bethel's gospel carries inspiration — an inspiration that has lifted the congregation well beyond its storefront origins.

If Bethel demonstrates ethnic continuity, the Roman Catholic parish of St. Joseph the Worker exemplifies ethnic change. Founded a century ago by Dutch immigrants, St. Joseph's has seen a whole parade of nationalities pass through its doors and is now the home of Grand Rapids' latest immigrants, from Latin America. One of its roles, therefore, looks familiar, as it must fortify its members against the hazards of the streets. But it faces a new challenge as well in the popularity of a storefront Pentecostalism (reminiscent of Bethel and First Assembly's origins) that can threaten but also enrich its own Catholic heritage. Intertwining freedom and restraint, innovation and loyalty, always has been the task of immigrant churches. If St. Joseph's confronts that calling most starkly, other churches must sense it too, for since the 1960s' revolution, all Americans have become displaced in mind if not in body, immigrants in their own land.

> *"People are tired of religion, tired of the dead, dry liturgy; they are looking for an expression of their love."*
>
> **— The Rev. Wayne Benson**

WARMTH AND WARFARE

In 1913, Pete and Iva Fairbairn were losing their son to spinal meningitis. Fairbairn, a farmer who had relocated from Alanson (near Petoskey) to Wyoming Township, was accustomed to meeting challenges head on, with either enormous strength or volcanic temper. Neither promised much now. So he turned to God, swearing eternal devotion should his son be spared. When his prayer was granted, Fairbairn kept his vow. Along the river in downtown Grand Rapids, he found a little mission where people believed in miracles. His devotion was confirmed 14 years later when their minister laid hands on the Fairbairns' granddaughter and saved her from convulsions. This time the family decided to begin prayer meetings in their own home, to bear witness to God's power among their neighbors.[1]

From this house-church of 10 families has emerged the First Assembly of God which today claims 2,000 members, an average Sunday morning attendance of 4,000, and a 5,000-seat sanctuary that is twice as large as any other church building in West Michigan. The contrast is a fair measure of the congregation's vision, of its appeal, and of

FIGURE 4

An aerial view of First Assembly of God in 1984, before its present auditorium was built.

the paradoxes that seem to underlie both.

Let's begin with appearances. At first glance, First Assembly's physical plant resembles nothing so much as that centerpiece of modern society, the shopping mall. Two huge auditoriums anchor either end of long enclosed corridors which give access to a series of smaller spaces — not shops in this case, but offices and classrooms. The whole is climate controlled and surrounded by acres of free parking. The larger auditorium, in turn, calls to mind an amphitheater. Its 6,240-square-foot platform alone is larger than Grand Rapids' pioneer church buildings put together, but even at that looks out at another 130,000 square feet of floor space, at a 50-seat orchestra pit, and at a 200-seat choir. The hall features state-of-the-art audio and video equipment, most noticeably the two 16-by-12-foot television screens that dominate the front wall and cast a speaker or singer larger than life size. From its 19,800 square yards of carpeting to a $40,000 grand piano, the auditorium breathes a mood of quiet elegance.[2]

Sundays at 10 a.m. and 5 p.m., however, a throng assembles here not to shop but to praise, not to worship the wonders of high-tech but of a supernatural Savior. Anyone who has come for gimmicks or gorgeous robes, for strutting showmen or mystic revelations, will go home disappointed. The music is upbeat but not flashy, the prayers spontaneous but intent. After an hour of these has passed, another hour of earnest preaching begins. The message is as plain as the minister's business suit: it is Jesus Christ, not pastor or parishioner, who must be lifted up so that he can draw all people to himself. On this note, the audience and the auditorium come together, for just as the worshippers unabashedly lift their hands in praise, so the pillars ringing the auditorium entrance spell out high for all to see the biblical names of God, from the Revelation of St. John back to Job and Genesis.

Using the latest means to promote an ancient faith is an old tradition in Protestantism, stretching from Martin Luther's reliance on the printing press to John Wesley's field preaching before bedraggled coal miners to Billy Graham's rallies in baseball stadiums. First Assembly simply has adapted the practice to an electronic, suburban setting. Like these predecessors, the church aims to use the techniques of the age to attack the spirit of the age, adopts popular styles to steel people against worldly wiles

FIGURE 5
A baptism in Buck Creek in 1931 involved the Rev. Alex Rudenko, Mary Haight, and Robert Stocking.

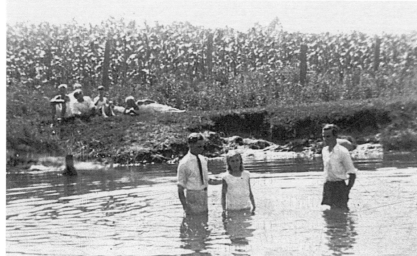

FIGURE 6
First Assembly of God congregation outside its first building around 1940.

and bond them together in a holy community. The formula runs great risks, as its critics always have pointed out, but it also opens enormous opportunities. How First Assembly has pursued that challenge is the essence of its story. Why this congregation in particular came to face the challenge in the first place leads back into the history of the Pentecostal movement of which First Assembly is a part.

Modern Pentecostalism traces its birth to the very first day of the 20th century, Jan. 1, 1901, when a prayer meeting at Bethel Bible School in Topeka, Kan., broke forth into the speaking of unknown languages. For those present, the gift of "tongues" marked a new outpouring of the Holy Ghost reminiscent of the first Pentecost, 50 days after Jesus' resurrection. It meant that the church was being restored on the original New Testament pattern, that a great wave of world evangelization was about to commence, and that Jesus' second coming was at hand. Many heard the news and were glad, especially those discounted by the world. They claimed the experience of New Testament miracles, including prophesying and healing as well as tongues; they spread the word to neighbor and stranger alike; they marked themselves off from worldliness by renouncing alcohol, tobacco, gambling, dancing, fashion, cosmetics, and adornment of every sort. Intimacy with God and gaining the next world made up for losing this one. But over time, much of the present world would come around. Pentecostalism today is the fastest-growing form of Christianity around the globe, and the majority brand in Africa

and Latin America.

As part of this boom, First Assembly has undergone the same passage as Wealthy Park Baptist and Calvary Undenominational; appealing to the disenchanted, it has prospered. First Assembly's growth simply came later. For its first 40 years, the church remained small and subject to ridicule. It quickly outgrew the Fairbairn house but could only afford a cinder-block basement with 10 wooden benches and a sawdust floor, built in 1930 on a donated lot at 52 Bellevue St. SW. Five years later the congregation bought a nearby house for $500 and recycled its materials — down to the nails — to raise a wooden structure over the basement. By the end of the 1930s the group

FIGURE 7
The Rev. Gene Hogan is surrounded by members of the 1966 South YMCA softball champions.

FIGURE 8
The Rev. Gene Hogan, pictured above with his wife, Vivian, was pastor at First Assembly of God from 1962 to 1969.

FIGURE 9
First Assembly of God's second building at 52 Bellevue St. SW in 1961.

Quakers: A Small but Powerful Group

FIGURE 10 A meeting of the Quakers.

In 1965, a small group of men and women quietly set up a display of "war toys" at area libraries.

Plastic tanks, toy machine guns, fierce-looking GI Joe dolls and other hints of destruction and violence were lined up for all to see. Nearby were alternative toys: puzzles, dolls, balls, coloring books, games. The contrast illustrated a sobering reality: children were being indoctrinated with a military mentality.

The group hoped the display would motivate parents to seek alternative presents for their children that Christmas.

"We were trying to emphasize the fact (that) many of the toys on the market were giving sanction to war," said Betty Ford, an organizer of the event sponsored by the Grand Rapids Meeting of the Society of Friends — the Quakers. "We wanted people in Grand Rapids to know that we believed violence is not something that can be tolerated or accepted."

It was the first of many public programs that the anti-war group would support or present in coming years.

Especially as the Vietnam War began in full force, the tiny but stalwart band of believers would give the community another way of viewing the matter of settling differences through bloodshed.

"The religious society of Friends is Christian based," said Ford (no relation to former President Gerald R. Ford and his wife, Betty). "Just about anyone can find a basis for worshipping with us. We don't have a doctrine. Some Friends do believe in the divinity of Christ; some don't."

Few at the start and still small today, the Grand Rapids Quakers have exerted a lasting influence. Begun in fall 1961 in a meeting room at the Central YWCA, the local society always has combined worship with social action.

In 1968, at the height of the Vietnam War, this action came in the form of peace protests. In August of that year, the Friends sponsored an anti-war rally outside the downtown federal building to "protest the alleged hypocrisy of the Paris Peace talks and urge a cease-fire in

FIGURE 11 Ethel Dungan on Calder Plaza silently protests the Vietnam War.

South Vietnam and an immediate end to the bombing of North Vietnam," Ford said.

In 1971, the local Friends helped establish the West Michigan American Friends Committee, a local chapter of the group's national social action organization. The AFC was the forerunner of what became the Institute for Global Education. With young Church of the Brethren intern Mark Kane as director, the group began to offer programs and seminars and to address issues close to the hearts of Quakers.

The AFC also helped to start walks for hunger, food pantries and food banks, peace alliances and peace rallies. It was instrumental in convincing Grand Rapids city officials to go on record as one of the first cities to divest funds from South Africa, said Kane, who eventually left the job and became a psychiatric social worker in Grand Rapids.

The AFC, Kane added, is only one aspect of Quakerism. Many members of the service committee aren't actually members of the society. Attraction to the principles of pacifism drew him to the group.

"One of the old quotes of Quakerism is that service begins after worship," he said. "Out of their faith came the committee. It was not formed to convert anybody."

Quakerism was founded in 17th century England by George Fox. From the start, Quaker beliefs brought persecution to members. Even locally, many Friends have had to remove their names from the phone book because of the vicious calls they would receive after participating in anti-war activities, Ford said.

A guiding force in the local group was Ethel Watts Dungan, who was born in England in December 1894. She was a dedicated Quaker all her days. After her husband, Eugene, retired as a teacher in the Chicago area, the couple moved to Alto and helped to begin the Friends meeting group.

For almost four years in the late 1960s, Ethel and Eugene stood in a silent vigil every Thursday at noon on the Calder Plaza in downtown Grand Rapids. They were there, grim and grieving, to protest the ongoing violence in Vietnam. Ethel Dungan died in December 1986.

Current members said they have no doubts the Dungans would have been on the front lines, carrying signs and candles, in January 1991 when the Friends organized protests against President George Bush's attack on Saddam Hussein's forces in Iraq.

Operation Desert Storm brought Quakers and their supporters into the streets again. As in most times of military crisis, the small society grew in numbers. The handful of core worshippers were joined in their Sunday meetings by a few others who also wanted to worship in silence for an end to the fighting.

But once the war ended, the numbers dwindled and the dozen or so members once again lapsed into their weekly silence alone.

"Silent worship, which we do, is not that easy," Ford said. "People seem to need more structure. They may agree with us as far as our testimonies, but they go to church elsewhere. Even so, we've probably been more active in this community than our numbers would indicate."

FIGURE 12 Calder Plaza Vietnam War protests.

had grown to 175 members, added on some classrooms, and joined the Assemblies of God, the largest national fellowship in the Pentecostal movement. But there it stayed. The spontaneous worship the members prized sometimes spilled over into confusion, as tongues-speaking, dancing in the Spirit, and the "fire baptism" of the Holy Ghost confirmed outsiders' opinion of them as a bunch of "holy rollers." Their all-night prayer vigils produced promises of a great future, but their present reality seemed rather middling.[3]

The church did grow some over the 1940s and 1950s with the suburban boom that doubled Wyoming's population, but in the process developed two different minds about its course. In 1955 the congregation bought a lot on 52nd Street SW and drew up blueprints for a 1,000-seat sanctuary, but fears of so large a financial burden undid the plan and the indecision caused some members to leave.

Instead, a new structure went up on the existing site in 1960–1961, with a capacity to seat 50 percent more than the 300 members on the books. By all tokens, First Assembly was looking at a normal, suburban future. Its pastor in the mid-1960s, Gene Hogan, stressed reverence and order in worship; their softball team won the South YMCA championship in 1966; their new kitchen and fellowship hall accommodated pleasant church suppers and youth gatherings. The same core families carried on as they had for years: the Bullises, Haights, Husseys, Millers, Stearnses, and Van Stees.[4]

Meanwhile, the nation was in tumult. Riots and racial acrimony, student rebellion and political corruption, all fueled by a bad war in southeast Asia, created a radical climate that affected religion, too. Theologians discussed the death of God and the relativity of morals; church executives designed programs relevant to social activists. In this unlikely context, Pentecostalism exploded. Thousands of youth in the streets, but also adults in the pews, found the divine intimacy of tongues-speaking. Miraculous healings did not seem so strange next to hippies, hashish, and the Hare Krishnas. Old-line Pentecostal churches reaped a good part of this harvest. After plateauing nationally at 400,000 members in the late 1950s, the Assemblies of God spurted to 600,000 by 1970, 1.5 million by 1980, and 2.2 million today.[5] Much of this growth came from the initiative of congregations like First Assembly.

First Assembly felt the boom in the early 1970s as attendance taxed the church's 450-seat capacity. Again the question of expansion arose, and again some members of the assembly left, including its minister, Burdette Faulk, who began a new church in Grandville in 1974. In calling 28-year-old M. Wayne Benson to replace him, the majority who remained found a leader with the vision for making the old prophetic promises come true.[6] "I don't want to knock what the other pastor [Faulk] had done," Benson recounted to The Grand Rapids *Press*, "but the church was just not alive" when he arrived. He encouraged the members to clap and raise their hands in worship

again — old Pentecostal gestures that had been subdued in the quest for reverence. As a former recording artist and minister of music at Brightmoor Tabernacle in northwest Detroit, Benson also tuned the congregation in to the new celebrative wave in Christian popular music. He had learned as well from his pastor at Brightmoor Tabernacle, Bond Bowman, to dissolve some of the old Pentecostal legalisms. The caricature of a gray-dressed, black-shoed lady with hair in a bun gave way to a more youthful style, permitting jewelry and make-up, shorter skirts and pants-suits, all formerly forbidden. The congregation's new freedom of praise and worship caught the national mood exactly. "People are tired of religion, tired of the dead, dry liturgy," Benson explained. "They are looking for an expression of their love. We allow that — no, we promote that — here." [7]

But in the mid-1970s people also were hungry for moral direction, and First Assembly's pulpit prescribed it with conviction. As much as personal life was to be filled with the Spirit, it was to follow the precise words of Scripture, taken to be infallible and unchanging. While the church's earlier leaders had gone by the old Pentecostal title, Brother, Benson was called Pastor from the start, befitting his authority in the congregation (who are known as "sheep"), over the associate ministers (who report to him), and over the elders (whom he appoints). Benson has been careful to avoid the potential abuses of this structure by sharing the pulpit with his associates, by deferring to their counsel

and expertise, and — especially — by leaving financial matters in the hands of congregationally elected deacons.[8] Yet this plural leadership has carried forward a single vision, a vision that divides the world into stark halves and defines the believers' duty with unmistakable clarity.

Believing that God directly touches lives also opens the possibility of devilish counterfeits. In fact, in the world view of First Assembly, Satan is a pressing force at all times and places, requiring the equal and opposite action of the Holy Spirit, cultivated by prayer, for protection. This spiritual warfare absorbs all of life, personal and national. The membership hears regular warnings against dabbling in the occult, against the demons (meant literally) of addiction, against the seductions of mysticism and rock music. On the national scene, the battle is against the secular humanism it sees in the teaching of evolution and the banning of formal prayer in public schools, in abortion and homosexual behavior, in radical feminism and other assaults on the two-parent, male-headed home.[9]

First Assembly provides a two-pronged message fit to the age: warmth and warfare, expressiveness and control, personal fulfillment and taut authority. The result has been a massive influx of people. By the assembly's account, half of them come from the ranks of the unchurched; the rest move from other churches after having caught the Pentecostal spirit. By Benson's third year, 1977, First Assembly had regained capacity crowds (attendance averaged 467) at the Bellevue

FIGURE 15
First Assembly of God held services in a tent when the City of Wyoming would not let the church open its new building on 44th Street SW due to code violations.

building, prompting the purchase of a 24-acre site on 44th Street SW. The next year they moved into a 1,500-seat sanctuary there and immediately felt a lift. Average attendance rose to 822 in 1979, 1,330 in 1980, 1,906 in 1981 (one morning service becoming two), 2,600 in 1982, 2,900 in 1983, 3,230 in 1984 (two becoming three). With mathematical regularity, attendance would level off at 80 percent of seating capacity and soar again when more services were added.[10] The latest plateau came in 1988 (at 3,830), spurring plans for the 5,000-seat sanctuary that was dedicated May 31–June 7, 1992. If this growth curve continues, First Assembly can expect attendance of 8,000 (80 percent of 5,000 at each of two morning services) sometime in the 1990s. That would accomplish its part of the national Assemblies' "Decade of Harvest" campaign which is designed to "thrust us into the year 2000 with a century-climaxing siege against the powers of darkness." [11]

If its growth curve continues, First Assembly can expect attendance of 8,000 (80 percent of 5,000 at each of two morning services) sometime in the 1990s. That would accomplish its part of the national Assemblies' "Decade of Harvest" campaign which is designed to "thrust us into the year 2000 with a century-climaxing siege against the powers of darkness."

All this "clothing for the body," as the buildings are called, costs money: $1.2 million for the 1978 structure; $5 million for a 31,000-square-foot office and educational complex completed in 1984; $12 million for the 1992 sanctuary, of which $4 million is paid and $2 million more pledged.[12] These sums have come in regularly as the congregation always has proceeded to its next proj-ect with its previous debts liquidated. The church's literature cites these figures and more — numbers about building dimensions, recorded salvations, and attendance averages — side by side with testimonies of revelations and healings, of miracles great and small. First Assembly is spirit and statistics, technology and transcendence, in one bubbling brew. Similar contrasts carry through all its life. On one

Sunday the congregation hears of a tender God who wants nothing more than to give his children a miracle. On another the picture changes to a righteous Judge who lets the unrepentant suffer pointedly for their sins. The mammoth services on Sunday offer anonymity for the casual and the encouragement of mass numbers for the committed, while small care groups (ideally, of 20 members each) meet twice a month in members' homes to give close attention to individual needs. From prayer to counseling to financial aid, First Assembly takes care of its own.[13] Care for the outside world takes the form of evangelism: "prayer warfare" against the forces of evil, elaborate Christmas and Easter pageants for the curious, a rescue mission for downtown street people, and bold prophecies of becoming a "fountainhead church in the greater Grand Rapids area impacting this community, in fact the world, with the life-changing message of Jesus Christ." [14]

First Assembly has come a long way toward that goal, but it also has left something behind. Its worship negotiates between rejoicing and respectability, still nervous about the holy-roller stigma. It expects but does not require water baptism, Spirit baptism (with tongues as initial evidence), and allegiance to behavioral taboos. To one of Pete Fairbairn's granddaughters, Donna Kamen, these amount to a fatal compromise that made her leave First Assembly for a stricter fellowship on the old model.[15] To others, these are the tensions of creative witness. Managing them without betraying the Spirit is the church's first challenge for the future. The second is measuring the next age as deftly as it has the latest one for the promise of the Great Day to come.

THE GOSPEL'S SONG

If Grand Rapids ever comes together as a city, it is in June at the downtown Festival. That event concludes to the singing of the Bethel Pentecostal Church gospel choir. The group has been bringing its message into churches of every denomination for more than 30 years, but on this occasion it stands at the heart of the entire city. Its style is black gospel, its theology is Pentecostal Christian, but its message of freedom, joy, and hope can cut across every color and creed.

Just that promise marked Pentecostalism at its birth when the fire of the Spirit burned through social prejudice as well as personal sin. The movement began its worldwide spread from a 1,000-day revival (1906–1909) at the Azusa Street mission in Los Angeles. Those meetings were led by an itinerant black preacher, William Seymour, and their interracial audience typified Pentecostal gatherings for some years to come. By the 1920s, however, the color line reasserted itself and the movement became as segregated as the denominational churches it scorned.

Pentecostals also fell into theological quarrels. The most seri-ous involved the doctrine of the Trinity, as some members rejected the orthodox formula adopted in the fourth century in favor of what they took to be the original Christian position of "Jesus only." This became known as the "apostolic" or "Oneness" teaching: God was one person (not three-in-one), manifest in creation as Father, in redemption as Son, and in the human soul as Holy Ghost, but was to be acknowledged by Christians simply as Jesus. Oneness fellowships, black and white, are set apart by their baptizing believers in the name of Jesus only.

In black America, Oneness teaching fared better in the volatile Midwest than in the

FIGURE 16
The Bethel Pentecostal Choir closes another Festival in downtown Grand Rapids.

FIGURE 17
A service at Elder Horace Young's home in the early 1950s.

longer-settled South. The predominantly black Oneness denomination, the Pentecostal Assemblies of the World (PAW), became centered from the 1920s on in Indianapolis; Columbus, Ohio; and Chicago.[16] For years it tried to be genuinely biracial in testimony to the unity of all believers in Christ. It maintained racial parity of bishops even after most whites had left the denomination. This stance brought the PAW honor later during the civil rights movement, but demographic realities also enabled it to further black dignity and cultural traditions.

All these forces played out in Grand Rapids in the formation of Bethel Pentecostal Church. Pentecostalism had arrived here very early, in the 1908 tour of Frank Bartleman, a missionary of the Azusa Street revival. By 1917 a Oneness church, the Apostolic Faith Assembly, was holding services on South Division Avenue; by 1923 it moved to the corner of Rena Street and Ionia Avenue SW where it still stands today.[17] In 1950 the members of the Rena Street Mission were mostly white but invited an African-American, Elder Horace Young from Springfield, Ohio, to hold a revival and, in effect, to be a candidate for their vacant pulpit. Young lost the congregational vote by a very slim margin to Lawrence E. Brisbin, a white pastor who would become Presiding Bishop of the PAW in the 1980s. The assembly's black families believed that racial bias had tilted the vote, so when Elder Young received permission from his regional supervisors to begin another church in town, they followed him. The group organized as Bethel Pentecostal Church in Young's home at 4639 Potter Ave. SE — as it happened, just a mile southeast of First Assembly.[18]

Few as they were (only 30), Bethel's members soon outgrew their pastor's quarters; besides, his bathtub was an adequate but hardly edifying baptistry. So they purchased Sinz's drugstore at Sherman Street and Eastern Avenue SE, adding one more entry to the notable roster of churches that neighborhood has produced.

If others noticed Bethel in the 1950s, it was as a typical storefront church. Its facilities were not much advanced beyond the Young home. As the church records note:

"One of the major problems, among many, was the furnace. The aging coal furnace had but one register in the center of the Church and during the frigid winter months, the saints found it as cold inside as out, due to the burned out fire. The Brothers would then raise the trap door to the basement and squeeze down in their white shirts and suits to build another fire, and more often than not, there would be more smoke than heat. In

FIGURE 20
Basting chicken on the grill at the Bar-Be-Q Hut in October 1969. Bethel Pentecostal Church operated the business to raise money for a new building.

spite of all the difficulties, the saints felt (and rightly so) they were highly blessed to have a place to worship their God." [19]

More annoying was the ridicule of passers-by who would peek in the open door on hot summer nights and laugh at the "primitive" goings-on. Nor could the congregation claim much status. Bethel's original board members were factory workers, a waiter, and a dealer in second-hand furniture; even 20 years later its associate ministers still worked full-time on the outside as custodian and produce manager at Meijer Inc.[20]

When Elder Young left for a San Antonio church in 1961, Bethel Pentecostal received its future in the person of William Abney, whom Young had tapped as his successor. Detroit-born (again, like First Assembly's Wayne Benson), Abney grew up as the oldest of 11 children, tutored by eminent PAW pastors and nurtured by a restaurateur father who also made the family adept at music.[21] Abney brought all these traits to Grand Rapids: a deep loyalty to the denomination, the people skills of the entrepreneur, a concern for young people which had distinguished his 12 years of service as the PAW's national youth director, and the musical talent that would put Bethel on the local map.

Abney first worked to improve the church facility, redecorating the interior to make it less an ex-drugstore and more a sanctuary. By 1968 the congregation set out to erect an entirely new building on site, raising money by taking over a day-old bakery outlet across the street and, more famously, selling chicken barbecue in supermarket parking lots around town. They even established the Bar-Be-Q Hut at 1300 S. Division Ave., a block east of the Rena Street church. After a year of construction, the new church was dedicated in April 1970 with two weeks of festivities featuring PAW dignitaries and local African-American preachers. These could well pay tribute; Bethel was on the move to becoming the

FIGURE 21
Bethel Pentecostal Church building at Cherry Street and Madison Avenue SE was purchased from Central Christian Church in 1972.

Grand Rapids' Link to Islam

Gathered in the easternmost corner of a building that once housed a Jehovah's Witnesses congregation, about 20 male followers of the prophet Muhammed offer prayers in Arabic to Allah.

As the men sink to their knees, bow low and continue their rituals of praise, a half-dozen women do the same in a room in the back of the Islamic Center of Grand Rapids.

The group of men and women are observing a form of worship that began in Grand Rapids in the late 1950s in a former dance hall on South Division Avenue.

From the start, the Muslim movement in West Michigan has been small and mostly quiet.

The groups worshipping in Grand Rapids for a time were divid-

FIGURE 22

Noah Seifullah at Madison Square in 1992.

ed into two strains — those following the tenets of the worldwide Islamic faith and those who adhered to the Nation of Islam, the so-called Black Muslim movement.

Islam was brought to West Michigan in the late 1950s by Black Muslim leader Malcolm X who was then traveling the country and establishing meeting centers for the Chicago-based Nation of Islam.

The Nation of Islam disappeared in Grand Rapids in the mid-1970s when the Honorable Elijah Muhammad, founder of the movement, died. Followers of the religion at that time joined the larger, worldwide Islamic movement. In the early 1990s, the Nation of Islam no longer had a formal worship place in Grand Rapids.

"When I first came here to this country in 1974 it was very rare to hear much about Islam," said Ghulam Malik, an early founder of the Islamic Center. "That is changing. Now a day doesn't go by that you don't read or hear about Islam. I've seen quite a turn. The response has been positive."

Malik came to the United States from Pakistan to study veterinary medicine. A veterinarian for the U.S. Department of Agriculture, he helped establish the Islamic Center of Grand Rapids by gathering a few of the faith's advocates in the basement of his home, and the homes of

a few others, for services and classes in the early 1980s.

Malik said many members of the center in 1993 were first-generation Americans. Of the 40 families who regularly attend services, the bulk were headed by men and women who moved to the United States from abroad. They are members of the Sunni sect of Islam and are connected to the Chicago-based Institute of Islamic Information and Education.

"We are practicing a way of life here," he said. "We are trying to say all of the prayers and perform all of our regular religious obligations and pass on our beliefs to our children."

The first Muslim meeting place in Grand Rapids was in a home on Baxter Street SE. From there, believers moved to a former dance hall on Division Avenue near Franklin Street SE. That group in turn moved to a building on Hall Street near Eastern Avenue SE and eventually landed for a few years in a storefront on Madison Avenue SE, south of Hall.

Najeeullah Muhammad is an African American who recalls attending one of the first Islamic services held in Grand Rapids.

"Most of the members at that time were African Americans, but it was very hard for us to grasp this faith," he said. "Islam was not something we pictured very easily in our minds."

One of the first leaders of that local group was Imam Noah A.A. Seifullah, a neighborhood activist and one of the people credited with transforming Madison Square, a decaying inner city business area, into a vital neighborhood again. In 1993, this group, which emerged out of the Nation of Islam, met in the board room of the Madison Square Co-operative with Seifullah as its leader.

"We've been nomads for many years. At one time in our transition, we had about 75 to 80 families worshipping with us," he said.

About 15 core families were attached to his group in 1993. Many others had moved to the Islamic Center. "There is no religious division between the Islamic Center and ourselves," Seifullah said. "We are people who have an affinity for the same beliefs but worship in different places."

Seifullah said he opened a masjid or mosque affiliated with the American Muslim Mission on Madison SE in the Madison Square Business District in 1982. A refurbished storefront, the mosque was closed in 1988 during a widespread renovation of the area.

> *"We are practicing a way of life here. We are trying to say all of the prayers and perform all of our regular religious obligations and pass on our beliefs to our children."*
>
> **— Ghulam Malik**

Seifullah credits his faith as the force that motivated him to work to convince the city to devote time and money to bring new life to the once-dilapidated area. "Our religion allowed us to take a broader view and we saw a way to turn around a destitute situation."

The Islamic Center of Grand Rapids emerged from the need of Middle Eastern immigrants to this country to worship as they were taught in their native lands.

From the basements of the founders, the center was moved in 1986 to a room at Fountain Street Church. Relations between the church and the center were strained, and the Muslims moved again, Malik said. The center found a permanent home in 1988 in the former Jehovah's Witnesses Kingdom Hall on Burton Street, east of Eastern SE.

The Islamic Center in 1993 had no imam, or official leader. The group was still small and hoped to grow and establish itself even more firmly into the spiritual fabric of Grand Rapids.

"As members of a non-Muslim society, we try to influence that society by the character of what we do," Malik said. "We don't cheat, don't lie, don't do drugs, don't eat pork. We hope we are contributing something positive by the way in which we live."

third-largest black congregation in town, behind True Light and Messiah Baptist. It achieved that rank by 1974, necessitating the purchase of its current structure at Cherry Street and Madison Avenue SE.[22] (The seller was Central Christian Church which had been founded a century before by emigres from the Cascade Disciples [see Chapter 8].)

Through it all the church became best known for its music. This is just, for music has been the crucible of black Pentecostal creativity and the heart of its worship.[23] After slavery, African Americans largely stopped singing spirituals, while its leading churches turned toward European hymnody. It was left to black commoners to find a new style, and that they did with the creation of gospel. Distilled out of secular jazz and blues, forged in the cauldron of Northern ghettoes, gospel voiced the struggle for hope and the joys of triumph in language that came out of

people's own lives. If elite churches frowned on rhythm and instrumentation, the black storefronts let fly with it all, without apology. If today's praise choruses at First Assembly sound like light-rock, Bethel's Pentecostals resound with a now-driving, now-weeping rhythm-and-blues. No worries about respectability here: Sundays witness slayings in the Spirit, holy dancing in the aisles, ecstatic trances, and testimonies of healing given with a twirl and shout to prove the point. If this verges on white stereotypes of "black," Bethel's people are not embarrassed as more elegant Negroes were 40 years ago. Today, charter member Dan Suttles notes, members of elite churches are clapping and raising their hands, too.[24] In any case, every form of behavior evident at Bethel was present 200 years ago in the great frontier revivals that birthed Protestant evangelicalism, black and white.

according to Donald Carew, chairman of Bethel's ruling board, "they got tired of their ho-hum '[high] society' services where they sat for an hour listening to a lecture." [25] The singing and preaching blend together to open the parishioners' souls to God's presence, fitting them for another week of combat with the forces of evil.

Today these forces confront Bethel in new as well as familiar forms. "The greatest challenge facing this church," says Carew, "is getting young people to grasp the education and hope that will lift them out of poverty and the culture of despair." That sounds a theme as old as Benjamin Franklin — and Booker T. Washington. But Bethel's vision goes a step farther. The second challenge, Carew adds, is to avoid "getting diluted with a waning spirituality" as a result of success.[26] That temptation has struck Pentecostals of every hue as the movement's own growth matches its members' prosperity. First Assembly was tainted with the fall of Assembly of God televangelists Jimmy Swaggart and Jim Bakker, the latter of whom dangled his handicapped second cousin, First Assembly member Kevin Whittum, as bait for donations during the worst of his scandal. Bethel was grieved by the tragedy of the DeBarge brothers, Elder Abney's nephews, who leaped from the church choir into a national recording career, only to have some of them fall over allegations of assault and convictions for drug-carrying.[27] Prosperity has another lure, too, as some of the church's youth have left for an easier Pentecostalism which does not demand, as Bethel still does, full Spirit-baptism and a strict behavioral code.

But prosperity also can bring opportunities. Elder Abney's long service to his denomination was recognized by the PAW's 1992 national convention which named him a suffragan (assistant) bishop. Locally, he has been urged more than once to run for

FIGURE 23
Bethel Pentecostal's choir performing at Fountain Street Church.

FIGURE 24
The map locates sites and other landmarks for Bethel Pentecostal Church and St. Joseph the Worker Catholic Church.

Bethel holds fast to an Afro-, indeed, to an all-American tradition, but not for tradition's sake. As Elder Abney says, "Fervent worship … is the cutting edge of the church everywhere today because that's how you meet and hold and affect people." Bethel Pentecostal believes just as much as First Assembly in the present threat of Satan and the necessity of the Spirit's Power to combat it. That Power has been the church's chief attraction from the start. Most of its members were not raised Pentecostal but converted from other denominations because,

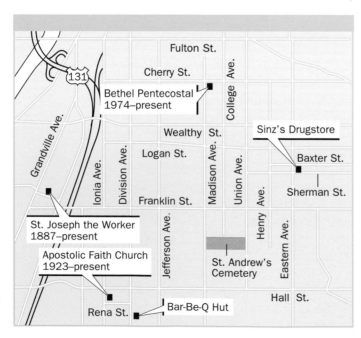

political office, and has preached on notable community occasions, such as the Martin Luther King commemoration in January 1993. But the congregation's civic involvement largely has followed the vision of a church-based, holistic social ministry. That vision now centers on a plan to address the challenges of both poverty and prosperity by building a new structure in the inner city. Besides a sanctuary for worship, it would offer a gymnasium, drug-rehabilitation facility, safe housing for single women and the elderly, and a day-care center for the children of working parents. Fittingly, the building's proposed name echoes Pentecostalism's original theme: Bethel, the "house of God," will become the Abundant Life Center.[28]

OLD CHURCH, NEW TIMES

At 9 o'clock on Sunday morning, 250 people pack themselves into St. Joseph the Worker Roman Catholic Church. They certainly have not come for architectural magnificence, for the little building at 333 Rumsey St. SW (near the Franklin Street exit of the U.S. 131 expressway) is but one story tall, clad in aluminum siding. The interior has more appeal, its simple stained glass windows and small statues creating a warm, close atmosphere. The attraction grows as the service begins to a trio of gui-

tar, accordion, and tambourine playing a lilting folk melody. Wherever these people have come from this morning — from the Grandville Avenue corridor to the southwest, from city neighborhoods three or four miles away, even from rural townships in northern Kent County — almost all of them have come within living memory from another country. They gather at St. Joseph's to worship in their native Spanish and to receive guidance for adapting to a new country amid straining circumstances.

As it is today at St. Joseph's, so it was at the beginning. The church, named after the

FIGURE 25
The Rev. Henry Frencken stands in front of St. Joseph's rectory in 1895.

FIGURE 26
St. Joseph's church and school in 1888.

Flights to Freedom

The Rev. Howard Schipper and his wife, Marybelle, were awaiting a flight home from California when they confronted a rare opportunity. Gathered at one end of the airplane were a half-dozen Vietnamese refugees recently rescued from dire circumstances in Southeast Asia. The children, the Schippers learned on that day in 1975, were bound for new, safer homes in the Boston area.

Almost immediately, Howard Schipper thought of the words the Rev. Robert Schuller had delivered only a day earlier at a conference in the Crystal Cathedral in Garden Grove. The popular Reformed Church in America telepreacher had been challenging the Schippers and the other men and women at the church-growth conference to put their Christian faith into practice. Dream big, he had told them, and do it with God's purpose in mind.

In their seats on the airplane roaring back to Grand Rapids, Howard and Marybelle Schipper gazed at the refugee children and did just that. They dreamed big. And between them was born one of the handful of successful resettlement programs to be established in the United States in the years following the Vietnam War.

"We were responding to pure, explosive need," said Schipper, pastor of Bethany Reformed Church in Grand Rapids at the time he launched the effort out of which was soon spawned the Freedom Flight Refugee Center. "We thought we would bring a few families to this country over the next year. We believed there was something we could do to help."

As it turned out, his prediction of helping only a few families was modest. The next year has turned into nearly two decades and a few families became several thousand families and individuals. By 1993, this church-sponsored program to give war-ravaged men, women and children a new start on life had helped bring more than 8,000 Southeast Asian refugees to West Michigan.

"Nearly every denomination in the Grand Rapids area became involved," said Marybelle Schipper, director of the refugee center, which operates out of a storefront on Alger Street SE.

For decades, refugees from war, famine and other disasters had been seeking a new start in this country. Grand Rapids had been the destination for many, especially Poles, Germans, Dutch, and some Slavs following World War II. In many instances, these people had come here under the sponsorship of an individual church.

In the early 1950s, dozens of Hungarian families came to West Michigan following a tumultuous uprising in their homeland. Soon after Soviet tanks rolled into Budapest, Hungarians who had been seeking a different political path found themselves in flight. A percentage of these, at the urging of a few RCA congregations, sought asylum in West Michigan. A few years later, the Chris-

FIGURE 27 The Rev. Howard Schipper and refugee family in 1975.

tian Reformed Church brought several Cuban refugees — those marked for death or imprisonment by Fidel Castro — to safety in Grand Rapids.

But none of these efforts was on the scale of that undertaken by Howard Schipper and the Freedom Flight Refugee Center in the wake of the fall of Saigon.

"The local community opened its heart and its home to my people," said Lai Tran, a refugee who came to this country in 1978 and eventually was named director of the refugee resettlement effort for the Catholic Diocese of Grand Rapids.

Early on, the U.S. government as well as many other groups and organizations in this county opposed resettlement of Southeast Asian refugees. The prevailing attitude was to keep them outside of U.S. borders and to offer them aid to be used elsewhere, preferably in their homeland. Schipper and others, however, believed this country and its people had an obligation to refugees who could no longer remain safely in their own country. Purges were commonplace; facing a life of torture in jail was reality for many who had supported the American cause in Vietnam.

"I was overwhelmed by the plight of the refugees, and vexed by the apathy of many Americans," said Schipper, who eventually became general secretary of the RCA in West Michigan.

Starting in June 1975 and running into the next few years, nearly 3,000 refugees were given a new start in the Grand Rapids area. Facing new language, customs, climate and other hardships, they worked to become part of the daily fabric of their new community. Those who came to West Michigan were among the initial refugees who fled South Vietnam after the war. Schipper and his supporters assumed once they were comfortable the job would end.

That wasn't the case. In subsequent years, the Freedom Flight Refugee Center and then the Catholic Human Development Office found themselves helping to locate and then reunite family members of those who came to West Michigan in the first wave. In addition, they dedicated themselves to finding homes for those Laotians, Cambodians, Thais and Vietnamese who fled their troubled countries in boats in the late 1970s and early 1980s. These "boat people" — many of whom escaped their dangerous homes only to face worse trauma at sea — also left behind families that eventually were brought over.

Reunification became in the years following the war an important dimension of the resettlement efforts.

"Our role has been to see to the complete resettlement task, to bring families back together. We offer all of the core services," said Lai Tran of the Catholic Human Development Office. "We are the go-between. We help them with their health, education, and employment."

By integrating into the population of West Michigan, the Southeast Asian refugees joined the many others — the East Europeans, the Latin Americans, and other Asians — who had come before them. And there were others whom churches helped set up in homes here in the years following Vietnam. Poles escaping the domination of the country by Communist influence, Ethiopians leaving behind famine, and Salvadorans fleeing the dreaded right-wing death squads found a roof, food, and a new start.

Many of these refugees found jobs, started businesses, went to college and began congregations, not all of them Christian. Two Buddhist temples, for example, sprang up in the region following the movement of Southeast Asian peoples from one side of the world to another.

In all, refugees varied in how well they melded into the pot that was America. Some thrived; others languished. Some churches shined in the works they performed; others decided to play little or no role in the effort, deciding instead that their faith called them to other forms of action or inaction.

The Freedom Flight Refugee Center has continued to offer its mission of mercy and amalgamation. Although the numbers have slowed in the early 1990s, the center was still open, providing valuable immigration service to those in need.

Howard Schipper credits many in West Michigan, from politicians to school superintendents, from social service agencies to businesses, with making the process a success. For him, the arms of Christ opened and those suffering the after-effects of a particularly unpopular war were given another chance by churches across Grand Rapids.

"It is a marvel that the resettlement process has worked as well as it has, even if it is adjudged to be greatly lacking," Schipper once wrote. "The success is a tribute to the continuing assistance given primarily by the compassionate church and individual sponsors, and to the few organizations that responded with help."

> *"We were responding to pure, explosive need ... We believed there was something we could do to help."*
>
> **— The Rev. Howard Schipper, Freedom Flight Refugee Center**

patron of labor and protector of the poor, remains a working-class parish struggling to absorb immigrants. Two major differences apply. A hundred years ago the worshippers were Dutch observing the traditional Mass. Today they are Latinos participating in a folk service, courtesy in part of the broader latitude offered by the Second Vatican Council. Like these immigrants, American Catholicism as a whole is seeking to renew an old faith in an altered world.

St. Joseph's was born in 1887 as the fifth Roman Catholic congregation in Grand Rapids and as one of the few Dutch-language parishes in the nation. Bishop Henry Richter had commissioned Father Cornelius Roche to lay the foundation of the church the year before, and that he did — a 74-by-42-foot rectangle set only 18 inches deep, allowing Calvinist rascals in the neighborhood to steal the cornerstone. This and a $69 kitty greet-

ed Father Henry Frencken when he arrived in town from his native Belgium, 27 years old and newly ordained, on Sept. 14, 1887.[29]

For the next 20 years Frencken struggled to collect money, erect buildings, and answer charges that St. Joseph's, as an ethnic church, was stealing members from territorial parishes. Money was the perennial problem. For his constant appeals to every source, Frencken noted, "they can call me rightly 'St. Joseph's beggar.'" He had to take the parish's $1,800 debt onto his personal account to get the bishop to consecrate the church in 1889. To get the building finished at all, he had added his own sweat to that of his parishioners.

"As the people wanted to see something done," Frencken recalled, *"we did not do anything to the poor foundation but Mr. [Peter] Workman [a carpenter in the parish] started the upper structure which was to be veneered. Soon*

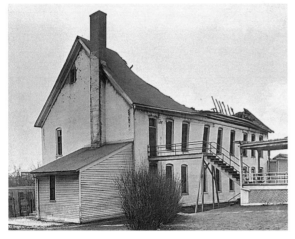

FIGURE 29
Rear view of St. Joseph's Church after a fire in 1943.

FIGURE 31
The interior of St. Joseph's
Church on Easter 1938.

the first story rose, but the difficulty was, how to get all the lumber, rafters, joists, shingles, in fact all that was necessary to build the second story and the roof. As most parishioners were working men, they were asked to come to the building evenings after supper and help Mr. Workman hoist all that was necessary for the second story and the roof. This went on fine for 20 or 25 strong men came, whenever we wanted them; there was no prohibition and a glass of beer was all they received as temporal reward, whilst God, Who saw their zeal to build a house for Him, surely would reward them spiritually. Of course, I was always present such evenings, and in the day time I used the hammer and the saw as good as a carpenter." [30]

The building was a combination church, school, and rectory. Frencken got separate quarters in 1891 to get away from the school noises and gave his old rooms to the nuns who taught there. Holding evening parish meetings upstairs from the sisters' quarters fueled Protestant gossip, however, so a separate fellowship hall came next. The sisters finally got their convent in 1903. All these struggles were tolerable; the friction over parish boundaries was not. When in 1906 Frencken got wind of the diocese's plans to start Holy Name parish farther down Grandville Avenue, he quit and returned to Belgium. Apparently life there was less aggravating; he died in 1953, aged 93. [31]

Its neighborhood offered St. Joseph's a constant change of fortunes. The number of Dutch on the near Southwest Side increased 80 percent between 1880 and 1900 to constitute some half of the area's residents. When the Grand Rapids & Indiana Railroad arrived (almost simultaneously with Frencken), the center of the Dutch community shifted south to Franklin and Grandville, close by the new church. But most of the newcomers were Protestant. Although Catholics composed 40 percent of the Netherlands' population, they were only 20 percent of Dutch immigrants and tended to head for Wisconsin rather than Michigan. Besides, the Franklin-Grandville enclave had the second-highest rate of renters in Dutch Grand Rapids, which fueled an exodus over the next decades toward Clyde Park. [32] This, along with Frencken's exit, complicated St. Joseph's future. Four Franciscan priests of German descent served the parish from 1906 through 1928, steering it through the language change. After 1928, pastors were appointed by the diocese and reflected the arrival of other ethnic groups onto the parish roster. Fewer than half the children baptized in the 1930s had Dutch surnames; Germans, Irish, and Poles supplied the rest, and these were joined in the 1940s by many Italians. [33]

The group faced its sternest test on April 15, 1943, when a fire destroyed its main building. The lower floor, housing the school, had held 130 pupils but an hour before the fire was discovered; the church on

FIGURE 32
The Rev. Steven D.
Cron came to St.
Joseph's in 1985.

the upper floor was destroyed, and the collapse of the roof nearly killed fireman and St. Joseph's parishioner Peter Dutmers. For the next nine years, the congregation worshipped in the fellowship hall next door. It salvaged the old structure for the school and finished the present church building in 1952. In between came the events that signaled the parish's future — a Hispanic baptism in 1948 and a Hispanic wedding in 1950.[34]

That future was sealed by a steady flow of Latino arrivals over the next 25 years. By 1975, parish membership was two-thirds Hispanic; it is 95 percent Hispanic today. A few of that number are Cubans who fled to the United States after Fidel Castro's revolution in 1959. Nearly half are Mexicans — or more often Mexican-Americans — who started coming to the Midwest as seasonal farm workers in the 1950s and eventually left the migrant stream to settle here. Just as many are Puerto Ricans who gravitated to Grand Rapids from larger cities, usually Chicago.[35]

The people who have found their way to St. Joseph's form a fraction of the Latino influx into the area. The U.S. census counted 10,588 people of Spanish origin or descent in Kent County in 1970, 14,684 in 1990. St. Joseph's Sunday attendance averages 450: 250 at the 9 a.m. Spanish service and 200 at the 11 a.m. English. About 300 families attend services at least occasionally; 700 to 800 families have a loose affiliation with the parish. Even counting the 200 souls who attend the Guadalupe chapel at St. Andrew's Cathedral and, perhaps, a like number worshipping in outlying townships, only a small percentage of the area's Hispanics are participating institutionally in the religion of their birth.[36]

Latino history and culture account for some of this estrangement. Historically, Roman Catholic officials in Latin America lived at the top of a two-tier society, creating suspicion among the common people. The latter readily identified themselves as Catholics but practiced the faith in their own way. Catholicism meant personal devotion to one's patron saint. It meant family cohesion. It meant being part of the pueblo — the people or community — in its festivities and allegiances. It did not necessarily include formal structures, doctrine, or sacramental observances. As in other traditional cultures, for Latinos the sacred was not a separate space but a lively presence in everyday activities.[37]

American culture, however, is anti-traditional: impersonal, segmented, bureaucratic, competitive. Adjusting from one culture to another has challenged every immigrant group, but Hispanics — especially those of Mexican or Puerto Rican origins — more than most. Less compelled to change languages, not separated from their home country by an ocean, many Hispanic Americans continue to live between or across two worlds, prolonging their first-generation stage. St. Joseph's, says its pastor, Father Steve Cron, must be the only church in town that reduces services at Christmas because so many parishioners have gone "home" for the holidays.[38]

These continuities enrich life, keep traditions strong, and resonate with Latino values. They also have tended in the past to reduce commitment to local projects and public life. Not just religiously but politically and socially, Grand Rapids' Hispanics have kept a low profile. This tendency has economic as well as cultural roots. While the Dutch arrived during the rise of the industrial system, Latinos have come in its decline.

St. Joseph's parishioners hold typical blue-collar jobs — at laundries, bakeries, food-processing plants, car-repair shops — and some still do seasonal farm labor; but the route out of such a way of life is narrower than ever. The consequences hit the church daily. A booming drug trade along Grandville Avenue ravages bodies, multiplies robberies to maintain habits, and triggers murders. Father Cron is on call at hospitals to visit shooting and drug overdose victims who have rarely been in church but count him as their pastor. Indeed, Cron says, "given a broad definition of 'parish,' our jail ministry wasn't really 'outreach' but a parish ministry. Unfortunately, we had to give it up because so many of our volunteers, though now clean, had records and so were considered security risks." Sometimes the threat of the street has cut very close indeed, as in the 1988 fire set by an arsonist in St. Joseph's sanctuary.[39]

Against these conditions, the parish has worked valiantly. As he has for all 15 years of his ministry (since 1985 at St. Joseph's), Father Cron regularly visits migrant labor camps during harvest season to hold services. The parish lends facilities to Alcoholics and Narcotics Anonymous and to the public schools for community education, all in the Spanish language. On its own it runs an emergency food and clothing outlet, a church school program (preschool through eighth grade) enrolling 230, a high school youth group of 50, an adult leadership training course, and a half-dozen small devotional groups. Much of this work has been conducted by Sister Pat Lamb who, along with Sister Marilyn Furtaw (in charge of visiting the sick and aged), are subsidized by the Sisters of Mercy, continuing a pattern of women's ministry to immigrants that American

> *"Can the diocese afford a small parish like St. Joseph's? Will other churches continue to subsidize us? Should they?"*
>
> **— The Rev. Steven D. Cron**

Catholicism has carried on for 200 years.[40]

Such resolution comes from challenges. St. Joseph's test today equals that of 100 years ago. Money is still a problem. Weekly offerings, the annual parish festival, and a food booth at the downtown Festival in June bring in about half of what the parish needs; the rest comes from the diocese and other parishes. Like Henry Frencken, Steve Cron worries about the future his successors will face. Finding a successor is the first challenge. While Frencken was one of six children, all of whom took religious vocations, today recruits into the American priesthood lag far behind retirements. Furthermore, where might such a successor work? "Can the diocese afford a small parish like St. Joseph's?" Cron wonders. "Will other churches continue to subsidize us? Should they?"

Perhaps little St. Joseph's will be merged with St. Andrew's Cathedral, mighty in the days of Frencken's Bishop Richter but numbering a smaller, more multi-ethnic membership today. Will Latinos be willing to leave their enclaves for a downtown church that, psychologically, seems far away? Will

FIGURE 33
St. Joseph's Church in the 1960s.

The Legacy of Vatican II

FIGURE 34

Bishop Breitenbeck was bishop of the Diocese of Grand Rapids for two decades.

Even in his retirement as spiritual leader of the Roman Catholic Diocese of Grand Rapids, Joseph Breitenbeck continued to think regularly of the days that most shaped his ministry in West Michigan.

What the bishop remembered was his attendance at the Second Vatican Council — a monumental gathering of church officials that changed the lives of all Catholics.

Especially clear in the bishop's memory was the rain that fell for several days before the last scheduled meeting of the Council. In Rome as the newly consecrated auxiliary bishop of the Detroit Archdiocese, Breitenbeck recalled that tempers were short and spirits were damp. But on the morning of Dec. 8, 1965, bright sun broke through, washing the Vatican with a heavenly glow.

Joining his fellow bishops, archbishops and cardinals from around the world, Breitenbeck that day signed a document entitled "The Church in the Modern World."

Called to order and given its direction by Pope John XXIII, the Second Vatican Council was held to review church practices and bring some of them into line with contemporary thought, lifestyle and beliefs.

After the Council, the use of the Latin language diminished; priests were told to face the people instead of the wall when saying Mass; the ritual of Confession, in which a penitent spoke alone to a confessor, was broadened and people were asked to speak of their sins together, in public, instead of in the dark. Some prayers were dropped; others added. Statues and paintings — long traditional trappings of the church — were in some places removed. In their stead came more up-to-date furnishings and liturgical decorations.

At the time, Breitenbeck — who became bishop in Grand Rapids in 1969 and retired in 1989 — had no idea how the document would thoroughly disrupt a denomination that until then had been steeped, some said trapped, in tradition.

He spoke about the Second Vatican Council as well as his 40 years with the church in an interview with co-author Chris Meehan.

What was your reaction as you sat among the church hierarchy in Rome during the sessions of the Second Vatican Council?

This Vatican Council was totally different than any others. It spoke to everybody, not just Catholics, of goodwill. For the first time, we were speaking not just to our own but to the whole world. We were to make use of the medicine of mercy, rather than of severity. The basic statement in the whole document is dignity of the human person.

Were you surprised by the direction in which the Council moved the church?

I couldn't believe what I was hearing when I was over there (in Rome). We were learning that we might not have to have the Pope breathing down our backs. We were learning that we could start to think for ourselves. They were throwing out a church based on so much legalism — with authority here and authority there. For me it opened up a whole new vista.

Did you grow up as a Catholic hoping and praying for a change in the church's rigid structure?

My background was canon law. I was from the old school. I liked how it was. But as I made contacts with theologians at the Council, I began to see how much change was in store. They were talking about changing the liturgy to make it appeal more to the people. They were talking about opening up the whole church. I remember the time when it was almost forbidden to go to a Protestant funeral. Later on, I presided over the funeral of (Union Bank President) Ed Frey at St. Mark's Episcopal Church.

What is the biggest lesson that you took from the Council?

That we were to be friendly to people of other faiths. We had to ask what can we do to better our relationships with people of other faiths. The Council prompted me to go to Hope College once every year for a dialogue. We threw all of our differences on the table and talked them over. We wanted to know what made each other tick.

Back home, what did the Council mean in the parishes?

It was a big change. We were asked to set up parish councils to handle the affairs of the parish. These were all new ideas and some people, especially older pastors, couldn't understand why they were being asked to give up that responsibility. The people were actually beginning to run the churches for the first time. Some of the priests had a hard time adjusting. Also, there was the Mass in English. Some people didn't like that.

Some of the changes caused much dissension among the people in the pews.

That did happen. For example, there was a struggle over changing the inside of St. Andrew's Cathedral. There was a core group who wanted to run it and not change the altar or other things. They didn't want us to take down the Stations

of the Cross. I sat with that crowd a number of times. In the end we made the changes and the hard-core group left for somewhere else.

What was the hardest part of the changes for you?

One of the hardest things was trying to build up the morale of my priests. I wish I could have done more of that. I wish I could have spent more time out in the parishes, but there just wasn't the time to resolve all of the things that mushroomed into problems. There were times when I asked for ventilation, and I got a lot of ventilation coming back my way.

Near the end of your tenure as bishop, some of the people at St. Isidore's Church in Grand Rapids took you to court to block some of the changes being proposed for the inside of their church. Even though they lost and you won, was that painful?

Very much so. I have regretted that it had to go that way. When I listened to those people, even though many of them made it very personal, I had to say to myself that they weren't attacking me. They were attacking what I was doing. It was a hard time. There were even threats on my life. But I was just acting out the call of the Vatican Council. There were many changes and I was glad to be part of some of them.

FIGURE 35
Bishop Breitenbeck at nurses' graduation.

FIGURE 36

Grand Rapids' middle-class Catholics allow "their" cathedral to go Hispanic? What will happen to the neighborhood if St. Joseph's is empty? These are the local versions of a momentous national question. American Catholics today number some 60 million; the Latin-American population is 17 million and growing rapidly via migration and a high birth rate. Concerned clergy from Cron to the National Conference of Catholic Bishops insist that, much as Hispanics might need the church, the American church needs Hispanics. Anglo pride or neglect spells a constricted Catholic future, but the better alternative requires catalyzing people who have been reluctant to get involved.[41] On the other hand, since religious and civic involvement tend to rise with upward social mobility, the higher profile Latinos have

recently taken in local politics might augur a strong future for St. Joseph's.

The Pentecostal storefronts that dot the streets of the parish show another method of galvanizing devotion. They also testify to the campaign that evangelical groups have launched among Latinos in Grand Rapids as across the nation. Henry Frencken faced Protestant prejudice; Steve Cron faces proselytizing besides. For some in the neighborhood, Cron believes, the storefronts may be the only route back to the gospel; on the other hand, they divide families and the community's scarce resources. The storefronts' appeal lies partly in their democratic structure, since these are churches that Latinos can own and lead. Southern Baptists, for instance, ordain three times as many Hispanic pastors as do American Catholics.

FIGURE 36
One parting view of Grand Rapids taken in September 1991 just before the construction of Bridgewater Place. St. Adalbert's and St. Mary's stand boldly in the forefront as survivors of urban renewal and freeway construction.

Moreover, their pentecostal piety appeals to the personal orientation of Latino religion by its intimate connection with supernatural powers, its emotional sense of the faith, and its absolute moral standards.[42] All of these, some proselytes complain, have slipped in Catholicism since Vatican II.

At the same time, many American bishops have encouraged a charismatic renewal in their own territories. Cron's predecessor at St. Joseph's, the Rev. James Bozung, made it the centerpiece of his ministry. Some half dozen small groups in the parish still meet in each other's homes to carry on the cause today. For Cron the movement is a solid part, but only a part, of the whole. Like traditional Latino piety, the pentecostal type too must "get beyond self-absorption into service for others, into knowledge of the faith, and into the full life of the community." [43]

That life centers on the Sunday morning service, but the service points beyond the Sunday sanctuary to the rest of life. In keeping with the mandates of Vatican II, the bulletin lists Scripture readings for daily devotions; the entire service proceeds in the language of the people; the elements for the Eucharist are kept in the middle of the church until consecrated, then are distributed by laymen — and women. The homily lasts longer, too. This Sunday it happens to be based on Luke 13:22–30. Strive to enter in by the narrow door, the pastor says, echoing Jesus' words. Walk the proper way, *el camino bueno*. Use the gifts you have been given — prayer, Scripture, and sacraments — in honor of the Giver and on behalf of the needy all around you, in the pews and on the streets. For of such, the passage concludes, is the kingdom of God: "on the final day, the first shall be last, and the last first." [44]

As I write these words, the world is commemorating the 500th anniversary of Columbus' first voyage across the Atlantic. Over the 325 years following that event (1492–1817), six out of every seven people who followed him came from Africa; their legacy is present today at Bethel Pentecostal Church. The Spanish who made the crossing intermingled with the native peoples here; some of their descendants gather today at St. Joseph's.[45] There they worship in a church built by Europeans, who dominated the Atlantic crossing for another 125 years (1817–1942). The buildings were erected by Dutchmen for the sake of a faith that was pioneered here by Frederic Baraga, from Slovenia. In the week I wrote his story, that region was breaking away from Yugoslavia. Over the past 20 years, the First Assembly of God has flourished in the suburbs as First Methodist, First (Park) Congregational, and First (Fountain Street) Baptist did a century ago downtown.

Thus, if history does not exactly repeat itself, it certainly recycles and renews itself in the present, touching upon our lives every day. History does not save us but might, if we attend to it, grace us with some wisdom, with a better comprehension of our ancestors' legacy and of our own future. What that future holds for Grand Rapids and its congregations, God only knows. We honor that God and our future alike if we take from the past the better part of the faith that has animated thousands of people and the public life they built in this region. For the Odawa and the French, Hispanic and Hollander, Irish and Pole, German and generic American can acknowledge together, as have Christians and Muslims of all ages, the mandate of the ancient Jewish prophet: "What does the Lord require of you, but to do justice, to love mercy, and to walk humbly with your God?"

Directory of Congregations

The following is a directory of congregations in the Grand Rapids metropolitan area. It is not intended to give a complete history of each congregation, nor to provide a complete list of all pastors. These are skeleton outlines which, it is hoped, will enable the individual congregational researcher to flesh out the history more quickly. Here can be found the congregation's name (extant congregations are in bold print); last or current address; phone number; year organized; names by which the congregation was previously known; previous locations (in parentheses); the year the house of worship was built; the architect's name, if known; and the names and dates of service of the first pastor, the current pastor, and of pastors who had a particularly long or significant tenure in the community.

Every attention has been paid to try to incorporate the suggestions and additions received from the various congregations, but it was impossible to accommodate every request while keeping the format consistent and without appearing to show favoritism. Local church personnel were of great assistance in the compilation of the directory. Much of the original research material for this directory can be found in the Local Historical Collections at the Grand Rapids Public Library.

ABERDEEN REFORMED

1000 Aberdeen St. NE 49505; Phone: 361–0341.
RCA; Organized: 1925 as Aberdeen Street
Mission; Built: 1948; Addition: 1980.

1925–28	Rev. Garrett Flikkema
1928–43	Rev. John J. Fryling
1990–	Rev. Roger E. Eernisse

ADA BIBLE CHURCH

6015 Ada Drive SE 49546; Phone: 676–3137.
Undenominational; Organized: 1974; Built:
1990 (Perry & Associates).

1974–82	Rev. Joseph Smith
1983–	Rev. Jeff Manion

ADA CHRISTIAN REFORMED

7152 Bradfield St. SE 49301; Phone:
676–1698. Organized: 1909; Built: 1909 (J. &
G. Daverman); Built: 1958 (Dan Vos).

1911–15	Rev. Martin M. Schans
1921–42	Rev. H. Dekker
1990–	Rev. Douglas R. Fauble

ADA COMMUNITY REFORMED

7239 Thornapple River Drive SE 49301;
Phone: 676–1032. RCA; Organized: 1902;
Built: 1969 (Dan Vos).

1903–05	Rev. Seine J. Menning
1988–	Rev. Thomas J. Bartha

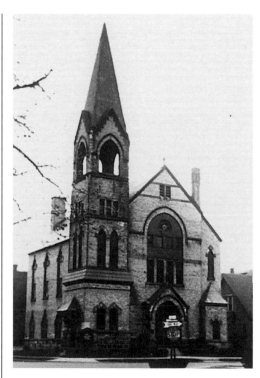

FIGURE 1

This structure at the southeast corner of Scribner Avenue and Second Street NW served the German Methodist Episcopal Church (1888–1920), the Ahavas Israel Congregation (1920–1949), and Unity Church (1949–1961) until it was removed for freeway construction in August 1961.

ADA CONGREGATIONAL
See **FIRST CONGREGATIONAL CHURCH OF ADA**

AFRICAN METHODIST EPISCOPAL
See **FIRST COMMUNITY AFRICAN METHODIST EPISCOPAL**

AHAVAS ISRAEL CONGREGATION
2727 Michigan St. NE 49506;
Phone: 949–2840. Conservative;
United Synagogue of America;
Organized: 1911; 1911–38 Ahavas
Achim Congregation; merged with
Congregation Beth Israel in 1938; (428
Scribner Ave. NW 1911–20; 528
Scribner NW 1920–52; 44 Lafayette
Ave. NE 1952–70); Built: 1970 (Henry
Pestka).
1911–20   Rabbi Zachary Kramer
1986–   Rabbi Michael L. Rascoe

ALDERSGATE UNITED METHODIST
4301 Ambrose Ave. NE 49505;
Phone: 363–3446. Organized: 1959;
Built: 1962 (William Vandenhout).
1959–64   Rev. Charles E. Fry
1981–92   Rev. William Johnson
1992–   Rev. Ellen A. Brubaker

ALEXANDER STREET
CHURCH OF GOD
See **NEW COVENANT COMMUNITY CHURCH**

ALGER PARK CHRISTIAN REFORMED
2655 Eastern Ave. SE 49507; Phone:
452–9686. Organized: 1952; Built: 1952
(Daverman).
1954–56   Rev. Anthony A. Hoekema
1987–   Rev. Ecko DeVries
1989–   Rev. Larry M. Fryling

ALL AMERICAN CITY'S FIRST BAPTIST
441 Bradford St. NE 49503; Phone:
363–6482. Organized: 1983; Built: 1903
as Bradford Street Mission.
1983–   Rev. David F. Franks

ALL NATIONS LILLIE WHITE
PENTECOSTAL MISSION
907 Logan St. SE. 1965–75.
1975   Rev. H.T. Turner

ALL–NATIONS PRAYER BAND
SPIRITUAL CHURCH
638 Ionia Ave. SW. 1965–72.

ALL NATIONS ST. JUDE
MISSION OF PRAYER
744 Grandville Ave. SW. 1955–83
(53 Buckley St. SW 1955–59; 639
Thompson Ave. SE 1959–65; 131
Antoine St. SW 1965–66; 666
Grandville SW 1966–67).
1955–83   Rev. Mrs. Rosetta A.
           Webb/Johnson

ALL NATION'S SPIRITUAL
See **NEW COVENANT COMMUNITY CHURCH**

ALL SOULS UNIVERSALIST
See PEOPLES CHURCH OF
GRAND RAPIDS

ALLEN ROAD GOSPEL CHAPEL
See **THIRTY SIXTH STREET CHRISTIAN REFORMED**

ALLIANCE CHAPEL
See CHRISTIAN MISSIONARY
ALLIANCE

ALPINE AVENUE
CHRISTIAN REFORMED
960 Alpine Ave. NW; Organized:
1881; Built: 1904 (Sidney J. Osgood).
1882–86   Rev. William H. Frieling
1886–1905 Rev. Peter Ekster
1966–90   Rev. John H. Bergsma
1990 Merged with Highland Hills
Christian Reformed to become
WESTEND CHRISTIAN REFORMED.

AMAZING GRACE CHURCH
922 Cherry St. SE 49506; Phone:
454–0922. Lutheran Missouri
Synod/ELCA; Organized: 1992.
1992–   Rev. Louis J. Miller

AMBASSADOR BAPTIST TEMPLE
1001 56th St. SW Wyoming 49509;
Phone: 538–0790. International Baptist
Bible Fellowship; Organized: 1969;
Built: 1972.
1969–71   Rev. John McKinny
1971–   Rev. Thomas E. Koon

AMBASSADOR CHURCH OF GOD IN CHRIST
640 Eastern Ave. SE 49503; Phone:
243–8540; Organized: 1992.
1992–   Rev. William Walton

AMERICAN INDIAN CHURCH
See **PA–WA–TING MA–GED–WIN UNITED METHODIST**

AMERICAN INDIAN GOSPEL CHURCH
127 Meerse St. SE. 1969–73.

AMERICAN MUSLIM MISSION
See **MASJID MUHAMMAD**

AMERICAN REFORMED CHURCH
3179 68th St. SE Caledonia 49316;
Phone: 698–6360; Organized: 1955
(1331 Franklin St. SE 1955–59; 858
Grandville Ave. SW 1959–79); Built:
1913 as Dutton Christian Reformed.
1957–62   Rev. Sybren Cnossen
1979–91   Rev. Peter Kingma

AMES METHODIST EPISCOPAL
See **ST. PAUL UNITED METHODIST**

APOSTOLIC ASSEMBLY OF FAITH IN JESUS CHRIST
1600 Buchanan Ave. SW 49507;
Phone: 245–9504; Organized: 1980.
1980–86   Rev. Aaron Loreto Martinez
1992–   Rev. Adam Temperbier

APOSTOLIC CHURCH
See **NEW APOSTOLIC CHURCH**

APOSTOLIC FAITH ASSEMBLY
See APOSTOLIC FAITH MISSION

APOSTOLIC FAITH CHURCH
57 Rena St. SW 49507; Phone:
243–9719. Pentecostal Assemblies of
the World Inc; Organized: 1911 (IOOF
Hall 1238 Madison Ave. SE 1915; 515
S. Division Ave. 1916–20); Built: 1923.
1915–37   Rev. Baba M. David
1951–   Bishop Lawrence E. Brisbin

APOSTOLIC FAITH MISSION
273 Market Ave. SW. 1915–26 (957
Ottawa Ave. NW 1915–18);
1924–25   Rev. Alfred J. Cousineau
1925–26   Rev. Robert F. Tobin

APOSTOLIC FAITH MISSION
See **FAIRVIEW APOSTOLIC**

APOSTOLIC FAITH TABERNACLE
See **FAIRVIEW APOSTOLIC**

APOSTOLIC GOSPEL
TABERNACLE/TEMPLE
See **FAIRVIEW APOSTOLIC**

APOSTOLIC HOLINESS CHURCH
417 Front Ave. NW. 1912–13.

ARCADIA CHRISTIAN REFORMED
3601 Plainfield Ave. NE; Organized:
1950 as mission, 1958 as church; Built:
1962 (1414 Four Mile Road NE 1947).
1947–58   Rev. Henry Buikema
1959–62   Rev. Paul Holtrop
1978–85   Rev. Jay J. DeVries
1985 Merged with Plainfield CRC to
become Arcadia–Plainfield CRC.

ARCADIA–PLAINFIELD
CHRISTIAN REFORMED
See **BLYTHEFIELD
CHRISTIAN REFORMED**

ARNETT CHAPEL
See **FIRST COMMUNITY
AFRICAN METHODIST
EPISCOPAL**

ASBURY AME ZION
CHURCH MISSION
See **HILLIARD CHAPEL AME ZION**

ASBURY METHODIST CHAPEL
See JOY MEMORIAL METHODIST

ASCENSION LUTHERAN
2627 44th St. SE 49508; Phone:
455–8108. ELCA; Organized: 1961;
Built: 1962.
1961   Rev. Kenneth H. Graquist
1991–   Rev. Gary R. Soop

ASSEMBLIES OF GOD
See **CENTRAL ASSEMBLY OF GOD**

ASSEMBLY OF GOD MISSION
401 Eleventh St. NW; 1958–59.
1958–59   Rev. Juan J. Martinez

ASSEMBLY OF SAINTS PENTECOSTAL
1455 Grandville Ave. SW 49509;
Phone: 776–0128. National
Pentecostal, Milwaukee, Wis.;
Organized: 1975 as Assembly of Saints
of Biogenetic Holiness Concepts No 2.
(449 S. Division Ave. 1982–88).
1975–   Bishop Roosevelt Robinson

**ASSOCIATED BIBLE STUDENTS
OF GRAND RAPIDS**
830 North Park St. NE 49505; Phone:
361–1110. Independent/autonomous
Bible fellowship; Organized: 1933.
Church purchased 1990 (240 N.
Division Ave. 1945–48; Maccabees
Hall, 126 Sheldon Ave. SE; West
YMCA, 902 Leonard St. NW).

ASSOCIATION OF HOUSE CHURCHES
See **NEW CHURCH OF
THE HOLY SPIRIT**

AVERY CHAPEL
920 Lyon St. NE.
1896–1928; Congregational.
1898   W.F. Holmes

BAHA'I FAITH—GRAND RAPIDS
2057 Wyndham Hill Drive NE 49505;
Phone: 364–9200. Organized: 1954.
1992–   Elizabeth Herth

**BANNER OF CHRIST
COMMUNITY CHURCH**
1111 68th St. SW Byron Center 49315;
Phone: 538–1313. United Brethren;
Organized: 1919; 1924–90 Banner Street
United Brethren; (64 Banner St. SW
1924–90. Wyoming Senior Citizen
Center, 165 54th St. SW, Wyoming,
1990–91) Built: 1991.
1919   Rev. Andrew Hoffman
1948–61   Rev. Duane A. Reahm
1989–   Rev. Bruce E. Strine

BAPTIST
1837–42.
1837   Rev. S.D. Wooster

BAPTIST CHURCH OF THE CITY
OF GRAND RAPIDS
See **FOUNTAIN STREET**

BAPTIST MISSION
South side Bridge Street NW on west
bank of Grand River. 1822–36;
Organized: 1822 as Thomas Station.
1826–27   Rev. Isaac McCoy
1827–36   Rev. Leonard Slater
1836 moved with Odawa to
Gull Prairie/Prairieville, Barry County.

BAPTIST TEMPLE
See TEMPLO BAUTISTA

BARKER MEMORIAL CONGREGATIONAL
See **WALLIN
CONGREGATIONAL UCC**

BAXTER STREET GOSPEL HALL
952 Baxter St. SE. 1948–56.

BEACON LIGHT CHAPEL/MISSION
4614 Walton Ave. SW Wyoming.
CRC; 1937–67; Built: 1937. (4620
Buchanan Ave. SW Wyoming 1937–41)

**BECKWITH HILLS
CHRISTIAN REFORMED**
2100 Chelsea Road NE 49505; Phone:
458–0150. Organized: 1875 as Fourth
Reformed; 1880–1963 Coldbrook
Christian Reformed; (Barnett Street
and Ionia Avenue NW 1875–1910; 7

FIGURE 2
The old Coldbrook Christian Reformed
Church at Barnett and Taylor NW. This
1910 J. & G. Daverman structure was
torn down in 1975. Its original
congregation had relocated as
Beckwith Hills CRC in 1963.

Barnett St. NW 1910–63 (J. & G. Daverman); Built: 1963 (James K. Haveman).
1882–1906 Rev. Lammert J. Hulst
1954–69   Rev. Richard R. Rienstra
1989–   Rev. L. Bryce Mensink

BELMONT MISSION
See **SUNSHINE MINISTRIES**

BENJAMIN AVENUE BAPTIST
See **NORTH SIDE COMMUNITY BAPTIST**

BEREAN BAPTIST
1574 Coit Ave. NE 49505; Phone: 363–9824. General Association Regular Baptist; Organized: 1892 (New England Hall, 1593 Plainfield Ave. NE 1892.); Built: 1929 (J. & G. Daverman)
1895   Rev. B.P. Hewitt
1936–58   Rev. Howard A. Keithley
1993–   Dr. Gary L. Hauck

BEREAN BIBLE CHURCH
1040 26th St. SW Wyoming 49509; Phone: 532–3609. Nondenominational; Organized: 1920 as Beree Gereformierdekirk (622 Sherman St. SE 1920–37. 858 Grandville Ave. SW 1937–59); Built: 1959 (Lenger Construction Co).
1920–29   Rev. Henry J. Bonnema
1935–53   Rev. Bert A. Baker
1990–   Rev. Craig Apel

BEREAN CHURCH
See **BEREAN BIBLE CHURCH**

BEREAN REFORMED
See **BEREAN BIBLE CHURCH**

BERKLEY HILLS PILGRIM
See **BERKLEY HILLS WESLEYAN**

BERKLEY HILLS WESLEYAN
1666 Ball Ave. NE 49505; Phone: 364–9505. Organized: 1928 as First Pilgrim Tabernacle (401 Ionia Ave. NW 1932–37; Peoples' Church, 100 Sheldon Ave. SE 1937–39; 70 Bostwick Ave. NE 1939–59); Built: 1991 (Jeffrey Parker).
1928–37   Rev. Edward Boone
1987–   Rev. William F. Kinnan Jr.

FIGURE 3
Thomas Benjamin & Son were the architects for the unusual Bethel Christian Reformed Church at 724 Shamrock St. SW in 1914. This 1931 view shows the original building before a later addition.

BETHANY BIBLE CHURCH
3900 E. Fulton St. 49546; Phone: 949–9020. Organized: 1968; Built: 1970 (Ritsema & TerHaar);
1968–91   Rev. Raymond E. Befus

BETHANY REFORMED
834 Lake Drive SE 49506; Phone: 451–2895. Organized: 1893 (739 Baldwin St. SE 1894–1924); Built: 1924 (Pierre Lindhout).
1893–98   Rev. John Lamar
1944–56   Rev. Henry Bast
1963–72   Rev. Henry Bast
1990–   Rev. Curry M. Pikkaart

BETHEL ASAMBLEA DE DIOS
832 Grandville Ave. SW 49503; Phone: 245–3718. Organized: 1954 (109 Gold Ave. SW 1954–55; 35 National Ave. SW 1955–75); Built: 1918 as Joldersma Funeral Home.
1954–58   Rev. Rodolfo Martinez Munoz
1989–   Rev. John A. Vega

BETHEL ASSEMBLY OF GOD
200 Griggs St. SW. 1963–71.
1963–65   Rev. C.E. DeWitt

BETHEL BAPTIST
4050 44th St. SW Grandville. Independent Baptist; 1958–86; Built: 1959 (Chris Steketee).
1958–64   Gerrold Pell
1985–86   Rev. Rudy J. Hillesheim

BETHEL CHRISTIAN METHODIST EPISCOPAL MISSION
1060 Cass Ave. SE. 1959–70.
1959–70   Rev. Dahlia A. Anderson

BETHEL CHRISTIAN REFORMED
724 Shamrock St. SW 49509; Phone: 243–6827. Organized: 1912; Built: 1914–17 (Thomas Benjamin & Son).
1913–26   Rev. Gerrit Hoeksema
1926–45   Rev. Garret Hofmeyer
1987–   Rev. Rodger J. Buining

BETHEL CHRISTIAN REFORMED MISSION
254 Hall St. SW.
1919–56 (1967 Grandville Ave. SW Wyoming 1919–24).

BETHEL LUTHERAN
3655 Wilson Ave. SW Grandville
49418; Phone: 534–3364. Missouri
Synod; Organized: 1954; Built: 1956
(Eldon Peroh).

1958–60	Rev. Charles Pool
1960–68	Rev. Ralph W. Carey
1968–77	Rev. Theodore Pflug
1980–	Rev. Ralph W. Carey

BETHEL PENTECOSTAL
200 Madison Ave. SE 49503; Phone:
454–5654. Organized: 1948
(559 Eastern Ave. SE 1948–51; 556
Eastern SE 1955–72); Built: 1921 as
Central Christian (Harvey H.
Weemhoff).

1948–61	Rev. Horace M. Young
1961–	Rev. Dr. William C. Abney

BETHEL REFORMED
1700 Coit Ave. NE 49505; Phone:
363–3919. Organized: 1906; Built: 1927
(J. & G. Daverman).

1908–10	Rev. Peter C. DeJong
1986–	Rev. Jay Sowers

BETHEL SEVENTH DAY ADVENTIST
1024 Adams St. SE 49507; Phone:
243–3182. Organized: 1960 (109
Graham St. SW 1960–74); Built: 1920
as Oakdale Park Reformed (Benjamin
& Weemhoff).

1975	Rev. Robert L. Jones
1985–	Rev. Emanuel Foxworth
1992–	Elder Ronald Bell

BETHESDA NORWEGIAN EVANGELICAL LUTHERAN
645 Front Ave. NW.
1900–16; (12 Michigan St. NE 1900–01).

1900–03	Rev. J.J. Lee
1903–05	Rev. Thor O. Sigmond.

BETHLEHEM LUTHERAN
330 Crescent St. NE 49503; Phone:
456–1741. ELCA; Organized: 1873 as
Swedish Evangelical Lutheran (428
Sinclair Ave. NE 1874–89; 237
Scribner Ave. NW 1889–1929); Built:
1929 (Colton & Knecht).

1874–80	Rev. N.A. Yongberg
1930–46	Rev. George A. Fahlund
1948–78	Rev. Wesley A. Samuelson
1979–	Rev. Robert W. Mueller

BETHLEHEM MISSIONARY BAPTIST
858 Grandville Ave. SW 49503;
Phone: 452–0762. National Baptist
Convention of America Inc;
Organized: 1960 (714 S. Division Ave.
1960–61; 708 Cass Ave. SE 1961–69);
Built: 1937 as Berean Bible Church.

1960–62	Rev. Willie M. McCain
1962–	Rev. Robert L. Johnson

BETHSEDA NORWEGIAN EVANGELICAL LUTHERAN
See **BETHESDA NORWEGIAN EVANGELICAL LUTHERAN**

BEVERLY CHRISTIAN REFORMED
Calvin Christian Junior High School,
2500 Newport St. SW Wyoming
49509; Phone: 534–0006. Organized:
1953 (1854 Porter St. SW Wyoming
1953–57; 2019 Porter SW 1957–92).

1954–61	Rev. Richard Wezeman
1986–92	Rev. Arthur J. Besteman
1992–	Rev. John Blankespoor

FIGURE 4
The Swedish Evangelical Lutheran
Church (now Bethlehem Lutheran)
worshipped at 237 Scribner Ave. NW
from 1889 to 1929. The U.S. 131
freeway now occupies the site.

BEVERLY INDEPENDENT CHRISTIAN REFORMED
2019 Porter St. SW Wyoming 49509;
Phone: 534–0006. Organized: 1992;
Built: 1958 as Beverly Christian
Reformed (Kammeraad Stroup,
Holland).

1992–	Rev. Arthur J. Besteman

BEVERLY REFORMED
2141 Porter St. SW Wyoming 49509;
Phone: 532–2871. Organized: 1915
(1858 Porter SW 1914–53); Built:
1953.

1916–20	Rev. Arie J. Van den Heuvel
1932–44	Rev. John H. Vos
1985–	Rev. Eugene H. Voss

BIBLE MISSIONARY CHURCH
2501 Bristol Ave. NW Walker 49504;
Phone: 784–5202. Organized: 1958
(1007 Leonard St. NW 1958–86.)
Built: 1975 as Bristolwood Christian
Reformed.

1958–63	Rev. Paul E. King
1982–	Rev. Harold R. Hart.

BIBLE SPIRITUALIST CHURCH
See **ASSOCIATED BIBLE STUDENTS OF GRAND RAPIDS**

BIBLE TRUTH HALL
2060 Johanna Ave. SW Wyoming 49509.
Plymouth Brethren; Organized: 1929
(1170 Madison Ave. SE 1929–34; 8
Holland Ave. NE 1934–61); Built:
1927 as Reorganized Church of Jesus
Christ of LDS.

BLESSED HOPE BIBLE
737 Baldwin St. SE 49503; Phone:
774–9296. Organized: 1979; Built: 1894
as Bethany Reformed.

1979–91	Rev. James L. Pittman Sr.
1991–	Rev. Stanley Floyd

FIGURE 5

The old Roxy Theater at 2150 Plainfield Ave. NE served as Blessed Sacrament Church from 1946 to 1951.

BLESSED SACRAMENT

2275 Diamond Ave. NE 49505;
Phone: 361–7339. RC; Organized:
1946. (Roxy Theater, 2150 Plainfield
Ave. NE 1946–51); Built: 1989
(Richard C. Koprowski). School 1950.

1946–50	Rev. John W. Collins
1950–71	Msgr. Anthony P. Arszulowicz
1971–74	Rev. Eugene S. Golas
1974–83	Rev. Louis L. LaSarge
1983–91	Rev. Henry J. Dondzila
1991–	Rev. Robert A. Hart

BLYTHEFIELD CHRISTIAN REFORMED

6350 Kuttshill Drive NE Rockford
49341; Phone: 866–2962. Organized:
1985 as merger of Arcadia CRC and
Plainfield CRC; 1985–88
Arcadia–Plainfield CRC; Built: 1964 as
Plainfield CRC.

1986–88	Rev. Jay J. DeVries
1988–	Rev. Andrew A. Gorter

BOLD GOSPEL PENTECOSTAL

1225 S. Division Ave.; 1984–85.

BOSTON SQUARE CHRISTIAN REFORMED

1803 Kalamazoo Ave. SE 49507;
Phone: 241–1245. Organized: 1942
(1603 Kalamazoo Ave. SE 1942–51);
Built: 1951 (James K. Haveman).

1943–50	Rev. Vincent C. Licatesi
1987–	Rev. Alfred S. Luke

BOSTON STREET GOSPEL CHAPEL

1515 Boston St. SE; 1929–35.

BOWEN CONGREGATIONAL

Paris Township Hall, 3151 Kalamazoo
Ave. SE; 1955–57.

1955–56   Rev. Larry Voss
1957 Merged with **PLYMOUTH CONGREGATIONAL UNITED CHURCH OF CHRIST**

BRADFORD STREET MISSION

441 Bradford St. NE. CRC; 1903–83;
Built: 1903.

1920   John W. Kiel

BRETHREN MISSION

See CALVARY GRACE CHURCH

BRETON ROAD BAPTIST

5040 Breton Ave. SE Kentwood 49508;
Phone: 698–7751. Independent;
Organized: 1988; Built: 1968–71 as
Good Shepherd Missionary Church
(Church Builders).

1988–	Rev. Don E. Cooper
1992–	Rev. Mark Hertstein

BRETON VILLAGE BAPTIST

See VILLAGE BAPTIST

BRIDGE CHURCH MINISTRIES

923 Douglas St. NW 49504; Phone:
454–3905. Autonomous
undenominational evangelistic
traveling church; Organized: 1987.

1987–   Rev. Douglas Wood

BRIDGE STREET CHAPEL

See BRIDGE STREET
GOSPEL MISSION

BRIDGE STREET GOSPEL MISSION

340 Bridge St. NW. CRC; 1939–51
(359 Scribner Ave. NW 1940–48.);
Merged with **GOLD AVENUE CHURCH.**

BRIDGE STREET METHODIST EPISCOPAL

See **FAITH UNITED METHODIST**

BRISTOL AVENUE CHAPEL

2021 Bristol Ave. NW Walker; 1959–60.

BRISTOLWOOD CHRISTIAN REFORMED

2501 Bristol Ave. NW Walker.
1948–85; 1948–61 Front Avenue
Gospel Chapel; 1961–66 Bristolwood
Chapel (1133 Front Ave. NW
1948–61); Built: 1961.

1966–84   Rev. Marion D.
           Groenendyk

BROADWAY AVENUE CHRISTIAN REFORMED

See **WESTVIEW CHRISTIAN REFORMED**

BROADWAY BAPTIST CHURCH OF GRAND RAPIDS

1142 Broadway Ave. NW. American
Baptist Churches in USA; 1962–76.

1962–63	Rev. Donald E. Williams
1974–76	Rev. William A. Harrington

BROADWAY CHRISTIAN REFORMED

See **WESTVIEW CHRISTIAN REFORMED**

**BROADWAY CHURCH
OF GOD IN CHRIST**
1142 Broadway Ave. NW 49504;
Phone: 451–8853. Organized: 1979;
Built: 1904 as Broadway Avenue CRC
(Sidney J. Osgood); Add 1914 (J. & G.
Daverman).
1979–   Rev. Benjamin M.
             Matthews

BROADWAY METHODIST EPISCOPAL
1416 Broadway Ave. NW.
1889–95; Organized: 1889 as Myrtle
Street Mission (Turner Avenue and
Webster Street NW 1889); Built: 1889.

BROOKSIDE CHRISTIAN REFORMED
3600 Kalamazoo Ave. SE 49508;
Phone: 452–3191. Organized: 1959;
Built: 1972 (J. & G. Daverman).
1960–68   Rev. Donald J. Drost
1969–77   Rev. Richard Hertel
1978–92   Rev. Dale W. VanderVeen
1985–   Rev. Benjamin Becksvoort
1986–   Rev. Robert W. Vance
1993–   Rev. Norman Meyer

BUCKLEY STREET CHAPEL
See **GRACE
CHRISTIAN REFORMED**

BUDDY BEAR MINISTRY
See **SABAOTH MINISTRIES**

**BURLINGAME CONGREGATIONAL
UNITED CHURCH OF CHRIST**
1841 Havana Ave. SW Wyoming
49509; Phone: 243–6896. Organized:
1924; Built: 1925 (Harvey H.
Weemhoff).
1925–29   Rev. Arden Johnson
1957–71   Rev. Homer E. Dalrymple
1981–   Rev. David Lee Smith

BURTON AVENUE MISSION
See BURTON STREET MISSION

BURTON BAPTIST
2010 Plymouth Ave. SE 49506;
Phone: 452–1681. American Baptist
Churches in USA; Organized: 1905 as
Burton Avenue Baptist (1974 Horton
Ave. SE 1905–59; 101 Burton St. SE
1959–61); Built: 1961.
1905   Rev. Edgar L. Killiam
1992–   Rev. Edward E. Pikey

BURTON FAITH MISSION
644 Burton St. SW; 1932–41.

BURTON HEIGHTS BAPTIST
301 Burton St. SW 49507; Phone:
534–7352. Independent; Organized:
1972 as Iglesia Bautista Hispana or First
Spanish Baptist; Built: 1912 as Church
of the Brethren.
1972–75   Rev. Justo P. Pratt
1984–   Rev. Tad Gates

BURTON HEIGHTS BAPTIST
See **BURTON BAPTIST**

BURTON HEIGHTS BIBLE CHURCH
1600 Buchanan Ave. SW; 1973–77.
1973–77   Rev. Alden J. Wyma

**BURTON HEIGHTS
CHRISTIAN REFORMED**
1970 Jefferson Ave. SE 49507;
Phone: 243–5319. Organized: 1905
(2106 Horton Ave. SE 1905–22.); Built:
1922 (J. & G. Daverman).
1906–10   Rev. William Bode
1921–29   Rev. Henry J. Mulder
1958–78   Rev. Arnold Brink
1985–   Rev. Douglas M. MacLeod

BURTON HEIGHTS CHURCH OF CHRIST
See **SOUTHSIDE
CHURCH OF CHRIST**

BURTON HEIGHTS CHURCH OF GOD
See **SUNSET PARK
CHURCH OF GOD**

**BURTON HEIGHTS
UNITED METHODIST**
100 Burton St. SE 49507; Phone:
245–9237. Organized: 1892; 1892–1909
Feakin Memorial Methodist Episcopal.
(200 Griggs St. SW 1895–1909 [C.O.
Thompson]); Built: 1910; Add 1915
(J.R. Lakie).
1895–96   Rev. O.E. Wightman
1907–10   Rev. Alvin O. Carman
1975–80   Rev. Ronald M. Fassett
1991–   Rev. Dr. Zawdie K. Abiade

BURTON MISSION
See BURTON STREET MISSION

BURTON STREET BAPTIST
See **BURTON BAPTIST**

BURTON STREET FELLOWSHIP
1113 Burton St. SW Wyoming 49509.
Organized: 1990.

BURTON STREET MISSION
640 Burton St. SW. 1906–12;
Organized: 1905 as Burton Mission.
1905–06   William S. Shoup
1910–11   Jacob Dykehouse

**BUTTERWORTH STREET
FELLOWSHIP**
755 Butterworth St. SW 49504;
235–3218. InterCity Planting Mission
— Southern Baptist; Organized: 1989.
1991–   Rev. Terry LaDuke

CALVARY BAPTIST
1200 28th St. SE 49508;
Phone: 243–3674. General Association
Regular Baptists; Organized: 1889
(Ringuette's Hall, 800 S. Division Ave.
1889; 826 Ionia Ave. SW 1890–1926;
700 Burton St. SE 1926–80); Built:
1981 (Bill Papke & Associates).
1889–97   Rev. Jabez Snashall
1924–40   Rev. William Headley
1967–88   Rev. John White Jr.
1989–   Rev. James E. Jeffery

CALVARY CHRISTIAN REFORMED
3500 Byron Center Ave. SW Wyoming
49509; Phone: 534–0934; Organized:
1959; (West Newhall School, 1585
36th St. SW Wyoming 1959–61);
Built: 1967.
1959–63   Rev. Jacob W. Uitvlugt
1982–   Rev. Dr. Douglas A.
             Kamstra

CALVARY CHURCH
777 E. Beltline Ave. NE 49506; Phone:
956–9377. Independent; Organized:
1929 as Calvary Undenominational
(426 Michigan St. NE 1929–86); Built:
1986 (Design Plus, Jim Reminga).
1929–38   Rev. Dr. Martin R.
             DeHaan
1952–64   Rev. Louis P. Lehman
1970–83   Rev. George E. Gardiner
1983–86   Rev. Louis P. Lehman
1987–   Rev. Dr. Edward G.
             Dobson

CALVARY GOSPEL CENTER

61 Sheldon Ave. SE.
1938–49 (24 Ransom Ave. NE 1938–40).
1940   Rev. W.E. Pietsch
1945   Rev. Donald G. Hescott

CALVARY GRACE CHURCH

301 Burton St. SW.
Brethren (Dunkard); 1905–72;
Organized: 1905–10 Brethren Mission;
1910–58 Church of the Brethren (122
Burton St. SW 1905–10; 8 Burton SW
1911–12).
1912–14   Rev. C. Walter Warstler
1970–72   Rev. G. Robert Petrovich

CALVARY GRACE
See **COMMUNITY BIBLE**

CALVARY MEMORIAL ASSEMBLY OF GOD

2220 Three Mile Road NE 49505;
Phone: 363–3929. Organized: 1966.
1966–74   Rev. Daniel D. Roehl
1974–88   Rev. Jack E. Rowe
1989–92   Rev. Rick D. Pasquale
1992   Rev. Ken Hubbard
1992–   Rev. Daniel D. Jenkin

CALVARY REFORMED

1513 E. Fulton St. 49503;
Phone: 454–0126. Organized: 1915;
Built: 1924 (Harvey H. Weemhoff).
1916   Rev. Clarence P. Dame
1980–   Rev. James G. DeWitt

CALVARY TABERNACLE

2100 Horton Ave. SE.
1968–71 (356 Spencer St. NE
1968–69).
1969–71   Rev. Robert David Haner

CALVARY UNDENOMINATIONAL
See **CALVARY CHURCH**

CALVIN CHRISTIAN REFORMED

700 Ethel Ave. SE 49506;
Phone: 451–8467. Organized: 1946
(Calvin College, 1331 Franklin St. SE
1946–55); Built: 1955 (Daverman).
1948–83   Rev. Clarence Boomsma
1986–   Rev. Harvey Kiekover

FIGURE 6
The Catholic Information Center at 329 Monroe Ave. NW (1948 to 1965). Operated by the Paulist Fathers, it was relocated for urban renewal. This became the site of the Hall of Justice and police headquarters.

CANAL STREET MISSION

222 Monroe Ave. NW.
1903–05; Organized: 1903 as Lyon
Street Mission.
1903–05   Rev. Abram H. Kauffman

CASCADE CHRISTIAN

2829 Thornapple River Drive SE
49546; Phone: 949–1360.
Disciples of Christ (2798 Orange Ave.
SE 1864–1979); Organized: 1865; 1864
Brother Alanson Wilcox, Zebulon
Stow; Chapel built 1880; Built: 1964.
1881–98   Rev. Elias Sias
1958–89   Rev. Raymond Gaylord
1989–   Rev. Dr. Clayton
           Klingenfus

CASCADE CHRISTIAN REFORMED

6655 Cascade Road SE 49546;
Phone: 949–4342. Organized: 1952;
Built: 1962.
1953–57   Rev. Jacob P. Boonstra
1990–   Rev. Gerard L. Dykstra

CATHOLIC INFORMATION CENTER
See **CHAPEL OF ST. PAUL**

CENTER CHURCH
See **NEW CHURCH OF THE HOLY SPIRIT**

CENTRAL ASSEMBLY OF GOD

2660 Breton Ave. SE 49546;
Phone: 942–6320. Organized: 1935;
1935 Assemblies of God; 1935–38
Front Avenue Full Gospel Church;
1951–68 Woodmere Gardens
Tabernacle; 1968–76 Evangel Temple
(645 Front Ave. NW 1935–38;
154 Gold Ave. NW 1939–51; 953
Spencer St. NE 1951–76); Built: 1976.
1939–43   Rev. Frederick H.
           Neubauer
1943–46   Rev. Paul Evans
1957–65   Rev. J. Herbert Meppelink
1983–   Rev. Carl J. Halquist Jr.

CENTRAL CHRISTIAN

2525 Leonard St. NE 49505;
Phone: 458–4662. Disciples of Christ;
Organized: 1874 as Church of Christ
(201 N. Division Ave. 1874–87;
northwest corner Lyon Street and
Barclay Avenue NE (Sidney J. Osgood)
1887–1919; 24 Ransom Ave. NE
1919–22; 200 Madison Ave. SE
1922–74); Built: 1974 (VanCurler
Associates).
1875–76   Rev. Dr. S.E. Pearre
1985–   Rev. Paul L. Channels

FIGURE 7
Sidney J. Osgood designed this building for the Church of Christ (now Central Christian) at northwest corner of Lyon Street and Barclay Avenue NE. Built in 1887, it was replaced by an apartment house about 1920.

**CENTRAL CHURCH
OF CHRIST (DISCIPLES)**
See **CENTRAL CHRISTIAN**

CENTRAL CHURCH OF THE NAZARENE
See **FULLER AVENUE CHURCH
OF THE NAZARENE**

CENTRAL REFORMED
10 College Ave. NE 49503;
Phone: 456–1773. Organized: 1918 as merger of First Reformed and Second Reformed (164 Fountain St. NE 1918–53); Built: 1956 (Eggers & Higgins, New York, N.Y.).
1919–54   Rev. Dr. John A. Dykstra
1971–83   Rev. Dr. Herman J. Ridder
1988–   Rev. Dr. Robert W.
           Bedingfield Sr.

CENTRAL SEVENTH-DAY ADVENTIST
100 Sheldon Ave. SE 49503;
Phone: 774–0171. Organized: 1887 (Ringuette's Hall, 800 S. Division Ave. 1887–89; Good Templars Hall, 19–27 S. Division 1889–99; 328 Cass Ave. SE (Thomas Benjamin & Son) 1899–1929); Built: 1892 as All Souls Universalist (William G. Robinson).
1887–88   Rev. H.W. Miller
1990–   Rev. John B. Fortune

CHABAD HOUSE
2619 Michigan St. NE 49506;
Phone: 957–0770. Jewish; Organized: 1978; Built: 1987 (Dennis Johnson).
1978–   Rabbi Josef Y. Weingarten

CHAPEL OF ST. PAUL
246 Ionia Ave. NW 49503;
Phone: 459–7267. RC; Organized: 1948; 1948–84 Catholic Information Center/Christ the King Chapel (329 Monroe Ave. NW 1948–65.).
1948–49   Rev. Paul V. Maloney CSP
1992–   Rev. Robert L. Pinkston
           CSP

**CHARLES STREET
MISSIONARY BAPTIST**
See **WEALTHY PARK BAPTIST**

CHILDREN OF ZION
903 Scribner Ave. NW.
1875–1914; Organized: 1875 as mission, 1878 Messiah Temple of the Children of Zion (Lincoln Hall, northeast corner Bridge Street and Scribner NW 1875–81); Built: 1881.
1878–86   Bishop David D. Patterson
1888–1911 Rev. Henry A. Olmsted

CHRIST CHURCH
Northeast corner Cannonsburg Road and Northland Drive NE.
Episcopal; 1852–78.

CHRIST CHURCH
2500 Breton Ave. SE 49546;
Phone: 949–9630. Presbyterian Church in America; Organized: 1965 (1432 Wealthy St. SE 1965–82); Built: 1982 (Don Fritz).
1967–85   Rev. Allan M. Baldwin
1991–   Rev. Walter Lorenz

CHRIST COMMUNITY CHURCH
Calvin Theological Seminary, 3201 Burton St. SE 49546; Phone: 949–5156. International Council of Community Churches; Organized: 1992.
1992–   Rev. Dr. John Tobian

CHRIST LUTHERAN
2350 44th St. SW Wyoming 49509;
Phone: 532–2774. ELCA; Organized: 1964 as American Lutheran congregation; Built: 1963.
1963–67   Rev. Victor Wenger
1980–   Rev. Wilson Fleming

CHRIST NEW COVENANT
See **CHRIST'S COVENANT**

**CHRIST TABERNACLE CHURCH
OF GOD IN CHRIST**
53 Canton St. SW; 1972–74.

CHRIST TEMPLE
405 Diamond Ave. SE.
Apostolic Faith; 1935.

CHRIST TEMPLE OF ETERNAL TRUTH
25 Sycamore St. SE 49503; (53 Canton St. SW 1968–74).
1976–   Rev. Retha Earles

CHRIST TEMPLE UNITED PENTECOSTAL
934 Eleventh St. NW; 1977–84.
1977–84   Rev. Jerry Julien

CHRIST THE KING CHAPEL
See **CHAPEL OF ST. PAUL**

CHRIST THE KING LUTHERAN
1261 Beckwith Ave. NE 49505;
Phone: 456–5620. Missouri Synod; Organized: 1977; Built: 1979 (Sam Gray).
1977–80   Rev. Allen Fanning
1989–   Rev. Philip Florip

**CHRISTELIJKE
GEREFORMEERDE KERK**
See **OAKDALE PARK
CHRISTIAN REFORMED**

CHRISTIAN CRUSADE MISSION
288 Leonard St. NW; 1951.

**CHRISTIAN EVANGELICAL
MISSION CHURCH**
See **EVANGELICAL COVENANT
CHURCH OF GRAND RAPIDS**

CHRISTIAN MISSION
CHURCH OF GOD IN CHRIST
523 LaGrave Ave. SE; 1980–83.
1980–82   Rev. J.W. Christian
1982–83   Rev. C.W. Hines

CHRISTIAN MISSIONARY ALLIANCE
704 Wealthy St. SE.
1901–10; 1901–03 Alliance Chapel
(201 N. Division Ave. 1901–03; 230
Michigan St. NE 1904–09).
1901–09   Rev. F.L. Allen
1910   Myron A. Dean

CHRISTIAN REFORMATION
1001 33rd St. SE 49508;
Phone: 243–9477. Independent;
Organized: 1970; Built: 1974.
1970–76   Rev. Vincent C. Licatesi
1976–91   Rev. Claude DePrine
1992–   Rev. Mark A. Scholten

CHRISTIAN REFORMED
See **FIRST PROTESTANT
REFORMED**

CHRISTIAN REFORMED (English)
See **LA GRAVE AVENUE
CHRISTIAN REFORMED**

CHRISTIAN REFORMED MISSION
(11 Gold Ave. SW)
See **GOLD AVENUE CHURCH**

CHRISTIAN SPIRITUALIST CHURCH
1107 Sheldon Ave. SE.
1929–59; 1929–42 Christian
Spiritualist Temple; 1944–48
Spiritualist Temple; Also Covenant
Church (4 Library St. NE 1929–42; 126
Sheldon SE 1944–46).
1929–30   Rev. Alson D. Miller
1935–41   Rev. Mrs. Lucille M.
           MacFee

CHRIST'S COMMUNITY
1019 Wealthy St. SE; 1985–89.
1985–89   Rev. A. Gene Beerens

CHRIST'S COVENANT
647 Jessie St. NE 49505;
Phone: 361–1545. Independent;
Organized: 1981 (Wyoming Seventh-
Day Adventist, 2580 44th St. SW
Wyoming 1981–85; Reformed Bible
College, 1869 Robinson Road SE
1985–88); Built: 1957 as North Park
Mennonite Chapel.
1981–   Rev. Steven W. Holladay

CHURCH OF CHRIST
1158 Burton St. SW Wyoming; 1953–55.

CHURCH OF CHRIST
638 Ionia Ave. SW
See **EASTERN AVENUE
CHURCH OF CHRIST**

CHURCH OF CHRIST
15 Janet St. SE Wyoming 49548; 1992.

CHURCH OF CHRIST
418 Lake Michigan Drive NW;
1954–56.

CHURCH OF CHRIST
224 Houseman Building, 41–51 Pearl
St. NW; 1964–65.

CHURCH OF CHRIST
(4435 Potter Ave. SE Kentwood)
See **GRACE TABERNACLE
CHURCH OF GOD IN CHRIST**

CHURCH OF CHRIST
219 Walter St. SE Wyoming; 1934–36.

CHURCH OF CHRIST, THE
See **SOUTHSIDE CHURCH
OF CHRIST**

CHURCH OF CHRIST (DISCIPLES)
See **CENTRAL CHRISTIAN**

CHURCH OF DELIVERANCE
1320 Madison Ave. SE; 1975–76.
1975–76   Rev. Isaiah Hacket

CHURCH OF DELIVERANCE IN JESUS
3651 Coit Ave. NE 49505.
Organized: 1975.

CHURCH OF DIVINE LIGHT
226 Leonard St. NE 49503;
Phone: 451–9788. Independent
Spiritual Association; Organized: 1950
(1107 Sheldon Ave. SE 1960); Built:
1932 as Creston Protestant Reformed;
Purchased 1962.
1950–56   Rev. Jesse McClintock
1956–89   Rev. Mrs. Ann Lumsden
1992–   Rev. Joanne Kwiatkowski

CHURCH OF DIVINE TRUTH
1053 Madison Ave. SE.
Spiritualist. 1937–42.
1937–42   Rev. Mrs. Katherine Miller

CHURCH OF GOD
(401 Eleventh St. NW)
See **SPANISH CHURCH OF GOD**

CHURCH OF GOD
526 B St. SW.
1948–61 (815 S. Division Ave. 1948–53)
1948–61   Rev. Clyde P. Hardiman Jr.

CHURCH OF GOD (7 Barnett St. NW)
See **LEONARD STREET
CHURCH OF GOD**

CHURCH OF GOD
(1803 Buchanan Ave. SW)
See **SUNSET PARK
CHURCH OF GOD**

CHURCH OF GOD (328 Cass Ave. SE)
See **NEW COVENANT
COMMUNITY CHURCH**

CHURCH OF GOD
(16 Coolidge St. SW Wyoming)
See **WYOMING CHURCH OF GOD**

CHURCH OF GOD
1811 S. Division Ave.; 1978–85.
1979–85   Rev. C.L. Anderson

CHURCH OF GOD
300 Graceland St. NE/2051 Lafayette
Ave. NE; 1954–63.
1958–60   Rev. Robert H. Flinchum

CHURCH OF GOD
(312 Jefferson Ave. SE)
See **LEONARD STREET
CHURCH OF GOD**

CHURCH OF GOD
(588 Jefferson Ave. SE)
See **SUNSET PARK
CHURCH OF GOD**

CHURCH OF GOD
(1009 Kalamazoo Ave. SE)
See **NEW COVENANT
COMMUNITY CHURCH**

CHURCH OF GOD
(1961 Leonard St. NE)
See **LEONARD STREET
CHURCH OF GOD**

CHURCH OF GOD
(140 National Ave. SW)
See **LEONARD STREET
CHURCH OF GOD**

CHURCH OF GOD
(2400 Plainfield Ave. NE)
See **ORCHARD VIEW
CHURCH OF GOD**

CHURCH OF GOD, THE
(645 Front Ave. NW)
See **LEONARD STREET
CHURCH OF GOD**

CHURCH OF GOD IN CHRIST
(329 Bartlett St. SW)
See **NEW BEGINNING
CHURCH OF GOD IN CHRIST**

CHURCH OF GOD IN CHRIST
1001 Baxter St. SE; 1954–69.
1954–69   Rev. Theodore S.
                Matthews

CHURCH OF GOD IN CHRIST
267 Canton St. SW; 1959–60.

CHURCH OF GOD IN CHRIST
736 Cornwall Ave SE; 1974–77.

CHURCH OF GOD IN CHRIST
(116 Delaware St. SW)
See **DAVIS CHAPEL MEMORIAL
CHURCH OF GOD IN CHRIST**

CHURCH OF GOD IN CHRIST
305 S. Division Ave.; 1977–78.
1977–78   Elder George A. McSwain

CHURCH OF GOD IN CHRIST
569 S. Division Ave.; 1966–67.

CHURCH OF GOD IN CHRIST
(814 S. Division Ave.)
See **GRACE TABERNACLE
CHURCH OF GOD IN CHRIST**

CHURCH OF GOD IN CHRIST
(1225 S. Division Ave.)
See **DAVIS CHAPEL MEMORIAL
CHURCH OF GOD IN CHRIST**

CHURCH OF GOD IN CHRIST
(123 Franklin St. SE)
See **GRACE PENTECOSTAL
CHURCH OF GOD IN CHRIST**

CHURCH OF GOD IN CHRIST
327 Grandville Ave. SW; 1923–24.

CHURCH OF GOD IN CHRIST
734 Grandville Ave. SW; 1954–61.

CHURCH OF GOD IN CHRIST
254 Hall St. SW.
1954–62 (1222 Randolph Ave. SW
1954–55).
1958–59   Rev. Boyd Johnson

CHURCH OF GOD IN CHRIST
(1009 Hermitage St. SE)
See **GRACE PENTECOSTAL
CHURCH OF GOD IN CHRIST**

CHURCH OF GOD IN CHRIST
1013 Kalamazoo Ave. SE; 1967–68.

CHURCH OF GOD IN CHRIST
(18 LaBelle St. SE)
See **FAITH TEMPLE CHURCH
OF GOD IN CHRIST**

CHURCH OF GOD IN CHRIST
1721 Madison Ave. SE 49507.
Organized: 1992.
1992   Rev. Levi Dent

CHURCH OF GOD IN CHRIST
25 Pleasant St. SE; 1959–61.

CHURCH OF GOD IN CHRIST
(108 Pleasant St. SW)
See **DAVIS CHAPEL MEMORIAL
CHURCH OF GOD IN CHRIST**

CHURCH OF GOD IN CHRIST
(4435 Potter Ave. SE Kentwood)
See **GRACE TABERNACLE
CHURCH OF GOD IN CHRIST**

CHURCH OF GOD IN CHRIST
711 Sheldon Ave. SE; 1953–61.
1953–60   Rev. Jenus H. Houston

CHURCH OF GOD IN CHRIST
626 Sherman St. SE 49503;
Phone: 243–5271. Organized: 1935
(2786 Woodward Ave. SW Wyoming
1935); Built: 1920 as Berean Bible
Church.
1935–62   Rev. John J. Burns
1967–82   Rev. Master DeBose
1982–   Rev. Virgil W. Hurt

CHURCH OF GOD IN CHRIST
(742 Thompson Ave. SE)
See **GRACE PENTECOSTAL
CHURCH OF GOD IN CHRIST**

CHURCH OF GOD IN PROPHECY
807 Butterworth St. SW; 1954–55.

CHURCH OF GOD MISSION
See **ORCHARD VIEW
CHURCH OF GOD**

CHURCH OF GOD
OF DELIVERANCE IN JESUS
806 Butterworth St. SW; 1970–75.

CHURCH OF GOD OF PROPHECY
1320 Ashland Ave. NE.
1966–84 (109 Gold Ave. SW 1966–69)
1973–75   Rev. Shelly S. Sullivan
1981–82   Rev. Roy L. Hayes

CHURCH OF GOD PENTECOSTAL
1326 Ashland Ave. NE 49505;
Phone: 456–8669. Organized: 1973 (53
Canton St. SW 1973–76; 1130 S.
Division Ave. 1976–83; 227 Bartlett St.
SW 1983–89);
1973–76   Rev. Henry Keller
1976–   Rev. Roosevelt Beville

CHURCH OF GOD
SPANISH INDEPENDENTS
1106 Grandville Ave. SW; 1968–69.

CHURCH OF GRAND RAPIDS
25 Commerce Ave. SW; 1972–75.
1972–75   Rev. Donald VanderMolen

CHURCH OF JESUS CHRIST IN GOD
815 S. Division Ave.
1939–56 (448 Lake Michigan Drive NW
1939; 317 N. Division Ave. 1940; 649
Ottawa Ave. NW 1941; 626 Ottawa NW
1942; 435 Michigan St. NE 1943–44; 649
Ottawa NW 1945–46; 736 Ottawa NW
1948–54.)
1940–52   Rev. Charles L. Graham
1952–56   Rev. H. Archie Phillips

**CHURCH OF JESUS CHRIST
OF LATTER DAY SAINTS**
212 Bellevue St. SE Wyoming; 1979.
1979   Bishop Russell A. Figueira

**CHURCH OF JESUS CHRIST
OF LATTER DAY SAINTS**
2780 Leonard St. NE 49505;
Phone: 949–3343. Organized: 1908
(249 Hall St. SE 1909–12; 346 Hall SE
1912–13; 342 Hall SE 1914; 817 Coit
Ave. NE 1915; 1007 S. Division Ave.
1916–17; 1208 S. Division 1917–25.
439 Ottawa Ave. NW 1929–33; 4
Library St. NE 1933–36; 746 Scribner
Ave. NW 1936–38; 242 Carlton Ave.
SE 1945–61; 3181 Bradford St. NE
1961–85); Built: 1985 (WBDC).
1922–25   Rev. Egerton K. Evans
GRAND RAPIDS WARD:
1991–   Bishop Charles Stoddard
GRAND VALLEY WARD:
1989–   Bishop Jarakal (Claude)
              Jensen
GRAND RIVER BRANCH:
1991–   Jeffrey L. Lewis

**CHURCH OF JESUS CHRIST
OF LATTER DAY SAINTS**
324 Prospect Ave. NE.
Florentine Sisters/missionary residence;
1979–81.

CHURCH OF THE ALCOHOLIC
See **NEW LIFE CHURCH**

CHURCH OF THE BRETHREN
1723 44th St. SE; 1966–67.

CHURCH OF THE BRETHREN
See **CALVARY GRACE CHURCH**

CHURCH OF THE FULL GOSPEL
2100 Horton Ave. SE.
United Pentecostal; 1967–75 (766
Seventh St. NW 1967–71).
1967–75   Rev. Maurice R. Gordon

CHURCH OF THE GOOD SHEPHERD
501 Michigan St. NE.
Episcopal; 1873–1912; 1886–1900
Trinity Episcopal; Built: 1873.
1873–75   Rev. Seth Smith Chapin
1886–89   Rev. Sidney H. Woodford
1889–98   Rev. Henry H. Johnston
1911–12   Rev. William B. Guion

CHURCH OF THE LIVING GOD
See **GREATER ELIEZER TEMPLE
OF THE APOSTOLIC FAITH**

CHURCH OF THE NAZARENE
See **FULLER AVENUE
CHURCH OF THE NAZARENE**

CHURCH OF THE NEW COVENANT
126 Sheldon Ave. SE; 1945–46.
1945   Rev. Elam E. Branch

CHURCH OF THE OPEN DOOR, THE
1730 Burlingame Ave. SW Wyoming
49509; Phone: 452–3378.
Independent Fundamental Churches of
America; Organized: 1929 (441 Burton
St. SW 1929–34; 1508 Grandville Ave.
SW 1934–50); Built: 1950.
1929–32   Rev. Albert H. Waalkes
1970–80   Rev. J. Bruce Slack
1992–   Rev. Roger Walcott

CHURCH OF THE REDEEMER
1072 Jefferson Ave. SE.
United Methodist; 1966–75.
1966–68   Rev. James D. Cochran
1968–74   Rev. William Carter

CHURCH OF THE SERVANT
3835 Burton St. SE 49546;
Phone: 241–3905. CRC; Organized:
1973 (Oakhill Presbyterian Church,
1930 Leonard St. NE. Creston
Christian School, 1031 Page St. NE;
Mulick Park School, 1761 Rosewood
Ave. SE; Seymour Christian School,
2550 Eastern Ave. SE.); Built: 1993
(Gunnar Birkerts).
1974–82   Rev. John Vriend
1983–   Rev. Jack Roeda

CHURCH OF THE SEVEN STARS
20 Burton St. SW 49507;
Phone: 241–2128. Spiritual, Chicago
IL; Organized: 1975 (756 Wealthy St.
SE 1975–85).
1975–86   Rev. Robert W. Curry
1986–   Rev. Essie B. Curry

CHURCH OF TRUTH
See **SPIRITUAL TEMPLE SOCIETY
FIRST CHURCH OF TRUTH**

CITY MISSION
See **MEL TROTTER
MINISTRIES INC.**

CITY MISSION
See **TRINITY UNITED METHODIST**

CITY MISSION (South Branch)
See **GALEWOOD GOSPEL CHAPEL**

CITY RESCUE MISSION
See **MEL TROTTER
MINISTRIES INC.**

CITY RESCUE MISSION (branch)
8 Burton St. SW; 1910.

CITY RESCUE MISSION
(Galewood/South Branch)
See **GALEWOOD GOSPEL CHAPEL**

CITY VIEW CHURCH
960 Alpine Ave. NW 49504;
Phone: 235–1533. Independent Baptist;
Organized: 1989 (663 Bridge St. NW
1989–91); Built: 1904 as Alpine
Avenue Christian Reformed (Sidney J.
Osgood).
1989–92   Rev. Kenneth E. Stone
1992–   Rev. Luke P. Wilson

FIGURE 8
Bethel CRC Mission erected this building at 254 Hall St. SW in 1919 and used it until 1956. From 1962 to 1974 it was the Grace and Truth Chapel, now the Community Bible Church of Grandville. The building was torn down in 1976 for the parking lot of Amway's Hall Street plant, now the Benteler Corp.

CLANCY STREET MINISTRIES
816 Clancy Ave. NE 49503;
Phone: 235-2195. RCA youth
ministry; Organized: 1988.
1988–93   Gordon Brouwer
1993–   Rev. Carol Faas, Steve Faas

CLARK MEMORIAL
METHODIST EPISCOPAL
1530 Sherman St. SE; 1908–20.
1910   Rev. A.T. Luther
1912–14   Rev. Gilbert Stensell.

CLYDE PARK CHURCH
OF THE NAZARENE
2545 Clyde Park Ave. SW Wyoming
49509; Phone: 534-1433. Organized:
1941 as East Church of the Nazarene
(1144 Hazen St. SE 1941–54); Built:
1962.
1941–42   Rev. Dr. William G.
           Heslop
1953–67   Rev. Keith C. St. John
1992–   Rev. Ed Kateskey

COIT COMMUNITY
CHRISTIAN REFORMED
600 Lafayette Ave. NE 49503;
Phone: 458-2398. Organized: 1967 as
Livingston Chapel (607 Livingston
Ave. NE 1967–77); Built: 1895 as
Epworth Methodist Episcopal.
1967   Rev. Marvin VanderVliet
1977–85   Rev. Peter J. Kooreman
1990–   Rev. Henry Perez.

COLDBROOK CHRISTIAN REFORMED
See **BECKWITH HILLS
CHRISTIAN REFORMED**

COLLEGE AVENUE GOSPEL HALL
See **FOREST HILLS
BIBLE CHAPEL**

COLORED MISSION CHURCH
732 Cornwall Ave. SE.
Methodist Episcopal; 1915–17.

COLORED MISSION
SUNDAY SCHOOL
See MISSION SUNDAY SCHOOL
(422 Coldbrook St. NE)

COMMERCE STREET
METHODIST EPISCOPAL
See **FIRST COMMUNITY AFRICAN
METHODIST EPISCOPAL**

COMMUNITY BIBLE BAPTIST
811 Wealthy St. SE 49506;
Phone: 451-8237. Independent;
Organized: 1973 (737 Baldwin St. SE
1973–84); Built: 1912 as Wealthy
Street Baptist (Pierre Lindhout).
1973–84   Rev. Starlon Washington
1986–   Rev. Melvin L. Upchurch

COMMUNITY BIBLE CHURCH
2687 Ivanrest Ave. SW Grandville
49418; Phone: 531-1260. Grace
Gospel Fellowship; Organized: 1954 as
Grace Assembly; 1960 Calvary Grace;
1962–74 Grace and Truth Chapel
(1132 Cass Ave. SE 1955; 254 Hall St.
SW 1962–74; 5047 Burlingame Ave.
SW Wyoming 1974).
1954–80   Rev. Bert A. Baker
1988–   Rev. Gary T. Cloud

COMMUNITY
CHRISTIAN REFORMED
150 Burt St. SE Wyoming 49548;
Phone: 534-1779. 1944–70 Godwin
Gospel Chapel; Organized: 1984 as
church; Built: 1945; Addition: 1989
(Richard Postema).
1944–46   Rev. J. Vredevoogd
1976–85   Rev. Peter E. Brink
1986–   Rev. David A. Struyk

COMMUNITY FELLOWSHIP
1121 Madison Ave. SE; 1985–88.
1985–88   Rev. Phillip J. Holmes

COMSTOCK PARK BAPTIST
Comstock Park; 1909–15.
1909   Rev. William F.. Cuthbert

COMSTOCK PARK CHAPEL
See **COMSTOCK PARK
CHRISTIAN REFORMED**

COMSTOCK PARK
CHRISTIAN REFORMED
5070 Pine Island Drive NE Comstock
Park 49321; Phone: 784-6851.
1946–50 Comstock Park Gospel
Mission; 1950–57 Comstock Park
Chapel (3920 West River Drive NW
Comstock Park 1946–50; 4485 West

River NW 1950–67); Built: 1968.

1952–60	Rev. William Swierenga
1961–75	Rev. Paul J. Veenstra
1975–84	Rev. John H. Looman
1984–89	Rev. Mike J. Meekhof
1991–	Rev. Gerald A. Koning

COMSTOCK PARK GOSPEL MISSION/CHAPEL
See **COMSTOCK PARK CHRISTIAN REFORMED**

COMSTOCK PARK UNITED CONGREGATIONAL CHURCH OF CHRIST
62 Lamoreaux Drive NE Comstock Park 49321; Phone: 784–5545. Organized: 1910 (IOOF Hall, Comstock Park 1910–14); Built: as Comstock Park Baptist; 1915 moved to present site.

1910–14	Rev. S.P. Morris.
1927–41	Rev. Estle C. Barnes
1986–	Rev. Lawrence Brosseit

CONFERENCE MEETING
See SPIRITUALISTS

CONGREGATION BETH ISRAEL
438 Ottawa Ave. NW. 1894–1938 (338 Bridge St. NW 1894; 300 Bridge NW 1894–96; 822 Ottawa Ave. NW 1896–1903).

1894	Rabbi Abraham Wohlkuen
1933–38	Rabbi Solomon Gross
1938	Merged with Congregation Ahavas Achim to form Ahavas Israel.

CONGREGATION EMANUEL
1715 Fulton St. E 49503; Phone: 459–5976. Organized: 1857 (Pierce Block, southwest corner Monroe Avenue and Erie Street NW 1872–75; Godfrey Block, 65–67 Monroe Ave. NW 1875–82; 72 Ransom Ave. NE 1882–1954 (David S. Hopkins); Built: 1954 (Eric Mendelsohn).

1872–74	Rabbi Wolf Weinstein
1921–36	Rabbi Philip Waterman
1937–47	Rabbi Jerome Folkman
1972–	Rabbi Albert M. Lewis

CONGREGATIONAL CHURCH OF CASCADE
See **FIRST CONGREGATIONAL CHURCH OF ADA**

FIGURE 9
Built by Catholic philanthropist John Clancy in 1889, St. John's Home at 385 Leonard St. NE served (1894–1922) as the first motherhouse for the Dominican Sisters in Grand Rapids. They established Marywood in that year, but continued to operate the home until its demolition in 1960.

CONTINENTAL BAPTIST MISSIONS
5900 Alpine Ave. NW Comstock Park 49321; Phone: 784–7190. 1977–83 Hiawatha Baptist Missions (1526 Plainfield Ave. NE 1977–85; 1520 Plainfield NE 1985–87).

| 1977–83 | Rev. Arthur B. Cunningham |
| 1983– | Charles E. Vermilyea |

CONVERSATIONAL, THE
See SPIRITUALISTS

CORNERSTONE COMMUNITY
2415 Porter St. SW Wyoming 49509. 1985–92.

| 1985–92 | Rev. Kenneth H. Myers |

COTA CHURCH OF THE ALCOHOLIC
See **NEW LIFE CHURCH**

COVENANT CHURCH
See CHRISTIAN SPIRITUALIST

CRESTON CHRISTIAN REFORMED
238 Spencer St. NE 49505; Phone: 459–2401. Organized: 1915 (Page Hall, 1431 Plainfield Ave. NE 1915–17; Shanahan Hall, 1418 Plainfield NE 1917); Built: 1917 (J. & G. Daverman).

1916–23	Rev. Karst Bergsma
1926–46	Rev. Henry Verduin
1983–	Rev. Donald J. VanBeek

CRESTON CHURCH OF CHRIST
Children's Bible Hour building, 1331 Plainfield Ave NE 49505; Phone: 361–6990. Independent; Organized: 1989.

| 1989– | Rev. Douglas Doyle. |

CRESTON PROTESTANT REFORMED
224 Leonard St. NE. 1932–62 (Creston Christian School, 1031 Page St. NE 1958–60).

1932–36	Rev. John J. VanderBreggen
1957–61	Rev. Lambert Doezema
1957–59	Rev. Bernard Woudenberg at 224 Leonard St. NE

CRESTON UNDENOMINATIONAL
See EAST LEONARD BAPTIST

FIGURE 10
The present-day Eastern Avenue Church of Christ worshipped in this humble structure at 638 Ionia Ave. SW from 1949 to 1969.

CRIMINAL JUSTICE CHAPLAINCY
345 State St. SE 49503;
Phone: 454–4925. CRC; Organized:
1980 (25 Commerce Ave. SW 1985).
1980–   Rev. James VanderSchaaf

CROSBY STREET
CHRISTIAN REFORMED
See **WEST LEONARD**
CHRISTIAN REFORMED

DANISH LUTHERAN
South side Travis St. East of Coit Ave.
NE; 1895–1905.
1905   Rev. J.P. Lilleso

DANISH–NORWEGIAN
CONGREGATIONAL
401 Ionia Ave. NW; 1895–97.
1895–97   Rev. P. Peterson

DAVIS CHAPEL MEMORIAL
CHURCH OF GOD IN CHRIST
111 Griggs St. SE 49507;
Phone: 243–9071. Organized: 1945
(108 Pleasant St. SW 1945–49; 116
Delaware St. SW 1949–61; 1225 S.
Division Ave. 1961–79); Built: 1928
(Harvey H. Weemhoff) as Griggs Street
Evangelical.
1945–75   Rev. Mack M. Davis
1980–85   Rev. Isaac G. Morgan
1992–   Rev. Earl J. Wright

DEEPER LIFE TABERNACLE
9894 64th Ave. Allendale.
1947–68 Forest Ridge Park Mission
(3653 Coit Ave. NE 1947–73; 142
National Ave. SW 1973–75).
1973–75   Rev. John W. Woods

DEGAGE MINISTRIES
11 Cherry St. SE 49503;
Phone: 454–1661. Organized: 1967 (67
Barclay Ave. NE 1967–68; 25 S.
Division Ave. 1968–75; 10 Weston St.
SE 1975–92).
1967   Richard Bigelow
1992–   James Courey

DELIVERANCE TEMPLE
704 Jefferson Ave. SE 49503;
Phone: 1980–90. 1980–84 Pentecostal
Deliverance Church of Apostolic Faith
(451 Jefferson SE 1980–84).
1980–90   Rev. Eugene Sacus

DENNIS AVENUE
CHRISTIAN REFORMED
See **MAYFAIR**
CHRISTIAN REFORMED

DICKINSON AVENUE
METHODIST EPISCOPAL
Northwest corner Dickinson Street and
Paris Avenue SE; 1892–1907.
1893–94   Rev. Thomas Boone
1906   Rev. J.W. Hart.

DISCOVERY
CHRISTIAN REFORMED
Meadow Pointe Mall, 1425 60th St. SE
Kentwood 49508; Phone: 281–5170.
Organized: 1991.
1991–   Rev. James Hoogeveen

DIVERSE MINISTRIES
ENTERPRISES
834 Union Ave. NE 49503;
Phone: 454–5897. Organized: 1967.
1967–   Frank Bush

DIVINE LIGHT MISSION (ASHRAM)
541 College Ave. SE; 1975.

DIVISION AVENUE REFORMED CHAPEL
60 Brown St. SW; 1924–25.
1924–25   Rev. Garrett Flikkema

DIVISION STREET FELLOWSHIP
229 S. Division Ave. 49503;
Phone: 774–0890. Independent;
InterCity Planting Mission —
Southern Baptist; Organized: 1980 as
Division Street Ministries (Herkimer
Hotel, 323 S. Division 1980–85).
1980–   Rev. Daniel A. Schutte

DIVISION STREET
METHODIST EPISCOPAL
See **FIRST UNITED METHODIST**

DOMINICAN CHAPEL/MARYWOOD
2025 E. Fulton St. 49503;
Phone: 454–1241. RC; Organized: 1894
as Dominican Sisters of Grand Rapids
(385 Leonard St. NE 1894–1922);
Built: 1922. Chapel renovated 1985
(INAI Studios, Adrian).
1942–74   Rev. Charles P. Wilson OP
1985–   Rev. Gregory Heille OP
1990–   Michelle Rego–Reatini

DRIVE–IN CHURCH
3500 Remembrance Road NW Walker
49504; 1966–80.

DUTCH REFORMED
See **NETHERLANDS REFORMED**
CHURCH OF GRAND RAPIDS

DUTCH REFORMED
See SECOND REFORMED

EAST CHURCH OF THE NAZARENE
See **CLYDE PARK CHURCH
OF THE NAZARENE**

EAST CONGREGATIONAL
1005 Giddings Ave. SE 49506;
Phone: 245–0578. UCC; Organized:
1894 (Wealthy Street near Reeds Lake,
East Grand Rapids 1894; Shannon's
Hall, Lovett Avenue and Wealthy
Street SE East Grand Rapids 1894–96;
362 Norwood Ave. SE (Osgood &
Osgood) 1896–1929); Klise Memorial
Chapel built 1929 (Ralph Adams Cram
& Ferguson, Boston); Built: 1953 (Ralph
Adams Cram, Boston).

1894–98	Rev. William H. Underhill
1951–63	Rev. Dr. Joseph Q. Mayne
1971–85	Rev. Dr. Seymour VanDyken
1992–	Rev. Laurel TenHave–Chapman

EAST LEONARD BAPTIST
1441 Leonard St. NE.
1933–87; Organized: 1933 as Creston
Undenominational; Built: 1934;
Addition: 1954.

1952–67	Rev. R. Glenn Warner
1984–87	Rev. Don A. Krise

EAST LEONARD
CHRISTIAN REFORMED
1027 Leonard St. NE 49505;
Phone: 454–4444. Organized: 1925;
Built: 1929 (J. & G. Daverman).

1926–30	Rev. B.H. Spalink
1940–50	Rev. John G. VanDyke
1989–	Rev. Terry D. Slachter

EAST LEONARD GOSPEL MISSION
1124 Leonard St. NE; 1931–35.

EAST PARIS CHRISTIAN REFORMED
3065 E. Paris Ave. SE Kentwood
49512; Phone: 949–3462. Organized:
1902 (3350 E. Paris Ave. SE Kentwood
1902–59); Built: 1959 (David Post).

1905–07	Rev. Ymen P. DeJong
1990–	Rev. Gerrit W. Sheeres

EAST PARIS CONGREGATIONAL
West side of East Paris Avenue, south
of 28th Street SE; 1902–20.

EAST PARIS REFORMED
Paris Township (Kentwood); 1913–18.

EAST SIDE CHURCH OF GOD IN CHRIST
1001 Baxter St. SE; 1976–77.

1976–77	Rev. Eddie J. Matthews

EAST STREET CHRISTIAN REFORMED
See **EASTERN AVENUE
CHRISTIAN REFORMED**

EAST STREET METHODIST EPISCOPAL
See **TRINITY UNITED METHODIST**

EAST STREET TRUE
HOLLAND REFORMED
See **EASTERN AVENUE
CHRISTIAN REFORMED**

EASTERN AVENUE BAPTIST
See **SOUTH EASTERN
BIBLE CHURCH**

EASTERN AVENUE
CHRISTIAN REFORMED
514 Eastern Ave. SE 49503;
Phone: 454–4888. Organized: 1879 as
East Street True Holland Reformed;
Built: 1887; Remodeled 1916 (J. & G.
Daverman).

1881–87	Rev. J. Post
1900–19	Rev. Johannes Groen
1920–24	Rev. Herman Hoeksema
1925–41	Rev. William P. VanWyk
1987–	Rev. Rolf Bouma

EASTERN AVENUE
CHURCH OF CHRIST
658 Eastern Ave. SE 49503;
Phone: 241–1797. Organized: 1949 as
Ionia Avenue Church of Christ (638
Ionia Ave. SW 1949–69; Franklin
Street Church of Christ 909 Franklin
St. SE 1970–84); Built: 1916 as
Immanuel Reformed (Harvey H.
Weemhoff).

1949–54	Brother Elmer Hogan
1978–90	Rev. Norman L. Evans
1991–	Rev. Milton E. Hopkins

EASTERN AVENUE FREE METHODIST
5665 Eastern Ave. SE Kentwood
49508; Phone: 455–2710. Organized:
1929 as Godwin Heights Free
Methodist Episcopal (15 Janet St. SE
Wyoming 1929–62); Built: 1962 (Vos
Construction).

1929–30	Rev. Quitman Smith
1985–	Rev. Richard J. Keep

EASTERN AVENUE GOSPEL CHAPEL
See **FOREST HILLS
BIBLE CHAPEL**

EASTMINSTER PRESBYTERIAN
1700 Woodward Ave. SE 49506;
Phone: 247–8833. Presbyterian Church
(USA); Organized: 1952; Built: 1954
(James K. Haveman, Chris Steketee).

1953–81	Rev. Edward A. Brigham
1990–	Rev. Kurt J. Kremlick
1993–	Rev. Craig Seitz.

EASTMONT BAPTIST
5038 Cascade Road SE 49546;
Phone: 949–0540. General Association
of Regular Baptists; Organized: 1954;
Built: 1902 as East Paris Christian
Reformed; moved 1959; Add 1966.

1954–57	Rev. Alfred Mersman
1984–92	Rev. James F. Middleton
1992–	Rev. Dwane McNeil

EASTMONT REFORMED
See FOREST HILLS
COMMUNITY REFORMED

EASTOWN CHRISTIAN
Room 4, 1331 Lake Drive SE; 1982–85.

1982–85	Rev. Chris Rollstone

EBEN HAEZER
NETHERLANDS REFORMED
See **NETHERLANDS REFORMED
CHURCH OF GRAND RAPIDS**

EBENEZER
NETHERLANDS REFORMED
See **NETHERLANDS REFORMED
CHURCH OF GRAND RAPIDS**

ECCLESIAN CHURCH
450 Sligh Blvd. NE; 1969–70.

1969–70	Rev. Samuel Saltar

EDGEWOOD BAPTIST MISSION
Southeast corner Edgewood Avenue
and Eleanor Street NE; 1918–29.
1926   John Alta

EIGHTH REFORMED
851 Burton St. SW Wyoming 49509;
Phone: 452–9417. Organized: 1891;
Built: 1913 (Pierre Lindhout).
1892–96   Rev. Roelof Duiker
1965–75   Rev. Wilbur R. Ringnalda
1977–92   Rev. Howard E. Davis
1992–   Rev. Kenneth L. Westrate

**ELIEZER CHURCH
OF APOSTOLIC FAITH**
See **GREATER ELIEZER TEMPLE
OF THE APOSTOLIC FAITH**

ELIM BAPTIST
154 Gold Ave. NW.
1890–1939; 1890–1933 Swedish Baptist
(Third Street and Lane Avenue NW
1890–93; 701 Turner NW 1893–94;
Bridge Street and Gold NW 1894–95).
1891–92   Rev. Henry Nelson
1929–32   Rev. Carl A. Anderson

EMANUEL BAPTIST MISSION
See **IMMANUEL BAPTIST**
(434 College Ave. NE)

EMANUEL CHRISTIAN REFORMED
See **IMMANUEL
CHRISTIAN REFORMED**

EMANUEL CHURCH
See **IMMANUEL INDEPENDENT
CHURCH OF COMSTOCK PARK**

EMANUEL IGLESIA PENTECOSTAL
See **IGLESIA DE DIOS
PENTECOSTAL**

EMERALD LAKE CHAPEL
3133 Amon Ave. NE 49505.
Organized: 1960.

EMMANUEL BAPTIST
1144 Quarry Ave. NW 49504;
Phone: 776–1352. Independent;
Organized: 1981 (Pinery Park
Elementary School, 2550 Rogerslane
Ave. SW Wyoming 1981–83;
Tallmadge Township Hall, 1451
Leonard St. Marne 1983–85); Built:
1892 as Holland Baptist.
1981–   Rev. Terry L. Garner

EMMANUEL WESLEYAN
1144 Quarry Ave. NW.
1873–1985; Organized: 1873 as First
Wesleyan Methodist (341 Crosby St.
NW 1874–1961).
1873–75   Rev. H.R. Stevens
1960–65   Rev. Bruce W. Densmore
1985   Rev. Lynn A. Ensign
1985 Merged with Fairview Wesleyan
to become **FIRST WESLEYAN.**

EPWORTH UNITED METHODIST
600 Lafayette Ave. NE; 1895–1977.
1896   Rev. B.E. Paddock
1973–75   Rev. Robert L. Hinklin.

ETERNAL LIFE CENTER
1127 Wealthy St. SE; 1985.
1985   Tommy L. Walker

EVANGEL HALL
See **NORTHWEST GOSPEL HALL**

EVANGEL TEMPLE
See **CENTRAL ASSEMBLY OF GOD**

**EVANGELICAL COVENANT
CHURCH OF GRAND RAPIDS**
1933 Tremont Blvd. NW 49504;
Phone: 453–6346. Organized: 1880 as
Swedish Mission (507 Broadway Ave.
NW 1880–1964); 1945 Mission
Covenant Church; Built: 1964.
1879   Rev. Peter Wadin
1977–89   Rev. Wesley C. Swanson
1990–   Rev. Donald E. Logue

EVANGELICAL LATVIAN LUTHERAN
See **LATVIAN
EVANGELICAL LUTHERAN**

EVANGELICAL UNITED BRETHREN
See **NORTHLAWN
UNITED METHODIST**

EVANGELICAL WESLEYAN
See **WYOMING WESLEYAN**

EVANGELISTIC CENTER, THE
1255 Broadway Ave. NW 49504;
Phone: 451–8503. Organized: 1988.
1988–   Rev. Harry Dunn

EVANGELISTIC HOLINESS CHURCH
109 Gold Ave. SW; 1969–71.

EVERGLADE REFORMED
940 Everglade Drive SE.
Organized: 1951; Built: 1955.
1952–57   Rev. Norwood K. Reck
1969–74   Rev. Bernard Daniel
            Hakken Jr.
1974   Merged with Oakdale Park
Reformed to become **NEW LIFE
REFORMED**

EXCEEDING FAITH MINISTRIES
900 Michigan St. NE 49503;
Phone: 459–8883. Organized: 1992
(Best Western Midway Hotel, 4101
28th St. SE 1992–93).
1992–   Rev. Terrence Redmond

FAIR GROUND UNION SUNDAY SCHOOL
See **ST. PAUL
UNITED METHODIST**

FAIR HAVEN BAPTIST
2828 Richmond St. NW Walker
49504; Phone: 453–3482.
Organized: 1895 as Scribner Avenue
Baptist; 1961–63 Broadway Baptist
(1236 Scribner NW 1895–1961; 1142
Broadway Ave. NW 1961–63; 1320
Ashland Ave. NE 1963–72); Built:
1972 (VanWienen & Postema).
1895   Rev. C.W. Barber
1957–86   Rev. Donald E. Williams
1990–   Rev. Thomas M.
            Cavanaugh

FAIRMONT BAPTIST
See **NORTH PARK BAPTIST**

FAIRMOUNT BAPTIST
See **NORTH PARK BAPTIST**

FAIRMOUNT PARK MISSION
See **NORTH PARK BAPTIST**

FAIRVIEW APOSTOLIC

2391 Hillside Drive NW Walker
49504; Phone: 364–9564.
United Pentecostal; Organized: 1930 as
Apostolic Faith Mission (325 Murray
St. SW Wyoming 1931–54); 1954–74
Apostolic Gospel Tabernacle/Temple
(212 Bellevue St. SE Wyoming
1954–79); Built: 1926 as Fairview
Reformed (Harvey H. Weemhoff).

1931–43	Rev. Perry Sigourney
1950–74	Rev. Arthur L. Colegrove
1974–	Rev. Charles W. Colegrove

FAIRVIEW REFORMED

1465 Three Mile Road NW Walker
49504; Phone: 784–4060.
Organized: 1918 (2391 Hillside Drive
NW 1918–24 (Frank P. Allen & Sons);
1926–79 (Harvey H. Weemhoff); Built:
1979 (VanWienen & Papke).

1918	Rev. Philip G. Meengs
1920–23	Rev. Edward Huibregtse
1960–75	Rev. Emo Ausema
1976–90	Rev. Ralph E. Robrahn
1990–	Rev. Dr. Richard J. Bates

FAIRVIEW WESLEYAN

1091 Three Mile Road NW Walker.
1867–1985; Organized: 1867 as First
Wesleyan Methodist Church of Walker
(Wait School, 2683 Alpine Ave. NW
Walker 1867–70; 883 Three Mile NW
Walker 1870–1960).

1867–70	Rev. L.J. Francisco
1985	Rev. Ivan L. Morse
1985	Merged with Emmanuel

Wesleyan to become **FIRST
WESLEYAN.**

FAIRWAY CHRISTIAN REFORMED

Fairway Golf Course, 4120 Chicago
Drive SW Grandville 49418; Phone:
531–9009. Organized: 1992.

1992–	Rev. Jeffrey Sajdak

FAITH BAPTIST

1412 44th St. SE Kentwood 49508;
Phone: 538–1680. General Association
of Regular Baptists; Organized: 1954
(2738 Breton Ave. SE 1954–55;
American Legion Hall, Breton and

FIGURE 11

Local architect Sidney J. Osgood was kept busy by local congregations. Although the parsonage was removed in 1977, this landmark church at 535 Church Place SW, still stands. It has been occupied by Fifth Reformed (1886–1957), Pleasant Hill Reformed (1960–67), Faith Missionary Baptist (1968–88), and currently by Faith Temple Apostolic Church.

Burton Street SE 1955–57); Built: 1957
(Daverman).

1954–56	Rev. John Afman
1980–92	Rev. David Phillips
1992–	Rev. Timothy D. Gunderson

FAITH CHRISTIAN ACADEMY
See **FAITH TABERNACLE**

FAITH CHRISTIAN REFORMED

1701 Kalamazoo Ave. SE.
1960–78; Built: 1952 as Fourth
Protestant Reformed.

1960–62	Rev. Andrew B. Cammenga
1968–75	Rev. Jerome M. Julien
1975–78	Rev. G.H. Stoutmeyer

FAITH CHURCH OF GOD IN CHRIST
See **FAITH TEMPLE CHURCH OF GOD IN CHRIST**

FAITH COMMUNITY CHRISTIAN REFORMED

Byron Center Avenue and 52nd Street
SW Wyoming 49509; Phone:
532–5432. Organized: 1919; 1919–93

Wyoming Park CRC (2733 Byron
Center Ave. SW Wyoming 1919–93;
built 1928 (J. & G. Daverman); Built:
1993 (Ted Faber).

1921–25	Rev. Edward B. Pekelder
1926–29	Rev. John P. Battema
1971–84	Rev. Leonard C. Bossenbroek
1990–	Rev. Kenneth L. Havert

FAITH DELIVERANCE PENTECOSTAL CHURCH OF GOD IN CHRIST

1326 Ashland Ave. NE 49505.
Organized: 1985.

1985–	Rev. Floyd D. Flippin

FAITH FELLOWSHIP

3931 Leland Ave. NE Comstock Park
49321; Phone: 784–5222.
Independent; Organized: 1983
(Cummings School, 4261 Schoolcraft
St. NW Walker 1983–85; Kenowa
Junior High School, 4252 Three Mile
Road NW Walker 1985–88); Built:
1940 as Emanuel Church.

1992	Rev. Ronald G. Diehl

FAITH LUTHERAN
2740 Fuller Ave. NE 49505;
Phone: 361–2679. ELCA; Organized:
1952 (928 Aberdeen St. NE 1952–56);
Built: 1956; Add 1964.
1952–87	Rev. Robert J. Lignell
1992–	Rev. Daniel B. Ward, senior pastor
1989–	Rev. Pauline Standley, assistant pastor

FAITH MINISTRIES CENTER
2317 Sylvan Ave. SE 49506;
Phone: 245–7301. Church of God,
Anderson, Ind.; Organized: 1984; Built:
1965 as Shawnee Park CRC Cadet
Building.
1984–	Rev. David Spearman, Rev. Donna Spearman

FAITH MIRACLE CENTER CHURCH INC. USA
447 Worden St. SE.
1978–80 (305 S. Division Ave. 1978–9).
1978–80	Rev. B.T. Kilgore

FAITH MISSIONARY BAPTIST
See **NEHEMIAH BAPTIST**

FAITH REFORMED
618 32nd St. SW Wyoming 49509;
Phone: 532–0206. Organized: 1947
(2822 Woodward Ave. SW Wyoming
1947–51); Built: 1951.
1947–57	Rev. James Vos
1988–	Rev. Eildert D. Zwart

FAITH TABERNACLE
953 Spencer St. NE 49505;
Phone: 361–9300. United Pentecostal;
Organized: 1968 as First United
Pentecostal (2100 Horton Ave. SE
1968–86); Built: 1956 as Woodmere
Gardens Tabernacle.
1968–75	Rev. Maurice R. Gordon
1975–88	Rev. Nathan Rose
1988–	Rev. Carl E. McKellar

FAITH TEACHING MISSION
See **NEW LIFE CHRISTIAN FELLOWSHIP**

FAITH TEMPLE APOSTOLIC
535 Church Place SW 49503;
Phone: 458–3185. Pentecostal Church
of Apostolic Faith; Organized: 1980
(750 Wealthy St. SE 1982–85; 451
Jefferson Ave SE 1986–88); Built: 1886
as Fifth Reformed (Sidney J. Osgood).
1982–86	Bishop Willie Duncan.
1988–	Elder Fred L. Jorden Sr.

FAITH TEMPLE CHURCH OF GOD IN CHRIST
18 LaBelle St. SE 49507;
Phone: 245–6378. Organized: 1960 as
Faith Church of God in Christ.
1960–	Rev. John H. Matthews

FAITH UNITED CHURCH OF GOD
3290 Walker Ave. NW Walker 49504;
Phone: 363–4834. Church of God,
Anderson, Ind.; Organized: 1984 (2396
Hillside Drive NW Walker 1984–90;
Walker Station School, 3971 Richmond
St. NW Walker 1990–93); Built: 1993
(Design Forum).
1985–	Rev. Paul M. Stover, Rev. Diana Stover

FAITH UNITED METHODIST
2600 Seventh St. NW 49504;
Phone: 453–0693. Organized: 1977;
Built: 1961 as Second Methodist.
1977–84	Rev. Eugene A. Lewis
1987–	Rev. Douglas L. Pedersen

FAMILY WORSHIP CENTER
3809 Lake Eastbrook Blvd. SE 49546;
Phone: 243–2436. Independent
Interdenominational; Organized: 1986
(Holiday Inn East, 3333 28th St. SE
Kentwood 1986; Jordan College, 1925
Breton Ave. SE 1986–87; 68 Banner
St. SW 1987–91; Calvin College Fine
Arts Center auditorium, 3201 Burton
St. SE 1991–92); Remodeled 1992
(Jeffrey Parker Associates).
1986–	Rev. Harvey L. Hester Jr. Rev. Mrs. E. Jacqueline Hester

FE ESPERANZA Y AMOR CHRISTIAN REFORMED
Burton Heights Christian Reformed,
1970 Jefferson Ave. SE 49507;
Phone: 454–9271. Organized: 1988.
1990–	Rev. Luis Pellecer

FEAKIN MEMORIAL METHODIST EPISCOPAL
See **BURTON HEIGHTS UNITED METHODIST**

FELLOWSHIP BIBLE
735 Buth Drive NE Comstock Park
49321; Phone: 784–4978.
IFCA; Organized: 1982 as merger of
Belmont Bible and Immanuel
Independent; Built: 1982.
1982–85	Rev. Patrick Deja

FELLOWSHIP CHAPEL.
637 Michigan St. NE 49503.
Organized: 1992.

FELLOWSHIP CHRISTIAN REFORMED
4375 Ivanrest Ave. SW Grandville
49418; Phone: 532–2350. Organized:
1975 (3934 Wilson Ave. SW Grandville
1975–84); Built: 1984 (PAG).
1976–83	Rev. Daniel G. Bos
1984–87	Rev. Dennis W. Boonstra
1988–	Rev. Gerald D. Postema

FELLOWSHIP YOUTH CRUSADE FOR CHRIST
1132 S. Division Ave.; 1969–70.

FIFTH AVENUE CHRISTIAN REFORMED
See FRANKLIN STREET CHRISTIAN REFORMED

FIFTH AVENUE CHURCH OF CHRIST
See **WOODVIEW CHRISTIAN**

FIFTH REFORMED
2012 Griggs St. SE 49506;
Phone: 245–9247. Organized: 1886
(535 Church Place SW 1886–1957);
Built: 1957 (James K. Haveman).
1886–89	Rev. Rense Henry Joldersma
1953–65	Rev. Chester J. Droog
1989–	Rev. David Bast

FIRST ADVENTIST
See **CENTRAL SEVENTH–DAY ADVENTIST**

FIRST ASSEMBLY OF GOD
2100 44th St. SW Wyoming 49509;
Phone: 531–2100. Organized: 1929 as
Full Gospel Assembly (52 Bellevue St.
SW Wyoming 1929–78); Built: 1978
(Brady Barnes Neil); Addition: 1992.
1930–39   Rev. Beauford F. Miller
1974–   Rev. M. Wayne Benson

FIRST BAPTIST
(3568 Alpine Ave. NW Walker)
See **GREENVIEW BAPTIST**

FIRST BAPTIST (301 N. Division Ave., 24 Fountain St. NE)
See **FOUNTAIN STREET**

FIRST BAPTIST (1164 Lafayette Ave. SE, 1121 Madison Ave. SE)
See **FIRST MISSIONARY BAPTIST**

FIRST BAPTIST CHURCH OF ALPINE AND WALKER
Four Mile Road and Peach Ridge
Avenue NW.
Organized: 1856; Built: 1859; 1909
Merged with First Congregational of
Alpine and Walker to become **TRINITY
CONGREGATIONAL UCC**

FIRST BEREAN REFORMED CHURCH OF GRAND RAPIDS
See **BEREAN BIBLE CHURCH**

FIRST CHRISTIAN REFORMED
650 Bates St. SE 49503;
Phone: 452–4370. Organized: 1857 as
True Protestant Dutch Reformed.
(Northwest corner Ionia Avenue and
Weston Street SW 1857–67; 58
Commerce Ave. SW 1867–1912
(William G. Robinson); Built: 1912 (J.
& G. Daverman).
1857   Rev. Hendrik G. Klyn
1873–76   Rev. Gerrit E. Boer
1908–18   Rev. Peter Ekster
1985–   Rev. Morris N. Greidanus

FIRST CHURCH OF CHRIST SCIENTIST
48 Lafayette Ave. SE 49503;
Phone: 459–3633. Organized: 1893
(Good Templars Hall, 23 S. Division
Ave. 1895; Ladies Literary Club,
61 Sheldon Ave. SE 1898; St. Cecilia
Building, 24 Ransom Ave. NE 1900);
Built: 1905 (SS Beaman, Chicago).

FIGURE 12
The Liberty Theater at 1028 S. Division Ave. entertained thousands of moviegoers from 1916 until the mid-1950s. It was used for worship by First Community Church of Christ from 1955 to 1960, and was destroyed by fire on April 14, 1961.

FIRST CHURCH OF THE NAZARENE
3765 Kalamazoo Ave. SE 49508;
Phone: 245–2151. Organized: 1910 as
Pentecostal Church of the Nazarene
(200 Griggs St. SW 1910–23;
2100 Horton Ave. SE 1923–63); Built:
1963.
1910–12   Rev. Charles L. Bradley
1953–68   Rev. Fletcher Galloway
1974–90   Rev. Branson E. Roberts
1990–   Rev. Dr. Walter Crow

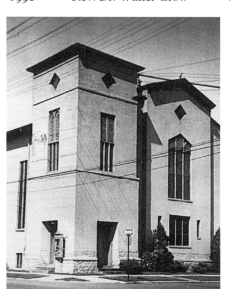

FIRST COMMUNITY AFRICAN METHODIST EPISCOPAL
500 James Ave. SE 49503;
Phone: 459–0151. Organized: 1874.
(Northwest corner Commerce Avenue
and Goodrich Street SW 1874–82;
Ionia Avenue and Cherry Street SW
1882–83; 341 Commerce Ave. SW
1883–1922); Built: 1922 (Robinson &
Campau).
1874   Rev. A.Y. Hall

FIGURES 13, 14
First Presbyterian, left, was located at the northeast corner of First and Scribner NW from 1868 to 1961. Its new house of worship, below, at 2825 Leonard NW, built in 1963, escaped the wrecking ball for less than 20 years. It was replaced by the Country Club Green Condominiums in 1980.

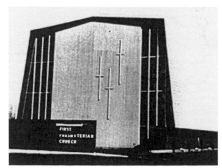

1898–1900 Rev. Lewis Pettiford
1918–26 Rev. Lewis Pettiford
1966–86 Rev. Lyman S. Parks
1989– Rev. Dr. Robert J. Eckert

FIRST COMMUNITY
CHURCH OF CHRIST
27 Pleasant St. SE 49503;
Phone: 243–0023. Independent;
Organized: 1951 (422 Grandville Ave.
SW 1951–55; 1028 S. Division Ave.
1955–60).
1951–85 Rev. Mrs. Althea Dennis
Rev. Medrick Dennis

FIRST CONGREGATIONAL
See **FIRST (PARK)**
CONGREGATIONAL

FIRST CONGREGATIONAL
CHURCH OF ADA, UCC
6330 Ada Drive SE 49546;
Phone: 676–2166. Organized: 1849;
1849–60 Congregational Church of
Cascade; Built: 1988 (Paul Pushnik).
1849–59 Rev. R.J. Hess
1986– Rev. Gary L. Burdick

FIRST CONGREGATIONAL
CHURCH OF ALPINE AND WALKER
2725 Four Mile Road NW.
Organized: 1869; Built: 1873.
1909 Merged with First Baptist of Alpine
and Walker to become **TRINITY**
CONGREGATIONAL UCC.

FIRST DUTCH REFORMED
See **CENTRAL REFORMED**

FIRST EVANGELICAL
See HOPE EVANGELICAL
UNITED BRETHREN

FIRST EVANGELICAL FREE
3950 Burton St. SE 49546;
Phone: 949–5690. Organized: 1962;
Built: 1954 as Murphy School;
Purchased 1965; Sanctuary built 1982
(Walter Carlson, Glenview, Ill.).
1966–68 Rev. Kenneth Hasper
1973–83 Rev. Denis Johnson
1990– Rev. Dr. Frederick C.
Moore

FIGURE 15
Like the nearby Ladies Literary Society , the St. Cecilia building at 24 Ransom
Ave. NE has hosted many churches on a temporary basis since its construction in
1894. First Methodist Episcopal (now First United Methodist) (1913–16) and
Central Christian (1919–22) met here while they were between churches.

FIRST FREE METHODIST
800 Maryland Ave. NE 49505;
Phone: 454–2720. Organized: 1886
(329 Bridge St. NW 1895; 1320
Ashland Ave. NE 1900–63); Built:
1963 (Dan Vos).
1886–87 Rev. H.D. Gaffin
1991– Rev. Elton O. Smith Jr.

FIRST FREE WILL BAPTIST
See **SOUTH EASTERN**
BIBLE CHURCH

FIRST GERMAN EVANGELICAL
LUTHERAN CHURCH EMANUEL
See **IMMANUEL LUTHERAN**

FIRST METHODIST (Grandville)
See **GRANDVILLE**
UNITED METHODIST

FIRST METHODIST EPISCOPAL
See **FIRST UNITED METHODIST**

FIRST MEXICAN BAPTIST
See IGLESIA BAUTISTA
PRIMERA MEXICANA

FIRST MISSIONARY BAPTIST
1164 Lafayette Ave. SE 49507;
Phone: 452–2520. Organized: 1966
(1121 Madison Ave. SE 1966–67; 1175

Lafayette Ave. SE 1967; 1121 Madison
SE 1967–79); Built: 1951 as Madison
Square Christian Reformed. Purchased
1979.
1966– Rev. Leslie L. Hudnell

FIRST NETHERLANDS REFORMED
540 Crescent St. NE 49503;
Phone: 456–8802. Organized: 1870
(201 N. Division Ave. 1870–73; 322
N. Division 1873–1951); Built: 1951
(James K. Haveman); Hastings Street
Christian School 1908–55; Plymouth
Christian School 1955.
1870–76 Rev. Cornelius Kloppenburg
1877–91 Rev. Cornelius Vorst
1892–93 Rev. Martin VanderSpek
1896–1904 Rev. Gerrit J. Wolbers
1906–09 Rev. Cornelius Pieneman
1911–22 Rev. Hendrik A.
Minderman
1947–84 Rev. William C. Lamain
1986– Rev. Joel R. Beeke

FIRST ORTHODOX
PROTESTANT REFORMED
Calvin College, 1546 Franklin St. SE.
1955–61.
1955–61 Rev. Hubert DeWolf

FIRST (PARK) CONGREGATIONAL

10 E. Park Place NE 49503;
Phone: 459-3203. UCC; Organized:
1836 as First Presbyterian (1 Monroe
Ave. NW 1841–68); Built: 1868
(Asahel Barrows Jr., Chicago); Chapel
built 1915 (Osgood & Osgood);
Addition: 1929 (Cram & Ferguson,
Boston; William Kenneth Rindge).

1837–38	Rev. A.D. McCoy
1839–47	Rev. James Ballard
1863–83	Rev. J. Morgan Smith
1916–33	Rev. Dr. Charles W. Merriam
1933–52	Rev. Dr. Edward Archibald Thompson
1962–71	Rev. Dr. Ned Burr McKenney
1972–90	Rev. Dr. William F. Allinder
1992–	Rev. Dale C. Nelson

FIRST PILGRIM TABERNACLE
See **BERKLEY HILLS WESLEYAN**

FIRST PRESBYTERIAN
2825 Leonard St. NW.
1855–1978 (502 Front Ave.. NW
1855–68; 317 First St. NW 1868–1961
(PRL Peirce); Built: 1963.

1855–61	Rev. Courtney Smith
1889–1905	Rev. L.H. Davis
1941–46	Rev. William H. Sill
1964–73	Rev. William H. Sill

FIRST PRESBYTERIAN
See **FIRST (PARK) CONGREGATIONAL**

FIRST PROTESTANT REFORMED
2800 Michigan St. NE 49506;
Phone: 942-0332. Organized: 1924
(Franklin Park community building,
900 Fuller Ave. SE 1925–26; St.
Cecilia, 24 Ransom Ave. NE 1926; 755
Fuller SE 1926–53; Grand Rapids
Christian High School, 415 Franklin
St. SE 1953–55; 755 Fuller SE
1955–84; St. Cecilia, 24 Ransom NE
1984–85); Built: 1985 (Tom Newhof).

1924–53	Rev. Herman Hoeksema
1953–55	Rev. George M. Ophoff
1955–64	Rev. Herman Hoeksema
1965–77	Rev. Gise J. VanBaren
1987–	Rev. Meindert W. Joostens

FIRST REFORMED
164 Fountain St. NE.
1840–1918 (Southwest corner
Michigan Street and Ottawa
Avenue NW 1861–72. West side
North Division Avenue between Pearl
Street and Lyon Street 1872–92;
164 Fountain St. NE 1894–1918).

1840–42	Rev. Hart E. Waring
1873–92	Rev. Peter Moerdyke DD
1907–18	Rev. John A. Brown

1918 Merged with Second Reformed to
form **CENTRAL REFORMED.**

FIRST REFORMED OF GRANDVILLE
3060 Wilson Ave. SW Grandville
49418; Phone: 534-5465. Organized:
1859; Built: 1959 (James K. Haveman);
Add 1983 (Stan Jager).

1867–70	Rev. Mannes Kiekintveld
1946–61	Rev. Henry J. TenClay
1977–90	Rev. Ronald Zartman
1991–	Rev. Douglas VanBronkhorst

FIRST SEVENTH DAY ADVENTIST
See **CENTRAL SEVENTH-DAY ADVENTIST**

FIRST SOCIETY OF SPIRITUALISTS OF GRAND RAPIDS
See **SPIRITUALISTS**

FIRST UNITARIAN SOCIETY OF GRAND RAPIDS
See **UNITARIAN CHURCH**

FIRST UNITED BRETHREN CHURCH OF GRAND RAPIDS
See **OLIVET UNITED METHODIST**

FIGURES 16, 17

Schaafsma Heating Co., below, occupies the structure at 1140 Ionia Ave. NW, which was built as Fourth Reformed Church in 1875. From 1888 to 1956, Fourth Reformed worshipped in this early Daverman church, left, at 1031 Ionia NW where the Autodie plant stands today.

FIRST UNITED HOLINESS
15 Janet St. SE Wyoming; 1967–84.
1967–74   Rev. Bliss E. Scott
1976–84   Rev. Gary E. Dougherty

FIRST UNITED METHODIST
227 E. Fulton St. 49503; Phone
451–2879. Organized: 1835 as the
Grand River Mission of the Methodist
Episcopal Church (Southwest Bond
Avenue between Michigan Street and
Crescent Street NW 1835–40; Court
House, Fulton Street Park 1840–43;
Old white church, 60 N. Division Ave.
1843–1869; 2nd church 1869–1913
(David S. Hopkins); St. Cecilia
Auditorium, 24 Ransom Ave. NE
1913–16); Built: 1916 (Robinson &
Campau).
1835–36   Rev. Osbond Monnett
1935–57   Rev. Dr. Lester A.
           Kilpatrick
1993–   Rev. Gary Haller,
           Rev. Laurie Haller

FIRST UNITED METHODIST (Grandville)
See **GRANDVILLE**
UNITED METHODIST

FIRST UNITED MISSIONARY
See GOOD SHEPHERD MISSIONARY

FIRST UNITED PENTECOSTAL
See **FAITH TABERNACLE**

FIRST UNIVERSALIST
See ALL SOULS UNIVERSALIST

FIRST WESLEYAN
1091 Three Mile Road NW Walker
49504; Phone: 784–9280.
Organized: 1985 as merger of Emmanuel
Wesleyan and Fairview Wesleyan.
1985   Rev. Ivan L. Morse
1992–   Rev. Philip W. Mitchell

FIRST WESLEYAN METHODIST
See EMMANUEL WESLEYAN

FIRST WESLEYAN METHODIST
CHURCH OF WALKER
See FAIRVIEW WESLEYAN

FISHER–OF–MEN
962 E. Fulton St.; 1979–80.

FLORENTINE SISTERS
See CHURCH OF JESUS CHRIST
OF LATTER DAY SAINTS
(324 Prospect Ave. NE)

FOREST HILLS BIBLE CHAPEL
4623 Ada Drive SE 49546;
Phone: 942–5550. Plymouth Brethren;
1890–1924 College Avenue Gospel
Hall. 1924–58 Eastern Avenue Gospel
Hall. 1958–76 Eastern Avenue Gospel
Chapel. Organized: 1890 as College
Avenue Gospel Hall (432 College Ave.
NE 1890–1924; 737 Baldwin St. SE
1924–76); Built: 1957 as Forest Hills
Community Reformed.
1890–1910 George VanderMeulen
1945   Charles E. Lacey
1970–85   Russell J. VanRyn
1990–   Russell J. VanRyn
1990–92   Don Mitchell

FOREST HILLS
COMMUNITY REFORMED
4623 Ada Drive SE.
1955–75; 1955–74 Eastmont Reformed;
Built: 1957.
1956–62   Rev. Collins D. Weeber
1971–75   Rev. Simon Nagel

FOREST HILLS PRESBYTERIAN
7495 Cascade Road SE 49546;
Phone: 942–2751. PCUSA; Organized:
1979 (Forest Hills Central High
School, 5901 Hall St. SE 1979–82);
Built: 1982 (Dow, Midland); Addition:
1990 (DSO).
1979–   Rev. Thomas D. Keizer

FOREST RIDGE PARK MISSION
See DEEPER LIFE
TABERNACLE MISSION

FORTY FOURTH STREET
CHRISTIAN REFORMED
See **WEST FORTY FOURTH**
CHRISTIAN REFORMED

FOUNTAIN STREET CHURCH
24 Fountain St. NE 49503;
Phone: 459–8386. Independent Liberal;
Organized: 1842 as First Baptist;
1869–77 Baptist Church of the City of
Grand Rapids; 1877–1965 Fountain
Street Baptist (301 N. Division Ave.
1848–65; 24 Fountain St. NE 1865–70;

111 N. Division 1870–73; 24 Fountain
NE 1873–1917 (G.P. Randall,
Chicago); Powers Theater, 123 Pearl
St. NW 1917–24); Built: 1924
(Coolidge & Hodgdon, Chicago).
1842–44   Rev. T.Z.R. Jones
1870–85   Rev. Samuel Graves DD
1890–96   Rev. John L. Jackson DD
1897–1906 Rev. John Herman
           Randall DD
1906–33   Rev. Alfred W.
           Wishart DD
1933–43   Rev. Milton M. McGorrill
1944–79   Dr. Duncan E. Littlefair
1983–   Dr. David O. Rankin

FOUR SQUARE FREE SPIRIT
16 Coolidge St. SW Wyoming.
Pentecostal; 1980–82.
1980–82   Rev. James Ausbrook

FOURTH HOLLAND
CHRISTIAN REFORMED
See **LA GRAVE AVENUE**
CHRISTIAN REFORMED

FOURTH PROTESTANT REFORMED
See **SOUTHEAST**
PROTESTANT REFORMED

FOURTH REFORMED
1226 Union Ave. NE 49505;
Phone: 454–1561. Organized: 1875
(1140 Ionia Ave. NW 1875–81;
Coldbrook Street between Ottawa
Avenue and Ionia Avenue NW
1881–88; 1031 Ionia NW 1888–1955
(J.H. Daverman & Son); Ladies
Literary Club, 61 Sheldon Ave. SE
1955–56. Built: 1955 (James K.
Haveman).
1876–81   Rev. Lammert J. Hulst
1882–91   Rev. Peter DePree
1929–41   Rev. James D. Ellenbrook
1949–58   Rev. Henry P. Kik
1959–68   Rev. Russell E. Horton
1991–   Rev. Terry Thole

FRANKLIN STREET
CHRISTIAN REFORMED
460 Franklin St. SW.
Organized: 1887 as Holland Christian
Reformed; 1910–12 Fifth Avenue
Christian Reformed; Built: 1886;

Addition: 1889; Built: 1921.
1887–1902 Rev. W.R. Smidt
1907–18 Rev. Lambertus Veltkamp
1926–37 Rev. Henry Baker
1963–66 Rev. Jerome M. Julien
1966 Merged with **ROGERS HEIGHTS CHRISTIAN REFORMED.**

**FRANKLIN STREET
CHURCH OF CHRIST**
See **EASTERN AVENUE
CHURCH OF CHRIST**

**FRANKLIN STREET
CHURCH OF CHRIST**
See **WOODVIEW CHRISTIAN**

**FREE HOLLAND
CHRISTIAN REFORMED**
See **FIRST NETHERLANDS
REFORMED**

FREE HOLLAND REFORMED
(924 Clancy Ave. NE)
See **HOLLAND REFORMED**

FREE HOLLAND REFORMED
(1044 Turner Ave. NW)
See **NETHERLANDS REFORMED
CHURCH OF GRAND RAPIDS**

FREE METHODIST
See **FIRST FREE METHODIST**

FREE REFORMED
903 Scribner Ave. NW.
1929–44.
1930–44 Rev. James Wielhouwer
1944 Merged with Rehoboth Reformed.

**FREE REFORMED CHURCH
OF NORTH AMERICA**
950 Ball Ave. NE 49503;
Phone: 456–5910. Organized: 1944 as
Rehoboth Reformed; 1951–75 Old
Christian Reformed (St. Cecilia
Building, 24 Ransom Ave. NE 1944;
1124 Leonard St. NE 1944;
903 Scribner Ave. NW 1944–60);
Built: 1961 (Dan Vos).
1948–54 Rev. Gerrit A. Zijderveld
1990– Rev. Pieter VanderMeyden

FREE WILL BAPTIST
French's Store near Leonard Street
1870–72 (201 N. Division Ave. 1870).
1871–72 Rev. Mr. Jones.

FREE WILL BAPTIST
15 Janet St. SE Wyoming; 1963–67.
1963–64 Rev. A.J. Varney

FREE WILL BAPTIST
See **SOUTH EASTERN
BIBLE CHURCH**

**FRIENDS & NEIGHBORS
GOSPEL MISSION**
559 Michigan St. NE; 1951–53.

FRIENDSHIP CHAPEL
See **FELLOWSHIP CHAPEL**

FRIENDSHIP COMMUNITY CHAPEL
436 Leonard St. NW 49504;
Phone: 451–9025. RCA; Organized:
1974 (448 Leonard St. NW 1974–80);
1974–79 Henry P. Spalink,
Kent Kelley.
1979–87 Evangelist Gerben Malda
1987– Rev. Rodney S. Thole

FRIENDSHIP MISSIONARY BAPTIST
865 Baxter St. SE 49506;
Phone: 458–0637. Organized: 1976.
1976–77 Rev. G. David May
1977– Rev. Erskin Robertson

**FRONT AVENUE FULL
GOSPEL CHURCH**
See **CENTRAL ASSEMBLY OF GOD**

FRONT AVENUE GOSPEL CHAPEL
See BRISTOLWOOD
CHRISTIAN REFORMED

FRUIT RIDGE COMMUNITY
1470 Three Mile Road NW Walker
49504; Phone: 785–7371.
Christian & Missionary Alliance.
1992– Rev. Michael D. Scott

FULL GOSPEL ASSEMBLY
See **FIRST ASSEMBLY OF GOD**

FULL GOSPEL DELIVERANCE CHURCH
See **MC SWAIN TEMPLE
CHURCH OF GOD IN CHRIST**

FULL GOSPEL MISSION
227 Bartlett St. SW.
Pentecostal; 1965–89; Organized: 1965
as Pentecostal Full Gospel Mission.
1974 Elder George W. Barnwell
1981–89 Bishop Darvis Beene

FULL GOSPEL MISSION
894 Caulfield Ave. SW.
Pentecostal; 1969–90; Organized: 1969
as Pentecostal Church in Jesus (1001
Baxter St. SE 1969–70; 1000
Grandville Ave. SW 1970–72; 300
Wealthy St. SE 1974–80).
1969–90 Bishop Darvis Beene

FULL GOSPEL MISSION
(S. 1056 Division Ave.)
See PENTECOSTAL MISSION

FULL GOSPEL MISSION
1011 Wealthy St. SE.
Pentecostal; 1939–40.
1939–40 Rev. John J. Bloem

FULL GOSPEL
PENTECOSTAL TABERNACLE
See **FIRST ASSEMBLY OF GOD**

**FULLER AVENUE
CHRISTIAN REFORMED**
1239 Fuller Ave. SE 49506;
Phone: 241–1679. Organized: 1925;
Built: 1927 (J. & G. Daverman).
1925–29 Rev. E.F.J. VanHalsema
1950–62 Rev. George Gritter
1988– Rev. Archie VanderHart

**FULLER AVENUE
CHURCH OF THE NAZARENE**
869 Fuller Ave. NE 49503;
Phone: 459–2773. Organized: 1934;
1934–39 North Side Nazarene;
1939–49 Central Church of the
Nazarene (701 Knapp St. NE 1934–39;
438 Ottawa Ave. NW 1939–49); Built:
1949; Addition: 1956; Addition; 1962.
1934–38 Rev. Charles E. Lang
1975–90 Rev. James C. Brillhart
1990– Rev. Paul Robert Evans

FUNDAMENTAL BAPTIST TEMPLE
3450 E. Beltline Ave. NE.
Independent; 1963–88 (356 Spencer
St. NE 1963–67);
1963–67   Rev. Earl Koon
1985–88   Rev. Don E. Cooper
See **BRETON ROAD BAPTIST**

GALEWOOD GOSPEL CHAPEL
1154 Burton St. SW Wyoming 49509;
Phone: 241–5628. Undenominational;
Organized: 1924 as Galewood/South
branch of Mel Trotter Ministries (1204
Burton SW 1924–31; 1100 Burton SW
1931–45); Built: 1945.
1924–31   Rev. Patrick Colegrove
1931–75   Rev. Louis J. Shy
1989–   Rev. Brenton Sutliffe

GALEWOOD MISSION
See **GALEWOOD
GOSPEL CHAPEL**

GARDEN PARK CHURCH OF GOD
5615 Madison Ave. SE Kentwood
49548; Phone: 532–2400.
Abrahamic Faith; Organized: 1964
(350 Nancy St. SE Kentwood
1964–71); Built: 1971 (Orie Martin).
1966–68   Rev. Francis Burnett
1974–   Rev. Ray M. Hall

GARFIELD PARK REFORMED
1975 Jefferson Ave. SE.
1917–90; 1917–26 Zion Reformed;
Built: 1926 (Harvey H. Weemhoff).
1917–19   Rev. Ralph Bloemendal
1957–71   Rev. Theodore Schaap
1971–84   Rev. Robert L. Bast
1985–90   Rev. James D. Knol

**GERMAN EVANGELICAL LUTHERAN
CHURCH OF IMMANUEL**
See **IMMANUEL LUTHERAN**

GERMAN EVANGELICAL ZION
See HOPE EVANGELICAL
UNITED BRETHREN

GERMAN LUTHERAN
See **IMMANUEL LUTHERAN**

GERMAN METHODIST EPISCOPAL
See VALLEY AVENUE
UNITED METHODIST

**GETHSEMANE CHURCH
OF GOD IN CHRIST**
451 Jefferson Ave. SE.
1974–80; Organized: as Gethsemane
Garden Church of God in Christ.
1974–80   Rev. Marcus Blackmore

**GETHSEMANE CHURCH
OF GOD IN CHRIST**
1701 Kalamazoo Ave. SE 49507;
Phone: 452–9522. Organized: 1986;
Built: 1952 as Fourth Protestant
Reformed.
1986–   Rev. Nathaniel Hollie

GETHSEMANE LUTHERAN
3152 Clyde Park Ave. SW Wyoming
49509; Phone: 538–5220.
ELCA; Organized: 1956 (North
Godwin School, 161 34th St. SW
Wyoming 1955–57; 16 Coolidge St
SW Wyoming 1957–61); Built: 1961.
1955–59   Rev. Frank Starkey
1959–67   Rev. Dale Hallberg
1967–77   Rev. Gary L. DesJardin
1977–92   Rev. Kenneth G. Johnson
1993–   Rev. Paul G. Phelps

GLAD TYDINGS GOSPEL TABERNACLE
200 Griggs St. SW; 1972–78.
1963–65   Rev. C.E. DeWitt
1974   Rev. Wallace Cook

GLORIOUS CHURCH OF CHRIST
645 Grandville Ave. SW.
Apostolic Faith; 1964–78 (651
Grandville SW 1964–65; 649
Grandville SW 1965–67).
1974–78   Rev. James L. Chesbro

GODWIN BAPTIST
See **MAPLELAWN BAPTIST**

GODWIN GOSPEL CHAPEL
See **COMMUNITY
CHRISTIAN REFORMED**

GODWIN GOSPEL MISSION
3749 S. Division Ave. Wyoming.
1929–32 (3759 S. Division 1929–31).

**GODWIN HEIGHTS
CHRISTIAN REFORMED**
225 32nd St. SW Wyoming 49548;
Phone: 452–0990. Organized: 1927
(3565 Jefferson Ave. SE Wyoming
1927–55); Built: 1955 (James K.
Haveman).
1929–32   Rev. Henry Rikkers
1963–70   Rev. Vincent C. Licatesi
1971–87   Rev. Harry J. Kwantes
1990–   Rev. Harold E. Veldman

GODWIN HEIGHTS FREE METHODIST
See **EASTERN AVENUE
FREE METHODIST**

**GODWIN HEIGHTS
GOSPEL TABERNACLE**
See **MAPLELAWN BAPTIST**

GOLD AVENUE BACK TO GOD CHAPEL
See GOLD AVENUE CHURCH

**GOLD AVENUE
CHRISTIAN REFORMED**
See GOLD AVENUE CHURCH

GOLD AVENUE CHURCH
49 Gold Ave. NW 49504;
Phone: 454–8833. Christian Reformed;
Organized: 1929 as West Fulton Street
Gospel Mission (632 W. Fulton St.
1930; 620 W. Fulton 1935; 11 Gold
SW 1940–89); Built: 1883 and
remodeled 1953 as Second Baptist.
1929–43   Rev. John VanDeWater
1944–51   Andrew VanderVeer
1951–64   Elias Dykstra
1965–74   Peter Doot
1975–86   Michael Knierim
1982–91   William Ridley
1992–   Rev. Robert Offringa

**GOOD NEWS
COMMUNITY REFORMED**
4319 Byron Center Ave. SW Wyoming
49509; Phone: 532–7755. Organized:
1978 as mission; 1982 as church
(Ramblewood Apartments, 4277
Stonebridge Road SW; Gerribee Party
Place, 4050 Chicago Drive SW; school,
Jenison; Pinery Park senior center, 2380
DeHoop Ave. SW, 1978–92.)
1978–82   Rev. Stanley Hagemeyer
1982–87   Rev. Donald Topp
1987–   Rev. H. Arlan TenClay

GOOD SHEPHERD CHURCH

737 Eastern Ave. SE 49503;
Phone: 243–2283.
Nondenominational; Organized: 1954
(738 Thomas St. SE 1954–70).
1954–72   Rev. Robert L. Lowe
1987–   Rev. Anderson Cooperwood

GOOD SHEPHERD EPISCOPAL
See CHURCH OF THE
GOOD SHEPHERD

GOOD SHEPHERD MISSIONARY CHURCH

5040 Breton Ave. SE Kentwood.
Missionary, Fort Wayne, Ind.; 1950–85;
Organized: as United Missionary
Church (312 Jefferson Ave. SE
1950–55; 1144 Hazen St. SE 1958–64;
2100 Horton Ave. SE 1964–68;
Valleywood Middle School, 1110 50th
St. SE Kentwood 1968–69); Built:
1968–71 (Church Builders).
1950   Rev. John Tuckey
1955–59   Rev. Roscoe E Burk
1968–85   Rev. Arthur J. Taylor

GOOD SHEPHERD MISSIONARY BAPTIST
See GOOD SHEPHERD CHURCH

GOSPEL BELLS MISSION

617 Jefferson Ave. SE.
1929–65; Organized: as Gospel Bell
Missionary Evangelists (834 Ionia Ave.
SW 1929–31; 947–49 S. Division Ave.
1931–32; 849 S. Division 1932–33).
1929–50   Rev. Samuel William
            Glover
1950–65   Mrs. Ada M. Glover

GOSPEL CHAPEL
See GRIGGS STREET
CHRISTIAN REFORMED

GOSPEL CHAPEL
See MADISON SQUARE
CHRISTIAN REFORMED

GOSPEL FELLOWSHIP

4809 Eastern Ave. SE Kentwood
49508; 1990.
1990   Rev. Vincent C. Licatesi

FIGURE 18
The Franklin Theatre at 814 S. Division Ave. was converted into a reception hall, the Rose Room, after World War II. Muhammad's Mosque No. 61 was located here (1970–1979), and it is now home to the Grace Tabernacle COGIC.

GOSPEL FELLOWSHIP

368 Norwood Ave. SE; 1938–54.
1940–48   Rev. Otis Q. Sellers
1949–54   Rev. Gerritt Hazekamp

GOSPEL HALL (735 Baldwin St. SE., 432 College Ave. NE.)
See FOREST HILLS BIBLE CHAPEL

GOSPEL HALL

434 Sixth St. NW; 1940–45.
1944–45   Rev. Henry Stadt

GOSPEL MEETING HALL

1649 Preston Ave. NW.
Organized: 1960.

GOSPEL MISSION

348 Bartlett St. SW; 1913–23.

GOSPEL MISSION

449 S. Division Ave.; 1973–74.

GOSPEL MISSION CHAPEL/HALL

737 Ionia Ave. NW; 1930–65.
1951   Bert DeKorte

GOSPEL TABERNACLE
See MAPLELAWN BAPTIST

GOSPEL TEMPLE MISSIONARY BAPTIST

460 Franklin St. SW 49503;
Phone: 245–2619. Organized: 1956
(508 Ottawa Ave. NW 1959–60; 523
LaGrave Ave. SE 1961–69); Built: 1921
as Franklin Street Christian Reformed
(J. & G. Daverman).
1957–58   Rev. William Perry
1961–   Rev. Leonard Gant

GRACE AND TRUTH CHAPEL
See COMMUNITY BIBLE

GRACE ASSEMBLY
See COMMUNITY BIBLE

GRACE BIBLE

3715 Wilson Ave. SW Grandville
49418; Phone: 538–9350.
IFCA; Organized: 1933 (3087 Wilson
SW Grandville 1933–56); Built: 1956
(Daverman); Addition: 1969;
Addition: 1986.
1933–47   Rev. George Tuinstra
1956–76   Rev. Paul Boger
1976–   Rev. Kenneth E. Hasper

GRACE CHAPEL
See GRACE CHURCH
OF GRAND RAPIDS

GRACE CHRISTIAN REFORMED

100 Buckley St. SE 49503;
Phone: 452–8920. Organized: 1949 as
Buckley Street Chapel, 1962 as church;
Built: 1949; Addition: 1978.

1949–62	Albert Veen, evangelist
1962–65	Rev. Martin Toonstra
1966–69	Rev. Peter Huiner
1968–74	Rev. Paul W. Brink
1976–	Rev. Roger E. VanHarn

GRACE CHURCH OF GRAND RAPIDS

1815 Hall St. SE East Grand Rapids
49506; Phone: 241–4631.
Episcopal; Organized: 1873 as Grace
Chapel, 1875 as church (Public school,
northeast corner Wealthy Street and
Prospect Avenue SE 1873–78; 305
Cherry St. SE/150 Lafayette Ave. SE
1878–1956 (built 1892 William G.
Robinson; remodeled 1926 Harvey H.
Weemhoff); Built: 1953 (Edward I.
Schulte, Cincinnati).

1873–74	Rev. Samuel Earp
1874–75	Rev. Seth S. Chapin
1927–36	Rev. Lewis B. Whittemore
1936–68	Rev. Donald V. Carey
1991–	Rev. Edward R. Rich III

GRACE EPISCOPAL

See **GRACE CHURCH OF GRAND RAPIDS**

GRACE LUTHERAN

150 50th St. SW Wyoming 49548;
Phone: 534–0805. Missouri Synod;
Organized: 1949 (4023 S. Division
Ave. Wyoming 1949–50); Chapel
built: 1950. Church built: 1962.

1949–58	Rev. Carl L. Moellman
1967–	Rev. Noble P. Lach

GRACE MINISTRIES INTERNATIONAL INC.

2125 Martindale Ave. SW Wyoming
49509; Phone: 241–5666.
Nondenominational; Organized: 1939 in
Chicago. Moved to Grand Rapids 1960.

1960–67	Henry J. Sonneveldt
1967–74	Dan Bultema
1987–	Dr. Samuel R. Vinton Jr.

GRACE MISSION

3838 S. Division Ave. Wyoming; 1935.

FIGURE 19

The Greater Eliezer Temple of the Apostolic Faith at 909 Franklin St. SE was destroyed in a spectacular fire on Sunday, Aug. 9, 1992. An early design of Pierre Lindhout, it was home to Plymouth Congregational from 1893 to 1959.

GRACE PENTECOSTAL CHURCH OF GOD IN CHRIST

1441 Leonard St. NE 49505;
Phone: 454–1694. Organized: 1950
(123 Franklin St. SE 1950–65;
1001 Hermitage St. SE 1965–88);
Built: 1934 as Creston
Undenominational; Addition: 1954.

1950–	Rev. James Holloway

GRACE REFORMED

3330 Burlingame Ave. SW Wyoming
49509; Phone: 538–3100.
Organized: 1897 (Reelman's Hall, 710
Grandville Ave. SW 1897–98;
Klondyke Church, 1898–99;
892 Caulfield Ave. SW 1899–1963);
Built: 1964 (J. & G. Daverman).

1897–1901	Rev. John Van de Erve
1912–38	Rev. Cornelius H. Spaan
1938–45	Rev. Theodore Schaap
1949–53	Rev. Abraham Rynbrandt
1954–59	Rev. James W. Schut
1959–65	Rev. Rodger H. Dalman
1966–72	Rev. Harry L. Brower
1973–85	Rev. Mark D. DeWitt
1986–	Rev. Louis H. Benes III
1988–	Rev. Brian K. Taylor

GRACE TABERNACLE CHURCH OF GOD IN CHRIST

814 S. Division Ave.
Organized: 1964 as Church of Christ
(4435 Potter Ave. SE Kentwood
1964–78).

1974–	Rev. Jake Lipsey

GRAND CHRISTIAN CENTER

See GOOD SHEPHERD
MISSIONARY CHURCH

GRAND RAPIDS BIBLE STUDENTS

126 Sheldon Ave. SE.
Undenominational; 1949–67.

GRAND RAPIDS FRIENDS MEETING

IGE, 415 Ethel Ave. SE 49506;
Phone: 774–7701. Quaker;
Organized: 1962.

1962	Eugene and Ethel Dungan

GRAND RAPIDS IMMANUEL BAPTIST

1935 44th St. SE 49508;
Phone: 455–2610. Southern Baptist
Convention; Organized: 1956 (Central
Seventh Day Adventist Church, 100
Sheldon Ave. SE 1956–58; 909

FIGURE 20

A commercial structure added to an old dwelling at 533 Jefferson Ave. SE was the first home (1963–68) for the Guiding Light Church of God in Christ.

Franklin St. SE 1958–64); Built: 1965 (Glass, DeWitt, Mich.); Addition: 1986.

1957–62	Rev. John W. Nichol
1985–92	Rev. Floyd E. Hughes
1993–	Rev. Scott Johnson.

GRAND RAPIDS ISLAMIC CENTER AND MOSQUE
See **ISLAMIC CENTER OF WEST MICHIGAN**

GRAND RAPIDS LATVIAN EVANGELICAL LUTHERAN
1780 Knapp St. NE 49505; Phone: 361–6003. Organized: 1950 (111 Burton St. SE 1950–86); Built: 1986 (Aivars Linde).

1950–65	Rev. Janis Ozols
1965–77	Rev. Kristaps Hermanis
1977–	Rev. Janis V. Mednis

GRAND RAPIDS MARANATHA SPANISH SEVENTH–DAY ADVENTIST
See **IGLESIA ADVENTISTA MARANATHA**

GRAND RAPIDS SPIRITUAL ASSOCIATION
See **SPIRITUAL SOCIETY**

GRAND RAPIDS UNITY CENTER/SOCIETY
See **UNITY CHURCH OF PRACTICAL CHRISTIANITY**

GRAND RAPIDS WEST CHURCH OF THE NAZARENE
1313 Bristol Ave. NW 49504; Phone: 453–5550. Organized: 1964 (West YMCA, 902 Leonard St. NW 1964–73); Built: 1973.

| 1964–65 | Rev. Kenneth Culver |
| 1991– | Rev. Kenneth L. Anderson |

GRAND RIVER MISSION
See **FIRST UNITED METHODIST**

GRANDVILLE ASSEMBLY OF GOD
3260 52nd St. SW Wyoming 49509; Phone: 531–0010. Organized: 1974 (West Elementary School, 3777 Aaron Ave. SW Grandville 1975–77); Built: 1977 (Walter J. Perry).

| 1974–83 | Pastor Burdette L. Faulk |
| 1983– | Pastor John F. Godfrey |

GRANDVILLE AVENUE CHRISTIAN REFORMED
811 Chicago Drive SW Grand Rapids 49509; Phone: 243–5875. Organized: 1891 (1537 Grandville Ave. SW 1891–1950; Remodeled 1915 (Thomas Benjamin & Son); Built: 1951 (J. & G. Daverman).

1893–96	Rev. William Greve
1917–45	Rev. Dr. Ymen P. DeJong
1991–	Rev. P. Wayne Townsend

GRANDVILLE BAPTIST
4325 40th St. SW Grandville 49418; Phone: 534–8681. General Association of Regular Baptists; Organized: 1957 (3087 Wilson Ave. SW Grandville 1958–67); Built: 1967 (Dan Vos).

| 1957–60 | Rev. Hollis Tiffany |
| 1988– | Rev. C. Powers Payton |

GRANDVILLE BIBLE
4122 44th St. SW Grandville 49418; Phone: 532–3118. IFCA; Organized: 1986; Chapel built: 1959 as Bethel Baptist (Chris Steketee); Church built: 1990 (W.L. Perry Associates).

| 1988–91 | Rev. Ernest H. Baker |
| 1992– | Rev. Bryan Jones |

GRANDVILLE CHURCH OF CHRIST
3725 44th St. SW Grandville 49418; Phone: 534–8884. Independent; Organized: 1962 (West Elementary School, 3777 Aaron Ave. SW Grandville 1962–63); Built: 1963 (Edward W. Koerber).

| 1962–69 | Rev. Ivan E. Wilkerson |
| 1980– | Rev. Russell R. Holden |

GRANDVILLE–JENISON CONGREGATIONAL UNITED CHURCH OF CHRIST
3900 Henry St. SW Grandville 49418; Phone: 534–5552. Organized: 1949 as merger of First Congregational Church of Jenison (Main Street, Jenison 1905–35) and First Congregational Church of Grandville (organized: 1838); (Church Avenue and Oakes Street SW Grandville 1855–1917; Superior Street and Barrett Avenue SW Grandville 1917–44); Built: 1949. Addition: 1964 (Kammeraad Stroop).

| 1837–43 | Rev. James Ballard |
| 1991– | Rev. William T. Curnow |

GRANDVILLE
PROTESTANT REFORMED
4320 40th St. SW Grandville 49418;
Phone: 538–6176. Organized: 1984
(Grandville High School, 3535 Wilson
Ave. SW Grandville 1984–89).

1984–92	Rev. Jason Kortening
1992–	Rev. Audred P. Spriensma

GRANDVILLE UNITED METHODIST
3140 Wilson Ave. SW Grandville
49418; Phone: 538–3070. Organized:
1869 as First Methodist (Prairie and
Washington SW Grandville
1869–1923); Built: 1970 (Edgar Robert
Firant).

1868–69	Rev. Cowan
1988–	Rev. Dr. J. Melvin Bricker,
Rev. Kim Gladding

GRANT STREET MISSION
310 Grant St. SW. Christian
Reformed; 1915–22.

1920	John Butt

GREATER ELIEZER TEMPLE
OF THE APOSTOLIC FAITH
Aquinas College, 1607 Robinson Road
SE 49506; Phone: 245–1531.
The Church of Our Lord Jesus Christ;
Organized: 1979 as Church of the
Living God (1121 Madison Ave. SE
1980–82; 926 Wealthy St. SE 1982–83;
755 Eastern Ave. SE 1983–91; 909
Franklin St. SE 1991–92).

1979–80	Bpisho Raymond Dunlap
1980–	Rev. Larry D. Weaver

GREATER HARVEST
CHURCH OF GOD IN CHRIST
1007 Cooper Ave. SE 49507.
Organized: 1990 (1154 Sheldon Ave. SE
1990–91; 1721 Madison Ave. SE 1992).

1990–	Elder Keith Flowers

GREENVIEW BAPTIST
1030 Four Mile Road NW Walker
49504; Phone: 784–0555. Organized:
1957; 1957–67 First Baptist Church of
Comstock Park (3943 West River
Drive NE Comstock Park 1958–60;
3568 Alpine Ave. NW Walker
1960–68); Built: 1968.

1957–60	Rev. James Carmichael
1965–70	Rev. Gene H. Schafer
1988–	Rev. Michael Sikora

GRIGGS STREET CHRISTIAN REFORMED
See GRIGGS STREET
GOSPEL CHAPEL

GRIGGS STREET EVANGELICAL
UNITED BRETHREN
See GRIGGS STREET
UNITED METHODIST

GRIGGS STREET GOSPEL CHAPEL
306 Griggs St. SW.
CRC; 1948–77.

1955	Peter VanderKamp
1972–77	Rev. Herbert J. Kramer

GRIGGS STREET
ORTHODOX PRESBYTERIAN
See **HARVEST
ORTHODOX PRESBYTERIAN**

GRIGGS STREET UNITED METHODIST
111 Griggs St. SE.
Organized: 1907 as Second Evangelical;
1928–49 Griggs Street Evangelical;
1949–68 Griggs Street Evangelical
United Brethren.

1908–10	Rev. Edward Frye
1968–76	Rev. G. Allen Steeby
1979	Merged with **WESLEY
PARK UNITED METHODIST**

GUIDING LIGHT CHURCH
OF GOD IN CHRIST, THE
1223 Madison Ave. SE.
1963–78 (533 Jefferson Ave. SE 1963–68;
1204 Madison SE 1969–71).

1963–78	Rev. Henry Flowers

GUIDING LIGHT MISSION
1019 Wealthy St. SE 49506;
Phone: 771–0236.
Christian Reformed mission for women;
Organized: 1989; (15 S. Division Ave.
1989–90).

1989–	Wanda VanKlumpenburg

GUIDING LIGHT MISSION, THE
255 S. Division Ave. 49503;
Phone: 451–0236. CRC; Organized:
1957 (50 S. Division 1957–59; 101 S.
Division 1959–79; 25 Commerce
Ave. SW 1979–86).

1957–66	Rev. Andrew VanDerVeer
1984–	Herman Koning

HARVEST CHURCH
OF OUR LORD JESUS CHRIST
755 Eastern Ave. SE 49503.
Organized: 1993.

1993–	Pastor Stephen Collins

HARVEST FULL GOSPEL CHURCH
6025 28th St. SE; 1980–81.

HARVEST ORTHODOX
PRESBYTERIAN
Calvin Christian School, 601 36th St.
SW Wyoming 49509; Phone: 531–2700.
(306 Griggs St. SW 1977–91).

1977–78	Rev. Herbert J. Kramer
1990–92	Rev. R. Calvin Malcor
1992–	Terry Gray

HAVEN OF REST RESCUE MISSION
302–04 Bridge St. NW.
1952–71 (312 Bridge NW 1952–60).

1952–56	Arnold J. VanderMeulen
1957–71	Herbert P. Newhouse

HAZEN STREET MISSION
See **SEYMOUR
CHRISTIAN REFORMED**

HEARTSIDE CHAPEL
54 S. Division Ave. 49503;
Phone: 235–7211.
Ecumenical; Organized: 1983.

1983–92	Dr. George G. Beukema
1987–	Rev. George K.
Heartwell Jr.
1992–	Rev. Barbara A. Pekich

HERITAGE BAPTIST
1570 60th St. SE 49508;
Phone: 698–6111. Independent;
Organized: 1979 (Dutton Elementary
School, 3820 68th St. SE 1979; East
Kentwood High School, 6178 Campus
Park Drive SE 1979–84); Built: 1984
(Barnes Construction Co).

1979–84	Rev. David Wood Sr.
1986–	Rev. E.H. Moore

HIAWATHA BAPTIST MISSIONS
See **CONTINENTAL
BAPTIST MISSIONS**

HIGHLAND HILLS BAPTIST

1415 Northrup Ave. NW 49504;
Phone: 453–2845. General Association
of Regular Baptists; Organized: 1894;
1894–1944 Holland Baptist; 1944–61
Quarry Avenue Baptist
(848 McReynolds Ave. NW 1895–1905;
1144 Quarry Ave. NW 1905–61); Built:
1961 (J. & G. Daverman).

1894–1944	Rev. Douwe Laansma
1945–58	Rev. Robert G. Dice
1959–68	Rev. Gordon F. Cook
1968–85	Rev. Richard J. Woodworth
1986–	Rev. Stanley L. Mohr

HIGHLAND HILLS CHRISTIAN REFORMED

1015 Westend Ave. NW.
Organized: 1950.

1950–54	Rev. Jacob D. Eppinga
1984–89	Rev. John Hofman Jr.
1990	Merged with Alpine Avenue

Christian Reformed to become
WESTEND CHRISTIAN REFORMED

HILLCREST COMMUNITY CHURCH

850 Norwich Ave. SW 49503;
Phone: 452–2720. CRC; Organized:
1946 as Hillcrest Chapel (Way of Life
Chapel, 315 Grant St. SW 1942–46;
907 Dorchester Ave. SW 1947–49);
Built: 1949 (Joseph Hoort); Addition:
1971.

1942–55	Rev. Miner Tanis
1976–	Rev. Louis K. Toering

HILLIARD CHAPEL AME ZION

Olivet United Methodist Church, 1933
Buchanan Ave. SW 49507;
Phone: 245–9270. Organized: 1976 as
Asbury AME Zion Church Mission
(841 Sheldon Ave. SE 1976–86; 839
Madison Ave. SE 1987–88).

1976–85	Rev. Ebenezer James
1987–	Rev. Ernest G. Brewster Sr.

HISPANIC APOSTOLATE
See **OUR LADY OF GUADALUPE**

HISPANIC UNITED METHODIST
See **IGLESIA METODISTA UNIDA HISPANA**

HOLINESS GOSPEL MISSION

11 Wealthy St. SW; 1951–61.

HOLINESS MISSION

115 S. Division Ave.; 1914–15.

1914–15	Rev. Jacob Bos

HOLLAND BAPTIST
See **HIGHLAND HILLS BAPTIST**

HOLLAND CHRISTIAN REFORMED
(Crosby Street NW)
See **WEST LEONARD CHRISTIAN REFORMED**

HOLLAND CHRISTIAN REFORMED
(48 Dennis Ave. SE)
See **MAYFAIR CHRISTIAN REFORMED**

HOLLAND CHRISTIAN REFORMED
(460 Franklin St. SW)
See **FRANKLIN STREET CHRISTIAN REFORMED**

HOLLAND CHRISTIAN REFORMED
(1537 Grandville Ave. SW)
See **GRANDVILLE AVENUE CHRISTIAN REFORMED**

HOLLAND CHRISTIAN REFORMED
(111 LaGrave Ave. SE)
See **LAGRAVE AVENUE CHRISTIAN REFORMED**

HOLLAND CHRISTIAN REFORMED
(Powers and Ohio)
See **OAKDALE PARK CHRISTIAN REFORMED**

HOLLAND CONGREGATIONAL

657 Leonard St. NW; 1893–97.

1893–97	Rev. John W. Poot

HOLLAND REFORMED
(1024 Adams St. SE)
See **OAKDALE PARK REFORMED**

HOLLAND REFORMED

924 Clancy Ave. NE.
1889–1915. (Finn's Hall, 1153
Plainfield Ave. NE 1889.) Built: 1889.

1890–1910	Rev. John Van den Broek

HOLLAND REFORMED
(1044 Turner Ave. NW)
See **NETHERLANDS REFORMED CHURCH OF GRAND RAPIDS**

HOLLAND UNITARIAN

401 Ionia Ave. NW.
1885–1920; Independent (Universalist
Church, Pearl Street between Ionia
Avenue and Ottawa Avenue NW
1885–86); Built: 1886.

1885–99	Rev. Frederick W.N. Hugenholtz
1899–1916	Rev. Bernard A. VanSluyters

HOLLANDSCHE CHURCH
See **FIRST CHRISTIAN REFORMED**

HOLY CROSS EPISCOPAL

4252 Breton Ave. SE Kentwood 49512;
Phone: 949–7034. Organized: 1962
(Meadowlawn School, 4939 Burgis
Ave. SE Kentwood 1962–63; YWCA,
4550 Eastern Ave. SE Kentwood
1963–65); Built: 1965.

1962–65	Rev. Gary A. Garnett
1978–	Rev. Charles F. Homeyer

HOLY NAME OF JESUS

1630 Godfrey Ave. SW Wyoming
49509. RC; Organized: 1908; Built:
1961 (Stapert Pratt Bulthuis Sprau &
Crothers Inc., Kalamazoo); School
1908.

1908–17	Rev. Thomas J. Reid
1917–32	Rev. Oswald T. McGinn
1985–93	Rev. Thomas C. Niedzwiecki
1993–	Rev. Donald E. Weber

HOLY NAZARENE TABERNACLE

64 Stormzand Place NE 49503.
1953–58 (815 S. Division Ave.
1953–54).

1953–58	Rev. Mrs. Clyde Crane

HOLY SPIRIT

2230 Lake Michigan Drive NW 49504.
RC; Organized: 1952; Built: 1953;
School 1953.

1952–76	Rev. Bernard L. Sikorski
1984–	Rev. David E. LeBlanc

HOLY TRINITY
1200 Alpine Church St. NW
Comstock Park 49321;
Phone: 784–0677. RC; Organized: 1848
(Five Mile Road and Baumhoff Avenue
NW 1848–82); Built: 1957 (Humbrecht
Associates, Fort Wayne, Ind.) Built:
1967 (Edgar Robert Firant); School 1923.
1852–57   Rev. Julian Maciejewski
1923–63   Msgr. Charles F. Bolte
1963–73   Msgr. William J. Hoogterp
1987–   Rev. John J. Wisneski

HOLY TRINITY EPISCOPAL
5333 Clyde Park Ave. SW Wyoming
49509; Phone: 538–0900. Organized:
1957 (3403 Burlingame Ave. SW
Wyoming 1957–62); Built: 1962
(Russell F. Donker Associates);
Addition: 1990 (Lakewood Inc.).
1958–66   Rev. Everett Francis Ellis
1967–73   Rev. Roderic Duncan Wiltse
1973–76   Rev. Peter Hanson Gray
1976–   Rev. D. Edward
    Emenheiser

**HOLY TRINITY
EVANGELICAL LUTHERAN**
4201 Burlingame Ave. SW Wyoming
49509; Phone: 538–1122.
Wisconsin Synod; Organized: 1963
(East Newhall School, 1585 36th
St. SW Wyoming 1963–64); Built:
1985 (Richard Postema); School 1964.
1963–70   Rev. Harold A. Hempel
1980–   Rev. Frederick S. Adrian

HOLY TRINITY FELLOWSHIP CENTER
513 Eastern Ave. SE 49503;
Phone: 776–0230. Baptist; Organized:
1992 (Sheldon Complex, 121 Franklin
St. SE 1992–93).
1992–   Rev. Harold Tyler Jr.,
    Rev. Cy Young Sr.

HOLY TRINITY GREEK ORTHODOX
330 Lakeside Drive NE 49503;
Phone: 454–6563. Organized: 1927
(1000 Cherry St. SE 1927–49; 72
Ransom Ave. NE 1949–76); Built:
1976 (Lou Cordogan).
1929–31   Rev. Asterios Asteriou
1952–65   Rev. Polykarpos G.
    Gryfakis
1984–   Rev. James A. Bogdan

HOLY ZION CHURCH
OF GOD IN CHRIST
904 Logan St. SE; 1971–80.
1971–80   Rev. Edward H.J. Haralson

HOME ACRES MISSIONARY BAPTIST
128 44th St. SE Kentwood.
1952–66 (15 Murray St. SW Wyoming
1952–53); Built: 1953.
1952–54   Rev. Edward F. Rodgers
1957–60   Rev. Thomas M. Hayes
1962–64   Rev. Kelley Campbell

HOME ACRES REFORMED
21 Murray St. SE Kentwood 49548;
Phone: 534–0527. Organized: 1925;
Built: 1928.
1926–32   Rev. Bert Brower
1969–81   Rev. Elton L. VanPernis
1991–   Rev. Dr. George Kroeze

HOME OF HOPE MISSION
See **NORTH PARK BAPTIST**

HOME SPIRITUALIST CHURCH
304 Cherry St. SE; 1939–40
1939–40   Rev. Mrs. Belle Fuller

HOMESTEAD BIBLE CHAPEL
See **MAPLE CREEK COMMUNITY**

HOPE CHRISTIAN REFORMED
3110 Barrett Ave. SW Grandville
49418; Phone: 534–8901.
Organized: 1916 (4551 Hall St.
SW/4790 River Bend Drive SW
Walker 1917–37; Caldwell Building,
Chicago Drive and Franklin Avenue
SW Grandville 1937–39); Built: 1940.
1917–24   Rev. George M. Ophoff
1971–83   Rev. Sebastian T.
    Cammenga
1991–   Rev. Curtis A. Walters

HOPE EVANGELICAL
UNITED BRETHREN
754 Bridge St. NW.
1883–1964; Organized: 1883 as Zion
German Evangelical Church; Built: 1884.
1884–85   Rev. L.V. Soldan
1960–64   Rev. Arthur C. Bauman

HOPE LUTHERAN
100 Packard Ave. SE 49503;
Phone: 459–2941. Missouri Synod;
Organized: 1914 as Hope Evangelical
Lutheran (903 Scribner Ave. NW
1913–21; 401 Ionia Ave. NW
1921–29); Built: 1929 (Charles M.
Norton).
1914–15   Rev. Ernst Ross
1916–53   Rev. Emil L. Schwan
1953–67   Rev. Ralph H. Young
1983–   Rev. Allen A. Gartner

HOPE METHODIST INDIAN MISSION
754 Bridge St. NW; 1964–66.
1964–66   Rev. Lewis Church

HOPE MISSION (654 Eastern Ave. SE)
See **IMMANUEL REFORMED**

HOPE MISSION
420 Scribner Ave. NW; 1943–45.

HOPE PROTESTANT REFORMED
1580 Ferndale Ave. SW Walker 49504;
Phone: 453–1791. Organized: 1916 as
Hope Christian Reformed; Organized:
1924–26 as Hope Protestant Reformed
(Blair School, 4790 River Bend Drive
SW Walker 1924–30; 1545 Wilson
Ave. SW Walker 1930–65). Built:
1965 (James K. Haveman).
1924–29   Rev. George M. Ophoff
1986–   Rev. James D. Slopsema

HOPE REFORMED
2010 Kalamazoo Ave. SE 49507;
Phone: 241–3421. Organized: 1942;
Built: 1950.
1943–54   Rev. John L. VanHarn
1955–61   Rev. Henry J. Vermeer
1962–72   Rev. Harland H. Steele
1974–81   Rev. Richard A. Welscott
1982–91   Rev. Vernon D.
    Hoffman Sr.
1991–   Rev. Robert J. Baird

HOPE RESCUE MISSION
330 Bridge St. NW; 1945.

HOUSE OF PRAYER
25 Sycamore St. SE 49503.
1960–89; (227 Bartlett St. SW
1960–65; 28 Buckley St. SE 1965–89).
1960–89   Rev. Mrs. Beatrice A. Bates

FIGURE 21
Architect Sidney J. Osgood's sketch book contained this drawing of his Immanuel Presbyterian Church on Madison at Oakdale Street SE. Erected in 1889, this building burned in the early morning hours of April 30, 1955. The site is now occupied by Madison Square Christian Reformed Church.

HOUSE OF PRAYER FOR ALL PEOPLE
See HOUSE OF PRAYER

HOUSE OF PRAYER MINISTRIES
1007 Wealthy St. SE 49506;
Phone: 245–1042; Organized: 1991.
1991–   Rev. Lemar Hill

HOUSE OF PRAYER
SPIRITUAL CHURCH
See **HOUSE OF PRAYER**

HOUSE OF THE LORD, THE
1522 Plastico Ave. SW Wyoming;
1954–60.

HOUSEHOLD OF FAITH TABERNACLE
645 Front Ave. NW. 1939–53.
Organized: 1939 as Household of
Faith Mission (643 Stocking Ave.
NW 1939–40).
1940–46   Rev. Algie E. Sanford

HUNTINGTON WOODS BAPTIST
4550 Byron Center Ave. SW Wyoming
49509; Phone: 532–5383. Southern
Baptist Convention; Organized: 1963
(Southwest Newhall Elementary
School, Clyde Park Avenue and 44th
Street SW Wyoming 1961–65); Built:

1965 (Peter DeVos, Kalamazoo).
1961–63   William Varnell
1963–73   Rev. David B. Ray
1985–   Rev. Michael D. Painter

IDEAL PARK CHRISTIAN REFORMED
320 56th St. SW Wyoming 49548;
Phone: 532–2204. Organized: 1947 as
Lamar Plat Gospel Chapel; 1951 as
Ideal Park Chapel; 1961 as church;
Built: 1963 (Randal Cooper).
1960–62   Rev. Vincent C. Licatesi
1962–67   Rev. Sidney A. Werkema
1967–90   Rev. John M. Hofman
1990–   Rev. Zachary G. Anderson

IGLESIA ADVENTISTA DE SEPTIMO DIA
See IGLESIA ADVENTISTA
HISPANA DE GRAND RAPIDS

IGLESIA ADVENTISTA DE WYOMING
3880 Jefferson Ave. SE Wyoming
49548; Phone: 247–1230. Organized:
1975 (Central Seventh Day Adventist
Church, 100 Sheldon Ave. SE
1971–75; Burton Heights United

Methodist Church, 100 Burton St. SE
1975–77; 700 Burton SE 1977–84;
4614 Walton Ave. SW Wyoming
1984–91).
1971   Rev. Oswald Scully
1990–   Rev. Eduardo Valdez

IGLESIA ADVENTISTA
HISPANA DE GRAND RAPIDS
700 Burton St. SE 49507;
Phone: 243–3405. Organized: 1977
(Burton Heights United Methodist
Church, 100 Burton St. SE 1977–83).
1977–78   Rev. Jose Guillen
1990–   Rev. Eduardo Valdez

IGLESIA ADVENTISTA MARANATHA
68 Banner St. SW 49507;
Phone: 452–6003. Organized: 1988
(Jefferson Ave. SE 1988–90; 306 Griggs
St. SW 1990–92).
1988   Luis Leonor
1990–91   Pastor David Garcia
1992–   Pastor Hector Jurado

IGLESIA ASAMBLEAS CRISTIANAS
354 Fuller Ave. SE 49506.
1992 (892 Caulfield Ave. SW 1992).
1992   Eduardo Terrero

IGLESIA BAUTISTA HISPANA
See **BURTON HEIGHTS BAPTIST**

IGLESIA BAUTISTA
PRIMERA MEXICANA
140 National Ave. SW; 1955–69.
1957–60   Rev. Leonard M. Ortiz

IGLESIA BETHEL ASAMBLEA DE DIOS
See **BETHEL ASAMBLEA DE DIOS**

IGLESIA BIBLICA EL CALVARIO
SPANISH SPEAKING CHURCH
2007 Eastern Ave. SE; 1978–85.

IGLESIA BIBLICA ENMANUEL
Church of the Open Door, 1730
Burlingame Ave. SW Wyoming 49509;
Phone: 452–5648. Organized: 1991
(Calvary Undenominational Church,
777 E. Beltline Ave. NE 1991–92).
1991–   Rev. Lorenzo Miguel

IGLESIA CATOLICA
DE SAN JOSE OBRERO
See **ST. JOSEPH THE WORKER**

IGLESIA CRISTIANA
144 Burton St. SW; 1974–77.
1974–77   Rev. Juan M. Vasquez

IGLESIA DE CRISTO MISIONERA
200 Griggs St. SW 49507;
Phone: 241–4708. Pentecostal;
Organized: 1973 (1102 Grandville Ave.
SW 1973–76; South Division Avenue
1976–79; Madison Avenue SE
1979–80); Built: 1953 as Burton
Heights Church of God.
1973–75   Rev. Salvatore Morales
1982–   Rev. Israel Ausua,
           Rev. Carmen Ausua
1992–   Hilda Gonzalez

**IGLESIA DE DIOS
MANANTIAL DE VIDA**
1522 Plastico Ave. SW Wyoming
49509; Phone: 554–9308.
Pentecostal; Organized: 1975; Built:
1929 as New Apostolic Church.
1975–   Rev. Gregorio Saez

IGLESIA DE DIOS OMNIPRESENTE
See **IGLESIA PENTECOSTES
DEL DIOS OMNIPRESENTE**

IGLESIA DE DIOS PENTECOSTAL
1112 Grandville Ave. SW 49503;
Phone: 247–8200. Organized: 1986.
1986–   Rev. Lorenzo E. Ventura

**IGLESIA DE DIOS
PENTECOSTAL M.I. "EBENEZER"**
1132 S. Division Ave. 49507.
Organized: 1990.
1992–   Hugo E. Adulante

IGLESIA METODISTA UNIDA HISPANA
107 Burton St. SE 49507;
Phone: 241–2000. Organized: 1984
(Olivet United Methodist Church,
1933 Buchanan Ave. SW 1984–85).
1984–85   Rev. Miguel A. Rivera
1992–   Rev. Juan B. Falcon

**IGLESIA PENTECOSTAL
CASA DE DIOS**
1814 S. Division Ave. 49507.
Organized: 1989.
1992–   Wilfredo J. Dilbert Jr.

**IGLESIA PENTECOSTAL
PRINCIPE DE PAZ**
1955 S. Division Ave. 49507;
Phone: 235–7585.
Pentecostal, New York, N.Y.;
Organized: 1990.
1990–   Pastor Manuel A. Vazquez

**IGLESIA PENTECOSTES
DEL DIOS OMNIPRESENTE**
1009 Hermitage St. SE 49506;
Phone: 451–0187.
Built: 1875–86 as Third Reformed.
1990–   Rev. Eliazar Alonzo

IGLESIA RESURRECCION Y VIDA
2147 S. Division Ave. 49507;
Phone: 452–0032. Independent;
Organized: 1989 (515 S. Division
1990–91).
1989–90   Rev. Duane VanderKlok
1990–   Rev. Victor Morales

IMMACULATE HEART OF MARY
1935 Plymouth Ave. SE 49506.
RC; Organized: 1949; Built: 1966
(Charles Hannan, Farmington, Mich.);
School 1952.
1949–55; 1962–69 Rev. Charles A.
           Killgoar OMI
1989–   Rev. Leonard Sudlik OMI

IMMANUEL BAPTIST
434 College Ave. NE.
1889–97 (Swedish Lutheran Church,
428 Sinclair Ave. NE 1889); Built: 1889.
1889–94   W.C. Sheppard
1895–97   C..S. Osburn

IMMANUEL BAPTIST
See **GRAND RAPIDS
IMMANUEL BAPTIST**

IMMANUEL CHRISTIAN REFORMED
33 Elwell St. SW Wyoming 49548;
Phone: 531–6470. Organized: 1948;
Built: 1965.
1948–52   Rev. Henry A. Venema
1986–   Rev. E. Robert Tigchelaar

**IMMANUEL EVANGELICAL
LUTHERAN**
See **IMMANUEL LUTHERAN**

**IMMANUEL INDEPENDENT
CHURCH OF COMSTOCK PARK**
3931 Leland Ave. NE Comstock Park.
Organized: 1934; Built: 1943.
1934–68   Rev. George L. Youngs
1968–79   Rev. Robert Lee Buer
1979–82   Rev. Patrick Deja
1982   Merged with Belmont Bible
Church to become **FELLOWSHIP
BIBLE CHURCH**

IMMANUEL LUTHERAN
338 N. Division Ave. 49503;
Phone: 454–3655. Missouri Synod;
Organized: 1856; Built: 1890 (William
G. Robinson); School 1858.
1856–58   Rev. Frederick W.
           Richmann
1884–1910 Rev. Charles J.T. Frincke
1930–48   Rev. Walter C. Wangerin
1947–68   Rev. Martin W. Brauer
1972–   Rev. Dr. K. Frank Graves
1980–   Rev. Fred C. Krause

IMMANUEL PENTECOSTAL
831 Fremont Ave. NW; 1938–39.
1938–39   Rev. Frederick H.
           Neubauer

IMMANUEL PRESBYTERIAN
1441 Madison Ave. SE; 1889–1980.
1889–91   Rev. George Reynolds
1955–80   Rev. Eugene G. Slep

IMMANUEL REFORMED
1300 E. Beltline Ave. SE 49506;
Phone: 957–9117. Organized: 1907 as
Hope Mission (654 Eastern Ave. SE
1908–84); Built: 1984 (Kammeraad,
Holland).
1907–11   Rev. Ralph Bloemendal
1920–30   Rev. Jacob G. Brouwer
1958–71   Rev. Jerome B. DeJong
1992–   Rev. Dr. Robert Charnin

INDEPENDENT BIBLE MISSION
749 Lamoreaux Drive NW Comstock
Park 49321; Phone: 784–5606.
IFCA; Organized: 1952 (149 Lamoreaux
Drive NW Comstock Park 1952–91).
1952–67   Rev. Wright VanPlew
1981–   Rev. Paul R. Deal

INTERNATIONAL
EVANGELISM CHURCH
109 Gold Ave. SW; 1971–79.
1974–79   Manuel Avila

IONIA AVENUE CHURCH OF CHRIST
See **EASTERN AVENUE
CHURCH OF CHRIST**

ISLAMIC CENTER
OF WEST MICHIGAN
1301 Burton St. SE 49507;
Phone: 241–4555. Independent;
Organized: 1988; Built: 1956 as
Jehovah's Witnesses Kingdom Hall.
1988–   Dr. Ghulam Malik

IVANREST CHRISTIAN REFORMED
3777 Ivanrest Ave. SW Grandville
49418; Phone: 534–3114. Organized:
1926 as Ivanrest Gospel Chapel, as
church 1964; Built: 1966 (Visser Bros).
1943–48   Evangelist George
                Oppenhuizen
1952–61   Evangelist Willis Timmer
1964–72   Rev. L. Calvin Bergsma
1986–   Rev. George C. Vink

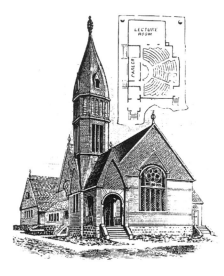

FIGURE 22
Osgood designed the Joy Memorial
Methodist Episcopal Church at 35
National Ave. SW in 1889. After 1950,
it was occupied by smaller
congregations, including the Bethel
Asamblea de Dios (1955–75).
Converted into apartments, the building
burned on Christmas Eve 1983.

N.B. Jehovah's Witnesses listings
are alphabetical by street. P.O.
designates Presiding Overseer.

JEHOVAH'S WITNESSES EAST
1320 36th St. SE 49508;
Phone: 247–6624. Organized: 1965
(1301 Burton St. SE 1965–89); Built:
1989.
1948–77   P.O. Delbert Starner
1987–   P.O. Theodis Harry

JEHOVAH'S WITNESSES CENTRAL
1320 36th St. SE 49508;
Phone: 247–6624. Organized: 1974
(2306 McKee Ave. SW 1974–89);
Built: 1989.
1974   P.O. Alva N. Bacon
1988–   P.O. Salvatore M.
                Mattaliano

JEHOVAH'S WITNESSES
SOUTH/WEST
2041 36th St. SW Wyoming 49509;
Phone: 532–8475. Organized: 1984
(1301 Burton St. SE 1956–72; 2306
McKee Ave. SW 1972–90); Built:
1990.
1951–   P.O. Charles B. Blackburn
1984–87   Elder Jeffery R. Clark
1987–   Elder James K. Engelkin

JEHOVAH'S WITNESSES WYOMING
2041 36th St. SW Wyoming 49509;
Phone: 532–8475. Organized: 1984
(2306 McKee Ave. SW 1984–90.)
Built: 1990.
1984–87   P.O. Jeffery R. Clark
1987–   P.O. James K. Engelking

JEHOVAH'S WITNESSES ALPINE
4483 Fruit Ridge Ave. NW 49504;
Phone: 784–3040. Organized: 1951
(578 Stocking Ave. NW 1951–56;
3564 Alpine Ave. NW Walker
1956–72); Built: 1972.
1951   P.O. Lionel E. Corkins
1988–   P.O. Marc S. Razmus

JEHOVAH'S WITNESSES KENTWOOD
7033 Hammond Ave. SE Caledonia
49316; Phone: 698–6830. Organized:
1958. (4402 Magnolia Ave. SW
Wyoming 1957–73).
1958   P.O. Donald D. Frazine
1983–   P.O. William Meulenberg

JEHOVAH'S WITNESSES
SPANISH SOUTH
2306 McKee Ave. SW 49509;
Phone: 452–9005. Organized: 1979;
Built: 1972.
1979   P.O. Jose Santos
1993–   P.O. Antonio Sabater

JEHOVAH'S WITNESSES
SPANISH NORTH
2306 McKee Ave. SW 49509;
Phone: 452–9005.
Organized: 1988; Built: 1972.
1988–   P.O. Gonzales Carrera

JEHOVAH'S WITNESSES NORTH
2535 Michigan St. NE.
1883–1988 (Andrew Olson residence,
226 Ann St. NE 1883–1907; GAR
Hall, 1107 Sheldon Ave. SE 1907–20;
All Souls Universalist Church, 100
Sheldon SE 1920–36; AFRV Hall,
1538 Monroe Ave. NW 1936–40;
YMCA, 33 Library St. NE 1940–44;
Transportation Building, 44 Ionia Ave.
SW 1944–50; Majestic Theater, 34 N.
Division Ave. 1950; 578 Stocking Ave.
NW 1950–51; 322 N. Division Ave.
1951–53; Rowe Hotel, 201 Michigan St.
NW 1953–54; 1432 Michigan NE
1954–70); Built: 1970; Addition: 1987.
1951   Albert Tracy
1955–60   John C. Heyboer.

JEHOVAH'S WITNESSES CASCADE
2535 Michigan St. NE 49506;
Phone: 949–0251. Organized: 1988;
Built: 1970; Addition: 1987.
1988–93   P.O. Linley Rockwell
1993–   P.O. Randy Andrus

JEHOVAH'S WITNESSES
PLAINFIELD
6001 West River Drive NE Belmont
49306; Phone: 363–9735.
Organized: 1965 (3564 Alpine Ave.
NW Walker 1956–65; 2655 Dean Lake
Ave. NE 1965–90); Built: 1990.
1965   P.O. Martin H. O'Neill
1965–72   Elder Frank Razmus
1983–   P.O. Robert T. Needham

JEHOVAH'S WITNESSES KINGDOM HALL

5595 Wilson Ave. SW Grandville 49418; Phone: 534–1362. Organized: 1955 (2021 S. Division Ave. 1951–55; 4402 Magnolia Ave. SW Wyoming 1955–72); Built: 1972.

1972–88	P.O. Floyd B. Jackson
1989–	P.O. John M. Colburn Sr.

JESUS CHRIST APOSTOLIC
See **NEW LIFE APOSTOLIC ASSEMBLY**

JOHN KNOX PRESBYTERIAN

4150 Kalamazoo Ave. SE 49508; Phone: 455–5060. Organized: 1958 (Bowen Station School 1957–59; Old Paris Township Hall, 3151 Kalamazoo Ave. SE 1959–63; Bowen School, 4483 Kalamazoo SE 1963–64); Built: 1964.

1959–65	Rev. John M. VandenBosch
1965–74	Rev. Earl E. Davidson
1979–92	Rev. Randall R. Painter
1979–	Rev. Rodney W. Westveer

JOY MEMORIAL METHODIST

35 National Ave. SW. 1889–1950 (Lawton and Pomeroy's Hall, 632 W. Fulton St. 1889); Built: 1889 (Sidney J. Osgood).

1890	Rev. J.H. Brownell
1912–15	Rev. Floyd E. George
1945–46	Rev. Floyd E. George

KELLOGGSVILLE CHRISTIAN REFORMED

610 52nd St. SE Kentwood 49548; Phone: 534–0085. Organized: 1875; Built: Addition: 1914 (J. & G. Daverman); Built: 1920 (J. & G. Daverman); Built: 1954; Addition: 1970.

1881–87	Rev. P. Schut
1933–45	Rev. Edgar Boeve
1990–	Rev. Ronald L. Fynewever
1991–	Rev. Maurice L. DeYoung

KENT FELLOWSHIP CHURCH
See **SOUTH EASTERN BIBLE CHURCH**

KENTWOOD BAPTIST

2875 52nd St. SE Kentwood 49508; Phone: 698–6279. General Association of Regular Baptists; Organized: 1864 as Terrace Baptist; 1882–1961 Paris Baptist (Smith School District No. 10, Paris Township 1864–82; SE corner T.S. Smith farm 1882–1959); Built: 1959. Addition: 1967; Addition: 1990 (Dan Vos Construction).

1882–92	Rev. Butterfield
1985–	Rev. H. Jack Miller

KENTWOOD CHRISTIAN

5841 Kalamazoo Ave. SE Kentwood 49508; Phone: 455–1510. Non–denominational/Independent; Organized: 1964; Built: 1964 (Goodman Builders).

1964–69	Rev. Gene S. Carter
1969–83	Rev. Kent Hickerson
1984–	Rev. Lawrence L. Carter

KENTWOOD COMMUNITY CHURCH

1723 44th St. SE Kentwood; 1967–70

KENTWOOD COMMUNITY CHURCH

1200 60th St. SE 49508; Phone: 455–1740. Wesleyan Church, Indianapolis, Ind.; Organized: 1979 (Greenhouse, Breton Avenue north of 28th Street SE 1979–80; Valleywood Middle School, 1110 50th St. SE Kentwood 1980–83; 5820 Eastern Ave. SE Kentwood 1983–87); Built: 1987 (Jeffrey Parker).

1979–82	Rev. Richard R. Wynn
1979–	Rev. Wayne K. Schmidt Jr.

KING OF LIFE AMERICAN LUTHERAN

2143 Highbluff Drive NE; 1970–75.

1970–75	Rev. John W. Gast

KING PARK CHURCH

1145 Franklin St. SE 49506; Phone: 241–3050. Nondenominational; Organized: 1984; Built: 1926 as First Protestant Reformed (Harvey H. Weemhoff).

1984–	Rev. Charles VanderBeek

KINNEY STATION CHRISTIAN REFORMED
See **WALKER CHRISTIAN REFORMED**

KLISE MEMORIAL CHAPEL OF EAST CONGREGATIONAL

1005 Giddings Ave. SE; Phone: 245–0578. Built: 1929 (Ralph Adams Cram and Ferguson, Boston).

KNAPP STREET REFORMED

4025 Knapp St. NE 49505; Phone: 363–5078. Organized: 1915; Built: 1970.

1919–25	Rev. Thomas G. VandenBosch
1925–57	Rev. Paul E. Trompen
1985–	Rev. Mark A. Vanderson

KLONDYKE CHURCH
See **GRACE REFORMED**

KOINONIA CHURCH OF GRAND RAPIDS

954 Dunham St. SE 49506; Phone: 245–2334. Nondenominational; Organized: 1973 (655 Sherman St. SE 1973; 346 Wealthy St. SE 1973–77; 2125 Stafford Ave. SW 1977–87; 1725 Horton Ave. SE 1987–89; 1102 Lafayette Ave. SE 1989–90; 847 Sigsbee St. SE 1990–91).

1973–	Rev. Edward Jarvis Bottum

KOREAN CATHOLIC COMMUNITY

Our Lady of Sorrows Church, 101 Hall St. SE 49507; Phone: 243–0222. Organized: 1993.

1993	Rev. Young Kwon Ham

KOREAN CHRISTIAN REFORMED CHURCH OF GRAND RAPIDS, THE

Wyoming Park Christian Reformed Church, 2731 Byron Center Ave. SW Wyoming 49509; Phone: 532–2112. Organized: as undenominational 1975; CRC 1981 (Home Acres Reformed Church, 21 Murray St. SE Kentwood 1975–76; Burton Heights Christian Reformed Church, 1970 Jefferson Ave. SE 1976–81; 441 Knapp St. NE 1981–89; Grace Bible College Chapel, 2445 28th St. SW Wyoming 1989–91; 212 Bellevue St. SE Wyoming 1991–92; Grace Bible College Chapel, 2445 28th St. SW Wyoming 1992–93).

1975–78	Rev. Han Hum Oak
1988–	Rev. Youn-Kyoo Chung

KOREAN CHURCH OF GRAND RAPIDS, THE
See **KOREAN CHRISTIAN REFORMED CHURCH OF GRAND RAPIDS, THE**

LA GRAVE AVENUE CHRISTIAN REFORMED
107 LaGrave Ave. SE 49503;
Phone: 454–7204. Organized: 1887 as
Fourth Holland Christian Reformed;
Built: 1888 (Sidney J. Osgood); Built:
1960 (Daverman Associates).
1887–92	Rev. John Y. DeBaun
1899–1915	Rev. Dr. Henry Beets
1954–87	Rev. Jacob D. Eppinga
1978–	Rev. John J. Steigenga
1990–	Rev. Stanley Mast

LAKE DRIVE BAPTIST
2119 Lake Drive SE East Grand Rapids
49506; Phone: 451–8638.
General Association of Regular
Baptists; Organized: 1905 as mission,
1923 as church; 1905–23 Reed's Lake
Baptist Chapel/Church; Built: 1926
(George Brouwer).
1921–72	Rev. Gerard Knol
1972–92	Rev. Jay G. Dyksterhouse
1992–	Rev. James H. Lane

LATIN AMERICAN ASSEMBLY OF GOD
See **BETHEL ASAMBLEA DE DIOS**

LATVIAN APOSTOLATE
See **OUR LADY OF AGLONA**

LATVIAN EVANGELICAL LUTHERAN
See **GRAND RAPIDS LATVIAN EVANGELICAL LUTHERAN**

LAURA BAPTIST
See **ST. PAUL MISSIONARY BAPTIST**

LEE STREET CHRISTIAN REFORMED
1261 Lee St. SW Wyoming 49509;
Phone: 241–2105. Organized: 1926;
Built: 1940 (J. & G. Daverman).
1927–39	Rev. Joseph J. Steigenga
1989–	Rev. James M. Boer

LEONARD HEIGHTS BAPTIST
1273 Lamont Ave. NW 49504;
Phone: 453–3797. General Association
of Regular Baptists; Organized: 1956;
Built: 1956.
1956–60	Rev. Larry Asman
1992–	Rev. Douglas Beason

LEONARD HEIGHTS CHAPEL
See **REMEMBRANCE REFORMED**

LEONARD STREET CHURCH OF GOD
1961 Leonard St. NE 49505;
Phone: 454–6098. Church of God,
Cleveland, Tenn.; Organized: 1949 (312
Jefferson Ave. SE 1948–51; 140 National
Ave. SW 1951–53; 645 Front Ave. NW
1953–63; 7 Barnett St. NW 1963–75);
Built: 1976.
1949	Rev. O.C. Boatright
1992–	Rev. Gene B. Martin

LEONARD STREET MISSION
452 Leonard St. NW.
1942–45	(514 Leonard St. NW 1942).
1945	Supt. Joseph F. Gronski

LIBERAL HOLLAND CHURCH
See **HOLLAND UNITARIAN**

LIBERAL (HOLLAND) UNIVERSALIST
See **HOLLAND UNITARIAN**

LIFE LINE MISSION
77 Grandville Ave. SW.
1898–1901 (318 Bridge St. NW
1898–1900).
1898–1901	Rev. Franklin A. Perkins

LIGHT BURDEN CHURCH OF GOD
200 Griggs St. SW; 1978–80.
1979–80	Rev. Carl McKay

LIGHT HOUSE DELIVERANCE CENTER, THE
122 S. Division Ave. 49503; 1990.
1990	Rev. Charles J. Green

LIGHTHOUSE OF TRUTH
661 Turner Ave. NW.
Spiritualist; 1971–77.
1971–77	Rev. Vivian Patricia Kelley

LILLIE WHITE PENTECOSTAL
See ALL NATIONS LILLIE WHITE PENTECOSTAL MISSION

LIVING WORD FELLOWSHIP
Gerribee Party Place, 4050 Chicago
Drive SW Grandville 49418;
Phone: 532–0774.
Independent/Autonomous; Organized:
1988 (West Elementary School, 3777
Aaron Ave. SW Grandville 1988–89).
1988–	Rev. Dennis Brown, Rev. Susan Brown

LIVINGSTON CHAPEL
See **COIT COMMUNITY CHRISTIAN REFORMED**

LOVE AND FAITH CHURCH OF GOD IN CHRIST
1121 Madison Ave. SE; 1984–85.
1984–85	Rev. Johnnie A. Cutts

LOWELL BAPTIST
Calvin College, 1331 Franklin St. SE.
1943–46.
1943–44	Rev. Melbourne W. Stadt

LYON STREET MISSION
See CANAL STREET MISSION

MACEDONIA MISSIONARY BAPTIST
48 Dennis Ave. SE 49506;
Phone: 451–4132. Organized: 1962 as
Macedonia Nondenominational (1060
Cass Ave. SE 1962–80); Built: 1893 as
Dennis Avenue Christian Reformed
(Daverman).
1962–70	Rev. D.A. Anderson
1976–	Rev. Charlie Jones

MADISON AVENUE MISSIONARY BAPTIST
5757 Madison Ave. SE Kentwood
49548; Phone: 534–2963.
American Baptist Association;
Organized: as mission 1970, as church
1976; Built: 1970.
1970–76	Rev. Tom C. Hansen
1987–	Rev. Joseph W. Culberson

MADISON SQUARE CHRISTIAN REFORMED
1441 Madison Ave. SE 49507;
Phone: 245–7791. Organized: 1914 as
Madison Square Mission, as church
1970; 1940–41 Madison Square Gospel
Center. 1941–42 Gospel Chapel (340
Hall St. SE 1914–15; 1209 Madison SE
1919–21; 1164 Madison SE 1929–40;

1163 Madison SE 1941–42; 1230 Madison SE 1945–51; 1164 Lafayette Ave. SE 1951–80); Built: 1955 as Immanuel Presbyterian (Harvey H. Weemhoff); Addition: 1992 (DSO Architects).

1920	Elizabeth Smitter
1941–42	Henry Koets, Rev. Jennie Koets
1948–62	Rev. Walter G. Dubois
1967–74	Rev. Vernon F. Geurkink
1981–	Rev. Dante A. Venegas
1982–	Rev. David H. Beelen

MAPLE CREEK COMMUNITY

1881 52nd St. SE Kentwood 49508; Phone: 455–5050. Independent Plymouth Brethren; Organized: 1961 as Homestead Bible Chapel; Built: 1961 (Anderson & Associates).

1961–90	Elder Dr. Dean Smith
1990–	Elder Alexander J. Ruffin

MAPLE HILL CHURCH, UNITED BRETHREN IN CHRIST

3810 56th St. SW Grandville 49418; Phone: 532–3314. Organized: 1897; Built: 1897; Addition 1969.

1897–1902	Rev. S.G. Hall
1991–	Rev. Stephen O. Eastman

MAPLELAWN BAPTIST

124 Maplelawn St. SW Wyoming 49548; Phone: 532–5990. General Association of Regular Baptists; Organized: 1929 as mission, 1946 as church; 1929–46 Godwin Heights Gospel Tabernacle; 1946–57 Godwin Baptist (16 Coolidge St. SW Wyoming 1932–57); Built: 1957 (Harold Marsman).

1929–41	Rev. Mrs. Jennie Koets
1990–	Rev. Dann C. Green

MARANATHA BAPTIST

15 Murray St. SW Wyoming; 1946–51.

1948	Rev. Adrian E. Freyling
1951	Rev. Carl E. Sadler

MARANATHA BIBLE CHURCH

4426 Stoney Creek Ave. NW Comstock Park 49321; Phone: 784–5905. IFCA; Organized: 1970 (149 Lamoreaux Drive NW Comstock Park 1970–75); Built: 1975 (Buffinga Bros).

1970–73	Rev. Martin Uppendal
1970–91	Rev. Richard C .Gordon
1991–	Rev. John J. Campbell

MARANATHA MINISTRIES

5353 Wilson Ave. SW Grandville 49418; Phone: 530–8484. Charismatic nondenominational; Organized: 1973 (Gerribee Party Place, 4050 Chicago Drive SW Grandville 1974–89); Built: 1989 (Jeffrey Parker).

1973–75	Elder Calvin Burgsma
1985–	Rev. Merle Bremer

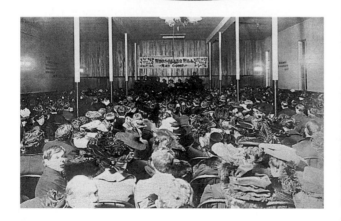

FIGURES 23, 24, 25
These views of the Mel Trotter Ministries show, at top left, the second mission building (1905–51) at 60 Market St. NW; an interior view, lower left, of a mission assembly; and the old Kent Theatre at 322 Monroe Ave. NW, which served as the mission auditorium from 1955 until its removal for urban renewal in 1965.

MARANATHA SPANISH SEVENTH–DAY ADVENTIST
See **IGLESIA ADVENTISTA MARANATHA**

MARTIN LUTHER KING JR. MISSIONARY BAPTIST
758 Wealthy St. SE 49503;
Phone: 451–8311. Organized: 1972
(111 Graham St. SW 1972–76.)
1972–   Rev. Alvin Hills Sr.

MARTIN LUTHER KING MISSIONARY MISSION
1214 Madison Ave. SE; 1974.

MARYWOOD/DOMINICAN CHAPEL
See **DOMINICAN CHAPEL/MARYWOOD**

MASJID MUHAMMAD
Madison Square Co–Operative Inc.,
1167 Madison Ave. SE 49507;
Phone: 245–2563. World Community
of Al–Islam in the West No. 61;
Organized: 1958; 1965–74
Muhammad's Mosque (571 S. Division
Ave. 1965–67; 1166 Madison Ave. SE
1968–70; 814 S. Division 1970–79;
1004 Hall St. SE 1979–81; 1229
Madison SE 1981–90).
1979–   Imam Noah A.A. Seifullah

MATTHEWS TEMPLE CHURCH OF GOD IN CHRIST
444 Pleasant St. SW 49503;
Phone: 454–6393. Organized: 1949
(60th Street and Eastern Avenue SE
1949–68); Built: 1968 (Chuck
Lawson).
1949–   Rev. Edward J. Matthews

MAYFAIR CHRISTIAN REFORMED
1740 Lyon St. NE 49503;
Phone: 454–8878. Organized: 1893 as
Dennis Avenue Christian Reformed
(Fulton Street near Diamond Avenue
SE 1893; 48 Dennis Ave. SE
1893–1955); Built: 1955 (James K.
Haveman).
1896–1903 Rev. Edward VanderVries
1942–52   Rev. Dr. Lubbertus
           Oostendorp
1954–69   Rev. Henry DeMots
1976–93   Rev. Wilmer R. Witte
1992–   Rev. Peter Verhulst

MAYFLOWER CHAPEL
See **FIRST FREE METHODIST**

MAYFLOWER CONGREGATIONAL
1320 Ashland Ave. NE; 1894–1900.
Became **FIRST FREE METHODIST**

MAYFLOWER CONGREGATIONAL
2345 Robinson Road SE 49506;
Phone: 459–6255. National
Association of
Congregational–Christian Churches;
Organized: 1958 (Lakeside School,
2325 Hall St. SE East Grand Rapids
1958–61); Built: 1960 (Rindge Rindge
Eggers & Higgins, New York, N.Y.).
1958–72   Rev. Dr. Bruce H.
           Masselink
1972–87   Rev. Dr. Maurice A. Fetty
1989–   Rev. Dr. Kenneth W.
           Gottman

MC SWAIN TEMPLE CHURCH OF GOD IN CHRIST
311 Hall St. SE 49507.
Organized: 1972 as Full Gospel
Deliverance Church (715 S. Division
Ave. 1972–74).
1972–74   Rev. Peggy M. Wheeler
1976–87   Rev. John H. McSwain

MEADOW SPRINGS COMMUNITY CHURCH
Wedgewood Acres, 3300 36th St. SE
Kentwood 49512; Phone: 455–5672.
Orthodox Presbyterian, Philadelphia;
Organized: 1991.
1991–   Rev. Gerald J. Neumair

MEL TROTTER MINISTRIES
225 Commerce Ave. SW 49503;
Phone: 454–8249. Organized: 1900
(317 Monroe Ave. NW 1900; 60
Market Ave. NW 1905–51; 346
Monroe NW 1951–65; Auditorium,
322 Monroe NW 1955–65).
1900–40   Rev. Melvin E. Trotter
1992–   Dr. John J. Willock

MEL TROTTER MINISTRIES
(Galewood/South Branch)
See **GALEWOOD GOSPEL CHAPEL**

MEL TROTTER MISSION
704 Jefferson Ave. SE; 1964–70.

MESSIAH BAPTIST
See **MESSIAH MISSIONARY BAPTIST**

MESSIAH LUTHERAN
2727 Five Mile Road NE 49505;
Phone: 363–2553. Missouri Synod;
Organized: 1964; Built: 1966 (Kellogg
& Kiefer).
1964–66   Rev. Henry C. Lubben
1966–81   Rev. Gordon Goltz
1981–90   Rev. Alvin R. Garchow
1991–   Rev. Terry E. Hoese

MESSIAH MISSIONARY BAPTIST
513 Henry Ave. SE 49503;
Phone: 458–2651. Organized: 1889
(Ringuette's Hall, 800–802 S. Division
Ave. 1889–90; 138 Grandville Ave.
SW 1890–96; 457 Henry SE 1896–97;
559 Eastern Ave. SE 1897–99); Built:
1922 (Harvey W. Jackson and Alfonso
Williams); Built: 1979.
1889   Rev. J.W. Johnson
1890   Catherine Carter,
           Rev. Jacob Holt
1890–95   Rev. John Rookus
1895–99   Rev. Robert Gillard
1933–69   Rev. Albert Keith
1972–   Rev. Clifton Rhodes Jr.

MESSIAH TEMPLE
See CHILDREN OF ZION

METHODIST CHURCH OF WALKER
See FAIRVIEW WESLEYAN

METHODIST EPISCOPAL (German)
See VALLEY AVENUE UNITED METHODIST

METHODIST UNION CHAPEL
See **SOUTH UNITED METHODIST**

METROPOLITAN BAPTIST TEMPLE
See **NEW TESTAMENT BAPTIST**

MEXICAN CHAPEL
See **OUR LADY OF GUADALUPE**

FIGURE 26
J. & G. Daverman designed this fine structure at 1044 Turner Ave. NW for the west side Netherlands Reformed Church of Grand Rapids in 1908. Freeway construction forced the congregation to abandon it in 1960, and a new church was built on Covell Avenue in 1963.

MID CITY MISSIONARY BAPTIST
892 Caulfield Ave. SW 49503; Phone: 247–1866. Organized: 1986 (934 Cass Ave. SE 1986–87; 1000 Prospect Ave. SE 1987–88; King Park Church, 755 Fuller Ave. SE 1988; Martin Luther King Jr. Missionary Baptist Church, 758 Wealthy St. SE 1988–89; 1434 Madison Ave. SE 1989); Built: 1899 as Grace Reformed. Remodeled 1926 (Harvey H. Weemhoff).
1986–   Rev. David G. May

MILLBROOK
CHRISTIAN REFORMED
3661 Poinsettia Ave. SE 49508; Phone: 243–9203. Organized: 1954; Built: 1956 (Randy Cooper).
1956–62   Rev. Gerrien Gunnink
1976–92   Rev. James E. DeVries

MIRACULOUS TIMES CHURCH
460 Franklin St. SW; 1974–75.
1974   Mother A.B. Nesbitt

MISSION CHURCH
See WAYSIDE BIBLE/MEMORIAL/ MISSION CHURCH/CHAPEL

MISSION COVENANT CHURCH
See **EVANGELICAL COVENANT CHURCH OF GRAND RAPIDS**

MISSION HOUSE
1848 Godfrey Ave. SW Wyoming. RCA; 1946–63.
1951   Rev. Hendrich M. Veenschoten

MISSION LATINO AMERICANO
See INTERNATIONAL EVANGELISM CHURCH

MISSION SUNDAY SCHOOL
422 Coldbrook St. NE.
1932–46; Organized: 1932 as Colored Mission Sunday School.

MISSION SUNDAY SCHOOL
123 Shelby St. SW.
1915; Affiliated with Madison Square Mission

MISSIONARY CHURCH OF CHRIST
(Spanish)
See **IGLESIA DE CRISTO MISIONERA**

MISSIONARY RESIDENCE
See MISSION HOUSE

MORNING GLORY CHURCH
OF GOD IN CHRIST
2316 S. Division Ave. 49507.
Organized: 1993.

MORNING STAR
CHURCH OF GOD IN CHRIST
1130 S. Division Ave. 49507; Phone: 247–3685. Organized: 1985.
1985–   Rev. Adam Green

MOSES CHAPEL
MISSIONARY BAPTIST
1060 Cass Ave. SE 49507; Phone: 245–9945. Organized: 1980; Built: 1967 as Macedonia Nondenominational.
1980–89   Rev. William H. Curry
1989–   Rev. Johnny Bolden

MOUNT OLIVE LUTHERAN
3950 Leonard St. NW Walker 49504; Phone: 453–0803. Missouri Synod; Organized: 1956; Built: 1968.
1956–63   Rev. Richard J. Scholz
1964–66   Rev. Kenneth Fischer
1966–91   Rev. Arthur C. Krueger
1993–   Rev. Steven C. Helms

MOUNT OLIVE MISSIONARY BAPTIST
1072 Jefferson Ave. SE.
1965–84; 1965–66 Mount Olivet Missionary Baptist; 1966–74 Tabernacle Church of God (38 Buckley St. SW 1965–74; 826 Ionia Ave. SW 1968–69).
1965–66   Rev. Daniel Perry
1966–72   Rev. Peggy W. Wheeler
1972–83   Rev. Charles W. Blackmore

MOUNT ZION BAPTIST
826 Ionia Ave. SW.
1960–70 (736 Cornwall Ave. SE 1960).

MOUNT ZION
CHURCH OF GOD IN CHRIST
718 Lafayette Ave. SE 49503; Phone: 245–2526. Organized: 1968 (123 Franklin St. SE 1968–70; 1320 Madison Ave. SE 1970–75); Built: 1975 (Smizt, Lowell).
1968–   Rev. Dank Tyler

MOUNT ZION
MISSIONARY BAPTIST
2100 Horton Ave. SE 49507; Phone: 247–8211. Organized: 1964 (739 Union Ave. SE 1964; New Hope Baptist Church, 257 Finney Ave. SW 1964–71; Grandville Ave. SW 1971; 865 Baxter St. SE 1971–81); Built: 1907 as Burton Heights Christian Reformed (J. & G. Daverman).
1964–68   Rev. Charlie Jones
1986–   Rev. Richard C .Clark

MUHAMMAD'S TEMPLE
OF ISLAM NO. 61
See **MASJID MUHAMMAD**

MYRTLE STREET MISSION
See BROADWAY METHODIST EPISCOPAL

NATIONAL EVANGELISTIC ASSOCIATION

528 Ottawa Ave. NW. Organized: 1935.

1935 Cornelius Quartel

NATIVE AMERICAN ASSEMBLY OF GOD

441 Knapp St. NE 49505; Phone: 774–5900. Organized: 1986 (17 S. Division Ave. 1986–92).

1986–   Rev. Michael W. Peters

NATIVE AMERICAN MINISTRY

See SABAOTH MINISTRIES

NATIVITY CHURCH OF GOD IN CHRIST

1634 S. Division Ave. 49507; Phone: 247–7759. Organized: 1990.

1990–   Rev. Dennis R. Robinson

NEDERDUITSCH REFORMED

See FIRST NETHERLANDS REFORMED

NEDERDUITSCHE GEREFORMEERDE GEMEENTE

See NETHERLANDS REFORMED CHURCH OF GRAND RAPIDS

NEHEMIAH BAPTIST

1975 Jefferson Ave. SE 49507; Phone: 241–2471. Woodland Southern Baptist; Organized: 1968 as Faith Missionary Baptist (535 Church Place SW 1968–88; King Park Church, 755 Fuller Ave. SE 1988–89; Grand Rapids School of the Bible and Music, 1331 Franklin St. SE 1989–90); Built: 1926 as Garfield Park Reformed (Harvey H. Weemhoff).

1968–69   Rev. Dr. Theodore H. Rankin
1985–   Rev. Rory R. Marshall

NELAND AVENUE CHRISTIAN REFORMED

940 Neland Ave. SE 49507; Phone: 245–0669. Organized: 1915; Built: 1916 (J. & G. Daverman).

1917–26   Rev. H. Henry Meeter
1926–28   Rev. D.H. Kromminga
1929–44   Rev. Henry J. Kuiper
1945–57   Rev. Ralph J. Danhof
1957–63   Rev. John O. Schuring

1964–70	Rev. Seymour VanDyken
1972–81	Rev. Tymen E. Hofman
1983–86	Rev. Richard J. Hamstra.
1982–	Rev. Carl L. Kammeraad
1988–	Rev. Duane K. Kelderman

NETHERLANDS EVANGELICAL

See NETHERLANDS REFORMED (337 Ottawa Ave. NW)

NETHERLANDS REFORMED

337 Ottawa Ave. NW. 1922–47; (350 Leonard St. NW 1922–23).

1922–44   Rev. Jacob C. Wielhouwer moderator. English–speaking congregation merged in 1947 with NETHERLANDS REFORMED to form FIRST NETHERLANDS REFORMED in 1950

NETHERLANDS REFORMED

See FIRST NETHERLANDS REFORMED

NETHERLANDS REFORMED CHURCH OF GRAND RAPIDS

1255 Covell Ave. NW 49504; Phone: 453–6916. Independent; Organized: for worship 1876; as church 1887 (Hall/Bridge Street NW 1876–88; 1044 Turner Ave. NW 1888–1960; 2nd church built 1908 [J. & G. Daverman]; West Side Christian School, 1138 Pine Ave. NW 1960–63); Built: 1963 (Jacques Kocker, Holland).

1883–87	Elder M. Donker
1887–91	Rev. Teunis Meysters
1896–1913	Rev. Titus Hager
1917–44	Rev. Jacob C. Wielhouwer
1966–86	Rev. Benjamin Densel

NEW APOSTOLIC CHURCH

1140 Hazen St. SE 49507; Phone: 534–0354. Organized: 1906 (667 Hogan St. SW 1906–11; 709 Shamrock St. SW 1911–26; 1928 Huizen Ave. SW Wyoming 1926–29; 1522 Plastico Ave. SW Wyoming 1929–54; 312 Jefferson Ave. SE 1954–64); Built: 1934 as Hazen Street Mission.

1906–25	Rev. Adrian Tromp
1925–43	Rev. Maurice A.L. Eman
1972–	Rev. Marinus Donze

NEW BEGINNING CHURCH OF GOD IN CHRIST

1045 Cass Ave. SE 49507; Phone: 245–6332. Organized: 1924 (329 Bartlett St. SW 1924–63).

1924–27	Rev. A.D. Johnson
1929–32	Rev. Andrew G. Griffin
1950–	Rev. James Holloway
1962–81	Rev. James C. Richardson
1981–85	Rev. Adam Green

NEW BEGINNING PENTECOSTAL CHURCH OF JESUS CHRIST

1100 S. Division Ave. 49507. 1992–93 (755 Eastern Ave. SE 1992).

NEW CHURCH

See ZION TABERNACLE

NEW CHURCH OF THE HOLY SPIRIT

1422 Wealthy St. SE 49506; Phone: 774–0520. Independent; Organized: 1958 as Religious Counseling Center Church; 1966–77 Plainfield Center Church; 1977–87 Association of House Churches (5055 Plainfield Ave. NE 1958–70; 1164 Forest Hill Ave. SE 1970–74; 1153 Giddings Ave. SE 1974–78).

1958–   Rev. H. Walter Yoder

NEW COMMUNITY OF WEST MICHIGAN

Suite E, Eastbrook Mall, 3525 28th St. SE 49512; Phone: 940–3030. Independent; Organized: 1991 (President Inn, 3221 Plainfield Ave. NE 1991; school, Kentwood 1991–92); East location worship site at Eastbrook Mall, 3525 28th SE. West location worship site at Grand Village Mall, 3501 Fairlanes Ave. SW Grandville.

1991–   Rev. Lewis R. VanderMeer

NEW COVENANT CHURCH

1107 Sheldon Ave. SE. 1950–61; Christian Spiritualist and Covenant.

1955   Rev. Irvin E. Runk

NEW COVENANT COMMUNITY CHURCH

1000 Kalamazoo Ave. SE 49507; Phone: 452–6770. Church of God in Michigan, Anderson, Ind.; Organized: 1931 as Universal Hagar's Spiritualist

Church; 1938–40 All Nations Spiritual Church; 1940–72 Church of God; 1972–90 Alexander Street Church of God (307 Grandville Ave. SW 1931–32; 756 S. Division Ave. 1932–33; 303 Grandville SW 1934–36; 431 Grandville SW 1936–37; 307 Grandville SW 1938–45; 109 Graham St. SW 1945–56; 328 Cass Ave. SE 1956–68; 1009 Kalamazoo SE 1968–72); Built: 1972 (James Stewart).

1932–33	Rev. Mrs. Bennie Alexander
1939–60	Rev. Chester A. Craig
1970–75	Rev. W. Frank Steward
1979–89	Rev. Lewis Livingston
1990–	Rev. Dr. Maurice A. Collins

NEW GOOD SHEPHERD CHURCH
257 Finney Ave. SW 49503. Organized: 1992 (1518 Eastern Ave. SE 1992–93).

1992–	Rev. Virgie N. Young

NEW HOPE CHURCH
15 Diamond Ave. NE 49503; Phone: 454–3900. Interfaith; Organized: 1980 as COTA Church of the Alcoholic (Sunshine Christian Reformed Church, 3305 E. Beltline Ave. NE 1980).

1980–83	Rev. Dwight D. Keller
1984–	Rev. Herman J. Teitsma

NEW HOPE MISSIONARY BAPTIST
130 Delaware St. SW 49507; Phone: 452–4278. National Baptist Convention of America Inc.; Organized: 1934 (325 Grandville Ave. SW 1934–37; 257 Finney Ave. SW 1937–64; 882 Caulfield Ave. SW 1964–83); Built: 1983 (Dan Vos).

1934–44	Rev. Joshua Haynes
1949–87	Rev. Dr. John V. Williams
1988–	Rev. Donnell Smith

NEW JERUSALEM CHURCH
See ZION TABERNACLE

NEW JERUSALEM
CHURCH OF GOD IN CHRIST
439 S. Division Ave. 49503; Phone: 241–3736. Organized: 1978.

1978–	Rev. Mrs. Annie L. Welford

NEW LIFE APOSTOLIC ASSEMBLY
1550 Ellen Ave. SW Wyoming 49509; Phone: 243–7516. United Pentecostal, St Louis, Mo.; Organized: 1964; 1964–66 Wyoming United Pentecostal; 1966–76 Jesus Christ Apostolic Church (Galewood Theater, 1051 Burton St. SW Wyoming 1964–66; 1710 Kreft St. NE 1966–76).

1964–66	Rev. James A. Lawrence
1984–	Rev. Dennis L. Kleiman

NEW LIFE CHRISTIAN CHURCH
2449 Camelot Court. SE 49546; Phone: 949–3344. Covenant Ministries International; Organized: 1978 (Russell Street, Middleville 1978–81; West Elementary School, Middleville 1981–87; Dutton Elementary School, 3820 68th St. SE Dutton 1987–).

1978–	Rev. Gary L. Finkbeiner

NEW LIFE CHRISTIAN FELLOWSHIP
2777 Knapp St. NE 49505; Phone: 364–7043. Nondenominational; Organized: 1971 as Faith Teaching Mission (2800 Michigan St. NE 1971–82; Beckwith School, 2405 Leonard St. NE 1982–85); Built: 1986.

1971–81	Rev. Morris Robert Steere
1977–	Rev. Lonnie D. Shields

NEW LIFE CHURCH
See NEW HOPE CHURCH

NEW LIFE CHURCH
OF GOD IN CHRIST
1072 Jefferson Ave. SE 49507; Phone: 247–0250. Organized: 1980 (525 LaGrave Ave. SE 1980; 1721 Madison Ave. SE 1980–82); Built: 1908 as St. Paul Methodist Episcopal (WEN Hunter, Detroit); Addition: 1955.

1980–	Rev. Robert Dean

NEW LIFE FELLOWSHIP
See NEW LIFE
CHRISTIAN FELLOWSHIP

NEW LIFE FELLOWSHIP CHURCH
700 Burton St. SE 49507; Phone: 452–6080. Pentecostal, Indianapolis; Organized: 1989 (King Park Church, 755 Fuller Ave. SE 1989); Built: 1930 as Calvary Baptist.

1989–	Dr. Albert Norris Duke

NEW LIFE REFORMED
973 28th St. SE 49508; Phone: 241–3173. Organized: 1974 as merger of Everglade Reformed and Oakdale Park Reformed; Built: 1955 as Everglade Reformed; Addition: 1977.

1974–78	Rev. Bernard Daniel Hakken Jr.
1974–76	Rev. Henry J. Boekhoven
1978–84	Rev. Gene A. Poll
1986–	Rev. Edward W. Schmidt

NEW LIFE TABERNACLE
CHURCH OF GOD IN CHRIST
815 Grandville Ave. SW 49503; Phone: 243–2254. Organized: 1978 (930 Union Ave. SE 1978–79; Franklin–Hall Complex, 400 Franklin St. SW 1979–81; Moses Chapel Baptist Church, 1060 Cass Ave. SE 1981–83).

1978–	Rev. Jeffrey Stokes

NEW ST. MARK
MISSIONARY BAPTIST
26 Shelby St. SW 49507; Phone: 243–9451. Organized: 1953 (708 Cass Ave. SE 1953–60); Built: 1881 at South Division Ave. and Albany Street SW as Ames Methodist Episcopal; in the late 1890s, moved to present site.

1953–65	Rev. Leslie L. Hudnell
1975–	Rev. Charles H. Hudson

NEW TESTAMENT BAPTIST
137 36th St. SE Wyoming 49548; Phone: 452–7981. 1955–86 Metropolitan Baptist Temple; 1986–89 Metropolitan Baptist Church.

1955–74	Rev. Walter Eldridge
1982–92	Rev. Edward R. Quackenbush

NEWHALL BAPTIST
3434 Hubal Ave. SW Wyoming 49509;
Phone: 538–1500. General Association
of Regular Baptists; Organized: 1953 as
mission, 1954 as church (3434 Taft
Ave. SW Wyoming 1953;
3403 Burlingame Ave. SW Wyoming
1953–55); Built: 1955 (Harold
Marsman); Addition: 1963.

1957–65	Rev. Wayne K. Anderson
1991–	Rev. Bruce R. Sparks

NEWHALL REFORMED
3746 Byron Center Ave. SW Wyoming
49509; Phone: 534–0203. Organized:
1956; Built: 1956.

1957–62	Rev. Raymond DeVries
1963–74	Rev. Robert J. VanZyl
1975–88	Rev. Brook B. Stephens
1988–	Rev. Scott A. Summers

NINTH REFORMED
57 Deloney Ave SW.
1892–1978; Built: 1892.

1892–95	Rev. Henry K. Boer
1937–47	Rev. Rense Dykstra
1948–62	Rev. John Minnema
1964–73	Rev. Richard J. TerMaat
1974–78	Rev. Harry P. Mencarelli

NORSK EVANGELICAL LUTHERAN
40 National Ave. NW; 1893–1913.

1894–95	Rev. M. Nelson

NORTH GRAND RAPIDS
PROTESTANT EPISCOPAL MISSION
See ST. MATTHEW MISSION

NORTH KENT PRESBYTERIAN
See **OAKHILL PRESBYTERIAN**

NORTH PARK BAPTIST
3365 Coit Ave. NE 49505;
Phone: 364–9532. Organized: 1909 as
Fairmount Park/Home of Hope
Mission; 1946–63 Fairmount Baptist
(300 Graceland St. NE 1909–55);
Built: 1955 (Post McMillan Palmer);
Addition: 1964.

1907–33	Rev. A.B. Goudzwaard
1933–45	Rev. Wilhelmina Wiarda
1965–75	Rev. George B. White
1986–	Rev. Carl M. Kresge.

NORTH PARK CHAPEL
645 Jessie St. NE; 1958–69.

1964–66	Howard L. Bielema
1966–68	R. Kamroth

NORTH PARK MENNONITE CHAPEL
645 Jessie St. NE; 1969–85.

1969–75	Rev. Orie Schrock
1984–88	Rev. Monty D. Ledford

NORTH PARK PRESBYTERIAN
500 North Park St. NE 49505;
Phone: 363–6864. Organized: 1914
(Old North Park School, NW corner
Coit Avenue and Kendalwood Street
NE 1910–21); Built: 1921 (John
VandenBogert, George V.E. Thebaud);
Addition: 1952; Addition: 1963 (N.J.
Westra & Son).

1914–15	Rev. D. Vincent Blayney
1918–19	Rev. C.L. Austin
1992–	Rev. David R. Anson

NORTH SIDE COMMUNITY BAPTIST
3864 Benjamin Ave. NE 49505;
Phone: 363–7893. Southern Baptist;
1964–80 Oakview Baptist; 1980–92
Benjamin Avenue Baptist; Built: 1957
as Oakview Reformed.

1965–67	Rev. Loren Ames
1991–	Rev. Michael R. Van Der Walle

NORTH SIDE NAZARENE
See **FULLER AVENUE
CHURCH OF THE NAZARENE**

NORTHLAND BAPTIST
4162 Hunsberger Ave. NE 49505;
Phone: 364–6101. General Association
of Regular Baptists; Organized: 1954
(4056 Plainfield Ave. NE 1954–63);
Built: 1963.

1956–59	Rev. Harold Legant
1990–	Rev. Larry D. Green

NORTHLAWN EVANGELICAL
UNITED BRETHREN
See **NORTHLAWN
UNITED METHODIST**

NORTHLAWN UNITED METHODIST
1157 Northlawn St. NE 49505;
Phone: 361–8503. Organized: 1950 as
Northlawn Evangelical United
Brethren; Built: 1953 (Chris Steketee).

1950–57	Rev. James A. Lange
1992–	Rev. Stanley Finkbeiner

NORTHSIDE CHRISTIAN
See NORTHSIDE
CHURCH OF CHRIST

NORTHSIDE CHURCH OF CHRIST
1739 Providence St. NE; 1957–80.

1970–77	Rev. William P. Cook

NORTHSIDE COMMUNITY BAPTIST
See **NORTH SIDE
COMMUNITY BAPTIST**

NORTHVIEW ALLIANCE CHURCH
5110 Plainfield Ave. NE 49505;
Phone: 363–7171. Christian and
Missionary Alliance; Organized: 1987
(Movies at North Kent Mall,
4180 Jupiter Ave. NE 1987); Built:
1990 (Walter Perry).

1987–92	Rev. Michael D. Scott
1992–	Rev. Larry J. Mosher

NORTHVIEW CHURCH OF CHRIST
26 Burton St. SW 49507;
Phone: 534–9025.
Undenominational; Organized: 1977
(West Side Christian School, 1138 Pine
Ave. NW 1977–80; St. Cecilia
Auditorium, 24 Ransom Ave. NE 1980).

1977–	Rev. Leon F. Groendal

NORTHWEST GOSPEL HALL
1350 Garfield Ave. NW 49504;
Phone: 456–9166. Organized: 1922 as
Evangel Hall (1007 Leonard St. NW
1922–58); Built: 1956.

1922–80	Rev. Peter J. Pell Jr., William Pell
1990–	Elder Frank Dietrick

NORWEGIAN EVANGELICAL
LUTHERAN
See NORSK EVANGELICAL
LUTHERAN

FIGURE 27

The Italian Catholic parish of Our Lady of Sorrows worshipped in this small brick building at 1154 Sheldon SE from 1921 to 1957. It was enlarged and converted into a parish school, and in 1970 became the first location for the Southeast Academic Center. It is now leased by the parish to Green Street Head Start.

NORWEGIAN LUTHERAN
Immanuel Lutheran Church, 338 N. Division Ave.
1880–84 (Swedish Lutheran Church, 428 Sinclair Ave. NE 1880–82).
1883–84   Rev. A. Anderson

OAK VIEW CONGREGATIONAL
Plainfield Township, four miles north of Leonard Street NE.
Organized: 1886 as mission, 1888 as church.
1886   H.A. Shearer
1888   Rev. M.S. Angell

OAKDALE PARK CHRISTIAN REFORMED
1313 E. Butler Ave. SE 49507;
Phone: 452–5764. Organized: 1890 (961 Hancock St. SE 1891–1963); second church built 1905 (J. & G. Daverman); Built: 1963 (Daverman Associates).
1891–95   Rev. G.A. DeHaan
1911–22   Rev. William P. VanWyk
1979–   Rev. William VandenBosch

OAKDALE PARK EPISCOPAL
Cottage Grove Street and Blaine Avenue SE. 1889–94.

OAKDALE PARK METHODIST EPISCOPAL
See OAKDALE UNITED METHODIST

OAKDALE PARK REFORMED
1024 Adams St. SE.
1889–1974; 1889–95 Holland Reformed; 1895–1924 Sixth Reformed.
1890–93   Rev. John M. Lumkes
1929–43   Rev. Arthur Maatman
1951–66   Rev. Lawrence J. Borst
1968–74   Rev. Henry J. Boekhoven
1974   Merged with Everglade Reformed to become NEW LIFE REFORMED

OAKDALE UNITED METHODIST
1005 Evergreen St. SE 49507;
Phone: 452–7118. Organized: 1917; second church built 1927 (Harvey H. Weemhoff); Built: 1959 (William Vanderbout).
1917–23   Rev. John A. DeGraff
1934–49   Rev. John R. Gregory
1987–   Rev. Jane B. Shapley

OAKHILL PRESBYTERIAN
1930 Leonard St. NE 49505;
Phone: 456–5626. Presbyterian Church in USA; Organized: 1957 as mission, 1963 as church; (Beckwith School, 2405 Leonard NE 1963–65); Built: 1969 (Thomas B. Browne Associates).
1959   Rev. Alexander S. Unguary
1961–65   Rev. Frank A. Beattie
1966–85   Rev. James R. Rea
1987–   Rev. Jeffrey S. Carlson

OAKVIEW BAPTIST
See NORTH SIDE COMMUNITY BAPTIST

OAKVIEW REFORMED
4242 Plainfield Ave. NE 49505;
Phone: 363–0744. Organized: 1957 (Coit Ave. NE 1957–58; 3864 Benjamin Ave. NE 1958–66); Built: 1966 (Robert Reed).
1958–61   Rev. Dr. Harris John VerKaik
1961–67   Rev. E. Donald Teusink
1967–80   Rev. Gerald VanderVelde
1981–89   Rev. Richard Borst
1990–   Rev. William H. Fennema

OAKWOOD PARK EPISCOPAL
See OAKDALE PARK EPISCOPAL

OLD CHRISTIAN REFORMED
See FREE REFORMED CHURCH OF NORTH AMERICA

OLD TIME GOSPEL MISSION
4 Leonard St. NE; 1961–76.
1961–76   Rev. Neva E. Thurkettle

OLD TIME METHODIST MISSION
1426 Grandville Ave. SW; 1961–63.

OLIVET EVANGELICAL UNITED BRETHREN
See OLIVET UNITED METHODIST

OLIVET REFORMED
3085 Wallace Ave. SW Grandville 49418; Phone: 534–0436.
Organized: 1948 (Wyoming Park Seventh Day Adventist Church, 2447 Byron Center Ave. SW Wyoming 1948–49); Built: 1949–53 (Daverman).
1949–52   Rev. William A. Swets
1984–   Rev. John F. Ornee

OLIVET UNITED METHODIST

1933 Buchanan Ave. SW 49507;
Phone: 245–3903. Organized: 1890 as
First United Brethren Church of Grand
Rapids. (Griggs Street near Buchanan SW
1889–90; 1948 Buchanan SW 1890–1910
(George Lohman); Built: 1910.

1889–91	Rev. Howard S. Schaeffer
1891–1910	Rev. William D. Stratton
1931–46	Rev. Irvin E. Runk
1989–	Rev. Barry T. Petrucci

OPEN BIBLE CHURCH

3065 Alger St. SE 49546;
Phone: 949–3940. Undenominational;
IFCA; Organized: 1925 (Ladies Literary
Club, 61 Sheldon Ave. SE 1925–26; St.
Cecilia Auditorium, 24 Ransom Ave.
NE 1926–27; 18 LaBelle St. SE
1927–64; 1456 Ellen Ave. SW
Wyoming 1964–68); Built: 1965.

1925–30	Rev. Dr. John T. Mitchell
1963–80	Rev. William R. Swanger
1992–	Rev. Daniel J. Spaulding

FIGURE 28
Although the congregation much later
became the Peoples Church of Grand
Rapids, this building on the north side
of Pearl Street between Ottawa and
Ionia avenues was known as the
Universalist Church (1868–92) to
earlier generations of Grand Rapidians.

FIGURE 29
Calvary Baptist (1890–1926) and Pilgrim Rest Missionary Baptist (1928–1966)
worshipped in this church at the northeast corner of Ionia and Antoine SW.

ORCHARD VIEW CHURCH OF GOD

2777 Leffingwell Ave. NE 49505;
Phone: 361–1669. Church of God,
Anderson, Ind.; Organized: 1931 as
Church of God Mission; 1955–78
Pasadena Park Church of God
(Knapp Street and Lafayette Avenue
NE 1931–32; 2456 Plainfield Ave. NE
1932–39; 841 Hollywood St. NE
1939–78); Basement church built 1939;
completed 1955.

1935	Rev. Mrs. Alice Raab
1937–39	Rev. Floyd Bowman
1958–70	Rev. Forrest M. Plants
1972–	Rev. Donald K. Dillon

ORTHODOX REFORMED

1900 Greenleaf Court SE 49508;
Phone: 452–6295. Unaffiliated;
Organized: 1970 (Shawnee Park CRC
Cadet Building, 2325 Sylvan Ave. SE
1970–78); Built: 1978 (Fred Renaud).

1970–84	Rev. Gerald Vandenberg
1984–92	Rev. Peter J. Breen
1992–	Rev. Harrison A. Newhouse

OTTAWA AVENUE MISSION

958 Ottawa Ave. NW; 1935.

1935	Rev. Cornelius Quartel

OUR LADY OF AGLONA

507 Broadway Ave. NW 49504;
Phone: 454–5921. RC; Organized: 1951
as Latvian Apostolate (307 LaGrave Ave.
SE 1951–56; 348 Mount Vernon Ave.
NW 1956–61); Built: 1883.

1951–81	Rev. Stanislaus Matiss
1981–93	Rev. Edward Statkus

OUR LADY OF GUADALUPE

7 Maple St. SE 49503;
Phone: 452–3555. RC; Organized: 1950
(307 LaGrave Ave. SE 1950–54).

1950–53	Rev. Titas Narbutas
1962–65	Rev. Theodore J. Kozlowski
1981–	Rev. Theodore J. Kozlowski

OUR LADY OF SORROWS

101 Hall St. SE 49507;
Phone: 243–0222. RC; Organized:
1908 (St. Andrew Cathedral basement,
267 Sheldon Ave. SE 1908–21; 1154
Sheldon SE 1921–57); Built: 1957
(Humbrecht Associates, Fort Wayne
Ind.); School 1922–70.

1908–53	Msgr. Salvatore Cianci
1955–62	Rev. Efrem Davanzo IMC
1966–70	Rev. Efrem Davanzo IMC
1978–85	Rev. Julian Reginato IMC
1988–93	Rev. Dennis W. Morrow

OUR SAVIOR LUTHERAN
2900 Burton St. SE 49546;
Phone: 949–0710. Missouri Synod;
Organized: 1961 (Martin Luther
School, 1916 Ridgewood Ave. SE
1961–66); Built: 1966 (Thomas
Browne Associates).

1961–92	Rev. Eugene L. Krieger
1992–	Rev. Charles Pool

PARIS BAPTIST
See **KENTWOOD BAPTIST**

PARK CONGREGATIONAL
See **FIRST (PARK)
CONGREGATIONAL**

PASADENA PARK CHURCH OF GOD
See **ORCHARD VIEW
CHURCH OF GOD**

PA–WA–TING MA–GED–WIN
UNITED METHODIST
441 Knapp St. NE 49505;
Phone: 364–6445. Organized: 1984 as
American Indian Church mission,
1988 as church (West Side Complex,
215 Straight Ave. NW 1984–87;
Olivet United Methodist Church, 1933
Buchanan Ave. SW 1987–88); Built:
1942 as St. James Lutheran (Harry L.
Mead).

1988–92	Rev. Joseph Sprague
1992–	Rev. David G. Knapp

PENNELLWOOD CHURCH OF GOD
3459 Reiser Ave. SW Wyoming 49548;
Phone: 452–3119. Abrahamic Faith;
Organized: 1935 (3055–57 S. Division
Ave. Wyoming 1935; 28 36th St. SW
1935–49); Built: 1949 (Arlie G.
Townsend).

1935–36	Brother F.L. Austin
1952–56	Rev. E. Milan Hall
1961–68	Rev. E. Milan Hall
1989–	Rev. Larry W. Mayberry

PENTECOSTAL ASSEMBLY
See **PENTECOSTAL MISSION**

PENTECOSTAL CHURCH IN JESUS
See **FULL GOSPEL MISSION** (894
Caulfield Ave. SW)

PENTECOSTAL CHURCH
OF THE NAZARENE
See **FIRST CHURCH
OF THE NAZARENE**

PENTECOSTAL DELIVERANCE
CHURCH OF APOSTOLIC FAITH
See **DELIVERANCE TEMPLE**

PENTECOSTAL FULL
GOSPEL MISSION
See **FULL GOSPEL MISSION**
(227 Bartlett St. SW)

PENTECOSTAL HOLINESS CHURCH
5427 Crippen Ave. SW Wyoming.
1957–74.

PENTECOSTAL MISSION
645 Front Ave. NW.
1909–35; (1056 S. Division Ave.
1909–12; 242 Pearl St. NW 1913–15).

1911	Fannie Knoll

PENTECOSTAL TABERNACLE
535 LaGrave Ave. SE; 1971–72.

1971–72	Rev. Peggy M. Wheeler

PEOPLE'S CHURCH
See **RESURRECTION LIFE
FULL GOSPEL CHURCH**

PEOPLES' CHURCH, THE
Lockerby Hall, NW corner Ionia
Avenue and Fountain Street NW.
Undenominational; 1893–96.

1893–94	Rev. H. Digby Johnson
1894–95	Rev. C.K. Gibson

PEOPLES CHURCH, THE
1654 Monroe Ave. NW.
1951–62 (35 National Ave. SW 1951–56).

PEOPLES CHURCH OF GRAND RAPIDS
100 Sheldon Ave. SE.
Universalist. 1858–1939; Organized:
1858 as First Universalist; 1892–1933
All Souls Universalist (Luce's Hall, 101
Monroe Ave. NW 1858–68; North side
Pearl Street between Ottawa Avenue
and Ionia Avenue NW 1868–92);
Built: 1892 (William G. Robinson).

1858–59	Rev. H.L. Hayward
1875–94	Rev. Charles Fluhrer
1930–39	Rev. James W. Hailwood

PHILIP HOOD MISSION
See **WOODVIEW CHRISTIAN**

PILGRIM REST
MISSIONARY BAPTIST
510 Franklin St. SE 49507;
Phone: 241–3315. National Baptist
Convention USA; Organized: 1927
(422 Ionia Ave. SW 1927–28; 826
Ionia SW 1928–66); Built: 1966 (Case,
Flint).

1927–30	Rev. William M. Moss
1930–37	Rev. William H. Thompson
1937–61	Rev. Emmett H. Hill
1963–	Rev. Dr. Maurice Jones

PLAINFIELD AVENUE
CHURCH OF CHRIST
315 Sweet St. NE.
1912–31; Organized: 1912 as Sweet
Street Church of Christ.

1912–13	Rev. George T. Stansbury
1915–20	Rev. John Calvin Meese

PLAINFIELD AVENUE
METHODIST EPISCOPAL
See **PLAINFIELD
UNITED METHODIST**

PLAINFIELD CENTER CHURCH
See **NEW CHURCH
OF THE HOLY SPIRIT**

PLAINFIELD CHRISTIAN REFORMED
6350 Kuttshill Drive NE Rockford.
Organized: 1908.

1908–10	Rev. Henry J. Mulder
1926–39	Rev. H.S. Koning
1977–85	Rev. Jacob P. Boonstra

(4435 Cannonsburg Road NE 1911–64
(J. & G. Daverman)
1985 Merged with Arcadia CRC to
become ARCADIA–PLAINFIELD
CHRISTIAN REFORMED.
See **BLYTHEFIELD CHRISTIAN
REFORMED**

PLAINFIELD UNITED METHODIST
214 Spencer St. NE 49505;
Phone: 454–7625. Organized: 1879
(New England Hall, 1337 Plainfield
Ave. NE 1878–80); Built 1882; Built:
1910; Addition: 1961.
1878–79	Rev. A.D. Newton
1879–80	Rev. S.G. Warner
1946–62	Rev. Leroy M. Whitney
1991–	Rev. Lynn Pier–Fitzgerald

PLEASANT HILL CHAPEL
409–11 Pleasant St. SW.
RCA; 1957–75.

PLEASANT HILL REFORMED
527 Church Place SW; 1960–67.
| 1960–65 | Rev. H. Herbert Taylor |

PLYMOUTH BRETHREN
See **FOREST HILLS
BIBLE CHAPEL**

**PLYMOUTH CONGREGATIONAL
UNITED CHURCH OF CHRIST**
4010 Kalamazoo Ave. SE 49508;
Phone: 455–4260. Organized: 1892 as
Plymouth Congregational (909
Franklin St. SE 1893–1959 (Pierre
Lindhout); Built: 1959 (David Post,
Brice McMillen).
1895	Rev. Robert M. Higgins
1919–26	Rev. James W. Hailwood
1933–57	Rev. Albert E. Potts
1958–63	Rev. Dean Dalrymple
1978–	Rev. Douglas N. VanDoren

**PLYMOUTH HEIGHTS
CHRISTIAN REFORMED**
1800 Plymouth Ave. SE 49506;
Phone: 243–5638. Organized: 1951
(Sylvan Christian School, 1630 Griggs
St. SE 1951–52); Built: 1953 (James K.
Haveman).
1953–64	Rev. Edward E. Heerema
1964–86	Rev. Wilbert M. VanDyk
1988–	Rev. Peter J. VanElderen Jr.
1989–	Dr. Russell L. Palsrok

POLISH FULL GOSPEL MOVEMENT
711 Watson St. SW; 1954–60.
| 1954–60 | Rev. Julius Gicz |

POTTER TEMPLE
See **CHURCH OF GOD IN
CHRIST (814 S. Division Ave.)**

**PRAYER COMMUNITY OF
ST. FRANCIS & ST. JOHN**
300 Graceland St. NE; 1982–83.
| 1982–83 | Rev. Thomas Kroon |

**PRAYING HANDS
CHURCH OF GOD IN CHRIST**
Redeemer Lutheran Church,
1905 Madison Ave. SE 49507;
Phone: 454–3301. Organized: 1991
(Burton Heights United Methodist
Church, 100 Burton St. SE 1991–93).
| 1991– | Rev. Walter C. Durham |

**PREPARED WAY PENTECOSTAL
ASSEMBLY & DIOCESAN**
1402 S. Division Ave. 49507;
Phone: 452–0237. Independent;
Organized: 1982.
| 1982– | Rev. Ann Winfield |

PRIMERA IGLESIA BAUTISTA HISPANA
See **BURTON HEIGHTS BAPTIST**

PRINCE OF PEACE LUTHERAN
3020 Lake Michigan Drive NW 49504;
Phone: 453–1164. ELCA; Organized:
1962 (Shawmut Hills School, 2250
Burritt St. NW 1962–64); Built: 1964
(Edgar Robert Firant).
1962–69	Rev. Vernel A. Lundeen
1969–80	Rev. Lowell L. Anderson
1990–	Rev. John P. Wiig

**PRINCE OF PEACE
MISSIONARY BAPTIST**
715 Evergreen St. SE 49507;
Phone: 452–2023. National Baptist
Convention USA; Organized: 1979
(4500 Potter Ave. SE Kentwood
1979–80); Built: 1990.
| 1979– | Rev. Moses A. Garmon |

**PRINCETON
CHRISTIAN REFORMED**
5330 Kalamazoo Ave. SE Kentwood
49508; Phone: 455–0110. Organized:
1963; Built: 1963 (Marvin DeWinter).
1965–70	Rev. Henry B. VandenHeuvel
1972–91	Rev. John C. Medendorp Jr.
1987–91	Rev. Thomas Wolthuis
1991–93	Rev. Sierd Woudstra
1993–	Rev. Berton VanAntwerpen

PROTESTANT CHRISTIAN REFORMED
See **SOUTHWEST
PROTESTANT REFORMED**

PROTESTING CHRISTIAN REFORMED
See **SOUTHWEST
PROTESTANT REFORMED**

QUAKERS
See **GRAND RAPIDS
FRIENDS MEETING**

QUARRY AVENUE BAPTIST
See **HIGHLAND HILLS BAPTIST**

**RECONCILIATION METROPOLITAN
COMMUNITY CHURCH**
300 Graceland St. NE 49505;
Phone: 364–7633. Universal Fellowship
of Metropolitan Community Churches;
Organized: 1981 (1108 Wealthy St. SE
1980–82; Fountain Street Church, 24
Fountain St. NE 1982–85); Built: 1909;
purchased 1986.
1981–83	Rev. Samuel P. Kader
1987–91	Rev. Bruce A. Roller
1993–	Rev. Marlene L. Casmero

REDEEMER LUTHERAN
1905 Madison Ave. SE 49507;
Phone: 452–1529. Missouri Synod;
Organized: 1928 as mission, 1929 as
church (1954 S. Division Ave.
1928–29); Built: 1929 (Harry L. Mead).
1928–56	Rev. Herbert P. Dorn
1957–71	Rev. Edwin V. Fitz
1992–	Rev. Roberto A. Becerra

**REED'S LAKE BAPTIST
CHAPEL/CHURCH**
See **LAKE DRIVE BAPTIST**

REFORMED BAPTIST
3181 Bradford St. NE 49506;
Phone: 940–0554. Independent;
Organized: 1972 (South YMCA, 2222
44th St. SW Wyoming 1975–77;
1701 Kalamazoo Ave. SE 1977–86).
1972–	Rev. James A. Hufstetler
1982–	Rev. Samuel E. Waldron
1987–	Rev. David W. Merck
1989–	Rev. Mark J. Chanski

FIGURE 30
This mission-style basement structure was St. Francis Xavier Church at Brown Street and Lafayette Avenue SE from 1920 to 1955. Its walls serve as the foundation for the present church.

REHOBOTH REFORMED
See **FREE REFORMED CHURCH OF NORTH AMERICA**

RELIGIO–PHILOSOPHICAL SOCIETY
See **SPIRITUALISTS**

RELIGIOUS COUNSELING CENTER CHURCH
See **NEW CHURCH OF THE HOLY SPIRIT**

REMEMBRANCE REFORMED
1915 Maplerow Ave. NW Walker 49504; Phone: 453–7709.
Organized: 1952 as Leonard Heights Chapel, 1956 as church; Built: 1958 (Larry VanMullen).
1958–62   Rev. Jack VanDyken
1993–   Rev. Tom Schwanda

RENAISSANCE CHURCH OF GOD IN CHRIST INC.
306 Griggs St. SW 49507;
Phone: 243–2074. Organized: 1992.
1992–   Rev. Dennis J. McMurray

REORGANIZED CHURCH OF JESUS CHRIST OF LATTER DAY SAINTS (GRAND VALLEY)
4790 Jacob St. SW Wyoming 49418;
Phone: 534–3413. Organized: 1970 (Grandville City Hall, 3195 Wilson Ave. SW Grandville 1970–73; Masonic

Temple Crescent Lodge 322, 3782 Crystal St. SW Grandville 1973; Red Carpet Inn, 3300 28th St. SW Grandville 1973–75); Built: 1975 (Larsen).
1970–73   Rev. William A. Dodds
1988–   Rev. David L. Johnson

REORGANIZED CHURCH OF JESUS CHRIST OF LATTER DAY SAINTS
2060 Johanna Ave. SW Wyoming.
1927–56 (2024 Johanna SW 1927–33).
1937   Elder William H. Dodds

REORGANIZED CHURCH OF JESUS CHRIST OF LATTER DAY SAINTS (NORTHVIEW)
4875 Palenque Court NE 49505;
Phone: 364–4339. Organized: 1966 (Northview High School, 4451 Hunsberger Drive NE 1966–68); Built: 1968 (Edgar Robert Firant).
1966–68   Rev. William Griffin
1992–   Rev. Robert Wilson

REORGANIZED CHURCH OF JESUS CHRIST OF LATTER DAY SAINTS
8 44th St. SE Kentwood; 1939–41.
1941   Elder William H. Dodds

REORGANIZED CHURCH OF JESUS CHRIST OF LATTER DAY SAINTS (UNION)
2140 Union Blvd. SE 49507;
Phone: 452–1801. Organized: 1895 (1575 S. Division Ave. 1895; Luce Block, 101 Monroe NW 1896; 1056 S. Division 1896–1900; 1204 S. Division 1918; 1225 S. Division 1923–52; Frank

P. Allen & Son); Built: 1953.
1895   L. Phelps
1900–18   Rev. Egerton K. Evans
1953   Rev. James C. Phillips
1970–80   Rev. Alma Dieterman
1991–   Rev. Thomas A. Reynolds

RESURRECTION CHURCH INTERNATIONAL EVANGELISM
35 National Ave. SW; 1976–77.

RESURRECTION FELLOWSHIP CHURCH
Box 68004 Grand Rapids 49516.
Organized: 1992.
Gary Hankins ThM, Eric Moore

RESURRECTION LIFE FULL GOSPEL CHURCH
5100 Ivanrest Ave. SW Wyoming 49509; Phone: 534–4923.
Nondenominational; Organized: 1967; 1967–85 People's Church (By Pass Motel/Red Carpet Inn, 3300 28th St. SW 1967–68; 2687 Ivanrest Ave. SW 1968–75; South Elementary School, 3650 Navaho Court SW Grandville 1975; 4270 44th St. SW 1975–93);
Built: 1993 (Sluiter VandenBosch).
1967–84   Rev. James E. Bugg
1984–   Rev. Duane G VanderKlok

RESURRECCION Y VIDA IGLESIA HISPANA
See **IGLESIA RESURRECCION Y VIDA**

REVIVAL CENTER
750 Wealthy St. SE; 1974.
1974   Rev. Benjamin Matthews

RICHMOND HILL MISSION
1725 Hanchett Ave. NW; 1929–30.

RICHMOND REFORMED
1814 Walker Ave. NW 49504;
Phone: 453–9211. Organized: 1927;
Built: 1952; Addition: 1959 (1708 Richmond St. NW 1927–52).
1928–33   Rev. Jerry A. Veldman
1956–69   Rev. Charles B. Wissink
1990–   Rev. James Van Zetten

RISING STAR MISSIONARY BAPTIST
257 Finney Ave. SW; 1982–85.
1982–85   Rev. J.H. Whiteside

RIVER OF LIFE MINISTRIES

4248 Kalamazoo Ave. SE 49508;
Phone: 245–1584. Independent;
Organized: 1980 (301 Burton St. SE
1980–83; 2317 Sylvan Ave. SE
1984–88; Midway Hotel, 4101 28th St.
SE Kentwood 1988–89; 2143 S.
Division Ave. 1990–92).

1980–	Rev. Robert J. Barnes,
	Rev. Rosemary Barnes

RIVERBEND BIBLE BAPTIST

1667 Wilson Ave. SW Walker 49504;
Phone: 453–6443. Organized: 1942 as
mission, 1962 as church; 1962–79
Riverbend Bible Church; Built: 1964.

1962–67	Rev. Wesley Perschbacher
1981–	Rev. David J. Piell

RIVERLIFE MINISTRIES
See **RIVER OF LIFE MINISTRIES**

RIVERSIDE CHRISTIAN REFORMED

604 Comstock Blvd. NE 49505;
Phone: 361–0604. Organized: 1953
(Fairmount School, 2042 Oakwood
Ave. NE 1953–54; Riverside School,
2420 Coit Ave. NE 1954–55); Built:
1957 (Daverman); Addition: 1976
(Robert Amor).

1955–60	Rev. Winston C. Boelkins
1969–77	Rev. Leonard Greenway
1979–87	Rev. Harlan G.
	VandenEinde Jr.
1989–	Rev. Matthew A. Palsrok

ROGERS HEIGHTS
CHRISTIAN REFORMED

3025 Michael Ave. SW Wyoming
49509; Phone: 532–3174. Organized:
1958 (1219 Buckingham St. SW
1958–65); Built: 1965; Merged with
Franklin Street CRC 1966.

1959–65	Rev. Floyd R. DeBoer
1979–86	Rev. Roger A. Kok
1987–	Rev. David L. Smit

ROOSEVELT PARK
PROTESTANT REFORMED
See **SOUTHWEST**
PROTESTANT REFORMED

FIGURE 31
St. Jude's parish held services in this quonset hut on Plainfield Avenue NE from
1948 until it burned on July 4, 1953.

SABAOTH MINISTRIES

2100 44th St. SW Wyoming 49509.
Meets at Seidman Center, 139 Crofton
St. SE; Phone: 774–5900. Assembly of
God; Organized: 1988.

1988–   Rev. Richard LaBelle
Includes Buddy Bear Ministry and
Native American Ministry.

SACRED HEART

156 Valley Ave. SW 49504;
Phone: 459–8362. RC; Organized:
1904; Built: 1924 (Brielmaier,
Milwaukee; Harry L. Mead); School
1905.

1904–14	Rev. Ladislaus P. Krakowski
1957–73	Msgr. Edmund F. Falicki
1990–	Rev. Joseph W. Kenshol

ST. ADALBERT BASILICA

654 Davis Ave. NW 49504;
Phone: 458–3065. RC; Organized:
1881; Built: 1913 (Henry J. Harks,
Cleveland; Christian G. Vierheilig);
School 1884; 1980 designated basilica.

1883–84	Rev. Casimir Jablonowski
1904–35	Msgr. Casimir Skory
1935–70	Msgr. John A.
	Maksymowski
1982–	Rev. Leo S. Rosloniec

ST. AGNES

502 Wilson Ave. NW.
RC; 1950–52; Worshipped in Rosedale
Memorial Park chapel.

1950–52   Rev. Bernard L Sikorski
See **HOLY SPIRIT**

ST. ALPHONSUS

224 Carrier St. NE 49505;
Phone: 451–3043. RC; Organized:
1888; Built: 1909 (Harry J. Rill,
Detroit; Christian G. Vierheilig);
School 1889.

1888–92	Rev. Theodore Lamy CSsR
1987–93	Rev. John F. Dowd CSsR
1993–	Rev. Daniel Lowery CSsR

ST. ANDREW CATHEDRAL

267 Sheldon Ave. SE 49503;
Phone: 456–1454. RC; Organized: 1833
as St. Mary's Mission at the Grand
River Rapids (Butterworth Street and
Gelock Avenue SW); (Monroe
Avenue and Ottawa Avenue NW
1849–75); Built: 1876 (John Grady);
School 1874.

1833–35	Rev. Frederic Baraga
1835–53	Rev. Andrew Viszoczky
1893–1917	Rev. John A. Schmitt
1917–51	Msgr. Dennis E. Malone
1956–68	Msgr. Charles W. Popell
1975–80	Msgr. Hugh M. Beahan
1984–	Msgr. Gaspar F. Ancona

ST. ANDREW EPISCOPAL
1025 Three Mile Road NE 49505;
Phone: 361–7887. Organized: 1953
(VanStrien–Alman Funeral Home,
1833 Plainfield Ave. NE 1953–56);
Built: 1956 (Chris Steketee); Addition:
1960 1965 (Charles Hornbach).
1953–85   Rev. Lester B. Thomas Jr.
1992–   Rev. Michael C. Fedewa

ST. ANDREW SYRIAN CHAPEL
St. Andrew Cathedral basement, 267
Sheldon Ave. SE. RC; 1927–35.
1927–28   Rev. Gabriel Khouri

ST. ANTHONY OF PADUA
1776 Acacia Drive NW 49504;
Phone: 453–8229. RC; Organized: 1906
(461 Richmond St. NW 1906–59; built
1914 (John F. Smith); Built: 1959
(Humbrecht Associates, Fort Wayne,
Ind.); School 1907.
1907–08   Rev. Anthony Eickelmann
1988–   Rev. Bernard Zajdel
           OFM Conv.

ST. BEDE MISSION FOR DEAF MUTES
St. Mark's Episcopal Church, 134 N.
Division Ave. Episcopal.
1893–1960.
1893–1911 Rev. Austin W. Mann,
           John E. Nash
1911–20   Rev. B.R. Allabaugh
1936   Rev. Horace B. Waters
1960   Rev. Arthur Leisman

ST. DOMINIC
50 Bellevue St. SW Wyoming 49548;
Phone: 531–1480. RC; Organized: 1974
(3860 S. Division Ave. 1974–78);
Built: 1961 as First Assembly of God.
1974   Rev. Robert J. Maternoski
1990–   Rev. Thomas J. DeYoung

ST. FRANCIS XAVIER
250 Brown St. SE 49507;
Phone: 241–2485. RC; Organized:
1914; Built: 1914 (Christian G.
Vierheilig); Built: 1960 (Brielmaier,
Milwaukee); School 1914.
1917–23   Rev. Thomas J. Reid
1923–43   Rev. John J. McAllister
1953–69   Msgr. Francis M. Schultz
1987–   Rev. Charles R. Antekeier

FIGURE 32

St. Mary Temple of Peace Spiritual Church expects to leave its old church at 1107 Sheldon SE behind when it moves into new quarters across the street in 1993. Bearing the marks of an Osgood design, the structure was originally built as Oakdale Park Episcopal at Cottage Grove and Blaine SE. It was moved to its present site in 1894 and served as St. John's Episcopal until 1909. It was being used as a labor union hall when its present congregation purchased it in 1965.

ST. GEORGE
ANTIOCHIAN ORTHODOX
334 LaGrave Ave. SE 49503;
Phone: 454–7558. Organized: 1910 as
St. George Syrian Orthodox (219
Williams St. SW 1910–25); Built: 1925
(James Price).
1905–20   Rev. Philipous Abou–assali
1941–57   Rev. John G. Mickel
1962–   Rev. John Estephan

ST. IMMANUEL
See **IMMANUEL LUTHERAN**

ST. ISIDORE
628 Diamond Ave. NE 49503;
Phone: 459–4731. RC; Organized:
1897; Built: 1912–17 (Christian G.
Vierheilig); School 1901.
1900–12   Rev. Marion Matkowski
1912–52   Msgr. Joseph S. Pietrasik
1970–81   Msgr. Joseph J Podhajski PA.
1984–87   Rev. Stephen E. Vesbit
1987–   Rev. Donald E.
           Lomasiewicz

ST. JAMES
733 Bridge St. NW 49504;
Phone: 458–3213. RC; Organized:
1870; Built: 1872 (John Grady,
William G. Robinson); School 1886.
1872–76   Rev. James C. Pulcher
1881–98   Rev. James C. Pulcher
1898–1922 Rev. Robert W. Brown
1938–61   Msgr. Raymond H. Baker
1962–68   Bishop Charles A.
           Salatka DD
1986–   Rev. Richard J. Host

ST. JAMES CHURCH OF TRUTH
144 Grant St. SW; 1945–52.

ST. JAMES
EVANGELICAL LUTHERAN
2040 Oakwood Ave. NE 49505;
Phone: 363–7718. Missouri Synod;
Organized: 1929 as mission, 1930 as
church (407 Knapp St. NE 1929–42;
441 Knapp NE 1942–69); Built: 1969.
1930–39   Rev. Edward C. Meyer
1939–55   Rev. Edward M. Lang
1984–   Rev. James H. Blain

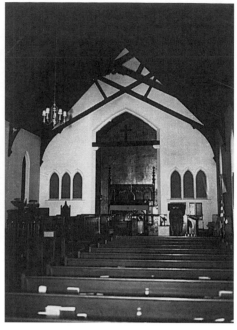

FIGURES 33, 34

St. Paul Memorial Episcopal Church was designed by David S. Hopkins in 1869, and stood at 610 Turner NW across from the old Union High School until freeway construction caused its relocation in 1961. Exterior above, interior at right.

ST. JAMES MISSION
Southwest Grand Rapids.
Episcopal; 1895–97.

ST. JOHN CHRYSOSTOM RUSSIAN ORTHODOX

40 National Ave. NW 49504;
Phone: 454–1166. Organized: 1916;
Built: 1893 as Norsk Evangelical
Lutheran.

1916–17	Rev. Anton Diachenko
1919–28	Rev. John Tertichny
1928–38	Rev. Nikolai Bellavin
1992–	Rev. Michael St. Andrew

ST. JOHN EPISCOPAL
1107 Sheldon Ave. SE.
1891–1909; Church purchased from
Oakdale Park Episcopal and moved 1894.

1891–97	Rev. J. Brewster Hubbs
1895–96	Rev. Abraham Reeves

ST. JOHN MISSIONARY BAPTIST

1132 Cass Ave. SE 49507;
Phone: 245–3921. Organized: 1965
(Ionia Ave. SW 1965–66); Built: 1900
as Grand Rapids Women's Club.

1965–89	Rev. Willie M. McCain
1989–	Rev. Roy L. Hampton

ST. JOHN UNITED CHURCH OF CHRIST

1934 Bridge St. NW 49504;
Phone: 453–2497. Organized: 1880 as
St. John's German Evangelical;
1934–57 St. John's Evangelical and
Reformed Church (348 Mount Vernon
NW 1881–1956); Built: 1956 (J. & G.
Daverman/Roger Allen).

1880–84	Rev. Frederick Mueller
1898–1938	Rev. F. Robert Schreiber
1972–84	Rev. Nelson H. Andres
1989–	Rev. Michael R. Ott

ST. JOHN VIANNEY

4101 Clyde Park Ave. SW Wyoming
49509; Phone: 534–5449. RC;
Organized: 1942 (3860 S. Division
Ave. Wyoming 1942–51; chapel
1951–74); Built: 1951; School 1952.

1942–53	Rev. Francis M. Schultz
1953–70	Rev. John C. Klonowski
1988–	Rev. James C. Kowalski

ST. JOSEPH THE WORKER

333 Rumsey St. SW 49503;
Phone: 456–7982. RC; Organized:
1887; Built: 1955 (Mead & Norton);
School 1888–1970.

1889–1906	Rev. Henry G. Frencken
1947–61	Msgr. William J. Murphy
1985–	Rev. Steven D. Cron

ST. JUDE

1120 Four Mile Road NE 49505;
Phone: 363–6885. RC; Organized: 1946
(3150 Plainfield Ave. NE 1946–56);
Built: 1964 (George Rafferty); School
1957.

1946–52	Rev. Ralph J. Kelly
1952–88	Msgr. Charles D. Brophy
1988–	Rev. Patrick T. Cawley

ST. LUKE AFRICAN METHODIST EPISCOPAL ZION

101 Delaware St. SE 49507;
Phone: 452–7227. Organized: 1863 as
mission, 1878 as church (123 Franklin
St. SE 1875–1950); Built: 1886 as South
Congregational (Sidney J. Osgood);
Addition: 1914 (Frank P. Allen &
Son).

1869, 1881	Rev. David Butler
1875	Rev. Baron William Ford
1878	Rev. Luke Miles
1957–86	Rev. Henry V. Hutcherson
1986–93	Rev. George A. Stewart
1993–	Rev. Gwendolyn Harris Strickland

ST. LUKE LUTHERAN
3215 Four Mile Road NE 49505;
Phone: 363–2381. ELCA; Organized:
1981 (Orchard View School, 2770
Leffingwell Ave. NE 1981–84); Built:
1984 (VanWienen & Papke);
Addition: 1989 (VanWienen &
Papke).

1981–	Rev. Mark A. Hellmann
1989–92	Scott Vana, associate pastor
1992–	Keith Lomen, associate pastor

ST. LUKE MISSION
Norsk Evangelical Lutheran Church,
40 National Ave. NW. Episcopal;
1895–1909.

1895–97	Rev. Dr. Campbell Fair
1904–08	Rev. Charles Donohue

ST. MARGARET MARY OF THE SACRED HEART CHAPEL
4616 Walton Ave. SW Wyoming
49548; Phone: 532–4290.
Traditional Catholic. Society of St.
Pius X, Kansas City, Mo.; Organized:
1980 (Gaines Township Hall, 1685
68th St. SE Dutton 1980–90); Built:
1937 as Beacon Light Mission.

1980–92	Rev. Leo Carley
1992–	Rev. James Haynes

ST. MARK EPISCOPAL
134 N. Division Ave. 49503;
Phone: 456–1684.
Organized: 1836 (Northeast corner
Monroe Avenue and Crescent Street
NW 1839–40; northwest corner
Division Avenue and Crescent Street
NW 1840–48); Built: 1848; Addition:
1871 (David S. Hopkins); Addition:
1893 (A.W. Rush & Sons); Addition:
1916 (Christian G. Vierheilig); Seat of
Bishop of Diocese of Western Michigan
1875–1964.

1839–42	Rev. Melancthon Hoyt
1843–61	Rev. Francis H. Cuming
1886–97	Rev. Dr. Campbell Fair
1897–1906	Rev. Dr. John Newton McCormick
1922–33	Very Rev. Charles E. Jackson
1933–50	Very Rev. H. Ralph Higgins
1971–	Rev. Joseph A. Howell

ST. MARK LUTHERAN
1934 52nd St. SE Kentwood 49508;
Phone: 455–5320. Missouri Synod;
Organized: 1966; Built: 1987
(Progressive Engineer).

1966–73	Rev. Wayne H. Pohl
1973–81	Rev. Robert Hoehner
1981–	Rev. Rodney D. Otto
1990–	Rev. John C. Pitcher

ST. MARY
423 First St. NW 49504;
Phone: 459–7390. RC; Organized:
1857; Built: 1874 (Hempel, New York
NY); School 1866–1990.

1857–62	Rev. Mathias M. Marco
1870–86	Rev. John G. Ehrenstrasser
1900–11	Bishop Joseph Schrembs DD
1940–65	Msgr. Bernard J. Hansknecht
1970–75	Msgr. Hugh M. Beahan
1975–88	Msgr. Joseph E. Murphy
1988–	Rev. Bernard A. Hall

ST. MARY MAGDALEN
1213 52nd St. SE Kentwood 49508;
Phone: 455–9310. RC; Organized:
1956; Built: 1965 (Gordon Cornwell,
Traverse City).

1956–71	Rev. John A. Breitenstein
1988–	Rev. Michael G. McKenna

ST. MARY MISSION AT THE GRAND RIVER RAPIDS
See **ST. ANDREW CATHEDRAL**

ST. MARY SPIRITUAL CHURCH
See **ST. MARY TEMPLE OF PEACE SPIRITUAL CHURCH**

ST. MARY TEMPLE OF PEACE SPIRITUAL CHURCH
1106 Sheldon Ave. SE 49507;
Phone: 452–5405. Spiritual, Kansas
City, Mo.; Organized: 1948 (Grant
Street SW 1948–49; Graham
Street SW 1949; 419 Grandville Ave.
SW 1951–59; 114 Grant St. SW
1960–64; 1107 Sheldon Ave. SE
1965–93); Built: 1993 (VanDyke).

1948–72	Rev. Roberta Heard/Hunter
1970–	Rev. Jessie M. White

ST. MATTHEW LUTHERAN
5125 Cascade Road SE 49546;
Phone: 942–9091. Missouri Synod;
Organized: 1969 mission, 1971 church
(Forest Hills Middle School, 5810 Ada
Drive SE 1969–71); Built: 1971.

1971–91	Rev. James E. Henning
1992–	Rev. Daniel E. Lochner

ST. MATTHEW MISSION
1431 Coit Ave. NE.
Episcopal; 1888–1908 (Monroe
Avenue and Travis Street NW
1888–91; 1126 Plainfield Ave. NE
1891–92; SW corner Quimby Street
and North Avenue NE 1892–1901
(Frank P. Allen).

1891–97	Rev. Dr. Campbell Fair
1893–96	M.C. Burch
1901–08	Rev. Charles Donohue

ST. MATTHIAS EPISCOPAL
See ST. MATTHEW MISSION

ST. MICHAEL BYZANTINE-SLAVONIC RITE CATHOLIC
See **ST. MICHAEL UKRAINIAN CATHOLIC**

ST. MICHAEL EPISCOPAL
2965 Wycliff Drive SE 49546;
Phone: 949–1223. Organized: 1960;
Built: 1961 (Sandy Grant).

1960–62	Rev. Frank G. Ireland
1991–	Rev. William G. Smith II

ST. MICHAEL UKRAINIAN CATHOLIC
154 Gold Ave. NW 49504;
Phone: 531–9360. Diocese of St.
Nicholas in Chicago for Ukrainians;
Organized: 1949; Built: 1895 as
Swedish Baptist; Church bought 1951.

1949–59	Rev. Andrew Kuzma
1991–	Rev. Mykhailo Kuzma, Rev. James A. Chelich

ST. NICHOLAS ORTHODOX
2148 Boston St. SE East Grand Rapids
49506; Phone: 452–2700.
Antiochian Orthodox Christian
Archdiocese; Organized: 1923 as St.
Nicholas Syrian Orthodox (328 Cass
Ave. SE 1923–57); Built: 1957.

1923–40	Rev. Philipous Abou–assali
1943–70	Rt. Rev. Ellis R. Khouri
1985–	Rev. Elias L. Mitchell

ST. PAUL

2750 Burton St. SE 49546;
Phone: 949–6633. RC; Organized: 1961
as St. Stephen Precursor mission, 1965
as church; Built: 1991 (Robert
Wassenaar); School 1962.

1965–69	Msgr. William E. Powers
1979–87	Rev. John W. McGee
1987–	Msgr. John J. Giammona

ST. PAUL ANGLICAN CATHOLIC

2560 Lake Michigan Drive NW 49504;
Phone: 791–2187. Anglican Catholic,
Athens, Ga.; Organized: 1978
(Tallmadge Township Fire Station,
O–1451 Leonard St. 1978–85; 1530
40th St. SW Wyoming 1985–87;
English Hills Country Club, 1200 Four
Mile Road NW Walker 1987); Built:
1987 (Alexander Dempsey).

1978–83	Rev. James R. Sharp
1989–	Rev. Ellwood Dean Poling

ST. PAUL BAPTIST
See **ST. PAUL**
MISSIONARY BAPTIST

ST. PAUL CHAPEL
See **CATHOLIC**
INFORMATION CENTER

ST. PAUL EPISCOPAL

3412 Leonard St. NW Walker 49504;
Phone: 791–2060. Organized: 1870
(610 Turner Ave. NW 1869–1961
(David S. Hopkins); Built: 1961 (Roger
Allen).

1870–79	Rev. Sidney Beckwith
1899–1908	Rev. Charles Donohue
1923–39	Rev. Clarence M. Farney
1964–75	Rev. John L. English
1980–	Rev. John L. English

ST. PAUL LUTHERAN

4041 44th St. SW Grandville.
1971–87; LCA.

1973–76	Rev. Robert L. Hansen
1983–87	Rev. Terry Graunke

ST. PAUL MEMORIAL EPISCOPAL
See **ST. PAUL EPISCOPAL**

ST. PAUL METHODIST
See **ST. PAUL**
UNITED METHODIST

ST. PAUL MISSIONARY BAPTIST

556 Eastern Ave. SE 49503;
Phone: 451–0719. National
Association Baptists USA, Nashville
Tenn.; Organized: 1952; 1952–55 Laura
Baptist; 1955–68 St. Paul Baptist
(53 Canton St. SW 1952–68; 311 Hall
St. SE 1965–74); Built: 1970 as Bethel
Pentecostal.

1952–61	Rev. A.K. Claybren
1972–	Rev. William E. Townsend

ST. PAUL UNITED METHODIST

3334 Breton Ave. SE Kentwood 49512;
Phone: 949–0880. Organized: 1876;
1877 Fair Ground Union Sunday
School; 1877–83 South Division Street
Methodist Episcopal; 1883–1896 Ames
Methodist Episcopal; 1896–1907 Tenth
Avenue Methodist Episcopal; (Mrs.
C.H. Fox home, 45 Graham St. SW
1876–77; Dr. Watts' drug store, 847 S.
Division 1877; Houseman Fair
Grounds, South Division 1877–78; St.
Luke AME Zion, 123 Franklin St. SE
1878–81; South Division and Albany
Street SW 1881–1900; 26 Shelby St.
SW 1900–09; 207 Highland St. SE
1909–55; 1072 Jefferson Ave. SE
1955–65); Built: 1965 (James K.
Haveman).

1880	Rev. Archer
1989–	Rev. Theron E. Bailey

SS PETER & PAUL

520 Myrtle St. NW 49504;
Phone: 454–6000. RC; Organized:
1904; Built: 1924 (J.J. Wernette &
Co.); School 1907.

1904–12	Rev. Wenceslaus V. Matulaitis
1925–61	Msgr. Joseph A. Lipkus
1992–93	Rev. Thomas F. Boufford
1993–	Rev. Dennis W. Morrow

ST. PHILIP EPISCOPAL

558 Henry Ave. SE 49503;
Phone: 451–9865. Organized: 1911
(557 Henry Ave. SE 1911–18); Built:
1918 (Frank P. Allen & Son).

1911–12	Rev. Lincoln R. Vercoe
1920–29	Rev. Ellis A. Christian
1935–38	Rt. Rev. John M. Burgess
1950–69	Rev. George A. Stams
1979–87	Rev. Thomas Smith Jr.
1990–	Rev. Dr. Margaret J. Neill

ST. PIUS X

3937 Wilson Ave. SW Grandville
49418; Phone: 532–9344. RC;
Organized: 1953 (Grand Theater, 3574
Chicago Drive SW Grandville
1953–56); Built: 1956 (J. & G.
Daverman); Built: 1988 (Richard
Drury, Traverse City).

1954–59	Rev. John N. McDuffee
1968–73	Rev. John W. McGee
1980–89	Rev. Michael A. Danner
1989–	Rev. John A. Najdowski

ST. ROBERT OF NEWMINSTER

6477 Ada Drive SE Ada 49301;
Phone: 676–9111. RC; Organized: 1951
(7300 E. Fulton St. 1951–70); Built:
1970 (Jude T. Fusco Associates).

1951–56	Rev. Frederick J. Voss
1956–66	Rev. M. Donald Farrell
1966–73	Rev. Henry J. Niedzwiecki
1973–79	Rev. John W. McGee
1979–88	Rev. David L. Hawley
1988–	Msgr. Ernest P. Schneider.

ST. STEPHEN

750 Gladstone Ave. SE East Grand
Rapids 49506; Phone: 243–8998.
Organized: 1924; Built: 1925 (J.J.
Wernette & Co); School 1925.

1924–36	Rev. Leo J. Farquharson
1936–50	Msgr. Robert W. Bogg
1950–61	Msgr. James A. Bryant
1961–66	Msgr. Arthur J. LeRoux
1966–71	Msgr. Edward N. Alt
1971–77	Bishop Joseph C. McKinney
1977–82	Rev. George J. Fekete
1982–85	Rev. Joseph M. Malewitz
1985–	Rev. Thomas S. Vesbit

ST. STEPHEN MISSION
Eastern Grand Rapids.
Episcopal; 1905–07.

1906	Rev. W.M. Warlow

ST. STEPHEN PRECURSOR
See **ST. PAUL**

FIGURE 35
Scribner Avenue Baptist, 1236 Scribner NW, 1895–1961. The congregation is now known as Fair Haven Baptist on Richmond Street in Walker.

ST. THOMAS
1449 Wilcox Park Drive SE 49506; Phone: 459–4662. RC; Organized: 1924; Built: 1954 (Roger Allen & Associates) School 1925.

1924–26	Rev. Aloysius M. Fitzpatrick
1940–70	Msgr. Raymond J. Sweeney
1987–	Rev. Donald J. Heydens
1993–	Rev. James A. Chelich

N.B. Salvation Army listings are alphabetical by street.

SALVATION ARMY HOMELESS ASSISTANCE PROGRAM RECEPTION CENTER
40 S. Division Ave. 49503; Phone: 454–5840 (6 Weston St. SE 1990–93).

1990–93	Lt. Col. Eric Britcher
1993–	Major William A. Roberts

SALVATION ARMY (ADULT REHABILITATION CENTER)
1491 S. Division Ave. 49507; Phone: 452–3133. Organized: 1906 as Salvation Army (Men's Industrial Home); 1963–75 Salvation Army (Men's Social Service Center); (226 Grandville Ave. SW 1906–07; 43 Williams St. SW 1907–28; 225 Commerce Ave. SW 1928–64).

1928–64	Adj. Calhoun.
1965	Major William T. Gant
1990–	Major David Carr

SALVATION ARMY BURTON HEIGHTS CORPS NO. 3
2244 S. Division Ave. 1940–75 (26 Burton St. SW 1940–50; 12 Quigley Blvd. SW 1950–52; 144 Burton St. SW 1952–80).

1945	Capt. L. Geer
1970	David H. Riches

SALVATION ARMY BURTON HEIGHTS CORPS COMMUNITY CENTER

See **SALVATION ARMY DICKINSON PARK CORPS COMMUNITY CENTER**

SALVATION ARMY (MEN'S SOCIAL CENTER)
609–11 Eastern Ave. SE. 1976–80; 1950–76 Salvation Army Store.

1965	Mrs. Lucinda D. Hillard
1980	Evelyn DeLaughter

SALVATION ARMY HERITAGE HILL CORPS
160 Fountain St. NE 49503; Phone: 454–1459. Organized: 1989 as combination of Citadel Corps and Temple Corps.

1989–90	Major John McCarty
1991–	Major Melville R. James
1993	Linda Glover, director, Booth Family Services

SALVATION ARMY CITADEL CORPS
1215 E. Fulton St. 49503. 1883–1989; 1883–1935 Salvation Army Corps No. 1 (south side Pearl Street NW at Grand River 1883–87; Hall, 80 Market Ave. NW 1887–88; Barracks, 249 Pearl NW 1888–89; 231 Pearl NW 1889–1901; Barracks, 124 Monroe Ave. NW 1901–02; 315 Monroe NW 1902–04; 218 Pearl NW 1904–05; 634 Sheldon Ave. SE 1905–06; 114–116 Pearl NW 1906–11; 240 Pearl NW 1911–15; 242 Pearl NW 1915–22; 227 Pearl NW 1922–59; 67

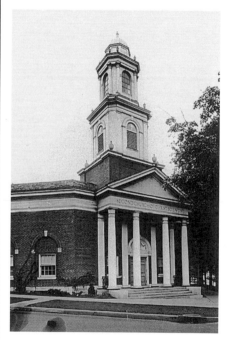

FIGURE 36
The Second Christian Science Church at 70 Bostwick Ave. NE was a Colton & Knecht design in 1929. It later served as the First Pilgrim Tabernacle (1939–59) and then as the Michigan Room of the Grand Rapids Public Library until it was removed for library expansion in 1966.

FIGURE 37
Built in 1870, Second Reformed Church at 154 Bostwick Ave. NE burned on the afternoon of May 23, 1895. The photo includes the old Central High School in the background and one steeple of St. Mark's Episcopal at right.

Barclay Ave. NE 1959–89).
1883	Capt. Jane McCracken
1895	Adj. Henry C. Kernahan
1985–89	Major Carl C. Amick
1989	Combined with Temple

Corps to form **SALVATION ARMY HERITAGE HILL CORPS**

SALVATION ARMY BOOTH SERVICES
1215 E. Fulton St. 49503;
Phone: 459–9468. Organized: 1887 as Salvation Army Rescue Home; 1912–75 Salvation Army (Evangeline Home); (NW corner Second Street and Pine Avenue NW 1887–90; 1018 Second NW 1890–91; 1022 Second NW 1891–92; College Avenue and Walnut Street NE 1892–96; 726 Sinclair Ave. NE 1896–98; 1950 S. Division Ave. 1898–1912); Building donated 1912 by Edward and Susan Lowe; Built: 1967.
| 1887 | Capt. Lottie Collier |
| 1993– | Major William A. Roberts |

SALVATION ARMY
(RECREATION CENTER)
570–72 Grandville Ave. SW; 1944–53.

SALVATION ARMY (MISSION)
315 Grant St. SW; 1953–76.

SALVATION ARMY THRIFT STORE
2740 Hague Ave. SW Wyoming 49509; Phone: 530–8020.
Organized: 1991.
1991	Major Brian Merritt
1991–	Major David Carr
1992–	Carolyn E. Priester

SALVATION ARMY TEMPLE CORPS
441 Knapp St. NE.
1915–80; Organized: 1915 as Salvation Army (Swedish Branch); 1920–30 Salvation Army (Scandinavian Branch); 1935–55 Salvation Army Corps No. 2 (419 Stocking Ave. NW 1915; 934 Bridge St. NW 1920; 924 Leonard St. NW 1935–67).
1920	Capt. Christian Pedersen
1980	Major George Hogg
1989	Combined with Citadel

Corps to form **SALVATION ARMY HERITAGE HILL CORPS.**

SALVATION ARMY
(MEN'S SOCIAL CENTER)
500 Leonard St. NW.
1976–83; 1963–76 Salvation Army Store
| 1980 | Judy Rush |

SALVATION ARMY DICKINSON PARK CORPS COMMUNITY CENTER
1632 Linden Ave. SE 49507;
Phone: 241–3723. Organized: 1941; 1941–89 Salvation Army Burton Heights Corps Community Center (2244 S. Division Ave. 1941–89); Built: 1988 (Newhof & Winer).
| 1941–89 | Lt. Herbert Jensen |
| 1991– | Capt. Lonneal Richardson |

SALVATION ARMY (DIVISIONAL HEADQUARTERS)
1345 Monroe Ave. NW 49505;
Phone: 459–3433. Organized: 1883 (south side Pearl Street NW at Grand River 1883–87; Hall, 80 Market Ave. NW 1887–88; Barracks, 249 Pearl NW 1888–89; 231 Pearl NW 1889–1901; Barracks, 124 Monroe Ave. NW 1901–02; 315 Monroe NW 1902–04; 218 Pearl NW 1904–05; 634 Sheldon Ave. SE 1905–06; 114–116 Pearl NW 1906–11; 240 Pearl NW 1911–15; 242

FIGURE 38
One of the earliest designs of architect William G. Robinson was Second Street Methodist Episcopal in 1871. Facing Second Street on the northeast corner of Turner Avenue, it was removed for the U.S. 131 freeway in 1961.

Pearl NW 1915–22; 227 Pearl NW
1922–59; 67 Barclay Ave. NE 1959–78;
1215 E. Fulton St. 1978–91).

1895	Adj. Henry C. Kernahan
1990–93	Lt. Col. Eric Britcher
1993–	Major William A. Roberts

SAMARITAN MISSION
1128 S. Division Ave.
1934–45; 1934–35 Samaritan Army
Mission (843 S. Division 1934–35).

SANCTIFIED CHURCH
718 Lafayette Ave. SE; 1974–75.

SCHOOL OF LIFE TRUTH HEALING MINISTRY
344 Washington St. SE; 1944–55.

| 1944–55 | Thomas H. Holtrop |

SCIENCE CHRISTIANS OF UNITED TRUTH CHURCH (WORLD HEADQUARTERS)
3860 S. Division Ave. Wyoming.
1979–86.

| 1984–85 | Rev. Eugene A. Stinson |

SCIENCE CHRISTIANS OF UNITED TRUTH CHURCH (NEW TRUTH PARISH)
3931 Leland Ave. NE Comstock Park.
Plainfield Branch; 1984–88.

| 1984–85 | Rev. Franklyn S. Taylor |

SCIENCE HALL LECTURE ASSOCIATION
See SPIRITUALISTS

SCRIBNER AVENUE BAPTIST
See FAIR HAVEN BAPTIST

SECOND BAPTIST
North Division Avenue between
Fountain and Pearl streets NW.
1861–69; Built: 1865.

1861–63	Rev. C.C. Miller, Rev. A. Stanwood
1863–67	Rev. C.B. Smith DD
1867–69	Rev. Nathan A. Reed
1869	Merged with First/

FOUNTAIN STREET Baptist.

SECOND BAPTIST
840 Wilson Ave. NW Walker 49504;
Phone: 791–9370. Organized: 1883 (49
Gold Ave. NW 1883–1989); Built:
1988 (Reid); Addition: 1991.

1883–89	Rev. Edward H. Brooks
1915–38	Rev. Isaac VanWestenbrugge
1978–	Rev. Kenneth J. Lindsey

SECOND CHRISTIAN REFORMED
See WESTVIEW
CHRISTIAN REFORMED

SECOND CHRISTIAN SCIENCE CHURCH
1431 Robinson Road SE.
1921–39; (All Souls Universalist
Church, 100 Sheldon Ave. SE
1921–29; 70 Bostwick Ave. NE
1929–38 (Colton & Knecht).

SECOND CHURCH OF CHRIST SCIENTIST
830 North Park St. NE.
1958–90 (3022 Coit Ave. NE
1958–62); Church purchased and
moved from Plainfield Avenue and
Four Mile Road NE 1962.

SECOND CONGREGATIONAL
525 Cheshire Drive NE 49505;
Phone: 361–2629. UCC; Organized:
1869 as mission, 1870 as church
(Monroe Avenue north of Leonard
Street NW 1869–74; 1331 Plainfield
Ave. NE 1874–1950 (Grove Proctor);
Built: 1950 (Daverman).

1869	Rev. John Holloway
1948–63	Rev. John E. Felible
1964–76	Rev. Edwin J. Arnold
1977–	Rev. Dr. Dewey A. Peterson

SECOND EVANGELICAL
See GRIGGS STREET
UNITED METHODIST

SECOND METHODIST EPISCOPAL
See SECOND
UNITED METHODIST

SECOND PRESBYTERIAN
See WESTMINSTER
PRESBYTERIAN

SECOND PROTESTANT REFORMED
See SOUTHWEST
PROTESTANT REFORMED

SECOND REFORMED
154 Bostwick Ave. NE.
1849–1918; Organized: as Dutch
Reformed; Built: 1870; Built: 1889
(William G. Robinson).

1854–57	Rev. H.G. Klyn
1860–73	Rev. Cornelius VanderMeulen
1883–95	Rev. Egbert Winter DD
1910–18	Rev. Henry Hospers
1918	Merged with First Reformed

to form CENTRAL REFORMED.

SECOND STREET METHODIST
See SECOND
UNITED METHODIST

SECOND TRUE DUTCH REFORMED
See EASTERN AVENUE
CHRISTIAN REFORMED

SECOND UNITED BRETHREN
Scribner Avenue near Tenth Street
NW; 1900–05.

| 1900 | Rev. Eli Good |
| 1905 | Rev. Charles E. Kriebel |

SECOND UNITED METHODIST
2600 Seventh St. NW 49504;
Organized: 1855 as Bridge Street
Methodist Episcopal (Northeast corner
Bridge Street and Front Avenue NW
1855–71); 1862–71 Second Methodist
Episcopal; 1871–1961 Second Street
Methodist (345 Second NW
1871–1961 (William G. Robinson);
Built: 1961; 1961–77 Second United
Methodist.

1855–56	Rev. Amos Wakefield.
1960	Rev. James E. Leach
1975	Rev. James W. Lavengood
1977	Merged with Valley

Avenue United Methodist to form
FAITH UNITED METHODIST

SERVANTS COMMUNITY REFORMED
57 Deloney Ave. SW 49504;
Phone: 451–2418. Organized: 1981;
Built: 1892 as Ninth Reformed.

| 1981–86 | Rev. Richard J. Termaat |
| 1990– | Rev. StevenVanBronkhorst |

FIGURE 39
Gracious old downtown mansions like the former Sidney F. Stevens residence at 126 Sheldon Ave. SE afforded many clubs and societies large rooms for meeting space. As the Maccabees Hall, this elegent dwelling was the home of the Spiritual Lighthouse of Truth from 1945 to 1967.

SEVEN POINTS OF
THE DIVINE MIND CHURCH
610 Sheldon Ave. SE 49503.
Nondenominational; Organized: 1972
(426 Paris Ave. SE 1972–80; 814
Jefferson Ave. SE 1980–85; 126 S.
Division Ave. 1990).

| 1972–93 | Rev. Mother Elsie Collins |
| 1980–85 | Bishop Harold S. Collins |

SEVENTH DAY ADVENTIST
2015 Kalamazoo Ave. SE; 1943–49.

SEVENTH DAY ADVENTIST
CHURCH OF WYOMING
2580 44th St. SW Wyoming 49509;
Phone: 532–3418. Organized: 1927
(2445 Byron Center Ave. SW
Wyoming 1927–73; Olivet Reformed
Church, 3085 Wallace Ave. SW
Grandville 1973–74); Built: 1974
(Charles VanderWoude).

| 1930 | Rev. Don A. Courville |
| 1991– | Rev. William A. Cook |

SEVENTH REFORMED
950 Leonard St. NW 49504;
Phone: 459–4451. Organized: 1890
(838 Leonard NW 1892–52 (J.H.
Daverman & Son); Built: 1951
(Daverman).

1891–93	Rev. John Lamar
1957–80	Rev. Gordon H. Girod
1980–90	Rev. Charles W. Krahe
1993–	Dr. John R. de Witt

SEYMOUR CHRISTIAN REFORMED
840 Alger St. SE 49507;
Phone: 245–8726. Organized: 1934 as
Hazen Street Mission, 1938 as church
(1144 Hazen SE 1934–41); Built: 1941.

1940–53	Rev. Richard J. Frens
1953–62	Rev. Jacob Hasper
1964–75	Rev. John A. DeKruyter
1973–92	Rev. Henry Admiraal
1991–	Rev. Alan A. Arkema

SHAWNEE PARK
CHRISTIAN REFORMED
2255 Tecumseh Drive SE 49506;
Phone: 452–6971. Organized: 1961;
Built: 1966 (Edgar Robert Firant).

| 1962–74 | Rev. Lawrence E. Veltkamp |
| 1990– | Rev. Roger A. Kok |

SHERMAN STREET
CHRISTIAN REFORMED
1000 Sherman St. SE 49506;
Phone: 452–7034. Organized: 1907;
Built: 1908 (J. & G. Daverman).

1908–11	Rev. John L. VanTielen
1956–67	Rev. John A. Mulder
1980–87	Rev. Harold E. Botts
1984–	Rev. Mark D. Vermaire

SIXTH REFORMED
See OAKDALE PARK REFORMED

SMITH MEMORIAL
CONGREGATIONAL
631 Hall St. SW 49503;
Phone: 243–1093. UCC; Organized:
1886 as mission, 1887 as church (305
Wealthy St. SW 1888–1912 (Sidney J.
Osgood); Built: 1912 (Henry H.
Turner).

1886–87	Rev. E.F. Goff
1887–90	Rev. H.A. McIntyre
1907–38	Rev. Herbert McConnell
1969–78	Rev. Edward Jarvis Bottum
1986–91	Rev. Margaret Beretz
1991–	Rev. Richard D. Rowlands

SOUTH CONGREGATIONAL
2415 Madison Ave. SE 49507;
Phone: 241–1639. UCC; Organized:
1874 as South Mission Sabbath School,
1878 as church (St. Luke AME Zion
Church, 123 Franklin St. SE 1874–76;
Delaware Street near Jefferson Avenue
SE 1876–86; 938 Sheldon Ave. SE
1886–1951); Built: 1950. Rebuilt 1968.

1874	Rev. Frederick York
1877–79	Rev. E.C. Olney
1880–89	Rev. Benjamin F. Sargent
1909–26	Rev. Charles O. Grieshaber
1931–41	Rev. Harold N. Skidmore
1950–66	Rev. Charles W. Scheid
1966–77	Rev. Richard L. Ford
1977–88	Rev. Philip Reikow
1989–	Rev. Ronald C. Skidmore

SOUTH DIVISION STREET
METHODIST EPISCOPAL
See **ST. PAUL**
UNITED METHODIST

SOUTH EASTERN BIBLE CHURCH

4915 Eastern Ave. SE Kentwood 49508; Phone: 538–2562. IFCA; Organized: 1960; 1960–84 First Free Will Baptist; 1984–89 Eastern Avenue Baptist; 1989–91 Kent Fellowship Church (Old Paris Township Hall, 3167 Kalamazoo Ave. SE 1960–62); Built: 1962.

1960–75	Rev. John N. Vick
1991–	Rev. Mark J. Highman

SOUTH END MISSION

1274 Burton St. SW Wyoming; 1928–30.

1928–29	James L. Colville

SOUTH GRAND RAPIDS METHODIST EPISCOPAL

See **SOUTH UNITED METHODIST**

SOUTH GRANDVILLE CHRISTIAN REFORMED

4130 Wilson Ave. SW Grandville 49418; Phone: 532–5413. Organized: 1954; Built: 1963 (James K. Haveman).

1956–64	Rev. Paul C. Zylstra
1972–89	Rev. Leonard H. VanDrunen
1990–	Rev. Robert D. Ritsema

SOUTH KENT FREE WILL BAPTIST

4614 Walton Ave. SW Wyoming. 1967–68.

SOUTH LAWN PARK CHURCH OF GOD

See **SOUTHLAWN CHURCH OF GOD**

SOUTH MISSION SABBATH SCHOOL

See **SOUTH CONGREGATIONAL**

SOUTH UNITED METHODIST

4500 S. Division Ave. Kentwood 49548; Phone: 534–8931. Organized: 1929 as Methodist Union Chapel; 1940–59 South Grand Rapids Methodist Episcopal; Built: 1954–55 (Donker Engineering); Addition: 1970 (VandenBout).

1929–31	Rev. Floyd George Jr.
1988–	Rev. Thomas M. Pier–Fitzgerald

SOUTH WYOMING UNITED METHODIST

5603 Byron Center Ave. SW Wyoming 49509; Phone: 532–0131. Organized: 1885 as mission, 1899 as church (Emmons School, 5600 Byron Center Ave. SW Wyoming 1885–99); Built: 1899.

1991–	Rev. Arthur Jackson

SOUTHEAST CHURCH OF CHRIST

1915 Nelson Ave. SE 49507; Phone: 243–1410. Nondenominational; Organized: 1990 (1759 Chamberlain Ave. SE 1990; Sylvan Christian School, 1630 Griggs St. SE 1990–91).

1990–	Rev. Dr. Paul Hubbard Jr.

SOUTHEAST PROTESTANT REFORMED

1535 Cambridge Drive SE 49506; Phone: 245–6931. Organized: 1944; 1944–59 Fourth Protestant Reformed; Built: 1959; (1701 Kalamazoo Ave. SE 1944–59; Adams Street Christian School, 1150 Adams SE 1959).

1944–62	Rev. Richard Veldman
1962–78	Rev. Marinus Schipper
1992–	Rev. Dale H. Kuiper

SOUTHEAST VALLEY ASSEMBLY OF GOD

2060 43rd St. SE 49508; Phone: 281–0500. Assembly of God, Dearborn; Organized: 1991.

1991–	Rev. Dean J. Elliott

SOUTHLAWN CHURCH OF GOD

3880 Jefferson Ave. SE Wyoming 49548; Phone: 534–9111. Organized: 1914; 1927–60 Southlawn Park Church of God; Built: 1927 (200 Abbie St. SE Wyoming 1927–80).

1927	Rev. James A. Patrick
1983–	Rev. Charles E. Jones

SOUTHSIDE CHURCH OF CHRIST

1304 36th St. SE 49508; Phone: 452–8017. Organized: 1930; 1930–41, 1945–67 The Church of Christ; 1941–45 Burton Heights Church of Christ (4559 S. Division Ave. Wyoming 1930–36; 203 Janet St. SE Wyoming 1936–41; 10 Quigley Blvd. SW 1941–45; 1225 S. Division

1945–53; 127 Meerse St. SE 1953–67); Built: 1967.

1930–60	Evangelist C.L. Puryear
1986–	Evangelist Charles S. Young

SOUTHWEST PROTESTANT REFORMED

4875 Ivanrest Ave. SW Grandville 49418; Phone: 532–6876. Organized: 1925; 1932–41 Roosevelt Park Protestant Reformed; 1941–58 Second Protestant Reformed (1514 Roosevelt Ave. SW 1925–39; 1456 Ellen Ave. SW Wyoming 1939–57; 2019 Porter St. SW Wyoming 1957–60; 1854 Porter SW Wyoming 1960–78); Built: 1978.

1925–26	Rev. Herman Hoeksema
1927–37	Rev. Bernard Kok
1939–41	Rev. Marinus Schipper

SPANISH ADVENTIST CHURCH OF GRAND RAPIDS

See **IGLESIA ADVENTISTA HISPANA DE GRAND RAPIDS**

SPANISH ADVENTIST CHURCH OF WYOMING

See **IGLESIA ADVENTISTA DE WYOMING**

SPANISH CHRISTIAN REFORMED

2445 Byron Center Ave. SW Wyoming 49509; Phone: 534–3836. Organized: 1962 as mission, 1981 as church (460 Franklin St. SW 1962–69; Calvin Seminary, 3201 Burton St. SE 1969–72; Beverly Christian Reformed Church, 2019 Porter St. SW Wyoming 1972–74).

1962–65	Rev. Juan Boonstra
1973–	Rev. Domingo G. Romero

SPANISH CHURCH OF GOD

300 Graceland St. SE. 1959–78 (401 Eleventh St. NW 1959–63).

1959–66	Rev. Alfred G. Galvan
1966–68	Rev. Miguel Corzo

SPANISH CHURCH OF GOD

See **IGLESIA DE DIOS MANANTIAL DE VIDA**

FIGURE 40
Trinity Baptist worshiped in this church at 1331 Plainfield Ave. NE from 1950 to 1965. It was built for Second Congregational in 1874.

SPANISH SEVENTH-DAY ADVENTIST
See **IGLESIA ADVENTISTA HISPANA DE GRAND RAPIDS**

SPIRITUAL AND LIBERAL ASSOCIATION OF GRAND RAPIDS, THE
See SPIRITUALISTS

SPIRITUAL LIGHTHOUSE OF TRUTH
1038 Lake Michigan Drive NW 49504. Organized: 1931 as Spiritual Mission of USA (439 Ottawa Ave. NW 1931–33; 240 N. Division Ave. 1933–45; 126 Sheldon Ave. SE 1945–67).
1932–33   Mrs. Frances Pearson, secretary
1933–61   Rev. Ernest A. Gleason
1992–   Rev. Bernard F. Gicz

SPIRITUAL MISSION
237 Scribner Ave NW; 1933–34.
1933–34   Myrtle Chamberlain, secretary

SPIRITUAL MISSION CHURCH
362 Norwood Ave. SE; 1931–33.
1931–33   Rev. Emma M. Farrington

SPIRITUAL MISSION
CHURCH OF DIVINE SCIENCE
1107 Sheldon Ave. SE.
Christian Science; 1929–36.
1930–31   Mrs. Emma M. Farrington

SPIRITUAL SOCIETY
Lincoln Hall, 110 Pearl St. NW.
1892–1906; 1892–1904 Grand Rapids Spiritual Association.
1893–95   Dr. J.C. Batdorf
1905–06   Rev. D.A. Herrick

SPIRITUAL TABERNACLE CHURCH
415 Ottawa Ave. NW; 1933–35.

SPIRITUAL TEMPLE SOCIETY
FIRST CHURCH OF TRUTH
127 Meerse St. SE 49507;
Phone: 241–3387. Spiritualist;
Independent Spiritual Association, Lansing; Organized: 1903 (26 Shelby St. SW 1909–61; Townsend Hall, 1577 Plainfield Ave. NE 1961–71).
1903–40   Rev. Amanda C. Flower
1940–56   Rev. Annie L. Carpenter

SPIRITUAL UNION OF
GRAND RAPIDS, THE
See SPIRITUALISTS
SPIRITUALIST CHURCH
351 King Court SW; 1930–31.
1930–31   Mrs. Sylvia Wright

SPIRITUALIST CHURCH
1224 Madison Ave. SE; 1945–48.

SPIRITUALIST TEMPLE
See CHRISTIAN SPIRITUALIST

SPIRITUALISTS
Kennedy's Block, Market Avenue and Louis Street NW. 1862–92; 1862 Religio–Philosophical Society; 1868 First Society of Spiritualists of Grand Rapids; 1879 The Spiritual and Liberal Association of Grand Rapids; 1884–87 Science Hall Lecture Association; 1886 The Conversational / Conference Meeting; 1888 Religio–Philosophical Society; 1889 The Spiritual Union of Grand Rapids; (Mills and Clancy's Hall, 184 Monroe Ave. NW 1865–70; Luce's Hall, 101 Monroe NW 1875–80; Good Templars' Hall, Pearl St. NW 1881–83; Science Hall, 233–35 Monroe

NW 1884; Independence Hall, 111 Monroe NW 1886; 84 Market Ave. NW 1888; Good Templars' Hall, 23 S. Division Ave. 1888–89).
1865   Wright L. Coffinberry, president
1868   Ira Jones, president
1884–87   Joseph Tompkins, president
1886   Mrs. Julia A. Stowe
1888   J.B. Josselyn, president
1889   L.V. Moulton

SPRING STREET CHRISTIAN REFORMED
See **FIRST CHRISTIAN REFORMED**

SPRING STREET
METHODIST EPISCOPAL
See **FIRST COMMUNITY AFRICAN METHODIST EPISCOPAL**

STANDALE BAPTIST
3714 Lake Michigan Drive NW Walker 49504; Phone: 453–4489. General Association of Regular Baptists; Organized: 1957 as mission, 1963 as church (Zinser School, 1234 Kinney Ave. NW Walker 1957–60); Built: 1960; Addition: 1964 (Dan Vos).
1957–60   Rev. David Gardner
1988–   Rev. Douglas Bartlett

STANDALE CHAPEL
See **STANDALE REFORMED**

STANDALE REFORMED
202 Cummings Ave. NW Walker 49504; Phone: 453–0005. Organized: 1952 (Rosedale Memorial Park Chapel, O-50 Lake Michigan Drive 1952; Cummings School, 4261 Schoolcraft St. NW Walker 1952–56); Built: 1957; Addition: 1972.
1953–58   Rev. David C. TerBeest
1969–76   Rev. J. Robert Steegstra
1978–86   Rev. Ronald J. Verwys
1988–   Rev. Randall L. Weener

STREET LIGHT OUTREACH
515 S. Division Ave. 49503;
Phone: 235–1209. Undenominational ministry of Resurrection Life Full Gospel Church; Organized: 1988.
1988–   Daniel J. Champion, Susan L. Champion

FIGURE 41
This 1888 Osgood design was a landmark at Wealthy and Finney SW for nearly 90 years. It saw service as Smith Memorial Congregational (1888–1912), Finney Elementary School (1912–45), and finally as True Light Baptist (1945–65). The Grand Rapids Area Transit Authority has occupied the site since 1977.

SUNSET PARK CHURCH OF GOD
3450 Michael Ave. SW Wyoming 49509. Organized: 1913; 1913–23 Church of God; 1923–63 Burton Heights Church of God (558 Jefferson Ave. SE 1913–23; 1803 Buchanan Ave. SW 1923–53; 200 Griggs St. SW 1953–63); Built: 1963 (Kammeraad Stroup, Holland).

FIGURE 42
William G. Robinson designed this church for Trinity Evangelical Lutheran at the southeast corner of Crescent Street and Bostwick Avenue NE. It served from 1898 to 1961.

1921–27	Rev. Allen G. Pontious
1928–45	Rev. Martin J. Raab, Rev. Alice Raab
1946–53	Rev. William Todd
1953–61	Rev. Estel Perry, Rev. Ocie Perry
1961–76	Rev. Paul H. Rider
1977–86	Rev. Richard Shockey
1987–	Rev. Calvin C. Bloom

SUNSHINE MINISTRIES
3300 E. Beltline Ave. NE 49505; Phone: 364-4242. CRC; Organized: 1923 as mission, 1971 as church; 1923–31 Sunshine Gospel Hall; 1931–49 Belmont Mission; 1949–71 Sunshine Back to God Chapel; 1971–89 Sunshine Christian Reformed (1219 Bradford St. NE 1923–49; 918 Benjamin Ave. NE 1949–79; 3295 E. Beltline NE 1979–89); Built: 1988 (VanWienen & Papke).

1961–65	Rev. Edwin Visscher
1972–91	Rev. Lewis R. VanderMeer
1993–	Rev. Matthew Heard

SWEDENBORGIAN
See ZION TABERNACLE

SWEDISH ASSEMBLY OF CHRIST
645 Front Ave. NW.
1914–19 (40 National Ave. NW 1914–15).

SWEDISH BAPTIST
See ELIM BAPTIST

SWEDISH EVANGELICAL LUTHERAN
See **BETHLEHEM LUTHERAN**

SWEDISH EVANGELICAL MISSION CHURCH
See **EVANGELICAL COVENANT CHURCH OF GRAND RAPIDS**

SWEDISH LUTHERAN
See **BETHLEHEM LUTHERAN**

SWEDISH MISSION CHURCH
See **EVANGELICAL COVENANT CHURCH OF GRAND RAPIDS**

SWEET STREET CHURCH OF CHRIST
See PLAINFIELD AVENUE CHURCH OF CHRIST

TABERNACLE BAPTIST
315 Sweet St. NE; 1910–11.

1910	Rev. Robert Gray
1911	Rev. Leonard Dunne

TABERNACLE BAPTIST
1320 Madison Ave. SE; 1974–75.

1974–75	Rev. J. Pulliam

TABERNACLE CHURCH
1856–60.

1856	Rev. L. Woodruff
1856–60	Rev. S.F. Holt
1860 Merged with FIRST BAPTIST.	

TABERNACLE CHURCH OF GOD
See MOUNT OLIVE MISSIONARY BAPTIST

TEMPLE BETH ISRAEL
See CONGREGATION BETH ISRAEL

TEMPLE EMANUEL
See **CONGREGATION EMANUEL**

TEMPLE MISSION
839 S. Division Ave.
1939–49 (715 S. Division 1939–42).

1949	Rev. Lewis Retan

TEMPLE OF CHRIST PRAYER BAND
See **CHRIST TEMPLE OF ETERNAL TRUTH**

FIGURE 43

The Ladies Literary Society at 61 Sheldon Ave. SE has been a temporary home for many churches, including (1920–42) the Grand Rapids Unity Center, now Unity Church of Practical Christianity. Built in 1887, it was designed by noted Grand Rapids architect William G. Robinson and was the first building in Michigan constructed specifically as a women's club.

TEMPLE OF PEACE
523 LaGrave Ave. SE; 1970–80.
1971–80   Rev. J.A. Davies

TEMPLO BAUTISTA
4614 Walton Ave. SW Wyoming.
1968–83; 1968–69 Baptist Temple.

TEMPLO BETHEL ASAMBLEA DE DIOS
See **BETHEL ASAMBLEA DE DIOS**

TEMPLO BETHEL HISPANO
See **BETHEL ASAMBLEA DE DIOS**

TENTH AVENUE
METHODIST EPISCOPAL
See **ST. PAUL**
UNITED METHODIST

TERRACE BAPTIST
See **KENTWOOD BAPTIST**

THE PEOPLES' CHURCH
See PEOPLES' CHURCH, THE

THIRD PRESBYTERIAN
140 National Ave. SW.
1875–1949; 1875–94 Mission Wood Presbyterian; Organized: 1875 as mission, 1883 as church; Built: 1876; Addition: 1891.
1883–85   Rev. Marcus L. Bocher
1896–1904 Rev. Reuben S. Smith
1917–31   Rev. Dr. Iman Wisse

THIRD REFORMED
2060 Michigan St. NE 49503;
Phone: 458–3089. Organized: 1875 (1009 Hermitage St. SE 1875–1968); Built: 1969 (Kammeraad Stroup).
1876–1902 Rev. Adrian Kriekaard
1906–18   Rev. Albert VandenBerg
1918–39   Rev. Nicholas Boer
1991–   Rev. Kent A. Fry

THIRTY SIXTH STREET
CHRISTIAN REFORMED
1265 36th St. SW Wyoming 49509;
Phone: 532–0393. Organized: 1930 as mission, 1953 as church; 1930–48 Allen Road Mission; 1948–53 Allen Road Gospel Chapel); Chapel built 1948 (Neil Hoek); Church built 1955 (Chris Steketee).
1954–61   Rev. Sidney A. Werkema
1989–   Rev. Robert L. Bierenga

THOMAS STATION
See BAPTIST MISSION

THORNAPPLE
COMMUNITY CHURCH
3260 Thornapple River Drive SE 49546;
Phone: 942–0821. RCA; Organized: 1980 (Cascade School, 6590 Cascade Road SE 1979–80; Thornapple Elementary School, 6932 Bridgewater Drive SE 1980–82; Cascade School, 1982–83); Built: 1983 (John Kwekel).
1979–86   Rev. Dale D. Matthews
1987–   Rev. Paul D. Wesselink

THORNAPPLE EVANGELICAL
COVENANT CHURCH OF CASCADE
6595 Cascade Road SE 49546;
Phone: 957–0580. Organized: 1979 (Pine Ridge School, 3250 Redford Ave. SE 1979–86); Built: 1986 (Architectural Group of Grandville).
1979–   Rev. Steven W. Armfield

THORNWOOD BAPTIST
971 Buttrick Ave. SE Ada 49301;
Phone: 676–9690. Sovereign Grace Fellowship, Flint; Organized: 1969 (Thornapple School, 6932 Bridgewater Drive SE 1969–70); Built: 1970.
1969–80   Rev. Robert C. Nelson
1992–   Rev. Norman A. Street

TOGETHER IN FAITH
1159 Madison Ave. SE 49507;
Phone: 452–5945.
Nondenominational; Organized: 1984.
1984–   Rev. Michael Townsend

TRINITY BAPTIST
2050 Aberdeen St. NE 49505;
Phone: 361–2802. General Association of Regular Baptists; Organized: 1948 (Stryker Hall, 1420 Plainfield Ave. NE 1948–50; 1331 Plainfield NE 1950–65); Built: 1965 (Dan Vos).
1948–53   Rev. W. Herbert Scott
1985–   Rev. Dr. Kent A. Pool

TRINITY COMMUNITY
METHODIST EPISCOPAL
See **TRINITY**
UNITED METHODIST

TRINITY CONGREGATIONAL UCC

2725 Four Mile Road NW 49504;
Phone: 784–2450. Organized: 1909 as
merger of First Baptist Church of
Alpine and Walker and First
Congregational Church of Alpine and
Walker; Built: 1967 (McMillen
Palmer).

1909–11	Rev. Reuben S. Smith
1937–39	Rev. Reuben S. Smith
1939–59	Rev. Herbert McConnell
1980–	Rev. Robert L. Kittendorf

TRINITY EPISCOPAL

See CHURCH OF
THE GOOD SHEPHERD

TRINITY EVANGELICAL LUTHERAN

2700 E. Fulton St. 49506;
Phone: 949–2510. ELCA; Organized:
1896 (102 Crescent St. NE 1898–1961
(William G Robinson); Addition: 1915
(Robinson & Campau); Built: 1961
(Harold E. Wagoner).

1896–1900	Rev. C.J. Kiefer
1926–54	Rev. Ralph J. White
1963–80	Rev. Dr. Raymond A. Heine
1989–	Rev. Marvin J. Schumacher

TRINITY LILY WHITE PENTECOSTAL

618 Jefferson Ave. SE; 1964–69.

1964–69	Elder L. Lee

TRINITY METHODIST

See **TRINITY UNITED METHODIST**

TRINITY PRESBYTERIAN

Wyoming Park; 1925.

1925	Rev. Jacob Klaasse

TRINITY REFORMED

1224 Davis Ave. NW 49504;
Phone: 451–4131. Organized: 1908
(Laroy Wagon Works, northeast corner
Alpine Avenue and Myrtle Street NW
1908–16); Built: 1913–16 (Thomas
Benjamin & Son); Addition: 1915 (J.
& G. Daverman).

1908–11	Rev. Teunis W. Muilenburg
1914–26	Rev. John G. VanZomeren
1936–49	Rev. Stanley D. Schipper
1978–88	Rev. Robert A. Wierenga
1989–	Rev. Victoria M. Menning, Rev. Bruce A. Menning
1991–	Rev. Bradley R. Olson

TRINITY UNITED METHODIST

1100 Lake Drive SE 49506;
Phone: 456–7168. Organized: 1874 as
City Mission. 1874–1908 East Street
Methodist Episcopal (116 Eastern Ave.
SE 1874–1920; Built: 1874 (David S.
Hopkins); Built: 1884; Built: 1922.

1874–75	Rev. H.J. VanFossen
1984–89	Rev. Charles Fry
1989–	Rev. Dr. Gerald A. Pohly

TROTTER MINISTRIES

(Galewood/South Branch)
See **GALEWOOD
GOSPEL CHAPEL**

TRUE HOLINESS CHURCH

581 Grandville Ave. SW.
1960–70; 1960–64 True Holiness
Mission (651 Grandville Ave. SW
1960–64).

TRUE HOLINESS CHURCH
OF GOD IN CHRIST

1001 Baxter St. SE; 1970–76.

1970–76	Rev. William Brown

TRUE HOLINESS CHURCH OF JESUS

715 S. Division Ave.
1969–78 (38 Buckley St. SW 1969–76;
1002 Grandville Ave. SW 1969–74).

1974	Rev. Rayford Richardson
1974–76	Rev. C.H. Blackmore

TRUE HOLINESS MISSION

See TRUE HOLINESS CHURCH

TRUE LIGHT BAPTIST

900 Thomas St. SE 49506;
Phone: 247–8072. Progressive National
Baptists, Detroit; Organized: 1922
(Goodrich Street and Finney Avenue
SW 1922; Bartlett Street and Ney
Avenue SW 1922; Grandville Avenue
and Goodrich SW 1923; 221 Williams
St. SW 1923–40; 305 Wealthy St. SW
1945–65); Built: 1966 (George B.
Savage).

1922–24	Rev. Paul L. Woodson
1924–33	Rev. Miller P. Parish
1933–35	Rev. L. Douglas Bunn
1935–37	Rev. Melzar D. Ware
1938–54	Rev. Haywood C. Toliver
1954–	Rev. Willie L. Patterson

TRUE REFORMED

Leppig's Hall, south side of Lyon Street
east of Monroe Avenue NW; 1887.

1887	Rev. E.L. Meinders

TRUTH & GRACE CHAPEL

300 Graceland St. NE; 1978–82.

1978–82	Rev. D.A. Baker

TURNER AVENUE
NETHERLANDS REFORMED

See **NETHERLANDS REFORMED
CHURCH OF GRAND RAPIDS**

TURNER AVENUE REFORMED

See **NETHERLANDS REFORMED
CHURCH OF GRAND RAPIDS**

TURNER MISSION (Methodist)

See FAIRVIEW WESLEYAN

TWELFTH STREET
CHRISTIAN REFORMED

950 Twelfth St. NW 49504;
Phone: 458–4998. Organized: 1917;
Built: 1922 (J. & G. Daverman).

1918–20	Rev. William M. Trap
1929–43	Rev. Jan K. VanBaalen
1972–85	Rev. John W. Dykstra
1987–	Rev. Henry G. Entingh

UNION TABERNACLE CHURCH OF GOD

706 Jefferson Ave. SE; 1964–65.

UNITARIAN CHURCH

Ladies Literary Club, 61 Sheldon Ave. SE.
1883–1899 (Powers Opera House, 123
Pearl St. NW 1883–85; WCTU, 231
Pearl NW 1885; Congregation
Emanuel, 72 Ransom Ave. NE
1885–86).

1883–85	Rev. Henry Powers
1885–86	Rev. John E. Roberts

UNITED BRETHREN

South Grand Rapids school house, near
South Division Avenue; 1889–90.

1889–90	Rev. Howard S. Shaeffer

UNITED BRETHREN MISSION

2129 S. Division Ave.; 1918–23.

1919–21	Mrs. Matilda Jordan
1921–22	Rev. Ernest Wheeler

FIGURE 44
Wallin Congregational Church, 1053 First St. NW from 1906–1962, was razed to make way for construction of Int. 196.

UNITED METHODIST
HISPANIC CHURCH
See **IGLESIA METODISTA
UNIDA HISPANA**

UNITED MISSIONARY
See GOOD SHEPHERD MISSIONARY

UNITED WESLEYAN
5440 Wilson Ave. SW Wyoming
49418; Phone: 534–0303. Wesleyan
Church, Indianapolis, Ind.; Organized:
1987 as merger of Wilson Avenue
Wesleyan and Wyoming Wesleyan;
Built: 1968 as Wilson Avenue
Wesleyan.
1987–88   Pastor Carl F. Aarett
1987–   Pastor Christopher DeBlaey

UNITY CHURCH OF PEACE
Lexington Hotel Suites, 5401 28th St.
SE 49546; Phone: 676–5540.
Undenominational; Organized: 1992.
1992–   Rev. Ann Haveman-Ashby,
          Rev. James T. Ashby

**UNITY CHURCH
OF PRACTICAL CHRISTIANITY**
1711 Walker Ave. NW 49504;
Phone: 453–9909. Unity School of
Christianity, Unity Village, Mo.;
Organized: 1920; 1920–42 Grand Rapids
Unity Center; 1942–48 Grand Rapids

Unity Society; 1949–63 Unity Church of
Christ; 1963–80 Unity Chapel in the
Pines (Ladies Literary Club, 61 Sheldon
Ave. SE 1920–42; 63 Jefferson Ave. SE
1942–49; 528 Scribner Ave. NW
1949–62); Built: 1963.
1920–51   Rev. Ida M. Bailey
1951–61   Rev. Leon I. Miller
1981–88   Rev. Richard L. Tweedy
1989–   Rev. Nathaniel R. Carter,
          Rev. Suzanne C. Carter

UNITY LATVIAN LUTHERAN
48 Dennis Ave. SE; 1950–80.
1950–80   Rev. Janis V. Lazda
1980   Merged with Latvian
Evangelical Lutheran to become
**GRAND RAPIDS LATVIAN
EVANGELICAL LUTHERAN**

UNITY LILY WHITE PENTECOSTAL
618 Jefferson Ave. SE; 1963–64.

UNITY REFORMED
4450 Poinsettia Ave. SE Kentwood
49508; Phone: 538–2340. Organized:
1956 (Bowen School, 4471 Kalamazoo
Ave. SE Kentwood 1956–57); Built:
1957 (Kellogg & Kiefer, Battle Creek);
Addition: 1965.
1957–61   Rev. Richard A. Evers
1980–   Rev. Mark J. Bergsma

UNITY SPIRITUALIST
Ladies Literary Club, 61 Sheldon Ave. SE.
1932–40 (37 Coldbrook St. NE 1932–35).
1932–40   Rev. Annie L. Carpenter

**UNIVERSAL CHURCH
OF THE RISEN CHRIST**
1320 Madison Ave. SE 49507;
Phone: 245–8701. Christ Temple,
Saginaw; Organized: 1967 (449 S.
Division Ave. 1974–75).
1967–   Rev. Lawyer Eckford
1967–   Rev. Julia B. Tolbert
1993–   Minister Davis

UNIVERSAL CHURCH OF TRUTH
433 S. Division Ave.
1975–78; 1975–76 Universal Church of
Jesus.
1975–78   Rev. Albert Franklin

UNIVERSAL HAGAR SPIRITUAL
See **NEW COVENANT
COMMUNITY CHURCH**

UNIVERSAL SPIRITUAL
CHURCH OF TRUTH
50 Grant St. SW; 1947–73.
1947–73   Rev. Elizabeth F.. McCoy

UNIVERSALIST
See PEOPLES CHURCH
OF GRAND RAPIDS

UNIVERSALIST CHURCH
OF GOOD WILL
802 Wealthy St. SE.
1953–67 (632 Wealthy SE 1953–57).
1953–67   Rev. Emma Farrington

UPTOWN ASSEMBLY OF GOD
Burton Heights United Methodist
Church, 100 Burton St. SE 49507;
Phone: 776–0696. Organized: 1992
(Iglesia Metodista Unida Hispana, 107
Burton St. SE 1992–93).
1992–   Rev. William J. Trim

URBAN MINISTRIES OUTREACH
17 S. Division Ave.; 1986–92.
VALLEY AVENUE
UNITED METHODIST
321 Valley Ave. NW.
1858–1977; 1858–1921 German
Methodist Episcopal (Hovey's Block,
Bridge Street and Scribner Avenue NW

1858–62; northwest corner Bridge and Turner Avenue NW 1862–88; 528 Scribner NW 1888–1921); Built: 1921.

1858–59	Rev. Gustav Laas
1974–77	Rev. Arthur D. Jackson
1977	Merged with Second

United Methodist to become **FAITH UNITED METHODIST.**

VIETNAMESE CATHOLIC COMMUNITY

Holy Name Church, 1630 Godfrey Ave. SW Wyoming 49509; Phone: 241–0131. Organized: 1977 (St. John Vianney Church, 4101 Clyde Park Ave. SW 1977–78; St. Pius X Church, 3937 Wilson Ave. SW 1978–79; St Joseph Center, 600 Burton St. SE 1979–83; Our Lady of Aglona Church, 507 Broadway Ave. NW 1983–85; St. James Church, 733 Bridge St. NW 1985–86; St Francis Xavier Church, 250 Brown St. SE 1986–88).

1980–83	Rev. Peter Hoang X. Nghiem
1987–	Rev. Peter Hoang X. Nghiem

VIETNAMESE EVANGELICAL
See **VIETNAMESE REFORMED CHRISTIAN CHURCH**

VIETNAMESE REFORMED CHRISTIAN CHURCH

1881 52nd St. SE Kentwood 49508; Phone: 452–2632. CRC/RCA; Organized: 1984 (Breton Avenue SE

FIGURE 45
Designed by architect Sidney J. Osgood, this ornate structure served the congregation of Wealthy Avenue (now Wealthy Park) Baptist Church for only 25 years, 1887–1912.

1984; Garfield Park Reformed Church, 1975 Jefferson Ave. SE 1984–89; Burton Heights CRC, 1970 Jefferson Ave. SE 1989–93).

1984–93	Rev. Howard E. Schipper, Rev. Donald J. Griffioen
1993–	Rev. Viet Tran

VIETNAMESE UNITED METHODIST
212 Bellevue St. SE Wyoming 49548; Phone: 940–4721. Organized: 1987 (Reformed Bible College, 3333 E. Beltline Ave. NE 1987; Olivet United Methodist, 1933 Buchanan Ave. SW 1987–92).

1987–	Rev. Vinh Quang Tran

VILLAGE BAPTIST
2600 Breton Ave. SE.
1972–76; 1972–74 Breton Village Baptist.

1972–73	Rev. Doyle McDaniel
1973–76	Rev. William H. Redman

VISION OUTREACH PENTECOSTAL
3653 Coit Ave. NE; 1973–75.

VOICE OF VICTORY CHURCH, THE
1250 Madison Ave. SE 49507; Organized: 1992.

1992–	Rev. Arthur A. Sheaud

VOLUNTEERS OF AMERICA GOSPEL MISSION
400 Bridge St. NW. 1896–1966. (auditorium, northeast corner Ionia Avenue and Fountain Street NW 1896–1900; southwest corner Front Avenue and Bridge Street NW 1900–01; 10 E. Fulton St. 1901–05; 182 Monroe Ave. NW 1905–06; 143 Pearl St. NW 1906–07; 430 Bond Ave. NW 1907–08; 131 Lyon St. NW 1908–09; 128 Lyon NW 1913–14; 225 Bond NW 1915–17; 223 Bond NW 1917–18; 116 Pearl NW 1918–20; 116–18 Pearl NW 1920–31; 124 Lyon NW 1931–50; 232 Bond NW 1950–55).

1905	Capt. John W. Cook
1912–54	Major Belle C. Hubbell
1954–65	Major Cyrus T. Green
1965–66	Howard W. Melvin, Evelyn I. Melvin.

Outlet Stores in 1965 at 878 Grandville Ave. SW, 1205 Madison Ave. SE, 662 Wealthy St. SE.

WALKER CHRISTIAN REFORMED
1941 Randall Ave. NW Walker 49504; Phone: 453–2960. Organized: 1912; 1911–58 Kinney Station Christian Reformed (Three Mile Road and Kinney Avenue NW Walker 1911–61); Built: 1961 (Jacques J. Kocher, Holland); Addition: 1991 (Richard Postema).

1912–16	Rev. J.R. Brink
1928–47	Rev. Peter Vos
1992–	Rev. Joel A. VanderKooi

WALLIN CONGREGATIONAL CHURCH UCC
1550 Oswego St. NW 49504; Phone: 453–5461. Organized: 1894 as mission, 1896 as church; 1895–1906 Barker Memorial Branch Chapel; 1906–62 Wallin Congregational; (East side of Lincoln Avenue north of Bridge Street NW 1895–1906; 1053 First St. NW 1906–62; Westwood Hills Elementary School, 1525 Mount Mercy Drive NW 1962–64); Built: 1964 (Gordon Cornwell, Traverse City).

1896–97	Dr. Charles T. Taylor
1954–82	Dr. John C. Whitcomb
1984–91	Rev. Isaias Paniamogan
1992–	Dr. Gerald R. Wick

WAY OF LIFE CHAPEL/MISSION
315 Grant St. SW.
1919–53; CRC; (723 S. Division Ave. 1919–20).

1942–46	Rev. Peter Doot

See **HILLCREST COMMUNITY CHURCH**

WAYSIDE BIBLE/MEMORIAL/ MISSION CHURCH/CHAPEL
1150 Lincoln Ave. NW.
1926–54; Undenominational; 1926–30 Wayside Gospel Mission (1156 Walker Ave. NW 1926–27; 1183 Walker NW 1928–30).

1926–28	Supt. Rockwell Martin
1951	Rev. Virgil C. Swanson

FIGURE 46
Woodview Christian Church was long known as Franklin Street Church of Christ. This frame building at 462 Franklin St. SE was its home from 1901 to 1959.

WEALTHY PARK BAPTIST

2233 Michigan St. NE 49503; Phone: 456-8506. General Association of Regular Baptisits; Organized: 1875 as mission, 1885 as church; 1875-87 Charles Street Missionary Baptist; 1887-1912 Wealthy Avenue Baptist; 1912-50 Wealthy Street Baptist Temple; 1950-82 Wealthy Street Baptist (346 Charles Ave. SE 1875-87; 811 Wealthy St. SE 1887-1912 (Sidney J. Osgood); 811 Wealthy SE 1912-82; Michigan Oak School, 2233 Michigan NE 1982-88); Built: 1988 (Decker Construction Co.).

1885-88	Rev. E.R. Bennett
1909-34	Rev. Dr. Oliver W. VanOsdel
1934-74	Rev. Dr. David Otis Fuller
1990-	Rev. Dr. John M. Polson

WEALTHY STREET BAPTIST CHURCH/TEMPLE
See **WEALTHY PARK BAPTIST**

WEALTHY STREET CHURCH OF GOD IN CHRIST

750 Wealthy St. SE 49503; Phone: 235-0137. Organized: 1968.

| 1983-85 | Rev. Henry Flowers |
| 1993 | Rev. Robert Angelo |

WESLEY PARK UNITED METHODIST

1150 32nd St. SW Wyoming 49509; Phone: 534-4411. Organized: 1955 (West Godwin Elementary School, 3546 Clyde Park Ave. SW Wyoming 1955-58); Built: 1958 (David E Post).

| 1955-61 | Rev. Clarence Hutchens |
| 1985- | Rev. Dr. Myron K. Williams |

WESLEYAN CHAPEL

15 Janet St. SE Wyoming 49548. Organized: 1984; Built: 1930 as Godwin Heights Free Methodist.

| 1990-92 | Rev. Edward O. Nelson |

WESLEYAN CHURCH

4122 44th St. SW Grandville. 1964-71; 1964-68 Wesleyan Methodist.

| 1964-66 | Rev. Arthur W. Ruder |
| 1966-71 | Rev. William E. Foster |

WESLEYAN METHODIST
See **EMMANUEL WESLEYAN** and **FAIRVIEW WESLEYAN**

WESLEYAN METHODIST EPISCOPAL
Northeast corner Sibley Street and Marion Avenue NW; 1884-86.

| 1884-86 | Rev. S.B. Shaw |

WEST CHURCH OF THE NAZARENE
See **GRAND RAPIDS WEST CHURCH OF THE NAZARENE**

WEST FORTY FOURTH CHRISTIAN REFORMED

1029 44th St. SW Wyoming 49509; Phone: 534-2454. Organized: 1954 as mission, 1975 as church; Built: 1956.

1953-58	Evangelist George Oppenhuizen
1958-76	Evangelist Kenneth Navis
1978-84	Rev. John Morren
1985-	Rev. Ronald Goudzwaard

WEST FULTON STREET BACK TO GOD CHAPEL
See **GOLD AVENUE CHURCH**

WEST LEONARD STREET CHRISTIAN REFORMED

1053 Leonard St. NW 49504; Phone: 456-1994. Organized: 1888; 1889-1908 Crosby Street CRC (north side of Crosby near Garfield Avenue NW 1889-1908); Built: 1912 (J. & G. Daverman).

1889-1904	Rev. Geert Broene
1905-14	Rev. Frank Doezema
1927-48	Rev. Richard Veldman
1989-92	Rev. Arlan W. Koppendrayer

WEST SIDE CHURCH OF CHRIST
903 Scribner Ave. NW. 1918-25 (282 Leonard St. NW 1918-20).

| 1920-21 | Rev. William J. Gillmore |

WEST SIDE MISSION
645 Front Ave. NW; 1928-32.

| 1928-31 | Rev. Edward Boone |

WESTEND CHRISTIAN REFORMED

1015 Westend Ave. NW 49504; Phone: 453-3077. Organized: 1991 as merger of Highland Hills and Alpine Avenue CRC; Built: 1950 as Highland Hills CRC (James K. Haveman).

| 1991-92 | Rev. Charles Terpstra, Rev. Eugene Bradford |
| 1992- | Rev. Henry Admiraal |

WESTGATE UNITED METHODIST
4505 Bekinshire Drive NW Comstock Park. 1963-80; Built: 1966.

| 1963-66 | Rev. Lyle Chapman |
| 1974-78 | Rev. Brent K. Phillips |

WESTMINSTER PRESBYTERIAN
47 Jefferson Ave. SE 49503;
Phone: 456–1456. Organized: 1861;
1861–67 Second Presbyterian
(Swedenborgian Church, 201 N.
Division Ave. 1861–65; southwest
corner North Division and Lyon Street
NW 1865–76 (C.J. Dietrich); Built:
1876–85 (Sidney J. Osgood).

1861–65	Rev. Courtney Smith
1949–66	Rev. Frederick Wyngarden
1974–88	Rev. John W. Stewart
1990–	Rev. William A. Evertsberg

WESTSIDE BAPTIST CHAPEL
753 Butterworth St. SW 49504.
Organized 1989.

WESTVIEW CHRISTIAN REFORMED
2929 Leonard St. NW 49504;
Phone: 453–3105. Organized 1893;
1894-1962 Broadway Avenue CRC
(Scribner Avenue Baptist Church,
1236 Scribner NW 1893–94; 1142
Broadway NW 1894–1962); Built: 1962
(Daverman).

1895–99	Rev. G.D. DeMott
1919–29	Rev. Henry J Kuiper
1929–45	Rev. John DeHaan Jr.
1953–62	Rev. G.J. Rozenboom
1983–	Rev. Charles S. Steenstra

WHOSO LIGHTHOUSE MISSION
900 Grandville Ave. SW; 1970–74.
1974	Rev. Edmonia Worley

WHOSOEVER MISSION
640 Burton St. SW; 1914–17.

WILSON AVENUE WESLEYAN
5440 Wilson Ave. SW Wyoming
49418; 1972–87.
1974	Rev. Ronald L. DePung

Merged 1987 with Wyoming Wesleyan
to become **UNITED WESLEYAN**

WOOD BROOK CATHEDRAL
1739 Providence St. NE 49505;
Phone: 361–1701.
Interdenominational; Organized: 1972
(3797 28th St. SE 1972–80); Built:
1957 as Northside Church of Christ.
1972–	Rev. Jesse Benjamin Stutts

WOODLAND DRIVE–IN CHURCH
2600 Breton Ave. SE 49546;
Phone: 942–5980. RCA; Organized:
1970 (Woodland Drive-In Theater,
2945 E. Beltline Ave. SE 1970–87);
Built: 1987.

1970–76	Rev. Raymond Rewerts
1984–	Rev. Verlyn D. VerBrugge

WOODLAWN CHRISTIAN REFORMED
Calvin College Chapel, 3201 Burton
St. SE 49546; Phone: 942–8406.
Organized: 1968.

1968–70	Rev. William K. Stob
1971–80	Rev. Dick M. Stravers
1980–	Rev. Dr. John Timmer

WOODMERE GARDENS TABERNACLE
See **CENTRAL ASSEMBLY OF GOD**

WOODVIEW CHRISTIAN
3785 Woodview Ave. SW Wyoming
49509; Phone: 532–5303. Organized:
1899 as Philip Hood Mission, 1901 as
church; 1901–12 Fifth Avenue Church
of Christ; 1912–60 Franklin Street
Church of Christ; 1961–75 Woodview
Church of Christ (462 Franklin St. SE
1901–29; 801 College Ave. SE 1929–59
(Harvey H. Weemhoff) West Godwin
Elementary School, 3546 Clyde Park
Ave. SW Wyoming 1958–61); Built:
1961 (Barnes Construction Co.);
Addition: 1983 (Dan Vos).

1901–02	Rev. W.E. Colegrove, Rev. F.P. Arthur
1902–03	Rev. J. Frank Green
1971–	Rev. Richard D. Robinson

WOODWARD AVENUE BAPTIST
2786 Woodward Ave. SW Wyoming
49509; Phone: 532–0906. General
Association of Regular Baptists;
Organized: 1920 as mission, 1938 as
church; 1920–38 Clyde Park Hills
Mission; Built: 1963 (Marsman).

1939–48	Rev. Frank Goulooze
1949–65	Rev. Frank Thatcher
1967–87	Rev. Arvle O. DeVaney
1988–	Rev. Jack J. Delaney

WYOMING CHURCH OF GOD
1854 Porter St. SW Wyoming 49509;
Phone: 532–3765. Church of God,
Cleveland, Tenn.; Organized: 1972
(3813 Michael St. SW Wyoming
1972–73; Newhall Junior High School,
1840 38th St. SW Wyoming 1973–74;
16 Coolidge St. SW Wyoming
1974–77); Built: 1915 as Beverly
Reformed (Oosterheert & Sons).

1973–80	Rev. Franklin D. Rose
1988–	Rev. Dale R. Cross

WYOMING FOUR SQUARE GOSPEL CHURCH
1550 Ellen Ave. SW Wyoming.
1968–76.
1968–72	Rev. Joe K. Adcock
1972–76	Rev. Paul D. Griffis

FIGURE 47
Organized in 1947, Zion Baptist Church
worshipped at the West Side Ladies
Literary Club at 518 Scribner Ave. NW
until 1952. This historic structure was
originally built as No. 3 Engine House in
1859, and served in that capacity until
1887. It was removed for freeway
construction in August 1961.

WYOMING PARK BAPTIST
2260 Porter St. SW Wyoming 49509;
Phone: 532–5183. Independent;
Organized: 1929; 1929–32 Wyoming
Park Undenominational; 1932–50
Wyoming Park Gospel Tabernacle;
1950–55 Wyoming Park Tabernacle;
(2445 Byron Center Ave. SW Wyoming
1929–31; 2417 Wyoming Ave. SW
Wyoming 1931–50); Built: 1955.
1929–31	Rev. John P. Battema
1939–58	Rev. Peter H. Elgersma
1990–	Rev. Philip A. Miller

WYOMING PARK
CHRISTIAN REFORMED
See **FAITH COMMUNITY
CHRISTIAN REFORMED**

WYOMING PARK
COMMUNITY UNITED BRETHREN
See **WYOMING PARK
UNITED METHODIST**

WYOMING PARK
EVANGELICAL UNITED BRETHREN
See **WYOMING PARK
UNITED METHODIST**

WYOMING PARK
GOSPEL TABERNACLE
See **WYOMING PARK BAPTIST**

WYOMING PARK
SEVENTH DAY ADVENTIST
See **SEVENTH DAY ADVENTIST
CHURCH OF WYOMING**

WYOMING PARK TABERNACLE
See **WYOMING PARK BAPTIST**

WYOMING PARK
UNDENOMINATIONAL
See **WYOMING PARK BAPTIST**

WYOMING PARK UNITED BRETHREN
See **WYOMING PARK
UNITED METHODIST**

**WYOMING PARK
UNITED METHODIST**
2244 Porter St. SW Wyoming 49509;

Phone: 532–7624. Organized: 1912;
1912–45 Wyoming Park United
Brethren; 1945–68 Wyoming Park
Evangelical United Brethren; Built:
1914 (Rev. James Albert Blickenstaff);
Built: 1957.
1912	Rev. Fred Clark
1988–	Rev. Donald Eddy

WYOMING PILGRIM CHURCH
See WYOMING WESLEYAN

WYOMING PRESBYTERIAN
1530 40th St. SW Wyoming.
1964–84; Built: 1965.
1965–68	Rev. Richard E. Wylie
1968–78	Rev. Russell Brandt

WYOMING
SEVENTH DAY ADVENTIST
See **SEVENTH DAY ADVENTIST
CHURCH OF WYOMING**

WYOMING SPANISH
SEVENTH DAY ADVENTIST
See **IGLESIA ADVENTISTA
DE WYOMING**

WYOMING UNITED PENTECOSTAL
See **NEW LIFE
APOSTOLIC ASSEMBLY**

WYOMING WESLEYAN
2040 36th St. SW Wyoming.
1959–87; 1959–70 Wyoming Pilgrim
Church (West Newhall School, 3610
Byron Center Ave. SW 1959–61).
1959–70	Rev. Ernest W. Klein
1981–86	Rev. Robert E. Miller
1987	Merged with Wilson
Avenue Wesleyan to become
UNITED WESLEYAN.

ZION BAPTIST
1706 Richmond St. NW 49504;
Phone: 791–9626. Independent; Gospel
Standard Baptist in England;
Organized: 1947 (West Side Ladies
Literary Club, 518 Scribner Ave. NW
1947–52).
1952–60	Rev. W. Sinclair Taylor
1960–76	Rev. Ebenezer J. Knight
1976–	Rev. Jay K. Stehouwer

ZION EVANGELICAL
See HOPE EVANGELICAL
UNITED BRETHREN
ZION GERMAN
EVANGELICAL LUTHERAN
See HOPE EVANGELICAL
UNITED BRETHREN

ZION HALL
See CHILDREN OF ZION

ZION LUTHERAN
582 Lamoreaux Drive NW Comstock
Park 49321; Phone: 784–7151.
ELCA; Organized: 1963 (Stoney Creek
Elementary School, 200 Lantern Drive
NW Comstock Park 1963–65); Built:
1965 (Stapert Pratt Bolthuis Sprau &
Crothers Inc.); Addition: 1992
(VanWienen & Papke, Kalamazoo).
1963–67	Rev. Theodore C. Melinat
1967–	Rev. Walter Thomas Zollman

ZION LUTHERAN
See HOPE EVANGELICAL
UNITED BRETHREN

ZION REFORMED
See GARFIELD PARK REFORMED

ZION REFORMED
4457 36th St. SW Grandville 49418;
Phone: 534–7533. Organized: 1954
(Bursley Elementary School, 1195 Port
Sheldon Road Jenison 1955–56); Built:
1956 (Johnson Construction Co.).
1955–61	Rev. John H. Maassen
1974–87	Rev. Harris J. Verkaik
1988–	Rev. Dr. Ronald L. Geschwendt

ZION TABERNACLE
201 N. Division Ave.
1849–1907; Swedenborgian; Built: 1852.
1850–53	Rev. Henry Weller
1900	Rev. James R. Adams

ZION TEMPLE CHURCH
OF GOD IN CHRIST
1031 Grandville Ave. SW; 1965–70.
1965–70	Elder Jeffrey Stokes

Chapter and Vignette Notes B

CHAPTER 1

1. James M. McClurken, "Strangers in Their Own Land," *Grand River Valley Review* 6/1 (1986), p. 9; Albert Baxter, *History of the City of Grand Rapids, Michigan* (New York and Grand Rapids, 1891), pp. 51–52.

2. The incident was recorded by McCoy in his *History of Baptist Indian Missions* (New York and London, 1970 [orig. ed., 1840]), p. 303. The larger context is described in James A. Clifton, George L. Cornell, and James M. McClurken, *People of the Three Fires: The Ottawa, Potawatomi, and Ojibwa of Michigan* (Grand Rapids, 1986), pp. 25–27.

3. Bruce G. Trigger, ed., *Handbook of North American Indians*, Vol. 15: *Northeast* (Washington, D.C., 1978), pp. 44–57; Helen Hornbeck Tanner, ed., *Atlas of Great Lakes Indian History* (Norman, Okla., 1987), p. 25; and McClurken, *People of the Three Fires*, p. iii–v.

4. The terminology in this book reflects the subjects' current preference. The following treatment of Odawa history relies on McClurken, *People of Three Fires*, pp. 3–36; Tanner, *Atlas*, pp. 29–35, 62–66, 132–35; and Johanna E. Feest and Christian F. Feest, "Ottawa," in Trigger, ed., *Handbook*, pp. 772–86.

5. Tanner, *Atlas*, pp. 29–35; McClurken, *People of Three Fires*, pp. 13–16.

6. McClurken, *People of Three Fires*, pp. 3–6; A. Irving Hallowell, "Ojibwa Ontology, Behavior, and World View," in Dennis Tedlock and Barbara Tedlock, *Teachings from the American Earth* (New York, 1975), pp. 170–72.

7. Hallowell, "Ojibwa Ontology," pp. 150–53, 169; McClurken, *People of the Three Fires*, pp. 6–11.

8. Hallowell, "Ojibwa Ontology," pp. 163–65, 171; McClurken, *People of the Three Fires*, pp. 9–10; Trigger, ed., *Handbook/Northeast*, pp. 605–06.

9. Tanner, *Atlas*, p. 29.

10. McClurken, *People of the Three Fires*, pp. 17–21; Mary M. Lewis Hoyt, "Life of Leonard Slater," *Michigan Pioneer Historical Collections* 35 (1907): 146.

11. Trigger, ed., *Handbook/Northeast*, p. 780; Tanner, *Atlas*, pp. 133–35.

12. For McCoy's character and exploits, I have relied upon *History of Baptist Indian Missions*, his memoirs; the "Introduction" to the reprinted edition, by Robert F. Berkhofer, Jr.; and George A. Schultz, *An Indian Canaan: Isaac McCoy and the Vision of an Indian State* (Norman, Okla., 1972).

13. Schultz, *Indian Canaan*, pp. 3–31; Berkhofer, "Introduction," pp. vi–vii.

14. Schultz, *Indian Canaan*, pp. 33–35, 54–6.

15. Schultz, *Indian Canaan*, pp. 56–65; McCoy, *History*, pp. 189–95.

16. McCoy, *History*, pp. 196–201, 217 (quotation, p. 197); Schultz, *Indian Canaan*, pp. 67–68.

17. Schultz, *Indian Canaan*, p. 67; see also Berkhofer, "Introduction," p. viii.

18. McCoy, *History*, pp. 200–01; Schultz, *Indian Canaan*, p. 96.

19. McCoy, *History*, pp. 224, 227, 249 (quotation).

20. McCoy, *History*, pp. 249–50.

21. McCoy, *History*, p. 251.

22. McCoy, *History*, pp. 258–59, 274–76 (quotations, pp. 275–76).

23. McCoy, *History*, pp. 293–96.

24. McClurken, "Strangers," pp. 9–10.

25. McCoy, *History*, pp. 308, 317, 329, 339, 390 (quotation). See also Schultz, *Indian Canaan*, pp. 99, 128.

26. McCoy, *History*, pp. 390–91, 396; Schultz, *Indian Canaan*, pp. 85, 154–56, 199.

27. Robert F. Berkhofer, Jr., *Salvation and the Savage* (Lexington, Ky., 1965).

28. McClurken, *People of the Three Fires*, pp. 33–35; Robert Bolt, "Rev. Leonard Slater in the Grand River Valley," *Michigan History* 51/3 (Fall 1967): 251.

29. John W. McGee, *The Catholic Church in the Grand River Valley, 1833–1950* (Grand Rapids, 1950), pp. 26–29.

30. McGee, *Catholic Church*, pp. 34–40, 44–47; Baxter, *History*, p. 52.

31. Baraga letter of July 26, 1833, quoted in McGee, *Catholic Church*, p. 38; letter of Oct. 12, 1833, quoted idid., p. 60.

32. Baraga letter of Dec. 1, 1833, quoted in McGee, *Catholic Church*, p. 60. On Christmas celebration, see ibid., p. 74.

33. McGee, *Catholic Church*, pp. 56–57, 63–65.

34. Baxter, *History*, p. 52; McGee, *Catholic Church*, pp. 52–53.

35. McGee, *Catholic Church*, pp. 53–56, 68–69, 72–73.

36. Quotation from Baraga letter of Feb. 1, 1834 (in McGee, *Catholic Church*, p. 63); on colonization, ibid., pp. 67, 69–70.

37. Baraga letter of Feb. 20, 1835, quoted in McGee, *Catholic Church*, p. 75.

38. McGee, *Catholic Church*, pp. 84–85, 88, 94.

39. McGee, *Catholic Church*, pp. 90–92.

40. Baxter, *History of Grand Rapids*, p. 288.

41. John Ball's reminiscence, recorded in Baxter, *History*, p. 74.

42. McGee, *Catholic Church*, pp. 93, 128–29; Baxter, *History of Grand Rapids*, p. 340.

43. Trigger, *Handbook*, p. 780; Baxter, *History of Grand Rapids*, p. 28; Coe Hayne, "Leonard Slater," *Michigan History* 28/3 (July 1944): 391–93; Hoyt, "Leonard Slater," pp. 154–55.

44. Berkhofer, "Introduction," pp. xx–xxv; McCoy, *History*, p. 555.

45. McClurken, *People of the Three Fires*, pp. 22, 33–35; McGee, *Catholic Church*, p. 98.

CAUGHT BETWEEN CULTURES, REJECTED BY BOTH

Albert Baxter, *History of the City of Grand Rapids, Michigan*, "Indian Intractability," (New York and Grand Rapids, 1891), pp. 34–36.

CONFUSING BAPTISM

Harold D. Burpee, "Fresh out of the Attic," Hastings *Banner*, July 30, 1964, p. 5. He quotes Mrs. Hoyt writing for the *Michigan Pioneer and Historical Collections*, Vol. 35, 1907.

WILD WHISKEY: BISHOP BARAGA LETTER

Portion of Baraga letter on file in Local Historical Collections at Grand Rapids Public Library.

CHAPTER 2

1. James Van Vulpen, *A Faith Journey* (Grand Rapids, 1985), p. 1; Mrs. W.H. Kinney and Mrs. F.A. Baldwin, eds., *Park Congregational Church: The Story of One Hundred Years, 1836–1936* (Grand Rapids, 1936), p. 4; Marian L. Withey, personal reminiscence, entry #44 in "Park Has Touched Me — I Have Grown!", loose-leaf collection from the 150th anniversary of Park Congregational Church.

2. The classic account is Whitney Cross, *The Burned-Over District: The Social and Intellectual History of Enthusiastic Religion in Western New York* (Ithaca, N.Y., 1950). A more recent version is Paul E. Johnson, *A Shopkeeper's Millennium: Society and Revivals in Rochester, New York, 1815–1837* (New York, 1978).

3. Data on laity are gathered from Albert Baxter, *History of the City of Grand Rapids, Michigan* (New York and Grand Rapids, 1891); on the clergy from Van Vulpen, *Faith Journey*, and Kinsey and Baldwin, *PCC: 100 Years*.

4. Van Vulpen, *Faith Journey*, pp. 4–9; Baxter, *History*, pp. 220–23.

5. Van Vulpen, *Faith Journey*, pp. 10–12.

6. Smith's sermon of November 18, 1869, "Farewell to the Old Church," echoes the themes his mentor, Horace Bushnell, sounded in his classic *Christian Nurture* (1847). On Smith's background, see Van Vulpen, *Faith Journey*, p. 13.

7. Van Vulpen, *Faith Journey*, pp. 14–16; Kinsey and Baldwin, *PCC: 100 Years*, pp. 17–19 (quotation p. 19).

8. Kinsey and Baldwin, *PCC: 100 Years*, pp. 93–95 (quotation p. 95); Van Vulpen, *Faith Journey*, p. 9.

9. "Park Has Touched Me," p. 91; see also Marian Withey's memoir, entry #44 in same collection. Baxter, *History*, pp. 247, 252, 353–54.

10. Baxter, *History*, pp. 131, 135, 199–202, 357–59.

11. See the remarkable 102-page "Informal History of the Tens" in "Park Has Touched Me" (quotation p. 42).

12. Kinsey and Baldwin, *PCC: 100 Years*, p. 35.

13. On the British visitor, "Park Has Touched Me," entry #51. On Merriam, Van Vulpen, *Faith Journey*; Kinsey and Baldwin, *PCC: 100 Years*, pp. 57–65. On pastimes, "Park Has Touched Me," #34, #35, and #42; and Kinsey and Baldwin, pp. 51, 123.

14. Data and connections derived from biographical entries in Baxter, *History*; Kinsey and Baldwin, *PCC: 100 Years*, pp. 27, 28, 120–21.

15. Baxter, *History*, pp. 674–78; David Halberstam, *The Best and the Brightest* (New York, 1972), pp. 47–50.

16. Van Vulpen, *Faith Journey*; "William Haldane Script" in the records of the 150th anniversary services, Park Congregational Church archives.

17. Joseph B. Ware, *History: First Methodist Episcopal Church, Grand Rapids, Michigan: 1835–1911* (Grand Rapids, 1911), pp. 2–7; Margaret Burnham Macmillan, *The Methodist Church in Michigan: The Nineteenth Century* (Michigan Area Methodist Historical Society, 1967), p. 153.

18. Ware, *History*, pp. 2, 7; Macmillan, *Methodist Church*, p. 125.

19. Baxter, *History*, p. 118.

20. Macmillan, *Methodist Church*, pp. 125–26; Ware, *History*, pp. 3, 9, 15 (quotation).

21. Ware, *History*, pp. 5 (quotation), 10.

22. Ware, *History*, pp. 11, 15, 16, 24.

23. Data derived from biographical and commercial entries in Baxter, *History*, and Ware, *History*, p. 6.

24. Ware, *History*, pp. 19–24.

25. Baxter, *History*, pp. 345, 356–59, 439; Ware, *History*, pp. 20, 24, 30.

26. Grand Rapids *Evening Press*, Jan. 1, 1916, p. 10; "Dedication Program," First Methodist Church, April 9–16, 1916; "First United Methodist Church, Grand Rapids, Michigan, Volume II: 1911–1976" (Grand Rapids, 1976), pp. 3–6.

27. "First United Methodist, Volume II," pp. 6–11, 40, 48.

28. "First United Methodist, Volume II," pp. 12–16, 25–30.

29. "First United Methodist, Volume II," pp. 18–19.

30. Van Vulpen, *Faith Journey*, p. 1; *Census of Religious Bodies*, 1906 (Washington, D.C., 1906).

31. The sponsors are listed in John W. McGee, *The Catholic Church in the Grand River Valley, 1833–1950* (Grand Rapids, 1950), p. 213.

32. Quoted in McGee, *Catholic Church*, p. 111.

33. McGee, *Catholic Church*, pp. 100–10.

34. McGee, *Catholic Church*, pp. 125–35.

35. McGee, *Catholic Church*, pp. 146–62, 188.

36. Data derived from biographical entries in Baxter, *History*; see also p. 355.

37. McGee, *Catholic Church*, pp. 185–95; quotation from Grand Rapids *Daily Morning Democrat*, in McGee, p. 211.

38. McGee, *Catholic Church*, pp. 205–12.

39. McGee, *Catholic Church*, pp. 287, 478, 464; "Souvenir of the Centennial of the First Mass in Grand Rapids" (Grand Rapids, 1933), p. 32.

40. McGee, *Catholic Church*, pp. 310–15; quotation, McGee, "St. Andrew's Church, 1876–1976" (Grand Rapids, 1976), p. 14; Van Vulpen, *Faith Journey*, p. 22.

41. McGee, *Catholic Church*, pp. 332, 348.

42. McGee, *Catholic Church*, p. 354; quotation from Msgr. Charles Popell in McGee, "St. Andrew's Church," p. 25.

43. McGee, *Catholic Church*, pp. 387–89.

44. McGee, "St. Andrew's Church," pp. 27–28, 34.

45. McGee, "St. Andrew's Church," pp. 25, 31–36.

CHURCH WOMEN HELPED HEAL THE NEEDY, SICK

Grand Rapids *Evening Leader*, April 26, 1890, p. 3.

Grand Rapids *Democrat*, Feb. 8, 1891, p. 2.

"St. Mark's Hospital Report," 1890, p. 47.

A TALE OF TWO CHURCHES

Author's interview with Ms. Mary Edmond, Feb. 22, 1991.

"The African Methodist Episcopal Zion Church," a history of the church by Ms. Mary A. Love.

The Rev. George A. Steward, "Souvenir Journal Sketches," Oct. 9, 1988, in church archives.

"The Animated Annals of South Congregational Church from 1878 to 1948," compiled by the Rev. Harry Pollard, in church archives.

CHAPTER 3

1. Quoted in Albert Baxter, *History of the City of Grand Rapids, Michigan* (New York and Grand Rapids, 1891), pp. 123–24.

2. Jacob De Jager, *The Hundredth Anniversary [of First Christian Reformed Church, Grand Rapids, Michigan], 1857–1957* (Grand Rapids, 1957), p. 10.

3. Peter Moerdyk, "History of the First Reformed Church, Grand Rapids, Michigan: A Discourse" (Grand Rapids, 1880), pp.

2–10; John A. and Irene Dykstra, *A History of Central Reformed Church, Grand Rapids, Michigan* (Grand Rapids, 1968), pp. 16–19.

4. Moerdyk, "History," pp. 10–13; Dykstra, *History*, pp. 19–21.

5. James D. Bratt, *Dutch Calvinism in Modern America: A History of a Conservative Subculture* (Grand Rapids, 1984), pp. 6–10.

6. Moerdyk, "History," pp. 14–18; Baxter, *History*, pp. 326–27.

7. Frans van Driele, "First Experiences," in Henry S. Lucas, ed., *Dutch Immigrant Memoirs and Related Writings* (Assen, 1955), vol. I, pp. 332–37. See also the anonymously written "In Memoriam: Frans van Driele" (n.p., n.d.) in the Central RCA archives.

8. Baxter, *History*, pp. 326–27.

9. Baxter, *History*, pp. 327–28.

10. See typescript summary of Second Reformed Church consistory minutes, 1873–1918, in the Central RCA archives.

11. Van Driele, "First Experiences," pp. 334–35.

12. Moerdyk, "History," pp. 20–33; quotation p. 31. See also Moerdyk's autobiographical statement in Baxter, *History*, pp. 324–25.

13. Baxter, *History*, pp. 323–24; Moerdyk, "History," pp. 25–33; First Reformed Church, *Church Record*, November 1894, in the Central RCA archives.

14. Baxter, *History*, pp. 323–24.

15. Consistory minutes, Second Reformed Church; Dykstra, *History*, pp. 33–35.

16. Dykstra, *History*, pp. 35–54. For Dykstra's pulpit messages, see his *Heavenly Days* (Grand Rapids, 1944).

17. Dykstra, *History*, pp. 55–81.

18. Henry Beets, *The Christian Reformed Church in North America* (Grand Rapids, 1923), pp. 44–49.

19. De Jager, *Hundredth Anniversary*, pp. 5–9, 91–93.

20. De Jager, *Hundredth Anniversary*, pp. 11–13; Beets, *The CRC*, pp. 59–62.

21. Beets, *The CRC*, pp. 62–67; Bratt, *Dutch Calvinism*, pp. 39–40.

22. Baxter, *History*, p. 335; De Jager, *Hundredth Anniversary*, pp. 11–12, 20–21.

23. De Jager, *Hundredth Anniversary*, pp. 13–26.

24. Quoted in De Jager, *Hundredth Anniversary*, p. 29.

25. De Jager, *Hundredth Anniversary*, pp. 33–37.

26. John Hage's reminiscences, quoted in De Jager, *Hundredth Anniversary*, pp. 94–95.

27. De Jager, *Hundredth Anniversary*, pp. 40–50.

28. De Jager, *Hundredth Anniversary*, pp. 51–52.

29. De Jager, *Hundredth Anniversary*, pp. 54–56; Bratt, *Dutch Calvinism*, pp. 126, 142–50, 153–55, 189.

30. Dale Van Kley and John LaGrand, "A History of First Christian Reformed Church, Grand Rapids, Michigan, 1957–1982" (Grand Rapids, 1982), Calvin College Archives.

31. *Geschichte der Deutschen Evangelische-Lutheran Immanuels Gemeinde U.A.C. zu Grand Rapids Michigan* (Grand Rapids, 1906), p. 7.

32. E. Clifford Nelson, ed., *The Lutherans in North America* (Philadelphia, 1975), pp. 150–59, 178–82.

33. Wilhelm W. Seeger, "The German-Americans in Grand Rapids, Michigan: An Historical Survey" (paper presented to the 10th annual Symposium of the Society for German-American Studies, Cincinnati, April 1986), p. 12.

34. *Geschichte Immanuel*, pp. 5–7.

35. *Geschichte Immanuel*, pp. 7–10; Nelson, *Lutherans*, p. 228.

36. *Geschichte Immanuel*, pp. 10–11; *History of Immanuel Evangelical Lutheran Congregation U.A.C. of Grand Rapids, Michigan* (Grand Rapids, 1931), pp. 9–10; Baxter, *History*, pp. 302–04.

37. *History of Immanuel*, p. 11; *Geschichte Immanuel*, pp. 14–15.

38. *Geschichte Immanuel*, pp. 15–17.

39. *History Immanuel*, pp. 11–15.

40. Seeger, "German-Americans," p. 17. For the national context, see Frederick Luebke, *Bonds of Loyalty: German-Americans and World War I* (DeKalb, IL, 1974).

41. Wilhelm W. Seeger, "The Braumeisters of Grand Rapids," *Grand River Valley Review* 8/1 (1988): 3–13; Baxter, *History*, p. 203.

42. Baxter, *History*, pp. 203 (source of quotation), 207.

43. John W. McGee, *The Catholic Church in the Grand River Valley, 1833–1950* (Grand Rapids, 1950), pp. 411–14; *Golden Jubilee Memories of St. Mary's Church, Grand Rapids, Michigan, 1857–1907* (Grand Rapids, 1907), pp. 91–94, 119–20.

44. *Golden Jubilee*, pp. 98–99.

45. *Golden Jubilee*, pp. 99–102 (quotation, p. 100).

46. *Golden Jubilee*, pp. 102–06.

47. *Golden Jubilee*, pp. 101–05, 113–14.

48. Rev. James Pulcher, quoted in *Golden Jubilee*, pp. 122–23.

49. *Golden Jubilee*, pp. 109–16, 141.

50. *Golden Jubilee*, pp. 152–66.

51. Details supplied by Ms. Marcia A. Guile.

MEN OF STRAIGHTFORWARD DEALING

Michigan Tradesman, July 2, 1902, Oct. 13, 1909, April, 17, 1912, and May 27, 1925.

Z.Z. Lydens, editor, *Story of Grand Rapids*, (Grand Rapids, 1966), pp. 244–245

Albert Baxter, *History of the City of Grand Rapids, Michigan*, (New York and Grand Rapids, 1891), pp. 484–485, 682–683.

"Oldest Clothing Store Traced to Earliest Jewish Settler," Grand Rapids *Press*, Sept. 11, 1980, p 20.

CHAPTER 4

1. Dee Brown, *The Year of the Century: 1876* (New York, 1966), pp. 112–37. John G. Cawelti, "America on Display: The World's Fairs of 1876, 1893, 1933," in Frederic C. Jaher, ed., *The Age of Industrialism in America* (New York, 1968), pp. 317–363. Frank E. Ransom, *The City Built on Wood: A History of the Furniture Industry in Grand Rapids, Michigan, 1850–1950* (n.p., 1955), pp. 17, 25.

2. Ransom, *City Built on Wood*, pp. 13, 17–27, 52. Jeffrey Kleiman, "The Rule From Above: Businessmen, Bankers, and the Drive to Organize in Grand Rapids, 1890–1906," *Michigan Historical Review* 12/2 (Fall 1986): 45–57.

3. F.M. Ten Hoor, *De Gereformeerde Amerikaan* 1 (February 1897): 13.

4. David Vander Stel, "The Dutch of Grand Rapids, Michigan, 1848–1900: Immigrant Neighborhood and Community Development in a Nineteenth Century City" (unpublished Ph.D. dissertation, Kent State University, 1983), p. 460. Robert P. Swierenga, "Dutch Immigration Patterns in the Nineteenth and Twentieth Centuries," in Swierenga, ed., *The Dutch in America: Immigration, Settlement, and Cultural Change* (New Brunswick, 1985), pp. 27–36. Henry S. Lucas, *Netherlanders in America* (Ann Arbor, 1955).

5. Vander Stel, "The Dutch of Grand Rapids," p. 124.

6. See Jacob Vanden Bosch, "Lammert Jan Hulst," *Reformed Journal* 7 (December 1957): 17–21; and Hulst's autobiography, *Drie en Zestig Jaren Prediker* (Kampen, 1913), the American half of which is available in English translation in the Calvin College Archives.

7. Elton J. Bruins, "The Masonic Controversy in Holland, Michigan, 1879–1882," in Peter De Klerk and Richard De Ridder, eds., *Perspectives on the Christian Reformed Church* (Grand Rapids, 1983), pp. 53–71. Henry Beets, *De Christelijke Gereformeerde Kerk in Noord Amerika* (Grand Rapids, 1918), pp. 174–186. Hulst's unpublished memoir of the Masonic controversy in his congregation is available in English translation in the Calvin College Archives.

8. *Souvenir: Fiftieth Anniversary, 1882–1932, Coldbrook Christian Reformed Church* (Grand Rapids, 1932), p. 3.

9. This is evident from the L.J. Hulst papers, Calvin College Archives, and is drolly recounted in Hulst's autobiography.

10. Vanden Bosch, "L.J. Hulst."

11. A good example is Hulst's sermon, "De Overwinning der Wereld," in *Uit Eigen Kring: Twee-en-vijftig Leeredenen* (Grand Rapids, 1903), pp. 55–71.

12. *A Century of Faithfulness: Beckwith Hills Christian Reformed Church, Grand Rapids, Michigan, 1882–1982* (Grand Rapids, 1982), pp. 42, 43.

13. Quoted in *The Yearbook of the Christian Reformed Church, 1923* (Grand Rapids, 1923), pp. 127–28. For more detail and context, see James D. Bratt, *Dutch Calvinism in Modern America: A History of a Conservative Subculture* (Grand Rapids, 1984), pp. 47–50. Hulst co-authored (with Calvin Seminary professor Gerrit K. Hemkes) a whole book on this point: *Oud- en Nieuw-Calvinisme* (Grand Rapids, 1913).

14. Vander Stel, "The Dutch in Grand Rapids," pp. 205–10, 258, 270–71, 339.

15. *Souvenir, Coldbrook CRC*, pp. 5, 6; *Beckwith Hills CRC*, p. 3, 17–22.

16. Victor Greene, "Poles," *Harvard Encyclopedia of American Ethnic Groups*, pp. 787–93.

17. Eduard A. Skendzel, *The Sacred Heart Story* (Grand Rapids, 1981), pp. 41, 42. For the history of Grand Rapids Polonia, I am indebted to this work and to many other pieces by Professor Skendzel collected in *Polonian Musings* (two-volume MS in the Local Historical Collections of the Grand Rapids Public Library) and summarized in "The Polanders," *Grand River Valley Review* 4/2 (1983): 2–11.

18. Skendzel, *Polonian Musings*, pp. 334–35, 402–03; *Sacred Heart Story*, pp. 119–20.

19. Victor Greene, *For God and Country: The Rise of Polish and Lithuanian Ethnic Consciousness in America, 1860–1910* (Madison, Wis., 1975), pp. 103–10; Greene, "Poles," p. 794; Skendzel, *Sacred Heart Story*, pp. 47–51 ("church of silence" quotation, p. 130).

20. Skendzel, *Polonian Musings*, p. 405–06, 417. Grand Rapids *Evening Press*, June 23, 1899, p. 3; Aug. 28, 1899, p. 3.

21. Skendzel, *Sacred Heart Story*, pp. 45–47, 53, 70–71.

22. Eduard Skendzel, *The Basilica of St. Adalbert, Grand Rapids, Michigan* (Grand Rapids, 1980; unpaginated). Skendzel, *Sacred Heart Story*, pp. 104–12.

23. Skendzel, *Sacred Heart Story*, pp. 83–84, 89, 108; *Polonian Musings*, pp. 339, 413, 473.

24. Ransom, *City Built on Wood*, p. 40.

25. Skendzel, *Sacred Heart Story*, pp. 128–38.

26. Skendzel, *Polonian Musings*, p. 340; *Sacred Heart Story*, pp. 103, 333.

27. Philip R. Vander Meer, "Religious Divisions and Political Roles: Midwestern Episcopalians, 1860–1910," in Vander Meer and Robert P. Swierenga, eds., *Belief and Behavior: Essays in the New Religious History* (New Brunswick, 1991), p. 222. I am indebted to Professor Vander Meer for calling the St. Mark's case to my attention and for sharing with me research data he gathered on the parish.

28. *Semi-Centennial Services at St. Mark's Church* (Grand Rapids, 1886), pp. 41–43. Hoyt's letter on the occasion of St. Mark's 50th anniversary is quoted on p. 69.

29. Paul E. Johnson, *A Shopkeeper's Millennium: Society and Revivals in Rochester, New York, 1815–1837* (New York, 1978), pp. 65, 68, 91.

30. *St. Mark's Semi-Centennial*, pp. 35–41, 45. Z.Z. Lydens, *The Story of Grand Rapids* (Grand Rapids, 1966), pp. 24, 324, 536. Albert Baxter, *History of Grand Rapids, Michigan* (New York and Grand Rapids, 1981), pp. 102, 191–2, 389, 669, 764.

31. S.L. Fuller, quoted in *St. Mark's Semi-Centennial*, p. 62.

32. *St. Mark's Semi-Centennial*, pp. 47–57.

33. *St. Mark's Semi-Centennial*, p. 58. Ransom, *City Built on Wood*, p. 39.

34. Vander Meer, "Religious Divisions," p. 224.

35. *St. Mark's Semi-Centennial*; "Hitherto" (sermon of Jonathan M. McCormick, bishop of Episcopal diocese of West Michigan, delivered on the 75th anniversary of St. Mark's); and Roger Allen, *The Story of St. Mark's* (Grand Rapids, 1936).

36. Data compiled from *Census of Religious Bodies, 1906* (Washington, D.C., 1906) by Philip Vander Meer.

37. Vander Meer, "Religious Divisions," p. 225.

38. Vander Meer, "Religious Divisions," p. 226.

39. Vander Meer, "Religious Divisions," p. 226. Skendzel, *Polonian Musings*, p. 471.

40. Allen, *Story of St. Mark's*, p. 45.

CHRISTIAN SOLDIERS DERAIL SECULAR SYMBOL

"Diamond Jubilee History of Eastern Avenue Christian Reformed Church." Church history, on file at church.

Tom LaBelle column, Grand Rapids *Press*. March 12, 1967, pp. 3–4.

A TESTAMENT TO THEIR FAITH

Author's interview with Eduard Adam Skendzel, May 4, 1991.

Philip Young, "The First 100 Years: Basilica of St. Adalbert: 1881–1981."

Grand Rapids *Evening Press*, June 19, 21 and 23, 1906.

SECRET SOCIETIES VERSUS THE CHURCHES

Lynn Dumenil, *Freemasonry and American Culture, 1880–1930* (Princeton, 1984), p. 225.

Mark C. Carnes, *Secret Ritual and Manhood in Victorian America* (New Haven, 1989), pp. 17–21, 149.

Albert Baxter, *History of the City of Grand Rapids, Michigan*, pp. 134–135, 629–635.

CHAPTER 5

1. Philip Buchen, *The Only Church With a History Like This* (Grand Rapids, 1959), vol. 3, p. 31.

2. Z.Z. Lydens, *The Story of Grand Rapids* (Grand Rapids, 1966), pp. 57–65.

3. Jeffrey D. Kleiman, "The Great Strike: Religion, Labor, and Reform in Grand Rapids, Michigan, 1890–1916" (unpublished Ph.D. dissertation, Michigan State University, 1985), quotation p. 97, church affiliation p. 81.

4. Buchen, *The Only Church*, vol. 3, pp. 29–33. The best historical account of this theology is William R. Hutchison, *The Modernist Impulse in American Protestantism* (New York, 1976).

5. Buchen, *The Only Church*, vol. 3, pp. 13–25.

6. For details on Graves, see Buchen, *The Only Church*, vol. 2, pp. 41–66, and the Samuel Graves folder in the Fountain Street Church archives. Regarding evangelicalism in 19th-century America, see William McLoughlin, *Revivals, Awakenings, and Reform* (Chicago, 1978) and Ronald G. Walters, *American Reformers, 1815–1860* (New York, 1978).

7. Grand Rapids *Herald*, Nov. 25, 1906.

8. Kleiman, "The Great Strike," p. 83.

9. Kleiman, "The Great Strike," quotation p. 99; account of the entire strike, pp. 97–126.

10. Grand Rapids *Press*, May 11, 1911.

11. Grand Rapids *Herald*, Sept. 7, 1908.

12. Kleiman, "The Great Strike," quotations pp. 86, 87; discussion of Wishart's social philosophy, pp. 83–88. For the national context of this line of thought, see Robert Wiebe, *The Search For Order, 1877–1920* (New York, 1967 and William L. O'Neill, *The Progressive Years: America Comes of Age* (New York, 1975).

13. Grand Rapids *News*, May 20, 1911.

14. Grand Rapids *News*, May 12, 1911.

15. Grand Rapids *Press*, May 18, 1911; see also Grand Rapids *News*, May 20, 1911.

16. Kleiman, "The Great Strike," pp. 46–48.

17. Henry Zwaanstra, *Reformed Thought and Experience in a New World: A Study of the Christian Reformed Church and Its American Environment, 1890–1918* (Kampen, 1973), pp. 239–94; James D. Bratt, *Dutch Calvinism in Modern America: A History of a Conservative Subculture* (Grand Rapids, 1984), pp. 74–76.

18. Kleiman, "The Great Strike," p.114.

19. *Banner*, Aug. 17, 1911, p. 510.

20. Quoted in Mike Johnston, "The Outspoken Viva Flaherty and Her Search for Social Justice," unpublished paper, pp. 4, 5.

21. Grand Rapids *News*, Dec. 7, 1911.

22. Kleiman, "The Great Strike," pp. 129FF. Anthony B. Travis, "Mayor George Ellis: Grand Rapids Political Boss and Progressive Reformer," *Michigan History* 58/2 (1974): 110–11, 120–22.

23. Travis, "George Ellis," pp. 110–11, 127–30.

24. Kleiman, "The Great Strike," pp. 151–56.

25. Dorr Kuizema, *De Calvinist*, Dec. 21, 1911 and April 15, 1912 (my translation). This insight fits well with the historian Samuel P. Hays' analysis of changes in city government in this era; see Hays, *American Political History as Social Analysis* (Knoxville, 1980), pp. 205–32.

26. Grand Rapids *News*, Feb. 26, 1917 and March 3, 1917; Wishart quotations from Henry Beets, "What We Dutch Calvinists really stand for, and Why," *Banner*, March 22, 1917, p. 184.

27. Beets, "Dutch Calvinists," *Banner*, March 22, 1917, and March 29, 1917, pp. 184–86, 200–01.

28. E. A. Stowe, *Michigan Tradesman*, March 6, 1918, and letter to Henry Beets, Feb. 15, 1918, Beets papers, Calvin College Archives. See more generally Bratt, *Dutch Calvinism*, pp. 83–90.

29. Johnston, "Viva Flaherty," pp. 6, 7; Buchen, *The Only Church*, vol. 3, p. 41.

30. Buchen, *The Only Church*, vol. 3, p. 55; Grand Rapids *Press*, May 22, 1917.

31. Grand Rapids *Herald*, Jan. 11, 1918.

32. Buchen, *The Only Church*, vol. 3, pp. 58, 59.

33. Buchen, *The Only Church*, vol. 3, pp. 51–54.

34. Oct. 11, 1931 sermon quoted in Buchen, *The Only Church*, vol. 3, p. 44.

35. Buchen, *The Only Church*, vol. 3, p. 72.

A MATTER OF DECENCY

"Tirades, Holy War Doomed Demon Rum," Grand Rapids *Press*, Aug. 27, 1967, p. 34.

"Prohibition Promoted an Illegal Ingenuity," Grand Rapids *Press*, p. 35.

Garry Boulard, "No Time for Teetotalers," Grand Rapids *Press*, Wonderland Magazine, Jan. 12, 1988, pp. 4–5.

Bruno Laskr, "Prohibition & Prosperity," The *Survey*, Nov. 6, 1920, pp. 186–222

"Grand Rapids Disregard for Prohibition Enforcement," on file, Local Historical Collections, the Grand Rapids Public Library.

"Billy Sunday Slams Home Run Against Booze While Thousands Cheer," Grand Rapids *Press*, Nov. 6, 1916, p. 1.

A DIFFERENT VIEWPOINT

Viva Flaherty, "History of the Grand Rapids Furniture Strike with Facts Hitherto Unpublished," (Grand Rapids, October 1911). Copy in Local Historical Collections at the Grand Rapids Public Library.

CHAPTER 6

1. Albert Baxter, *History of the City of Grand Rapids, Michigan* (New York and Grand Rapids, 1891), pp. 283–84; William T. Commons, "Wealthy St. Baptist Church: The First Half Century" (unpublished paper, May 1965, Miller Library, Grand Rapids Baptist College and Seminary), pp. 6–7.

2. Ruth van der Maas, "The Emergence of Fundamentalism Among the Baptists of Grand Rapids, Michigan, 1900–1925" (unpublished paper, Michigan State University, June 1987), pp. 9, 33; Sam Wanner, "Requested Re-evaluation: Wealthy St. Baptist Church Retrospectively Reexamined" (unpublished paper, History Department, Calvin College, May 1974), pp. 15–16. The church's membership in the 1930s continued in this pattern, being composed of 34% skilled and 27% unskilled workers, 22% clerical/sales/small proprietors, 11% business and 6% professionals (research notes of Joel Carpenter). I am indebted to Professor Carpenter for his assistance on Wealthy Street and Calvary Undenominational Church's history [see also Chapter 7].

3. Grand Rapids *Press*, March 6, 1907, p. 8; Dec. 19, 1907, p. 14; Nov. 2, 1908, p. 3.

4. Commons, "WSBC," pp. 13–15; John O. Wilson, "The Life of Dr. Oliver W. Van Osdel and the Influence of His Ministry" (unpublished paper, 1958); and Edgar B. Van Osdel's memoir of his father, especially pp. 6–7; all in Van Osdel papers, Miller Library, Grand Rapids Baptist College and Seminary.

5. Grand Rapids *Press*, June 1, 1909, p. 3 (source of quotation), and Oct. 20, 1917, p. 3; Grand Rapids *Herald*, Feb. 26, 1911, p. 1 'Editorial' section; program of the "Dedicatory Services of the Wealthy Street Baptist Church," Oct. 28–31, 1917, pp. 10–16.

6. Wilson, "Life of Van Osdel;" van der Maas, "Emergence of Fundamentalism," pp. 11–12, 21; letter from the Grand River

Valley Baptist Association to the Grand Rapids Baptist Association, September 1909 (source of quotation; Wealthy Street Baptist Church papers, Miller Library, Grand Rapids Baptist College and Seminary).

7. Grand Rapids *Press*, Oct. 6, 1917, p. 3; "Dedicatory Services," p. 7.

8. Wilson, "Life of Van Osdel," pp. 15–23; Stewart G. Cole, *The History of Fundamentalism* (New York, 1931), pp. 65–97, 292–94.

9. Kevin Bauder, "How Firm a Foundation: A History of the General Association of Regular Baptist Churches" (unpublished M. Div. thesis, Denver Baptist Theological Seminary, 1982), pp. 34–39, 52, 79, 91; George W. Dollar, *A History of Fundamentalism in America* (Greenville, S.C., 1973), pp. 221–23.

10. Membership statistics compiled by Joel Carpenter from annual "Report of the Church Historian," Wealthy St. Baptist Church. On missions, see James F. Larkin, "The Missions Program of Wealthy St. Baptist Church" (unpublished paper, April 1968, Miller Library, Grand Rapids Baptist College and Seminary), pp. 7–8.

11. Quoted in Grand Rapids *Press*, Jan. 19, 1974, p. A–3.

12. On Riley, Grand Rapids *Press*, June 15, 1923, p. 2; on Bryan, ibid., May 21, 1924, p. 15; Bob Jones, address to Grand Rapids Association of Regular Baptist Churches, reported in *Baptist Bulletin* III/4 (November 1937), p. 13.

13. Larkin, "Mission Program," pp. 7–8; chronology of the life of David Otis Fuller, supplied by James W. Spees; brochure of the Institute for Biblical Textual Studies, Grand Rapids, Michigan; author's interview with the Institute's associate director, Peter Van Kleeck, Jan. 21, 1992.

14. David Otis Fuller, ed., *Valiant for the Truth: A Treasury of Evangelical Writings* (New York, 1961), pp. ix–xi.

15. Joel Carpenter statistics compiled from "Annual Report;" Fuller interviewed in Grand Rapids *Press*, Jan. 19, 1974, p. A–3; author's interview with Wealthy Park Baptist Church's current pastor, John Polson, Jan. 21, 1992.

16. Author's interviews with Polson and Van Kleeck, Jan. 21, 1992.

17. Baxter, *History of Grand Rapids*, pp. 335–36; David Vander Stel, "The Dutch of Grand Rapids" (unpublished Ph.D. dissertation, Kent State University, 1983), pp. 229–34.

18. *One Hundred Years in the Covenant* [centennial history of Eastern Ave. Christian Reformed Church] (Grand Rapids, 1979), pp. 20–23; James D. Bratt, *Dutch Calvinism in Modern America* (Grand Rapids, 1984), pp. 52–54.

19. *One Hundred Years*, pp. 68–72; Bratt, *Dutch Calvinism*, pp. 76–79.

20. Bratt, *Dutch Calvinism*, pp. 103–4. Clear statements of this position by Hoeksema at the time came in a series in the CRC's weekly magazine, the *Banner*, April 10–May 22, 1919; also from the stand in subsequent court proceedings: *State of Michigan Supreme Court Records*, W. Hoeksema et al. v. H. Hoeksema et al., 1925, pp. 149–53.

21. Gertrude Hoeksema, *Therefore I Have Spoken: A Biography of Herman Hoeksema* (Grand Rapids, 1969), gives an intimate portrait of Hoeksema's youth, pp. 15–61. I have followed her characterization of Hoeksema's personality and theology; see, e.g., pp. 108, 136, 146, 186.

22. G. Hoeksema, *Therefore*, pp. 81–90, 133–43; Bratt, *Dutch Calvinism*, pp. 88–89, 105–10.

23. Bratt, *Dutch Calvinism*, pp. 110–15. *One Hundred Years* presents the story from the loyalists' perspective, pp. 30–36; Herman Hoeksema, *The Protestant Reformed Churches in America* (Grand Rapids, 1947), gives Hoeksema's exhaustive rendition, pp. 11–98.

24. Karen Hanko, "'Less than the Least': The Life of Cornelius Hanko" (unpublished paper, History Department, Calvin College, December 1991), p. 6.

25. Grand Rapids *Press*, Dec. 22, 1925, p. 1, chronicles the entire process. For Hoeksema's account, see his *PRC*, pp. 99–226; for the loyalists', *One Hundred Years*, pp. 36–40.

26. Grand Rapids *Press*, Feb. 9, 11–14, 21, 25, 1925. For Hoeksema's protest, see Feb. 11, 1925, pp. 1–2; regarding synodical president Idzaard Van Dellen, Feb. 14, 1925, p. 1.

27. *Supreme Court Record*, Hoeksema v. Hoeksema, pp. 92–95; G. Hoeksema, *Therefore*, pp. 155–59; Gertrude Hoeksema, *God's Covenant Faithfulness: The 50th Anniversary of the Protestant Reformed Churches in America* (Grand Rapids, 1975), p. 14.

28. G. Hoeksema, *God's Covenant Faithfulness*, pp. 15–25, 93; H. Hoeksema, *PRC*, pp. 268–87.

29. G. Hoeksema, *God's Covenant Faithfulness*, pp. 31–38; *Therefore*, pp. 177, 257–62, 295–300, 310–20.

30. G. Hoeksema, *Therefore*, pp. 322–33, quotation, p. 330. Statistics calculated from *Acts of Synod of the Protestant Reformed Churches in America* (Grand Rapids), 1950 and 1954.

31. G. Hoeksema, *God's Covenant Faithfulness*, pp. 70–77, 80–81, 92–95. Statistics derived from *Acts of Synod PRC* for the years mentioned.

32. Author's interview with William R. and Annette Byl, Nov. 10, 1992.

33. G. Hoeksema, *God's Covenant Faithfulness*, pp. 94–95.

34. Baxter, *History of Grand Rapids*, pp. 318–20; *First Presbyterian Church of Grand Rapids, 1855–1955: One Hundred Years of Christian Service* (Grand Rapids, 1955), pp. 4–7; Florence McCutcheon McKee, *Westminster Presbyterian Church, Grand Rapids, Michigan: A History of the Church ... to 1938* (Grand Rapids, 1938), pp. 1–9.

35. McKee, *WPC*, pp. 6–18; John Comin, *History of the Presbyterian Church in Michigan* (Ann Arbor, 1950), p. 108; Baxter, *History of Grand Rapids*, pp. 319–20.

36. Baxter, *History of Grand Rapids*, p. 320; McKee, *WPC*, pp. 20–38; Comin, *History of Presbyterian Church in Michigan*, p. 108; vertical file on Westminster Presbyterian Church, Local Historical Collections at the Grand Rapids Public Library.

37. McKee, *WPC*, pp. 35, 53, 65, 70, Appendix 25–26; "Westminster Presbyterian Church: The First 100 Years: 1861–1961" (Grand Rapids, 1961), pp. 6–7.

38. Vertical file, "WPC," Grand Rapids Public Library.

39. Grand Rapids *Press*, Feb. 12, 1920, p. 1; McKee, *WPC*, pp. 70–79.

40. George Marsden, *Fundamentalism and American Culture* (New York, 1980), pp. 117, 173–75, 180–81; Grand Rapids *Press*, May 22, 1924, p. 2.

41. Lefferts A. Loetscher, *The Broadening Church: A Study of Theological Issues in the Presbyterian Church Since 1869* (Philadelphia, 1957), p. 121; Grand Rapids *Press*, May 22, 1924, pp. 1–2.

42. See respective sections in the Grand Rapids *Press*, May 22 and 23, 1924; speeches recorded in issues of May 23–26, 1924.

43. Grand Rapids *Press*, May 23, 1924, pp. 1–2; May 24, 1924, p. 2.

44. On morals resolutions, see Grand Rapids *Press*, May 27 and 28, 1924, pp. 1–2 each issue. Theater advertisements are from the issue of May 24, 1924.

45. Grand Rapids *Press*, May 29, 1924, pp. 1–3. On the entire 1924 General Assembly, see Loetscher, *Broadening Church*, pp. 121–24.

46. Grand Rapids *Press*, May 29, 1924, pp. 1–3; Loetscher, *Broadening Church*, pp. 113–15.

47. Robert D. Towne, Grand Rapids *Press*, May 26, 1924, p. 3; Marsden, *Fundamentalism and American Culture*, pp. 183–84, 191–92; Loetscher, *Broadening Church*, pp. 125–36.

48. McKee, *WPC*, p. 78; Cole, *History of Fundamentalism*, pp. 116–19.

49. McKee, *WPC*, p. 93, Appendix p. 11; *WPC: 100 Years*, pp. 8–9; *WPC, 1861–1946* (source of quotation).

50. The mobility is evident throughout McKee, *WPC*, Appendix; on World War II service, *WPC: 1861–1946*; Prominent Dutch–named laity are listed in the ranks of church officers throughout the 1920s and 1930s in the pertinent pages of McKee.

ONE FAMILY, DIFFERENT WORLDS

Author's interview with Dr. Duncan Littlefair, June 15, 1990.

Jon Halvorsen, "Of Sinners and the saved and David Otis Fuller," Grand Rapids *Press*, Oct. 31, 1971, p. 7.

The Rev. Robert Gage, "Valiant for the Truth: David Otis Fuller, 1903–1988," The Baptist Bulletin, May 1988, pp. 20–21.

Roland Wilkerson, "Preacher David Fuller dies at age 84," Grand Rapids *Press*, Feb. 22, 1988.

A NEW AGE RELIGION

Beverly Pearson, "History of Unity Church," submitted to Local Historical Collections at the Grand Rapids Public Library.

Author's interview with Beverly Pearson, May 10, 1992.

Wilfred A. Peterson, "Ida M. Bailey," self-published. Submitted by Beverly Pearson.

RELIGIOUS PUBLISHING WAS ALL IN THE FAMILY

James E. Ruark and Ted W. Engstrom, "Dawn at the Farm," (Grand Rapids, Zondervan Publishing House, 1981), pp. 16–22.

Chris Meehan, "Printing the Word: Local religious publishers share common past, bright future," Grand Rapids *Press*, Jan. 20, 1988, p. 1C.

Gerald Elliott, "Peter J. (Pat) Zondervan: Religion's Stellar Publisher," Grand Rapids *Press*, p. 11A.

Chris Meehan, "Religious Book Houses Thrive," Grand Rapids *Press*, July 29, 1979, p. 1D.

Gerald Elliott, "Herman Baker: Book Seller and Publisher," Grand Rapids *Press*, Oct. 20, 1982, p. A13.

MEL TROTTER'S ORDINATION

Grand Rapids *Herald*, April 12, 1905.

SOUP, SOAP, AND SALVATION

"Death takes evangelist," Grand Rapids *Press*, Sept. 11, 1940.

Fred C. Zarfar, "Mel Trotter: a Biography," (Grand Rapids, Zondervan Publishing House, 1950).

CHAPTER 7

1. *Public Papers of the Presidents of the United States: Herbert Hoover … 1929* (Washington, D.C., 1974), pp. 7, 11.

2. Grand Rapids *Press*, March 4, 1929, p. 26.

3. Grand Rapids *Press*, Aug. 3, 1915, p. 2; Feb. 21, 1919, p. 11; Aug. 23, 1919, p. 1; Dec. 8, 1923, p. 10. James R. Adair, *M.R. De Haan: The Man and His Ministry* (Grand Rapids, 1969), pp. 62–63.

4. Adair, *De Haan*, pp. 72–74, 81; Thomas Boslooper, *Grace and Glory Days* (Clearwater, Fla., 1990), pp. 4, 5, 14; Grand Rapids *Press*, Feb. 18, 1928, p. 15.

5. Boslooper, *Grace and Glory*, pp. 6–9. Grand Rapids *Press*, Feb. 26, 1929, pp. 1, 2; Feb. 28, 1929, pp. 1–3; March 4, 1929, p. 16; March 5, 1929, p. 4; March 6, 1929, p. 29; April 4, 1929, p. 1.

6. Boslooper, *Grace and Glory*, pp. 9–12.

7. Boslooper, *Grace and Glory*, pp. 9–13. Grand Rapids *Press*, March 4, 1929, pp. 1, 2; March 11, 1929, p. 19; April 25, 1929, p. 1; Jan. 27, 1930, p. 18. Calvary Church, Undenominational, *Fifty Years of Blessing, 1929–1979* (Grand Rapids, 1979), p. 4.

8. Adair, *De Haan*, pp. 72–75. De Haan's views are laid out in detail in his dozen books; see, for example, *The Second Coming of Jesus* (Grand Rapids, 1944); *The Jews and Palestine in Prophecy* (Grand Rapids, 1950); and *The Days of Noah* (Grand Rapids, 1963). The best scholarly analysis of such thinking is Timothy P. Weber, *Living in the Shadow of the Second Coming: American Premillennialism, 1875–1925* (New York, 1979).

9. Albertus Pieters, *Jonah, the Whale, and Dr. M.R. De Haan* (Grand Rapids, n. d.), is a refutation by a Western Seminary professor.

10. Boslooper, *Grace and Glory*, pp. 51–57; Adair, *De Haan*, p. 84; *Calvary Undenominational Church: Dedication …* (Grand Rapids, Jan. 29–31, 1930), n.p.; Calvary Church, Undenominational, *Fifty Years*, p. 19; Grand Rapids *Herald*, July 27, 1925; July 10, 1930; Grand Rapids *Press*, July 25, 1927, p. 17; Jan. 2, 1929, p. 24.

11. Grand Rapids *Herald*, Sept. 7 and Oct. 5, 1933 (sources of

quotations); Grand Rapids *Press*, Sept. 14, 21, 1933, pp. 8, 13, respectively.

12. Grand Rapids *Herald*, Oct. 12, 1933; Grand Rapids *Press*, Oct. 27, 1936, p. 10.

13. For example, see De Haan, *The Days of Noah*.

14. Boslooper, *Grace and Glory*, pp. 87–91; Adair, *De Haan*, pp. 85–88; Grand Rapids *Press*, May 23, 1938, p. 20.

15. Boslooper, *Grace and Glory*, pp. 93–95.

16. These data are found in Calvary Church's various anniversary publications, unfortunately unpaginated: "These Forty Years: Calvary Church, 1929–1969;" *Fifty Years* [pp. 18–19]; "From the Hill to the Crossroads" (program of the Aug. 3, 1986 dedication of the church's new building); and *Calvary Church: 60th Anniversary, 1929–1989*.

17. Budget figures available in "From the Hill" and *Fifty Years*; current figure given in author's interview with Dr. Edward G. Dobson, March 13, 1992.

18. Author's interview with Dr. Edward G. Dobson, March 13, 1992.

19. Title of program at the new building's dedication, Aug. 3, 1986.

20. Although "temple" technically refers to the building and "congregation" to the body that gathers there, this chapter follows common usage in using the two terms interchangably.

21. The details of this and subsequent events in the first century of the congregation's history are well portrayed in *History of Temple Emanuel: 1857–1954* [June Horowitz, ed.; Grand Rapids, 1954]. The book is not paginated but proceeds in clear sequential order so that materials below can be readily referenced by chronology.

22. Horowitz, *History TE*; Albert Baxter, *History of the City of Grand Rapids, Michigan* (New York and Grand Rapids, 1891), pp. 300–302; "Souvenir: Diamond Jubilee, Julius Houseman Lodge B'nai B'rith, Grand Rapids, Michigan" (Grand Rapids, 1952).

23. Quoted in Grand Rapids *Eagle* (photostat in *History TE*).

24. In fact, Temple Emanuel is Michigan's oldest Jewish congregation to have been Reform from its beginning, and the fifth oldest such in the United States. Letter from June Horowitz to the author, April 11, 1992.

25. *History TE*. On Reform Judaism, see Nathan Glazer, *American Judaism*, 2nd ed. (Chicago, 1972), pp. 22–59.

26. All quotations from Horowitz, *History TE*.

27. *Dedication: Congregation Ahavas Israel* (Grand Rapids, Jan. 23–25, 1953), pp. 9–16.

28. Quoted in Horowitz, *History TE*.

29. Rabbi Charles J. Freund, quoted in Grand Rapids *Press*, June 16, 1917, p. 8. On Zionist meetings in Grand Rapids and their sponsorship, see Grand Rapids *Press*, Jan. 30, 1929, p. 33.

30. Horowitz, *History TE*.

31. See Waterman's reminisence in Horowitz, *History TE*; on Jewish relief needs, author's interview with June Horowitz, Feb. 10, 1992.

32. Horowitz, *History TE*.

33. Quotation from *Temple Emanuel Bulletin*, Sept. 9, 1950, n.p.

On merger, *Ahavas Israel*, pp. 16–21. On refugee settlement, author's interview with June Horowitz, Feb. 10, 1992.

34. Horowitz, *History TE*; *Ahavas Israel*, pp. 21–31.

35. United Jewish Appeal campaign scrapbook and file, Temple Emanuel archives.

36. "Study of Recreational and Educational Resources … Jewish Community of Grand Rapids, Michigan, July 1944" (in Local Historical Collections at the Grand Rapids Public Library), pp. 10–11.

37. Letter of June Horowitz to author, April 11, 1992; and *History TE*.

38. Z.Z. Lydens, ed., *The Story of Grand Rapids* (Grand Rapids, 1966), p. 411; Grand Rapids *Press*, Feb. 5 and May 21, 1951; Jan. 25, 1952.

39. Author's interview with June Horowitz, Feb. 10, 1992.

40. Grand Rapids *Press*, Nov. 5, 1908, p. 10; Dec. 21, 1908, p. 11; Jan. 6, 1909, p. 6; Jan. 11, 1909, p. 3; July 20, 1912, p. 1. Paul N. Chardoul, ed., *Grand Rapids' Greek Heritage* (Grand Rapids, 1986), pp. 2–3, 15, 18.

41. *The Living Stones of St. George Antiochian Orthodox Church at Grand Rapids: 50th Anniversary, 1926–1976*, n.p.; Chardoul, *Greek Heritage*, pp. 9–10. Grand Rapids *Press*, March 22, 1924, p. 18; Feb. 11, 1926, p. 2; Feb. 14, 1926, p. 23; April 17, 1926, p. 18; June 15, 1926, p. 4.

42. Chardoul, *Greek Heritage*, pp. 1–4.

43. St. John Chrysostom Russian Orthodox Church, "Questionnaire" (Grand Rapids Area Council for the Humanities, Church History project, 1991; Local Historical Collections at the Grand Rapids Public Library), pp. 5, 11–12.

44. Ibid., pp. 6, 14; Grand Rapids *Herald*, Nov. 29, 1942; Sept. 12, 1948.

45. "Questionnaire," pp. 10, 12 (with addenda), 19, 21; letter of Ludmilla Kucher to Marie Ogaeko, Nov. 3, 1990, in ibid.

46. "Questionnaire," pp. 3, 13, 16, 20, 22–23.

47. "Questionnaire," pp. 15 (with addenda), 21; Grand Rapids *Press*, Jan. 8, 1978; Jan. 7, 1982.

48. "Questionnaire," p. 15 (with addenda); Grand Rapids *Press*, May 14, 1983.

SOLDIERS AND SONG

Col. Jack Chene, "Corps History: Grand Rapids Centennial Temple Corps."

"Salvationists Celebrate Centennial This Weekend," Grand Rapids *Press*, Wonderland Magazine, Sept. 25, 1983.

"NOT SOUVLAKI HEAVEN"

Author's interviews with Paul N. Chardoul and the Rev. James Bogdan, April 9, 1993.

Paul N. Chardoul, "Grand Rapids Greek Heritage," (Grand Rapids, 1986).

CHAPTER 8

1. Figures taken from the U.S. population census of the respective years.

2. The following two paragraphs rely principally on an account written by Adeline Jefferson, Catherine Carter's daughter, in a pictorial directory of Messiah that is undated but, by internal evidence, comes from the mid-1970s. Supplementary sources are "Eighty-Fourth Anniversary, Messiah Baptist Church: 1890–1974" [Grand Rapids, 1974], p. 4; "100 Years: Messiah Missionary Baptist Church" [Grand Rapids, 1980], p. 3; Grand Rapids *Evening Leader*, Jan. 30, 1890, p. 4; Grand Rapids *Evening Press*, April 11, 1899, p. 3; and Dwight Goss, *History of Grand Rapids and its Industries* (Chicago, 1906), Vol. II, p. 1174.

3. Grand Rapids *Evening Press*, March 11, 1899, p. 11; *Grand Rapids City Directory*, 1900.

4. Grand Rapids *Evening Press*, April 7, 1913, p. 10; May 5, 1913, p. 2; July 8, 1912, p. 7.

5. Grand Rapids *Press*, Nov. 2, 1917, p. 22; Dec. 3, 1917, p. 12.

6. Grand Rapids *Press*, May 24, 1919, p. 8; Sept. 20, 1922, p. 13; Oct. 2, 1922, p. 9; March 24, 1923, p. 16; July 27, 1923, p. 6; Aug. 10, 1923, p. 8; Aug. 25, 1923, p. 5.

7. Grand Rapids *Press*, Oct. 22, 1922; Grand Rapids *Herald*, Oct. 29, 1922; p. v-12; Adeline Jefferson, op. cit.

8. "The Negro Population of Grand Rapids, Michigan: 1940" (survey by Department of Research, National Urban League, April, 1940), pp. 19–21, 93.

9. "Negro Population of Grand Rapids," pp. 42–45; Adeline Jefferson, op. cit.; Grand Rapids *Press*, July 22, 1933, p. 10; May 17, 1930, p. 4; June 10, 1930, p. 4; July 25, 1930, p. 6.

10. Grand Rapids *Press*, March 10, 1978, p. c9. The individuals named were all members of the Omega Psi Phi fraternity in Ann Arbor. I am indebted to Randal M. Jelks for this information.

11. Adeline Jefferson, op. cit.; author's interview with Mrs. Sara Glover, Jan. 16, 1992.

12. Grand Rapids *Press*, Feb. 1, 1943, p. 11; Feb. 22, 1943, p. 6; June 5, 1943, p. 18; Aug. 13, 1943, p. 8; Sept. 30, 1943, p. 10.

13. "Negro Population of Grand Rapids," pp. 22–37.

14. Adeline Jefferson, op. cit.; Grand Rapids *Press*, May 25, 1956, p. 8.

15. United Community Services, "Anatomy of a Riot, 1967" (Grand Rapids, 1967); Grand Rapids *Press*, July 30, 1967, pp. 23.

16. Grand Rapids *Press*, July 30, 1967, p. 23; Aug. 26, 1967, p. 5; Sept. 14, 1969, magazine p. 6.

17. "Eighty-Fourth Anniversary," p. 4; *Grand Rapids City Directory*, 1969.

18. "Eighty-Fourth Anniversary," p. 4; "100 Years: Messiah MBC," p. 4.

19. Author's interview with Rev. Eric Williams, July 7, 1992.

20. "100 Years, MBC," pp. 2, 12–13; Jack Palecki, "Spiritual Spotlight," *Afro-American Gazette* [Grand Rapids], April 1992, p. 13.

21. "100 Years, Messiah MBC," pp. 4, 15; author's interview with Rev. Eric Williams, July 7, 1992.

22. Marjorie M. Wykes, *Cascade Chronicles* (Cascade Historical Commission, 1987), p. 35.

23. Much of this account rests upon the church's centennial chronicle, "Open Doors, Open Hearts, Open Minds," written by Marjorie M. Wykes.

24. Albert Baxter, *History of the City of Grand Rapids, Michigan* (New York and Grand Rapids, 1891), pp. 293–94; "Open Doors," pp. 4–5.

25. *Cascade Christian Church: 125 Years* (n.p., 1989), pp. 12, 19–20, 23, 41; "Open Doors," p. 16.

26. "Open Doors," p. 7.

27. "Open Doors," pp. 11, 16.

28. "Open Doors," pp. 12, 16.

29. "Open Doors," p. 14; author's interview with Rev. Raymond Gaylord, June 16, 1992.

30. Raymond Gaylord, "Three Decades Plus" (personal memoir), pp. 11–12; *Cascade Christian Church*, pp. 49–50; author's interview with Rev. Raymond Gaylord, June 16, 1992.

31. Gaylord, "Three Decades," pp. 4–5, 13–15.

32. Gaylord, "Three Decades," pp. 9–10; "1991 Annual Report: Operation Santa Claus," p. 2.

33. Gaylord, "Three Decades," pp. 13–14; "ACCESS-6, 1982–1992: Nine-Year Financial Statement," pp. 1–2.

34. Gaylord, "Three Decades," pp. 6–8.

35. Author's interview with Rev. Raymond Gaylord, June 16, 1992; Cascade Christian Church brochure, "To Our Visitors."

36. Baxter, *History of Grand Rapids*, p. 304.

37. Ibid.; "St. John's Evangelical Church, Grand Rapids, Michigan: 50th Anniversary, 1880–1930" (Grand Rapids, 1930), unpaginated.

38. "St. John's 50th Anniversary."

39. Ibid.; St. John's Evangelical Church, "Greetings from Your Church and Loved Ones" (pamphlet of letters, 1945).

40. "St. John's United Church of Christ, Centennial: 1880–1980" (Grand Rapids, 1980, unpaginated); Grand Rapids *Press*, May 7, 1949, p. 5; Feb. 18, 1956, p. 5; Jan. 7, 1961, p. 5; Jan. 14, 1961, p. 6.

41. St. John's United Church of Christ, "Questionnaire," Grand Rapids Area Council for the Humanities, Church History Project, 1991; Local Historical Collections at the Grand Rapids Public Library, pp. 7, 8, 16–20, 22–23.

42. "Golden Anniversary, Seventh Reformed Church, 1890–1940" (Grand Rapids, 1940), pp. 3–13; "Seventh Reformed Church 1890–1990" (Grand Rapids, 1990), pp. 1–5.

43. "Golden Anniversary," pp. 8, 10–14; author's interviews with Mr. George Mulder and Rev. Morris Folkert, June 12, 1992.

44. "Seventy Five Years, Seventh Reformed Church: 1890–1965" (Grand Rapids, 1965, unpaginated); "Seventh Reformed Church, 1890–1990," pp. 9, 11–12.

45. James D. Bratt, *Dutch Calvinism in Modern America* (Grand Rapids, 1984), pp. 197–98; author's interview with Rev. Morris Folkert, June 12, 1992.

46. See, for example, Girod's columns in the congregational newsletter, "The Voice of Seventh," throughout the 1960s

and 1970s.

47. "Seventh Reformed Church, 1890–1990," pp. 14–16, 20.

48. "Seventh Reformed Church, 1890-1990," p. 23; Bratt, *Dutch Calvinism*, pp. 204–05; Gordon Girod, "Our Song of Hope: A Doctrinal Hodge-Podge," *Voice of Seventh* 19(June 4, 1978), pp. 3–5; Gordon Girod, "What About a CRC-RCA Merger?," *Torch & Trumpet* 19(October 1969), pp. 2–6.

49. "Seventh Reformed Church, 1890–1990," pp. 16–17, 23–26.

50. Ibid., pp. 17–18, 20–22, 35.

A PREACHER STORMS CITY HALL

J. Lamberts, "History of First AME Church."

Sonya Vann, "Coalition salutes GR's first black mayor and others," Grand Rapids *Press*, Oct. 31, 1992, p. A3.

Author's interview with Gene Proctor, Oct. 25, 1992.

A TOUCH OF GRACE

Author's interview with the Rev. David Baak, co-director of the Grand Rapids Center for Ecumenism, Nov. 22, 1992.

"20 Years of GRACE," *GRACE Notes*, (newsletter of the Grand Rapids Center for Ecumenism), November-December 1992, pp. 6–7.

"GR Church Council's Rev. Prescott: 'A witness to our oneness,'" Grand Rapids *Press*, Feb., 28, 1965, p. 21.

"Grand Rapids Area Center for Ecumensism," annual report for 1972.

HELPING ON THE HILL

Author's interview with the Rev. Wesley Samuelson, Feb. 10, 1993.

Author's interview with Barbara Roelofs, March 3, 1993.

"New Group Coordinates Historic Building Preservation," Grand Rapids *Press*, June 6, 1969, p. 2D.

"To meet the growing needs of Bethlehem," a church history published for parish house drive in 1953. Local Historical Collections at the Grand Rapids Public Library.

FATHER MIKE: MESSENGER FOR THE MASSES

Sister Marie Michael Jacobs, "Biographical Sketch: Monsignor Hugh M. Beahan (1920–1980)."

Author's interview with Sister Marie Michael Jacobs, April 16, 1992.

The Rev. Gaspar Ancona, "The Genius of Father Mike," Feb. 12, 1985.

"Father Mike Dies," Grand Rapids *Press*, April 18, 1981.

CHAPTER 9

1. "First Heritage: Grand Rapids First Assembly of God" (n.p., April 22, 1990), pp. 7–9; Leo Huisman, "The First Assembly of God in Grand Rapids: A Congregational History" (senior seminar paper, History Department, Calvin College, April 1992), pp. 2–3; Melissa Lettinga, "First Assembly of God" (senior seminar paper, History Department, Calvin College, December 1986), p. 5.

2. Statistics taken from "Dedication 1992," the program for the new sanctuary's opening May 31–June 7, 1992 (unpaginated).

3. "First Heritage," pp. 9–10; Lettinga, "First Assembly," pp. 6–9; First Assembly of God, "Dedication 1992."

4. Lettinga, "First Assembly," pp. 9–11; Huisman, "First Assembly," p. 14; First Assembly of God, "Scrapbook," vol. 1.

5. Margaret Poloma, "Charisma and Institution: The Assemblies of God," *Christian Century* 107 (Oct. 17, 1992): 932–34; Margaret Poloma and Brian F. Pendleton, "Religious Experience, Evangelism, and Institutional Growth in the Assemblies of God," *Journal of the Scientific Study of Religion* 28/4 (December 1989): 415.

6. "First Heritage," pp. 10–12; Lettinga, "First Assembly," pp. 11–12; Charles Vaughn and Dorothy Simon, *The City of Wyoming: A History* (Wyoming, MI, 1984), pp. 286–87.

7. "First Heritage," pp. 11–12; Lettinga, "First Assembly," pp. 12–15; author's interview with Mr. Rick Wilson, communications director at First Assembly of God, Aug. 12, 1992; quotations from Grand Rapids *Press*, Nov. 29, 1980, p. A4.

8. Huisman, "First Assembly," pp. 15–17; author's interview with Mr. Rick Wilson, Aug. 12, 1992.

9. This is evident in numerous First Assembly publications and addresses, from the 1981 issues of the congregational newsletter, *Lamblight*, to the sermon at the evening service, July 19, 1992.

10. Author's interview with Mr. Rick Wilson, Aug. 12, 1992; "First Heritage," p. 12; "Dedication 1992."

11. Quotation from M. Wayne Benson, "Harvest 2000" brochure, p. 20. See also Paul Tinlin and Edith Blumhofer, "Decade of Decline or Harvest?," *Christian Century* 108 (July 10–17, 1991): 684–87.

12. "First Heritage," pp. 12–14; Grand Rapids *Press*, March 28, 1992, pp. B1–2.

13. Sermon themes taken from the morning service of Aug. 9, 1992 and the evening service of July 19, 1992. Description of care groups taken from author's interview with Mr. Rick Wilson, Aug. 12, 1992, and First Assembly, "1986 Ministry Report."

14. Benson, "Harvest 2000," pp. 10, 15; author's interview with Mr. Rick Wilson, Aug. 12, 1992; Lettinga, "First Assembly," p. 15.

15. Interview with Ms. Donna Kamen, recorded by Huisman in "First Assembly," pp. 9–11.

16. The history of this group is told in Morris E. Golder, *History of the Pentecostal Assemblies of the World* (Indianapolis, 1973) and in the February 1992 issue (68/2) of its magazine, *The Christian Outlook*.

17. Frank Bartleman, *Azusa Street* (n.p., 1925), pp. 118–19, 124–25; *Grand Rapids City Directory, 1917 & 1925.*

18. "The History of Bethel Pentecostal Church," in *Bethel Pentecostal Church Dedication* (n.p., April 13-26, 1970), unpaginated; author's interview with Mr. Donald Carew, chair of Bethel Pentecostal's board, Aug. 20, 1992.

19. "History of BPC."

20. "History of BPC;" author's interview with Mr. Donald Carew; *Grand Rapids City Directory, 1950 and 1970.*

21. "History of BPC;" "Biographical Sketch of Our Pastor," in Bethel Pentecostal Church bulletin, July 19, 1992; author's interview with Elder William C. Abney, Aug. 21, 1992.

22. "History of BPC;" *BPC Dedication*; Grand Rapids *Press*, Oct. 5, 1974, p. A4.

23. The following is based on Joseph R. Washington, Jr., "The Black Holiness and Pentecostal Sects," in C. Eric Lincoln, ed., *The Black Experience in Religion* (Garden City, N.Y., 1974), pp. 196–212.

24. Author's interview with Mr. Dan Suttles, July 22, 1992.

25. Quotations from author's interviews with Elder William Abney and Mr. Donald Carew, Aug. 20–21, 1992.

26. Author's interview with Mr. Donald Carew, Aug. 20, 1992.

27. On Whittum, Grand Rapids *Press*, Aug. 12, 1992, p. A1; on DeBarge brothers, ibid., Oct. 26, 1988, p. A1; Jan. 19, 1989, p. E4; Jan. 27, 1989, p. D1; Feb. 19, 1989, p. A17; March 16, 1989, p. E1; Oct. 21, 1989, p. A4.

28. Author's interview with Elder William Abney, Aug. 21, 1992.

29. Albert Baxter, *History of Grand Rapids, Michigan* (New York and Grand Rapids, 1891), p. 344; Father Henry Frencken, "A History of St. Joseph the Worker Church" (compiled from letters to his successors and published upon the parish's centennial in 1989), pp. 1–2.

30. Frencken, "SJW," p. 2.

31. Frencken, "SJW," pp. 2–7; Grand Rapids *Press*, April 15, 1912, p. 9; Rev. Steve Cron, bulletin of parish's centennial service, July 30, 1989.

32. David G. Vander Stel, "The Dutch of Grand Rapids, Michigan, 1848–1900" (unpublished Ph.D. dissertation, Kent State University, 1983), pp. 185–88.

33. Bulletin of parish centennial; baptismal records of SJW.

34. Grand Rapids *Press*, April 15, 1943, p. 1; June 21, 1952, p. 4; author's interview with Rev. Steve Cron, Aug. 11, 1992.

35. Author's interview with Rev. Steve Cron, Aug. 11, 1992.

36. *U.S. Population Census 1970, 1990*; author's interview with Rev. Steve Cron, Aug. 11, 1992.

37. Joseph P. Fitzpatrick, *One Church, Many Cultures: The Challenge of Diversity* (Kansas City, 1987), pp. 132–35.

38. Author's interview with Rev. Steve Cron, Aug. 11, 1992.

39. Ibid.

40. Bulletin of parish centennial.

41. Ibid.; Fitzpatrick, *One Church*, pp. 129, 158–59; Isidro Lucas, *The Browning of America: The Hispanic Revolution in the American Church* (Chicago, 1981).

42. Author's interview with Rev. Steve Cron, Aug. 11, 1992; Lucas, *Browning of America*, pp. 89–90.

43. Author's interview with Rev. Steve Cron, Aug. 11, 1992.

44. Service at St. Joseph the Worker Roman Catholic Church, 9 a.m., Sunday, Aug. 23, 1992.

45. Gary B. Nash, *Red, White, and Black: The Peoples of Early North America*, 3rd ed. (Englewood Cliffs, N.J., 1992), pp. 63–65, 144.

GRAND RAPIDS' LINK TO ISLAM

"Minister aims to restore pride in his people," Grand Rapids *Press*, July 31, 1982, p. E1.

Author's interview with local Muslim leaders Ghulam Malik and Najeeullah Muhammad at Islamic Center of Grand Rapids, Feb. 5, 1993.

Interview with Noah Seifullah, Feb. 16, 1993.

FLIGHTS OF FREEDOM

Interview with the Rev. Howard and Marybelle Schipper on Feb. 4, 1992.

Interview with Ms. Lai Tran on Jan. 25, 1992.

Pastoral letter on subject of refugee resettlement, by Bishop Robert J. Rose, March 7, 1990.

QUAKERS: A SMALL BUT POWERFUL GROUP

Interview with Mrs. Betty Ford, Nov. 12, 1991.

Interview with Mr. Mark Kane, Dec. 2, 1991.

"Quakers, Friends remember Ethel W. Dungan," Grand Rapids *Press*, Dec. 12, 1986. p. 1D.

"Grand Rapids Friends Meeting: An Historical Perspective (1962–1989)," Local Historical Collections (church history project collection) at the Grand Rapids Public Library.

THE LEGACY OF VATICAN II: BISHOP BREITENBECK

Interview with Bishop Joseph Breitenbeck, July 22, 1991.

"Bishop Breitenbeck's Homily," given during his installation ceremonies in Grand Rapids on Dec. 2, 1969.

Picture and Map Credits C

CHAPTER 1

1. Grand Rapids Public Library, *Grand River Valley Review*, Vol. V. Number II.
2. Grand Rapids Public Library, *Grand River Valley Review*, Vol. V. Number II.
3. *Famous Indians*, Bureau of Indian Affairs 1966, p. 11.
4. *Famous Indians*, Bureau of Indian Affairs 1966, p. 15.
5, 8, 12, 17. The Grand Rapids Press library, hereafter referred to as GR Press.
6. University of Oklahoma, *The Potowatomis*, R. David Edmunds, University of Oklahoma Press 1978, p. 136. Photo courtesy of the Kansas State Historical Society Library in Topeka, Kan.
7, 10, 11. Grand Rapids Public Library, Local Historical Collections, hereafter referred to as GRPL.
9. Grand Rapids Public Library, *Six Months Among Indians*, Darius B. Cook 1889, reprinted 1974, p. 10.
13. *The Catholic Church in the Grand River Valley 1833–1950*, John W. McGee, Grand Rapids, Mich., 1950, p. 15.
14. *The Catholic Church in the Grand River Valley 1833–1950*, John W. McGee, Grand Rapids, Mich., 1950, p. 55.
15. Albert Baxter, *History of the City of Grand Rapids, Michigan*, New York and Grand Rapids, 1891, p. 761, hereafter referred to as Baxter.
16. *The Catholic Church in the Grand River Valley 1833–1950*, John W. McGee, Grand Rapids, Mich., 1950, p. 82.
18. First (Park) Congregational Church.

CHAPTER 2

1, 2, 8, 14, 39, 40. GR Press.
3, 4, 6–7, 13. First (Park) Congregational Church.
5. *Legislative Manual and Official Directory of the State of Michigan for the Year 1885*, Harry A. Conant, W.S. George 7 Co., State Printers and Binders, 1885, p. 531.
9–11, 15, 17–18, 23, 26–29, 33, 35, 41. GRPL.
12. Saint Mary's Hospital.
16, 32. Catholic Diocese of Grand Rapids Archives, hereafter referred to as Catholic Diocese Archives.
19–22, 25, 31. First Methodist Church.
24. *Publications of the Historical Society of Grand Rapids*, No. 5, Vol. 1, Part 5, 1909.
38, 42. St. Andrew's Cathedral.
34. *The Catholic Church in the Grand River Valley 1833–1950*, John W. McGee, Grand Rapids, Mich., 1950, p. 300.
36. *Grand Rapids Illustrated 1888*, E.B. Fisher.

CHAPTER 3

1. Booklet by the Grand Rapids Board of Trade, *Grand Rapids, Mich. as it is 1894*, courtesy of the Harris Paper Co., p. 28.
2, 16, 43. GR Press.
3–5, 8–13, 15. Central Reformed Church.
6, 14, 31, 33, 40, 41. GRPL.
7. *Reformed Review*, Winter 1977, Vol. 30 No. 9.
17–22. Calvin College and Theological Seminary Archives, hereafter referred to as Calvin College Archives.
23–32. Immanuel Lutheran Church.
34. *History of Temple Emanuel*, 1954.
35–37. *Golden Anniversary of St. Mary's Church 1907*.
40. St. Mary's Roman Catholic Church.
38. *Grand Rapids Illustrated 1888*, E.B. Fisher.
39. St. Andrew's Cathedral.

CHAPTER 4

1, 6–7, 17, 20, 22, 28. GRPL.
2, 24, 27, 29–30. GR Press.
3–5. Calvin College Archives.
8–9. St. Andrew's Cathedral.
10–11. Aaron Phipps.
12–16, 19. Eduard Adam Skendzel Polonian

Historical Collection.

18. *The First 100 Years Basilica of St. Adalbert's 1881–1981*, Philip Jung, p. 107.

21. *The Story of St. Mark's 1836–1936*, Roger Allen, 1936.

22, 25–26. St. Mark's Episcopal Church.

CHAPTER 5

1–11, 13–14. GRPL.

12. *Kathetos Annual of the Central High School of Grand Rapids, Michigan, for the year 1904.*

15. *The Only Church With a History Like This*, Vol. 3, Philip Buchen, 1960, Fountain Street Baptist Church, p. 65.

16. GR Press.

CHAPTER 6

1–4, 6, 8, 10, 12. Wealthy Park Baptist Church.

5, 7, 13–15, 19, 26–27, 30–35. GRPL.

9, 11, 24, 36, 38, 39. GR Press.

16–18, 20–22. Calvin College Archives.

23. *God's Covenant Faithfulness: The 50th Anniversary of the Protestant Reformed Churches of America*, 1975 Reformed Free Publishing Association.

25. William B. Eerdmans Publishing Company.

28, 39. Westminster Presbyterian Church.

29. *Grand Rapids Illustrated 1888*, E.B. Fisher.

37. Booklet by the Grand Rapids Board of Trade, *Grand Rapids, Mich. as it is 1894*, courtesy of the Harris Paper Co.

CHAPTER 7

1, 4–6, 19, 25, 29. GRPL.

2, 7, 11–14. Calvary Undenominational Church.

3, 9–10, 15–17, 21, 26–27, 31. GR Press.

8. Western Michigan/Northern Indiana Salvation Army Division.

18, 20, 22–24. Temple Emanuel.

28, 36. Paul Crouse.

30, 35, 37. St. John Chrysostom Russian Orthodox Church.

CHAPTER 8

1, 2, 4–7. Messiah Missionary Baptist Church.

3, 16, 38, 44, 45. GRPL.

8–13, 27–29. GR Press.

14–15, 17–26. Cascade Christian Church.

30–32, 34–37. St. John's United Church of Christ.

33. Paul Crouse.

39–42, 46–48. Seventh Reformed Church.

43. Catholic Diocese Archives.

CHAPTER 9

1, 4–9, 13, 15. First Assembly of God.

2, 24. GRPL.

3, 11–12, 14, 16, 19–23, 27, 32, 36. GR Press.

10. Grand Rapids Society of Friends.

17–18. Bethel Pentecostal Church.

25–26, 28–31, 33. St. Joseph the Worker Roman Catholic Church.

34–35. Catholic Diocese Archives.

DIRECTORY OF CONGREGATIONS

1, 3, 6, 8, 10, 12–14, 18–21, 23–26, 28–30, 33–42, 44, 46–47. GRPL.

2. Calvin College Archives.

4. Baxter, p. 305.

5, 9, 31. Catholic Diocese Archives.

7. Baxter, p. 293.

11. Baxter, p. 332.

15, 17, 27, 32, 43. Paul Crouse.

16. Baxter, p. 330.

22. Baxter, p. 339.

45. Baxter, p. 284.

Colophon

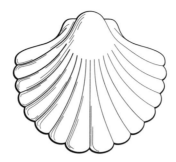

The scallop shell was worn by the palmer as a symbol of his journey to the Holy Land during the Crusades. St. James the Great is often associated with the shell because of the number of pilgrimages to Santiago de Compostela, a shrine in Spain containing a relic of him. Because of this, the scallop shell in Christian art has come to signify pilgrimage in general. Hence it is a fitting symbol denoting the journeys of faith undertaken by the people of Grand Rapids.

❧ This book was produced on a Macintosh® IIfx using QuarkXPress® 3.11, Adobe® Illustrator 3.2 and Adobe® Photoshop™ 2.5. Reflective prints were digitized using a UMAX UC630 flatbed scanner; others were photographed and the film transferred to Eastman Kodak's Photo CD™.
❧ All serif fonts are from the Goudy Old Style family. Body copy is Goudy 10.5pt on 13pt leading. The sans serif face used is Franklin Gothic. ❧ The electronic pages were output to negative film for stripping at William B. Eerdmans Publishing Company.